INTERNATIONAL ACCLAIM FOR THE BERLITZ COMPLETE GUIDE TO CRUISING AND CRUISE SHIPS

"One way to find the right cruise is to get a copy of Berlitz...which rates all the cruise ships in the world, the facilities they offer and the kind of passengers you can expect to meet."

International Herald Tribune

"...helps you pick a ship that most closely meets your needs."

The Travel Agent, New York

"...indispensable for choosing a ship the first time, or for experienced cruisers wanting to try a new ship."

Tourist Echo, Paris

"...a variety of knowledgeable advice and opinion."

Chicago Sun-Times

"Only once in many years does one find a book so very well done."

The Travel Store, Los Gatos, CA

"...informative about all aspects of cruising...sensible and comprehensive."

Sunday Telegraph, London

"...required reading when selecting a cruise ship."

Travel & Enjoyment, Hamburg

"...the do's and don'ts of taking a cruise."

The Housto͏ ͏

"...includes simply everything about...crui͏

Knight-Ridder͏

GW00696070

"...extensively describes ships in oceangoing vessels, giving star ratings a͏nd numerical scores to ͏eac͏

Chicago Tribune

STOP PRESS

The very nature of a book such as this, which contains so much factual information, is always subject to change, just as many parts of the cruise industry itself changes constantly. It was up to date and as accurate as possible up to June 1996, when this book was completed, but last minute changes received are noted below.

Cunard has announced that **Queen Elizabeth 2** is scheduled to undergo several changes following her 1997 World Cruise. Transatlantic crossings will be reduced to 18 from the present 24, with a duration of six days, instead of five days. The ship's capacity will be reduced to 1,500 (from the present 1,800), with lower grade accommodations being removed from service. All restaurants will feature one-sitting dining (formerly the Mauritania Restaurant, the ship's largest, featured two sittings). In addition, the Mauritania and Caronia restaurants will be reversed once again. Details of all the changes were not available when this book was completed. All gratuities are now included in the fare (this was commenced in April 1996).

American Hawaii Cruises' **Constitution** was permanently withdrawn from service following an extensive survey which found that the cost of bringing the vessel up to the latest safety standards was too high.

P&O Cruises' venerable **Canberra**, long a favorite of British mass-market passengers, will be withdrawn at the end of 1997. She will, in all probability, be replaced by **Star Princess**, presently being operated by U.S.-based sister company Princess Cruises.

Awani Dream is the name of the former **World Renaissance**, now operating in the burgeoning domestic Indonesian cruise market (this information was not received in time for this ship to be included in Part Three, however).

Star Clippers' two ships will sail in European waters during the summer of 1997, instead of one in the Caribbean and one in Europe.

World Explorer Cruises' **Enchanted Seas** has been renamed **Universe Explorer**. The ship is the subject of a long-term charter from Commodore Cruise Line.

Cunard's classic **Sagafjord** was chartered by the German company Transocean Tours, and entered service in July, 1996, as **Gripsholm**. The ship is not included in this edition, as it was thought that she would by totally withdrawn from service (the ship given as **Gripsholm**, ex-**Regent Sea**, in not in service for Transocean Tours).

Delphin Seereisen's **Kazakhstan II** has been renamed **Delphin**, and has been reflagged from Cyprus to Malta.

Costa Cruises' **Daphne** has been sold to Leisure Cruises, who will operate her starting March 1997 after an extensive refit. She will be renamed **Switzerland**.

THE NEXT EDITION OF THIS BOOK WILL BE PUBLISHED IN SEPTEMBER 1997

All evaluations of cruise ships in this book were made without bias. partiality, or prejudice. In almost all instances the ships have been visited recently by the author in order to update earlier ratings or assess current status. Much of the information contained in the profiles in Part Three was supplied and checked by the cruise lines and shipowners themselves. Any errors, or updated information should be sent to:
Mr Douglas Ward, The Maritime Evaluations Group, Canada House, 1 Carrick Way, New Milton, Hampshire BH25 6UD, ENGLAND.

BERLITZ®
1997 Complete Guide to

and Cruise Ships

by
DOUGLAS WARD

President
The Maritime Evaluations Group (MEG)

Berlitz Publishing Company, Inc.
Princeton, NJ

ACKNOWLEDGMENTS

The ship silhouettes and cabin layouts were drawn
by Oxford Illustrators.

The black and white photographs were kindly
supplied by the cruise lines concerned.

Photographs on pp. 147, 217 supplied by the author.

Cover art taken from a photograph by Claude
Mougin.

1997 Edition

PUBLISHER'S NOTE

The Maritime Evaluations Group (MEG) has
evaluated cruise ships since 1980, issuing
annual reports on the world's cruise fleet.
All professional opinions and ratings are
strictly those of the author and not of the
publisher, Berlitz, which makes this survey
available in bookstores.

Copyright ©1996, 1995, 1994, 1992, 1989, 1986
Berlitz Publishing Company, Inc.,
400 Alexander Park, Princeton,
NJ 08540-6306.

All rights reserved. No part of this book may be
reproduced or transmitted in any form or by any
means, electronic or mechanical, including
photocopying, recording, or by any information
storage and retrieval system without permission in
writing from the publisher.

Berlitz Trademark Reg. U.S. Patent Office and other
countries – Marca Registrada

ISBN 2-8315-6052-7

Printed in the United States of America

Contents

Contents

Where To?

With over 500 destinations to choose from, today's cruise ships do indeed roam all over the world. For the sake of simplicity, some of the major cruise areas are grouped together on the following pages, together with the names of the companies and, in most cases, the ships that will take you there.

Note that large cruise lines that operate several ships tend to switch ships to operate certain itineraries from year to year, and so the names of the ships are not provided. When it was compiled, the list was as accurate as it was possible to make it, given that many companies had not released their 1997 itineraries.

Finally, some ships just seem to roam the world constantly, on long cruises, with no fixed base ports.

KEY (*) = Year-Round

BAHAMAS

AquaMarin Cruises
Canaveral Cruise Line (*)
Carnival Cruise Lines (*)
Celebrity Cruises
Costa Cruises
Crystal Cruises
Cunard
Disney Cruise Line (*)
Dolphin Cruise Line (*)
Holland America Line (*)
Majesty Cruise Line (*)
Norwegian Cruise Line (*)
Premier Cruise Line (*)
Princess Cruises (*)
Royal Caribbean Cruises (*)
Seetours

BERMUDA (SUMMER)

Only the four cruise lines (with five ships) that have long-term Bermuda government contracts for weekly summer season cruises to Bermuda are listed here, although several other companies operate cruises that include Bermuda infrequently.

Celebrity Cruises
Majesty Cruise Line
Norwegian Cruise Line
Royal Caribbean Cruises

EASTERN CANADA/NEW ENGLAND

These cruises are normally 7-day northbound voyages between New York and Montreal, or southbound voyages from Montreal to New York. Of course, these can be combined to make a 14-day roundtrip voyage.

American Canadian Caribbean Line
AquaMarin Cruises
CTC Cruise Lines
Clipper Cruise Line
Crystal Cruises
Cunard
Delphin Seereisen
Deutsche Seetouristik
Dolphin Cruise Line
Hanseatic Tours
Hapag-Lloyd Cruises
Holland America Line
Neckermann Seereisen
P&O Cruises
Phoenix Seereisen
Princess Cruises
Radisson Seven Seas Cruises
Seabourn Cruise Line

Seetours
Silversea Cruises
Transocean Tours

CARIBBEAN

Note that there are several more companies than those listed here whose ships visit the Caribbean infrequently, but their schedules are seldom known far enough in advance to be included here.

Airtours Cruises
American Canadian Caribbean Line
AquaMarin Cruises
Arcalia Shipping
CTC Cruise Lines
Carnival Cruise Lines (*)
Celebrity Cruises (*)
Clipper Cruise Line
Club Med Cruises
Commodore Cruise Line (*)
Compagnie des Isles du Ponant
Costa Cruises
Crystal Cruises
Cunard (*)
Deilmann Reederei
Delphin Seerederei
Deutsche Seetouristik
Dolphin Cruise Line (*)
Fred Olsen Cruise Lines
Holland America Line (*)
Mediterranean Shipping Cruises
Neckermann Seereisen
Nina Cruise Line
Norwegian Cruise Line (*)
P&O Cruises

Paquet Cruises
Phoenix Seereisen
Premier Cruise Lines (*)
Princess Cruises
Radisson Seven Seas Cruises
Regal Cruise Line
Renaissance Cruises
Royal Caribbean Cruises (*)
Royal Olympic Cruises
Royal Seas Cruise Line (*)
Sea Cloud Cruises
Seabourn Cruise Line
Seawind Cruise Line (*)
Seetours
Silversea Cruises
Star Clippers
Tall Ship Adventures (*)
Transocean Tours
Windjammer Barefoot Cruises (*)
Windstar Cruises

ALASKA

These cruises are operated generally between May and September.

Abercrombie & Kent
Alaska Sightseeing/Cruise West
Carnival Cruise Lines
Celebrity Cruises
Clipper Cruise Line
Crystal Cruises
Cunard
Hanseatic Tours
Hapag-Lloyd Cruises

Holland America Line
Marine Expeditions
Norwegian Cruise Line
Phoenix Seereisen
Princess Cruises
Royal Caribbean Cruises
Seabourn Cruise Line
Society Expeditions
Special Expeditions
Transocean Tours
World Explorer Cruises

MEXICAN RIVIERA - YEAR-ROUND (3/4/7 DAYS)

Base: US West Coast

Carnival Cruise Line (*)
Royal Caribbean Cruises (*)

HAWAII

Author's Note: A number of cruise lines have ships that call at Hawaii, but none on a regular basis, due to the archaic Jones Act (U.S. cabotage laws), which states that only a U.S.-flag ship can embark and disembark passengers in a U.S. port without first going to a foreign port.

American Hawaii Cruises (*)
Carnival Cruise Lines
Crystal Cruises
Cunard
Holland America Line
Princess Cruises
Royal Caribbean Cruises
Seabourn Cruise Line

MEDITERRANEAN (INCLUDING BLACK SEA/GREEK ISLES)

Airtours Cruises

AquaMarin Cruises

Arcalia Shipping

CTC Cruise Lines

Club Med Cruises

Compagnie des Isles du Ponant

Costa Cruises

Crystal Cruises

Cunard

Deilmann Seerederei

Delphin Seereisen

Deutsche Seerederei

Dolphin Hellas Cruises

Fantasy Cruises

Festival Cruises

Fred Olsen Cruise Lines

Grimaldi Crusies

Hanseatic Tours

Holland America Line

Louis Cruise Lines (*)

Majestic International Cruises

Mar Line

Mediterranean Queen Lines

Mediterranean Shipping Cruises

Neckermann Seereisen

Italia Prima

Nina Cruise Line

Orient Lines

P&O Cruises

Paquet Cruises

Phoenix Seereisen

Primexpress Cruises

Princess Cruises

Radisson Seven Seas Cruises

Renaissance Cruises

Royal Caribbean Cruises

Royal Hispania Cruises

Royal Olympic Cruises (*)

Seabourn Cruise Line

Seetours

Silversea Cruises

Soviet Danube Shipping

Star Line

SunFest Cruises

Swan Hellenic Cruises

Thomson Cruises

Transocean Tours

Travelwise Cruises

Windstar Cruises

NORTH CAPE/BALTIC SEA

AquaMarin Cruises

Arcalia Shipping

CTC Cruise Lines

Costa Cruises

Crystal Cruises

Cunard

Deilmann Reederei

Deutsche Seerederei

Fantasy Cruises

Festival Cruises

Fred Olsen Cruise Lines

Fritidskryss

Hanseatic Tours

Hapag-Lloyd Cruises

Holland America Line

Mediterranean Shipping Cruises

Noble Caledonia

P&O Cruises

Paquet Cruises

Phoenix Seereisen

Primexpress Cruises

Princess Cruises

Radisson Seven Seas Cruises

Renaissance Cruises

Royal Caribbean Cruises

Seabourn Cruise Line

Seetours

Silversea Cruises

Swan Hellenic Cruises

Transocean Tours

ATLANTIC ISLES (CANARY ISLES/MADEIRA)

Airtours Cruises

Club Med Cruises

Costa Cruises

Crystal Cruises

Cunard

Deilmann Reederei

Festival Cruises

Fred Olsen Cruise Lines

Grimaldi Cruises

Holland America Line

P&O Cruises

Phoenix Seereisen

Radisson Seven Seas Cruises

Renaissance Cruises

Royal Hispania Cruises

Seetours

Silversea Cruises

Star Clippers

Thomson Cruises

Transocean Tours

ARABIAN GULF (RED SEA)

Noble Caledonia

P&O Cruises

Phoenix Seereisen

Renaissance Cruises

Royal Olympic Cruises

Swan Hellenic Cruises

Thomson Cruises

INDIAN OCEAN

CTC Cruise Lines

Crystal Cruises

Cunard

Hanseatic Tours/Hapag-Lloyd Cruises

NYK Cruise Line

Noble Caledonia

Orient Lines

P&O Cruises

Primexpress Cruises

Princess Cruises

Radisson Seven Seas Cruises

Renaissance Cruises

Seabourn Cruise Line

Silversea Cruises

Star Line Cruises

Swan Hellenic Cruises

Transocean Tours

SOUTHEAST ASIA

CTC Cruise Lines
Club Med Cruises
Crystal Cruises
Cunard
Far East Shipping (*)
Hanseatic Tours
Lines International (*)
Mitsui OSK Passenger Line (*)
NYK Cruise Line (*)
New Century Tours (*)
Noble Caledonia
Orient Lines
P&O Spice Island Cruises (*)
Princess Cruises
Radisson Seven Seas Cruises
Renaissance Cruises
Royal Caribbean Cruises (*)
Seabourn Cruise Line
Seetours
Showa Line (*)
Siam Cruise Line (*)
Silversea Cruises
Star Cruise (*)
Swan Hellenic Cruises
Transocean Tours
Venus Cruise Line
Windstar Cruises

AUSTRALIA/NEW ZEALAND/SOUTH PACIFIC

CTC Cruise Lines (*)
Celebrity Cruises
Club Med

Crystal Cruises

Cunard

Far East Shipping

Hanseatic Tours

Hapag-Lloyd Cruises

NYK Cruise Line

Orient Lines

P&O Holidays

P&O Cruises

Princess Cruises

Radisson Seven Seas Cruises

Seabourn Cruise Line

Silversea Cruises

Windstar Cruises (*)

AMAZON

Crystal Cruises

Cunard

Delphin Seereisen

Hanseatic Tours

Princess Cruises

Royal Olympic Cruises

Seabourn Cruise Line

Seetours

Silversea Cruises

Special Expeditions

Transocean Tours

ANTARCTICA

Author's Note: The Antarctic is no place for normal cruise ships. To operate in this region, where ice can easily crush a ship within the hour should the weather deteriorate (as it often does), a ship must have an "ice-strengthened" or "ice-hardened" hull" capable of breaking through pack ice in the formative stage. Rubber-inflatable Zodiac landing craft are used for venturing ashore (there so such thing as a dock on the Antarctic continent). All the companies listed here provide the right facilities, but some are better than others. The austral summer is the only time ships can get close to the Antarctic Peninsula (where many nations have their research stations), as the ice is so dense during the winter months that the continent (which, at its smallest, is the size of North America) swells to twice its summer size.

Abercrombie & Kent
Clipper Cruise Line
Hanseatic Tours
Hapag-Lloyd Cruises
Marine Expeditions
Noble Caledonia
Orient Lines
Quark Expeditions
Society Expeditions

AROUND BRITAIN

AquaMarin Cruises
Cunard
Curnow Shipping
Deilmann Reederei
Hapag-Lloyd Cruises
Noble Caledonia
Princess Cruises
Radisson Seven Seas Cruises
Raymond & Whitcomb
Royal Caribbean Cruises
Silversea Cruises
Swan Hellenic Cruises
Transocean Tours

AROUND AFRICA

Fred Olsen Cruise Lines

Phoenix Seereisen

SOUTH AMERICA (EAST COAST)

Arcalia Shipping

Celebrity Cruises

Costa Cruises

Crystal Cruises

Cunard

Delphin Seereisen

Hanseatic Tours

Holland America Line

Ivaran Lines

Marine Expeditions

Orient Lines

Phoenix Seereisen

Princess Cruises

Quark Expeditions

Royal Olympic Cruises

Seabourn Cruise Line

Seetours

Silversea Cruises

Transocean Tours

AROUND SOUTH AMERICA

Celebrity Cruises

Crystal Cruises

Cunard

Delphin Seereisen

Hanseatic Tours

Hapag-Lloyd Cruises
Holland America Line
Phoenix Seereisen
Princess Cruises
Seabourn Cruise Line
Seetours
Silversea Cruises
Transocean Tours

WORLD CRUISES (1997)

Crystal Cruises
Cunard
Hapag-Lloyd Cruises
Holland America Line
NYK Cruise Line
P&O Cruises
Peace Boat
Phoenix Seereisen
Transocean Cruise Lines

ROAMING SHIPS

You are just as likely to see the ships of the following companies in Nosy-Be (Madagascar) as in the Amazon, in Greenland, Barcelona, Oslo, Singapore, the Maldives or Seychelles. In fact, all they do all year long is roam the oceans of the world, mostly on non-repeating itineraries of varying cruise lengths.

Abercrombie & Kent
AquaMarin Cruises
Cunard Royal Viking
Delphin Seereisen
Deutsche Seetouristik
Hanseatic Tours

Hapag-Lloyd Cruises

Neckermann Seereisen

Phoenix Seereisen

Seetours

Society Expeditions

Transocean Tours

Northwest Passage

Hanseatic Tours	Hanseatic

Foreword

by David Mott
Passenger Ship Correspondent of Lloyds List

There has probably never been a better time to go cruising if you are looking for a vacation bargain while the cruise industry recovers from a temporary setback.

The North American cruise market, which accounts for more than 80 per cent of the worldwide total, was hit by a downturn in demand in the final few months of 1994 which was as unexpected as it was untypical.

Over the previous 15 years, growth in passenger numbers had been uninterrupted and had averaged just under 10 per cent each year. But the late dip in 1994 left that year with little or no growth; and 1995 fared little better, while 1996 showed more promise.

So 1996 and the following two or three years are crucial if the industry in North America is to return to the growth tack. The reasons for this relative decline are complicated economic factors which can probably be best summed up as the lack of a feel-good factor in a port-recession period which impinges on discretionary spending, such as vacations.

Curiously, these factors have not hit the European or Asian markets which have continued to expand in spite of roughly the same economic considerations.

It is, perhaps, important at this point to put the whole thing in perspective. The industry has not lost ground; it has simply failed to live up to the highly impressive growth rate of the previous decade and a half. Many industry experts believe that such a hiccup was inevitable in an uncertain world. Few doubt that cruising is back on course now that we are approaching the millennium.

Given this scenario, the outlook for those intending to cruise could hardly be better—whether they are first-timers or have a whole string of cruises under their belts. Cruise lines, especially in North America, are bending over backwards to lure passengers to the industry with the sort of deals which would not be available in more certain times.

So the need for a cruise guide such as the Berlitz *Cruising and Cruise Ships* enabling readers to choose the ship best suited to their needs has never been greater, given the bewildering choice of more than 200 ships on which one can cruise.

There is another, more urgent reason why this guide will become increasingly important in the years to come. The current cruise industry order book for major new ships amounts to almost 30 ships, bringing on-line a staggering 50,000 new beds, built at a cost of close to $10 billion.

Major companies like Carnival Cruise Lines and its more upmarket subsidiary Holland America Line, Celebrity Cruises, P&O/Princess Cruises, and Royal Caribbean Cruises feature largely in this array of orders for new tonnage. All are different; all cater for very individual tastes. The only certain way to know which is which is to consult this authoritative and very informative cruise guide.

As we have seen, the problems encountered by the North American market have not occurred in Europe, which is the second largest cruise market providing more than 1.3 million passengers a year. By far the strongest part of this market has been the United Kingdom, followed by Germany, with 480,000 and 309,000 respectively. Although still a relatively small total, both countries have quadrupled their cruise passengers over the last decade.

Indeed, it is true to say that market growth was strong enough to induce P&O to build the prestigious new *Oriana* with an eye to the early years of the next century when UK passenger numbers could well approach one million. Much of this growth can be attributed to a heightened industry awareness. Walk down any British high street 10 years ago and cruising would have been perceived as a minority vacation for the relatively rich. Now travel agents have racks of cruise vacations, emphasizing, not least, the all-inclusive nature of a vacation which, with a little analysis, can be seen to compare favorably with the price of many land-based vacations.

The balance of the world total for cruising is expected to grow rapidly as Southeast Asia takes to the water. Indeed, the number of ships servicing this part of the world has grown rapidly in the last five years, and is set to become a boom marketplace.

There's no better time to consider a cruise vacation than now, and prices will only rise in the future. My advice: read this book thoroughly, go to your travel agent, and start packing for the vacation of a lifetime. See you aboard.

David Mott is the passenger ship correspondent of Lloyd's List, the world's preeminent source of daily shipping information for ship owners and operators. He previously worked for the London *Times* and *Sunday Telegraph*, and is based, not surprisingly, in London.

Why Take a Cruise?

Why is a cruise vacation so popular?

Cruising has become a popular vacation today because it takes one away from the pressures and strains of contemporary life ashore, and offers a means of escape from reality. Cruise ships are really self-contained floating resort cities, but without the crime, and can take you to many destinations in the space of just a few days. The sea has always been a source of adventure, excitement, romance and wonder. It is beneficial and therapeutic, and, because you pay in advance, you know what you will spend on your vacation without any hidden surprises. There's no traffic to deal with, no pollution, no telephone to answer. And the hassles of ordinary travel are almost completely eliminated in one pleasant little package. It's no wonder that 85% of cruisegoers want to go again. And again.

Just who takes a cruise?

Singles, couples, families, honeymooners, second or third honeymooners, groups of friends, are all cruisegoers. Some are probably your next door neighbors.

But isn't cruising for wrinkly old people?

Nothing could be further from the truth. Indeed, the average age of cruise passengers becomes younger each year. Although those of silver years have found cruising to be a very safe way to travel the world, the average age of first-time cruisegoers is now *well under 40*. But do remember that even wrinkly old people can have a lot of fun, too, and many of them have more get up and go than many people under the age of 40!

Won't I get bored?

Usually it's the men that ask this. But get them aboard, and it's almost guaranteed that there won't be enough time in the day to do all the things they want to do (as long as you choose the right ship, for the right reasons). So, whether you want to lie back and be pampered, or go non-stop, you can do it on a cruise vacation, and you'll only have to pack and unpack once.

Is cruising for singles?

Yes indeed. A cruise vacation is ideal for people travelling alone, because it is easy to meet other people in a non-competitive environment. Many ships also have special cabins for singles as well as special add-on rates for single occupancy of double cabins. Some cruise lines will even find a cabin-mate to share with, if you so desire.

Are cruises for honeymooners?

Couldn't be better. In fact, cruising's the ideal setting for romance, for shipboard receptions, and honeymoons. Most decisions are already made for you, so all you have to do is show up. Most ships have accommodations in double, queen, or king sizes, too. And for those on a second honeymoon, many ships now perform a "renewal of vows" ceremony.

Are cruises for children, too?

Absolutely. In fact, a cruise provides families with more quality time than any other type of vacation. Events on board are tailored to various age groups. In addition, a cruise is very educational, and allows children to interact in a safe, crime-free environment, and takes them to destinations in comfortable and familiar surroundings. In fact, you'll have difficulty getting them off the ship at the end of the cruise, if you choose the right ship. And you, as parents (or as a single parent), will be able to get time to enjoy life too. Again, choosing the right ship is most important.

Can I find a quiet, serene cruise, away from children and noise?

Yes, indeed. If you don't like crowds, noise, scheduled activities or long lines, there are some beautiful small ships that are only too ready to cater to your every whim. Perhaps a river or barge cruise would provide the right antidote. There are so many choices.

Are there different classes aboard ship?

Not any more. Gone are the class distinctions and the pretentions of formality of the past. Differences can be found, however, in the type of accommodations chosen, in the price you may be expected to pay for a larger cabin (or suite), and the location of your cabin (or suite).

Can I go shopping in ports of call?

Yes you can. In fact, many passengers engage in "retail therapy" when visiting ports of call such as Hong Kong, Singapore, St. Maarten and St. Thomas, among so many others. Just remember, though, that you'll have to carry all those purchases home at the end of your cruise, as the luggage companies know well enough.

Aren't all ships and cruises quite similar?

Indeed no, far from it. Look through this book and you'll see that ships range from under 200 feet to over 1,000 feet in length. They carry from under 100 to over 3,000 passengers, and facilities vary, quite naturally, according to the size of the ship. The ambiance ranges from ultra-casual to formal. Entertainment, likewise, ranges from amateur dramatics to full-fledged high-tech production shows, from corner cabaret to world-famous headliner, and everything in between.

Isn't cruising expensive?

Cruising can be an all-inclusive vacation, or an almost all-inclusive vacation. If you compare what it would cost on land to have all your meals and entertainment provided, as well as your transportation costs, fitness and sports facilities, and social activities, educational talks, parties and other functions, you'll soon realize the incredible *value* of a cruise vacation. And, remember, a ship is a destination in itself, which moves to other destinations. No land-based resort could ever do that! Ask anyone who has been on a cruise recently, and you'll see. Finally, give yourself a vacation budget, and go to your professional travel agent with it. The rest, as they say, will be taken care of.

Where can I go on a cruise?

Pick any one of 500 destinations in the world, and you'll find a ship and cruise to take you there. A cruise can also take you to places inaccessible by any other means, such as Antarctica, the North Cape, South Sea islands, and many other fascinating destinations.

How to Use this Guide

Why be land bound when you can be cruise bound? Ever since my first transatlantic crossing, in July 1965, aboard Cunard's 83,673-grt *RMS Queen Elizabeth*, the largest passenger ship ever constructed (until the entry in 1996 of Carnival Cruise Line's 100,000-grt *Carnival Destiny*), I have been captivated by passenger ships and the sea. More than 3,800 days, involving some 750 cruises, 140 transatlantic crossings and countless Panama Canal transits, shipyard visits, maiden voyages and ships later, I am even more fascinated by and absorbed in every aspect of cruising and passenger-ship travel.

Cruising is the vacation of the 1990s. For the vacationer, there is simply no better way to get away from it all than on a cruise. Speak to anyone who has taken a cruise before—they'll be very enthusiastic in their praise. So will you—that is, if you choose the "right" ship for the "right" reasons.

That brings me to the purpose of this book: it is intended to be a primary and comprehensive source of information about cruising and the ships and companies that offer to take you away from the pressures, stresses and confines of daily life ashore.

When you first look into taking a cruise, you will be confronted by an enormous and bewildering choice. Don't panic. Simply read through this book carefully. At the end you will be nearer to making the right choice and will leave for your cruise as well informed as most specialists in the industry! In fact, professional cruise sales agents will also find this book a valuable reference source on ships and cruising.

The book is divided into three distinct sections. Parts One and Two comprise 21 chapters and various charts and diagrams; introduce you to the world of cruising; help you define what you are looking for in a cruise; tell you how and where to book and what kind of accommodations to choose; and provide valuable advice on what you should know before you go.

There is a complete picture of life aboard ship and how to get the best from it: the well-known cuisine; the evolution of cruising; nautical terminology; amusing anecdotes; who's who on board, and advice about going ashore. If you are looking for the cruise with a difference—along a river or an adventurous expedition—there is a discussion of these aspects, too, culminating with that ultimate travel experience: the world cruise, and other grand voyages.

Part Three contains profiles of 215 oceangoing cruise ships of the world (including expedition, "soft" expedition cruise vessels and sail-cruise vessels). From large to small, from unabashed luxury to ships for the budget-minded, old and new, they're all here.

The ratings are a painstaking documentation of my personal work, much of it undertaken incognito. To keep this book up-to-date and as accurate as possible, I travel constantly throughout the world and inspect over 100 ships each year, including areas that passengers don't normally see, but which are a necessary part of the total evaluation. This translates to being "on the road" for more than ten months each year.

The ratings are best used selectively—according to your personal tastes and preferences. If cuisine is important to you, or your concern is for entertainment, then these aspects of the ratings will obviously be more significant for you than the overall score or number of stars achieved.

The attraction of cruising is in the variety of opportunities available. This book is intended to help you make an informed choice, given the enormous differences between ships, service standards and cruise lines today.

This book covers the state of the cruise industry through the end of 1996 with a look at 1997 and beyond. It is a tribute to everyone who has made my seafaring experiences possible. In addition, I would like to thank Tom and Gwen Ward (my parents), without whom I would never have gone cruising.

Douglas Ward
June 1996

During the early part of his sea-going career, which started in 1965, Douglas Ward worked on some 15 well-known liners (some of which are no longer in service) as follows:

Andes, 25,689 grt; scrapped in 1971.
Black Watch, 11,209 grt; withdrawn.
Blenheim, 10,420 grt; now *Discovery I*.
Calypso, 20,204 grt; now *OceanBreeze* .
Cunard Countess, 17,593 grt; still in service.
Cunard Princess, 17,495 grt; now *Symphony*.
Franconia, 22,637 grt; now *Fedor Shalyapin*.
Kenya Castle, 19,904 grt; now *Amerikanis*.
Ocean Monarch, 22,552 grt; withdrawn in 1966, scrapped at Kaohsiung in 1975.

Oronsay, 27,632 grt; withdrawn in 1973, scrapped at Kaohsiung in 1974.
Queen Elizabeth, 83,673 grt; withdrawn 1968; caught fire in Hong Kong under suspicious circumstances Feb. 9, 1972.
Queen Elizabeth 2, 70,327 grt; still in service.
Queen Mary, 81,237 grt; withdrawn in 1967, moored alongside at Long Beach, California.
Reina del Mar, 21,501 grt; withdrawn in 1975, scrapped at Kaohsiung in 1975.
Southern Cross, 20,204 grt; now *OceanBreeze*.

PART ONE

What's New in Cruising

The cruise industry continues to grow at a fairly healthy rate (more than 10 per cent a year in Europe, less in North America). For 1997 and beyond, the introduction of new ships will proceed at a dizzying pace (with some 18 new ships due for delivery between January 1997 and January 1999, at a cost of around $5 billion), partly fueled by the phasing out of subsidies to all European shipyards by 1998, and by the expected increase in demand for the high-value cruise vacation product.

New ships incorporate the latest in high-tech electronic equipment, and the best in advanced ship design and construction, and offer passengers an unprecedented choice of facilities, and dining and entertainment experiences.

Several new ships are being provided with either diesel-electric or diesel-mechanical propulsion systems, which propel them at speeds of about 25 knots (few ships can go faster, except for *QE2*, which has a service speed of 30 knots). This equips them for the more attractive long-distance itineraries, and gives them the capacity of having reserve speed when crossing vast stretches of water, such as those of the Atlantic, Indian and Pacific oceans. Among the new ships capable of 25 knots or more are *Grandeur of the Seas*, *Legend of the Seas*, *Oriana*, *Splendour of the Seas*, and *Vision of the Seas*. Diesel-electric power systems have become the power philosophy of choice because of their varied service profile and the tough requirements placed on power used by the various departments of the latest breed of floating hotel. However, it may not be long before gas turbine powerplants are introduced to cruise ships.

EXTERIORS

The curved, indented, and tiered after-decks of P&O Cruises' *Oriana* are stunning, overlooking the aft pool area (more dramatic, but no less practical, than the terraces on Norwegian Cruise Line's well-designed *Dreamward* and *Windward*). Other cruise ships take the "block" approach, and fill in their stern areas with cabins that have an aft-facing view (*Carnival Destiny*, *Century*, *Galaxy*), or multi-level dining rooms with a huge expanse of glass windows, or other public rooms and facilities. More glass areas are being created to provide a link between passenger and sea. *Dawn Princess*, *Enchantment of the Seas*, *Grandeur of the Seas*, *Legend of the Seas*, *Splendour of the Seas*, and *Sun Princess* all have great expanses of glass.

Golfers can enjoy the 6,000 sq. ft. (557.5 m^2), 18-hole miniature golf courses aboard *Legend of the Seas* and *Splendour of the Seas*. The courses are complete with the foliage, grass, sand traps, bridges, water hazards and other "trappings" of a traditional miniature golf course – although there is no room for caddies! Holes range from 155 to 230 sq. ft. (14.3-21.4 m^2). The courses were designed by the same firm that designed the course for the world's largest shopping center, the Mall of America in Bloomington, Minnesota.

Several ships feature electronic golf simulators (*Century*, *Dawn Princess*, *Galaxy*, *Royal Viking Sun*, *Sun Princess*), on which you can play some of the world's best golf courses (for a fee). *Dawn Princess* and *Sun Princess* feature a basketball court in the base of the huge funnel structure.

It's back to the future with the Stargazing Deck aboard Royal Caribbean Cruises' *Legend of the Seas* and *Splendour of the Seas*. Both feature a special starwheel, called a "plani-wheel," created specifically for the line. Located on a forward-facing outdoor deck, passengers can look at the night sky, with charts of the stars and planets in two sections, one each for the northern and southern hemispheres.

INTERIORS

Interiors include such things as a 10-deck-high atrium (*Legend of the Seas*, *Splendour of the Seas*), large theaters with revolving stages and hydraulic orchestra pits (*Carnival Destiny*, *Century*, *Dawn Princess*, *Galaxy*, *Oriana*, *Sun Princess*), and interactive television in cabins (Sony in conjunction with *Century*, *Galaxy*). *Oriana*'s showlounge even has individually air-conditioned seats (the air exiting from each seat-back), while the grand atriums in *Legend of the Seas* and *Splendour of the Seas* connect with a midship Viking Crown Lounge (day lounge/bar and nightclub) at the base of the funnel, a first on any ship. *Oriana* sports the first two-level shop at sea, appropriately called Knightsbridge, with the two levels linked by a spiral staircase.

Deitsche Seetouristik's Aida was introduced in 1996.

Some of the most stunning, bold and graphic interiors continue to be found in the latest ships built for Carnival Cruise Lines. Its *Imagination* has ancient mythological figures such as sphinxes, Medusas, and winged Mercury figures to reflect the refinement of civilizations past. Somehow, lilac neon, mosaics, and multi-colored carpeting all go together here. It's all a feast for the eyes and mind, but for many it could be sensory overkill, though an excellent advertisement for the fiber optic and lighting industries. Carnival Cruise Lines' newest ship, *Inspiration*, features interior decor celebrating the arts, music, painting and literature. Designer Joe Farcus calls it "entertainment architecture."

Indeed, the latest breed of ships have become floating museums, with collections of artwork costing several millions of dollars for each vessel. For example, $3.8 million (*Century*); $2.5 million (*Sun Princess*); $2 million (*Veendam*); $1 million (*Inspiration*). However, it's not the money spent that's important; it's the fact that artwork now forms a more integral part of the physical interior decor than ever before, and particularly so with large ships, with ever larger wall spaces to cover. Some ships (*Dawn Princess, Sun Princess*, for example) have artwork along the passenger accommodations hallways, whereas most other ships leave their hallways bare.

Many cruise lines can now be reached on the Internet. Royal Caribbean Cruises, for example, has over 100 pages for you to browse, including information about the ports of call (much more than is found in the company's brochures). Computers now link almost all departments and functions aboard today's new ships, and the latest in-cabin interactive systems let you order wine and shore excursions, play casino games, and order pay-per-view movies, all from the comfort of your cabin. The only thing computers can't do yet is pour you a drink, although you can order one, accompanied by a light snack. The leading interactive systems for cruise ships are produced by Sea-Vision, a U.S.-based company that is really a network provider.

Ships are now being built to include two atrium lobbies instead of just one (*Carnival Destiny, Galaxy*), while one new ship has a forward observation lounge complete with waterfall, spanning some four decks (*CostaVictoria*). In *Century*, the atrium contains a waterfall with a background of nine large video screens.

In *Dawn Princess* and *Sun Princess*, an aft swimming pool is "layered" over two decks, partly open, partly covered by glass. Several new ships now feature magrodomes, glass-enclosed structures that are used to cover swimming pools in case of inclement weather (*Carnival Destiny, Galaxy, Legend of the Seas, Splendour of the Seas*). These may not be new facilities (*Europa* has one, and *QE2* had one until removed in a 1994 refit), but they do make it possible for cruise passengers to enjoy all-weather swimming. Unlike the sliding multi-fold magrodomes on various other ships, the glass structures used on both *Legend of the Seas* and *Splendour of the Seas* are one-piece affairs.

Several cruise ships already have two-deck-high dining rooms (*Century, Dawn Princess, Galaxy, Legend of the*

DID YOU KNOW ...?

...that Verdi wrote an opera to commemorate the opening of the Suez Canal? Its name is *Aida*.

...that the average time for a ship to pass through the Panama Canal is 8 hours? The fastest transit time was set by the uss *Manley*, at 4 hours and 38 minutes.

...that the first passenger ship to be fitted with stabilizers was the 24,215 grt, 1949-built *Chusan* of the Peninsular & Oriental Steam Navigation Company (P&O)?

...that the first passenger ship to exceed 10,000 grt was the *City of New York* of 1888 (British)?

Seas, Maasdam, Nordic Empress, Ryndam, Splendour of the Seas, Statendam, Sun Princess, Veendam), and more will follow, complete with grand staircases that connect the two levels.

More ships now provide alternative dining spots. At the moment *Asuka, Crystal Harmony, Crystal Symphony, Langkapuri Star Aquarius, Star Pisces,* and *Vistafjord*) already have them, but several new ships will include more dining choices. *Dawn Princess* and *Sun Princess* each have five dining places (*Langkapuri Star Aquarius,* placed into service in 1993, has seven!). Coming in 1998/1999 are *SuperStar Leo* and *SuperStar Virgo*; both will have Chinese and Japanese restaurants, as well as a main dining room, informal lido café, and other dining options. Some ships also have special theme bars/lounges, serving delicacies such as caviar and champagne, cheese, dessert, and pastry items. *Imagination* and *Inspiration* sport 24-hour pizzerias, with an adjacent lounge to supply beer

round-the-clock. The latest Princess ships, *Dawn Princess, Grand Princess,* and *Sun Princess*, also have pizzerias, as will *Disney Magic* (1998).

The physically challenged will be pleased to know that 25 specially adapted cabins catering for their needs have been fitted in *Carnival Destiny.* All are fitted out to the Americans with Disabilities Act (ADA) standards.

Those who are left-handed might be interested to know that half of the cabins aboard *Century* and *Galaxy* have doors that open inward to the left, and half to the right.

Health and fitness spas are now one of the hottest passenger facilities in the latest cruise ships, with more space than ever devoted to them.

In recent years the basic sauna and massage facility has given way to specially designed marine spas providing the latest in high-tech muscle exercising, aerobic, and weight-training machines, and relaxation treatments in a completely "themed" environment. Close by will be the ship's swimming pools and whirlpools.

The latest shipboard spas contain a combination of all or several of these: reception desk, changing area, aerobics exercise room, gymnasium, sauna, steam room, massage and other treatment rooms. Facilities will include all or some of these: a hydrotherapy and thalassotherapy center, jet blitz, rasul (graduated steam and all-body mud cleansing), and other treatment rooms.

In some ships, the beauty salon is adjacent to the spa complex, or contained within it. The latest spas, with their personal treatments and affiliated beauty salon, have become significant revenue-producing areas for both cruise line and concession.

The most common (and popular) location for spas in the latest ships is on an upper deck area with windows that provide ocean views, particularly for exercise areas. Treatment rooms must be flexible so that they can be adapted to incorporate the latest trends (and gimmicks). Traditional Japanese design elements, including a rock garden and shoji screens, provide a serene environment for passengers in the 9,340 sq. ft. (867.6 m²) AquaSpa aboard Celebrity Cruises' *Century*.

What else? Telescopes for stargazing are featured in *Century*, in its forward-facing "Hemispheres" discotheque atop the ship, with its stainless steel "dome" above the dance floor raised in futuristic ceremony every night.

Carnival Cruise Lines was the first, in the spring of 1995, to introduce cash-dispensing ATMs (automated teller machines) aboard some of its largest ships.

Other unusual items include, for example, marine-quality binoculars for passengers in the top suites aboard *Oriana*, and in all passenger "club" category suites in *Asuka*. Umbrellas are provided in all cabins aboard *Silver Cloud*, *Silver Wind*, and *Song of Flower*. Electric shoe cleaning machines are found in all men's public toilets aboard *Kazakhstan II*. The day's weather is provided in each cabin every morning on the small luxury cruise ships such as *Oceanic Grace*, *Sea Goddess I*, *Sea Goddess II*, and *Song of Flower*. The Japanese cruise ships *Asuka*, *Fuji Maru*, *Nippon Maru*, and *Oceanic Grace* all have pull-out (spring-loaded) flashlights for emergency use.

"Standard" cabins *are* getting a little larger. For example, at 170 sq. ft. (15.7 m²) the cabins in *Legend of the Seas* and *Splendour of the Seas* are larger than in any other ships of Royal Caribbean Cruises to date. Those two ships have huge suites measuring some 1,148 sq. ft. (106.6 m²). But the *largest* living quarters aboard any current cruise ship are those in Celebrity Cruises' *Century* and *Galaxy*, where two penthouse suites of 1,173 sq. ft. (109.0 m²) can be expanded to an apartment-sized 1,515 sq. ft. (140.7 m²) by using the adjacent mini-suite and its lockable inter-connecting door. These penthouses also have built-in teleconferencing capabilities. In many ships, more cabins have private balconies than ever before. In *Sun Princess*, for example, there are 750 outside cabins with private balconies.

Cabin bathrooms in the new ship *Aida* (for German-speaking passengers) feature wall-mounted soap and shampoo dispensers, so there is no wastage of throwaway plastic bottles.

Holland America Line has discontinued the cigar humidor service for which they had been known for many years. Cigar smokers will be pleased to learn, however, that Celebrity Cruises has introduced it in *Century*, with all its attendant ceremony, performed by specialists in Michael's Club, a lovely room created just for smokers. Deutsche Seetouristik also has one aboard *Aida*. Non-smokers will be pleased that many ships (particularly those cruising in the Caribbean and Alaska areas) now feature totally non-smoking dining rooms.

Hot destinations? Apart from the usual Caribbean and Alaska cruising areas, there's Europe, with the Baltic and Russia, the Black Sea and the eastern Mediterranean. But the hottest "new" area to be discovered, particularly for European passengers, is perhaps the Arabian Gulf, with ships now calling at Dhahran (Saudi Arabia), Kuwait City (Kuwait), Manama (Bahrain), Abu Dhabi and Sharjah (United Arab Emirates), and Muscat (Oman), not to mention the Red Sea ports of Aqaba (Jordan), Aden and Hodeidah (Yemen). And then there is the mystical South-East Asia, including China, Japan, Thailand, Malaysia, Singapore, and Vietnam. Who said cruising was boring?

In another cruise industry first, Royal Caribbean Cruises has established a "Crown and Anchor Club" in St. Thomas and San Juan. This is to Royal Caribbean Cruises passengers what private lounges are to frequent flying business people. There's no charge for the use of the "club," located in Charlotte Amalie, where passengers can enjoy complimentary tea and coffee, rest in comfortable seating, be able to check their shopping purchases, pick up brochures, purchase spirits, and discuss shopping and tourism questions with the Royal Caribbean Cruises staff in attendance. The company, which has a reputation as an innovator, is expected to expand the program to other ports of call on its cruises. A fine, practical idea.

Another shoreside idea is a definite back to the future project. It is the terminal that is being constructed at Port Canaveral, Florida, in preparation for the two Disney Cruise Line ships on order. The terminal is a re-creation of The Ocean Terminal in Southampton, England, built in the post-war years for Cunard passengers for *Queen Elizabeth* and *Queen Mary*.

FOOD AND SERVICE

Note that on seven-day cruise ships, menu cycles are repeated each week, so if you are considering, for example, two back-to-back seven-day Eastern and Western Caribbean or Mediterranean cruises, the same menu will be repeated for the second week (and, more than likely, so will the whole entertainment program, the cruise director's spiel, jokes, and activities).

Generally, cruise ship food and service has suffered in the past two years, after deep discounting in the North American marketplace. Standards of food quality, presentation, delivery, and service have fallen little by little. Also, because of the acute shortage of waiters who speak good English (the majority of cruise passengers being North American), many cruise lines have had to train personnel from Caribbean basin and Central American countries, whose command of the English language is less than desirable.

While most of the major lines have now realized their mistakes and have made advances in upgrading the food and service aspect of the cruise experience, the large ships (those carrying over 1,000 passengers) cannot seem to deliver what is portrayed in the cruise brochures consistently.

Still on the dining theme, some 2,000 Methuselah-sized bottles (the equivalent of 8 bottles) of Cristal champagne will be specially made for Crystal Cruises' passengers to purchase for the eve of the year 2000. The cost, of course, will be $2,000 each!

WHAT'S NOT SO HOT

Sadly, the cruise industry seems to insist on creating floating resort hotels that travel at night, and are usually in port during the day. There is thus little connection with the sea and nature. Unfortunately, this floating hotel concept has spoiled the nature of the latest cruise ship designs—almost everything is designed to keep passengers *inside* the ship (hopefully to spend money and thus increase on-board revenue).

Keeping passengers inside the ship has created another problem—that of so-called "cruise directors" who insist on interposing themselves into every part of your cruise, both day and night. Public address systems are consistently overused by these aggressive, bouncy youngsters, and are often far too loud, which hardly makes for a restful cruise experience. Some of them

have learned well from past masters, but many of today's cruise directors seem to be unable to communicate with anyone over the age of 30!

Another problem with the homogenous new ships are the cabins. As cookie-cutter standard cabins are all the same basic size (good for incentive planners, but not for individual cruisegoers), they also tend to be the same basic color: eggshell white, off-white, or computer-colored light beige! While such colors are welcome after days in the sun, they are tedious on voyages over long stretches of water. Only the bold bedspreads or the occasional color prints that adorn a spare wall bring relief. Close to useless are the wall-mounted hairdryers in the bathrooms (they seldom have enough directed pressure). They should, instead, be located in the vanity desk or dressing area.

Cookie-cutter ships are also good at assuming that all passengers are of the same basic types. Few cruise lines remain flexible enough to accommodate different tastes and requirements.

Ships in the standard cruise market now charge for all sorts of things they never used to, such as bottled mineral water (few cruise lines make this clear in their brochures), cups of cappuccino and espresso coffees, use of electronic golf simulator, postcards, and pay-per-view movies. Prices seem to keep rising for such things as photographs and medical services (free only aboard Russian or Ukrainian-owned ships).

Non-U.S. cruise passengers sailing on ships catering to Americans should note that the air-conditioning tends to be powerful. Take a couple of sweaters, or some thermal underwear!

One thing that's almost gone by the wayside are the streamers and the free champagne provided at bon voyage parties on deck on sailing day (with the exception of world cruises). Now it's a case of waiters hustling for you to buy a "bon voyage" cocktail. Shame!

Finally, in the seven-day cruise market, particularly from U.S. ports, the disembarkation process still leaves much to be desired, with passengers on large ships complaining that they are unceremoniously dumped ashore with no help after the trying procedure of locating their luggage and customs inspection, and no representation once they get to their respective airport for check-in. Last impressions of these seven-day cruises, therefore, are poor. Worst offenders are: Ft. Lauderdale, Miami and San Juan, with Los Angeles and San Francisco marginally better.

YOUR FIRST CRUISE: WHAT TO EXPECT

If you've never been on a cruise before, allow me to take you through a typical initial embarkation process.

Let's assume that you've arrived at the airport closest to your ship's embarkation point, and retrieved your luggage. There will probably be a representative from the cruise line waiting. You will be asked to place your luggage in a cluster together with other passengers on the same flight as you, or perhaps with passengers on other flights of the same airline, arriving at roughly the same time as yours.

Alternatively, you could have driven to the port of embarkation, in which case you will hand over your luggage to a representative of the cruise line, or to a baggage handler (who may expect a tip). The next time you see your luggage should be aboard ship, where it will be delivered to your cabin.

Head to the registration (check-in) area in the terminal building. For large ships, several desks will be set up. Go to the desk that displays the letter of your surname, wait in line (having filled out all embarkation, registration, and immigration documents), and then check in.

If you are cruising from a U.S. port and you are a non-U.S. citizen or "Resident Alien," you will go to a separate desk to check in. You will be asked for your passport, which you leave with the check-in personnel, but remember to ask for a receipt for it.

If you are cruising from any other port in the world that is not a U.S. port, note that each country has its own check-in requirements, set-ups, and procedures. In any event, once you've checked in, you'll be only a few steps away from your ship and cruise.

Documents in hand, you'll probably go through a security screening device, for both your person and hand luggage. Next, you'll walk a few paces towards the gangway (this may be a covered, airport-type gangway, or an open gangway, hopefully with a net underneath it in case you drop something over the side). It could be flat or steep, depending on the location of the gangway, the tide, etc. When you get to the gangway, you'll probably be greeted by the ship's photographers, a snap-happy team ready to take your photograph. If you don't want to be photographed, say "no" firmly and proceed to the gangway.

Once on the gangway, you'll feel a heightened sense of anticipation. At the ship side of the gangway, you'll find a (hopefully) decorated entrance, and the comfortable feel of cool air-conditioning if the weather is hot. You should also be greeted by well-dressed young men and women of the cruise staff, probably accompanied by an officer or security personnel who will ask for your boarding pass, and your cabin number. Show them your cabin number and a steward should magically appear to take your carry-on luggage from you, and take you directly to your cabin. At last you've arrived.

The door to your cabin should be unlocked and open. If it is locked, ask the steward to obtain the key to open the door. On the newest ships, you'll probably be handed an electronically coded key card, which you insert into the door lock. Once inside the cabin, put down your personal effects and take a good look. Is it clean? Is it tidy? Are the beds properly made? Check under them to make sure the floor is clean. Make sure there is ice in the ice container. Check the bathroom, bath (if there is one), or shower. Make sure there are towels and soap.

If there are problems, bring them to the attention of your cabin steward immediately. Or call the purser's office (or reception desk), and explain the problem, then quietly, but quite firmly request that someone in a supervisory position see you to resolve it.

The housekeeping on cruise ships is generally very good, but sometimes when "turnaround" time is tight, when passengers disembark in the morning, and new passengers embark in the afternoon, little things get overlooked.

One thing you should do immediately is to learn the telephone number for the ship's hospital, doctor, or for medical emergencies, just so you know how to call for help should any medical emergency arise.

Your luggage probably won't have arrived yet (if it's a ship carrying more than 500 passengers), so don't sit in the cabin waiting for it. Once you've oriented yourself with the cabin and its features, put your hand luggage away somewhere, and, deck plan in hand, take a walk.

Familiarize yourself with the layout of the ship. Learn which way is forward, which way is aft, and how to reach your cabin from the main stairways. This is also a good time to learn how to get from your cabin to the outside decks, in case of an emergency. It is likely that a Passenger Lifeboat Drill will be held *before* the ship sails, which is good as your cruise won't be disturbed. In any case, the drill *must* take place within 24 hours after the ship sails from the port of embarkation.

After the drill (you'll find your lifejacket in the cabin, and directions to your assembly station will be posted on the back of the cabin door), you can take off the lifejacket and *relax*. By now your luggage should have arrived.

Unpack, then go out out on deck just before the ship sails. It's always a magical moment, and a good time to meet some new faces. Now, enjoy yourself—you're on a wonderful cruise vacation. You'll soon be ready for that first night dinner. It's just amazing how the sea air gives you an appetite, although there's no truth to the rumor that the sea air seems to shrink your clothes by the end of the cruise.

Cruising: A Backgrounder

In 1835 a curious advertisement appeared in the first issue of the *Shetland Journal*. Under the heading "To Tourists," it proposed an imaginary cruise from Stromness in Scotland, round Iceland and the Faroe Islands, and went on to suggest the pleasures of cruising under the Spanish sun in winter. So it is said that the journal's founder, Arthur Anderson, invented the concept of cruising. Just two years later, Anderson, along with his partner Brodie Wilcox, founded the great Peninsular Steam Navigation Company (later to become P&O).

Sailing for leisure soon caught on. Even writers such as William Makepeace Thackeray and Charles Dickens boarded ships for the excitement of the voyage, and not just to reach a destination. The Victorians had discovered tourism, and they promoted the idea widely. Indeed, Thackeray's account of his legendary voyage in 1844, from Cornhill to Grand Cairo by means of the P&O ships of the day, makes fascinating reading, as does the account by Dickens of his transatlantic crossing in a Cunard ship in 1842. P&O's *Tagus*, which journeyed from London to the Black Sea in 1843, was the subject of Mark Twain's *The Innocents Abroad*, which was published in 1869.

In 1881 P&O's 2,376-ton *Ceylon* was sold to the newly formed Oceanic Yachting Company for conversion into a commercial pleasure yacht capable of sailing round the world—the first pas-

Cunard's Royal Viking Sun *one of the two most highly rated cruise ships in the world.*

senger ship to do so. The ship continued its cruising career after it had been sold to the Polytechnic Touring Association.

Cruising in its more modern sense eventually got underway on March 12, 1889, when the 33,847-ton Orient liners *Chimborazo* and *Garrone* were taken from their normal services to Australia and employed for seasonal cruises to the Norwegian fjords. By 1893 seasonal cruises were also being offered to the Mediterranean, and in 1895 a third vessel, *Lusitania*, was sent on a 60-day cruise around the West Indies, Madeira, Tenerife and the Azores. A year later, Hapag's *Columbia* sailed from Genoa to the West Indies. From then on, both the Orient Line and the Royal Mail Steam Packet Company featured regular cruises for the wealthy. In 1912 the former Orient Line's *Ortona* emerged after refit, operating under Royal Mail as the 8,939-ton *Arcadian* (ex-*Asturias*). With beds for 320 first-class passengers (there was no other class), facilities included a 35-foot-long swimming pool and a three-deck-high dining room.

The first vessel to be built exclusively for cruising was Hamburg America Line's two-funnel yacht, the 4,409-ton *Prinzessin Victoria Luise*. This luxury vessel even included a private suite for the German Kaiser.

Following World War I there was a shortage of ship tonnage, and cruising activities were curtailed, but with one notable exception—Royal Mail's *Arcadian*, which built up an enviable reputation as a British cruise vessel. Among her facilities were a tiled swimming pool and hot and cold running water supplied to every cabin.

One of the first round-the-world cruises was made in 1922-3 by Cunard's *Laconia* (19,680 grt)—a three-class ship that sailed from New York. The itinerary included many of the ports of call that are still popular with world-cruise travelers today. The vessel accommodated 350 persons in each of its first two classes, and 1,500 in third class, giving a total capacity of 2,200 passengers—more than most of the ships of today.

In the 1920s, cruising became the thing to do for the world's well-to-do. Being pampered in such grand style was "in," and is still the underlying concept of cruising. The ship took you and your belongings anywhere, and fed you, accommodated you, relaxed you, and entertained you. At the same time, it even catered for your servants who, of course, accompanied you.

The cruise idyll was helped greatly by Prohibition in the 1930s. After all, just a few miles out at sea you were free to consume as much liquor as you wanted. And cheap three- and four-day weekend "booze cruises" out of New York were preferable to "bathtub gin." Then came short cruises, with destinations as well as booze. In time, the short cruise was to become one of the principal sources of profit for the steamship companies of the day.

During the late 1920s and well into the 1930s ships became floating luxury palaces, offering every amenity imaginable in this era of social elegance. One of the most beautiful flowing staircases ever built was aboard the French liner *Paris* (35,469 grt), constructed in 1921. It is reported that seagulls made this ship their five-star favorite because of its *haute cuisine* garbage.

In the 1930s a battle raged between the giant cruising companies of the world, with Britain, France, Germany and the United States building liners of unprecedented luxury, elegance, glamor, and comfort. Each country was competing to produce the biggest and best afloat. For a time, quality was somehow related to smokestacks: the more a ship had, the better. Although speed had always been a factor, particularly on the transatlantic run, it now became a matter of national ambition.

The first ship designed specifically for cruising from the United States after World War II was *Ocean Monarch* (Furness Withy & Company Ltd.), which was awarded a gold medal by the U.S. Academy of Designing for the "outstanding beauty and unusual design features of a cruise ship." Her maiden voyage was from New York to Bermuda on May 3, 1951. I worked aboard her for a short time.

One of the most renowned cruise liners of all time was Cunard's *Caronia* (34,183 grt), which was conceived in 1948. She was designed and built to offer a transatlantic service in the peak summer months only and then spend the rest of the year doing long, expensive cruises. One of her outstanding features was a single giant mast and one smokestack—the largest of her time—and her hull was painted four shades of green, supposedly for the purposes of heat resistance and easy identification. Known for making extensive world cruises, she was one of the first ships to provide a private adjoining bathroom for every cabin—a true luxury. Lovingly known as the "Green Goddess,"

she was sometimes called the "millionaires' ship."

In June 1958 the first commercial jet aircraft flew across the Atlantic and completely altered the economics of transatlantic travel. It was the last year in which more passengers crossed the North Atlantic by sea than by air. In the early 1960s the passenger shipping directories listed more than 100 ocean-going passenger ship lines, with more than 30 ships featuring transatlantic crossings for the better part of each year. Up until the mid-1960s, it was cheaper to cross the Atlantic by ship than by plane, but the appearance of the jet aircraft changed that rapidly, particularly with the introduction of jumbo jets in the early 1970s.

Today, one major superliner still offers a regular transatlantic service— Cunard's elegant *Queen Elizabeth 2* (70,267 grt). Built in 1969, re-engined and extensively refurbished in 1987, with a major interior refit in 1994, *QE2* offers more than two dozen crossings each year between the ports of New York and Southampton. Occasional calls are made at other U.S. east coast ports, as well as Cherbourg in France and Hamburg in Germany. Besides *QE2*, there are another two dozen or so cruise ships that periodically offer transatlantic crossings, usually twice a year when relocating between cruise areas, such as the Caribbean and the Mediterranean.

The success of the jumbo jets created a fleet of unprofitable and out-of-work passenger liners that appeared doomed for the scrap heap. Even the famous big "Queens," which were noted for their regular weekly transatlantic service, found themselves at risk.

Cunard's *Queen Mary* was withdrawn in September 1967. Her sister ship, *Queen Elizabeth*, at 83,673 grt (until 1990 the largest passenger liner ever built) made her final crossing in October 1968. I was aboard for the last few voyages of this great ship.

The transatlantic shipping companies searched desperately for new ways to employ their aging vessels, but few survived the ever-successful growth of the jet aircraft. Ships were sold for a fraction of their value, and many lines simply went out of business.

Those that did survive attempted to mix transatlantic crossings with voyages south to the sun, drawing on the growing popularity of the Caribbean. Cruising became an alternative, and an entire new industry was born, with new lines being formed exclusively for cruising.

Then came smaller, highly specialized ships, which were capable of getting into the tiny ports of developing Caribbean islands (there were no commercial airlines taking vacationers to the Caribbean then), and which were built to carry a sufficient number of passengers in one single-class arrangement to make money.

Instead of cruising long distances south from northerly ports such as New York, the new lines established their headquarters in Florida. This move enabled them to avoid the cold weather and rough seas of the northern ports and to save on fuel costs with shorter runs to the Caribbean. So, cruising was reborn. California became the base for cruises to the Mexican Riviera, and Vancouver on Canada's west coast became the focus for summer cruises to Alaska.

Flying passengers to embarkation ports was the next logical step, and there soon emerged a working relationship between the cruise lines and the airlines. The air/sea package therefore came into being, with the cruise lines using the jumbo jets for their own purposes. The concept of fly-cruising was introduced in 1960 by Chandris Cruises in the Mediterranean cruise area; these days passengers are flown to almost anywhere in the world to join up with cruises.

Next came the "sail 'n' stay" packages, which are joint cruise and hotel vacations that were all included in the cruise fare. Cruising had become an integrated part of tourism, with ships and hotels offering comfort and relaxation and the airlines providing quick access. Some of the old liners came out of mothballs—purchased by emerging cruise lines. These ships have been refurbished for warm-weather cruising operations, often with their interiors being almost entirely redesigned and refitted.

One of the best examples of the refurbishment of a famous transatlantic liner is Norwegian Cruise Line's *Norway*, formerly the liner *France* (and owned by Compagnie Générale Transatlantique). It has been successfully converted into a Caribbean cruise liner and is a striking sight with its bold redesigns and vibrant colors.

During the late 1970s the cruise industry grew at a rapid rate. It is still expanding today and is, in fact, the fastest-growing segment of the travel industry. Several brand new cruise ships enter service each year, and the growth in new ships being built will continue well into the millennium.

CRUISING TODAY

Today's cruise concept hasn't changed a great deal from that of earlier days, although it has been improved, refined and expanded. Cruises now place more emphasis on destinations and feature more ports. Modern ships are larger, on the whole, than their counterparts of yesteryear, and yet cabin size has decreased in order to provide more space for ship entertainment and other public facilities.

Today's ships boast air-conditioning to keep heat and humidity out, stabilizers to keep the ship on an even keel, an excellent high level of maintenance, safety and hygiene, and more emphasis on health and fitness facilities.

Cruise ship design has moved from the traditional, classic, rounded profiles of the past to extremely boxy shapes with square sterns and towering superstructures. Although ship lovers lament the changes in design, many of these were brought about by a need to fit as much as possible in the space provided—you can squeeze more in a square box than you can in a round one, although it may be less aesthetically appealing. Form follows function, and ships have changed in function from ocean transportation to floating vacation resorts.

With new ships being introduced at the rate of one every few months to cater for the increase in demand for cruises, and old tonnage in the process of being converted, reconstructed or upgraded in order to comply with the latest international safety and hygiene regulations, the choice for cruise vacations has never been more comprehensive, nor more bewildering.

Whatever you enjoy doing, you'll find it on a cruise. Although ships have long been devoted to eating and relaxation in comfort (promulgating the maxim "Traveling slowly unwinds you faster"), cruise lines now offer a great deal more in the way of activities as well as learning and life-enriching experiences than they did several years ago. Also, there are now many more places you can visit on a cruise: from Antarctica to Acapulco, Bermuda to Bergen, Dakar to Dominica, Shanghai to St. Thomas, or if you wish, *nowhere at all*. All told, more than 500 ports are visited by the world's cruise fleet (including 115 in the Aegean/Mediterranean area and 145 in Northern Europe alone).

Although small when compared to the figures for tourism in general, the cruise industry is a $12 billion business worldwide (over $7 billion in the United States alone) and is growing steadily each year. Clearly, cruising is in the mainstream of the vacation industry.

With well over 5 million gross registered tonnes of ships, the global cruise industry provides employment to an increasing number of personnel, both directly (there are over 60,000 shipboard officers, staff and crew, as well as about 15,000 employees in the cruise company head offices) and indirectly (as in the case of suppliers of foodstuffs and mechanical and electrical parts, port agents, transport companies, and also a wide variety of other peripheral workers).

The spin-off effect on tourism in those areas that are adjacent, or close to, the world's principal ports for the embarkation and disembarkation of cruise passengers is tremendous, with direct and indirect benefits to both mainland and island destinations, airlines, railways, bus firms, other transportation systems, hotels, car rental companies, and so on.

In 1996 more than 7 million people worldwide took a cruise, packaged and sold by cruise lines through tour operators and travel agents or cruise consultants. By far the greatest number of passengers were Americans and most of the cruising took place from North American ports. While four times as many Americans still prefer to visit Europe on vacation, cruising is clearly emerging as a highly attractive value-for-money escape.

The most recent (1996) breakdown of passengers by nationality choosing to take cruise vacations is provided below (taken from figures that have been supplied by the Maritime Evaluations Group):

United States	4,600,000
U.K.*	480,000
Asia (not including Japan)	450,000
Germany**	309,000
Canada	250,000
Italy	250,000
Rest of Europe	250,000
Japan	225,000
France	200,000
Australasia	150,000
Cyprus***	75,000
Total	7,239,000 *

*This figure includes the 130,000 British passengers that take 2- to 7-day cruises from Cyprus in conjunction with a resort/hotel stay.
**Includes 91,000 river cruise passengers.
***Local Cyprus market.

In terms of popularity, the Caribbean (including the Bahamas and Bermuda) is still at the forefront of warm-weather cruising, followed closely by Europe (including the Aegean, Mediterranean and Baltic, all of which offer not only sunshine but also historical, cultural and archeological interest). Following this comes Alaska, then comes South-East Asia.

As more and more ships are built, it is likely that some will have to move out of the Caribbean and develop new ports of call or home bases. This expansion promises to make a wider range of cruises available to cruisegoers everywhere.

Ship cruising has come of age. No longer the domain of affluent, retired people, the industry today is vibrant and alive with passengers of every age and socio-economic background. Also, cruising is no longer the shipping business, it is the *hospitality* industry.

CONSTRUCTING A MODERN CRUISE SHIP

More than any other type of vessel, a cruise ship has to fulfill fantasies and satisfy exotic imaginations. It is the job of the shipyard to take those fantasies and transform them into a steel ship— without unduly straining the laws of naval architecture and safety regulations, not to mention budgets.

While no perfect cruise ship exists, turning ship owners' dreams and concepts into ships that embody those ideals is the job of specialized marine architects and shipyards, as well as consultants, interior designers, and a mass of specialist suppliers. Computers have simplified this complex process, which seems to be mostly successful, though shipboard management and operations personnel very often become frustrated with shoreside designers who are more idealist than they are practical.

At one time ships were constructed in huge building docks by being put together from the keel (backbone) up. Today's ships are built in huge sections, then joined together in an assembly area (as many as 50 sections for one of the current ships). The sections may not even be constructed in the shipyard, but they will be assembled there.

Cost is the predominant factor in all ship design and size today. The larger the ship, the more cabins can be incorporated, hence the greater the potential in earnings, both in bookings and on-board revenue. It is said that a 2 per cent increase in cabin capacity on a 1,400-passenger ship could mean an increase of $1–$1.5 million in annual income. But adding more facilities and cabins does increase the weight and cost of a ship.

Ships today represent a compromise between ideals and restrictions of space and finance; the solution, according to some experts, is to design ships for specific conditions of service. That means making a ship to fit a specific operating niche and cruise area, rather than for general use.

Traditionally, passenger spaces have been slotted in wherever there was space within a given hull. Today, however, computers provide the possibility of highly targeted ship design. CAD (computer-aided design) is standard, and enables a new ship to be built

Building a cruise ship. This view shows the keel of the 72,000-grt Galaxy *being laid. Behind her is the 70,606-grt* Century *nearing completion in the massive covered building hall at the Meyer Werft shipyard in Papenburg, Germany.*

within a period of two years, compared to the four or five years needed in the 1950s.

The maximum noise and vibration levels in the accommodations spaces and recreational areas are stipulated in any owner's contract with the shipyard. Global vibration tests are carried out once the ship is built and launched, using what is termed a finite method element of evaluation, which embraces analyses of prime sources of noise and excitation: the ship's propellers and main engines.

In the outfitting of a large cruise ship today, prefabricated cabin modules, including *in situ* bathrooms with toilets, are used. When the steel structure of the relevant deck is ready, with the main lines and insulation already installed, a specific cabin module is then affixed to the deck, and power lines and sanitary plumbing are swiftly connected. All the waste and power connections, together with hot/cold water mixing valves, are arranged in the service area of the bathroom, and can be reached from outside the cabin module from the passageway for maintenance purposes.

While accommodations modules in ships can be successfully systemized, the public spaces cannot. Areas such as food preparation galleys and pantries can, however, be supplied on a turnkey arrangement by outside contractors. They install these highly specialized areas during the fitting out period. Electrical wiring is another area that is normally subcontracted today. In the building of the liner *France* (now called *Norway*), some 18,000 miles of electrical cabling had to be installed.

Numerous contractors and subcontractors are involved during the fitting out period of one of today's cruise ves-

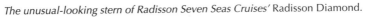

The unusual-looking stern of Radisson Seven Seas Cruises' Radisson Diamond.

sels, the whole being a massive effort of coordination and timing. If just one or two contractors or subcontractors fall behind schedule, it can put the entire shipbuilding process behind, causing as many problems as, for example, a fire or strike would.

CRUISING TOMORROW

A report by the Maritime Evaluations Group (MEG) states that less than 10 per cent of any national population has discovered cruising, but more ships are being constructed every year because of the expected, and growing, increase in popularity. This has led to an over-capacity of (or rather, less demand for) berths in some cruising areas during certain "soft" periods each year, which has kept prices modest and extremely competitive in favor of passengers (in 1995 several cruise lines offered two for one discounts). Since 85 per cent of people who take cruises are eager to go again, the overcapacity should decline as the margin increases.

The average age of all cruisegoers is decreasing, with almost 40 per cent of new passengers under the age of 35. Clearly, this has meant a revamping of on-board facilities and activities for many ships, the provision of more and better health and fitness facilities and programs, and a higher, more international standard of entertainment.

There is a definite trend toward "specialty" cruising, on smaller ships which are equipped to cater to young, active passengers pursuing their hobbies or special interests, such as watersports. Cruise areas are developing for the islands of the South Pacific, the Far East, South America, and around East and West Africa.

As for ship design, current thinking in the industry follows two distinct avenues, both based on the "economy of scale" and on market forces. The economy of scale helps the operator to keep down the cost per passenger. This is the reason for the move toward either large ships that can carry 2,000 passengers or more (*Carnival Destiny, Ecstasy, Fantasy, Fascination, Grand Princess, Imagination, Inspiration, Majesty of the Seas, Monarch of the Seas, Norway, Rhapsody of the Seas, Sensation,* and *Splendour of the Seas,* for example), or smaller luxury vessels that do not accommodate more than 250 passengers (*Oceanic Grace, Renaissance 1-8, Sea Goddess I, Sea Goddess II, Seabourn Legend, Seabourn Pride, Seabourn Spirit, Song of Flower,* for example).

This presumes that some passengers will think "bigger is better," whereas others will think "small and exclusive." Somehow, it is difficult to make a profit out of medium-sized ships in an economically variable environment as in the U.S. (Caribbean) market (but they are ideal for the small ports of the Aegean and the Mediterranean cruise areas); ships that have been delivered during the past few years are either large-capacity mega-ships or small-capacity yacht-like vessels, with only a sprinkling of medium-sized ships.

True, large ships can offer more facilities than small ships, but they can't get into so many ports; and a metropolis at sea, while it might be good for large conventions and meetings, poses a challenge for the individual cruise passenger who simply wants to have a quiet, restful vacation.

SAFETY

Safeguards for cruise passengers include lifeboats and life rafts. Since the introduction of the 1983 amendments to Chapter III of the *Safety of Life at Sea* (SOLAS) *Convention 1974* (which actually came into effect in 1980), much attention has been given to safety, particularly to ships' lifeboats, their design and effectiveness. All cruise ships built since July 1, 1986 have either totally enclosed or partially enclosed lifeboats. The totally enclosed lifeboats have diesel engines that will still operate when inverted.

The latest life rafts, called Hydrostatic Release Units (HRU), were designed in Britain and approved by the Royal Navy, and are now compulsory on all British-registered ships. Briefly, an HRU is capable of automatically releasing a life raft from its mountings when a ship sinks (even *after* it sinks), but can also be operated manually at the installation point, saving precious time in an emergency.

The 1990 SOLAS standards on stability and fire protection (mandating the installation of sprinkler systems) for new ship construction are taking effect in 1997. Existing ships have another five years to comply (the retro-fitting of sprinkler systems is an expensive measure that may not be considered viable by owners of older ships).

A lifeboat drill must be conducted on board within 24 hours of leaving port. You will hear an announcement from the bridge, which goes something like this:

"*Ladies and Gentlemen, may I have your attention, please. This is the captain speaking to you from the bridge. In fifteen minutes time, the ship's alarm bells will signal emergency lifeboat drill for all passengers. This is a mandatory drill, conducted in accordance with the requirements of the Safety of Life at Sea Convention. There are no exceptions.*

"*The emergency signal is a succession of seven or more short blasts followed by one long blast of the ship's whistle, supplemented by the ringing of the electric gongs throughout the ship. On hearing this signal, you should make your way quickly but quietly to your cabin, put on some warm clothing and your lifejacket, then follow the signs to your emergency boat station, where you will be kept fully informed over the loudspeakers through which I am speaking to you now.*"

However, with two cruise companies, Carnival Cruise Lines and Princess Cruises, launching three ships between them that measure over 100,000 grt, the "bigger is better" principle is being pursued for all it's worth, even though these ships might be limited to the Caribbean as they are too wide to transit the Panama Canal.

The "small is exclusive" concept, on the other hand, has now gained a strong foothold, particularly in the luxury category. New specialist lines offer very high quality ships of low capacity. A small-draft vessel can enter ports larger ships can't even approach, and it can provide a highly personalized range of quality services. However, small ships aren't as stable in bad weather, which is why they tend to follow itineraries close to shore.

Some cruise lines have expanded by "stretching" their ships. This is accomplished by taking a ship into dry dock, literally cutting it in half, and inserting a newly constructed midsection. This instantly increases the vessel's capacity, enabling it to add more accommodations space and enlarge public room facilities, with the advantage of maintaining the same draft.

One interesting example of such a ship stretch can clearly be seen in Holland America Line's *Westerdam* (ex-*Homeric*), where the midsection that was built and inserted has larger windows than the fore and aft sections which formed the original ship. *Westerdam* was, in fact, the first ship ever to be stretched in dry dock (in the world's largest covered building dock at Papenburg, Germany). Other examples of ships that have been stretched (all of them done in "wet" dock with

the ship in the water and the new midsection floated into place and then welded together) are: *Black Watch* (ex-*Royal Viking Star*), *Carousel* (ex-*Nordic Prince)*, *Golden Princess* (ex-*Royal Viking Sky*), *Royal Odyssey* (ex-*Royal Viking Sea*) and *Song of Norway*.

Besides the traditional monohull construction of all but one cruise vessel up to now, a switch to multihull and "swath" (small water area twin hull) is most unlikely. Although multihull vessels provide a sound, wide base on which a platform can be constructed, with both accommodations and public areas lying well above the water line, one such example being the twin semi-submersible-hulled *Radisson Diamond*, there has as yet been little attempt to extend this idea.

Whatever direction the design of cruise vessels takes in future, ships, and the companies that operate them, will have to become increasingly environmentally friendly, and passengers will need to be taught to behave accordingly. With growing concern about the environment, particularly in eco-sensitive areas such as Alaska and the South Pacific, better safeguards against environmental pollution will have to be built into the vessels themselves.

The cruise industry is quickly heading toward "zero discharge," whereby nothing is discharged into the world's oceans at all, at any time. This is, naturally, an easier objective to attain for the latest batch of ships (in particular for small vessels). Older ships will have a more difficult time of achieving zero discharge owing to now outdated equipment. The future, however, is in total environment protection through zero discharge.

Choosing Your Ship and Cruise

So, you've decided your next vacation will be a cruise. Good choice! But the decisions don't stop there. Bombarded with glossy cruise literature tempting you with every imaginable lure, and the prolific use of the words "luxury," "gourmet dining," and "fabulous destinations," you may find choosing the right cruise for you difficult.

Whether you are traveling alone, or with your loved one or family, there are different ships to suit different needs. Despite company claims that theirs has been named the "Best Cruise Line" or "Best Cruise Ship," *THERE IS NO SUCH THING*, only what's best, and right, for you.

WHAT A CRUISE IS

A cruise is a vacation. It is an antidote to the stresses and strains of life ashore. It offers you a chance to relax and unwind in comfortable surroundings, with attentive service, good food, and a ship that changes the scenery for you. It is virtually a hassle-free, and, importantly, a crime-free vacation. You never have to make blind choices. Everything's close at hand, and there are always polite people to help you.

WHAT A CRUISE IS NOT

Some cruises simply aren't relaxing, despite cruise brochures proclaiming that "you can do as much or as little as you want to." Watch out for the high-density mega-ships that carry 2,000 or more passengers—or older ships with limited public room space; they tend to cram lots of passengers into small cabins and provide non-stop activities that do little but insult the intelligence and taste buds, and assault the pocket.

How do you begin to select the right cruise for the right price? Price is, of course, the key factor for most people. The cost of a cruise provides a useful guideline to the ambiance, passengers, and degree of luxury, food and service that you'll likely find on board.

The amount you are prepared to spend will determine the size, location, and style of the shipboard accommodations you will be assigned. Be wary of cruise lines that offer huge discounts—it either means that the product was unrealistically priced at source, or that there will be a reduction in quality somewhere. Remember, discount the price, and you end up with discounted quality. Aside from cost, ships are as individual as fingerprints: each one can change its "personality" from cruise to cruise, depending on the character of passengers on the ship.

Fellow passengers encompass all types of personality and lifestyle, from affluent, reserved, mature, to active, fun-loving, and youthful, or family-oriented, or conservation-minded, or adventurous, or wild fun seekers. They could be well traveled or otherwise, or they may be honeymooners on their first cruise, or veteran cruisgoers who cruise several times a year.

WHERE TO?

With approximately 500 destinations available to cruise ships, there's almost certainly a ship to take you wherever you want to go. Because itineraries vary widely, depending on each ship and cruise, it is wise to make as many comparisons as you can by reading the cruise brochures for descriptions of the ports of call. If, for example, you would like a Caribbean or a Mediterranean cruise, it is possible to choose from over 100 itineraries.

Several ships may offer the same, or similar itineraries, simply because these have been successfully tried and tested. You can then narrow the choice further by noting the time spent at each port, and whether the ship actually docks in port or lies at anchor. Then compare the size of each vessel and its facilities.

Caribbean and Mediterranean Cruises

These are usually destination-intensive cruises that cram between four and eight ports into one week, depending on whether you sail from a Florida port, or from a port in the Caribbean, such as Barbados or San Juan. This means you could be visiting at least one port a day, with little time at sea for relaxation.

This kind of intensive "island hopping" leaves little time to explore a destination before you have to be back on board. While you see a lot of places in a week, by the end of the cruise you may need another week to unwind. Ultimately, this is not the best way to cruise, unless you really wish to cover a lot of ground in a short space of time.

Although not stated in any cruise line brochure, you should be aware that June to November in the Caribbean are the months of the hurricane season.

Private Islands

Several cruise lines with Caribbean itineraries have their own "private island" (often called an "out-island")—a small island in the Bahamas close to Nassau (or in the Turks and Caicos Islands) that is outfitted with all the

Crystal Cruises' Crystal Symphony, seen here alongside at Bermuda's West End. (Photo D. Ward)

ingredients to make an all-day beach party a memorable occasion. These are extremely popular with passengers, with watersports, scuba, snorkeling, crystal-clear waters, warm sands, even a hammock or two. And there are no reservations to be made, no tickets to purchase, no hassle with taxis.

Norwegian Cruise Line was the first to use an out-island, in 1977. But Disney Cruise Lines, whose first ship debuts in January 1998, promises to have the most extensive facilities of all on its private island (which is wholly owned, not leased, like most).

Cruise lines have their own inventive names for these islands, such as Blue Lagoon Island, Great Stirrup Cay, Princess Cays, Royal Isle. Some of the out-islands change names, depending on what day of the week it is, and what ship is in. You should note that the beaches, while idyllic for 200 passengers, can prove very noisy and crowded when filled with 2,000 or more passengers from one of the large ships, anchored for a "Beach Barbecue Day."

These private island beach days are not all-inclusive, and cruise lines now charge high rates for everything, including snorkeling gear (and mandatory swimvest), all pleasure craft, and such things as "banana" boat fun rides.

European Cruises

If you are planning to go to Europe (including the Baltic, Black Sea, Mediterranean, and Norwegian fjord areas), traveling there by cruise ship makes economic sense. So many of Europe's greatest cities—among them Amsterdam, Barcelona, Copenhagen, Genoa, Helsinki, Lisbon, London, Monte Carlo, Nice, Oslo, St. Peters-burg, Stockholm, and Venice—are on the water, and it is much less expensive to take a cruise than to fly and stay in decent hotels. Another advantage is that you won't have to try to speak or understand different languages when you are aboard ship as you would ashore (if you choose the right ship).

Ships with under 1,000 passengers are arguably better than large ships, as they will be able to get berthing space (larger ships may have to anchor in many small ports, which means it will take you more time to get to and from shore). On some itineraries, one company may give you more time ashore than another, so it pays to compare cruise brochures. On ships that cater to passengers of different nationalities, daily programs, and announcements, will be in as many as six languages.

Alaska Cruises

For a real cold rush, try an Alaska cruise. Some ships must anchor rather than dock in several ports of call, because of the limited amount of docking space. Some lines also may pay more in fees so that their ships can dock alongside, making it easier for passengers to go ashore; this is useful when the weather is poor. Most cruise brochures unfortunately don't indicate which ports are known to be anchor (tender) ports (European, and particularly German, brochures are much better at providing this information).

Two of the major cruise companies, Holland America Line and Princess Cruises, both have such comprehensive shoreside facilities—hotels, tour buses, and even trains—that they are committed to Alaska for many years. Holland America Line-Westours and

55

Holland America Line's 1,212-passenger Noordam, seen here in Glacier Bay, Alaska.

Princess Tours (a division of Princess Cruises) have invested between them over $250 million in Alaska (Holland America Line-Westours is the state's largest private employer). Other lines must therefore depend on what's left of the various forms of local transportation for their shoreside tours.

Sadly, there is now so much congestion in the tiny Alaskan ports (more than 400,000 cruise passengers visited Alaska in 1996), where there can be several ships in port on any one day, that avoiding crowded streets becomes an unpleasant part of the cruise experience. Even nature is retreating; with more humans around, wildlife is becoming harder to spot.

Transcanal Cruises

Transcanal cruises will take you through the Panama Canal, which was constructed by the United States after the failure of a French effort started by Ferdinand de Lesseps. The French labored for 20 years, beginning in 1880, but disease and financial problems defeated them. The United States took over the canal building effort in 1904 and the waterway opened just 10 years later on August 15 1914. The Panama Canal runs from northwest to southeast, and the best way to experience this engineering wonder is from the deck of a cruise ship.

Cruising from the Caribbean to the Pacific, your ship will be lifted 85 feet (26 m) in a continuous flight of three steps at Gatun Locks to Gatun Lake, through which it will travel to Gaillard Cut where the Canal slices through the Continental Divide. It will be lowered at Pedro Miguel Locks 31 feet (9.4 m) in one step to Miraflores Lake and then the remaining two steps to sea level at Miraflores Locks before passing into the Pacific Ocean. Ships move through the locks under their own power guided by towing locomotives, and the 50-mile (80-km) trip across the Isthmus of Panama takes about nine hours in all.

Australasia and Orient Cruises

If you like the idea of Australasia, South-East Asia and the Orient, and you live in Europe or North America, be aware that the flying time to your port of embarkation and ship will be long. It is advisable to arrive at least two days before the cruise, as the time changes and jet lag can be quite severe. The area has so much to offer that it's worth taking a cruise of a minimum of 14 days to make the most of it.

Choose an itinerary that appeals to you, and then read about the proposed destinations and their attractions. Your cruise or travel agent will be able to provide some of the essential background on destinations and help you select an itinerary. Australia, New Zealand, the islands of the South Pacific, Hong Kong, China, Japan, Indonesia, Malaysia, and Thailand offer superb cruise destinations.

HOW LONG?

On many ships, the standard of luxury, comfort, and service is generally in direct proportion to the length of the cruise. In order to operate long, low-density voyages, cruise lines must charge high rates to cover the extensive preparations, high food and transportation costs, port operations, fuel and other expenditures. The length of cruise you choose will depend on the time and money at your disposal and the degree of comfort you are seeking.

The popular standard length of cruise is seven days, although trips vary from two-day party cruises to a slow exotic voyage around the world lasting up to 180 days. If you are new to cruising and want to "get your feet wet," you might try a short cruise of three or four days first. This will give you a good idea of what is involved, the kind of facilities and the lifestyle on board. Note that a three- or four-day cruise from an American port such as Miami, Ft. Lauderdale, Los Angeles or San Juan, or from the Greek port of Piraeus, could end up as a bit of an endurance test. It's fine if you like non-stop activities, but it is hardly what you need if all you want to do is to relax.

WHICH SHIP?

Because cruise ships (particularly the larger ones) are self-sufficient resorts, there really is a cruise line, cruise, and ship to suit virtually everyone, so it is important to take into account your own personality when selecting a ship.

Ships are measured (not weighed) in gross register tonnes (grt) and come in a variety of sizes, as follows:

intimate, for up to 250 passengers (generally under 10,000 grt)
small, for 250-500 passengers (generally 10,000-20,000 grt)
medium, for 500-1,000 passengers (generally 20,000-35,000 grt)
large, for 1,000-2,000 passengers (generally 35,000-70,000 grt)
mega-ship, for over 2,000 passengers (generally 70,000-100,000-plus grt)

Whatever the physical dimensions, all cruise ships provide the same basic ingredients: accommodations, activities, entertainment, food, good service, and ports of call, although some of them do it much better than others.

There are a few "all-inclusive" ships where there really are no bar bills to pay, nothing to sign for, no gratuities to give, and no standing in line to sign up for shore excursions, but these tend to be the smaller "luxury" cruise ships that cost upwards of $500 per person, per day (although some suites on larger "standard" market cruise ships can easily cost that). Once you're on board, you may never have to ask "how much?" Most of the larger cruise ships, however, will entice you in many ways to spend money on board, which is one way that cruise lines manage to support their low fares.

If you want or need a lot of space around you, it is of little use booking a cruise on a small, intimate ship where you knock elbows almost every time you move. If you like intimacy, close contact with people and a homey ambiance, you may feel lost and lonely on a large ship.

To get an idea of the amount of space you'll have around you aboard ship, look at the Passenger Space Ratio given in the evaluation of each ship in Part Three of this book. A Passenger Space Ratio of 50 and above is the ultimate in terms of space per passenger; 30 and above can be considered very spacious; between 20 and 30 is moderately so; between 10 and 20 would be high density; and below 10, extremely cramped, as in "sardine-style."

THE BIG SIX CRUISE LINES

Cruise lines with large ships (those catering to more than 1,000 passengers) all offer one thing: a well-packaged cruise vacation (generally of seven days) that includes attractive itineraries, plenty of food, a good standard of entertainment and production shows, use of all the ship's facilities, and so on. Most ask you to pay port taxes, insurance, and gratuities to staff, over and above the actual cruise fare, as well as for many additional items.

Where they differ, however, is in the facilities, space, food, and service they offer, together with subtle differences in the delivery of the cruise product.

While it is impossible to detail all the differences between these and other cruise lines, here are some of the principal ones between the "Big Six" North America-based cruise lines. Please note that changes, upgrading and downgrading of products and services may have occurred since the completion of this book.

Carnival Cruise Lines

The largest cruise line in the world specializes in cruises for the young at heart, with constant upbeat music, and passenger participation games typical of an adult summer camp atmosphere. Some could be taken to be potentially degrading, but they are well liked by passengers who associate such noisy activities with "fun." No cushioned deck pads for deck chairs are available.

With cookie-cutter ships, the company does a fine job in providing activities to make you either a) thirsty or b) gamble. If you don't mind drinks in plastic glasses, and basic hamburger/hot dog-style fast foods in abundance, this line will provide it for you well. The company provides excellent "dazzle and sizzle" production shows and a lot of nighttime entertainment options for party people.

INTIMATE: UNDER 250 PASSENGERS
(BASIS 2, INCLUDING SINGLE CABINS)

	Number of Passengers Basis 2	Passenger Tonnage Ratio	Space
Alla Tarasova	100	3,985	39.8
Americana	88	19,203	218.2
Antonina Nezhdanova	96	3,941	41.0
Bali Sea Dancer	143	3,852	26.9
Bremen	164	6,752	41.1
Caledonian Star	120	3,095	25.7
Carina	168	7,127	42.4
Explorer	100	2,398	23.9
Hanseatic	184	8,378	45.5
Hebridean Princess	48	2,112	44.0
Hong Kong Dragon Star	250	7,560	30.2
Kapitan Dranitsyn	112	12,288	109.7
Klaudia Yelanskaya	104	3,941	37.8
Le Ponant	56	1,489	26.5
Lili Marleen	30	750	25.0
Megastar Aries	80	3,300	41.2
Megastar Taurus	80	3,300	41.2
Mikhail Sholokhov	234	9,878	42.2
Nantucket Clipper	102	1,471	14.4
Oceanic Grace	120	5,218	43.4
Orient Star	96	3,941	41.0
Polaris	82	2,214	27.0
Professor Khromov	38	2,142	56.3
Regina Maris	174	4,007	23.0
Renaissance One	100	3,990	39.9
Renaissance Two	100	3,990	39.9
Renaissance Three	100	3,990	39.9
Renaissance Four	100	3,990	39.9
Renaissance Five	114	4,280	37.5
Renaissance Six	114	4,280	37.5
Renaissance Seven	114	4,280	37.5
St. Helena	96	6,767	70.4
Sea Cloud	69	2,532	36.6
Renaissance Eight	114	4,280	37.5
Royal Star	222	5,360	24.1
Sea Goddess I	116	4,260	36.7
Sea Goddess II	115	4,260	36.7
Seabourn Legend	212	9,975	47.0

Seabourn Pride	204	9,975	48.8
Seabourn Spirit	204	9,975	48.8
Sir Francis Drake	28	450	16.0
Song of Flower	214	8,282	38.7
Star Clipper	170	3,025	17.7
Star Flyer	170	3,025	17.7
Wind Song	148	5,703	38.5
Wind Spirit	148	5,703	38.5
Wind Star	148	5,703	38.5
World Discoverer	138	3,153	22.8
Yamal	100	20,646	206.4
Yorktown Clipper	138	2,254	16.3

SMALL: 250-500 PASSENGERS
(BASIS 2, INCLUDING SINGLE CABINS)

Andaman Princess	276	5,097	18.4
Astra	282	5,635	19.9
Astra II	460	10,563	22.9
Atalante	484	13,113	27.0
Azerbaydzhan	460	15,065	32.7
Berlin	422	9,570	22.6
Black Prince	446	11,209	25.1
Club Med I	386	14,745	38.1
Club Med II	392	14,745	37.6
CostaPlaya	489	12,475	25.5
Daphne	412	9,436	22.9
Dimitriy Shostakovich	278	10,303	37.0
Don Juan	448	10,000	22.3
Fuji Maru	328	23,340	71.1
Funchal	439	9,563	21.7
Kareliya	472	15,065	31.9
Kazakhstan II	474	16,500	34.8
Konstantin Simonov	278	9,885	35.5
Kristina Regina	276	3,878	14.0
Minerva	392	12,000	30.6
Odysseus	454	12,000	26.4
Orient Venus	390	21,884	56.1
Orpheus	304	6,000	19.7
Princesa Amorosa	284	5,026	17.6
Queen Elini	416	6,497	15.6
Radisson Diamond	354	20.295	57.3
Royal Seas	452	15,402	34.0

Sapphire	500	11,125	22.2
Silver Cloud	296	16,800	56.7
Silver Wind	296	16,927	57.1
Stella Oceanis	300	6,000	20.0
Vistamar	295	7,478	25.3

MEDIUM: 500-1,000 PASSENGERS
(BASIS 2, INCLUDING SINGLE CABINS)

Aegean Dolphin	576	11,563	20.0
Albatros	940	24,803	26.3
Arkona	516	18,591	36.0
Astor	590	20,158	34.1
Asuka	584	28,717	49.1
Ausonia	506	12,609	24.9
Black Watch	832	28,078	34.2
Bolero	758	16,107	21.2
Calypso	502	8,000	15.9
Constitution	796	30,090	37.8
CostaAllegra	810	28,430	35.0
CostaMarina	772	25,441	32.9
CostaRiviera	924	31,500	34.0
Crystal Harmony	960	48,621	50.6
Crystal Symphony	960	50,202	52.2
Cunard Countess	812	17,593	21.6
Cunard Dynasty	800	19,089	23.8
Dolphin IV	588	13,000	22.1
Enchanted Isle	729	23,395	32.0
Europa	600	37,012	61.6
Fairstar	976	23,764	24.3
Gripsholm	714	22,785	31.9
Independence	809	30,090	37.1
Island Princess	610	19,907	32.6
Italia Prima	540	15,000	27.7
Ivan Franko	580	20,064	34.5
La Palma	648	11,608	17.9
Leeward	950	25,000	26.3
Leisure World	730	16,254	22.2
Marco Polo	848	20,502	24.1
Maxim Gorki	650	24,981	38.4
Mermoz	533	13,691	25.6
Monterey	600	21,051	35.0
Nautican	510	15,271	29.9

Nippon Maru	408	21,903	53.6
OceanBreeze	782	21,486	27.4
Ocean Majesty	535	10,417	19.4
Olympic	976	31,500	32.2
Pacific Princess	610	20,646	33.8
Princesa Marissa	628	10,487	16.6
Princesa Victoria	566	15,007	26.5
Princess Danae	544	17,074	31.3
Regal Empress	875	22,979	26.2
Rhapsody	804	17,495	21.7
Royal Viking Sun	740	37,845	51.1
SeaBreeze I	842	21,900	26.0
Seawind Crown	728	24,568	33.7
Seawing	754	16,607	22.0
Shota Rustaveli	493	20,499	41.5
Southern Cross	720	17,270	23.9
Star/Ship Atlantic	972	35,143	36.1
Stella Solaris	620	17,832	28.7
Sun Viking	714	18,556	25.9
Superstar Gemini	820	19,046	23.2
Symphony	664	16,495	24.8
Taras Shevchenko	574	20,027	34.8
The Azur	665	14,717	22.1
Triton	756	14,155	18.7
Universe Explorer	740	23,879	32.2
Victoria	714	28,891	40.4
Vistafjord	677	24,492	36.1

LARGE: 1,000-2,000 PASSENGERS
(BASIS 2, INCLUDING SINGLE CABINS)

Aida	1,186	38,600	32.5
Canberra	1,399	44,807	32.0
Carousel	1,062	23,200	21.8
Celebration	1,486	47,262	31.8
Century	1,750	73,606	42.0
CostaClassica	1,308	52,950	40.4
CostaRomantica	1,356	53,049	39.1
CostaVictoria	1,950	74,000	37.9
Crown Princess	1,590	70,000	44.0
Dawn Princess	1,950	76,500	39.2
Disney Magic	1,950	85,000	48.5
Dreamward	1,246	39,217	31.4

Enchantment of the Seas	1,950	74,000	37.9
EugenioCosta	1,012	32,753	32.3
Galaxy	1,908	74,000	38.7
Grandeur of the Seas	1,954	73,600	37.6
Holiday	1,452	46,052	31.7
Horizon	1,354	46,811	34.5
IslandBreeze	1,146	38,175	33.3
Jubilee	1,486	47,262	31.8
Langkapuri Star Aquarius	1,530	40,022	26.1
Legend of the Seas	1,804	70,950	39.3
Maasdam	1,264	55,451	43.8
Meridian	1,106	30,441	27.5
Nieuw Amsterdam	1,210	33,930	28.0
Noordam	1,210	33,930	28.0
Nordic Empress	1,600	48,563	30.3
Norwegian Crown	1,052	34,242	32.5
Oriana	1,828	69,153	37.8
Queen Elizabeth 2	1,756	70,327	40.0
Regal Princess	1,590	70,000	44.0
Rotterdam	1,114	38,645	34.6
Royal Majesty	1,056	32,396	30.6
Royal Princess	1,200	44,348	36.9
Ryndam	1,264	55,451	43.8
Seaward	1,534	42,276	27.5
Sky Princess	1,200	46,314	38.5
Song of America	1,402	37,584	26.8
Song of Norway	1,004	23,005	22.9
Splendour of the Seas	1,804	69,130	38.8
Star Pisces	1,530	40,022	26.1
Star Princess	1,470	63,564	43.2
Star/Ship Oceanic	1,180	38,772	32.8
Statendam	1,264	55,451	43.8
Sun Princess	1,950	77,000	39.4
Tropicale	1,022	36,674	35.8
Veendam	1,264	55,451	43.8
Viking Serenade	1,512	40,132	26.5
Westerdam	1,494	53,872	36.0
Windward	1,246	39,217	31.4
Zenith	1,374	47,255	34.3

**MEGA-SHIP: OVER 2,000 PASSENGERS
(BASIS 2, INCLUDING SINGLE CABINS)**

Carnival Destiny	2,642	100,000	26.4
Ecstasy	2,040	70,367	34.4
Fantasy	2,040	70,367	34.4
Fascination	2,040	70,367	34.4
Grand Princess	2,600	104,000	40.0
Imagination	2,040	70,367	34.4
Inspiration	2,040	70,367	34.4
Majesty of the Seas	2,354	73,941	31.4
Monarch of the Seas	2,354	73,941	31.4
Norway	2,044	76,049	37.2
Rhapsody of the Seas	2,000	75,000	37.5
Sensation	2,040	70,367	34.4
Sovereign of the Seas	2,354	73,192	31.0

The cabins throughout the fleet are of a good standard size. Bed linen is 50 per cent cotton/50 per cent polyester, while towels are 100 per cent cotton. The company delivers *exactly* what it states in its brochures – nothing more, nothing less. Carnival will help you have fun all the way, but don't expect the finesse you might find on other lines.

Celebrity Cruises

Celebrity Cruises has established an excellent reputation for its cuisine, although its daytime buffets are not nearly as good as when the line first started. However, all meals *are* made from scratch, and no pre-packaged or pre-prepared items are used at all, an admirable achievement. The waiters are well trained, and it's easy to communicate with them. There are several tables for two in the dining room. The dining room chairs, however, do not have armrests.

The line provides real glasses, and 100 per cent cotton towels in all cabin bathrooms, while bed linen is a 50 per cent cotton/50 per cent polyester mix. Bathrobes are supplied only to suite passengers. Three ships in its present five-ship fleet have outdoor wrap-around promenade decks (exceptions: *Century*, *Galaxy*). The ships are kept spotlessly clean, and passengers notice staff vacuuming and polishing almost every hour of the day and night. The artwork is of a very high standard.

Holland America Line

This line features teakwood outdoor promenade decks fleetwide, while many other cruise lines feature astro-turf, or some other form of indoor-outdoor carpeting. The ships are kept very clean.

The food is reasonable, but not memorable. Food quality, presentation and service has decreased somewhat in recent years. Dining room service is provided too fast by friendly Indonesian waiters. The line offers free ice cream at certain hours of the day and features Starbucks coffee, an American favorite. The company's claim to "five star" ships is misleading. Yes, the ships are extremely good, and have an elegant "feel" to them, but the product has suffered of late, due to lack of supervision and staff training.

Cabins are of good proportions, and nicely equipped. The towels are of 86 per cent cotton, 14 per cent polyester, while bed linen is 50 per cent cotton/50 per cent polyester. However, 100 per cent cotton face cloths are provided in the public restrooms.

Norwegian Cruise Line

This line provides a good product for a youthful, active, sports-minded audience. Most of the staff are from the Caribbean basin, and the service provided does not in general have the finesse of those ships with a greater percentage of European staff.

The cabins are generally very attractive, although closet and drawer space is somewhat limited in the newest ships. Towels are of 86 per cent cotton/ 14 per cent polyester (though face cloths are of 100 per cent cotton), while bed linen is a mix of 50 per cent cotton/50 per cent polyester.

While the dining room cuisine is generally non-memorable, light fare is available in an informal "bistro" setting aboard all ships in the fleet.

Costa Cruises' 810-passenger CostaAllegra cruises the Mediterranean, and offers a dramatic wall of glass in the restaurant at the stern of the ship.

Princess Cruises

Despite billing itself as "The Love Boat," Princess Cruises does not have any tables for two in its dining rooms (exceptions: *Dawn Princess, Grand Princess, Sun Princess*). The cuisine in general is not really memorable, but its pasta dishes are very good.

The well-equipped cabins are of generous proportions (exceptions: *Dawn Princess, Sun Princess*). Bathrobes are provided for all passengers, on all of the company's ships, as are real glasses in the bathroom. Towels are of 86 per cent cotton/14 per cent polyester (face cloths are, however, of 100 per cent cotton), while bed linen is 50 per cent cotton/50 per cent polyester.

The company's Shore Excursion Program is arguably the best run of any of the major companies noted here.

Royal Caribbean Cruises

Standard cabins are small (the latest two, *Legend of the Seas* and *Splendour of the Seas*, have much larger cabins). The company places more emphasis than most on passenger participation activities, such as a Passenger Talent Show, Masquerade Parade, Country & Western Jamboree, and so on.

While Royal Caribbean Cruises' food is of a better standard than that aboard Carnival Cruise Line ships, Carnival ships have larger cabins, as do the ships of Celebrity Cruises, Holland America Line and Princess Cruises.

Towels are of a mix of 84 per cent cotton and 16 per cent polyester; bed linen is a 50 per cent cotton/50 per cent polyester mix.

WHAT THE BIG SIX DON'T PROVIDE

- Bathrobes for all passengers (exception: Princess Cruises).
- Flowers in your cabin (unless you are in the top suites).
- Real glasses in the cabin bathrooms (exceptions: Celebrity Cruises and Princess Cruises). The others provide plastic glasses.

- Non-allergenic pillows.
- Tableside carving and flambeau items.
- Cappuccino and espresso coffees and bottled water in the dining room at no charge.
- Self-service launderettes (exceptions: Carnival Cruise Lines and Princess Cruises).

LARGE SHIPS vs SMALL SHIPS

Large Ships: Advantages

- Large ships have the widest range of public rooms and facilities, often an outdoor wrap-around promenade deck, and more space.
- Large, new ships have state-of-the-art electronic interactive entertainment facilities and options.
- They generally sail well in open seas in inclement weather conditions.
- There are more activities for people of all ages, particularly children.

Large Ships: Disadvantages

- Trying to find your way around the ship can prove frustrating.
- You'll find plenty of lines to wait in; for embarkation, purser's office, buffet meals, shore tenders, shore excursions, and disembarkation.
- The largest ships are like hotels, with many items at extra cost.
- Signage is often confusing; there is a lack of elevators at peak times.
- The larger the ship, the more impersonal the service (unless you have "butler" service in a penthouse suite).

- It's more difficult to meet people on different meal sittings.
- Dining room chairs will probably be close together, with waiters and bus boys buzzing constantly.
- The dining room staff will be so programmed to provide speedy service, it's almost impossible to sit and dine in a leisurely fashion.
- The food will probably be quite bland.
- Trying to phone for room service can be frustrating (particularly those ships with automatic telephone answering systems that state "your call will be answered by room service personnel in the order it was received").
- Room service breakfast is not generally available on the day of disembarkation.
- Almost all large ships close their swimming pools at 6:00 p.m. Some even take away all the deck chairs.
- When the ship is at anchor, you'll probably need to stand in line, or wait in a lounge, with a "tender ticket" to go ashore by ship-to-shore craft. This can take an hour or more on some ships!

Small Ships: Advantages

- They are more like small inns than mega-resorts.
- They are easy to find your way around, and signage is usually clear and concise.
- They are at their best in warm weather areas.
- They can truly cater to the highest degree of culinary excellence, with fresh foods cooked individually to order.

- If they provide an "open seating" in the dining room, you can sit with whomever you wish, whenever you wish, for all meals.
- They provide a totally unstructured lifestyle. They offer a level of service not found on most larger ships.
- They provide an "open bridge" policy, allowing passengers to go on the navigation bridge at almost any time (except during difficult maneuvers and in cases of difficult weather conditions).
- Some small ships have a hydraulic marina watersports platform located in the stern. They also carry equipment such as jet skis, windsurfers, a waterski power boat, and scuba and snorkeling gear.
- When the ship is at anchor, going ashore is easy and speedy, with a continuous tender service.

Small Ships: Disadvantages

- They do not have the bulk, length or beam to sail well in open seas in inclement weather conditions.
- They do not have the range of public rooms or open spaces that large ships can provide. Options for entertainment, therefore, are somewhat limited.

SMALL (INTIMATE) CRUISE SHIPS: THE CRÈME DE LA CRÈME

CUNARD
Sea Goddess I (4,260 grt; 116 passengers; PSR: 36.7)
Sea Goddess II (4,260 grt; 116 passengers; PSR: 36.7)

HANSEATIC TOURS
Hanseatic (8,378 grt; 160 passengers; PSR: 52.3)

RADISSON SEVEN SEAS CRUISES
Song of Flower (8,282 grt; 214 passengers; PSR: 38.7)

RENAISSANCE CRUISES
Renaissance 1/2/3/4 (3,990 grt; 100 passengers; PSR: 39.9)
Renaissance 5/6/7/8 (4,280 grt; 114 passengers; PSR: 37.5)

SEABOURN CRUISE LINE
Seabourn Legend (9,975 grt; 212 passengers; PSR: 47.0)
Seabourn Pride (9,975 grt; 204 passengers; PSR: 48.8)
Seabourn Spirit (9,975 grt; 204 passengers; PSR: 48.8)

SHOWA LINE
Oceanic Grace (5,218 grt; 120 passengers; PSR: 43.4)

COMPARABLE FEATURES

All the above ships have similar facilities and features, including an "open bridge" policy and totally unstructured environments, which means you are not asked to participate in any scheduled activities.

All feature outside cabins only (usually but incorrectly called "suites" by most "upscale" cruise companies, as they are really well-equipped luxury cabins), with two beds, which, when placed together, can form a queen-sized bed. The cabin accessories, which include fluffy cotton bathrobes, hairdryer, color television, VCRs, and flowers and fruit (replenished daily), are also common to all. On most of these ships, you can go from your cabin to other parts of the ship (apart from the restaurant) in your bathrobe during the day. But after 6 p.m., passengers become more formal,and enjoy dressing for dinner and social evenings.

Cabins in *Hanseatic, Oceanic Grace, Renaissance 1-8, Seabourn Legend, Seabourn Pride*, and *Seabourn Spirit* have the lounge sitting area adjacent to a large picture window. Aboard *Sea Goddess I* and *Sea Goddess II* the bedroom is adjacent to the window and the lounge area is adjacent to the picture window.

Cabin bathrooms in *Song of Flower* are smaller and more difficult to maneuver in than on the other ships (the "half-tubs" are deep and more difficult to get into and out of). Cabin bathrooms in *Seabourn Pride* and *Seabourn Spirit* have two washbasins. Those in *Hanseatic, Oceanic Grace, Renaissance 1-8, Seabourn Legend, Sea Goddess I, Sea Goddess II*, and *Song of Flower* have one.

Cabin windows in *Seabourn Pride* and *Seabourn Spirit* have electrically operated blinds. Those in *Hanseatic, Seabourn Legend, Sea Goddess I*, and *Sea Goddess II* are manually operated. *Oceanic Grace, Renaissance 1-8*, and *Song of Flower* have no blinds.

Aboard *Sea Goddess I, Sea Goddess II*, and *Song of Flower* all liquor, champagnes, wines, as well as soft drinks, are included in the cruise fare. Aboard *Seabourn Legend, Seabourn Pride* and *Seabourn Spirit*, only wines, spirits and soft drinks for in-cabin use are included when you first embark. Soft drinks are provided free afterwards, while everything else that is consumed in public rooms is charged for (at low prices). The Sea Goddesses aim to deliver an all-inclusive product—which they do—although port taxes and insurance are, strangely, extra.

Afternoon tea aboard *Sea Goddess I* and *Sea Goddess II* is superior to that on all the other small luxury ships. Most serve tea in a silver pot (quite incorrect, as tea should be served only from a bone china or porcelain teapot). *Seabourn Legend, Seabourn Pride*, and *Seabourn Spirit* provide individual bone china pots in the casual dining area, while in the more formal dining room, and for afternoon tea, silver pots (fine for coffee, never for tea) are used.

In the dining room, tableside flambeaus are featured aboard *Hanseatic, Seabourn Legend, Seabourn Pride, Seabourn Spirit, Sea Goddess I,* and *Sea Goddess II*, but not aboard *Oceanic Grace, Renaissance 1-8* or *Song of Flower*. All the ships mentioned above usually offer full room-service breakfast. This is not usually the case on large ships.

All have watersports facilities, but only *Seabourn Legend, Seabourn Pride*, and *Seabourn Spirit* feature a floating, enclosed aft marina pool, and air-conditioned mahogany shore tenders (the two tenders on *Oceanic Grace* also have a shower). However, the marinas are frequently impractical as they can be used only in flat calm sea conditions.

If you are thinking about a long cruise on one of these intimate-sized vessels, do remember that they are really like a tiny village rather than a large town. But if you like people, they can be the epitome of fine living at sea.

NEW VS OLD SHIPS

Some executives in the cruise industry, whose fleets comprise new tonnage, are often quoted as saying that all pre-1960 tonnage should be scrapped. Yet many passengers prefer the older-style ships. While it is inevitable that some older tonnage cannot match up to the latest in high-tech section-built ships, ships today are simply not constructed to the same high standards, or with the same loving care, as in the past. Below are some advantages and disadvantages of both.

New Ships—Advantages

- They incorporate the latest in high-tech electronic equipment and the best in advanced ship design and construction.
- They meet the latest safety and operating standards, as laid down by the international maritime conventions.
- They offer passengers more public room space, with public rooms and lounges built out to the sides of the hull, as open and closed promenade decks are no longer regarded as an essential requirement.
- They have public room spaces that are easier to convert if necessary.
- They offer more standardized cabin layouts and fewer categories.
- They are more fuel efficient.
- They manage to incorporate the latest advances in technology, as well as the latest in passenger and crew facilities and amenities.
- They do have a shallower draft, which makes it easier for them to enter and leave ports.

- They have bow and stern thrusters, so they seldom require tug assistance in many ports, in this way cutting operating costs.
- They have new plumbing and air-conditioning systems that work.
- They have diesel engines mounted on rubber to minimize vibration.
- They are usually fitted with the latest submersible lifeboats.

New Ships—Disadvantages

- They do not "take the weather" as well as older ships. Because of their shallow draft, these ships roll.
- They tend to have smaller standard cabins, which can mean narrow—and very often short—beds.
- Their thin hulls don't withstand bangs and dents as well as older, more heavily plated vessels.
- They have decor made mostly from synthetic materials (due to stringent fire regulations), which may cause problems for those passengers who are sensitive to such materials.
- They are powered by diesel engines, which inevitably cause some vibration; although on the latest vessels, the engines are mounted on pliable, floating rubber cushions and are therefore virtually vibration-free.
- They have cabin windows that are completely sealed instead of portholes that can be opened.

Older Ships (pre-1970)—Advantages

- They have very strong, plated hulls (often riveted) that can withstand tremendously hard wear and tear. They can "take the weather" well.

- They have large cabins with long, wide beds/berths.
- They have a wide range of cabin sizes, shapes, and grades.
- They are powered by steam turbines, which are virtually free of vibration or noise.
- They have portholes that, in many instances, actually open.
- Their interiors are built using more traditional materials such as wood and brass, with less use of synthetic fibers.
- They have deep drafts, which help them to achieve a smooth ride in the open seas.

Older Ships (pre-1970)— Disadvantages

- They are not so fuel efficient, and therefore they are more expensive to operate than the new ships.
- They need a larger crew, because of the more awkward labor-intensive layouts of the ships.
- They have a deep draft (necessary for a smooth ride), but need tugs to negotiate ports and tight berths.
- They have increasing difficulty in complying with the current international fire, safety, and environmental regulations.
- They are usually fitted with older-type open lifeboats.
- Any vessel that is over 10 years old may have problems with plumbing and air-conditioning.

The International Maritime Organization (IMO), a United Nations agency, was formed in the late 1940s to vote in legislation among its 130-plus member nations regulating the safety of life at sea. The IMO Safety Committee has voted to bring older ships up to date by making various safety features— such as smoke detectors—mandatory in all cruise vessels. From 1994, and covering an 11-year period, all vessels are required to fit sprinkler systems (this is an expensive retrofit for many older ships), and provide automatic navigation bridge control of fire doors.

THE CREW

A ship's country of registration or parent company location can be a clue to the atmosphere on board, although many ships are registered, for financial reasons, under a flag of convenience, such as Liberia or Panama.

You can estimate the standard of service by looking at the crew to passenger ratio. Better service will be found on those ships with a ratio of one crew member to every two passengers, or higher.

Except for those ships with a single-nationality crew, you can expect the language proportions on board to be something like as follows: 38 per cent European, 36 per cent North/South American, 26 per cent Asian.

MAIDEN/INAUGURAL VOYAGES

There is an element of excitement in taking the plunge on the maiden voyage of a new cruise ship, or in joining the inaugural voyage of a recently refurbished, or reconstructed, or stretched vessel, or in exploring a new cruising area. But although it can be exciting, there is usually an element of uncertainty in any first voyage. Of course many things can, and do, go awry. Then again, there are maiden voyages that have no major problems.

If you are a repeat cruisegoer who isn't phased by some inconvenience, fine; otherwise it is best to wait until the ship has been in service for at least two or three months. However, if you book a cruise on the third or fourth voyage, and the ship's introduction is delayed, you could find yourself on the maiden voyage! One thing is certain— any maiden voyage is a collector's item.

So, what exactly can go wrong?

- A strike, or fire, or a bankruptcy at a shipyard are possible causes of delay to a new ship or a completely new cruise line about to embark on its first venture. Ship introductions such as *Club Med I*, *Crown Monarch*, *Crown Dynasty* (now *Cunard Dynasty*), *Ecstasy*, *Fantasy*, *Marco Polo*, *Nieuw Amsterdam* as well as the eight small Renaissance vessels were all delayed by shipyard strikes and bankruptcies, while *Astor* (now called *Arkona*), *Crown Dynasty*, and *Monarch of the Seas* were delayed as a result of extensive fires while still being fitted out.
- Service on new or recently refurbished ships or a new cruise line is likely to be uncertain, and could be a complete disaster. An existing cruise line may use experienced crew from its other vessels to help "bring out" a new ship, but they may be unfamiliar with the ship's layout and have problems training other staff.

- Plumbing and electrical items tend to cause the most problems, particularly on reconstructed and refurbished vessels. For example, toilets don't flush, or don't stop flushing; room thermostats have mistakenly been fitted with reverse wiring; "automatic" telephones refuse to function, and so on.
- The galley (kitchen) of a new ship causes perhaps the most consternation. Even if everything does work, and the executive chef has ordered all the right ingredients and supplies, they could be anywhere other than where they should be!
- "Software" items such as menus or remote control units for television and/or video systems, door keys, towels, glassware, and perhaps even toilet paper, may be missing.

THEME CRUISES

If you still think that all cruises are the same, the following list will give you an idea of what is available in the way of special theme cruises:

Adventure	Fashion
Archeological	Food and Wine
Art Lovers	Gay/Lesbian
Backgammon	Holistic Health
Big Band Bridge	Jazz Festival
Chess Tournament	Maiden Voyage
Chocoholics	Movie Buffs
Classical Music	Murder Mystery
Computer Science	Naturalist
Cosmetology	Photographic
Country and Western	Singles
Diet and Nutrition	Square Dancing
Educational	Steamboat Race
Exploration	Theatrical

Sea Goddess I, and sister ship Sea Goddess II, are two of the highest-rated intimate cruise ships in the world. Sea Goddess I, is seen here going through London's famed Tower Bridge.

Perhaps the most successful theme cruise of all is the annual Classical Music Cruise aboard *Mermoz* (Paquet Cruises), organized by André Borocz, who is himself an accomplished musician. Famous classical musicians who have been engaged to perform (or sing) on the cruise have included Annie Fisher, Isaac Stern, James Galway, Jean-Pierre Rampal, Mystislav Rostropovich, Tamas Vasary, Maurice André and Vladimir Ashkenazy. Shore excursions consist of concerts in some of the world's most beautiful settings.

For jazz enthusiasts, the most comprehensive cruise is the Annual Floating Jazz Festival in October aboard *Norway* (Norwegian Cruise Lines), featuring performers such as Clark Terry, Gary Burton, Joe Williams, Jimmy McGriff, Lee Konitz, Lou Donaldson, Jimmy Giuffre, Stanley Turrentine, and Dick Hyman. Other music styles that are gaining popularity at sea include Country and Western, Rhythm 'n' Blues, and '50s and '60s music cruises.

Always check with your travel agent your proposed ship and sailing dates, particularly if you don't want to be with lots of theme cruise vacationers.

SIGNS YOU'VE CHOSEN THE WRONG SHIP

- When, after you've embarked, a waiter hands you a drink in a tall plastic glass from a whole tray of ones of identical color and froth, then gives you a bill to sign and doesn't even have the courtesy to say "Welcome Aboard."
- When the so-called "luxury" cabin you booked has walls so thin you can hear your neighbor combing his hair.
- When you wanted a quiet, restful cruise, but your travel agent has put you on a ship with 300 baseball fans (solution: read this book thoroughly first!)
- When you packed your tuxedo, but the ship's passengers take "formal" attire to mean clean cut-off jeans and a less stained T-shirt.
- When the "medical facility" consists of a box of plasters.
- When you have a cabin with an "obstructed view," and it is next to or below the disco. Or laundry.
- When the "Fresh Selected Greens" on the menu means a sprig of parsley on the entrée plate.

- When you have to buy shin pads to prevent injury in case 600 children run you over in the passageways.
- When the Evian water bottle on your dining room table comes with a bill ever so quickly if you dare open it.
- When "Fresh Catch of the Day" means the fish is so old that it would be best used as a door wedge.
- When the brochure says "Butler Service," but you have to clean your own shoes, get your own ice, and still tip him double the amount you would for a cabin steward.
- When the Beer Drinking Contest, the Hog Calling Contest, Knobbly Knees Contest, and Pajama Bingo are listed as "enrichment lectures."
- When the brochure says tipping is not required, but your waiter and cabin steward tell you otherwise, and threaten they'll break your kneecaps if you don't hand them a large sum of money.
- When, on the final day the words "early breakfast" mean 5:00 a.m., and "vacate your cabin by 7:30 a.m." means you spend about three hours sitting in the showlounge waiting for disembarkation, with 500 available seats, your hand luggage and 2,000 other passengers.
- When the Lifeboat Drill consists of some crew member handing you a lifejacket and asking you to teach him how to wear it, and then asking you what the whistle's for.
- When you're out on deck, you look up and notice a big hole in the bottom of one or more of the ship's lifeboats.
- When the cabin steward tries to sell you a time-share in his uncle's coal mine, at a reduced price, or go without soap and towels for a week.
- When the "five-course gourmet meal" turns out to be five courses of salty chicken soup.
- When the "Deck Buffet" literally means that there are no tables and chairs, only the deck, to eat off.
- When the brochure shows photos of smiling young couples, but you and your partner are the only ones under 80.
- When the library is located in the engine room.
- When the captain tells you he isn't licensed to sail the ship.

The 212-passenger Seabourn Pride, one of three sister ships in the Seabourn Cruise Line fleet, offers a superb, elegant environment for refined living at sea.

Booking Your Cruise

TRAVEL AGENTS

Many people think that travel agents charge for their services. They don't (perhaps they will, soon), but they do earn commission from cruise lines for booking their clients on a cruise.

Can I do my own booking direct with the cruise line? Yes and no. Yes, you can book your cruise direct with a small number of cruise lines (mostly in Europe/Asia/Japan), and no, because most of the cruise lines do not generally accept personal checks, thus in effect requiring you to book through a travel agent; in the United States, 95 per cent of cruise bookings are made by travel agents.

A good travel agent will probably ask you to complete a profile questionnaire. When this is done, the agent will go through it with you, perhaps asking you some additional questions before making suggestions about the ships and cruises that seem to match your requirements.

Your travel agent will handle all matters relevant to your booking, and off you go. You may even find a nice flower arrangement in your cabin on arrival, or a bottle of wine or champagne for dinner one night, courtesy of the agency.

Consider your travel agent as your business adviser, not merely as a ticket agent. As a business adviser, a travel agent should have the latest information on matters such as changes of itinerary, the cruise fares, fuel surcharges,

discounts, and any other related items, and should also be able to arrange insurance (most important) just in case you have to cancel prior to sailing. Some cruise lines now have a totally automated booking system by computer. Some are linked into the computer systems of major airlines and allow agents access to almost all shipboard information, and even displays details such as cabin dimensions and if there is a porthole or window.

10 Questions to ask your travel agent

1. Is air transportation included in the cabin rate quoted? If not, what will be the extra cost?
2. What extra costs will be involved? (These can include port charges, insurance, gratuities, shore excursions, laundry, drinks).
3. What is the cruise line's cancellation policy?
4. If I want to make changes to my air arrangements, routing, dates, etc., will the insurance policy cover me for everything in case of missed or canceled flights?
5. Does your agency deal with only one, or several different insurance companies?
6. Does the cruise line offer advance booking discounts or other incentives?
7. Do you have preferred suppliers, or do you book any cruise on any cruise ship?

8. Have you sailed on the ship I want to book, or that you are recommending?
9. Is your travel agency bonded and insured? If so, by whom?
10. If you book the shore excursions offered and recommended by the cruise line, what insurance cover is provided?

CRUISE CONSULTANTS

Remember, there is *no* "Best Cruise Line in the World," or "Best Cruise Ship," only the ship and cruise that's right for *you*. It's the job of your cruise agent or travel agent to find exactly the right ship for your needs. They're all out there, but there's a more bewildering choice than ever before.

A number of cruise-only agencies—often called "cruise consultants"—have sprung up in the last few years. While most are reputable, some sell only a limited number of cruises. These are "preferred suppliers" because they may be receiving special "overrides" on top of their normal commission. If you have chosen a ship and cruise, be firm and book exactly what you want, or change agencies. In the U.K., go to a member of the Guild of Professional Cruise Agents. PSARA (the Passenger Shipping Association of Retail Agents) provides in-depth agent training in the U.K., as well as a complete "bonding" scheme to protect passengers from failed agencies or cruise lines. In the United States, look for a member of NACOA—the National Association of Cruise Only Agents (note that in the U.S. most agencies are not "bonded" in case of failure).

Many traditional travel agencies now have a special cruise section, with a knowledgeable consultant in charge. A good agent will help you solve the problem of which cabin you should choose, but be firm in the amount you want to pay, or you may end up with a larger and more costly cabin than you had originally intended.

In the United States, CLIA (Cruise Lines International Association) is a marketing organization with about three dozen member lines, which does an admirable job providing training seminars for some 25,000 members of cruise/travel agents throughout North America.

CRUISE BROKERS

Cruise brokers (also known as cruise consolidators or cruise discounters) are useful for making last-minute bookings. They often have unsold cabins at substantially discounted rates. Most brokers have low overheads, being equipped with only a phone and automated message services. British cruise-goers can look at Teletext, on television channels 3 and 4, for information on travel companies offering discounts (Note: this is *not* an endorsement of these companies). Do not send any money to the cruise agency until you have received a written invoice which details all the key items.

If you're looking for full service, and help in choosing a cruise, then a cruise broker isn't for you; but if you *can* book at the last minute, a cruise broker may save you a substantial amount of money. But what you gain in price you may lose in choice—of dinner sittings,

DID YOU KNOW ...?

...that the first "en suite" rooms (with private bathroom in cabin) were on board Cunard Line's *Campania* of 1893?

...that the first ship-to-shore wireless telegraphy took place on an American passenger ship, *St. Paul*, in 1899?

...that the last three-funnel passenger ship was the Cunard/White Line's *Queen Mary* (1939–1967)?

cabin category and location, and other arrangements. You may also have to pay your airfare to join the cruise.

If you do book your cruise through a large consolidator or packager, you should find out exactly who is responsible for getting you where you are supposed to be at the right time. Read the fine print.

The cruise line/operator/packager may seem, initially, to be responsible, but there are no set standards within the industry at present and legal requirements vary from country to country. The best advice is to make sure you read the fine print when booking. If you have complicated travel arrangements, you must make sure that the cruise line provides you with a list of contacts for every stage of your journey.

RESERVATIONS

Rule number one: do plan ahead and book early. After you have chosen a ship, cruise, date, and cabin, the agency will ask for a deposit—roughly 10 per cent for long cruises, 20 per cent for short cruises (most cruise lines ask for a set amount, such as $250).

When you make your initial reservation you should also make any special dining request known, such as your seating preference, whether you would prefer the smoking or non-smoking sections or any special dietary requirements. The prices quoted in cruise brochures are based on tariffs current at the time the brochures are printed. All the cruise lines reserve the right to change these prices in the event of tariff increases, fluctuating rates of exchange, fuel surcharges, or any other costs which are beyond their control.

Confirmation of your reservation and cruise fare will be sent to you by your travel agent. The balance is normally requested 45 to 60 days prior to departure, depending on individual line policy. For a late reservation, you have to make payment in full as soon as space is confirmed. Shortly after full payment has been received by the line, your cruise ticket (if applicable) will be issued, along with baggage tags and other items.

When it arrives, check your ticket. In these days of automation, it is prudent to make sure that the ship, date, and cruise details you paid for are correctly recorded. Also it always is wise to verify that any connecting flight times are okay.

EXTRA COSTS

You will read brochures boldly proclaiming that "everything's included," but in most cases you'll find that this isn't strictly true.

Your fare covers things such as ship transportation, landing and embarkation charges, cabin accommodations, all meals, entertainment, and service on board. With very few exceptions, it does not include alcoholic beverages, laundry, dry cleaning or valet services, shore excursions, meals ashore, gratuities, port charges, cancellation insurance (this covers you only if the cruise itself is canceled by the cruise line or the tour operator), optional on-board activities such as skeet shooting, bingo or horse-racing and casino gambling, or special features or conveniences that were not mentioned in the cruise line's brochure.

On most cruise ships, you should expect to spend about $25 per day per person on extras, plus another $10-$12 per day per person in gratuities. This can add up to as much as $500 per couple on a seven-day cruise. Genuine exceptions are some of the intimate ships (those carrying fewer than 250 passengers), where just about everything *is* included.

Here are some examples of typical extra costs:

Cappucino/Espresso	$1.50-$2.50
Dry-Clean Dress	$3.00-$7.50
Dry-Clean 2-Piece Suit	$4.50-$7.50
Golf Simulator (30 mins)	$15.00
Hair Wash/Set	$17.00-$28.00
Haircut (men)	$20.00
Ice Cream	$1.00-$3.75
In-cabin movies	$6.95
Laundry Soap	$0.50-$1.00
Massage	$1.00 per minute (plus tip)
Satellite Phone/Fax	$6.95-$15.50 per minute
Souvenir Photo	$6.00-$8.00
Trapshooting (3 or 5 shots)	$5.00, $8.00
Wine/Cheese Tasting	$5.00
Wine with Dinner	$7.00-$500
Bottled Water	$2.50-$4.50

In order to calculate the total cost of the cruise you've chosen, not including any of the extra-cost services you might decide you want once on board, read the brochure and, with the help of your travel agent, make up a list of the costs that might be involved. Below are the approximate prices per person for a typical seven-day cruise on a well-rated medium or large cruise ship. This estimate is based on an outside two-bedded cabin:

Cruise fares	$1,500
Port charges	$100 (if not included)
Gratuities	$50
Total per person	$1,650

Divide this by seven and you get an average cost of $235 per person per day. For this price, you would not even find a half-decent hotel room in New York City!

DISCOUNTS AND INCENTIVES

Looking at the fares listed in current cruise line brochures is only just the starting point. Because of overcapacity in certain cruise markets at specified times of the year (such as at the beginning and at the end of the summer) cruise discounts and special incentives are widespread. It is wise to enlist the eyes and ears of a good travel agent and check out current discounts.

One way of saving any money is to book well ahead, so that you can profit from one of many variations on the "super savers" theme. Many cruise lines now offer larger discounts for those that book the farthest ahead, with discounts decreasing as the date of the cruise comes closer. Another method is to reserve a cabin grade, but not a specific cabin—booked as "tba" (to be assigned). Some lines will accept this arrangement and they may even upgrade (or possibly have to down-grade) you on embarkation day if all the cabins in your grade have been sold. It is useful to know that the first cabins to be sold out are usually those at minimum and maximum rates.

Another way of economizing is to wait for a "stand-by" cabin on sailing day or shortly earlier. Some lines offer stand-by fares 30 days before sailing (60 days for transatlantic crossings). They may confirm a cabin (some lines even assign the ship) on the day of embarkation.

Those who can go suitcase-in-hand to the dockside might be lucky enough to get on at a minimum rate (or less) and be assigned a last-minute cancellation of a high-grade cabin.

For cruises to areas where there is year-round sunshine, there is an "on" and an "off" season. Naturally, the best cruise buys are in the off season, while the on season commands the highest prices. Some lines offer a "shoulder" season, which is somewhere between the on and off seasons. Peak season is during the Christmas and New Year vacation. Check with your travel agent to get the best rate for the time you wish to go.

Many of the cruise lines offer highly reduced rates for third and fourth persons sharing a cabin with two full-fare adults. Individual policy varies, so ask your travel agent for current rates. On some sailings, they might even go free.

Many cruise lines also have their own versions of "frequent passenger" clubs. You can join most without a fee (some, like Celebrity Cruises' Captain's Club, make a charge of $25), and you will be notified first of any special offers that are being made. Discounts can frequently be as high as $1,500 per cabin, so it's worth belonging to a club, especially if you like cruising with a particular line.

Most cruise fares are listed as "per person double occupancy" or "ppd." If you are single and wish to occupy a double cabin on your own, you may have to pay a single supplement (see *Cruising for Romantics*).

However, many lines will let you share a cabin at the standard ppd rate. The line will find you a cabin partner of the same sex, and you can both save money by sharing. The line cannot, however, guarantee that you'll like your partner, but they will invariably specify which cabin categories they have available for sharing.

For those wishing to take their children on a cruise, there are some excellent bargains available for families (see *Cruising for Families*).

CANCELLATIONS AND REFUNDS

It is highly recommended that you take out full cancellation insurance (if it's not already included), as cruises (and air transportation to and from them) must be paid in full before your tickets are issued. Without such insurance, if you cancel at the last minute, even for medical reasons, it generally means that you will lose the entire amount. Insurance cover can be obtained from your travel agent for a nominal charge.

Cruise lines usually accept cancellations that are notified more than 30 days before sailing, but all charge full fare if you don't turn up on sailing day, whatever the reason. Other cancellation fees vary from 10 to 100 per cent, depending on the cruise and length of trip. Curiously, many cruise lines do not return port taxes, which are *not* part of the cruise fare.

If you cancel with sufficient notice due to serious medical problems, a doctor's letter should be obtained. This is usually regarded sympathetically by cruise lines.

MEDICAL INSURANCE

Whether you intend to travel overseas or cruise down a local river, and your present medical insurance does not cover you, you should look into extra coverage for your cruise. A "passenger protection program" is a service usually prepackaged by the cruise line, and the charge for same will appear on your final invoice unless you decline. This is worth every penny, and it typically covers such things as evacuation by air ambulance, high-limit baggage, baggage transfers, personal liability, and missed departure.

PORT TAXES/HANDLING CHARGES

These are assessed by individual port authorities and are generally shown with the cruise rates for each itinerary. Port charges will be part of the final payment for your cruise, although they can be changed at any time up to the day of embarkation. The most expensive port charge at the time of press was Bermuda, at $60 per passenger (in 1994, some 589,855 passengers visited this tiny island). The typical handling charges for a cruise ending in America, for example, include a U.S. Customs User/Federal Inspection Fee for each passenger.

AIR/SEA PACKAGES

When your cruise fare includes a one-way or round-trip air ticket, the airline arrangements usually can't be changed without having to pay considerably more toward the fare. This is because cruise lines often book space on aircraft on a special group basis in order to obtain the lowest rates. Changing your air ticket or flight within 30 days of your cruise will mean having to pay a surcharge to the cruise line of about $25 per person.

If you do change your ticket, remember that in the event of the airline canceling your flight, the cruise line is under no obligation to help you or return your cruise fare if you don't reach the ship on time. If you are joining a ship in a far-off country, allow several extra days (particularly during the winter) just to cover the risk that your domestic airline connections don't work as planned or are canceled altogether.

Because of the group-fare ticket basis by which cruise lines work, be aware that this can also mean that the airline routing to get you to your ship may not always be direct or non-stop. The airlines' use of this hub-and-spoke system can be extremely frustrating for cruise passengers. Because of changes to air schedules, cruise and air tickets are often not sent to passengers until a few days before the cruise. A small number of upscale cruise lines include business-class air tickets.

In Europe, air/sea packages generally start at a major metropolitan airport, while some include first-class rail travel to the airport from outlying districts. In the United States, it is no longer necessary for passengers to depart from a major city, since many cruise lines will include connecting flights from small suburban airports as part of the whole package.

There are many variations on the air/sea theme, but all have the same advantage of offering passengers an all-inclusive price, even down to airport-to-ship transfers and port charges.

Most cruise lines offer the flexibility of jetting out to join a ship in one port

and flying home from another. This is especially popular for Mediterranean, transcanal (Panama Canal) and long cruises. Cunard even has a transatlantic program that lets you cruise one way and then fly back the other. They have taken the idea even further by allowing you to return on specially selected, supersonic Concorde flights for a small additional charge.

Another advantage of almost every air/sea package is that you only have to check in your baggage once—at the departure airport—for even the baggage transfer from plane to ship is handled for you. This does not, however, include intercontinental fly/cruises, where you must claim your baggage at the airport on arrival in order to clear it through customs.

You may be able to hold an open return air ticket, which allows you to make either a pre- or post-cruise stopover. This depends on the type of contract that exists between a cruise line and its airline partner. Usually, however, you have no stopovers en route, nor can you even change flights.

Whenever the price of an air/sea package is all-inclusive, it is often presented as "free air" in publicity material. Of course, there really is no such thing as a free air ticket—the cost of the air fare is simply hidden in the overall cruise fare.

However, air tickets are not always included. Some cruise lines do not believe in increasing their rates to cover "free air" or they simply may wish to avoid subsidizing airline tickets. These are, for the most part, upmarket lines that operate long-distance cruises to some of the more exotic destinations. In some countries (such as Germany), the term "free air" cannot appear in advertisements by law.

PRE- AND POST-CRUISE PROGRAMS

To extend your cruise, it may be worth looking into the extra stay programs that are offered by many cruise lines. These can be taken either before or after your cruise, and can add another dimension to your cruise vacation.

Hotel add-ons are well noted in most cruise brochures, but you will need to look deeper in order to find some of the more unusual add-ons.

These can include some of the world's most famous and luxurious trains, for example. Such trains as the famed Orient Express (which travels between Venice, London or Paris), the Eastern and Oriental Express (which runs between Bangkok and Singapore), or the Royal Scotsman (which connects London and Edinburgh, with the possibility of additional train cruises around Scotland) can all add a welcome and extremely scenic land perspective to any luxury cruise.

THE COLOR OF SEAWATER

Seawater is colorless. We only see color in seawater because water plays with light. The dark blue of deep seawater is produced in part by the refraction of light particles in the water. Also, the color blue is absorbed least by seawater. The reflection of the sky is another factor. Green seas are found closer to land and are the result of suspended material carried in coastal waters, usually yellow pigments resulting from the decomposition of plant matter. The Red Sea was named for the periodic blooms of algae which stain its surface.

WAVES

Waves of water are produced when the air–sea surface interface is distorted by a force such as wind. Waves provide one of the most important mechanisms for transporting energy from one point to another on the surface of the sea. A restoring force such as gravity, surface tension, or the Coriolis Force then acts to return the surface to its equilibrium position.

Accommodations

You've got to feel at home when at sea. And to achieve this, choosing the right accommodations for you is the single most important decision you will have to make. So choose wisely, for if you find your cabin (incorrectly called a "stateroom" by some companies) is too small when you get to the ship, it may be impossible to change it or upgrade it to a higher price category, as the ship could well be completely sold out.

Although you may request a specific cabin when you book, most lines now designate cabins only when deposits have been received and confirmed. They will, however, guarantee the grade and rate requested. If this is not done automatically, or if you come across a disclaimer such as one spotted recently—"All cabin assignments are confirmed upon embarkation of the vessel"—then I would advise that you get a guarantee in writing stating that your cabin will not be changed upon embarkation.

There are really three main types of accommodations to choose from, but there are many variations on each theme: suites (often called penthouse suites, these are the largest of accommodations, with or without private balcony); outside cabins (with large picture window or one or more portholes; they can be either with or without private balcony); and inside cabins (so-called because there is no window or porthole). Here are some tips that you should take into consideration when making your choice.

ABOUT PRIVATE BALCONIES

Cruise lines have devised a new gimmick, and a welcome one—private balconies. A private balcony (also often called a "veranda") is just that: an outside balcony where you can sit, enjoy the view, or even dine. There's something quite wonderful about sitting on one's private veranda eating caviar and sipping champagne, or having breakfast à la deck in some exotic place. It's also pleasant to use to get fresh air, and to escape cold air-conditioned cabins. In warm weather areas, a private balcony will prove a delight.

Some private balconies are not so private, however. Those that are not separated by floor- to-ceiling partitions (as in the case of *Carnival Destiny*, *Maasdam*, *Norway*, *Oriana*, *Ryndam*, *Statendam*, and *Veendam* for example), don't quite cut it. You could get noise from your neighbor. You could also get mountains of smoke from a smoking neighbor in the cabin in front of your own. There is no guarantee. But, when all things are in your favor, a balcony is a wonderful extra. Some ships (*Century*, *Galaxy*, *Radisson Diamond*, for example) have balconies that have full floor-to-ceiling privacy partitions *and* a light as well, a real bonus. (Partitions on *Century* and *Galaxy* are full or partial, depending on deck and location.)

If you choose a ship with expensive suites that have forward-facing private balconies at the front of the ship (such

A standard cabin aboard Holiday *(Carnival Cruise Lines). This shows an "L"-shaped layout of two beds, one of which converts to a sofa for daytime use, plus a "foldaway" third, upper berth.*

as *Seabourn Legend, Seabourn Pride, Seabourn Spirit, Silver Cloud, Silver Wind*, for example), notice that although the forward view is excellent when the ship is moving forward, the wind speed can make these balconies all but unusable. In addition, be aware that when the ship drops anchor in ports of call, the noise can be very loud indeed).

Those ships with private balcony cabins (or suites) positioned along the port and starboard sides may be better (such as *Asuka, Century, Crystal Harmony, Crystal Symphony, Dawn Princess, Galaxy, Royal Princess, Royal Viking Sun, Silver Cloud, Silver Wind, Sun Princess*). If you really want sunshine, however, remember that this will depend on the direction the ship is traveling (and the time of day). The profiles in Part Three of this book gives you the number of cabins with private balconies on each ship. You should look at the ship's deck plan carefully with your travel agent to find where your chosen cabin is located.

All private balconies have railings to lean on, but some have solid steel plates underneath (between the railing and the deck), which prevent you from looking out to sea when seated (*Dawn Princess, Sun Princess*, for example). More satisfactory are those with clear glass (*Horizon, Nordic Empress, Zenith*, for example), or horizontal bars.

HOW MUCH TO PAY

The amount you pay for accommodations on most cruise ships is directly related to the size of the cabin, the location within the ship, the facilities provided and various other factors.

There are no set standards within the cruise industry; each line implements its own system according to ship size, age, construction, and the profit potential. Many lines still neglect to give cabin sizes in their brochures, but you'll find the size range in *The Ratings and Evaluations* section in Part Three of this book.

Before you select your cabin, decide how much you can afford to spend—including airfare (if applicable) and your on-board expenses (remember to include the estimated cost of shore excursions, port charges, and tips)—since this will determine the cabin categories available to you. It is advisable to choose the most expensive cabin you can afford, especially if it's your first cruise, as you will spend some time there. If it is too small (and most cabins are small), you just might suffer from "cabin fever," and so the cruise might fall short of your expectations. Alternatively, it is better to book a low-grade cabin on a good ship than book a high-grade cabin on a poor ship.

If you are in a party of three or more and don't mind sharing a cabin, you'll achieve a substantial saving per person, so you may be able to go to a higher-grade cabin without paying any extra money.

In general, you will get precisely the kind of cabin you pay for.

SIZE OF CABINS

Ships' cabins should be looked upon as hotel rooms in miniature, providing more or less the same facilities. With one difference—that of space. Ships necessarily have space limitations, and therefore tend to utilize every inch efficiently. Viewed by many owners and designers as little more than a convenient place for passengers to sleep, shower and change for dinner, a cabin's space is often compromised in favor of large public rooms and open areas. In some of the smaller inside and outside cabins, changing clothes is a challenge; and to take a shower, you'd need to be an acrobat!

There really is no such thing as an average cabin, as cabin size will depend

on the space that is allocated to accommodations within a ship of whatever tonnage measurement and principal dimensions. New ships are fitted with more standardized cabin sizes, because they are made in modular form. They also have integrated bathrooms, often made from noncombustible phenolic-glass-reinforced plastics, and fitted into the ship during construction.

Generally, the larger the ship, the more generous it will be with cabin space. Cabins can vary from the compact 121 sq. ft. (11.24 m²) standard cabins on several of the Royal Caribbean Cruises ships to a magnificent 1,515 sq. ft. (140.7 m²) penthouse suite on Celebrity Cruises' Century.

Remember that cruise ships are operated both for the pleasure of passengers and for the profit of the cruise companies. This is the reason why cabins on many new or modern ships are on the small side. The more cabins that a ship can provide, the more fare-paying passengers can be carried and the greater the on-board revenue.

Ships of yesteryear were able to offer passengers more spacious cabins simply because there were more days at sea, fewer ports of call, fewer entertainment rooms and the overall speed was much slower. This encouraged many to spend a great deal of time in their cabins, very often entertaining other passengers.

Although most modern ships have smaller cabins, they are certainly adequate for standard-length cruises, and allow maximum space in public rooms for entertainment and social events.

Some cruise brochures are more detailed and specific than others when it comes to deck plans and cabin layout diagrams. Deck plans do not normally show dimensions, but they are drawn to scale, unless otherwise noted.

You can get a good idea of the space in a cabin by examining the cabin plan of the cruise category you are interested in. By looking at the beds (each twin being between 2 feet and 3 feet wide and 6 feet long), you can quite easily figure out how much empty or utilized space (bathroom, closets and so on) there is.

If the cabins appear to be the same size on the deck plan, it's because they *are*, with the exception of suite rooms, which will be substantially larger.

Ask the cruise line, via your travel agent, for the dimensions of the cabin you have selected, if it is not indicated on the deck plan. Pace out a room at home as a means of comparison.

LOCATION OF YOUR CABIN

An "outside" cabin is preferable by far, especially if this is the first time you are to go cruising. An "inside" cabin has no portholes or windows, which makes it much more difficult to orient yourself or to gauge the weather.

Cabins that are located in the center of a ship are more stable, and they also tend to be noise- and vibration-free. Ships powered by diesel engines (this applies to most new and modern vessels) create and transmit some vibration, especially at the stern. For those who are technically minded, passenger cabins typically result in a noise level of 50-55 dBA (this affects the standard cabins) and 40-50 dBA (this affects the suites and upper-grade cabins).

Take into account your personal habits when choosing the location of your cabin. For example, if you like to go to bed early, don't pick a cabin close to the disco. And if you have trouble walking, select a cabin close to the elevator (and not on a lower deck, where there are none).

Generally, the higher the deck, the higher the cabin price and the better the service—an inheritance from the transoceanic times, when upper deck cabins and suites were sunnier and warmer.

Cabins at the bow (front) of a ship are slightly crescent-shaped, given that the outer wall follows the curvature of the ship's hull. But they are usually roomier and cheaper. However, these forward cabins can be exposed to early morning noises, such as the anchor being dropped at those ports where the ship cannot dock.

Connecting cabins are fine for families or close friends, but remember that the wall between them is usually thin, and conversations can be heard.

If you book a deluxe upper-deck cabin, check the deck plan carefully; the cabin could have a view of the lifeboats. Many cruise lines now indicate these "obstructed-view" cabins in the brochure. Make sure to read the fine print. Similarly, cabins on promenade decks may have windows easily looked into by passers-by on deck.

If you select a cabin that is on one of the lower decks, be advised that engine noise and heat become more noticeable, especially at the aft end of the vessel, and around the engine casing. Be aware that on many older ships, elevators will probably not operate to the lowermost decks.

FACILITIES

Cabins will provide some, or all, of the following features:

- Private bathroom (generally small and compact) fitted with shower, wash basin, and toilet. Higher-priced cabins and suites often have full-size bathtubs—some may even have a whirlpool bath and/or bidet, a hairdryer, and considerably more space.
- Electrical outlets for personal appliances, usually U.S. standard, sometimes both 110 and 220 volts.
- Multichannel radio; on some ships, television (on regular or closed circuit); video equipment.
- Two beds, or a lower and an upper berth (plus, possibly, another one or two upper berths), or a double, queen-, or king-size bed (usually in suites or deluxe accommodations). On some ships, twin beds can be pushed together to form a double.
- Telephone, for inter-cabin or ship-to-shore communication.
- Depending on cabin size, a chair, or chair and table, or sofa and table, or a lounge/sitting area (in higher-priced accommodations only).
- Refrigerator and bar (higher-priced accommodations only).
- Vanity/desk unit with a chair or stool.
- Personal safe.
- Closet space, some drawer space, plus storage room under beds for suitcases.
- Bedside night stand/table unit.
- Towels, soap, shampoo and conditioner. (Most of the "upscale" ships will provide a greater selection.)

Many first-time cruisers are surprised to find their cabins furnished with twin beds. Double beds were in fact a comparative rarity on the cruise ships except in the higher-priced suite rooms until recently. On some ships with small cabins (*Cunard Countess, Rhapsody, Song of Norway, Sun Viking*, for example), twin beds can be converted to sofas for daytime use, and at night are converted back by the steward.

The two beds are placed in one of two configurations: parallel (with little space in between) or, preferably, in an "L" shape, giving more floor space and the illusion that the cabin is larger.

On some of the ships (especially the older ones), you will find upper and lower berths. A "berth" is a nautical term for a bed held in a wooden or metal frame. A "pullman berth" tucks away out of sight during the day, usually into the bulkhead or ceiling. You climb up a short ladder at night to get into an upper berth.

THE SUITE LIFE

Suites are the most luxurious and spacious of all the shipboard accommodations. The definition of a suite is that it is a "suite of rooms" and comprises a lounge or sitting room separated from a bedroom by a solid door (not just a curtain), a bedroom with a double, queen- or king-size bed, or large, movable twin beds, and one or more bathrooms. Be advised, however, that many cruise lines inaccurately describe some accommodations as suites, when in fact they are simply nothing more than larger cabins with a curtain to divide the sitting from the sleeping area. The best suites ("owner's suite" or "penthouse suite") are located high and in the quietest part of the ship. Some ships have whole decks or sections of decks devoted to suites. Ship owners and cruise line marketing companies know that certain passengers will pay handsomely to stay in the largest and quietest of accommodations, and have preferential treatment.

Bathroom suites will be quite large (relatively speaking) and will have a large bath tub (often with a whirlpool tub) and a shower, hairdryer, plus a toilet, deluxe wash basin (or two) and, on some ships, a bidet. Some ships even boast gold bathroom fittings in their best suites! Although this is the exception and not the rule, bathrooms attached to suites are usually excellent.

Suites should also be equipped with a stereo system, television, VCR player, CD player, refrigerator and a partially or fully stocked bar, and occupants can command a 24-hour butler service.

In ships such as *Norwegian Crown* and *QE2*, each suite is decorated in a different style, with authentic or reproduction period furniture, beautiful drapes, and fine furnishings. In *Century*, *Crystal Harmony*, *Crystal Symphony*, *Galaxy*, *QE2* and *Royal Viking Sun*, you'll be attended by a personal butler (on some ships, however, the butler is nothing more than a waiter in a different uniform).

Suite rooms are obviously best for a long voyage, when the ship might cross stretches of ocean for five or more days at a time. They are particularly suitable for impressing a loved one and for entertaining in.

Most of the suites will have their own balcony or veranda, although it's wise to check the deck plan in case the veranda faces the lifeboats or some other obstructive apparatus. Suites are usually sheltered from the noise of the ship and the wind, and should provide considerable privacy. Some of the very

This is the Owner's Suite aboard Seabourn Legend *(Seabourn Cruise Line). It has a private balcony (not shown in the photo), and offers 554 sq. ft. (51.4m^2) of refined private living space.*

best suites are the exclusive and private owner's suites in *Seabourn Legend, Seabourn Pride, Seabourn Spirit* and *Vistafjord.*

19TH-CENTURY CRUISING

Cruising today is not the same as it used to be; on the first cruise ships there was little entertainment, and passengers had to clean their own cabins. Orders enforced on all ships sailing from Great Britain in 1849, for example, instructed all passengers to be in their beds by 10 p.m.!

READING A DECK PLAN

Learning to read a deck plan is relatively easy. It is always laid out so that the bow (front part of the ship) faces to your right or to the top of a page.

Traditionally, ships have designated the central deck (equivalent to the main lobby of a hotel) as the Main Deck. Here you'll find the purser's office and the other principal business offices. Some modern ships, however, do not use the term "Main Deck," preferring a more exclusive-sounding name. All ships also have a Boat Deck, where the lifeboats are stowed.

In the past, many cruise ships also had a Promenade Deck—an enclosed walkway along the length of the deck on one or both sides of the ship. This was popular with passengers crossing the Atlantic, for when the weather was cold or foggy, they could still take their stroll. It is located between the Main Deck and the Boat Deck, except on some modern ships where the Boat and Promenade decks are interchangeable. When the new generation of specialized cruise ships came into being in the 1970s, the Promenade Deck disappeared in favor of public entertainment lounges across the full beam of the ship, and the name of the deck was changed. Some of the ships that have been built recently have returned to the idea of a Promenade Deck.

The uppermost decks usually tend to be open and feature sunning space, multisports areas, and running or jogging tracks that may encircle the ship.

The Restaurant Deck has undergone a metamorphosis too. It used to be buried on one of the ship's lower decks so as to avoid the rolling motion of nonstabilized ocean liners. Even on the most luxurious liners, there were often no portholes, because the deck was placed below the waterline. As cruising replaced transportation as the prime source of revenue, newer ships were designed with restaurants set high above the waterline. Big picture windows provide diners with a panoramic view of the port or surrounding sea. The Restaurant Deck can therefore be either above or below Main Deck.

Traditionally, popular-priced cabins have been located below Main Deck, with the high-priced suites occupying space on one or two of the uppermost decks. In the latest ship designs, however, almost all accommodations areas are located above the Main Deck in order to cut down on the amount of disturbing engine noise and vibration. Older ships designated their accommodation decks A, B, C, D..., while modern ships have given them more appealing names, such as Acapulco, Bimini, Coral, Dolphin, and so on.

Note that on some ships, third- and fourth-person berths are available for families or friends wishing to share. These upper pullman berths, not shown on these cabin layouts, are recessed into the wall above the lower beds.

Large outside double with bed and convertible daytime sofabed, bathroom with shower, and good closet space.
(a)$1,750 (b)$2,450

Standard outside double with twin beds (plus a possible upper third/fourth berth), small sitting area, bathroom with shower, and reasonable closet space.
(a)$1,450 (b)$1,975

Inside double with two lower beds that may convert into daytime sofabeds (plus a possible upper 3rd/4th berth), bathroom with shower, and fair closet space.
(a)$1,250 (b)$1,750

The following rates are typical of those you can expect to pay for (a) a 7-day and (b) a 10-day Caribbean cruise on a modern cruise ship. The rates are per person, and include free roundtrip airfare or low-cost air add-ons from principal North American gateways.

Luxury outside suite with private verandah, separate lounge area, vanity area, extra-large double or queen-sized bed, bathroom with tub, shower, and extensive closet and storage space. (a)$2,750 (b)$4,000

Deluxe outside cabin with lounge area, double or twin beds, bathroom with tub, shower, and ample closet and storage space. (a)$2,250 (b)$2,850

Cruise Cuisine

The food is still the single most talked and written about aspect of the cruise experience. One of the most sensual pleasures in life is eating; who can fail to be aroused by the aroma of food being prepared, or be charmed by a delicious meal in fine surroundings, with a correctly laid table?

There is a special thrill of anticipation that comes with dining out in a fine restaurant. It is the same on board a luxury cruise ship, where gracious dining in elegant, friendly, and comfortable surroundings stimulates an appetite that is already sharpened by the bracing sea air. Some passengers do carry shipboard dining to the limit, however. Indeed, I've seen plenty of people eat more in one meal than most others do in two or three days!

Attention to presentation, quality, and choice of menu in the honored tradition of the transatlantic luxury liners has made the cruise ships justly famous. Cruise lines know that you'll spend more time eating on board than doing anything else, so their intention is to cater to your palate in every way possible, within the confines of a predetermined budget.

What is spent on food will range from about $7.50 to $30.00 a person a day, depending on the cruise line and standard of cuisine required, although there are exceptions at the higher end, particularly in the Japanese market, where fresh fish and seafood costs are exorbitantly high, and food costs of more than $50 per person per day are

normal. Most cruise ships catering to the standard (mass) market spend anything between $7.50 and $15.00 per person per day.

The "intelligent standardization" of the food operation and menus translates to cost-effectiveness in the process of food budgeting for any cruise line. Being able to rationalize expenditure *and* provide maximum passenger satisfaction is today almost a science.

Cruise lines tend to put maximum effort into telling passengers how good their food is, often to the point of being unable to deliver what is shown in their brochures, and thus anticipated by passengers. Generally, however, the level of food provided is good. The best rule of thumb is to ask yourself what you would expect, relative to what you are paying, if you were to eat out in a good restaurant. Does the ship's dining experience meet or exceed your expectations? Would you come back again for the food? If you would, then that particular cruise line has met its promise to feed you with fine food. While gourmet cuisine is enjoyed by a small percentage of people ashore, few ships have the facilities or availability of fresh foods to equal even those of a one-star Michelin-rated restaurant.

The cuisine will, inevitably, vary from one cruise line to another, and this will depend on the nationality and regional influence of the executive chef, his staff, and the ship's country of registry or ownership. Thus, choosing a cruise and ship also involves thinking about the kind of food that will be served on board—and how it is served.

There are perhaps as many different tastes as there are passengers. Some like plain food, some like spicy food. Some like *nouvelle cuisine*, some like meat and potatoes, and lots of it. Some like to try new things, some stick with the same old stuff. It's all a matter of personal taste. So, what the "standard" market cruise lines do is to cater for general tastes. Upscale cruise lines can offer food cooked more or less individually to your liking, but, as in a good restaurant, you get what you pay for. This is why cruise ship standards are so different. Some people are accustomed to drinking coffee out of styrofoam cups and eating food off paper plates at home. Others wouldn't dream of doing that, and expect fine dining, with food correctly served on fine china, just as they do at home.

Some ships have full place settings that include as many as 10 pieces of cutlery, while others provide the correct cutlery just before each course is served (this is more labor-intensive, but the time it takes to lay the cutlery gives the galley more time to get ready for the next course). If you don't know which knife and fork to use for which course, the rule is always to start at the outermost pair and work towards the innermost pair. The knife and fork closest to where the plate is set will be for the entree (main course). Some ships have special knives for fish courses; others do not, requiring you to use a standard (flat) knife.

While on the subject of place settings, if you are *left-handed*, make sure you tell your waiter at your first meal exactly how you want your cutlery placed, and to make sure that tea or coffee cup handles are turned in the correct direction. It would be even better if your right- or left-hand preferences were established at the time of booking, and the cruise lines passed on the information to the ship.

Menus for luncheon and dinner are usually displayed outside the dining room each morning so that you can preview the day's meals. On some of the more upmarket ships, menus will be delivered to your suite or cabin each day. When looking at the menu, one thing you'll never have to do is to consider the price—it's all included.

Depending on the ship and cruise, you could sit down to various gourmet specialties, such as duck à l'orange, beef Wellington, lobster thermidor, or prime roast rib of Kansas beef. Or maybe châteaubriand, veal scaloppini, fresh sea bass in dill sauce, or rack of roast English lamb. To top off the meal there could be crème brûlée, chocolate mousse, kiwi tart, or that favorite standby, the massed meringue—Baked Alaska—not to mention the tableside flambé choices such as Cherries Jubilee or Crêpes Suzette. And you can always rely on your waiter to bring you a double portion, should you so wish! Of course, these specialties may not be available on all ships. But if you would prefer something that is not on the menu, see the maître d', give him 24 hours' notice (plus a small tip) and, if the galley can cope, it could well be all your own.

Despite what the glossy brochures say, however, not all meals on all cruise ships are gourmet affairs by any stretch of the imagination. In general, cruise cuisine can be compared favorably to the kind of "banquet" food served in a good hotel or family restaurant. For a guide to the standard of cruise cuisine, service, and presentation on a particular ship, refer to the ratings in Part Three of this book, but remember that the rating of cruise cuisine is also determined in relation to the per diem cost averages paid by passengers.

Experienced passengers who "collect" cruises have seen it, smelled it, and tasted it all before on cruise ships: real rubber duck—foul (fowl) food, fit only to be stuffed, painted, and used as children's toys in their bathtubs! Talk about rock-hard lobster, leather fish, inedible month-old shrimp, third-world, veterinarian-rejected chicken, and grenade-quality meats. And not to mention teary-eyed or hammer-proof cheese, soggy, salty crackers, unripe fruits and coffee that looks (and tastes) like army surplus paint! Sadly, it's all there, in the cruise industry's global cafeteria.

One reason that the food on ships cannot always be a "gourmet" experience is that the galley (ship's kitchen) may be striving to turn out hundreds of meals at the same time. What you *will* find is a very fine selection of highly palatable, pleasing, and complete meals served in very comfortable surroundings, in the company of good friends (and *you* don't have to do the cooking!). Add to this the possibility of views out of huge picture windows that overlook a shimmering sea, and perhaps even dining by candlelight. Dining in such a setting is a delightful and relaxed way to spend any evening.

Many cruise lines with large ships now feature buffets for breakfast and luncheon (they don't require as much staff, cutlery, linen or cooked foods), one of the effects of discounted fares. Strangely, passengers don't seem to mind lining up for help-yourself food at the buffets (although it's informal, for the amount of money being paid, sitting down to a meal with service is surely better). Buffets look fine when they are fresh, but after a few minutes of hungry passengers serving themselves, they look a lot less appetizing. And one learns soon enough that the otherwise sweet little old ladies can become ruthlessly competitive when the buffet starting time comes round!

PLATE SERVICE VS SILVER SERVICE

Most fine restaurants ashore now have what is termed "plate service" rather than "silver service." Plate service is when the food is presented as a complete dish, the chef's total concept of how the food should look; its color combinations, the size of the component parts, and its positioning on the plate—all of it together representing the quality of his or her creativity.

In silver service, usually all component parts are brought to the table separately, so that the diner can make the choices regarding the food and what goes on the plate, not the chef. Silver service works best when there is plenty of time to deliver the product. In the setting of most cruise ships, however, silver service is now all but impossible. What some cruise lines class as silver service actually means silver service of vegetables only, with the main item, be it fish, fowl or meat, already positioned on the plate.

On most cruise ships, the "plate service" works well, and means that most people seated at a table will be served at the same time, and can eat together, rather than let their food become cold, as is often the case in silver service, unless several waiters are available to serve one table.

CAVIAR AND CHAMPAGNE

If it's the best caviar you're partial to, you might want to know that Cunard's *QE2* prides itself on being the world's largest single buyer of Beluga caviar (spending about half a million dollars annually), after the Russian and the Ukrainian governments. There are no mother-of-pearl caviar spoons on *QE2*, however, but you will find them on *Sea Goddess I*, *Sea Goddess II*, and *Song of Flower*.

Although it might seem like it from menu descriptions, most ships do not serve Beluga caviar, but serve the less expensive, and more widely available, Sevruga and Sevruga Malossol (low-salt) caviar. Even more widely served on less exclusive cruise ships, such as those of the Dolphin Cruise Line or Royal Caribbean Cruises, is Norwegian lumpfish caviar—quite different from the highly prized Beluga caviar. The price of caviar is a reflection of the growing rarity of the sturgeon, the fish from which it is derived.

For those who have not tasted good caviar, let me explain that you'll probably find it very salty. That's because the eggs are taken fresh from the female sturgeon, when she is said to be asleep (it takes about 20 years for a female beluga sturgeon to mature).

After the eggs are taken they are passed through a screen to separate them from other fibrous matter. They are then mixed with salt, which acts as a preservative and also promotes the taste. The more salt added, the better the caviar is preserved; the less salt added the finer the taste (Malossol means less salt). The process is done by highly skilled labor, which adds to its cost. The two countries that produce most of the world's caviar are Iran and Russia. In general, Russian caviar is more highly salted than caviar from Iran. And just as each vineyard produces different wines, so each fishery will produce different-tasting caviar.

The Caspian Sea is the spawning ground for 90 per cent of the world's caviar-producing sturgeon. There are three types that are fished for caviar.

1. The giant beluga is hardest to find and therefore the most expensive. It can weigh more than 1,500 lb (680 kg). One fish is capable of yielding as much as 20 lb (9 kg) of caviar, whose smoky-grey eggs are the largest (and also the most delicate).
2. The second most expensive caviar fish is the ossetra. This takes about 13 years to mature, and weighs up to about 40 lb (18 kg). These are the most durable eggs (they are also smaller), and range in color from a darkish brass to olive green.
3. The third caviar fish is the sevruga, which weighs about 6 lb (2.7 kg). It also has small eggs, ranging in color from soft grey to dark grey.

There is also a fourth type of sturgeon, known as a sterlet, which produces a translucent golden egg, although it is hard to find today (prior to 1917 all the golden caviar was sent to the Tsar in Russia).

There was a time when sturgeon was found in abundance—so much so that caviar was often placed on the bars of London and New York as a snack to promote the sale of beer and ale.

Caviar is a good natural accompaniment for good champagne, but good champagne (like anything else of high quality) doesn't come cheap. What most ships use as champagne—for the Captain's Welcome Aboard Party, for example—just about passes as champagne. Some ships (for example, the newer ships of Princess Cruises) feature a caviar and champagne bar on board, which offers several varieties of caviar, at extra cost of course. Champagne making is a real art (in France itself the production of Champagne is restricted to a very small geographical area). Unlike wine, it is bottled in many sizes, ranging from the minute to the ridiculously huge, and with a variety of names to match:

Quarter bottle:	18.7 centiliters
Half bottle (split):	37.5 centiliters
Bottle:	75 centiliters
Magnum:	2 bottles
Jeroboam:	4 bottles
Rehoboam:	6 bottles
Methuselah:	8 bottles
Salmanazar:	12 bottles
Balthazar:	16 bottles
Nebuchadnezzar:	20 bottles

There are three main grape-growing districts in Champagne: the Montagne de Reims, to the south and east of Reims; the Vallée de la Marne, surrounding the river: and the Côtes des Blancs, south of Epernay. The first two mainly grow the dark pinot-noir and pinot-meunier grapes, while the latter grows the white chardonnay variety. All are used in the making of champagne. Removing the husks before full fermentation prevents the dark grapes coloring the wine red. If a pink champagne is being made, however, the skins are left in the grape mix for a longer time to add color.

Afternoon tea served here in the Queens Room aboard Cunard's 1,740-passenger Queen Elizabeth 2.

Although the Champagne area has been producing wines of renown for a long time, its vintners were unable to keep their bubbles from fizzling out until a monk in the Abbey of Hautvilliers, whose name was Dom Perignon, came up with the solution. The bubbles—escaping carbonic acid gas—had always escaped, until Dom Perignon devised a bottle capable of containing the champagne without it exploding out of the bottle, which was a common occurrence in local cellars. The legacy of this clever monk is that the champagne bottle is the strongest bottle made today. Its thickness is concentrated around the bottle's base and shoulders. Dom Perignon's bottle was aided by the coincidental development of the cork.

Even after his work, champagne was not the perfect elixir we enjoy today. It was quite cloudy due to a residual sediment of dead yeast cells. Its bubbles, therefore, could not be truly relished visually—until la Veuve Cliquot (the Widow Cliquot) devised the system of *remuage* in the last century. Rather than laying the bottles down horizontally for their period of aging, she put them in a special rack, called a *pupitre*, which held them at a 45-degree angle, with the neck of the bottle down. Each day, the bottles are given a short, sharp, quarter turn so as to shake the sediment, which then gradually settles in the neck of the bottle. Once this is complete, a process called *dégorgement* freezes the neck of the bottle. It is then uncorked and internal pressure ejects the ice containing the sediment. Obviously, this means that the bottle is a little less than totally full, so the champagne is topped up with what is called the *dosage*, which is a sweet champagne liqueur. The degree of sweetness of this addition depends on the tastes of the market to which the champagne is ultimately destined. After the *dosage* is added the permanent cork is forced in and wired up. The bottles then remain in the cellar of the winery until they are ordered. Each of the bottles is then washed, labeled and shipped for sale to the consumer.

HEALTHY EATING

Nowadays, with more emphasis being placed on low-cholesterol and low-salt diets, many cruise ships feature "spa" menus—where the heavy, calorie-filled sauces have been replaced by *nouvelle cuisine* and spa cuisine.

Some cruise lines now include basic nutritional information, such as the calorie count, and fat, protein, and carbohydrate content, on their "spa" or "alternative" menus, or for selected "light" items on their regular menus. However, this is mostly for dinner, and very seldom for breakfast or luncheon.

If you are on any kind of restrictive diet, such as low salt, low fat, vegetarian, vegan, or macrobiotic diet, do let your travel agent know at the time of booking, and get them to confirm that the ship can actually handle your dietary requirements.

At the upper (expensive) end of the cruise spectrum, meals aboard ships such as *Royal Viking Sun, Sea Goddess I, Sea Goddess II, Seabourn Legend, Seabourn Pride,* and *Seabourn Spirit* can be memorable experiences, as they are cooked to the particular order of the individual passenger.

The difference between the most expensive and the least expensive cruises can frequently be found in attention to detail, such as the provision of high-quality biscuits made for eating with cheese, or the variety of fresh and exotic fruits and the general quality of meats and fish used.

NATIONAL DIFFERENCES

The different nationalities among passengers have their own special needs and requirements that have to be catered for. Here are a few instances of national characteristics which I have noticed and which you may also come across on a cruise:

- Asian, British, German and other European passengers like real china egg cups for their boiled eggs for breakfast. When North Americans eat boiled eggs, which is infrequently, they put the eggs into a bowl and eat them with a fork.
- German passengers want a wide choice of breads (especially dark breads), cold cuts, and cheeses for breakfast. And they also have an obvious liking for German draught or bottled beers rather than American canned beers.
- French passengers have a liking for soft, not flaky, croissants, and may request brioche and *confitures*.
- Japanese passengers will be looking for a "bento box" breakfast of fresh steamed Japanese rice (which is very different from Chinese rice), salmon, eel, and vegetable pickles.
- Southern Italians like to have red sauce with just about everything, while northern Italians like less of the red sauces and more flavorings, such as garlic, with their pasta.
- North Americans like weak coffee with everything—often before, during and after a meal. This is why, even on upscale ships, sugar is placed on tables (also for iced tea).
- Most passengers agree that cruise coffee is appalling, but often it is simply the chlorinated water that gives it a different taste. Europeans prefer strong coffee, usually made from the coffee beans of African countries like Kenya. North Americans usually drink the coffee from Colombia or Jamaica.
- European tea drinkers like to drink tea out of tea cups, not coffee mugs (very few cruise ships know how to make a decent cup of tea, so British passengers in particular, should be aware of this).

THE DINING ROOM

On many cruise ships, the running and staffing of dining rooms are contracted out to an outside catering organization specializing in cruise ships. Ships that are continually in waters away from their home country find that professional catering companies do an excellent job, and provide a degree of relief from the operation and staffing of their dining rooms. The quality is generally to a very high standard. However, ships that control their own catering staff and food are often those that go to great lengths to ensure that their passengers are satisfied.

Catering companies tend to change occasionally, so a complete list of them would probably soon become obsolete. However, here are just a few examples of the principal maritime catering companies:

Apollo Catering	USA
CFCS	Italy/USA
Century Catering	USA
Ligabue Catering	Italy
Stellar Maritime	USA
Trident Catering	USA
World-Wide Catering	USA
Zerbone Catering	Italy

DINING ROOM STAFF

The maître d' is an experienced host, with shrewd perceptions about compatibility; you can trust him when he gives you your table seating. If a table reservation has been arranged prior to boarding, you will find a table seating card in your cabin when you arrive. If this is not the case, you will need to make your reservations with the maître d' or one of his assistants. If you wish to reserve a special table or location in the dining room, do so as soon as possible after boarding.

Unless you are with your own group of friends, you will be seated next to strangers in the dining room. Tables for two are a rarity, except on some small ships and on some of the upmarket liners. Most tables seat six or eight people. It is a good idea to ask to be seated at a larger table, because if you are a couple seated at a table for four and you don't get along with your table partners, there's no one else to talk to. And remember, if the ship is full, it may be difficult to change tables once the cruise has started.

If you are unhappy with any aspect of the dining room operation, the earlier you complain the better. Don't wait until the cruise is over and then send a scathing letter to the cruise line, for then it is too late to do anything positive. See whoever is in charge—they are there to help you to enjoy your meals during the cruise. They want your comments—good or bad.

Each table has at least one waiter and one assistant waiter or busboy. On some ships, up to 30 nationalities may be represented among the dining room staff, who are taught to be courteous, charming, and helpful.

Many ships like to organize special incentive programs, such as a "waiter of the month" competition. This sort of thing helps to keep the staff on their toes, especially if they want to reach the "best" tables. The result is that passengers really do get fine service.

The best waiters are without doubt those who have been trained in the exclusive European hotels or in hotel and catering schools—like the Maritime Catering Institute in Salzburg, Austria. These highly qualified individuals will excel in silver service, and will always be ready with the next course when you want it. They will also know your likes and dislikes by the second night of the cruise. They normally work on the upmarket ships, where dignified professionalism is evident everywhere in the dining room.

SMOKING/NON-SMOKING

Several cruise line companies and their ships have totally non-smoking dining rooms. At the time of this book going to press they will include all the ships of these shipping cruise lines: CTC Cruise Lines, Carnival Cruise Lines, Commodore Cruise Line, Curnow Shipping, Fred Olsen, Hebridean Island Cruises, Majesty Cruise Line, Norwegian Cruise Line, Premier Cruise Lines, Princess Cruises, Royal Olympic Cruises, Transocean Tours, and Windstar Cruises. All other ships feature dining rooms that segregate the smokers from the non-smokers, and most ask that passengers smoke only cigarettes and not cigars or pipes. I expect many more ships will follow this example soon.

Non-smokers who wish to sit in a no-smoking area of the dining room should tell the maître d' or his assistants when reserving a table. Also, you should know that at open seating breakfasts and luncheons in the dining room (or informal buffet dining area), the smokers and non-smokers may be together. If you are bothered by smoke, demand a table in a non-smoking area.

THE CAPTAIN'S TABLE

The captain usually occupies a large table in or near the center of the dining room, the table seating eight or ten people who have been picked from the passenger or "commend" list by the maître d'. Alternatively, the captain may request personal friends or important company officials to dine with him. If you are invited to the captain's table for dinner, it is gracious to accept, and you'll have the chance to ask all the questions you've always wanted to ask about shipboard life.

The captain will not attend meals if he is required on the ship's bridge. When there are two sittings, the captain may have dinner at the first sitting one night, and at the second sitting the next night. On some ships, the captain's guests are changed daily so that more people have a chance to enjoy the experience.

Generally, senior officers also host tables, and being seated with them can be a fascinating experience, especially as they tend to be less formal.

WHICH SITTING?

The best cruise ships feature an open, or single, sitting for meals, where you may dine in unhurried style. "Open sitting" means that you can sit at any table with whom you wish, at whatever time you choose within dining room hours. "Single sitting" means you can choose when you wish to eat, but have regularly assigned tables for the entire cruise. The majority of ships operate a two-sitting arrangement.

The typical first-sitting passengers include: couples (those over 50), families, groups, early-risers, and those passengers who like to dine quickly, and at their normal dining hours at home.

The typical late-sitting passengers include: couples (those under 50), singles, honeymooners, late-risers, and those who like to dine in a leisurely and relaxed style over meals.

Those at the late sitting may not be hungry enough to eat again at the midnight buffet, since it begins about two hours later.

The standard meal times for a two-sitting ship are as follows:

Breakfast: 6:30 a.m./8:30 a.m.
Lunch: 12:00 noon/1:30 p.m.
Dinner: 6:30 p.m./8:30 p.m.

You should note that some ships that operate in Europe (the Mediterranean) may well have even later dinner sittings. Costa Cruises, for example, has its second dinner sitting at 9:00 p.m. instead of the more usual 8:15 p.m. or 8:30 p.m. Dinner hours may vary when the ship is in port to allow for the timing of shore excursions.

You may also find that some of the better seats for the shows and at the movie theater have been taken by those who were on the first sitting. Most ships resolve this problem by scheduling two performances for all the shows at night.

Most ships request that you enter the dining room 15 minutes after the meal has been announced. This is out of consideration for your fellow passengers, your table companions, and the dining room staff. This is especially true for those on the first sitting, but it provides little time to sit and linger over cocktails or after-dinner drinks—one of the drawbacks of the two-sitting arrangement.

SPECIAL REQUIREMENTS

If you are counting calories, are vegetarian or require a salt-free, sugar-restricted, macrobiotic or other diet, let the cruise line know when you first book. The line will then pass the information to the ship, so that your needs can be met. Some of the larger cruise lines, including Carnival Cruise Lines and Royal Caribbean Cruises, now fea-

ture a vegetarian entree on all their dinner menus.

Because the food on all the cruises is regarded as "international" or French cuisine, be prepared for dishes that are liberally sprinkled with salt. The vegetables are often cooked with sauces containing dairy products, salt, and sugar. If you want food more to your taste, have a word with the maître d'.

FIRST AND SECOND NIGHTS

For new and experienced cruisers alike, the first evening at sea is exciting—much as the opening night at the theater is. Nowhere is there more a feeling of anticipation than at that first casual dinner when you get a foretaste of the feasting to come.

By contrast, the second night of a cruise tends to be formal, as this is usually the ship captain's welcome-aboard dinner. For this the chef will pull out all the stops to produce a gourmet meal. The dinner follows the captain's cocktail party, which takes place in one of the ship's larger lounges and is an excellent opportunity to meet your fellow passengers and the ship's officers. Toward the end of the party, the captain will give his welcome aboard speech and may also introduce senior members of staff.

THEME NIGHTS

Some of the nights on the cruise will be organized as special theme nights, when waiters dress up fittingly and the menu is planned to suit the occasion.

A TYPICAL DAY

From morning till night, food is on offer to the point of overkill, even on the most modest cruise ship. In fact, on some ships you can eat up to seven meals a day.

Early risers will discover piping hot coffee and tea on deck from about as early as 6 a.m.

A full breakfast, of up to six courses and as many as 60 different items, can be taken in the main dining room. For a more casual meal, you may wish to eat al fresco or buffet style at the outdoor deck café (ideal after an early swim or if you don't wish to dress for the more formal dining room). The choice is obviously more restricted than in the main dining room, but good nonetheless. Times of dining will be set out in your daily program.

A third possibility, especially for romantics, is to have breakfast in your cabin. There's something rather special about waking up and eating breakfast without getting out of bed. Some ships do offer you a full choice of breakfast items, while others opt for the more simple, but usually well-presented, Continental breakfast.

On many ships, the mid-morning bouillon is an established favorite, often served up on one of the open decks—a legacy from the grand days of the transatlantic steamships. Bouillon aboard *Vistafjord* is served right at your chair-side from trolleys that parade around the promenade deck.

At lunch time, there are at least two choices: a hot lunch with all the trimmings in the dining room, or a buffet-style luncheon in the outdoor café, featuring light meals, salads, and one or two hot dishes. On some days, this could well turn into a lavish spread, with enough food for a feast (special favorites are the seafood and tropical fruits). And on some ships there will be a separate hot dog and hamburger stand or a pizzeria, where everything is cooked right in front of you, but usually presented with less style than at a McDonald's restaurant.

At around 4 p.m. another throwback to the heyday of the great liners takes place: afternoon tea—of course in the best British tradition—complete with finger sandwiches and cakes. This is often served in one of the main lounges to the accompaniment of live music (it may even be a "tea-dance") or recorded classical music. Afternoon tea usually lasts about an hour (although on some ships it is only half an hour, in which case it is best to be on time so as not to miss out).

Dinner is, of course, the main event of the evening, and apart from the casualness of the first and last nights, it is formal in style.

If you enjoy wine with your dinner, you will find an excellent choice on board. Upmarket ships will carry a selection of wines far more extensive than you will find even in the better restaurants ashore, while other ships will provide some excellent inexpensive wines from the country of the ship's registry or ownership. It is wise to order your wine for the evening meal at lunch time, or at the very latest as soon as you are seated; the wine stewards tend to be extremely busy during the evening meal, and need to draw their stock and possibly have it chilled. It is also worth noting that if you sail on one of the smaller ships, the selection of half-bottles of wine will be extremely limited, as most small ships have restricted space and would rather stock full bottles rather than half-bottles of wine.

A few hours after dinner, there's the midnight buffet—without doubt the most famous of all cruise ship meals. It really is at midnight (until 1 a.m.), and is a spread fit for royalty. Like dinner, it may be based around a different theme each night: a King Neptune seafood buffet one evening, an oriental buffet the next, a tropical fruit fantasy the third, and so on. And the desserts at these buffets are out of this world.

On one night (usually the penultimate evening) there will be a magnificent gala midnight buffet, for which the chefs pull out all the stops. Beautifully sculpted ice-carvings will be on display, each of them fashioned from a 300-lb (136-kg) block of ice. Some of the ships also demonstrate ice-carving.

Even if you are not hungry, stay up to see this display of culinary art—it's something most people never forget.

In addition—or as an alternative—to the midnight buffet, pizza may be served for the late-night disco dancers or the casino crowd.

On a typical day at sea, the ship's bars will be open from about 10 a.m. to late into the night, depending on the bar, its location, and the number of patrons. The details of bar hours are given in the ship's *Daily Program*.

THE EXECUTIVE CHEF

Each ship has its own executive chef who is responsible for planning the menus, ordering enough food (in con-

junction with the food manager), organizing his staff and arranging all the meals on the menus.

When a cruise line finds a good executive chef, it is unlikely that they will part company. Many of the best ships employ European chefs who are members of the prestigious Confrérie de la Chaîne des Rôtisseurs, which is the world's oldest gourmet society. The top food and beverage experts work together with their executive chefs, striving for perfection.

One of the principal aims of any good executive chef will be to make sure that menus are never repeated, even on long cruises. He will be inventive enough to offer his passengers dishes that will be new gastronomic experiences for them. On long voyages, the executive chef will work with specially invited guest chefs to offer the passengers a taste of the finest in regional cuisines. Sometimes, he may also purchase fish, seafood, fruit, and various other local produce in "wayside" ports and incorporate them into the menu with a "special of the day" announcement.

THE GALLEY

The galley ("kitchen" for landlubbers) is the very heart of all food preparation on board. At any time of the day or night, there is plenty of activity here—whether baking fresh bread at 2 a.m., making meals and snacks for passengers and crew around the clock, or decorating a special cake for a passenger's birthday celebration.

The staff, from executive chef to pot-washer, must all work together as a team, each designated a specific role—and there is little room for error.

The galley and preparation areas consist of the following sections:

Fish Preparation Area

This area contains freezers and a fully equipped preparation room, where fish is cleaned and cut to size before it is sent to the galley.

Meat Preparation Area

This area contains separate freezers for meat and poultry. These temperatures are kept at approximately 10°F. There are also defrosting areas (35°F to 40°F). Meat and poultry is sliced and portioned before being sent to the galley.

Soup, Pasta, and Vegetable Preparation Area

Vegetables are cleaned and prepared in this area, pasta is prepared and cooked, and soups are made in huge tureens.

Garde Manger (Cold Kitchen)

This is the area where all cold dishes and salads are prepared, from the simplest sandwich (for room service, for example) to the fine works of art that grace the most wonderful buffets. The area is well equipped with mixing machines, slicing machines and refrigeration cabinets where prepared dishes are stored until required.

Bakery and Pastry Shop

This area provides the raw ingredients for preparing food, and will contain dough mixers, refrigerators, proving ovens, ovens, and containers in all manner of shapes and sizes. Dessert items, pastries, sweets, and other confectionery are prepared and made here.

Dishwashing Area

This area contains huge conveyor-belt dishwashing machines. Wash and rinse temperatures are carefully controlled to comply with the relevant public health regulations. This is where all the special cooking utensils are scrubbed and cleaned, and where the silverware is scrupulously polished.

STANDARDS OF HYGIENE

Galley equipment is in almost constant use. Regular inspections and maintenance help detect potential problems.

Hygiene and correct sanitation are also vital in the galley, and there is continual cleaning of equipment, utensils, bulkheads, floors, and hands. All the staff are required to wear rubber-soled shoes or boots, and the senior officers conduct regular inspections of galleys, equipment, and personnel.

Passenger cruise ships sailing from U.S. ports or visiting them are all subject to sanitation inspections by officials from the United States Public Health (USPH) Department of Health and Human Services, under the auspices of the Centers for Disease Control. This is a *voluntary* inspection, not a *mandatory* inspection (it is based on 42 inspection items), and the whole program is paid for by the cruise lines. A similar process takes place in Britain under the Port Health Authority.

On board many ships, a hygiene officer oversees health and sanitation standards. A tour of the galley has proved to be a highlight for passengers on some smaller ships. On larger vessels, passengers are not usually allowed into the galley, due to constant activity and insurance restrictions. A video of *Behind the Scenes*, for use on in-cabin television, may be provided.

In accordance with internationally accepted standards, the potable water brought on board, or produced by distillation on cruise ships, should contain a free chlorine or bromine residual equal to or greater than 0.2 ppm (parts per million). This is why the drinking water served in the dining room often tastes of chlorine.

ENVIRONMENTAL CONCERNS

The cruise ships refine oil, treat human waste, and incinerate the garbage, but that's not enough today, as pressures continue to mount for clean oceans. Cruise ships and their operating companies have a unique position among all shipping interests. They are not likely to damage the ocean environment as compared with oil tankers, although spillage of any kind is regrettable. Because of ever-increasing regulations and environmental concern, many cruise lines are replacing plastics with more biodegradable and recyclable materials. For example, plastic plates used in certain areas on general market ships should be replaced by china plates, or washable and re-usable hard plastics; the plastic laundry bags should be replaced by paper bags; plastic bottles used for in-cabin amenities should be replaced by containers made of recyclable or re-usable materials. And the cruise lines should make a greater effort to purchase those products that have been produced from recycled paper.

WASTE DISPOSAL

Today's cruise ships need to be capable of efficient handling of garbage and waste materials, as trash generated by passengers and crew must be managed, stored, and disposed of efficiently and economically. The larger the ship, the more waste will obviously be created, and the greater the need for efficient, reliable disposal systems.

Trash includes bottles, cans, corrugated cartons, fabrics, foodstuffs, paper products, plastic containers, as well as medical waste, sludge oil, wet waste, and so on. The sheer magnitude of trash and waste materials can be highly problematic, especially on long cruises that have a large complement of passengers and crew. If solid waste is not burnable, or cannot be disposed of overboard (this type of waste must be bio-degradable), it must be stored aboard ship for later off-loading and disposal on land.

While some of the latest breed of cruise ships are already equipped with "zero-discharge" facilities, other, older, cruise ships still have a way to go when it comes to efficient and economical garbage handling. One method of dealing with food waste is to send it to a waste pulping machine that has been partially filled with water. Cutting mechanisms reduce the waste and allow it to pass through a special sizing ring to be pumped directly overboard or into a holding tank or an incinerator when within three-mile limits. Whichever method of waste disposal is chosen, it, as well as the ship, must meet the extremely stringent demands of Annex V of MARPOL 73/78 international regulations.

FOOD & BEVERAGE CONSUMPTION AND STORES

Consumption and stores required for just one transatlantic crossing of *QE2* (five days):

Food Consumption

Beef	9,000 lb
Veal	8,000 lb
Lamb	2,000 lb
Pork	2,500 lb
Chicken	3,500 lb
Duck	1,000 lb
Turkey	1,000 lb
Bacon	2,000 lb
Sausages	2,000 lb
Ham	8,000 lb
Caviar	75 lb
Foie Gras	15 lb
Fish	1,000 lb
Lobsters	1,500 lb
Crabs	800 lb
Tinned fish	1,500 cans
Fresh Vegetables	12,000 lb
Potatoes	3,000 lb
Cereals	800 lb
Rice/Other Grains	3,000 lb
Flour	5,000 lb
Cream	250 gallons
Milk	1,150 gallons
Ice Cream	450 gallons
Butter	2,500 lb
Eggs	43,000
Juices	3,000 gallons
Jam/Marmalade	300 dozen jars
Jam/Marmalade (bulk)	700 lb
Pickles/Condiments	200 bottles
Tea Bags	12,800
Kosher Food	800 lb
Biscuits	2,000 lb
Dog Biscuits	50 lb
Baby Food	600 jars

Bar Consumption

Champagnes	780 bottles
Assorted Wines	1,560 bottles
(the cellar contains 25,000 bottles)	
Whisky	500 bottles
Gin	600 bottles
Rum	240 bottles
Vodka	130 bottles
Brandy	240 bottles
Liqueurs	260 bottles
Port	120 bottles
Sherry	240 bottles
Beer (passengers)	5,230 bottles
Beer (crew)	8,530 cans
Fruit Juice	25,720 pints

The Laundry List

Tablecloths	2,932
Blankets	4,300
Oven Cloths	1,000
Sheets	11,600
Pillow Cases	13,100
Laundry Bags	3,250
Bath Mats	1,650
Hand Towels	15,500
Bath/Other Towels	13,000
Aprons	1,500
Deck Rugs	750

Cruising
for the Physically Challenged

The advantages of a cruise for the physically challenged are many: ideal place for self-renewal; pure air at sea; no smog; no pollen; no packing and unpacking; spacious public rooms; excellent medical facilities close at hand; almost any type of dietary requirements can be catered for; a helpful staff; relaxation; good entertainment; security; no crime on board; many different ports of call, and so on.

Cruise lines, port authorities, airlines, and various allied services are slowly improving their facilities so that those who are wheelchair-bound or otherwise handicapped can enjoy a cruise as fully as possible. At the last count, in the United States alone, some 43 million people—that is, one out of every five people over the age of fifteen—were registered as being physically handicapped, while in the U.K. over six million persons were registered disabled. Not all are in wheelchairs, of course, but all of them have needs that the cruise industry is (slowly) working to accommodate.

The main problem areas aboard cruise ships are:

a. the cabin itself: the entrance, configuration, the closet hanging rails, and the beds.
b. the cabin bathroom: the grab bars, wheel-in shower stall, toiletries cabinet should all be at an accessible height for the passengers.

c. elevator doorways: the width of the door is important for wheelchair passengers; elevator controls should be at a height suitable for operation from a wheelchair.
d. outside decks: access should be possible through electric-eye doors that open and close automatically rather than through doorways that have to be opened manually; any "lips" at doorways should be ramped.

The very design of ships has traditionally worked against mobility-limited people. To keep out water or to prevent it escaping from a flooded cabin or public area, raised edges (known as "coamings" or "lips") are often placed in doorways and across exit pathways. Also, cabin doorways are so often not wide enough to accommodate even a standard wheelchair. The "standard" cabin door is about 24 inches (61 cm) wide. Cabins designed for disabled people have doors that are about 30 inches (76 cm) wide. "Standard" bathroom doors are normally only about 22 inches (56 cm) wide, whereas those specifically designed for the disabled are about 28-30 inches (71-76 cm) wide. Do ask your travel agent to confirm the width of these two important access items, and do remember that, while the cabin door may be given as 30 inches (76 cm), you must allow for the fact that your knuckles on either side of a wheelchair can add 3 inches

(7.6 cm) to the width of your wheel-chair (the so-called industry "standard" size is 24.5 inches/62 cm wide, while a junior adult size is 22.5 inches/57 cm wide). The newest ships of Royal Caribbean Cruises, *Legend of the Seas* and *Splendour of the Seas,* for example, have cabin doorways that are 31 inches (79 cm) wide and elevator doorways that are 43 inches (109 cm) wide. And they also have cabins with verandas for passengers with disabilities.

Bathroom doors are a particular problem. Whether they open outward into the cabin or inward into the bath-room, the problems of maneuvering a wheelchair within a cramped space are only compounded. (Four cabins on *QE2,* however, have electrically oper-ated sliding doors into the bathroom, a completely level entrance into both the cabin and the bathroom, and remote-controlled lights, curtains, and doors, as well as a door intercom and alarm.) Remember also that bathrooms in most ships are normally small and are full of plumbing fixtures, often at odd angles—extremely awkward when you are trying to move about from the con-fines of a wheelchair. Bathrooms on newer ships are more accessible, except for the fact that their plumbing is very often located beneath the complete prefabricated module, making the floor higher than that in the cabin, which means a ramp must be fitted in order to "wheel" in.

Some cruise lines, such as Holland America Line, will, if given advance notice, remove a bathroom door and hang a fabric curtain in its place. Many lines will provide ramps for the bath-room doorway where a sill or "lip" is encountered.

It was once the policy of almost all cruise lines to discourage the mobility-limited from taking a cruise or indeed traveling anywhere by ship for reasons of safety, insurance, and legal liability. But it is now clear that a cruise is the ideal holiday for a physically chal-lenged person, as it provides a relaxed environment with plenty of social con-tact, and organized entertainment and activities. However, despite most cruise brochures declaring that they accept wheelchairs, few ships are well fitted to accommodate them. Some cruise lines, such as Carnival Cruise Lines, openly admit that all public restrooms and cabin bathrooms are inaccessible to wheelchair-bound passengers.

While on the subject of bathrooms, note that many ships have bathroom doors that open inward instead of out-ward, providing even less space for a wheelchair. An inward opening bath-room door is hard for even ambulatory passengers to cope with, but absolutely useless for anyone in a wheelchair. Many suites have bathroom doors that open inward, while standard-size cabin bathroom doors open outward. Ask your travel agent to check which one applies to your chosen ship and cabin.

The list at the end of this chapter pertains to all the ships presented in Part Three, and provides a guide as to their accessibility (the author person-ally wheels himself around each ship to check). Once you've decided on your ship and cruise, the next step is to select your accommodations. There are many grades of cabin, depending on size, facilities, and location. Select a cruise line that permits you to choose a specific cabin, rather than one that allows you to select a price category only, then assigns you a cabin immediately prior to your departure date or, worse still, actually at embarkation.

The following tips will help you choose wisely:

- If the ship does not have any specially equipped cabins for the handicapped, then book the best outside cabin in your price range or find a ship that *does* have cabins specially constructed or adapted for the disabled. However, be careful as you may find that even those cruise brochures that state that a ship has "wheelchair accessible" cabins fail to say whether the wheelchair will fit through the *bathroom* door, or whether there is a "lip" at the door. You should also find out whether your wheelchair can fit into the shower area. Get your travel agent to check, and re-check these details. Don't take "I think" as an answer. Get specific measurements.

- Choose a cabin that is close to an elevator. Not all elevators go to all decks, so check the deck plan carefully. For example, cabins for the physically challenged in *Radisson Diamond* are located far from the elevators. Smaller and older vessels may not even have elevators, making access to many areas, including the dining room, difficult and sometimes almost impossible.

- Avoid, at all costs, a cabin located down a little alleyway shared by several other cabins, even if the price is attractive. The space along these alleyways is extremely limited and trying to enter one of the cabins in a wheelchair is likely to be a frustrating experience.

- Since cabins that are located amidships are less affected by the motion of the vessel, look for something in the middle of the ship if you're concerned about rough seas, no matter how infrequently they might occur.

- The larger (and therefore the more expensive) the cabin is, the more room you will have to maneuver in. Nowhere does this assume more importance than in the bathroom.

- If your budget allows, pick a cabin that has a bath rather than just a shower, because there will be considerably more room, especially if you are unable to stand comfortably enough.

- Ships that exceed 20,000 grt will have far more spacious alleyways, public areas and (generally) bigger cabins. Ships under 20,000 grt tend to have cabins and passageways that are somewhat confining and therefore difficult to maneuver in, particularly past housekeeping carts.

- Meals on some ships may be served in your cabin, on special request—a decided advantage should you wish to avoid dressing for every meal. Few ships have enough space in the cabin for real dining tables, though.

- If you do want to join the other passengers in the dining room and your ship offers two fixed sittings for meals, choose the second rather than the first so that you can linger over your dinner.

- Space at dining room tables can be limited on many ships. When making table reservations, ask for a table that leaves plenty of room for your wheelchair, so that waiters, and other passengers, have enough room to get past.

109

- Even if you do find a cruise/travel agent who knows your needs and requirements, try to follow up on all aspects of the booking yourself so that there will be no slip-ups on the day of departure.
- Take your own wheelchair with you, as ships carry a very limited number of wheelchairs, meant for emergency hospital use only. An alternative is to rent an electric wheelchair, which can be delivered to the ship on your sailing date.
- Hanging rails in the closets on most ships are positioned too high for someone who is wheelchair-bound to reach, though some cruise ships do have cabins specially fitted out to suit mobility-limited passengers. Cabins in *QE2* and *Royal Viking Sun*, for example, are fitted with walk-in closets (the four special cabins on *QE2* have a pull-down facility to bring your clothes down to any height you want). In Part Three, the ships with special cabins are marked either with the number of cabins, or with a "Yes" alongside the entry for Wheelchair Cabins.
- Elevators may also be a source of difficulty for passengers in wheelchairs. Control buttons are often located too high to reach, especially those buttons for the upper decks.
- Doors on upper decks that open onto a Promenade or Lido Deck are very strong, are difficult to handle, and have high sills. Unless you are ambulatory, or can get out of your wheelchair, these doors can be a source of annoyance, even if there's help at hand, as they open inward or outward (they should ideally be electrically operated sliding doors).

- Advise any airline you might be traveling with of any special needs well ahead of time so that arrangements can be made to accommodate you without any last-minute problems.
- Advise the cruise line repeatedly of the need for proper transfer facilities, in particular buses or vans with wheelchair ramps.

EMBARKATION

Even if you've alerted the airline and arranged your travel according to your needs, there's still one problem area that can remain when you arrive at the cruise embarkation port to join your ship: the actual boarding. If you embark at ground level, the gangway to the ship may be level or inclined. It will depend on the embarkation deck of the ship and/or the tide in the port.

Alternatively, you may be required to embark from an upper level of the terminal, in which case the gangway could well be of the floating loading-bridge type, such as those used at major airports. Some of these have floors that are totally flat, while others may have raised lips an inch or so in height, spaced every 3 feet (0.9 m). These are awkward to negotiate in a wheelchair, especially if the gangway is made steeper by a rising tide.

TENDERING

I am constantly pressing the cruise lines to provide an anchor emblem in their brochures for those ports of call where ships will be at anchor instead of alongside. If the ship is at anchor, be prepared for an interesting but safe experience. The crew will lower you and your wheelchair into a waiting tender (a ship-to-shore launch) and then, after a short boat-ride, lift you out again onto a rigged gangway or integral platform. If the sea is calm this maneuver proceeds uneventfully; if the sea is choppy, your embarkation could vary from exciting to harrowing. This type of embarkation is fortunately rare, unless you are leaving a busy port with several ships all sailing the same day.

No two cruise lines seem to have the same wording in their policies with regard to tendering. In any event, you'll find it in the fine print at the back of a cruise brochure.

WHEELCHAIRS

Wheelchair cruise passengers with limited mobility should use a collapsible wheelchair. By limited mobility I mean a person who is able to get out of the wheelchair and step over a sill or walk with a cane, crutches or other walking device.

The chart on pages 110–111 indicates the best cruise ships for wheelchair accessibility.

Finally, remember to ask questions before you make a reservation. For example, some of the most important to ask are:

- Does the cruise line's travel insurance (with a cancellation/trip interruption) cover you for any injuries while you are aboard ship?
- Are there any public rooms or public decks on board the ship that

are inaccessible to wheelchairs (for instance, it is sometimes difficult to obtain access to the outdoor swimming pool deck)?

- Will you be guaranteed a good viewing place in the main showroom from where you can see the shows, if seated in a wheelchair?
- Will special transportation be provided to transfer you from airport to ship?
- If you need a collapsible wheelchair, will one be provided by the cruise line?
- Are passengers required to sign a medical release?
- Do passengers need a doctor's note to qualify for a handicapped cabin?
- Will crew members be on hand to help, or must passengers rely on their own traveling companions to assist them?
- Are the ship's tenders accessible to wheelchairs?
- How do you get from your cabin to the lifeboats (which may be up or down several decks) in an emergency, if the elevators are out of action and cannot be used?

WAIVERS

Passengers who do not require wheelchairs but are challenged in other ways, such as those who have impaired sight, hearing or speech, present their own particular requirements. Many of these can be avoided if the person is accompanied by an able-bodied companion, experienced in attending to their special needs. In any event, some cruise lines require physically challenged passengers to sign a waiver.

SAILING AS ONE OF THE CREW

For something really different and adventurous, how about sailing yourself? The square-rigged sts *Lord Nelson*, constructed in 1988, is a specially built barque sailing ship with three masts and a total of 18 sails. Designed for the physically challenged and able-bodied to share the challenge of crewing a ship at sea, the 141-foot-long (43-m) *Lord Nelson* is sailed in both the Caribbean and Mediterranean areas.

Aptly named after arguably Britain's most famous sailor, the ship was built at Wivenhoe, England, at a cost of $5 million for the Jubilee Sailing Trust, headquartered in Southampton, England. All decks are flat, without steps, and there are special lifts for you to get between them, as well as up the ship's side to get aboard. There is even a lift seat to go up the main mast.

Navigation aids include an audio compass and bright track radar screen for the blind or the partially sighted, and ship-to-shore radio and hydraulic-assist steering.

Down below, all accommodations are accessible to all the physically challenged or able-bodied crew, with specially fitted cabins and bathrooms. In addition, there is a saloon/bar, launderette, library, and workshop. *Lord Nelson's* flat decks, powered lifts, wide companionways and other facilities enable everyone on board to take part on equal terms as part of the crew.

Under a professional captain and sailing master, six permanent crew, including a qualified medical purser, guide and instruct the 40-strong crew on each "cruise."

HEARING-IMPAIRED

More than 6 million Americans suffer from hearing loss, and some 1.5 million Americans suffer from a hearing loss of more than 40 per cent. Those affected should be aware of some of the problems on board a ship:

* hearing the announcements on the public address system
* use of telephone
* poor acoustics in the key areas (for example, boarding shore tenders)

Remember to take a spare battery for your hearing aid. More and more new ships now have cabins specially fitted with colored signs to help those who are hearing-impaired, while Norwegian Cruise Line's *Dreamward* and *Windward* provide specially adapted cabins. Four of the cabins in *QE2* also have illuminated signs to assist those who are hearing-impaired. Crystal Cruises' *Crystal Harmony* and *Crystal Symphony*, as well as Celebrity Cruises' *Century* and *Galaxy*, are fitted with movie theaters that are equipped with special headsets for use by hearing-impaired passengers.

Many ships, particularly those that carry more than 500 passengers, make life difficult for the hearing-impaired by issuing a constant stream of irritating and repetitive announcements over the public address system. This often makes it difficult for the hearing-impaired to distinguish important announcements from the trivial ones.

Finally, when going ashore, for example on organized excursions, be aware that most destinations are not equipped for the hearing-impaired.

KEY:
✗ = Not suitable for wheelchair passengers
✓ = Acceptable for wheelchair passengers
✓✓ = Good for wheelchair passengers
✓✓✓ = Highly recommended as most suitable for wheelchair passengers

Aegean Dolphin ✗
Aida ✓✓
Albatros ✗
Alla Tarasova ✗
Americana ✗
Andaman Princess ✗
Antonina Nezhdanova ✗
Arkona ✓
Astor ✓
Astra ✗
Astra II ✗
Asuka ✓
Atalante ✗
Ausonia ✗
Azerbaydzhan ✗
Bali Sea Dancer ✗
Berlin ✓
Black Prince ✗
Black Watch ✗
Bolero ✗
Bremen ✗
Caledonian Star ✗
Calypso ✗
Canberra ✗
Carina ✗
Carnival Destiny ✓✓
Carousel ✗
Celebration ✗
Century ✓✓
Constitution ✗
CostaAllegra ✗
CostaClassica ✓✓
CostaMarina ✗
CostaPlaya ✗
CostaRiviera ✗
CostaRomantica ✓✓
CostaVictoria ✓✓
Crown Princess ✓✓

Crystal Harmony ✓✓✓
Crystal Symphony ✓✓✓
Cunard Countess ✗
Cunard Dynasty ✗
Daphne ✗
Dawn Princess ✓✓✓
Dimitri Shostakovich ✗
Dolphin IV ✗
Don Juan ✗
Dreamward ✓
Ecstasy ✓
Enchanted Isle ✗
Enchantment
  of the Seas ✓✓
EugenioCosta ✗
Europa ✓✓
Explorer ✗
Fairstar ✗
Fantasy ✓
Fascination ✓
Fuji Maru ✗
Funchal ✗
Galaxy ✓✓
Grand Princess ✓✓✓
Grandeur of the Seas ✓✓
Gripsholm ✗
Hanseatic ✗
Hebridean Princess ✗
Holiday ✗
Hong Kong Dragon Star ✗
Horizon ✓✓
Imagination ✓
Independence ✗
Inspiration ✓
Island Breeze ✗
Island Princess ✓
Italia Prima ✗
Ivan Franko ✗

INDEX TO SHIPS IN THIS BOOK (220 SHIPS)

Song of America ✗
Song of Flower ✗
Song of Norway ✗
Southern Cross ✗
Sovereign of the Seas ✓
Splendour of the Seas ✓✓
Star Pisces ✓
Star Princess ✓
Star/Ship Atlantic ✗
Star/Ship Oceanic ✗
Statendam ✓
Stella Oceanis ✗
Stella Solaris ✗
Sun Princess ✓✓✓
Sun Viking ✗
SuperStar Gemini ✗
Symphony ✗
Taras Shevchenko ✗
The Azur ✗
Triton ✗
Tropicale ✗
Universe Explorer ✗
Veendam ✓
Victoria ✓

Viking Serenade ✓
Vistafjord ✓
Vistamar ✗
Westerdam ✓
Windward ✓
World Discoverer ✗
Yamal ✗
Yorktown Clipper ✗
Zenith ✓✓

Sail-Cruise Ships

Club Med I ✗
Club Med II ✗
Le Ponant ✗
Lili Marleen ✗
Sea Cloud ✗
Sir Francis Drake ✗
Star Clipper ✗
Star Flyer ✗
Wind Song ✗
Wind Spirit ✗
Wind Star ✗

1. The following ships of Carnival Cruise Lines have double-width entertainment decks that are good for wheelchair passengers, but the public restrooms are not accessible. In addition, although the cabin bathrooms are equipped with shower stalls and grab bars, the bathrooms have a steep "lip" and are thus not accessible without stepping out of the wheelchair (*Celebration, Ecstasy, Fantasy, Fascination, Holiday, Imagination, Inspiration, Jubilee, Sensation*).

2. *Crystal Harmony* and *Crystal Symphony* (Crystal Cruises) are the only ships presently in operation that provide special access ramps from an accommodations deck directly to the ship's lifeboats.

3. *Crown Princess* and *Regal Princess* (Princess Cruises) both have large outside cabins for passengers with disabilities, but all have obstructed views.

Cruising for Romantics

TRAVELING SOLO OR SINGLE

Back in 1932, Warner Bros. released the film *One Way Passage*, a bittersweet story starring Kay Francis and William Powell. Then there was the shipboard affair kindled by Bette Davis and Paul Henried in *Now, Voyager*. Remember Irene Dunne and Charles Boyer in a film called *Love Affair*? Or the same couple in *An Affair to Remember*. All involved ocean-going passenger ships, and romance. Then there was *Gentlemen Prefer Blondes*, in which Marilyn Monroe and Jane Russell starred.

Even in the early 1950s Howard Hughes presented Jane Russell in an RKO movie called *The French Line*, which depicted life on board one of the great ocean liners of the time—the ss *Liberté*—as being exciting, frivolous, promiscuous, and romantic! The movie was, in fact, made on board the great ship. Today that same romantic attraction is still very much in vogue.

With more and more singles and solos (those who like to travel alone) in the world today, the possibility of a shipboard romance excites a special attraction. While you may not believe in the notion of mermaids, romance does happen—frequently. Cruise lines, long recognizing this fact, are now trying to help by providing special programs for single passengers. Unfortunately, many solos are turned off cruising because they find it hard to understand why so many lines charge a single occupancy supplement to the fare of someone traveling alone.

By far the most precious commodity aboard any cruise ship is space. Every square foot must be used for essential facilities or revenue-earning areas. Since a single cabin is often as large as a double, and uses the same electrical wiring, plumbing, and fixtures—and thus is just as expensive to build—cruise lines naturally feel justified in charging supplements or premiums for those who are occupying single cabins. Singles would probably not object to a smaller cabin, but don't like being charged a supplement or given a poor location.

Where they do exist, single cabins are often among the most expensive, when compared with the per-person rates for the double occupancy cabins. They are also less flexible. From the point of view of the crew, it takes as much time to clean a single cabin as it does a double. And there's only one tip instead of two.

One answer is to construct double cabins only, and then, whenever feasible, sell them as single-occupancy units—this is something that only a handful of cruise lines actually do. Guaranteed singles rates are offered by several lines, but the line and *not* the passenger picks the cabin. If the line doesn't find a roommate, the single passenger may get the cabin to him- or herself at no extra charge. Ideally, all lines would offer guaranteed singles rates, with no supplement.

DID YOU KNOW ...?

...that the first passenger ship to exceed 40,000 grt was the White Star Line's *Olympic* of 1911?

...that the first passenger ship to exceed 80,000 grt was the Compagnie Générale Transatlantique's *Normandie* of 1935 (built at 79,280, and later measured at 82,799 in 1936)?

More than *one million* cruise passengers traveled as singles in 1996! Cruise lines are only now realizing that about a quarter of calls to travel agents are made by singles, single parents, and solos. Singles tend to test the waters by taking short cruises at first. There are lots of singles on the three- and four-day cruises from several U.S. ports (Los Angeles, Miami, Port Canaveral, San Juan) as well as from the port of Piraeus in Greece.

Some cruise lines or tour operators advertise special cruises for singles, but remember that the age range could be anything from 7 to 70. One cruise line in Australia (CTC Cruises) operates 18 to 35 cruises—a nice touch for young people traveling as singles.

While there are some singles who travel with friends or family, many others like to travel alone. For this reason, the cruise lines have now established several programs to accommodate them. One is the "Guaranteed Single" rate, which provides a set price without having to be concerned about which cabin to choose.

A "Guaranteed Share" program is operated by some of the cruise lines.

This allows you to pay the normal double-occupancy rate, but the cruise line will provide another passenger of the same sex to share the double cabin with you.

Some cruise lines do not advertise a guaranteed-share program in their brochures, but will normally try to accommodate such bookings, particularly when demand for space is light. Sometimes, you may end up booking a guaranteed share basis only to find that you end up with a cabin all to yourself. As cruise lines are apt to change such things at short notice, it's best to check with your travel agent for the latest rates, and read the fine print.

Passengers who want to travel alone and not share a cabin can pay either a flat rate for the cabin, or a single "supplement" if they occupy a double cabin. Some cruise lines charge a fixed amount—$250, for instance—as a supplement, no matter what cabin category, ship, itinerary, or length of cruise you require. Single supplements, or solo occupancy rates, vary between lines, and sometimes between ships. It's advisable, therefore, to check with your travel agent, who will have up-to-date information on the latest rates.

CRUISING FOR SINGLE WOMEN

A single woman, a career woman—whether she is single or married—and a widow can take a cruise vacation knowing they are encapsulated in a safe, hassle-free environment. There is perhaps no better way to de-stress, and if you are seeking that special someone, cruising somehow brings people closer together. There's always someone to talk to, and cruising is not a "meat market" where you are always under observation. In the dining room, the maître d' will seat you with other singles, or a mix of singles and couples, as you wish.

If you *are* looking for romance, however, beware of the lure of the uniform, of an easy affair or fling with a ship's officer (or member of the crew). They get to see new faces every week (or every cruise), and so the possible risk of sexually transmitted conditions must be borne clearly in mind.

GENTLEMEN CRUISE HOSTS

Because the female to male passenger ratio is high (as much as eight to one on world cruises and other long voyages), especially for cruisers of middle to senior years, some lines employ male social hosts, generally about half a dozen, specially recruited to provide dance and bridge partners for passengers. First used to good effect aboard Cunard's QE2 in the late 1970s, gentlemen hosts are now employed by a number of cruise lines.

They also host a table in the dining room, appear as dance partners at all cocktail parties and dance classes, and accompany women on shore excursions. These gentlemen, usually over 55 years of age and/or retired, are outgoing, good minglers, well groomed, and enjoy traveling around the world free of charge.

If you are thinking that you'd like such a job, do remember that you'll have to dance for several hours most nights, and dance just about every kind of dance well! Crystal Cruises, Cunard, Ivaran Lines, Royal Cruise Line, and Silversea Cruises, among others, all provide gentlemen hosts, especially on the longer sea voyages or on world cruises.

THE LOVE BOAT CONNECTION

The two famous television shows *The Love Boat* (U.S.) and *Traumschiff* (Germany) have given a tremendous boost to the concept of cruising as the ultimate romantic vacation, although what is shown on the screen does not quite correspond to reality. Indeed, the captain of one of the ships featured on television, after being asked the difference between his real-life job as captain and that of master of *The Love Boat*, remarked: "On TV they can do a retake if things aren't quite right first time around, whereas I have to get it right first time!"

Ships are indeed romantic places. There is nothing quite like standing on the aft deck of a cruise ship with the object of your love—with hair blowing in the breeze—as you sail over the moonlit waters to yet another island paradise. Of course, a full moon only occurs once a month, so check the calendar to make sure the timing of *your* moonlit cruise is perfect.

But there is no doubt that cruises are excellent opportunities for meeting people of similar interests. So if you're looking for romance, and if you choose the right ship for your cruise, the odds are in your favor.

GETTING MARRIED ABOARD SHIP

Unlike in all those old black and white movies, a ship's captain can no longer marry you, with one exception—in Japan, where the law still allows Japanese couples to marry at sea.

You *can* get married aboard ship (though it must be alongside in port), provided you take along your own registered minister. Some lines, such as American Hawaii Cruises, Carnival Cruise Lines, and Majesty Cruise Lines, for example, offer a complete package, which includes the services of a minister to marry you, wedding cake, champagne and leis for the bridal party, a band to perform at the ceremony and an album of wedding photos. Carnival Cruise Lines' program includes a marriage ceremony on a beach in Grand Cayman or St. Thomas. Majesty Cruise Lines offers weddings aboard ship in Miami, and each of five price levels ($375–$825 at time of going to press) includes notary public services, witnesses and a beautifully designed marriage certificate.

Even if you can't get married aboard ship, you could consider having your wedding reception on one. Many of the cruise lines offer outstanding facilities and provide complete services to help you plan your reception. Contact the director of hotel services at the cruise line of your choice, and you'll be pleased with the way cruise lines go out of their way to help, especially if you follow the reception with a honeymoon cruise.

U.K.-based passengers should know that P&O Cruises has a series of cruises called the "Red-Letter Anniversary Collection" specially for those couples who are celebrating 10, 15, 20, 25, 30, 35, 40, 45, 50, 55 and 60 years of marriage. Gifts you'll receive with the compliments of P&O Cruises include a brass carriage clock, leather photograph album, free car parking at Southampton, or free first-class rail travel from anywhere in the U.K. (check with your travel agent for the latest details).

A cruise also makes not only a fine, no-worry honeymoon vacation, but a delightful belated honeymoon getaway if you had no time to spare when you were married. You'll feel like you're in the middle of a movie set as you sail away to fairytale places, though the ship's a destination in itself.

RENEWAL OF VOWS

There has recently been an upsurge in cruise lines performing the "renewal of vows" ceremonies. A cruise is a wonderful setting for re-affirming to one's partner the strength of commitment. A handful of ships even have a small chapel where this ceremony can take place, otherwise it can be anywhere aboard ship (a very romantic time is sunrise or sunset on the open deck).

The ceremony is conducted, usually by the ship's captain, in a non-denominational text that re-affirms the depth of the love and trust between "partners, lifetime friends and companions."

While some companies, such as Holland America Line, have complete packages that you can purchase, which include music, champagne, hors d'oeuvres, certificate, corsages for the women, and so on, other companies do not make a charge (yet). The ship's own photographer usually records the event (it is a revenue-generating photo opportunity) and will have special photo albums embossed with the cruise line's logo.

CRUISING FOR HONEYMOONERS

There is no doubt that cruising is becoming ever more popular as a honeymoon vacation. In fact, U.S.-based Premier Cruise Lines says that more than 5 per cent of its cruise passengers are honeymooners. And there are some real advantages to a honeymoon cruise: you pack and unpack only one time; it's a completely hassle-free and crime-free environment; and you'll get special attention, if you want it. What's more, it's also very easy to budget in advance, as one price often includes the airfare, the cruise, food, entertainment, several ports of call, shore excursions, and pre- and post-cruise hotel stays and other arrangements. And, once you are married, some cruise lines often offer discounts to entice you to book a future anniversary cruise.

Even nicer is the thought that you won't have to think about cooking

meals, as everything will be done for you. You won't have to think about where to eat, or what choice you will have. You can think of the crew as your very own service and kitchen staff.

Although no ship as yet provides bridal suites (hint, hint), many ships do provide cabins with queen-sized or double beds. Some, but by no means all, also provide tables for two in the dining room.

Some cruise ships feature Sunday or Monday departures (from Miami, San Juan, Venice, Singapore, for example), which allows couples to plan a Saturday wedding and reception, and a leisurely travel to the ship of choice. The pre- and post-cruise hotel accommodation can also be arranged by the cruise line.

While most large ships accommodate honeymoon couples really well, if you want to plan a more private, intimate honeymoon, then try one of the smaller, yacht-like cruise vessels, where you'll feel like it's your own private ship, and you have invited another 50 couples as guests. Highly recommended for a supremely elegant, utterly pampered honeymoon would be the ships of Renaissance Cruises, the Sea Goddess ships of Cunard, the ships of Seabourn Cruise Line, Radisson Seven Seas Cruises, Showa Line (whose *Oceanic Grace* specializes in weddings, and has huge electric chimes built into the topmost outside deck), Silversea Cruises, and Windstar Cruises. All of them have an open bridge policy, so you can join the captain on the bridge at almost any time.

While most of the passengers like to socialize in the evenings, it might be more romantic for the honeymooners to take a stroll by themselves on deck, to the forward part of the ship, above the ship's bridge. This will be the quietest (except perhaps for some wind noise), and most dimly lit part of the ship, an ideal spot for star gazing and romancing. Almost all ships are blessed with such places.

Cruise lines offer a variety of honeymoon packages, much as hotels and resorts on land do. Here's a list of some of the things you can expect from them (note that not all cruise lines provide all services):

- Private captain's cocktail party for honeymooners.
- Tables for two in the dining room.
- Set of crystal champagne or wine glasses.
- Honeymoon photograph with the captain, and photo album.
- Complimentary champagne (either imported or domestic) or wine.
- Honeymoon cruise certificate.

- Champagne and caviar served up for breakfast.
- Flowers in your suite or cabin.
- Complimentary cake.
- Special T-shirts.

Finally, before you go:

- Remember a copy of your marriage license or certificate, for immigration (or marriage) purposes, as your passports will not yet have been amended.
- Remember to allow extra in your budget for things like shipboard gratuities (tips), shore excursions, and spending money ashore.
- If you need to take your wedding gown aboard for a planned wedding somewhere along the way—perhaps in Hawaii, or Bermuda, for example—there is usually space to hang it in the dressing room next to the stage in the main showroom—especially on larger ships.

Cruising for Families

Yes, you *can* take children on a cruise. In fact, if you choose the right ship and cruise, you'll hardly see them at all once aboard. On a cruise, families can do different things, and parents don't have to be concerned about the whereabouts of their children. Where else can you go out on the town without having to drive, and be home in a moment if the babysitter needs you?

Dad can sleep in; mom can go for a swim; the kids can join in the organized activities that go on all day long. Whether you share a cabin with them or whether they have their own separate, though adjoining, cabin, there will be plenty to keep them occupied. On several of the ships which cruise in the Caribbean, you'll even find favorite life-sized cartoon characters on board.

Some cruise lines have token family programs, with limited activities and only a couple of general staff allocated to look after children, even though their brochures might claim otherwise. But the cruise lines that are serious about family cruise programs dedicate complete teams of children's "tweens and teens" counselors, who run special programs that are off-limits to adults. They also have specific facilities such as high chairs in the dining room, cots and playrooms. Most children's entertainment is designed to run simultaneously with adult programs. For those who cruise with very small children, baby-sitting services may also be available. Cunard's *QE2*, for example, has full-time children's nurses and even English nannies, while P&O Cruises' *Oriana* has a "night nursery" for children aged 2 to 5 years.

Parents, of course, have long realized that children cost more as they age. For example, children under 2 years old travel free on most cruise lines. But if they are over 2, then they cost money. In case they have to fly, those over 2 also cost more, as they must take up an airline seat.

But there's no doubt that families that cruise together, stay together! There's no better vacation for families than a ship cruise. Active parents can also enjoy the best of all worlds—family togetherness, social contact, and privacy. Cruise ships provide a safe, crime-free environment, and offer junior cruisers a great deal of freedom. Cruising has never been more child-friendly or affordable, as the emergence of new lines catering specifically to families has proven.

A cruise for children is an educational experience. They will tour the ship's bridge, meet senior officers and learn about the navigation, radar and communications equipment, as well as seeing how the ship operates. They will be exposed to different environments, experience many types of food, travel to and explore new places, and take part in exciting activities.

On the busiest ships, such as those of Premier Cruise Lines, adults will rarely get to use the swimming pools alone—they will be overwhelmed by lively children having a good time.

Junior cruisers enjoying one of many planned activities aboard one of the ships of Royal Caribbean Cruises.

Many cruise lines have added a whole variety of children's programs to their roster of daily activities. Some ships have separate swimming pools and play areas for children, as well as playrooms, junior discos, video rooms and teen centers. One cruise company—Carnival Cruise Lines—has created a "Camp Carnival" on its vessels. And Royal Caribbean Cruises has junior counselors on almost all its sailings. Other cruise lines generally have counselors sailing during the summer and other special holiday periods.

Cruise lines that are serious about children divide them into five distinct age groups, with various names to match, according to cruise line and program: Toddlers (ages 2-4); Juniors (ages 5-7); Intermediate (ages 8-10): Tweens (ages 11-13); and Teens (ages 14-17).

Children and junior cruisers are usually not permitted to participate in adult games, tournaments, quizzes and so on, but have their own versions. In compliance with international law, casinos and bars are reserved strictly for passengers aged 18 and over.

One North American cruise company that caters well to families with children is Premier Cruise Lines, which carries children's counselors on every cruise on each of its two red-hulled ships, *Star/Ship Atlantic* and *Star/Ship Oceanic*, as well as some well-known cartoon characters. Meanwhile, Carnival Cruise Lines has a 114-foot-long (35-m) water slide as part of the swimming pool on all its ships (it's even longer aboard *Carnival Destiny*).

In South-East Asia, Star Cruise, based in Singapore, has two ships, *Langkapuri Star Aquarius* and *Star Pisces*, out of a fleet of five (two new ships are also on order), that have incredible facilities for families with children, including a children's video arcade. There are also seven restaurants/dining places to choose from.

GENERAL INFORMATION

Parents with babies can rest assured that they will find selected baby foods on board ships that cater to children (along with cribs and high chairs—but do ask your travel agent to check first). If you need something out of the ordinary, or you need a special brand of baby food, do let your travel agent know well in advance. Most cruise lines are very accommodating and will do their best to obtain what is needed, provided enough notice is given, but parents using organic baby foods, such as those obtained from health food stores, should be aware that cruise lines buy their supplies from major general food suppliers and not the smaller specialized food houses.

Many ships have really full programs for children during days at sea, although these may be limited when the ship is in port. Ships expect you to take your children with you on organized shore excursions, and sometimes (though not always) there are special prices for children. If the ship has a playroom, it might be wise to find out if it is open and supervised on all days of the cruise. Don't expect your travel agent to know everything.

DISNEY'S COMING

In January 1998, Disney Cruise Line will enter the family cruise market with a bang. The giant entertainment company is building two mega-ships (each with two funnels) that will cater specifically to families with children. I anticipate that these two ships (which are designed to transit the Panama Canal) will be the supreme family cruise ships of the future. They will be in the 85,000 grt range, and cater to 1,750 adult passengers, plus up to 500 children, with the whole of the Disney organization to draw from for the shipboard entertainment program. The children's area will be a huge 15,000 sq. ft. (1,393.5 m²), and there will be more than 35 counselors on any given cruise. There will be a separate family/ children's pool, designated teen club and game arcade. A children's drop-off service in the evenings should prove popular, and a private babysitting service will be available, as will character "tuck-ins" for children, and character breakfast and lunch. Strollers (pushchairs) will also be available, at no charge. The cabins (880 of them) will range in size from 220 sq. ft. (20.4 m²) to 960 sq. ft. (89.1 m²). Some 73 per cent will be outside, and 44 per cent of those will have private verandas. As for dining, there will be three main restaurants, and one alternative restaurant. Disney will also have its own 1,000-acre private island, Gorda Cay (fully owned by Disney), which promises to be an outstanding facility. The first ship will feature three- and four-day cruises from Port Canaveral in Florida, combined with a three- or four-day stay at a Walt Disney World Resort. The ships have a stunning array of facilities for the following groups: (a) couples and single parents with children; (b) couples without children. The activities and entertainment will be innovative, as will be the range of accommodations.

When going ashore, remember that if you want to take your children swimming or to the beach, it is wise to phone ahead to a local hotel with a beach or pool. Whether it is in the Caribbean, the Mediterranean or the Orient, most hotels will be delighted to show off their property, hoping for future business.

Some cruise ships in the Caribbean area have the use of a "private" island for a day—ideal for children. A lifeguard will be on duty, and there will be watersports and snorkeling equipment you can rent. Note, though, that the beaches on some "private" islands are fine for 200, but with 2,000, they will be crowded. Standing in line for beach barbecues and toilet facilities is a necessary part of the experience.

While the sun and sea might attract the juniors to the warm waters of the Caribbean, children aged 7 and over will love a Mediterranean, Black Sea or Baltic cruise. They will find it easier to understand, remember and compare the differences between ports of call. They will also have a fine introduction to history and different cultures.

CHILDREN'S RATES

Most cruise lines offer special rates for children sharing their parents' cabin. The cost is often lower than third and fourth person share rates. To get the best possible rates, it is wise to book early. Don't overlook booking an inside cabin—you'll rarely be in it anyway.

While many adult cruise rates include airfare, most children's rates do not. Although some lines say children sail "free," they must in fact pay port taxes as well as airfare. The cruise line will get the airfare at the best rate, so there's no need to shop around for the lowest fare.

Unless they have plenty of things to keep them occupied, even the most placid children can become bored and restless. So try to choose a cruise where there are lots of other children, as they will be best equipped to provide the required entertainment.

SINGLE PARENTS

A single parent traveling with their child(ren) will have their own special needs, and needn't feel left out, either. Female single parents can also feel safe on a cruise, free of the unwanted advances of single men. Only a handful of cruise lines so far have introduced their own version of the "Single Parent Plan." This offers an economical way for single parents to go on a cruise, with parent and child sharing a two-berth cabin, or parent and children sharing a three-berth cabin. Single parents will pay approximately one-third the normal single person rate for their children.

CHILDREN-FRIENDLY CRUISE LINES

The following have been selected by the author for their excellent programs and care: Airtours Cruises, American Hawaii Cruises, Carnival Cruise Lines, Celebrity Cruises, Cunard, Norwegian Cruise Line, P&O Cruises, Premier Cruise Lines, Royal Caribbean Cruises, Star Cruise.

Before You Go

BAGGAGE

Cruise lines usually have no limit to the amount of baggage you take on your cruise ship, but as closet space is limited, take only the things you will use. Allow extra space in your luggage for purchases on the trip. Remember that towels, soap, shampoo, and shower caps are provided on board.

It is important that you properly tag all your baggage with your name, ship, cabin number, sailing date, and port of embarkation. Tags will be provided by the cruise line along with your ticket. Baggage transfers from airport to ship are generally smooth and problem-free when handled by the cruise line.

Liability for loss or damage to baggage is contained in the passenger contract. If you are not adequately covered for this, you should take out more insurance. The policy should extend from the date of departure until two or three days after your return home. Coverage can be obtained from your cruise/travel agent.

CLOTHING

If you think you might not wear it, don't take it: closet space on most ships is at a premium. Unless you are on an extended cruise, keep your luggage to a minimum. Most of the airlines have a limit of two suitcases at check-in (44 lb or 20 kg) per person, plus a tote bag or carry-all for small items.

For cruises to tropical areas, where the weather is warm to hot with high humidity, casual wear should include plenty of lightweight cottons and other natural fibers. Synthetic materials do not "breathe" as well and often retain heat. Clothes should, however, be as opaque as possible to counteract the ultraviolet rays of the sun. Also, take a lightweight cotton sweater or two for the evenings, when the ship's air-conditioning will seem even more powerful after a day in the sun.

The same is true for cruises to the Mediterranean, Greek Isles, or North Africa, although there will be little or no humidity most of the year. Certain areas may be dusty as well as dry. In these latitudes, the weather can be changeable and cool in the evenings October through March, so take extra sweaters.

On cruises to Alaska, the North Cape or to the Norwegian fjords, take some warm comfortable clothing, plus a raincoat or parka for the northernmost port calls. Cruises to Alaska and to the Land of the Midnight Sun only run during the peak summer months, when temperatures are pleasant and when the weather is less likely to be inclement. Unless you are traveling to northern ports such as St. Petersburg during winter, you won't need thermal underwear. However, you will definitely need it—and overcoats, too—if you are taking an adventure cruise to the Antarctic Peninsula or through the Northwest Passage.

In the Far East, what you wear will depend on the time of year. The information package that accompanies your tickets will give recommendations. For a cruise that sets off deep in winter from one of the northern ports (New York or Southampton, for example), and for cruises south to find the sun, you should take lightweight cottons plus a few sweaters.

Rainstorms in the tropics are infrequent and don't last long, but they can give you a good soaking, so take inexpensive but lightweight rain wear for excursions you go on.

In countries with a strong religious tradition, such as Venezuela, Haiti, Dominican Republic, Colombia, and countries in the Far East, do note that shorts or bare shoulders may cause local offense, so cover up.

Aboard ship, dress rules are relaxed during the day, but in the evening what you wear should be tasteful. Men should take a blazer or sports jacket and ties for the dining room and for any "informal" occasions. Transatlantic crossings are normally more elegant.

If you are the athletic type, pack sports clothes for the gymnasium. Shorts/jogging pants would also be useful for women who enjoy aerobics.

For formal nights (usually two out of every seven), women should wear their best long evening gown, elegant cocktail dress, or a smart pants suit. Gentlemen are expected to wear either a tuxedo or dark business suit. These "rules" are less rigid on short and moderately priced cruises.

There is sometimes a masquerade night on each cruise, so you may wish to take a costume. Or you can create something on board out of materials that are provided. One of the staff may help, and there may be photographs of past entries to give you ideas. Prizes are awarded for the most creative costume.

No matter where in the world you are traveling, comfortable low- or flat-heeled shoes are a *must* for women, except for formal occasions. Light, airy shoes are best for walking. If you are in the South Pacific or Caribbean and are not used to heat and humidity, your ankles may swell—so, tight shoes are not recommended. Rubber soles are best for walking on the deck of a ship.

FORMAL
Tuxedo (alternatively a dark suit) for men; evening gown or other appropriate formal attire for women.

INFORMAL
Jacket and tie for men; cocktail dress, dressy pants suit, or something similar, for women.

CASUAL
Slacks and jacket on top of sweater or open shirt for men; a blouse with skirt, slacks or similar comfortable attire for women.

On a typical 7-day cruise, the following is what you generally might expect as the dress code for each day:

Sat	Casual
Sun	Formal (Captain's Welcome Aboard Cocktail Party)
Mon	Casual/Informal
Tue	Casual/Informal
Wed	Casual/Informal
Thu	Formal (Captain's Farewell Cocktail Party)
Fri	Casual

DOCUMENTS

A passport is the most practical proof of your citizenship and identification. Although it is not required on all cruises, take it along, if you have one. A voter's registration card and a driver's license are normally acceptable, but are not considered as valid proof of your citizenship.

If you are a non-U.S. citizen taking a cruise from an American port, you must have a valid B-2 multiple-entry visitor's visa stamped in your passport in order to return to the United States at the end of your cruise.

Note: British passport holders do not need a visa to enter the U.S., as the Visa Waiver Program applies.

If you are cruising to areas other than those of the Bahamas, Bermuda, Caribbean, Alaska, Hawaii or Canada, and most of Europe, you may need a tourist visa. Your cruise/travel agent will advise you.

On cruises to the Orient particularly, but also to the Middle East and Africa, you may have to hand in your passport to the purser prior to landing. This helps the customs and immigration officials to "clear" the ship more quickly, and is standard practice. Your passport will be returned when the ship departs, or prior to its arrival in the port of disembarkation.

FLYING

For many people, flying to get to a port of embarkation has become the norm. Most cruise lines now include "free air" as part of the cruise ticket. The effects of rampant discounting, however, have resulted in cruise lines negotiating contracts with airlines that involve passengers sometimes having to travel on flights with absurd connections, even when direct flights are available. In the case of the United States, the introduction of deregulation has resulted in most airlines operating on a "hub and spoke" system, with flights feeding into major centers to connect with other flights. It is now more difficult to find non-stop coast-to-coast flights, as airlines prefer passengers to go through the system to ensure full domestic flights. This is not so prevalent in Europe, but distances are comparatively shorter given the size of each country.

FLYING AND AIR QUALITY

If you are joining a ship in a far-off port and your flight is over six hours' duration, you might want to consider paying a little more to move further forward into the Business Class or First Class, rather than go to the Economy Class at the back of the plane. The reason for making this recommendation is simply that the quality of fresh air is better at the front of the plane than it is at the back. There is also a dramatic difference in the quality of air in certain types of aircraft.

It is not easy to change cabin air frequently, because at 40,000 feet (12,192 m) the external air can be minus 75°F, and almost completely dry. This air must then be heated to 75°F, and the moisture must be added to the air before it is pumped into the cabin. This all uses fuel. The latest Boeing and Airbus aircraft have tried to cut down on waste by recycling some of the warm and somewhat moist cabin air. The air is filtered using a mesh to catch bacteria, but this adds to the time taken to change the air completely. What do you do if the air is bad? Tell the senior flight purser, who will ask the engineer to increase the circulation.

Smokers should be aware that in some countries, smoking is banned on certain flights.

FLYING AND JET LAG

If you are flying long distance to embark on your cruise or to fly home again, you should know that modern air travel is fast, safe, efficient, and comfortable (for the most part). Even experienced travelers, however, may occasionally find that the stresses of international travel persist long after the flight is over. Eastbound flights seem to cause more pronounced jetlag than westbound flights. And while jet aircraft are pressurized, they generally are done so only to some 8,000 feet (2,400 m) in altitude, causing discomfort in the ears and the stomach, and swollen feet. The air of the aircraft cabin is also slightly dry. A few precautions should help to reduce the less pleasant effects of flying around the world.

First, you should plan as well in advance of your cruise as you possibly can. It is preferable to take a daytime flight, so that you can arrive at, or close to, your normal bedtime. Try to remain as quiet as possible for the 24 hours prior to flying, and allow for another five hours of rest after any

flight which has crossed more than five time zones.

Enjoy the food and liquor offered during the flight—but in moderation. The best beverages are the nonalcoholic and nonsparkling ones. Smokers may wish to smoke less, as the reduced pressure (and reduced oxygen) means that the effect of carbon monoxide is greater, often resulting in a feeling of depression.

Babies and small children are less affected by changes in time because of their shorter sleeping and waking cycles. But adults generally need more time to adjust. The only way to experience a flight without jet lag is to fly the *Concorde* (London–New York or New York–London). At Mach 2 speed, such a flight does not produce the symptoms of jet lag.

MEDICATION

If you are planning a cruise that takes you away from your home country, make sure you take any medicines that you need, plus spare eyeglasses or contact lenses. In many countries it may be difficult to find certain medication. Others may be sold under quite different names. Those traveling on long cruises should ask their doctor for names of alternatives, in case the medicine they are taking is not available.

The ship pharmacy will stock some standard remedies, but don't expect it to have a supply of the more unusual or obscure medicines. Remember to take along a doctor's prescription for any medication you need, especially when you're flying into foreign countries to join a ship, as customs may be

129

difficult without documentation, particularly those in the Far East.

If you run out of medication and need to get another supply, most ships will require you to see the doctor, even if you have a prescription. There is a minimum charge of $15 for the visit, plus the cost of the medication.

Passengers who are diabetic should let spouses/companions carry a supply of insulin and syringes, as well as a quick source of glucose. Make sure you carry a sufficient supply with you, and don't pack it in any luggage that has to be checked in when flying.

MONEY MATTERS

Most of the cruise ships deal primarily in U.S. dollars but some take British pounds, or German marks, or Greek drachmas, or Australian dollars. Major credit cards and traveler's checks are widely accepted on board, but few lines take personal checks.

Most ships now allow passengers to sign for drinks and assorted other services. On some ships a convenient way to settle expenses is to set up a shipboard credit on embarkation. This is very useful on long voyages. Most lines now have a "cashless" cruising policy, allowing you to pay for all on-board expenses by pre-signed credit card.

PETS

Pets are not carried by cruise ships, with two exceptions. One is on the regular scheduled transatlantic services of *QE2*, which has 16 air-conditioned kennels, cat containers, plus several

special cages for birds. The other is on the regular scheduled South Atlantic service from England to Cape Town and the Ascension Islands aboard *St. Helena*. Quarantine and vaccination regulations can be obtained from the consulates of the relevant country.

PHOTOGRAPHY

Think about where you are going when buying film. It is best to use low-speed film in tropical areas such as the Caribbean or South Pacific, as high-speed film is easily damaged by heat. Take plenty of film with you; standard sizes are available in the ship's shop, but the selection is limited. If you purchase film on a port visit, try to buy it from an air-conditioned store, and check the expiry date.

Keep your film as cool as possible, as the latent image on exposed film is fragile and easily affected by heat. Professional photographers on board may develop film for you—for a fee.

When taking photographs at ports of call, respect the wishes of the local inhabitants. Always ask permission to photograph someone close-up.

WORK

If you need to work while on board, secretarial help and limited office facilities, including credit-card operated satellite-linked telephone and fax machines, as well as computers, may be available. Some ships, such as *Crystal Harmony*, *Crystal Symphony*, *Dawn Princess*, *Royal Viking Sun*, and *Sun Princess*, have business centers.

Life Aboard

AIR-CONDITIONING

On all modern cruise ships, cabin temperature is regulated by individually controlled thermostats, so that you can adjust it to suit yourself. The temperature in the public rooms is controlled automatically. On board the ship's air-conditioning is normally kept much cooler than you may be used to, so don't forget to take a sweater or scarf.

BABY-SITTING

On many cruise ships, stewards, stewardesses, and other staff may be available as sitters for an hourly charge. You can make whatever arrangements you need at the purser's office.

BEAUTY SALON/BARBER SHOP

It is advisable to make any appointments for the beauty salon or barber shop as soon after boarding as possible, especially on short cruises. Appointment times fill up rapidly, particularly before social events such as the captain's cocktail party. Charges are comparable to those ashore. The hours of opening will be posted at the salon, and also listed in the *Daily Program.*

BRIDGE VISITS

You should check the *Daily Program* for announcements of visits to the bridge, for which appointment cards can be picked up from the purser's office or cruise staff office. On some ships, bridge visits are not allowed for reasons of insurance and security. On others, although personal visits are forbidden, a *Behind the Scenes* video on how the ship is run may be shown on the in-cabin television system.

CASHLESS CRUISING

It is now quite common to cruise cash-free and settle your account with one easy payment. Often this is arranged by making an imprint of a credit card prior to departure, permitting you to sign for everything. Or you can pay by cash at the end of the cruise.

On most ships, it is no longer possible to pay using cash at the bar, in the beauty salon, or in the shops—a fact bemoaned by older passengers, many of whom often do not use or possess credit cards.

If your cruise ship includes a "private island" on its Bahamas/Caribbean itinerary, you will probably be asked to pay in cash for all beverages, watersports/scuba diving gear and any other items purchased ashore.

Before the end of the cruise, a detailed statement will be delivered to your cabin. Avoid lines by using a credit card for express check out. Some companies that use a "cashless" system may discontinue its use for the last day of the cruise, which can be most irritating for passengers without cash.

CASINO

A large number of cruise ships have a "full" casino, where a range of games are played, such as blackjack, roulette, craps, and baccarat. Playing chips and cash change are available.

Children under 18 are not allowed in the casino. The casino is closed in port due to international customs regulations, and taking photographs in the casino is usually forbidden. You will find that German and Japanese registered ships are not permitted to operate casinos that give cash prizes.

COMMENT CARDS

On the last day of the cruise you are asked to fill out a company "comment card." Some cruise lines offer "incentives" such as a bottle of champagne and even a free short cruise. Be honest when you fill out this important form, as it can serve as a way of communication between company and passenger. Be warned, however, that on many ships, dining room stewards present "sob" stories of how they will lose their station or section, or even their job, if you don't write "excellent" when you fill out your comment card. Some companies provide information on filling out the comment cards, inviting nothing short of an "excellent" rating.

If there *have* been problems with the service, don't write or mark "excellent." Instead, be realistic and mark "good," "fair," or "poor" as the case may be. Otherwise, the cruise line will never know that there are problems and that the service needs improving.

COMMUNICATIONS

Each cruise ship has been designated an internationally recognized call sign, which is made up of a combination of several letters and digits and can be obtained from the cruise line. For each of the ships listed in Part Three of this book, the radio call sign is provided where known (except for those ships

Fancy a flutter? Many ships operate gambling casinos, with blackjack, roulette, and craps among the most popular. There are also slot machines for those who like to do arm exercises. (Fred Olsen Cruise Lines)

which are not yet in service). To receive a call during your cruise, simply give the call sign and name of the ship to those concerned before you leave.

When the ship is at sea, you can call from your cabin (or the ship's radio room) to anywhere in the world:

- by radio-telephone (a slight/moderate background noise might be noticed);
- by satellite (which will be as clear as your own home phone).

The direct dial satellite calls, a service started in 1986, are more expensive, but they are usually completed without delay. Many ships now also have credit card telephones located in public areas aboard ship, which connect instantly at any time of the day or night, via satellite. Satellite calls can still be made when the ship is in port, but radio-telephone calls cannot be made. You could, however, use the local telephones (often at the local post office).

The satellite telephone calls will cost between $5 and $15 per minute, depending on the type of communications equipment the ship carries (the latest system, called Inmarsat-M, is digital and offers lower-priced calls). Cellular telephone calls, such as those operated by the Florida-based Cruise-Phone, typically range from $5.95 to $9.00 per minute. On ships that are equipped with CruisePhone, payment is made by a major credit card when you make your call. It is more difficult to pay cash for a satellite or cellular telephone call. (The cruise lines should take note of the fact that many of the older passengers, especially Europeans, do not own credit cards.)

It is also comforting to know that you can be contacted during your cruise through shore-to-ship calling. Your relatives and friends can reach you by calling the *High Seas Operator* in almost any country (in the United States, dial 1-800-SEA-CALL). Vessels equipped with satellite telephone links can be reached via the *Inmarsat* system; all the caller has to do is phone any local operator and ask for the Inmarsat Operator. When connected, the name of the ship should be given, together with the ocean code (Atlantic is 871; Pacific is 872; Indian Ocean is 873).

Telegrams, telexes, and faxes are all accepted at the purser's office or radio room for transmission when the ship is at sea. Your in-cabin phone can also be used to call any other part of the ship.

CUSTOMS REGULATIONS

All countries vary in the allowances granted by their own customs service, but you will be informed aboard your cruise ship of the allowable amounts for your nationality and residency.

DAILY PROGRAM

The *Daily Program* contains a list of the day's activities, entertainment, and social events, and is normally delivered to your cabin the evening before the day that it covers. It is important to read it carefully, so that you know what, when, and where things are happening. If you lose your copy, you can obtain another from the purser's office or your cabin steward/stewardess.

DECK CHAIRS

Deck chairs and cushions are available from the duty deck steward, and are free of charge on most ships. Specific locations cannot normally be reserved, except on the few ships where a charge is made, or by arrangement with the deck steward.

DEPARTURE TAX

If you are disembarking in a foreign port, and flying home, be advised that there may well be a departure tax to pay at the airport. Cruise lines often neglect to inform passengers of this, with embarrassing results, especially when you are normally required to pay the departure tax in cash in the local currency of wherever you are.

DISEMBARKATION

During the final part of your cruise, the cruise director will give an informal talk on the customs, immigration, and the disembarkation (sometimes called "debarkation") procedures. At least one member of each family should attend this important talk. This will help simplify and speed up the procedure and avoid confusion at arrival time.

The night before your ship reaches its final destination (in most cases this will be a return to the port you sailed from) you will be given a customs form to fill out. Any duty-free items bought from the ship's shop on board must be included in your allowance, so save the receipts just in case a customs officer wishes to see them.

The night before arrival, your main baggage should be packed and placed outside your cabin door on retiring or before 4 a.m. It will be collected, put in a central baggage area and off-loaded on arrival. Remember to leave out any fragile items and liquor, together with the clothes you intend to wear for disembarkation and onward

travel (it's amazing how many people have packed *everything*, only to find themselves in an embarrassing position on disembarkation day). Anything left in your cabin at this point will be considered hand baggage and has to be hand-carried off when you leave.

On disembarkation day, if you are on a two-sitting ship, be aware that breakfast is usually brought forward by one hour. This means that the first-sitting breakfast could well be as early as 5:30 a.m.! If you are flying home that same day, it's going to turn into a very long day. It might be better to miss breakfast and sleep later, providing announcements on the ship's public address system don't wake you (it is possible on many ships to turn off such announcements).

Even worse than the early breakfast is the fact that you'll be commanded (requested, if you're lucky) to leave your cabin early, only to wait for hours in the crowded public rooms. To add insult to injury, your cabin steward (after he's received his tip, of course) will knock on your door, saying he needs the sheets off the bed so that the cabin can be made up for the incoming passengers. Cruise on a small "upscale" ship and this won't happen.

Before leaving the ship, remember to claim any items you have placed in the ship's safety deposit boxes and leave your cabin key in your cabin. Passengers cannot go ashore until all baggage has been off-loaded, and the customs and/or immigration inspections or pre-inspections have been carried out on board.

In most ports, this takes two to three hours after arrival. Therefore, do not ask people to meet you at arrival time. They will not be allowed to go on board, and you can't get off until all formalities have been completed. Also, leave at least three hours from the time of arrival to catch a connecting flight or other transportation.

Listen for announcements about disembarkation procedures and try not to crowd into the main disembarkation gangway or lobby areas. Once off the ship, you must identify your baggage at the pierside before passing through any further customs (delays are usually minimal). Porters will be there to assist you.

DRUGSTORE

On some ships, there may be a separate drugstore in which a fairly extensive range of standard items will be available, while on others the drugstore will be a small section of the ship's main gift shop. The opening hours will be posted at the store and printed in the *Daily Program*.

ELECTRIC CURRENT

Most cruise ships operating in U.S. waters have standard American 110-volt AC current and sockets. Newer and refurbished ships have 110- and 220-volt AC (alternating current) outlets. A few of the older vessels have 220-volt DC (direct current) outlets; transformers/converters are available.

In general, electrical appliances may only be used on a ship if they operate on AC current. Check with your cabin steward or stewardess before plugging in any electrical appliance more powerful than an electric razor (such as a high-wattage hair dryer), just to make certain that the cabin's circuitry can handle the load.

ENGINE ROOM

On virtually all passenger ships, the engine room is off-limits to passengers, and visits are not allowed, for insurance and security reasons. On some ships, a technical information leaflet may be available from the purser's office. On others, a *Behind the Scenes* video may be shown on the in-cabin television system. For more specific or detailed information, you should contact a member of the ship's engineering staff via the purser's office.

GIFT SHOPS

The gift shop/boutique/drugstore will offer a selection of souvenirs, gifts, toiletries, and duty-free items, as well as a basic stock of essential items. You'll find duty-free goods, such as perfumes, watches, and so on, very competitively priced, and buying on board ship may save you the hassle of shopping ashore. Opening hours will be posted at the store and given in the *Daily Program*.

HEALTH/FITNESS/SPA FACILITIES

Depending on the size of the ship, the health and fitness facilities may include one or more of the following: a gymnasium, weight room, sauna, solarium, exercise classes and jogging track, parcours, massage, swimming pool(s) and whirlpool baths, nutrition lecture and herbal body wraps, and scuba and snorkel instruction. For information, check with your cruise/travel agent, or, when you are on board, contact the cruise director or the purser's office.

Some ships now have elaborate spas where (for an extra fee) entire days of treatments are on offer. Stress-reducing and relaxation treatments are practiced combined with the use of seawater, which contains minerals, micro-nutrients and vitamins. Personal massage might include Swedish remedial massage, shiatsu, the Alexander method, and aromatherapy treatments.

Few ships today run their own spa facilities, as finding quality personnel to provide consistency of product is time-consuming and difficult. A small number of concession companies now specialize in offering "turn-key" operations. The largest of these is Steiner Transocean, a company that emerged from the 1994 merger between Steiner of London and Coiffeur Transocean, also of London. Steiner Transocean operates the spa and beauty services on more than 130 ships. Good spa operations can be found aboard *Crystal Harmony*, *Crystal Symphony*, *Europa*, *Norway*, and *QE2*. All are operated by Steiner Transocean (the exception is *Europa*, which is run along the lines of a real German health spa, with medical services and treatments not available on any other cruise ship. This is operated by Polly's Vital Center, Austria). The spa on P&O's new *Oriana* is operated by Champneys, England.

LAUNCH (TENDER) SERVICES

Enclosed (or open) motor launches (called "tenders") are employed on those occasions when your cruise ship is unable to berth at a port or island. In these cases, a regular launch service is operated between ship and shore for the duration of the port call. Details of the launch service will be provided in the *Daily Program* and announced over the ship's P.A. system. When stepping on or off a tender, do remember to extend "forearm to forearm" to the person assisting you. Don't grip their hands because this simply has the effect of immobilizing the helper.

LAUNDERETTE

Some ships are fitted with self-service launderettes, equipped with washers, dryers, and ironing facilities, often at no charge. Full-time supervisory staff may be available to assist you, as in *QE2*. (Check the profile information for each individual ship in Part Three of this book.)

LAUNDRY AND DRY CLEANING

Most ships offer a full laundry and pressing service. Some ships may also offer dry-cleaning facilities. A detailed list of services (and prices) should be posted in your cabin. Your steward or stewardess will collect and deliver your laundry or dry cleaning.

LIBRARY

Most cruise ships are equipped with a library offering a large range of books, reference material and periodicals. A small deposit (refundable on return of a book) may sometimes be required for those wishing to borrow a book from the library. Note that on the small luxury ships, the library is open 24 hours a day, and no deposit is required. On the larger ships, you'll probably find that the library is open only a couple of hours each morning and afternoon.

SHIPS WITH THE LARGEST LIBRARIES

Enchanted Seas	15,000 books
Queen Elizabeth 2	6,000 books
Majesty of the Seas	6,000 books
Monarch of the Seas	6,000 books
Sovereign of the Seas	2,000 books
Crystal Harmony	1,500 books

Cunard's *QE2* is, at the present time, the only cruise ship with a full-time, fully qualified librarian.

Sadly, some of the Carnival Cruise Lines ships have superb library rooms and luscious, overstuffed armchairs, but, alas, few books! On many ships, the library is also the place where you can obtain games such as Scrabble, backgammon and chess.

LIFEBOAT DRILL

Safety at sea is the number one consideration of all members of the ship's crew. Standards are set by the Safety of Life at Sea (SOLAS) convention of the International Maritime Organization (IMO). For any evacuation procedure to be totally effective and efficient, passengers must know precisely where to go in the unlikely event that an emergency arises. For this reason, and to acquaint passengers with general safety procedures, a lifeboat drill is carried out at the start of the cruise. According to international maritime law, this must take place within 24 hours of embarkation. Some ships sensibly program the passenger lifeboat drill prior to sailing, so as not to take time away from passengers during the cruise.

There have been few recent incidents requiring the evacuation of passengers, although two cruise ships have been totally lost following collisions (*Jupiter*, 1988, and *Royal Pacific*, 1992). Travel by ship, however, still remains one of the safest means of transportation. Even so, it cannot be stressed strongly enough that attendance at lifeboat drill is not only required by the captain, but also makes sense; participation is mandatory. You must, at the very least, know your boat station, and how to get to it, in the event of an emergency requiring evacuation of the ship.

If others are lighthearted about the drill, don't let that affect your seriousness of purpose. Be sure to note your exit and escape pathways and learn how to put on your lifejacket correctly. The drill takes no more than about 15 minutes of your time and is a good investment in playing safe. (*Royal Pacific* actually sank in a mere 16 minutes following collision.)

Lifejackets are found in your cabin, and instructions as to how to get to your boat station are posted on the back of the cabin door.

LOST PROPERTY

You should contact the purser's office immediately if you lose or find something on the ship. Notices regarding lost and found property may be posted on the bulletin boards.

MAIL

You can buy stamps and post letters on most ships. Some ships use the postal privileges and stamps of their flag of registration, while others buy local stamps at ports of call. Mail is usually taken ashore by the ship's port agent just before the ship sails for the next port.

If you are sailing on an extended voyage (on a round-the-world cruise, for example), the cruise line will send you a list of all its agents and mailing addresses, together with your tickets and documents, before you leave for the cruise. In this way, you will be able to let your family and friends know where you will be and where you may be contacted at certain times.

MASSAGE

Make any appointments for massage as soon as possible after boarding, in order to get a time and day of your choice. Larger ships have more staff, and offer more flexibility in appointment times. The cost averages $1.00 per minute. On some ships, a massage service is available in your cabin, if it is big enough to accommodate a portable massage table.

MEDICAL SERVICES

All ships carrying over 50 passengers are required, by international maritime convention, to have a fully licensed physician aboard. Usually there is a reasonably equipped hospital in miniature, although the standard of medical practice and of the physicians themselves varies greatly from line to line. Most shipboard doctors are generalists; there are no cardiologists or neurosurgeons. And the doctors are often employed as outside contractors and therefore make charges for use of their services. British passengers should note that ships are not covered by the U.K. National Health Service scheme.

For example, Cunard's *QE2*, which carries up to 2,825 passengers and crew, has a fully equipped hospital with one surgeon, one doctor, a staff of six nurses and two medical orderlies; contrast this with Carnival Cruise Lines' *Sensation*, which carries up to 3,514 passengers and crew, with just one doctor and two nurses.

Regrettably, many cruise lines place a low priority on providing medical services (there are, however, some notable exceptions). Most shipboard physicians are not certified in trauma treatment or medical evacuation procedures, for example. Most ships that cater to North American passengers tend to carry doctors licensed in the United States, Canada, or Britain, but on many other ships, doctors come from a variety of countries and disciplines. Some medical organizations, such as the American College of Emergency Physicians, have created a special division for cruise medicine.

Although ships do have some facilities, there is wide variation between standards and equipment. Obviously, any vessel engaged in long-distance cruises, with several days at sea, should have better medical facilities and a better qualified staff than one that is engaged in a standard seven-day Caribbean cruise, with a port of call to make almost every day.

There is, at present, no agreed industry-wide standard relating to the standard of medical certification that is required by cruise ships. Most ship doctors are necessarily of the general practice type, but quite often, short-term contracts can mean poor continuity and differing standards.

Ideally, a ship's medical staff should be certified in Advanced Cardiac Life Support. The minimal standard medical equipment should include:

- Examination room
- Isolation ward/bed
- X-ray machine (to verify the existence of broken or fractured bones)
- ECG (electroencephalogram) cardiac monitor and defibrillator
- Oxygen-saturation monitor (used to determine blood-oxygen level)
- External pacemaker
- Oxygen, suction and ventilators
- Pulse oxymeter

- Hematology analyzer
- Culture incubator
- Mobile trolley intensive care unit.

Any existing health problems that will require treatment on board must be reported at the time you are booking. Finally, the doctor is the *only* ship's officer who is actually an independent contractor. Aboard ship, that means that standard fees are charged for treatment, including for seasickness shots (except on Russian and Ukrainian registered vessels, where the medical services are provided free).

MOVIES

On most cruise ships, a movie theater is an essential part of the ship's public-room facilities. The movies are recent, often selected by the cruise director or company entertainment director from a special film- or video-leasing service.

Some of the recently built or modified ships have replaced or supplemented the ship's movie theater with television sets in each cabin. News and events filmed on board are shown as well as video movie features.

NEWS AND SPORTS BULLETINS

The world's news and sports results are reported in the ship's newspaper or placed on the bulletin board—normally located near the purser's office or in the library. For sports results not listed, ask at the purser's office; it may be possible for the office to obtain the results for you.

PASSENGER LISTS

All ships of yesteryear provided passenger lists with each passenger's name and home town (or region). Few com-

panies carry on the tradition (perhaps some passengers are traveling with someone they shouldn't!). Among the companies that still compile a cruise passenger list are: Crystal Cruises, Cunard, Seabourn Cruise Line, Silversea Cruises, and Sun Line Cruises.

PHOTOGRAPHS

Professional photographers travel on board to take pictures of passengers throughout the cruise, including their arrival on board. They also cover all main events and social functions, such as the captain's cocktail party.

All the photographs can be viewed without any obligation to purchase (the price is likely to be in excess of $6.00 for a postcard-sized color photograph). They will all be displayed on photo boards either in the main foyer, or in a separate photo gallery. The color and quality of these pictures are usually excellent. Duplicates may be obtained even after your cruise, from the shore-based headquarters of the photographic concessionaire.

Photographers on board may also be able to develop your film, for a fee.

POSTCARDS AND WRITING PAPER

These are available from the writing room, library, purser's office, or from your room steward. On many ships, they are available for a modest sum.

PURSER'S OFFICE

This is also known as the reception office, guest relations desk, or information desk. Centrally located, this is the nerve center of the ship for general onboard information and problems. Opening hours are posted outside the office and given in the *Daily Program*.

On some ships, the purser's office is open 24 hours a day.

RELIGIOUS SERVICES

Interdenominational services are conducted on board, usually by the captain or staff captain. A few older ships (and the new ships of Costa Cruises) have a small private chapel. Sometimes denominational services are offered by specially invited or fellow-passenger members of the clergy.

ROOM SERVICE

Beverages and snacks are available at most hours; liquor is normally limited to the hours when the ship's bars are open. Your room steward will advise you of the services that are offered. There is no charge for room service.

SAFETY ABOARD

Passenger safety is a high priority for all cruise lines. Crew members must attend frequent emergency drills, the lifeboat equipment is regularly tested, and the fire-detecting devices, alarm and fire-fighting systems are checked throughout the ship. If you spot fire or smoke, use the nearest fire alarm box, alert a member of staff, or contact the bridge. Cruise lines should insist on a common language for all crew members, but this is far from the reality.

Be aware that slipping, tripping, and falling are the major sources of shipboard injury. This does not mean that ships are unsafe, but there are some things you can do to minimize the chance of injury.

If you *do* suffer from injury aboard a cruise ship, you may think it is the cruise line's fault and you may want to take some kind of legal action against

the cruise company concerned; you should be aware of the following:

In the United States, Appendix 46, Section 183(b) of the U.S. Civil Code requires that "the injured passenger notify the cruise line in writing within six months from the date of the injury to file a claim and suit must be filed within one year from the date of injury." Thus, if you file a claim after the one-year period, the cruise line will probably seek a summary judgment for dismissal, which will invariably be granted to it.

It is imperative that you first *read your ticket*. The passenger ticket is a *legal contract* between passenger and cruise line. It will invariably state that you must file suit in the state (or country) designated in the ticket. For example, if a resident of California buys a cruise, and the cruise line is based in Florida, then the suit must be filed in Florida. If you reside in the U.S. and you purchase a cruise in the Mediterranean and the cruise line is based in Italy, for example, then you would have to file suit in Italy. This is known as the Forum Clause.

There is usually a clause in the ticket that will read something like the following:

"The Carrier's legal responsibility for death, injury, illness, damage, delay or other loss or detriment of person or property of whatever kind suffered by the Passenger will, in the first instance, be governed by the Athens Convention relating to the Carriage of Passengers and their Luggage by Sea, 1974, with protocols and amendments, together with the further provisions of the International Convention on Limitation of Liability for Maritime Claims,

1976, with revisions and amendments (hereinafter collectively referred to as the "Convention"). The Carrier shall not be liable for any such death, injury, illness, damage, delay, loss or detriment caused by Act of God, war or warlike operations, civil commotions, labor trouble, interference by Authorities, perils of the sea, or any other cause beyond the control of the Carrier, fire, thefts or any other crime, errors in the navigation or the management of the Vessel, or defect in, or unseaworthiness of hull, machinery, appurtenances, equipment, furnishing or supplies of the Vessel, fault or neglect of pilot, tugs, agents, independent contractors, such as ship's Physician, Passengers or other persons on board not in the Carrier's employ or for any other cause of whatsoever nature except and unless it is proven that such death, injury, illness, damage, delay, loss resulting from Carrier's act or omission was committed with the intent to cause such loss or with knowledge that such loss would probably result therefrom and in that event the Carrier's liability therefore shall not exceed the specified limitations per Passenger in Special Drawing Rights (S.D.R.) as defined in the applicable conventions or in any further revision and/or amendment thereto as shall become applicable."

One area in which passengers may not be able to sue the cruise line is in the event of injury or accident when they are on a shore excursion advertised and sold aboard ship. This is because the tour operators of on-shore excursions are usually independently contracted, and do not belong to the cruise line. So, when you buy your shore excursion, ask whether the ship's insurance fully covers you under the terms of the passenger ticket contract.

IN YOUR CABIN
• Note that on many ships, particularly older vessels, there are raised lips separating the bathroom from the sleeping area.
• Do not use the fire sprinkler heads that are located on most cabin ceilings as a hanging place for clothes hangers, however light they are.
• On older ships, it is wise to note how the door lock works—some require a key on the inside in order to unlock the door. Leave the key in the lock, so that in the event of a real emergency, you do not have to hunt for the key.

ON DECK
• On older ships, look out for raised lips in doorways leading to open deck areas. Be alert and step, don't trip, over them.
• Wear sensible shoes, with rubber soles (not crepe) when walking on deck or going to pool and lido areas. Do not wear high heels.
• Walk with caution when the outer decks are wet after being washed, or if they are wet after rain—this warning applies especially to metal decks. There's nothing more painful than falling onto a solid steel deck.
• Don't throw a lighted cigarette or cigar end, or knock out your pipe, over the ship's side. The sea might seem like a safe place to throw such items, but the burning ash can easily be sucked into an opening in the ship's side or onto an aft open deck area, only to cause a fire.

HOW TO SURVIVE A SHIPBOARD FIRE
Shipboard fires generate heat, smoke, and often panic. In the unlikely event that you are in one, try to remain calm and think logically and clearly.

When you board the ship and get to your cabin, check the way from there to the nearest emergency exits fore and aft. Count the number of cabin doorways and other distinguishing features to the exits in case you have to escape without the benefit of lighting, or in case a passageway is filled with smoke and you can't see clearly. New ships will increasingly make use of the "low location" lighting systems, which are either the electroluminescent or photoluminescent type.

On many new ships, exit signs are located just above floor level, but on older vessels, exit signs may be above your head—virtually useless, as smoke and flames always rise.

You should also note the nearest fire alarm location and know how to use it in the event of dense smoke and/or no lighting. Indeed, all cabins should have pull-out flashlights, but as yet most of them do not.

If you are in your cabin and there is fire in the passageway outside, first put on your lifejacket and feel the cabin door handle. If the door handle is hot, soak a towel in water and use it to turn the handle of the door.

Check the passageway. If everything is clear, walk to the nearest emergency exit or stairway. If there is smoke in the passageway, crawl to the nearest exit. If the exit is blocked, then go to an alternate one.

It may take considerable effort to open a fire door to the exit, as they are very heavy. Never use the elevators, as they may stop at a deck that is on fire or full of smoke, and when the door opens, you may not be able to escape.

In the event of a fire beginning in your cabin, report it immediately by telephone. Then get out of your cabin if you can and close the door behind you to prevent smoke or flames from entering the passageway. Finally, sound the alarm and alert your neighbors.

SAILING TIME
In each port of call, the ship's sailing and all-aboard times will be posted at the gangway where you leave from. The all-aboard time is usually half an hour before sailing time (ships cannot wait for individual passengers who are delayed). On some ships, you will be given an identification card which has to be handed in at the gangway when you return from your visit ashore.

SAUNA
Many ships offer a sauna, which is usually small and compact, and occasionally unisex. In some cases there will be a small charge for its use, especially when it is combined with a massage. Towels are available at the sauna and there is also a small changing area. Opening times will be posted at the sauna and will appear in the information material in your cabin. Reservations are not normally necessary.

SEASICKNESS
Seasickness is rare these days, even in rough weather (less than 3 per cent of all passengers are seasick). Ships have stabilizers—large underwater "fins" on each side of the hull—to counteract any rolling motion. Nevertheless, it is possible to develop some symptoms—

anything from slight nausea to vomiting. What do you do?

Seasickness occurs when the brain receives confusing messages from the body's sensory organs; this causes an imbalance of a mechanism in the inner ear. The mind and brain are accustomed to our walking or riding on a nonmoving surface. If the surface itself moves in another direction, a signal is transmitted to the brain that something's wrong. Continuous mixed signals result in headaches, clammy skin, dizziness, paleness, and yawning, soon followed by bouts of nausea and vomiting. There is still no explanation for the great difference in individual susceptibility to seasickness.

Both old-time sailors and modern physicians have their own remedies, and you can take your choice or try them all:

1. When you notice the first movement of the ship, go out on deck and walk back and forth. You will find that your knees, which are our own form of stabilizer, will start getting their feel of balance and counteraction. This is the sign that you're "getting your sea legs."
2. When you are on deck, focus on a steady point, such as the horizon.
3. Get the breeze into your face, and if you're feeling nauseous, suck an orange or lemon.
4. Eat lightly. Don't make the mistake of thinking that a heavy meal will keep your stomach well anchored. It won't.
5. A recommended preventive for seasickness is ginger in powder form. (Mix half a teaspoon in a glass of warm water or milk, and drink it before sailing.) This is said to settle any stomach for a period of up to eight hours.
6. "Sea Bands" (or "Aquastraps") are a drug-free method of controlling motion sickness. These are slim bands (often in varying colors) that are wrapped around the wrist, with a circular "button" that presses against an acupressure point (*Nei Kuan*) on the lower arm. They should be attached a few minutes before you step aboard and should be worn on both wrists throughout the cruise.
7. Dramamine will be available in tablet form on board the ship.
8. If you are really distressed, the ship's doctor can give you an injection that will cure all discomfort. It may make you drowsy as well, but the last thing on your mind will be staying awake at the movie.

All of this being said, bear in mind that in addition to the stabilizers in the hull, most cruises are in warm, calm waters and most cruise ships spend much time along the coast or pull into port regularly. The odds are very much against being seasick.

SECURITY

After the tragedy of the hijacking of *Achille Lauro* in 1985, the United States House of Representatives Committee on the Security of Ports and Vessels, and the United Nations, have suggested ways by which passengers traveling by cruise ship could expect to receive the same level of protection as passengers traveling by air. It is satisfying to report that a progressive formulation of a recognized standard of passenger ship protection has been seen. The cruise lines have reached this recognized standard as a result of several factors: a moral obligation which, like safety, is inherent in the industry; the expectation of passengers; and now the firmer and more formal pressures that are being applied across the world by governments and coast guards.

But in spite of these pressures it is still true that the "recognized" standard can be interpreted widely by different companies and ports. The most conscientious cruise lines, ferry operators, and ports follow the standards laid down by International Maritime Security (IMS), a British company that is acknowledged as the world leader in cruise ship, ferry, and port security.

Increasingly, passengers find that at embarkation, as well as at way ports, they are required to go through metal detection devices at the gangway, and their baggage will be subject to more stringent inspection procedures. The question of security is now being taken into account during the final ratings and evaluation of the ships in Part Three of this book.

All cabins are provided with keys, and it is recommended that you keep your cabin door locked at all times when there is no one there. The usual keys are made of metal and operate a mechanical lock, whereas the newer and refurbished ships may have plastic "key cards," which operate electronically coded locks.

Cruise lines do not accept responsibility for any money or valuables left in cabins and suggest that you store them in a safety deposit box at the purser's office, or, if one is supplied, in your cabin personal safe.

You will be issued with a personal boarding pass when you embark. This serves as a form of identification and must be shown at the gangway each time you board. If you misplace or lose it, let the purser's office know immediately. The system of boarding passes is one of many ways in which cruise lines ensure passenger safety.

SHIPBOARD ETIQUETTE

Cruise lines want you to have a good vacation, but there are some rules that must be observed.

In public rooms, smoking and non-smoking sections are available. In the dining room, however, cigar and pipe smoking are not permitted at all.

If you do have a video camera with you, you must be aware that you will not be allowed to tape any of the professional entertainment shows and cabarets because of the international copyright infringement regulations.

Casual dress is of course fine when you're on vacation, but you will not be allowed to enter the ship's dining room in just your bathing suit. Bare feet, likewise, are not permitted.

SPORTS FACILITIES

The variety of sports facilities on board ship will obviously depend on how big the ship is. The facilities will include some of the following: badminton, basketball practice area, golf driving cage, horseshoes, jogging track, miniature putting green, paddle tennis, quoits, ring toss, shuffleboard, skeet shooting, squash (rarely), table tennis, and volleyball. Tournaments are also arranged by the sports director or the cruise staff. Check the *Daily Program* for times of events.

SUN

If your cruise takes you to the sun, remember that the closer you get to the equator, the more potent and penetrating are the sun's rays. These are most harmful from noon to 2 p.m., when the sun is directly overhead.

If you are taking a short cruise to the Bahamas, Caribbean, or Mexico, be wary of trying to get the best possible tan in the shortest space of time. You should always use a protective sun cream (15–30 factor range), and reapply it every time you go for a swim or soak in the pool or ocean.

It's best to begin with a short exposure time, no more than 15 minutes, then gradually work your way up to an hour or so. Always remember that it is better to go home with a suntan than with sunburn. If you do overdo it, you should seek immediate help from the ship's doctor.

SWIMMING POOLS

Depending on the ship, there will be indoor or outdoor swimming pools, or sometimes both. They may be closed when the ship is in port, either because of local health regulations or because they are being cleaned. Check the hours of opening in the *Daily Program*. Diving is not normally allowed, since pools are shallow. Parents should note that pools on most ships are not supervised. Be aware that some ships use excessive chlorine or bleaching agents for cleanliness, which could cause colors to run on your bathing wear.

TELEVISION

On most new and recently refurbished ships, in-cabin television is standard. Programming may be obtained by a mixture of satellite and video channels. Some ships can "lock-on" to live international news programs (such as those

Chess, anyone? This game of giant chess can be found on the open deck of the 11,209-grt, 446-passenger Black Prince *(Fred Olsen Cruise Lines).*

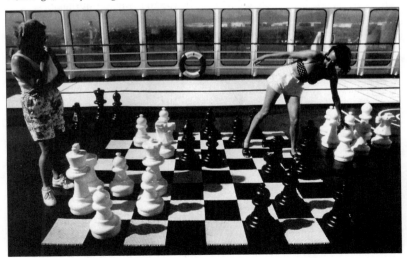

of CNN or BBC World News), or to *text-only* news services (like Oceansat News), for which cruise lines pay a subscription fee per cabin per month. Satellite television reception is often poor, however, because ships at sea are constantly moving out of an extremely narrow beam being downloaded from the satellite, and they therefore cannot "track" the signal as accurately as a land-based facility.

TIPPING (GRATUITIES)

Many people find the whole question of tipping awkward and embarrassing. The information given here is meant as a guideline; you should then add your own good judgment.

On some ships, subtle suggestions are made regarding tips, whereas on others, cruise directors, under the direction of the hotel manager, tend to get carried away, and are far too dictatorial as to the practice of tipping. Ships such as those of Princess Cruises offer hints on tipping via the in-cabin video system.

Some of the cruise brochures, such as those of Holland America Line, state that "tipping is not required." They may not be required, but they are most definitely expected by the ship's staff. The industry standard for cruises is roughly as follows:

- Dining room waiter: $3.00-$3.50 per person per day;
- Busboy: $1.50-$1.75 per day;
- Cabin steward/stewardess: $3.00-$3.50 per person per day.

Suite and penthouse passengers should tip $5.00 per person per day to each of the dining room waiters and the suite

stewards/stewardesses, as well as to the butler, if there is one (Cunard recommends $6 for the butler aboard *QE2*).

Any other gratuities should be given according to services rendered, just as you would tip in any good restaurant or hotel (for example, to the maître d', wine waiter, and barman). On many ships (those that belong to Carnival Cruise Lines, Cunard, Norwegian Cruise Line, and Royal Caribbean Cruises, for example), the tip for the barman or bar waiter is automatically added to your bar check, at a rate of 15 per cent.

Gratuities are usually given on the last evening of a cruise of up to 14 days' duration. For longer cruises, you normally extend half of the tip half way through the cruise and the rest on your last evening.

Note: On some Greek-staffed ships (Royal Olympic Cruises for example), gratuities are pooled and given to the chief steward, who shares them out at the end of each cruise. A daily amount of $8-$10 per person is the norm.

If you're traveling on a river cruise, you may be asked to tip the cruise director (who is actually more of a cruise manager), rather than approaching individual crew members.

Envelopes for tipping are available from the purser's office, where you can also ask for advice on tipping; otherwise envelopes may be placed in your cabin by your cabin steward or stewardess on the last night of the cruise.

On some of the best-rated ships, gratuities can be paid in advance, which means that you do not have to tip at all on board. In this instance, the ship's staff receive your tips direct from the company.

Gratuities are included in the cruise fare on the following ships, in which no extra tipping is permitted: *Asuka, Club Med I, Club Med II, Oceanic Grace, QE2, Radisson Diamond, Royal Viking Sun, Sea Goddess I, Sea Goddess II, Seabourn Pride, Seabourn Spirit, Silver Cloud, Silver Wind, Song of Flower* and *Vista Fjord.*

ORIGIN OF THE WORD "TIPS"

Before the introduction of postage stamps, coachmen who carried passengers were often asked to carry a letter or other package to its recipient. A small recompense was given for this service, called a "tip," which stands for "to insure personal service." Hence, when in future some special service was provided, particularly in the hospitality industry, the offering of tips became an accepted way of saying thank you for services rendered.

TWENTY-FOUR-HOUR CLOCK

On many European-based ships, the 24-hour clock is the standard way of referring to time, in keeping with the practicality of its use in international travel. In spite of the initial strangeness of this system of time-telling, you will soon find it not only simple to use, but far less likely to lead to confusion.

Up to midday, the hours are shown as 0100 to 1200. Thereafter they proceed from 1300 to 2400. Thus, 1400 is 2 p.m.; 1520 is 3:20 p.m.; and so on.

VALUABLES

A small number of ships have a lock box built into each cabin. However, items of special value should be stored

Informal deck buffets on Crystal Cruises' Crystal Harmony and Crystal Symphony include a wide selection of cheeses. (Photo: D. Ward)

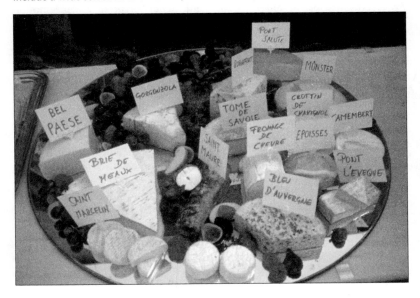

in a safety deposit box in the purser's office. You will then have simple and convenient access to all your valuables.

VISITORS

Passes for visitors to see you on board your ship must always be arranged in advance, preferably at the time you make your booking. Announcements will be made when it is time for all visitors to go ashore.

Sadly, Bon Voyage parties, such as those you may have seen in the movies, are virtually a thing of the past. They are no longer possible aboard ship (with the exception of those ships operating around-the-world cruises), owing to greatly increased security concerns and insurance regulations.

WATERSPORTS

Some of the small vessels, such as *Black Prince, Club Med I, Club Med II, Sea Goddess I, Sea Goddess II, Seabourn Pride, Seabourn Spirit, Silver Cloud, Silver Wind, Wind Song, Wind Spirit,* and *Wind Star,* have a watersports platform that is lowered from the ship's stern or side. These ships carry with them windsurfers, waterski boats, jet skis, waterskis, and scuba and snorkel equipment, usually at no extra charge. *Seabourn Legend, Seabourn Pride,* and *Seabourn Spirit* also feature an enclosed swimming "cage," which is needed for areas of the world where unpleasant fish might be lurking.

Although such facilities look good in the cruise brochures, in many cases

ships seem reluctant to make use of them. This is because many itineraries have too few useful anchor ports. Also, the sea must be in an almost flat, calm condition, which is seldom the case. Another more prosaic reason is simply because of strict insurance regulations.

WINE AND LIQUOR

The cost of drinks on board is generally lower than on land, since ships have access to duty-free liquor. Drinks may be ordered in the dining room, at any of the ship's bars or from the room service facility.

In the dining room, you can order wine with your meals from an extensive and reasonably priced wine list. If you want wine with your dinner, try to place your order at lunch time, as waiters are always at their busiest at the evening meal.

On some ships, a duty-free sales point will allow you to purchase wine and liquor for personal consumption in your cabin. Passengers are not normally permitted to bring these purchases into the dining room or into other public rooms, nor indeed any duty-free wine or liquor purchased in port. These regulations are obviously made to protect bar sales, which are a substantial source of on-board revenue for the cruise line.

Indeed, some lines have even introduced a "corkage" fee as part of their policy to deter passengers from bringing their own wines with them into the dining room.

WHAT TO DO IF...

1. Your luggage doesn't arrive at the ship.

If you are traveling as part of the cruise line's air/sea package, the airline is wholly responsible for locating your luggage and delivering it to the next port. If you arranged your own air transportation it is wholly *your* problem. Always have easy-to-read name and address tags both *inside* as well as *outside* your luggage. Keep track of claim documents and give the airline a detailed itinerary and list of port agents (usually included with your documents).

2. *You* miss the ship.

If you miss the ship's departure (due to late or non-performing flight connections, etc.), and you are traveling on an air/sea package, the airline will arrange to get you to the ship. If you are traveling "cruise-only" and have arranged your own air transportation, then *you* are responsible for onward flights, hotel stays, and transfers. Many cruise lines now have "deviation" desks, where, for a small fee, you can adjust airline flights and dates to suit personal preferences. If you arrive at the port just as your ship is pulling away, contact the ship's port agent immediately.

3. Your cabin is too small.

Almost all cruise ship cabins are too small! When you book a cruise, you pay for a certain category and type of cabin, but have little or no control over which one you actually get. See the hotel manager/purser as soon as possible, explaining what's wrong with the cabin. If the ship is full (and most are nowadays), it will be difficult to change. However, the hotel manager/purser will probably try to move you from known problem cabins, although they are not required to do so.

4. Your cabin has no air-conditioning, is noisy, or there are other problems.

If there is anything wrong in your cabin, or if the plumbing in your bathroom doesn't work, bring it to the attention of the cabin steward immediately. If nothing improves, complain to the hotel manager/purser. Some cabins may be located above the ship's laundry, generator, or galley (hot); others may be above the disco (noisy). If the ship is full, it may be difficult to change.

5. You have small children and the brochure implied that the ship has special programs for them, but when on board you find out it's not an all-year-round program.

In this instance, either the brochure was misleading, or your travel agent didn't know enough about the ship, or didn't ask the right questions. If you have a genuine cause for complaint, see your travel agent when you get home. Ships try to accommodate your young ones, but may not be covered by their insurance for "looking after" them throughout the day. Again, check thoroughly with your travel agent *before* you book.

6. You don't like your dining room sitting.

Most "standard" market ships operate two sittings for dinner (sometimes for all meals). When you book your cruise, you are asked whether you want first or second sitting. The line will make every attempt to please you. But if you want second sitting and are given first sitting, there may be little the maître d' can do.

7. You want a table for two and are put on a table for eight.

Again, see the maître d' and explain why you are not satisfied. A little gratuity may prove helpful.

149

8. A large group has taken over the ship.
Sometimes, large groups have blocked (pre-booked) several public rooms for meetings (seemingly every hour on the hour in the rooms you want to use). This means the individual passenger (that's you) becomes a second-class citizen. Make your displeasure known to the hotel manager/purser immediately, tell your travel agent, and write a follow-up letter to the line when you return home.

9. A port of call is deleted from the itinerary.
If you only took the cruise because the ship goes to the place you've wanted to go for years, then before you go, read the fine print in the brochure. A cruise line is under *no* obligation to perform the stated itinerary. For whatever reason (political unrest, weather, mechanical problems, no berth space, safety, etc.), the ship's captain has the ultimate responsibility.

10. You are unwell aboard ship
All cruise ships carrying more than 50 passengers are required to carry a fully qualified doctor and medical facilities, which will include a small pharmacy. You'll be well taken care of. The ship's medical doctor generally operates as a concession. So, although there are charges for medical services rendered, almost all cruise lines offer insurance packages that include medical coverage for most eventualities. It is wise to take out this insurance when you book.

11. You have a problem with a crew member.
Go immediately to the hotel manager or purser and explain the problem (for single women this could be a persistent cabin steward with a master door key). No one will do anything unless you let them know. Cruise ships try to hire decent staff, but, with 60,000 crew members aboard the world's cruise fleet, there are bound to be a few bad apples. Insist on a full written report of the

incident, which must be entered in the ship's daily log by the staff captain (or deputy captain).

12. You leave some personal belongings on a tour bus.
If you have left something on a tour bus, and you're back on board your ship, first advise the shore excursion manager. If he/she can't be located, advise the purser's office. The shore excursion manager will contact the tour operator ashore to ascertain whether any items have been handed in to their office. In many cases, items are in fact retrieved.

13. You have extra charges on your bill.
Check your itemized bill carefully. Then talk to the purser's office and ask them to show you the charge slips. Make sure you get a copy of your bill, *after* any modifications have been made.

14. The cruise airline's arrangements have you flying from Los Angeles via Timbucktoo to get to your cruise ship.
Well, it's fine if your cruise ship is in Timbucktoo (though it shouldn't be, as it's inland). Most cruise lines that have low rates also use the cheapest air routing to get you to your ship. That could mean charter flights from a central hub. It may also mean being dumped off the ship at the end of your cruise very early in the morning. Be warned, you get what you pay for. Ask questions *before* you book.

15. You are unhappy with your cruise experience.
You (or your travel agent) ultimately chose the ship and cruise. But if your ship doesn't meet your specific interests, or the ship performs less well than the brochure promises, then let your travel agent and the cruise line know as soon as possible. If your aggravation is valid, many cruise lines will offer a credit, good towards a future cruise. But do read the fine print on the ticket.

Entertainment

THAT'S ENTERTAINMENT!

After food, the most subjective (and talked-about) part of any *mainstream* cruise experience is the entertainment program. Menus always present you with a choice of several foods, whereas the same is not often possible with cruise ship entertainment, which has to be diversified and innovative, but never controversial. Ask 1,000 people what they would like to see as part of any evening's entertainment program, and 1,000 different answers will ensue. It's all a matter of personal taste and choice. Whatever one expects, the days have gone when you would have been entertained by waiters doubling as singers, although a few bar waiters are still known to perform tray-spinning effects to boost their tips!

Many passengers expect to see top notch entertainment, "headline" marquee name cabaret artists, that is, the world's most "popular" singers, and the most dazzling shows with slick special effects, just as one would find in the best venues in Las Vegas, London, or Paris. But there are many reasons why it's not exactly like that. International star acts invariably have an entourage that accompanies them to any venue: their personal manager, their musical director (often a pianist or conductor), a rhythm section (with bass player and drummer), even their hairdresser. On land, one-night shows are possible, but on a ship, an artist cannot always disembark after just one night, especially when it involves moving equipment, costumes, and baggage. They can also lose valuable money-making bookings, and telephone contact. Although they can be contacted at sea, it *is* more difficult, and the telephone number is not their own. This makes the whole business logistically and financially unattractive for all but the very largest ships on fixed itineraries, where a marquee name act might be considered a marketing draw.

When you are at home you can literally bring the world's top talent into your home via television. Cruise ships are a different matter altogether. Most entertainers do not like to be away from their "home base" for longish periods, as they depend so much on the telephone for their work. Most do not like the long contracts that the majority of ships must offer in order to amortize the cost over several weeks.

Entertainers on ships must also *live* with their audiences for several days (sometimes several weeks), something unheard of on land, as well as work on stages that are seldom designed for real live performances.

Many of the older (pre-1970) ships have extremely limited entertainment spaces, and very few ships provide proper dressing rooms and backstage facilities for the storage of costumes, props, or effects, not to mention the extensive sound and lighting equipment most live "name" artists demand or need. Indeed, only the latest ships provide the extensive facilities needed for presenting the kind of high-tech shows one would find in Las Vegas, London, or New York, for example, with elaborate electronic backdrops, revolving stages, orchestra pits, multi-slide projection, huge stageside video screens, pyrotechnic capabilities, and the latest light-mover and laser technology. Even the latest ships often lack enough dressing room and hanging space for the 150 costumes required in a single typical ship production show.

However, more emphasis has been placed on entertainment since the mid-1970s. Entertainment on today's large mainstream ships is market-driven. In other words, it is directed toward that segment of the industry that the cruise line's marketing department is specifically targeting (discounting notwithstanding). This is predominantly a family audience, so the entertainment must appeal to as broad an age range as possible—a tall order for any cruise line's director of entertainment.

A cruise line with several ships in its fleet will normally employ an entertainment department that is made up of an entertainment director and several assistants, and most cruise lines have contracts with one or more entertainment agencies that specialize in entertainment for cruise ships.

It is no use, for example, a company booking a juggler who needs a floor-to-ceiling height of 12 feet (3.6 m), but finds that the ship has a show lounge with a height of 7 feet (2.1 m). ("Couldn't he juggle sideways?" I've heard one cruise company executive ask!); or an acrobatic knife-throwing act (on a moving ship?); or a concert pianist when the ship only has an

Production show dancers in costume grace the stage of a Carnival Cruise Lines ship.

upright honky-tonk piano; or a singer who sings only in English when the passengers are all German-speaking, and so on.

Indeed, the most difficult audience to cater to is one of mixed nationalities (each of whom will expect entertainers to cater exclusively to their particular linguistic group). Given that cruise lines are now marketing to more international audiences in order to fill ships, the problem of finding the right entertainment is far more acute.

The more upscale cruise lines offer more classical music, even some light opera, and more fine guest lecturers and world-renowned authors than the seven-day package cruises heading for warm-weather destinations.

One area of entertainment that has become part of the experience, and is expected—particularly on the larger, mainstream cruise ships—is that of the glamorous "production show." This is the kind of show one would expect to see in any good Las Vegas show palace, with a team of singers and dancers, a production manager, lavish backdrops, extravagant sets, grand lighting, special effects, and stunning custom-designed costumes. Unfortunately, many cruise line executives, who know nothing about entertainment, regard plumes and huge peacock feathers paraded by showgirls who step, but can't dance, as being desirable. Some cruise ships have shows that are not becoming to either dancer or passenger. Shows that offer more creative costuming and real dancing win more votes today.

Passengers booking the back-to-back seven-day cruises (for example on alternating eastern and western Caribbean itineraries) should be aware that entertainment is generally geared to seven-day cruises. Thus, you will usually find the same two or three production shows and the same acts on the second week of your cruise. The way to avoid seeing everything twice is to pace yourself by just going to some of the events during the first week and saving the rest for the second week.

Regular cruisegoers will notice that they seem to see the same acts time after time on various ships. For the reasons given above, plus a few more, the criteria narrows the field even though there are many fine land-based acts. In addition, ship entertainers need to love socializing. Successful acts tend to be good mixers, are presentable when in public, don't do drugs or take excess alcohol, are not womanizers (or manizers?), are not late for rehearsals, and must cooperate with the cruise director and his staff, as well as the band. Sadly, with cruise lines forever looking for ways to cut costs, entertainment has of late been a major target for some companies (particularly the smaller ones). Cutting costs translates into bringing on, for example, lower-cost singers (who very often turn out to be non-reading, vocally challenged persons), and bands that can't read charts (musician-speak for musical arrangements) brought on board by cabaret acts.

SHOW BIZ AT SEA

In today's high-tech world, the putting together of a lavish 50–60-minute production show involves the concerted efforts of a range of experienced people from the world of show business, and a cost of $1 million per show is not unheard of. Weekly running costs (performers' salaries; costume cleaning and repair; royalty payments; replacement audio and video tapes, and so on) all add up to an expensive package for what is often a largely unappreciative and critical audience.

WHO'S WHO

Although production companies differ in their approach, the following list gives some idea of the various people involved behind the scenes.

Executive Producer

His or her task is to transfer the show's concept from design to reality. First, the brief from the cruise line's director of entertainments might be for one new ship production show (the average being two major shows per seven-day cruise). They must first plan the show. After deciding an initial concept, they may then call in the choreographer, vocal coach, and musical arranger for several lengthy meetings, so everyone agrees on the flow of the show, and the story line, or linkage.

Choreographer

The choreographer is generally responsible for auditioning dancers, and for the creation, selection, and teaching of all the dance routines. He or she will normally work in conjunction with the executive producer.

Musical Director

His or her job is to coordinate all musical scores and arrangements. He or she may also train the singers in voice and microphone techniques,

voice projection, accenting, phrasing, memory, and general presentation, and oversee all session singers and musicians for the recording sessions, click-track tapes, and so on.

Musical Arranger

After the music has been selected, the musical arrangements must be made. For just one song, this can come to a cost of as much as $2,000 for a single arrangement for a 12-piece orchestra.

Costume Designer

He or she must provide creative original designs for a minimum of seven costume changes in one 45-minute show. Costumes must also be practical, as they will be used repeatedly.

Costume Maker

He or she must purchase all materials, and be able to produce all of the costumes that are required by the costume designer, in the time frame allotted.

Graphic Designer

His or her job is to provide all the set designs, whether they are physical one-, two- or three-dimensional sets for the stage, or photographic images created on slide film, video, laser disk or other electronic media. The trend is for digital computer technology to play an increasingly important part in creating the images that are to be transferred via an electronic medium.

Lighting Designer

His or her task is to create the lighting patterns and effects for a production show. Sequences and action on stage must be carefully lit to the best advantage. The lighting designer will also present the completed lighting plot to the software company that will etch it into computer-controlled disks to be used every time the show runs.

PRODUCTION SHOWS: PUTTING THEM TOGETHER

A complete, new, large-scale production show, from conception to first performance, will take several months. Here is a breakdown of the time that's needed to put on a hypothetical show.

Month 1
- Production team create show concept.
- Write storybook and submit it to all concerned.
- Second and third meetings of the production team. The set designer provides sketches and graphics.
- Costume designer is contracted to design costumes for seven scene changes—different costumes for each lead singer (one male and one female), and for the dancers.
- Costume maker given order for 70 costumes to be delivered in April.

Month 2
- Advertise for dancers and singers.
- Book a rehearsal theater (with a wooden stage) for dancer auditions.
- Auditions and call-backs for the dancers.
- Book a rehearsal studio (equipped with a piano, microphones and amplifiers) for auditions for singers.
- Auditions and call-backs for the singers.
- Select the suitable talent, issue contracts on behalf of the cruise line

(usually five or six months). Talent will go back to their existing jobs while the new show is put together, making sure that they will be available for rehearsals. Measurements are taken for the costume designer.

Month 3
- Fine-tuning by production team; the timing of scene and costume changes.
- Order sets, backdrops, color slides. Video footage to be made.
- Go into the recording studio.
- Lay down: principal tracks, backing tracks, and click (SMPTE timing) track.
- Mix down and edit tape.
- Produce the "master" and "mother" tapes.
- Produce copies for use aboard ship, as well as backup copies.

Month 4
- Costume fitting; the first dress rehearsal.
- Second costume fitting.

Month 5
- Final rehearsals for intensive two- or three-week period.
- Give details of the ship's mailing address to all cast members, so that they can receive mail while working aboard ship.
- Obtain working visas for all cast members.

Month 6
- Crate and freight show costumes, sets, and backdrops.
- Provide the cruise line with details for booking flights and transportation for the performers etc.

155

- Provide the company's port agents with a name and flight list so they can meet and transfer the cast to the ship.
- Take the show on the high seas.
- After boarding and getting to know the layout of the ship, the entertainers will usually spend a week in intensive rehearsals, often working from midnight to about 5 a.m., while the cast due to come off the ship (for a vacation, or end of contract) is still doing a regular cruise entertainment show.

Month 7

- The opening night for the new show will probably be held on the first formal night of the cruise. No doubt all the ship's senior officers will be in attendance to "judge" the success of the show.

BANDS/MUSICIANS

Before the big production shows and artists can be booked, bands and musicians must be hired, often for long contracts. Polish musicians are favored for a ship's showband, as they are excellent music readers (necessary for all visiting cabaret artists, not to mention the big production shows).

American and British musicians are found on fewer and fewer ships, as cruise lines in the past have experienced too many problems with drugs, drink, and unions. Most musicians work to contracts of about six months. Entertaining lounge duos and solo pianists or singer/pianists are generally engaged through an entertainment agency specializing in cruise ships.

Steel bands are recruited from the Caribbean, while other specialist bands (such as popular Country and Western bands) may be invited aboard for special occasions or charters.

OTHER ENTERTAINMENT

Most cruise ships organize acts that, while perhaps not internationally recognized "names," can provide two or three different shows during a seven-day cruise. These will be male/female singers, illusionists, puppeteers, hypnotists, and even circus acts, with wide age-range appeal.

There are comedians, comediennes, and comedy duos who perform "clean" material that find employment year-round on what has become known as the "cruise ship circuit." These popular comics enjoy good accommodations, are stars while on board, and often go from ship to ship on a standard rotation every few days. There are raunchy, late-night "adults only" comedy acts on some of the ships with younger, "hip" audiences, but few of them seem to have enough material for two different shows.

The larger the ship, the larger the entertainment program. On certain ships, the cruise director may "double" as an act, but most companies prefer him or her to be strictly an administrative and social director, allowing more time to be with passengers. Whichever ship and cruise you choose to travel on, you'll find that being entertained "live" is an experience far superior to sitting at home in front of a television set, watching its clinical presentation. That's show business!

Nautical Notes

The world of ships is a world all its own, and associated with it is a whole language and culture that can at times seem confusing—though always fascinating—to the newcomer. Here are a few tidbits of nautical information that may help to contribute to the pleasure of your cruise.

RULES OF THE ROAD

Ships are subject to stringent international regulations. They must keep to the right in shipping lanes, and pass on the right (but there are certain exceptions). When circumstances raise some doubt or shipping lanes are crowded, ships often use their whistles, in the same way an automobile driver uses directional signals to show which way he will turn. When one ship passes another and gives a single blast on its whistle, this means it is turning to starboard (right). Two blasts means a turn to port (left). The other ship acknowledges by repeating the same signal.

Ships switch on their navigational running lights at night—with green for starboard, red for port. Also, they have two white lights on the masts, the forward one lower than the aft one.

Flags and pennants form another part of a ship's communication facilities and are displayed for identification purposes. Each time a country is visited, its national flag is shown. While entering and leaving a port, the ship flies a blue and vertical striped flag to request a pilot, while a half red, half white flag (divided vertically) indicates that a pilot is on board. Cruise lines and other passenger shipping lines also display their own "house" flag, proudly fluttering from the main mast.

A ship's funnel or smokestack is one other means of identification, each line having its own funnel design and color scheme. The size, height, and number of funnels were points worth advertising at the turn of the century. Most ocean liners of the time had four funnels and were called "four-stackers."

Today, perhaps the most distinctive funnel design belongs to those ships of Royal Caribbean Cruises; several of them actually have a nightclub or lounge perched partway up the stack itself. The view from these is spectacular, although in bad weather it's the room that will move most.

There are numerous customs at sea, many of them older than any maritime law. Superstition has always been an important element, as in the following example quoted in the British Admiralty Manual of Seamanship:

"The custom of breaking a bottle of wine over the stem of a ship when it is being launched originates from the old practice of toasting prosperity to a ship with a silver goblet of wine, which was then cast into the sea in order to prevent a toast of ill intent being drunk from the same cup. This was a practice that proved too expensive, and it was replaced in 1690 by the breaking of a bottle of wine over the stem."

ON THE WATCH

A ship's working day is made up of six four-hour time periods, known as "watches." In theory, a complement of officers and crew work the same watch round the clock: four hours on, followed by eight hours off during any 24-hour period.

To avoid working identical hours day after day, one of the four-hour periods is split further into first and second "dog watches" of two hours each, as follows:

0000-0400 hours	midwatch
0400-0800 hours	morning watch
0800-1200 hours	forenoon watch
1200-1600 hours	afternoon watch
1600-1800 hours	first dog watch
1800-2000 hours	second dog watch
2000-2400 hours	evening watch

On board ship, the tradition is to record time by the striking of bells to indicate the state of the watch. Each bell represents a half hour of time on watch and the duty is ended when eight bells are sounded at midnight, 0400, 0800, 1200, etc.

WIND SPEEDS

A navigational announcement to passengers is normally made once or twice a day, giving the ship's position, temperature and weather information.

Various winds affect the world's weather patterns. Such well-known winds as the Bora, Mistral, North wind, and Sirocco, among others, play an important part in the make-up of weather at and above sea level.

Wind velocity is measured on the Beaufort Scale, a method first devised in 1805 by Commodore Francis Beaufort for measuring the force of wind at sea. It became the official way of recording wind velocity in 1874, when it was adopted by the International Meteorological Committee.

You might be confused by the numbering system for wind velocity. There are 12 velocities, known as "force" on the Beaufort Scale. They are as follows:

Force	Speed (mph)	Description/Ocean Surface
0	0-1	Calm; glassy (like a mirror)
1	1-3	Light wind; rippled surface
2	4-7	Light breeze; small wavelets
3	8-12	Gentle breeze; large wavelets, scattered white-caps
4	13-18	Moderate breeze; small waves, frequent white-caps
5	19-24	Fresh breeze; moderate waves, numerous white-caps
6	25-31	Strong breeze; large waves, white foam crests
7	32-38	Moderate gale; streaky white foam
8	39-46	Fresh gale; moderately high waves
9	47-54	Strong gale; high waves
10	55-63	Whole gale, very high waves, curling crests
11	64-73	Storm; extremely high waves, froth and foam, poor visibility
12	73+	Hurricane; huge waves, thundering white spray, nil visibility

KNOTS AND LOGS

A knot is a unit of speed measuring one nautical mile. (A nautical mile is equal to one-sixtieth of a degree of the earth's circumference and measures exactly 6,080.2 feet/1,853.2 m.) It is about 800 feet (244 m), or one-seventh, which is longer than a land mile. Thus, when a ship is traveling at a speed of 20 knots (note: this is never referred to as 20 knots per hour), she is traveling at 20 nautical miles per hour.

This unit of measurement has its origin in the days prior to the advent of modern aids. At that time, sailors used a log and a length of rope in order to measure the distance which their boat had covered, as well as the speed at which it was advancing.

In 1574, a tract by William Bourne, entitled *A Regiment for the Sea*, records the method by which this was done. The log was weighted down at one end while the other end was affixed to a rope. The weighted end, when thrown over the stern into the sea, had the effect of making the log stand upright, thus being visible.

Sailors believed that the log stayed stationary at the spot where it had been cast into the water, while the rope unravelled. By measuring the length of rope used, they could ascertain how far the ship had traveled, and were thus able to calculate its speed.

Sailors first tied knots at regular intervals (eventually fixed at 47 feet 3 inches/14.4 m) along the rope, and counted how many knots had passed through their hands in a specified time (later established as 28 seconds), which was measured by the amount of sand that had run out of an hour glass.

They then used simple multiplication to clearly calculate the number of knots their ship was traveling at over the period of an hour. The data gathered in this way were put into a special record book—called a logbook. Today, a logbook is used to record the day-to-day details of the life of a ship and its crew, and other pertinent information.

LATITUDE AND LONGITUDE

Latitude signifies the distance north or south of the equator, while longitude signifies distance east or west of the 0 degree at Greenwich Observatory in London. Both are recorded in degrees, minutes, and seconds. At the equator, one minute of longitude is equal to one nautical mile, but as the meridians converge after leaving the equator, and meeting at the poles, the size of a degree becomes smaller.

PLIMSOLL MARK

The safety of ships at sea and all those aboard owes much to the 19th-century social reformer, Samuel Plimsoll, a member of the British parliament.

He was specially concerned about the frequent loss of ships due to overloading—certain ship owners would load their vessels down to the gunwales to squeeze every ounce of revenue out of them. They gambled on good weather, good fortune, and good seamanship to bring the ships safely into port. Many ships went to the bottom of the sea as a result of their buoyancy being impaired by overloading.

159

Samuel Plimsoll helped to enact the legislation that came to be known as the Merchant Shipping Act of 1875. This required all ship owners to mark all their vessels with a circular disc bisected with a line 12 inches (30.5 cm) long, bisected by a line 18 inches (45.7 cm) long, which would be observed as a measure of their maximum draft, that is, the depth to which a ship's hull could be safely immersed at sea. However, the Merchant Shipping Act of 1890 was even stricter, and required that the Plimsoll mark (or line) had to be positioned on the sides of vessels in accordance with tables that were drawn up by competent authorities. The Plimsoll mark is now found on the ships of every nation.

The Plimsoll mark indicates three different depths: the depth to which a vessel can be loaded in fresh water, which is less buoyant than salt water; the depth in summer, when seas are calmer; and the depth in winter, when the seas are rougher.

THE CHALLENGE OF THE BLUE RIBAND

No award has inspired as much rivalry between shipping lines as the coveted Blue Riband, given to the liner that makes the fastest transatlantic crossing in a particular year. Indeed, possession of the Blue Riband became—and still is—a source of national pride.

By the late 1800s references to the award were already being recorded, but the first real mention of it was made on August 1, 1900, when the *Illustrated London News* reported that the Blue Riband had been won by *Deutschland*, the Hamburg America Line passenger ship.

Although the great passenger liners of the North Atlantic raced to beat the speed record, there was no actual material award until 1935, when Harold K. Hales (1888-1942), a member of the British parliament, donated a silver challenge trophy to be awarded each year to the steamship line who won the Blue Riband. Speed became so important that newspapers carried

PREFIXES

ib – ice-breaker (diesel- or nuclear-powered)

ms – motor ship (diesel power)

mts – motor twin screw (diesel power), or motor turbine ship (steam turbine power)

mv – motor vessel (diesel power)

RMS – Royal Mail Ship

ss – steamship

ssc – semi-submersible craft (swath)

sts – sail training ship

tes – turbo-electric ship (steam turbine power)

ts – turbine steamer (steam turbine power), or twin screw vessel

tsmv – twin screw motor vessel

ys – yacht ship

daily records of distance steamed by major ships, as well as the duration of each crossing. Average speeds, although not revealed, could be calculated from the figures provided.

Naturally the distance covered can vary with each crossing of the Atlantic. Since 1900 the shortest distance that was recorded for Blue Riband purposes was the 2,807 nautical miles between Sandy Hook, New Jersey, and Queenstown (now Cobh) in Ireland, while the longest distance was 3,199 nautical miles, between Ambrose Light, New Jersey, and Cherbourg, France. Twelve ships have held the record westbound, and ten eastbound.

Some of the world's most illustrious passenger ships are listed among the holders of this prestigious award. For 22 years the Blue Riband was held by the U.K.'s *Mauretania*, passing briefly, in 1929, to Germany's *Bremen* and in 1930 to that country's *Europa*.

In 1933 Italy's *Rex* took over, only to lose it a mere two years later to France's *Normandie*. Then arrived the U.K.'s *Queen Mary* to vie for the award with *Normandie*. Both kept the award for a year each, in 1936 and 1937 respectively, until in 1938 Cunard firmly retrieved it with *Queen Mary*. In 1952, the prize was taken by the new U.S. liner, *United States*.

The liner *United States* has the distinction of being the fastest *real* liner ever to win the Blue Riband. Between July 3 and 7, 1952, during an eastbound crossing from Ambrose to Bishop Rock, the ship recorded an average speed of 35.59 knots, although it is claimed that in achieving such a speed, mechanical damage was caused to the extent that any attempt to repeat the performance was virtually out of the question.

No major passenger ship has been built since the early 1950s to challenge *United States'* record, although with the re-engining of Cunard's *QE2*, it is conceivable that she could attempt to make a Blue Riband crossing, given that she has achieved over 36 knots during her sea trials.

On June 22, 1990, the 243-foot-long (74-m), twin-hulled Sea Cat (catamaran-type) passenger ferry (not a cruise ship) *Hoverspeed Great Britain* made a successful, though somewhat unsporting, bid for the Blue Riband. The vessel, commissioned by Hoverspeed of England to bolster its fleet of hovercraft against anticipated competition from the Channel Tunnel, carried only one passenger, and had to refuel three times in mid-ocean, something that no really genuine ocean-going passenger liner has ever had to do. The trophy was awarded despite this, and is now back in England, the country where it first began.

THE BRIDGE

A ship's navigation bridge is manned at all times, both at sea and in port. Besides the captain, who is master of the vessel, other senior officers take "watch" turns for four- or eight-hour periods. In addition, junior officers are continually honing their skills as experienced navigators, awaiting the day when they will be promoted to master of a luxury cruise ship.

Besides the ship's captain, there is a qualified officer on duty at all times—even when the ship is docked in port.

The captain is always in command at times of high risk, such as when the ship is entering or leaving a port, when the density of traffic is particularly high, or when the visibility is severely restricted by poor weather.

Navigation has come a long way since the days of the ancient mariners, who used only the sun and the stars to calculate their course across the oceans. The space-age development of sophisticated navigation devices has enabled us to make giant strides from the less reliable techniques used long ago. Navigation satellites have enabled us to eliminate the guesswork of early navigation (the first global mobile satellite system came into being in 1979).

A ship's navigator today can establish accurately where the ship is in any weather and at any time. There follows a description of some of the navigation instruments, which will help you to understand the complexities of seamanship today.

System Control

The most sophisticated state of the art machinery and navigation systems are such technical marvels that sailors of yesteryear could not even conceive of their invention. The latest navigation and command system, which is known as the "Electronic Chart Precise Integrated Navigation System" (ECPINS), now combines the electronics of the most up-to-date satellite positioning methods (Global Positioning System) with automatic course plotting, video map displays of the oceans, gyro-compass, echo sounders, sonar doppler log, wind speed, and the various sensors to provide, in a single compact computer unit, a comprehensive at-a-glance display of the ship in relation to the rest of the world, contained in one "real-time" position on a single monitor's electronic chart.

The Compass

A compass is the instrument by which a ship may be steered on a pre-selected course, and by which bearings of *visible* objects can be taken in order to fix a ship's position on a navigation chart. There are two kinds of compass. The magnetic compass uses the inherent magnetic forces within and around the Earth; the gyro-compass, a relatively recent invention, uses the properties of gyroscopic inertia and precession—ideally used to align itself to a true north–south position.

Steering

There are two different methods that can be used to steer a ship:

- Electro-hydraulic steering uses the automatic (telemotor-type) transmission from the wheel itself to the steering gear aft. This is generally used in conditions of heavy traffic, during maneuvers into and out of ports, or on occasions when there is poor visibility.
- Automatic steering (gyro-pilot), a method which is used only in the open sea. This system eliminates the need for having someone at the wheel. However, on every ship, a quartermaster will always be at the wheel, as a backup to the system, for extra safety—and just in case a need should arise to switch from one steering system to another. This changeover from one to the other takes only a few seconds.

Satellite Navigator

Using this high-tech piece of equipment, the ship's officers can read, on a small television screen, the ship's position in the open ocean anywhere in the world, at any time, and in any weather, with pinpoint accuracy (that is, within plus or minus 600 feet/183 m).

The satellite navigator device uses the information transmitted by a constellation of up to six orbiting satellites. Each of these satellites is in a normal circular polar orbit at an altitude of 450 to 700 nautical miles, and orbits the Earth in about 108 minutes. Data from each give its current orbital position every two minutes.

Apart from telling the ship where it is, it can continuously provide the distance from any given point, calculate the drift caused by currents and so on, and tell the ship when the next satellite will pass.

The basis of the satellite navigation system is that of the U.S. Navy Satellite System (NNSS). This first became operational in January 1964 as the precision guidance system for the Polaris submarine fleet, and was made available for commercial use in 1967.

The latest system (and more accurate) is the GPS (Global Positioning System), which is now fitted to an increasing number of ships. This uses 24 satellites (18 of which are on-line at any given time) which can provide an accuracy in estimating a ship's position of plus or minus 6 feet (2 m). Another variation is the NACOS Navigational Command System. This collects information from a variety of sources: satellites, radar, gyroscopic compass, speed log, surface navigational systems as well as engines, thrusters, rudders, and human input. It then displays relevant computations and information on one screen controlled by a single keyboard.

Radar

Radar is one of the most important discoveries that has ever been made for the development of navigational aids, providing on screen a picture of all solid objects in a range that is selected by the navigator—which is from half a mile to a 72-mile (0.8-km to 116-km) radius. Its greatest asset is possibly as an invaluable aid to collision avoidance with other ships, although it has proven of value in finding a position at a distance when navigational marks or charted coastlines are within its range. Some ships have two or three radar sets with inter-switch units.

Engine Telegraph

These automatic signaling devices are used to communicate orders between the bridge and the engine room. There may be three—one on the bridge and on each bridgewing.

Bow Thruster

This small two-way handle is used to control the bow thrusters—powerful engines in the bow that push the ship away from the dockside without tugs. Some of the new ships may also have thrusters positioned at the stern.

Rudder Angle Indicator

This device is normally positioned in front of, and above, the quartermaster. It provides both the commanding officer and the quartermaster with a constant readout of the degrees of rudder angle, either to port (left) or to starboard (right).

Ships and the sea have their own special vocabulary. This list may be of use.

A

Abeam—off the side of the ship, at a right angle to its length

Aft—near, toward or in the rear of the ship

Ahead—something that is ahead of the ship's bow

Alleyway—a passageway or corridor

Alongside—said of a ship when it is beside a pier or another vessel

Amidships—in or toward the middle of the ship; the longitudinal center portion of the ship

Anchor Ball—black ball hoisted above the bow to show that the vessel is anchored

Astern—is the opposite of Ahead (i.e., meaning something behind, or astern, of the ship)

B

Backwash—motion in the water caused by the propeller(s) moving in a reverse direction (astern)

Bar—sandbar, usually caused by tidal or current conditions near the shore

Beam—width of the ship between its two sides at the widest point

Bearing—compass direction, expressed in degrees, from the ship to a particular objective or destination

Below—anything beneath the main deck

Berth—dock, pier, or quay. Also means bed on board ship

Bilge—lowermost spaces of the infrastructure of a ship

Boat Stations—allotted space for each person during lifeboat drill or any other emergency when lifeboats are lowered

Bow—the forwardmost part of the vessel

Bridge—navigational and command control center

Bulkhead—upright partition (wall) dividing the ship into compartments

Bunkers—the space where fuel is stored; "bunkering" means taking on fuel

C

Cable Length—a measured length equaling 100 fathoms or 600 ft (183 m)

Chart—a nautical map used for navigating

Colors—refers to the national flag or emblem flown by the ship

Companionway—interior stairway

Course—direction in which the ship is headed, in degrees

D

Davit—a device for raising and lowering lifeboats

Deadlight—a ventilated porthole cover to prevent light from entering

Disembark (also Debark)—to leave a ship

Dock—berth, pier, or quay

Draft (or Draught)—measurement in feet from the ship's waterline to the lowest point of its keel

E

Embark—to join a ship

F

Fantail—the rear or overhang of the ship

Fathom—distance equal to 6 ft (2 m)

Flagstaff—a pole at the stern of a ship where the flag of the ship's country of registry is flown

Free Port—port or place that is free of customs duty and regulations

Funnel—chimney from which the ship's combustion gases are propelled into the atmosphere

G

Galley—the ship's kitchen

Gangway—the stairway or ramp link between ship and shore

Gross Registered Tonnes (grt)—not the weight of the ship but the total of all permanently enclosed spaces above and below decks, with certain exceptions, such as the bridge, radio room, galleys, washing facilities, and other specified areas. It is the basis for harbor dues. New international regulations introduced in 1982 require ship owners to re-measure the grt of their vessels (1 grt = 100 cubic feet/2.83m³ of enclosed space)

H

Helm—the apparatus for steering a ship

House Flag—the flag denoting the company to which a ship belongs

Hull—the frame and body of the ship exclusive of masts or superstructure

L

Leeward—the side that is sheltered from the wind

M

Manifest—a list of the ship's passengers, crew, and cargo

N

Nautical Mile—one-sixtieth of a degree of the circumference of the earth, equal to 6,080.2 ft (1,853.2 m). It is about 800 ft (244 m), or one-seventh longer than a land mile

P

Pilot—a person licensed to navigate ships into or out of a harbor or through difficult waters, and to advise the captain on handling the ship during these procedures

Pitch—the rise and fall of a ship's bow that may occur when the ship is under way

Port—the left side of a ship when facing forward

Q

Quay—berth, dock, or pier

R

Rudder—a finlike device astern and below the waterline, for steering the vessel

S

Screw—a ship's propeller

Stabilizer—a gyroscopically operated retractable "fin" extending from either or both sides of the ship below the waterline to provide a more stable ride

Starboard—the right side of the ship when facing forward

Stern—the aftmost part of the ship which is opposite the bow

T

Tender—a smaller vessel, often a lifeboat, which is used to transport passengers between the ship and shore when the vessel is at anchor

W

Wake—the track of agitated water left behind a ship when in motion

Waterline—the line along the side of a ship's hull which corresponds to the surface of the water

Windward—the side toward which the wind blows

Y

Yaw—the erratic deviation from the ship's set course, usually caused by a heavy sea

VHF Radio

This is a radio receiver and transmitter, operating on VHF (Very High Frequency) with a "Line-of-Sight" range. It's used for communicating with other ships, pilots, port authorities, etc.

Radio Direction Finder

This operates on radio waves, enabling its operator to take bearings of shore radio stations. By crossing two or more bearings, you find the ship's position.

Depth Indicator

This equipment (which is an echosounder) provides a ship with a constant digital monitor readout, together with a printed chart.

Course Recorder

This records and prints all courses followed by the ship at all times.

Clearview Screen

This device makes simple but effective use of centrifugal force, where instead of having an automobile-type windshield wiper, a ship has circular screens that rotate at high speed to clear rain or sea spray away, providing those on the bridge with the best possible view in even the worst weather.

Engine Speed Indicators

These provide a reading of the number of revolutions per minute being generated by the engines. Each engine has a separate indicator, giving the speed in forward or reverse.

Facsimile Recorder

This is a special radio apparatus that is designed to receive meteorological and oceanographic maps, satellite pictures, and other pertinent weather information which is transmitted by maritime broadcast stations that are located all over the world.

Emergency Controls

These include control boards, electric circuits, and other devices to control flooding and fires on board ship.

Fire Control

If anyone sounds the fire alarm, an alarm is automatically set off on the bridge. A red panel light will be illuminated on a large plan of the ship, indicating the section of the ship that has to be checked so that the crew can take immediate action.

In the event of a fire, a ship is sectioned into several distinct zones, each of which can be tightly closed off. In addition, most of the cruise ships have a water-fed sprinkler system that can be activated at the touch of a button, or be automatically activated when sprinkler vials are broken by fire-generated heat.

New electronic fire-detection systems are also installed on ships in order to increase safety further.

Emergency Ventilation Control

This automatic fire damper system also has a manual switch that is activated to stop or control the flow of air (oxygen) to all areas of the ship, in this way reducing the fanning effect on flame and smoke via air-conditioning and fan systems.

Watertight Doors Control

Watertight doors throughout the ship can be closed off, in order to contain the movement of water flooding the ship. A master switch activates all the doors in a matter of seconds.

All the ships' watertight doors can be operated electrically and manually, which means that nobody can be trapped in a watertight compartment.

Stabilizers Control
The ship's two stabilizing fins can be extended, housed or controlled. They normally operate automatically under the control of a gyroscope located in the engine control room.

THE CRUISER'S PRAYER

"Heavenly Father, look down on us, Your humble, obedient cruise passengers who are doomed to travel the seas and the waterways of this earth, taking photographs, sending postcards, purchasing useless souvenirs and walking around in ill-fitting swimwear.

"We beseech You, oh Lord, to make sure that our plane is not hi-jacked, that our luggage is not lost, and that our over-sized carry-ons go unnoticed.

"Protect all of us from surly and unscrupulous taxi drivers, from avaricious porters and unlicensed, English-speaking guides in foreign places.

"Give us this day Divine guidance in the selection of our cruise ships and our travel agents—so that we may find our bookings and dining room reservations honored, our cabins of generous proportions, that our luggage arrives before the first evening meal.

"We pray that our cabin telephones work, the operator (human or electrical) speaks our tongue and that there are no phone calls from our children forcing us to abandon our cruise early.

"Lead us, dear Lord, to good, inexpensive eating places wherever in the world we go ashore—where the food is superb, the waiters friendly and the wine included in the price of a meal.

"Please grant us a cruise director who doesn't "cream" the spoils of bingo or horse racing, or doesn't stress that we visit only those jewelry stores from which he accepts an offering.

"Grant us the strength to take shore excursions—to visit museums, cathedrals, spice stalls and gift shops listed in the guidebooks.

"Give us the wisdom to tip correctly at the end of our voyage. Forgive us for under-tipping out of ignorance, and over-tipping out of fear. Please make the chief purser and ship's staff love us for what we are and not for what we can contribute to their worldly goods.

"Dear God, restrain our wives from shopping sprees and please protect them from bargains they do not need or cannot afford. Lead them not into temptation in St. Thomas or Hong Kong for they know not what they do.

"Almighty father, restrain our husbands from looking at foreign women and comparing them to us. Save them from making fools of themselves in cafés and nightclubs. Above all, please do not forgive them their trespasses for they know exactly what they do.

"And when our voyage is over and we return home to our loved ones, grant us the favor of finding someone who will look at our home videos and listen to our stories, so our lives as tourists will not have been in vain. This we ask you in the name of our chosen cruise line, and in the name of American Express, Visa, Mastercard, and our banks. Amen."

QUIPS AND QUOTES

Passengers cruising for the first time are the source of all the following questions:

"Do the crew sleep on board?"

"How far above sea level are we?"

"Does this elevator go up as well as down?"

"Will this elevator take me to my cabin?"

"What time's the midnight buffet?"

"Are there two sittings at the midnight buffet?"

"Is dinner in the dining room?"

"How many fjords to the dollar?"

"When the ship's at anchor tomorrow, can we walk ashore?"

"Do we have to stay up until midnight to change our clocks?"

"What time's the 2 o'clock tour?"

"Where's the bus for the walking tour?"

"Are the entertainers paid?"

"Will the ship wait for the tour buses to get back?"

"Will I get wet if I go snorkeling?"

"Do the Chinese do the laundry by hand?"

"Is the mail brought on by plane?"

"Does the ship dock in the middle of town?"

"Who's driving the ship if the captain is at the cocktail party?"

"Is the doctor qualified?"

"Is the island surrounded by water?"

"I'm married, but can I come to the Singles Party?"

"Should I put my luggage outside the cabin before or after I go to sleep?"

Overheard in the dining room:

"Waiter, this vichyssoise is cold."

"Was the fish caught this morning by the crew?"

Overheard on a British islands cruise:

"Windsor Castle is terrific. But why did they build it so close to the airport?"

Overheard on a Greek islands cruise:

"Why did the Greeks build so many ruins?"

Overheard on a round-Japan cruise, in Kagoshima, with Mount Suribaya in the background:

"Can you tell me what time the volcano will erupt—I want to be sure to take a photograph?"

Then there's the cruise line brochure which describes cabin layout: "cabins with double bed can accommodate a third passenger"! (Premier Cruise Lines)

And what about the saying "He let the cat out of the bag?" On board a square-rigger 150 years ago, this would have sent shudders through one's spine—for it meant that a sailor had committed an offense serious enough to have the "cat o' nine tails" extracted from its bag. The "cat" was a whip made of nine lengths of cord, each being about 18 inches long with three knots at the end, all fixed to a rope handle. It could inflict serious injuries, even death upon the victim. It is no longer carried on today's tall ships, having been outlawed by the U.S. Congress in 1850, and then by Britain's Royal Navy in 1879.

Who's Who on Board

Think of a cruise ship as a highly structured floating hotel, in which each of the crew members fills a well-defined role. A look at the chart on pages 170-171 will clarify the hierarchy aboard ship. The highest authority is the captain, and the chain of command works down through the ranks.

All members of the ship's company wear a uniform by which their station and function are instantly identifiable. Rank is also designated by the colors and insignia worn on the sleeves and epaulets of the uniform itself, although the colors in conjunction with the gold braid can vary somewhat. For example, throughout most of the industry, red generally signifies the medical department, but on ships of Italian registry, red signifies the purser's department.

CAPTAIN

The captain is the master of the ship and has absolute dictatorial rights and control over his vessel, officers, crew, and passengers. He is a seaman first, and manager of the ship second. He is also expected to be a generous and worthy host (the social aspect of a captain's job today requires an investment of about a quarter of his time spent with his passengers). When passenger ships are registered for insurance coverage (this is normally with Lloyd's of London), the captain's credentials and past record are reviewed, together with the seaworthiness of the vessel itself.

Although there may be several officers with a master's certificate on the bridge, the captain's authority remains unquestioned. He wears four gold bars on his sleeves and epaulets.

Every ship has a log, a daily record in which notes are recorded of all navigational and pertinent nautical data, details of reports from various department heads, and any relevant information on passengers or crew. Maritime law dictates that only the captain is allowed to sign that the daily entries in the log are correct, a necessary part of the job. If a ship was in trouble and had to be abandoned, the log would be the only record of the ship's operation, prevailing conditions, weather information, and the geographical locations that could be reviewed. The captain normally attends various social functions during the course of a cruise, hosts a table in the dining room, and is often seen during the day on walk-about inspection tours of the ship.

STAFF CAPTAIN

The staff captain is second in command and can take over at any time if needed. As the title suggests, the staff captain is concerned not only with what happens on the bridge, but is also involved in the day-to-day running of the ship, its staff and crew, and all the discipline.

In some companies the staff captain takes over when the captain is on leave;

in others there is a "floating" captain who takes all the relief commands. The staff captain also wears four gold bars.

The captain and staff captain work closely together, dividing the duties according to company policy and/or personal interest. At all times, one of these two officers must be on call when the ship is at sea, and most cruise lines insist that one or the other remains on board in any port of call.

The captain earns a top salary, and the staff captain is on almost the same scale. As a matter of interest, despite having as much expertise and responsibility for a passenger load often three times as great as a jumbo jet captain, a ship's captain earns roughly half the salary of that of the pilot.

The airline captain has the added advantage of being able to switch on an automatic pilot to handle almost every navigational task once aloft, and is guided down on to a runway with the assistance of computers and radar. His seagoing counterpart must be able to navigate manually and to negotiate hidden reefs, sandbars, sunken vessels, and marker buoys—including hazards not recorded on any chart.

The seagoing captain also has the very difficult responsibility of docking, maneuvering, and anchoring his ship, often in unfamiliar territory and sometimes in difficult weather conditions.

BRIDGE OFFICERS

Besides the captain and staff captain, other bridge officers include the chief officer, first officer, second officer, and several junior officers. Their job is to ensure the navigation and safe conduct

of the vessel at all times. The bridge is manned 24 hours a day, even in port.

Also on the bridge are the fire-detection systems and controls for the fire and watertight doors, which can be activated by "compartments" if there is a problem on the ship.

CHIEF ENGINEER

A ship's chief engineer (almost always referred to as "Chief") has the ultimate responsibility for the mechanical well-being of a cruise ship. This will include overseeing not only the main and auxiliary engines, but also the air-conditioning, generators, electrical systems, heating, plumbing, ventilation, refrigeration, and the water desalinization systems.

He is trained to handle a multiplicity of on-board systems, and is, in fact, the only person on board who can talk to the captain as an equal. With regard to engineering, he is a mechanical master. He wears four gold bars.

CHIEF RADIO OFFICER

The function of the chief radio officer is to keep the ship in constant touch with the outside world. The radio station is where all the radio, telegraph, telex, and the satellite communication equipment is found. The radio officer is also in charge of the automated telephone exchange.

Today, however, the job has become much simpler with the new automated satellite uplink/downlink systems, and is more concerned with maintenance of this high-tech equipment.

PRINCIPAL MEDICAL OFFICER

On the large cruise ships, the medical department can be very busy, with up to 2,700 passengers and 1,000 crew to attend to. Hopefully, you will meet the doctor socially, not professionally.

On many cruise ships, the hospital is a miniature version of a hospital on land, and may be fitted out with an operating theater, examination rooms, several beds, an X-ray room, and an isolation unit. There is at least one fully qualified doctor on board every cruise ship that is carrying 50 or more passengers, plus a small nursing staff. There may also be a physiotherapist, medical orderlies who may be petty officers, and maybe even a dentist.

HOTEL MANAGER

As head of a "floating hotel" involving almost two-thirds of the entire crew, the hotel manager is responsible for the passenger service, comfort, housekeeping, food, drink, and information services, plus the entertainment—just as in any first-class hotel ashore.

There will also be several junior hotel officers and other staff to whom responsibility for the day-to-day running of the various departments can be delegated.

A hotel manager's two most important associates and aides are the purser and the cruise director. At one time, the purser (called the chief purser on some ships) was responsible for the control of all passenger services. But due to the increasing emphasis that has been placed on food, recreation, comfort, and entertainment, the new position of hotel manager has been developed for the cruise ships.

On some ships, hotel managers are simply former chief pursers with a new title and added responsibilities.

If at any time during your cruise you have any unresolved problems or a request that has not been satisfactorily dealt with, contact the hotel manager or deputy hotel manager through the purser's office.

CHIEF PURSER

The chief purser's office is the financial, business, accommodations, and information hub of any ship, and will be located in a convenient location in the main lobby area.

The purser's department is responsible for all matters relating to money (including currency exchanges), mail, telexes, telegrams, and telefaxes; it also accepts valuables for safekeeping; and provides a complete information service, sometimes around the clock. The purser is also responsible for all passenger and crew accounts, purchasing and requisitioning of supplies, the shipboard concessions, the on-board printing of items such as the *Daily Program* and menus, and the manning of the telephone switchboard, if the ship does not have an automatic system. The purser's domain also includes relations with customs and immigration officials in all ports of call.

The purser has two main assistants: the hotel purser and the crew purser. The hotel purser is in charge of all passenger business, including accommodations (often under the direction of a

171

berthing officer), while the crew purser handles all matters relating to the ship's personnel and contracts.

If the cruise ship is based in foreign waters, the crew purser also oversees the crew changeovers and requests, and arranges the flights, baggage, and any other incidental crew matters. Many larger ships have two complete crews, one of which will be on leave while the other works the ship. Often, this works on a continuous rotation basis.

DEPUTY HOTEL MANAGER

The deputy hotel manager can take over from the hotel manager at any time, while his special domain is the food and beverage operation. On some ships, this is run by a concessionaire, who supplies not only the food, but also the dining room and bar staff, in which case the deputy hotel manager's role is that of an aide to both the hotel manager and the chief purser.

CONCIERGE

On some luxury cruise ships, such as those of Crystal Cruises and Cunard, the concierge acts as an invisible liaison officer between the ship and the passenger. The concierge's primary concern is for the well-being and satisfaction of the passengers, and the duties may include setting up private parties, obtaining opera or theater tickets for visits ashore, arranging any special transportation in ports of call, or simply being able to arrange to obtain any items that the passengers cannot find for themselves.

CRUISE DIRECTOR

Without any doubt, the most visible figure on board a ship is the cruise director, who has the ultimate responsibility of planning and operating the passenger entertainment, activities and sports programs, as well as acting as the master of ceremonies for all the shipboard functions and events. The cruise director oversees every area of leisure and recreation on the ship. The position is therefore highly demanding.

Before every ship cruise, the cruise director sketches in all projected activities, entertainment, and movies on a huge chart, showing the program in time slots throughout each day.

He has a number of helpers under his command; these will include the cruise staff and social hosts, the "headliner" and lesser entertainers, the bands and musicians, the lecturers, the recreation, sports and health instructors, and others.

On some larger ships, there may be one or more assistant cruise directors or an entertainment manager, a stage manager, and a social director. Cruise lines label their staff positions in different ways.

A cruise director must plan entertainment, movies and special theme nights with dexterity, taking care not to offend anyone in the process.

On the first day of the cruise, the cruise director will usually invite all the passengers to the main lounge and explain the entertainment program to them, at the same time urging the passengers to take advantage of the many events planned for the cruise. He may also introduce his staff and give a brief ship orientation soon after sailing.

At the start of each cruise, the cruise director usually gives a port lecture, often with audio-visual aids. In this, he will advise the passengers what to do ashore, describe the excursions available, and even offer advice on where to shop. But beware of the cruise director who oversells certain shopping stores, as he could well be on a healthy commission from them!

The cruise director may well be an officer, or a "nonsailor" with a showbiz background. A requirement for the job is certainly an ability to deal with difficult entertainers, crew, and passengers!

The cruise director has an office, together with members of his cruise staff, through which he can be reached for anything relating to the entertainment, activities, and sports programs on board. In Part Three of this book, you'll find an evaluation of the cruise director and his staff for each of the ships rated.

Note that on some ships, especially those operated by German companies, the cruise director is more of a cruise manager, and also deals with matters such as immigration, port clearances, and travel arrangements for passengers.

This is how a cruise director also functions on those Russian/Ukrainian-registered ships that are chartered to German tour operators.

SOCIAL HOSTESS

This position was created more for use on the larger cruise ships, where the cruise director needs a female counterpart to act as charming hostess at the various social functions and cocktail parties. The social hostess is not, however, the equivalent of being cruise director, and is not an officer, nor is she required to fulfill lifeboat command roles. She is, however, an important part of the social fabric on larger ships, and, on some, would be required to speak several languages.

She acts as hostess at the Captain's Welcome Aboard party, introducing passengers to the captain; writes invitations to the captain's table and officers' private parties; and would also be required to act as intermediary, in the event of death or serious injury of any passenger, between the ship, passengers and the family members on shore.

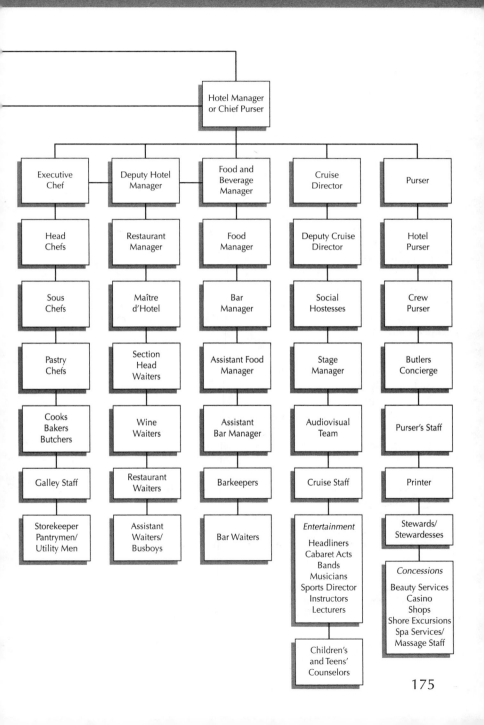

Hotel Manager
or Chief Purser

Executive Chef
Head Chefs
Sous Chefs
Pastry Chefs
Cooks Bakers Butchers
Galley Staff
Storekeeper Pantrymen/ Utility Men

Deputy Hotel Manager
Restaurant Manager
Maître d'Hotel
Section Head Waiters
Wine Waiters
Restaurant Waiters
Assistant Waiters/ Busboys

Food and Beverage Manager
Food Manager
Bar Manager
Assistant Food Manager
Assistant Bar Manager
Barkeepers
Bar Waiters

Cruise Director
Deputy Cruise Director
Social Hostesses
Stage Manager
Audiovisual Team
Cruise Staff

Entertainment
Headliners
Cabaret Acts
Bands
Musicians
Sports Director
Instructors
Lecturers

Children's and Teens' Counselors

Purser
Hotel Purser
Crew Purser
Butlers Concierge
Purser's Staff
Printer
Stewards/ Stewardesses

Concessions
Beauty Services
Casino
Shops
Shore Excursions
Spa Services/ Massage Staff

Shore Excursions and Shopping

SHORE EXCURSIONS

For some people the idea of a cruise might simply be to get away from it all. Indeed, no matter how many ports the ship visits, some never go ashore, preferring instead to revel in the complete ship-board aspect of cruising. For these people, the ship is the ultimate destination, and they could just as well be on a cruise to nowhere.

For the vast majority, however, the ports offered on a cruise itinerary are important considerations in choosing a cruise, the ship providing the transportation—a means to link the destinations together. The shore excursions, both a challenge and a bane to cruise lines, are proving to be one of the most vital and attractive aspects of the total cruise experience. They are organized so that they are varied enough to suit everyone, from the young and active to the elderly and infirm.

Today you need not feel the least bit uncomfortable or unsure in strange or unusual surroundings, or intimidated by languages other than your own. If you don't want to miss the major sightseeing attractions in each port, you'll find the organized shore excursions the perfect answer. Also, if you do not wish to be on your own, they provide an opportunity to get to know fellow passengers, perhaps with similar interests. Note: when you buy a shore excursion from the cruise line, you are fully covered by insurance; do your own excursion and you will not be covered.

The cruise lines generally plan and oversee shore excursions assuming that you have not seen a place. They aim to show you the most beautiful, striking, and fascinating aspects of a destination in a comfortable manner and at a reasonable price. The shore excursions are operated either by land, sea, or air, or sometimes a combination of all three. They are of varying duration: a half-day of sightseeing; full-day sightseeing, including lunch; evening outings, such as nightclub tours, including admission charges and one or more drinks; and overland excursions, often lasting several days and involving overnight stays in hotels.

On land, buses, rather than taxis or private cars, are so often the principal choice of transportation. This will cut costs and allow the tour operator to narrow the selection of guides to only those most competent, knowledgeable, and fluent in English (or in other languages), while providing some degree of security and control. In the case of air travel (often in small aircraft or by helicopter), the operating companies and all equipment must be thoroughly inspected, as must their safety record.

If shore excursions include travel overland and meals, the quality of any food to be served is taken into account, as are the food preparation areas and hygiene standards of personnel.

Shore excursions are categorized under the heading of "additional on-board expenses" for passengers, and are seen as sources of on-board revenue by the cruise lines. However, most of the money generated by the sale of shore excursions never reaches the coffers of the cruise lines, but instead goes to third parties—the tour operators in the ports of call. Only a handful of cruise products include shore excursions in the cruise fare, generally those lines that specialize in the "adventure" or "expedition" cruises to unusual and exotic destinations.

Interestingly, passengers often consider shore excursion prices as being high, but they are not aware of the tremendous behind-the-scenes organization required, and the costs involved locally. A considerable amount of time and money is spent by cruise lines setting up suitable shore excursion programs. And the last link in the chain of operation of a successful shore excursion program is the ship's shore excursion office.

SHORE EXCURSION DIRECTOR

In the head office of a cruise line is the shore excursion department, run by the director of shore excursions, who has the responsibility for setting up a successful program, sometimes worldwide. There may also be several staff members involved in the department. Without doubt the best shore excursions are provided by Hapag-Lloyd Cruises, Crystal Cruises, and Cunard.

Directors who work for lines operating worldwide have the greatest challenge, since each cruise undertaken may have a completely different itinerary. Those employed by lines that offer seasonal itineraries, such as those

to Alaska, the Mexican Riviera, the Caribbean, or the Mediterranean, have fewer problems because the itinerary remains unchanged during a complete cruising season.

Perhaps the most challenging of all jobs is that of setting up a comprehensive shore excursion program for a cruise round the world or for a long exotic voyage, where organizing shore excursions so often involves complex overland and flight arrangements and meetings with a number of government tourism officials.

One area that needs attention by the cruise lines is the description of shore excursions. Often, the language used can lead to disappointment and confusion. Ideally, all the cruise lines should adopt the following definitions in their descriptive literature and for their lectures and presentations:

- The term "visit" should be taken to mean actually entering the place or building concerned.
- The term "see" should be taken to mean viewing from the outside (as from a bus, for example).

SHORE EXCURSION OPERATOR

The shore excursion operator is the next link in the chain. Few lines run their own excursions, but instead contract a shore excursion operator for each port of call. They are responsible for providing the best means of transportation, local guides, food, entrance tickets to public buildings, gardens and nightclubs, and other attractions of the excursion.

177

Cruise lines and ground operators work together in planning or suggesting excursion itineraries, the operator offering the cruise line a "buying price per head" for the excursion or tour package. The margin between the buying price and the selling price to the cruise passenger can be as little as 50 cents or as much as 50 per cent. The average mark-up is about 20-25 per cent, an amount that is far lower than most cruisegoers imagine.

SHORE EXCURSION MANAGER

The cruise ship's representative supervising the entire operation of the shore excursion program is the shore excursion manager. As the eyes and ears of the cruise line, the shore excursion manager is free to recommend to head office that any excursion be suspended if it is not to his satisfaction—which gives him a good deal of authority with the local ground operators. Needless to say, some shore excursion managers can be bribed, to the detriment of passengers, in that some excursions will be downright poor.

The shore excursion manager and staff will be ready on the dockside dispatching the excursions in each port. Any last minute problems or questions you have should be raised then.

SHORE EXCURSION OFFICE

The shore excursion office is normally located in a central position on board, often close to the purser's office, in the main lobby area. This is where you should go for information about the ports of call or to purchase your shore excursion tickets, and where you will find the shore excursion manager and the other members of the department. Please note that the staff cannot normally act as guides or interpreters.

At the shore excursion office you will find details of the excursions and descriptive literature about the ports of call, with information on the history, language, population, currency, main sightseeing attractions, principal shopping areas, beaches and hotels, sports and watersports facilities, transportation, and the principal eating establishments. For more specific information, contact the shore excursion manager or visit the ship's library. On many of the ships, special full-color port booklets or cruise guides may be readily available. Shore excursion office opening times will be listed at the office, and in the *Daily Program*.

BOOKING EXCURSIONS

Early booking of excursions is highly recommended, especially if they are listed as "limited participation". This means that numbers will be restricted, and seats will be sold on a first come, first served basis. On some of the ships, excursions can be booked prior to the sailing date, but sellouts may occur. So, be sure to visit the shore excursion office as soon as you can after boarding and make your reservations early.

Payment for the excursion is normally made via a ship's central billing system, by cash, or traveler's check, or credit card. Note that on most ships, personal checks aren't accepted.

The shore excursion office usually attracts long lines shortly after the port lecture is given by the cruise director or the shore excursion manager. You can avoid a wait by reading through the descriptive literature and making your reservations before that talk.

On some cruise ships, prebooking forms for shore excursions will either be forwarded along with your cruise tickets and documents, or you may find them in your cabin on arrival. Prebooking means that you can reserve (and in some cases pay for) excursions before you board or before the shore excursion office is open for business.

As for any cancellations, most ships require a minimum of 24 hours' notice before the advertised shore excursion departure time. Refunds are at the discretion of the cruise line. Should you be unable to go on an excursion or if you change your mind, you will be able, in most cases, to sell your ticket to another passenger. Tickets do not normally have names or cabin numbers on them, except for those which involve air flights or overland arrangements. However, before attempting to resell any tickets, it is wise to check with the shore excursion manager.

CHOOSING THE RIGHT SHORE EXCURSION

As mentioned earlier, at the start of the cruise, the cruise director or the shore excursion manager will give passengers an informal audio-visual lecture on the ports of call on your cruise, together with a brief description of the shore excursions offered. Whether you are a novice or an experienced cruiser, make

an effort to attend this talk. Remember to take a pencil and paper with you to jot down any important points and list the excursions that interest you most.

Look carefully at the shore excursion literature and circle those places that most appeal to you. Then go to the shore excursion office and ask the staff any other questions you may want an answer to before you book.

Here are a few guidelines:
- Shore excursions are put together for general interest. If you want to see something that is not described in the excursion literature, don't take the excursion. Go on your own or with friends.
- In the Caribbean, many of the sightseeing tours cover the same ground. Choose one and then do something different in the next port. (The same is true of the history/archeology excursions operated in the Greek Isles.) It pays to avoid repeating a visit you've made already.
- If you are a history buff, remember that most excursions give very little in-depth history, and the guides are often not acquainted with details beyond a superficial general knowledge. So, pick up a pocket guidebook to the area or check what's on offer in the ship's library.
- City excursions are basically superficial. To get to know a city intimately, it is better to go it alone or with a small group of friends. Travel by taxi or bus directly to the places that are of most interest to you.
- If you enjoy diving or snorkeling, most of the Caribbean cruise ships operate dive-in excursions at a very

reasonable price that includes flippers, mask, and snorkel. Instruction for novices is offered on board, and underwater cameras can often be rented, too.

HELPFUL HINTS

Shore excursions are timed to be most convenient for the greatest number of participants, taking into account the timing of meals on board. Where ships operate two dining room sittings, passengers on the second breakfast sitting may find themselves having to rush their meal in order to participate in a morning excursion. Likewise, those on the afternoon excursions may have to hurry back to get to the first sitting at dinner on time.

Departure times are listed in the descriptive literature and in the *Daily Program*, and will be announced over the ship's public address system. Don't be late, or you may be too late. Note that there are absolutely no refunds if you miss the excursion.

If you are hearing-impaired, make arrangements with the shore excursion manager to assist you in departing for your excursions at the correct times.

Only take along what is necessary; leave any valuables in a safe place on the ship, together with any money and credit cards you do not plan to use. People in sightseeing groups are often targets for pickpockets in major cities such as Barcelona, Caracas, and Rio de Janeiro. Also, beware of the excursion guide who gives you a colored disk to wear for "identification"—he may be marking you as a "rich" tourist for local shopkeepers. You will find it easier—

and also cheaper—to remember your guide's name and the bus number.

Lost or misplaced excursion tickets should be reported immediately to the shore excursion manager. On most of the ships, excursion tickets, once sold, become the sole responsibility of the purchaser, and the cruise line is not generally able to issue replacements. If you place them on the dresser/vanity unit in the cabin, make sure they don't fall down the back, from where there may be no possibility of retrieval. Since tour tickets are not cheap, make sure you place them in a clearly marked envelope right away, and put them in your wallet or purse.

When in foreign ports, convert a little money into the local currency for minor expenses during any tour, or take a supply of U.S. one-dollar bills—useful if you wish to buy a soft drink, for example, or wish to take a taxi to the ship, if you prefer to go shopping rather than go back on the bus.

GOING INDEPENDENTLY

If you do not like to tour with groups of people, you can, of course, go ashore on your own, and in most places this is perfectly safe. In most areas of the world there are no restrictions on independent travel ashore, with the exception of the former countries of the Soviet Union, China, and areas of military importance, together with those countries that stipulate restrictions on individual visas, as in Myanmar (formerly known as Burma). Remember, however, that if you are not on one of the organized excursions, you are *not* covered by the ship's insurance.

Going ashore independently in the major ports of Alaska, the Bahamas, Bermuda, the Caribbean, the Mexican Riviera, the Mediterranean, Canary Islands, the Aegean, and the islands of the South Pacific is ideal for seeing what you want. But in many South American ports, it is wise to go with a friend, especially if you are unfamiliar with the language.

Indeed, in countries where the language is unknown to you, you should always carry some identification (but not your passport), the name of your ship and the area in which it is docked. If the ship is anchored and you take a launch tender ashore, make a note of exactly where the landing place is by observing nearby landmarks, as well as writing down the location. This will be invaluable if you get lost and need to take a taxi back to the launch.

On most ships you'll be given an identification tag or boarding pass at the purser's office or the gangway. This must be handed over every time you return to the ship. Remember that ships have schedules (and sometimes tides) to meet, and that they will not wait for any individual passengers who return late. If the ship is in a launch port in a tropical area and the weather changes for the worse, the ship's captain could well make a decision to depart early to avoid being hemmed in by an approaching storm—it has happened, especially in the Caribbean. If it does, locate the ship's agent in the port, who'll try to get you back on board (and the experience will provide dinner conversation for months).

If you are planning on going to a quiet, secluded beach to swim, first check with the cruise director or shore excursion manager, as certain beaches may be off-limits because of a dangerous undertow, drug pushers, or persistent hawkers. And, if you're thinking of going diving in the sea alone— don't! Not anywhere, not even if you know the area well. Always go diving with at least one companion.

Obviously, going ashore independently does not have to mean going alone. You'll more than likely meet up with others on board ship who prefer to go in their own group rather than with the organized excursion and you can travel with them.

Then again, you don't have to go off the ship in the ports of call at all. You are perfectly free to stay or go from the ship as you please. Sometimes, after several days at sea, you will simply feel like just staying aboard to enjoy the peace and calm while everyone else has left to rush around the port of call.

LOCAL TRANSPORT

In most ports, the same type of transportation is available for sightseeing. You can go by taxi, public bus, rental car, moped, motorcycle, or bicycle.

SIGHTSEEING BY TAXI

If you decide to hire a taxi for sightseeing, be prepared to negotiate the price in advance, and don't pay until you get back to the ship or to your final destination. If you are going with friends, hiring a taxi for a full- or half-day sightseeing trip can often work out far cheaper than renting a car, and you also avoid the hazards of driving. Of course, prices vary according to where in the world you are, but if you can find a driver who speaks English, or whatever your own national language is, and the taxi is comfortable, even air-conditioned, you're ahead.

Be wary of taxi drivers who wear a badge that claims, "I speak English," for it may be all the English they speak! To be sure, ask the driver a few questions, and make sure that the price you negotiate is clear to both of you. Better still, if your driver speaks only a little English, write down the agreed fare and show it to him. Be sure you know what currency the price represents.

TRAVELING BY BUS

Getting around by public bus can be an inexpensive method of sightseeing and of becoming immersed in the local life. In most countries, public transportation is very safe, but there are, of course, those places where it pays to keep an eye on your wallet or purse.

You will need a small amount of the local currency in order to travel on the bus system. You can usually get what you need on board your ship or from a local bank once at the port.

RENTAL CAR

If you are planning on renting a car for any specific ports of call, try to do so ahead of your cruise; book through your travel agent. This will not only save you much precious time on your arrival in port, but it will go a long way to ensuring that there will be a rental car available when you arrive.

Before departing for your cruise, check to see if your driver's license is valid for the destinations you will visit, as some countries may require you to obtain a local or visitor's license (for a fee) before allowing you to rent a car. Remember also to take along a major credit card, which you will need to make a deposit.

MOPED, MOTORCYCLE, AND BICYCLE

Mopeds and motorcycles are available for hire in many ports. In places such as Bermuda, remember that roadside walls are made of coral and limestone, and can give you nasty abrasions if you scrape them.

Bicycles are a favorite way of getting around in many ports of the world, especially in the Orient. They are inexpensive to rent and you will get some exercise as you pedal. One or two ships (and almost all canal barges) have bicycles on board for passenger use.

THE SHOPPING SCENE

For many cruise ship passengers, "retail therapy," or shopping, is a close second to eating. Indeed, one of the many joys of cruising is going ashore and shopping at leisure. Whether it's for local craftwork, handmade trinkets, articles of clothing, silk and cotton material, jewelry, or liquor, there is something special in store at each destination.

In some places, you will find shopping is a bargain compared with home, depending on the exchange rate, and your local duty and taxation structure.

The best ports for shopping are often those that are "duty free"—meaning that no customs duty is charged on the goods bought.

The best duty-free shopping in the world is in Hong Kong and Singapore, but the Caribbean, situated as it is on the "doorstep" of the United States, is also known for its good-value shopping, with St. Thomas, in the U.S. Virgin Islands, the best known spot. Indeed, there are many people who book a Caribbean cruise only if the itinerary includes St. Thomas.

Cruise lines are happy to go along with this. St. Thomas still offers prices that compare favorably with those on the mainland—particularly the liquor at duty-free prices. But don't forget that you'll have to carry that liquor home (the airlines will not accept it as part of your baggage).

GENERAL HINTS FOR SHOPPING

A good general rule for shopping is: know in advance just what you are looking for, especially if your time is limited. But if time is no problem, browsing can be fun.

When shopping time is included in shore excursions, be careful of those stores repeatedly recommended by the tour guides: the guides are likely to be receiving commissions from the merchants. Do shop around and compare prices before you buy. Excellent shopping hints and recommendations are often given in the cruise director's port lecture at the start of your cruise.

You should know that there are a number of cruise lines operating in the Bahamas, the Caribbean, and the Mexican Riviera who openly engage a company that provides the services of a "shopping lecturer" aboard all or some of their cruise ships. The shopping lecturer does nothing more than promote selected shops, goods, and services heavily, fully authorized by the cruise line (which gets a commission from the establishments they recommend). This relieves the cruise director of any responsibilities, together with any question about his involvement, credibility, and financial remuneration.

You will find in your cabin shopping maps that highlight "selected" stores. Often, they come with a "guarantee" such as that offered by Princess Cruises: "Shop with confidence at each of the recommended stores. Each merchant listed on this map has been carefully selected on the basis of quality, fair dealing and value."

When shopping for local handicrafts, make sure they have definitely been made in the country you are in. It may be that the so-called local product has in fact been made in Taiwan, Hong Kong, or some other country in the Far East. It pays to check.

If you have any specific questions about shopping, put them to the cruise director, shore excursion manager, or one of the cruise staff. Some shopping information may be available in the information literature about the port, and this should be available at the ship's shore excursion office.

Keep in mind that the ship's shops are also duty free, and, in most cases, competitive in price. The shops on board are closed while in port, however, in accordance with international customs regulations.

PART TWO

Coastal Cruises

EUROPE

There is year-round coastal cruising along the shores of Norway to the Land of the Midnight Sun aboard the ships of the Norwegian Coastal Express Line (Hurtig-Ruten). The fleet of 11 ships is comprised of six new 450- to 490-passenger vessels that are mini-cruise ships, together with some older vessels that are small yet comfortable, working express coastal packet steamers. Their principal job is the delivery of mail, packaged goods and foodstuffs, as well as passengers, to the communities along the shoreline, on the sea route known as "Highway 1."

This is a 2,500-mile (4,023-km) journey (from Bergen in Norway to Kirkenes close to the Russian border), half of which is north of the Arctic Circle, and takes 11 days, but you can join it at any of the 35 ports of call and stay as long as you wish. In 1994, the company carried a total of some 286,000 passengers.

The service started in 1893, and the three companies that combine to run it have 11 ships. Each ship is of a different size, and, with between 69 and 230 cabins, they can carry a maximum of between 144 and 490 passengers. The ships are: *Harald Jarl* (1960; 2,568 grt; 169 berths); *Kong Harald* (1993; 6,270 grt; 490 berths); *Lofoten* (1964; 2,597 grt; 233 berths); *Midnatsol* (1982; 4,200 grt; 322 berths); *Narvik* (1982; 4,073 grt; 308 berths); *Nordkapp* (1996; 11,204 grt; 490 berths); *Nordlys* (1994; 6,270 grt; 490 berths); *Nordnorge* (1997; 11,204 grt; 490 berths); *Polarlys* (1996; 11,204 grt; 490 berths); *Richard With* (1993; 6,270 grt; 490 berths); and *Vesteralen* (1983; 4,073 grt; 314 berths).

Archipelago hopping can be done on Sweden's east coast, too, by sailing in the daytime and staying in one of the many small hotels on the way. One vessel sails from Norrtalje, north of Stockholm, to Oskarshamn, near the Baltic island of Öland, right through the spectacular Swedish archipelago. You can now cruise from the Finnish city of Lappeenranta to the Estonian city of Viborg without a visa.

Indeed, the point-to-point coastal transportation between neighboring countries, major cities, and commercial centers is big business in northern Europe. Some of the larger cruise ferries could easily rival major cruise ships in other regions now. They're designed to operate in all weather, their facilities are virtually the same, but with much smaller cabins and with an emphasis on duty-free shopping.

Some would argue that ships such as *Silja Serenade* and *Silja Symphony,* which *are* designed for cruising but are used mainly as ferries, are constructed around their duty-free shopping centers. Nevertheless, these super-ferries are splendid as modes of transport and relaxation. And it would take a separate book to list them all, along with their owning companies, as they tend to change hands rather often.

SCOTLAND

The fishing town of Oban, some two hours west of Glasgow by road, is the base for one of the world's very finest vacation ships. The former MacBrayne ferry, *Hebridean Princess*, is a gem, and carries passengers around some of Scotland's most dramatic coastline and islands. Do remember to take plenty of warm clothing with you, however, as the weather can be somewhat unkind.

UNITED STATES

In the United States, coastal vessels offer a change of pace from the big oceangoing liners; informality is the order of the day. Accommodating up to 160 passengers, the ships tend to be more like a private party or club, and, unlike major cruise ships, these small vessels are rarely out of sight of land.

Their operators seek out lesser-known cruise areas, offering in-depth visits to places inaccessible to larger ships, both along the east coast, and in Alaska.

There has been little growth in this segment of the cruise market in recent years. If you prefer a small country inn to a larger resort, this type of cruise just might appeal to you. Each ship measures under 100 grt and each is classed as a "D"-class vessel.

You cruise in comfort at up to 12 knots. The public room facilities are limited, and because the vessels are of American registry, there's no casino on board. As far as entertainment goes, passengers are usually left to their own devices, although there may sometimes be a piano. Most of these vessels are in port during the evening, so you can go ashore for the local nightlife. Getting ashore is extremely easy; passengers can be off in a matter of minutes, with no waiting at the gangway.

The 138-passenger Yorktown Clipper *(Clipper Cruise Line) sails the inland waterways in North and Central America.*

Accommodations, though not elaborate, consist of all-outside cabins, each with its own large picture window and private bathroom. Closet space is very limited, so take only what you need. There is no room service. Some all-outside cabins open directly on to the deck—not convenient when it rains. Also, cabins are closer to the engines and generators, so noise is considerable. The quietest cabins are at the bow, and most cruising is done during the day so that passengers will be able to sleep better at night. Note that the overall length of beds on most of these vessels does not exceed 6 feet (2 m).

These vessels usually have three or four decks, and no elevators. Stairs can be steep, and are not recommended for people with walking difficulties.

Only two of the coastal and inland cruise vessels are featured in Part Three, since they are small and have limited facilities. You may have a linen change only once or twice a week, and you may not get a "turn-down" service. Typical cabin sizes range from 73 sq. ft. (6.7m²) to 232 sq. ft. (21.5m²).

COASTAL CRUISE SHIPS

SHIP	CABINS	CRUISE LINE
Ambassador I	45	Marco Polo Cruises
Bucanero	45	Galapagos Cruises
Caribbean Prince	38	American Canadian Caribbean Line
Isabella II	20	Metropolitan Touring
Mayan Prince	45	American Canadian Caribbean Line
Nantucket Clipper	51	Clipper Cruise Line
New Shoreham II	75	American Canadian Caribbean Line
Niagara Prince	42	American Canadian Caribbean Line
Reef Endeavor	75	Captain Cook Cruises
Reef Escape	59	Captain Cook Cruises
Santa Cruz	43	Metropolitan Touring
Sea Bird	35	Special Expeditions
Sea Lion	35	Special Expeditions
Spirit of Endeavor	51	Alaska Sightseeing
Spirit of Alaska	39	Alaska Sightseeing
Spirit of Discovery	43	Alaska Sightseeing
Spirit of Glacier Bay	25	Alaska Sightseeing
Temptress Explorer	50	Temptress Cruises
Temptress Voyager	33	Temptress Cruises
Tera Australis	50	Cruceros Australis
Yorktown Clipper	69	Clipper Cruise Line

River and Barge Cruises

Whether you want to cruise down the River Nile, along the mighty Amazon or along the lesser Orinoco, the stately Volga, the primal Sepik, the magnificent Rhine, the "blue" Danube, the mystical Irrawaddy (which has been renamed the Ayeyarwady), or along the "yellow" Yangtze—to say nothing of the Don and the Dnieper, the Elbe, or Australia's Murray—there's a cruise and vessel ready for you.

What sort of person enjoys cruising on river vessels? Well, cruise ship passengers who survive very well without dressing up, bingo, casinos, discos, and entertainment, and those who like a totally unstructured lifestyle.

RIVER CRUISING: EUROPE

Cruising down one of Europe's great waterways is an experience in itself—quite different from sailing on an open sea, where motion has to be taken into consideration (rivers are always calm). These cruises provide you with a constant change of scenery, often passing through several countries, each with their own history and architecture, in a week-long journey. The river vessels are always close to land and offer you the chance to visit cities and areas that are inaccessible to large ships. Indeed, watching stunning scenery slip past your floating hotel is one of the most relaxing and refreshing ways to absorb the beauty that has inspired poets and artists through the centuries. A cruise on the Danube, for example, will take you through four countries, and from the Black Forest to the Black Sea.

In 1840-41, the Marquess of Londonderry, a member of the British aristocracy, traveled across Europe along the Rhine and Danube rivers. He then wrote about these experiences, which were published in 1842 in a charming book entitled *A Steam Voyage to Constantinople*. And who could forget the romance implied in Johann Strauss's waltz "The Blue Danube"? The new Rhine-Main-Danube waterway is now open, and at 2,175 miles (3,500 km), it is the longest waterway in Europe. It connects 14 countries from Rotterdam on the North Sea to Sulina and Izmail on the Black Sea, and offers river travelers some of the most fascinating sights anywhere in the world.

River vessels are long and low in the water, and their masts must fold down in order to negotiate the low bridges found along most of Europe's rivers. Although they are small when compared to oceangoing cruise ships, these vessels do have a unique and friendly international atmosphere. The most modern of them do offer the discreet luxury of a small floating hotel, and some of them actually have several public rooms, including a large dining room. They typically have three or four decks. Most are air-conditioned, and the newest will also feature an observation lounge, bar, heated swimming pool (some of them may even have a heated indoor pool), a sauna, solarium, whirlpool, gymnasium, massage, hairdresser, and shop kiosk.

Although the cabins may be small, with limited closet space, they will be mostly outside (facing the river), have a private bathroom, and will be very comfortable for a one-week journey. Cabins are largest aboard *Mozart*, at 205 sq. ft. (19 m²), while most other river vessel cabins will be smaller. All of the cabins are generally clean and tidy, as well as functional. Many of the cabins on the most modern vessels feature a personal safe, a mini-bar, a television, and an alarm clock/radio. You will find that the ceilings are quite low, and that the beds are quite short, too. In general, shore excursions must be booked at the same time as you book your cabin, as only unsold space will be available on board the vessel.

In Europe, river cruising has now reached a very sophisticated level, and you can be assured of good service and meals of a consistently high European standard. The dining is quite pleasant, although not quite a gourmet experience (excepting those vessels that are catered by Austrian and Swiss companies). Lunch is normally a buffet affair. For dinner, a set menu, consisting of three or four courses, is the norm, except for the most upscale vessels. Without doubt the best cuisine can be found aboard *Danube Princess*, *Mozart*, and *Prussian Princess*, although reasonably decent cuisine is served on many other river vessels.

Typical rates for river cruises are from $800 to more than $3,000 per person for a one-week cruise (prices increase for the most popular periods), including meals, cabin with private facilities, side trips and airport/railway transfers. If you are already in Europe, many cruises can be purchased "cruise-only" for greater flexibility.

TIP: It's best to go for an outside cabin on a deck that doesn't have a promenade deck walkway outside it. Normally, cabins on the lowest deck have a four-berth configuration. It doesn't matter which side of the vessel you're on, as you'll see a river bank and scenery on both sides.

DID YOU KNOW ...?

...that the last four-funnel passenger ship was Cunard's *Aquitania* (1914-1949)?

...that Alaska has two time zones? Most of Alaska is one hour behind Pacific Standard Time, while the Aleutian Islands are two hours behind Pacific Standard Time.

...that the Pacific Ocean has a tide of 22 feet (6.7 meters), while the Atlantic Ocean has a tide of only 8 inches (20.3 cm)?

Informality is very much the order of the day, and, because rivers are calm by nature, you won't ever suffer from seasickness.

RIVER CRUISING: RUSSIA

Perhaps the best way to get to know Russia is on a river/inland waterways cruise. Often referred to as the "Waterways of the Tsars," the country benefits as a cruise destination from the well-developed network of rivers, lakes, and canals. Geographically, the river routes for tourists are divided into these three main areas:

• Those in Central European Russia.
• Those in Northwestern European Russia.
• Those in Asian Russia.

Rechtflot is the Russian government's management overlord. It consists of some 21 shipping companies, with the combined fleet made up of more than 5,000 vessels. The largest is the United Volga River Shipping Company, which alone has more than 2,000 river vessels. It carries more than 50 million passengers and about 100 million tons of cargo each year. The Moscow River Shipping Company is the next largest, operates more than 1,000 vessels, and transports as many as 11 million passengers and more than 60 million tons of cargo each year.

In the Central Basin, Moscow is the hub of river tourism, and the newly opened waterways between Moscow and St. Petersburg allow a seven-day cruise link between Russia's present and former capitals.

Best known Russian rivers are the Don, Moskva, Neva and Volga, but the lesser known Belaja, Dvina (and North Dvina) Irtysh, Kama, Ob (longest river in Siberia), Oka, Svir, Tura and Vyatka connect the great system of rivers and lakes in the vast Russian hinterland.

Many Russian vessels are chartered to foreign (non-Russian) cruise wholesalers and tour packagers. The vessels are well equipped, air-conditioned and almost always clean and tidy. I would advise you to choose one that has its food (especially the food) and hotel services catered by the Swiss company Flotel. *Kirov* is a good example.

One unusual Russian river vessel worth mentioning is *Rossiya*, which is used for state visits, and is extremely elegant and fitted throughout with exceptionally fine materials. Cruises include the services of a cruise manager and specialist lecturers, and some companies also specialize in "home stays" before or after the cruise as part of an attractive cultural package. A Russian entry visa is required for non-Russian visitors, and this can be obtained for you by the cruise/tour company.

RIVER CRUISING: THE NILE

A journey along the Nile—the world's longest (and historically the greatest) river—is a journey that takes you back in time, to over 4,000 years before the birth of Christ—when the Pharaohs believed they were immortal. Even though time has proved them mistaken, the people that lived along the river banks formed one of the greatest civilizations the world has ever known. The scenery has changed little in over

2,000 years, and the best way to see it is of course by river boat.

There are approximately 140 vessels cruising the Nile, many offering excellent standards of comfort, food, and service. Most have a swimming pool, lounge, piano bar, and a disco. A specialist lecturer in Ancient Egyptian history accompanies almost all sailings, which cruise the 140 miles (225 km) between Aswan and Luxor in four or five days. Extended cruises, typically of seven or eight days, cover about 295 miles (475 km), and visit Dendera and Abydos. The longest cruises, which take 10 to 12 days, cover 590 miles (950 km), and include visits to Sohag, El Amarna, Tuna El Gabal and Ashmuneim, ending in Cairo. In all, there are over 7,000 departures every year! If you're worried about terrorist attacks on passengers, note that these have only occurred on the Cairo to Aswan cruise section. But the best and most fascinating Nile cruising is between Aswan and Luxor, and this is normally not touched by the terrorist groups.

Most Nile cruises include all sightseeing excursions, which are accompanied by experienced, trained guides who may be resident on board, or who may meet the boat at each place of call. Multi-lingual guides also accompany each cruise.

RIVER CRUISING: CHINA

There are now several new river vessels featuring cruises along the Yangtze, the world's third longest river, particularly through the area known as the Three Yangtze River Gorges, which is a 100-mile (161-km) stretch between Nanjin Pass in the east and White King City in the west. The Three Gorges are the 47-mile-long (76-km) Xiling Gorge, the 25-mile-long (40-km) Wu Gorge, and the Qutang Gorge (known locally as "Wind Box Gorge"). Also, the Lesser Three Gorges (or Three Small Gorges) are, for many, a more impressive sight, sometimes part of the main cruise, but also reached by small river vessels from Wushan. Take a cabin with a balcony—it's worth the extra money, and the view is better. Note that in China, rats and rivers often go together, so be aware that rat poison may well be found under your bed.

Arguably, the best river vessels in China are the new *Elaine*, *Jeannie*, and *Sheena* (Regal China Cruises), a trio that cater superbly well to 258 passengers. The vessels have both Chinese- and Western-style restaurants, beauty salon, health club with sauna, and eight private mah-jong and karaoke rooms. Fine Asian hospitality and service prevail, and cabins are always supplied with fresh towels and hot tea. There are several other operators, but do check on the facilities, meet-and-greet service and the newness of the vessels before booking. The best time of the year to go is May–June, and late August–October (July and early August are extremely hot and humid).

If you do want to cruise this area sometime in the future, note that a $20 billion-plus hydro-electric Sanxia (three gorges) dam, the world's largest, is planned, essentially blocking off this major tourism attraction by creating a reservoir 370 miles (595 km) long. Construction is scheduled to start after the winter of 1997/1998, and is due for completion in 2009, which means that there will be no more river cruises after then if work goes ahead according to schedule.

IRAWADDY RIVER (MYANMAR)

How about the Road to Mandalay? For those visiting South-East Asia, Orient Express Hotels launched a new luxury river cruise vessel in Myanmar (formerly Burma) in January 1996.

The vessel, which has been named *Road to Mandalay*, operates weekly between Mandalay and Pagan, on the Ayeyarwady (Irrawaddy) River.

RIVER MURRAY (AUSTRALIA)

The fifth largest river in the world, the Murray was the lifeblood of the pioneers who lived in the driest continent on earth. Today the river flows for more than 1,250 miles (2,750 km) across a third of Australia. Paddlewheel boats such as *Murray Princess* offer all the amenities you'll find on America's *Mississippi Queen*. There are even six cabins for the physically challenged.

BARGE CRUISING: EUROPE

Smaller than river vessels, and more accurately called boats, "hotel barges" ply the inland waterways and canals of Europe April through November, when the weather is generally good. Barge cruises are usually of three, six, or 13 days' duration, and they offer a completely informal atmosphere, for up to a dozen passengers. These barges cruise along slowly in the daytime, and moor early each evening, to give you time to pay a visit to a local village, and to get a restful night's sleep.

Hotel barges are even more intimate than river vessels, and offer a different experience. You go ashore on your own during the day and at night. Shopping opportunities are limited, and evening entertainment is always impromptu. Most of the barges carry between eight and 24 passengers.

Hotel barges tend to be beautifully fitted out with rich wood paneling, full carpeting, custom-built furniture, and tastefully chosen fabrics. Each barge has a dining room/lounge-bar and is equipped with the passenger's comfort in mind. Each barge captain takes special pride in his vessel, often acquiring some rare memorabilia to be incorporated into the decor.

Locally grown fresh foods are usually purchased and prepared each day by a caring crew, allowing you to live well and feel like a house guest. Most of the barges can also be chartered for exclusive use—so you can just take your family and friends, for example.

The waterways of France, especially, offer beauty, tranquility and a diversity of interests, and barge cruising is an excellent way of exploring an area not previously visited. Most cruises include a visit to a famous vineyard and wine cellar, as well as side-trips to places of historic, architectural or scenic interests. You will be accompanied by a crew member familiar with the surrounding countryside. You can even go hot-air ballooning over the local countryside, and land to a welcome glass of champagne and your flight certificate.

Although ballooning is an expensive extra, the experience of floating within sight of châteaux, villages, and over pastoral landscapes, is something you can always treasure.

How you dine on board a barge will depend on which barge and area you choose; dining will range from home-style cooking to outstanding *nouvelle cuisine*, with all the trimmings. And the hotel barges will have English or English-speaking French crews.

Barging on the canals often means going through a constant succession of locks. Nowhere is this more enjoyable and entertaining than in the Burgundy region of France where, between Dijon and Macon, for example, a barge can negotiate as many as 54 locks during a six-day cruise. Interestingly, all lock-keepers in France are women!

Typical rates range from $600 to more than $3,000 per person for a six-day cruise. I don't recommend taking children. Rates include cabin with private facilities, all meals, excellent wine with lunch and dinner, other beverages, use of bicycles, side-trips and airport/railway transfers. Some operators also provide a hotel the night before or after the cruise. Clothing, by the way, is totally casual at all times, but at the beginning and end of the season, the weather can be unreliable, so make sure you take sweaters and rain gear.

STEAMBOATING: U.S.A.

The most famous of all river cruises in the United States are those aboard the steamboats of the mighty Mississippi River. Mark Twain, an outspoken fan of Mississippi cruising, at one time said: "When man can go 700 miles an hour, he'll want to go seven again."

The grand traditions of the steamboat era are maintained by the new *American Queen*, and by the older, smaller *Delta Queen* and *Mississippi Queen* (Delta Queen Steamboat Company), all of which are powered by steam engines that drive huge wooden paddlewheels at the stern.

The smaller and older of the three boats, the 180-passenger *Delta Queen*, was built on Scotland's Clydeside in 1926 and is now on the U.S. National

This is Mississippi Queen *(Delta Queen Steamboat Company), seen steamboating down the Mississippi River in the U.S.A.*

194

Register of Historic Places. She came to the nation's attention when President Jimmy Carter spent a week aboard in 1979.

Half a century younger, the 400-passenger *Mississippi Queen* was built at a cost of $27 million in Jefferson, Indiana, the place where nearly 5,000 steamboats were built during the 19th century. (*Mississippi Queen* itself was designed by the creator of Cunard's *QE2,* James Gardner of London.) Each of the steamboats features one of the rarest of musical instruments—a Caliope, or "steam piano," driven by the boat's engine.

A new, 222-cabin, 436-passenger American-built steamboat, which was named *American Queen* (Delta Queen Steamboat Company), debuted in June 1995. Built at a cost of $60 million by McDermott Shipyard, Morgan City, Louisiana, the riverboat is fitted out with vintage tandem compound horizontal reciprocating steam engines (circa 1930) that originally drove a steam dredge called *Kennedy.* The engines are used to drive the 60-ton stern paddle wheel, made up of individual bucket boards (the paddles) that measure 30 feet (9 m) in length and 2 feet (60 cm) in width. *American Queen* is the 30th steamboat built for the Delta Queen Steamboat Company.

Traveling aboard one of these steamboats makes you feel like you're stepping back into the past and into the world of American folklore. You will be surrounded by a certain charm and old-world graciousness, as well as by finely polished woods, brass, and sweeping staircases. And once every year, two boats challenge each other in the Great Steamboat Race—a 10-day extravaganza.

Steamboat cruises last from two to 12 days, and during the year there are several theme cruises, with big bands and lively entertainment. These boats cruise up and down the Mississippi and Ohio rivers.

As for food aboard the steamboats, it is generally very much "American" fare. That means you will be eating steak, shrimp, Creole sauces, fried foods, and few fresh vegetables.

Traveling on the river is a great way of taking a vacation and avoiding the crush of congested roads and airports. And of course there are no immigration or customs officials and procedures in the heartland of America.

Expedition and Nature Cruises

"The risk one runs in exploring a coast in these unknown and icy seas is so very great that I can be so bold to say no man will ever venture farther than I have done and that the lands to the south will never be explored."

So wrote Captain James Cook in 1774. His voyage was a feat of great courage, for not only did he take the risk of entering an unknown sea, but his ship, *Resolution,* was far too fragile a vessel (462 tons) to undertake such a trip. Yet there is no landscape quite so breathtaking and compelling as the polar regions of the south, and there is no experience so unforgettable as a visit there. Today's would-be Captain Cooks have the curiosity and drive to move into adventure cruising.

Given that we have so many opportunities to cruise in places such as Alaska and the Baltic, the Caribbean, the Mediterranean, and the Mexican Riviera areas, you may be surprised to discover a small but growing group of enthusiasts heading out for strange and remote waters. But there are countless virtually untouched areas to be visited by the more adventurous. Passengers tend to be more self-reliant and more interested in doing or learning than in being entertained.

On an expedition cruise, passengers play an active part in every aspect of the voyage, which tends to be intensively oriented toward visiting interesting destinations, exploring areas and studying nature. You will find naturalists, historians, and specialist lecturers, rather than entertainers, on board each ship to provide background information and observations about wildlife. Each participant receives his or her personal *log book*—which is illustrated and written by the renowned wildlife artists and writers who accompany each cruise. This log book documents the entire expedition and serves as a great source of information, as well as a complete *mémoire* of the voyage. All the companies that offer these adventure cruises provide expedition parka and waterproof boots.

Imagine walking on pack ice in the Arctic Circle, exploring a teeming penguin colony on Antarctica or the Falkland Islands, searching for the "lost" peoples in Melanesia, cruising close to the source of the Amazon, gazing at species of flora and fauna in the Galapagos Islands (Darwin's laboratory), or watching an authentic dragon (from a comfortable distance, of course). This is what expedition cruising is all about, and it is not really recommended for the novice cruisegoer.

Because of the briefings, the lectures, and the laboratory at sea, there is a strong cultural and intellectual aspect to these expedition cruises. There is no formal entertainment as such; passengers enjoy this type of cruise more for the camaraderie and educational experience than anything else. The vessels themselves are designed and equipped to sail through ice-laden waters, and yet have a shallow enough draft to glide over coral reefs.

Expedition cruise vessels can, nevertheless, provide comfortable and even elegant surroundings for as many as 200 passengers; they have a highly trained and knowledgeable staff, and they offer first-class food and service. Without traditional cruise ports to stop at, the ship must be self-sufficient, capable of long-range cruising, as well as being environmentally friendly.

Expedition cruising was inspired by people's desire to find out more about this remarkable planet we live on—its incredible animal, bird, and marine life. This type of cruise was pioneered in the late 1960s by Lars-Eric Lindblad, a Swedish-American who was determined to turn the experience of travel into adventure by opening up parts of the world that tourists had never visited.

After chartering several vessels for adventure cruises to Antarctica, Lindblad then organized the design and construction of a ship capable of going almost anywhere in comfort and safety. In 1969, this ship, *Lindblad Explorer*, was launched.

In the years that followed, the ship earned an enviable reputation in the adventure travel area. Lindblad's company sold the ship to Salen-Lindblad Cruising in 1982. They subsequently resold her to Society Expeditions, who renamed her *Society Explorer*. She is now operated by another adventure travel company, Abercrombie & Kent, as *Explorer*. (See Part Three, where details and ratings are provided.)

Today there is only a handful of adventure/expedition cruise companies that are in operation. They provide in-depth expertise and specially constructed vessels, usually with ice-hardened hulls that are capable of venturing into the vast reaches of the Arctic regions and Antarctica.

EXPEDITION AND NATURE CRUISE AREAS

Buddha was once asked to express verbally what life meant to him. For a moment he was still—then, without speaking, he held up a single rose. This is what several "destinations" on this planet are like, in that there are no words that can adequately describe them—they have instead to be experienced, just as a single rose.

The principal adventure cruise areas of the world at the moment are: Alaska and the Aleutians, Amazonia and the Orinoco, Antarctica, Australasia and the Great Barrier Reef, Chilean fjords, the Galapagos Archipelago, Indonesia, Melanesia, the Northwest Passage, and Polynesia and the South Pacific. Other adventure cruise destinations growing in popularity are Baha California and the Sea of Cortez, Greenland, the Red Sea, East Africa, the Réunion Islands and the Seychelles, West Africa and the Ivory Coast, and the South China Seas and China Coast.

In order to put together their special cruise expeditions, the staff at the various companies turn to knowledgeable sources and advisers. Scientific institutions are consulted, experienced world explorers are questioned, and naturalists provide up-to-date reports on wildlife sightings, migrations, and other natural phenomena. Although some days are scheduled for relaxation or preparing for the days ahead, participants are kept active both physically and mentally. And speaking of physical activity, it is unwise to consider such an adventure cruise if you are not completely ambulatory.

ANTARCTICA

Perhaps the most intriguing "destination" on earth is Antarctica, which was first sighted only in 1820 by the American sealer Nathaniel Palmer, British naval officer Edward Bransfield, and a Russian ship's captain Fabian Bellingshausen. For most, it's nothing but a wind-swept frozen wasteland (it has been calculated that the ice mass contains almost 90 per cent of the snow and ice in the world). For others, however, it represents the last pristine place on earth, empty of people, commerce and pollution, yet offering awesome scenery and a truly wonderful abundance of marine and bird life. There are no germs, and not a single tree. Over 6,000 people visited the conti-

nent during 1992—the first and only smoke-free continent on earth—and yet the first human to arrive did so within a generation of man landing on the moon. There is not a single permanent human inhabitant of the continent, whose ice is as much as 2 miles (3 km) thick. Its total land mass equals more than all the rivers and lakes on earth and exceeds that of China and India combined. The continent has a raw beauty and ever-changing landscape. Once part of the ancient land mass known as Gondwanaland (which also included Africa, South America, India, Australasia, and Madagascar), it is, perhaps, the closest we have to another planet, and has so fragile an ecosystem that it needs international protection.

Although visited by "soft" expedition cruise ships and even "normal"-sized cruise ships with ice-hardened hulls (capable of carrying as many as 800 passengers), the more remote "far side"—the Oates and Scott Coasts,

Hanseatic Tours' 160-passenger Hanseatic, seen here in Antarctica.

McMurdo Sound and the famous Ross Ice Shelf—can only be visited by "real" ice-breaker expedition ships such as *Kapitan Dranitsyn*, *Khlebnikov*, and *World Discoverer*, as the winds can easily reach more than 100 m.p.h. in this part of the continent. As there are no docks in Antarctica, venturing "ashore" is done by "wet" landings of Zodiac rubber inflatable craft—an integral part of the Antarctica experience.

GALAPAGOS

A word of advice about the Galapagos Islands: don't even think about taking a cruise with a "foreign-flag" expedition ship. The Ecuadoreans jealously guard their island, and prohibit the movement of virtually all the non-Ecuadorean-registered cruise vessels within its boundaries. Thus, the best way to get to see this place that Charles Darwin loved is to fly to Quito and then cruise on an Ecuadorean-registered vessel such as *Isabella II* (no doctor on board) or *Santa Cruz* (which does have a doctor on board).

GREENLAND

The world's largest island, Greenland, in the Arctic Circle, is technically a desert that is 82 per cent covered with ice (actually it is compressed snow), which can be as thick as 11,000 feet (3,353 m). This country's rocks are among the oldest in the world (the 3.8 billion-year-old Isukasia formations), and its ecosystem is one of the newest. The glacier at Jacobshavn (also known

as Ilulissat) is the fastest moving in the world, and creates a new iceberg every five minutes. Greenland is said to have more dogs than people, and these provide the principal means of transport for the Greenlanders.

THE ENVIRONMENT

Since the increase in people's environmental awareness, cruise adventurers have banded together to protect the environment from further damage. In future, only the ships that are capable of meeting new "zero discharge" standards, like those introduced in the Arctic by the Canadian Coast Guard, will be allowed to proceed through environmentally sensitive areas.

Expedition companies themselves are concerned about the environment, and they invest time and money in educating both crews and passengers about safe environmental procedures.

An "Antarctic traveler code" has been created, whose rules are enforced by all the expedition cruise companies, based on the Antarctic Conservation Act of 1978, and adopted by the U.S. Congress to protect and preserve the ecosystem, the flora, and the fauna of the Antarctic continent. By law, every U.S. citizen who travels to Antarctica must adhere to the Act.

Briefly, the Act makes it unlawful to take native animals or birds, to collect any special native plant or to introduce species, to enter certain special areas (SPAs), or to discharge or dispose of any pollutants, unless authorized by regulation or permit issued under the Act. To "take" a native mammal or a bird means to remove, harass, molest,

Explorer *(Society Expeditions)* anchored off South Georgia island, close to a nearby rookery of 75,000 King penguins.

harm, pursue, hunt, shoot, kill, trap, capture, restrain, or to tag any such wildlife, or to attempt to do as such.

Under the Act, violations are subject to civil penalties, including a fine of up to $10,000 and a term of one year's imprisonment for each violation. A copy of the Act is found in the library of each adventure/expedition ship that visits the continent.

THE COMPANIES

Abercrombie & Kent
This is a well-known company that operates the older, but still highly suitable *Explorer* (ex-*Society Explorer*).

Hanseatic Tours
This is the company that operates *Bremen* (ex-*Frontier Spirit*) as well as *Hanseatic*, which are the latest in high-tech luxury expedition cruise vessels.

Both vessels offer destination-intensive itineraries. The ships have truly luxurious appointments, and are targeted to appeal to both English-speaking and German-speaking passengers.

Marine Expeditions
This Canadian company charters several Russian vessels for "soft" expedition cruises to popular areas, including Antarctica. The company applies its own ship names for the charters (they are often the same ships used by other operators).

Quark Expeditions
This company, which was formed by the former president of Salen Lindblad Cruising (which was purchased by NYK of Japan in 1991), is the U.S. general sales agent for one or more of the Russian-owned nuclear- or diesel-powered icebreakers, which are fitted with a range of outstanding amenities

200

and creature comforts for up to 100 passengers. Among the vessels available for charter are *Kapitan Dranitsyn* and *Yamal*. In the U.K. the company is represented by Noble Caledonia Limited of London.

Society Expeditions

This company operates the more luxurious *World Discoverer*—a fine expedition cruise vessel, which features full creature comforts and a range of fascinating itineraries. In addition, the ship is often available for charter.

Special Expeditions

This company operates *Polaris*, a small expedition vessel, featuring splendid appointments and all the creature comforts (see profile section in Part Three for details). In addition, it has two small vessels, *Sea Bird* and *Sea Lion* (ex-Exploration Cruise Lines vessels), which operate "soft" expedition cruises along some of the specially protected coastal areas in the United States, including Alaska.

THE NORTHWEST PASSAGE

In 1984, Salen Lindblad Cruising made maritime history by successfully negotiating a westbound voyage through the Northwest Passage—a 41-day epic that started from St. John's, Newfoundland, in Canada, and ended at Yokohama in Japan. The expedition cruise had taken its organizers two years of planning, and was sold out just days after it was announced.

The search for a Northwest Passage to the Orient attracted brave explorers for more than four centuries. Despite numerous attempts and some loss of life, including Henry Hudson in 1610, a "white passage" to the East remained an elusive dream. Amundsen's 47-ton ship *Gjoa* eventually navigated the route in 1906, taking three years to do so. It was not until 1943 that a Canadian ship, *St. Roch*, became the first vessel in history to make the passage in a single season. *Lindblad Explorer* became the 34th vessel, and the first cruise vessel, to complete the journey through the Northwest Passage.

THE NORTHEAST PASSAGE

Quark Expeditions had the good fortune of making maritime history in July/August 1991 when a Russian icebreaker, *Sovetskiy Soyuz*, made a spectacular 21-day voyage to negotiate a passage from Murmansk, Russia, to Nome, Alaska, across the North Pole. The ship followed the trail which had been set in 1909 by Admiral Peary, who crossed the North Pole accompanied by 56 Eskimos, setting out on his journey by sled from Ellesmere Island. Although the polar ice cap had been navigated before by U.S. nuclear submarines *Skate* and *Nautilus*—as well as by dirigible and airplane—this was the first passenger ship to make the hazardous crossing. The planning for this expedition took over two years.

Sail-Cruise Ships

Thinking of a cruise but really want to sail? Been cruising on a conventional Caribbean cruise ship that is more like an endurance test? Whatever happened to the *romance* of sailing? Think no more, for the answer, to quote a movie title, is "back to the future."

If you're active, think about cruising under sail, with towering masts and washing-powder-white sails to power you along. There's simply nothing that beats the thrill of being aboard a multi-masted tall ship, sailing under thousands of square feet of canvas through waters that mariners have sailed across for centuries.

This is what cruising in the old traditional manner is all about, on board authentic sailing ships, on contemporary copies of clipper ships, or on the very latest high-tech cruise-sail ships. Even the most jaded of cruise passengers will love the exhilaration of being under sail.

Tall ships provide either a genuine sail-powered experience like those of the past (*Lili Marleen, Sea Cloud, Sir Francis Drake, Star Clipper, Star Flyer*), or they are contemporary vessels built to emulate sail-powered vessels, but which are actually *sail-assisted* vessels in an ultra-chic form (*Club Med I, Club Med II, Le Ponant, Wind Song, Wind Spirit, Wind Star*).

Whichever you choose, there are no rigid schedules, and life aboard equates with a wholly unstructured lifestyle, apart from meal times. Weather conditions often dictate whether a scheduled port visit will be made or not, but passengers sailing on these vessels are usually unconcerned with being ashore. They would rather savor the thrill of being one with nature, albeit in a comfortable, civilized setting, and without having to do the hard work.

REAL TALL SHIPS

While we have all been dreaming of adventure, a pocketful of designers and yachtsmen have committed their pen to paper, hand in pocket and rigging to mast, and come up with a pot-pourri of stunning vessels to delight the eye and refresh the spirit.

Ships of the Star Clippers company, *Star Clipper* and *Star Flyer*, are *working* four-masted barentine clipper ships that rely on the wind about 80 per cent of the time. Their diesel engines are used only as a backup in emergencies, for generating electrical power, and for desalinating approximately 40 tons of seawater each day for shipboard needs. The crew perform almost every task aboard these ships, including hoisting, trimming, winching, and repairing the sails. The whole sail-cruise experience evokes the feeling of sailing aboard some famous private yacht at the turn of the century. Star Clippers' two modern clipper ships were conceived in the mind of a ship-loving owner, Mikaël Krafft.

When growing up, Krafft, himself a yachtsman (he sails a 128-foot/39-m schooner) in his native Sweden, was told tales of the four-masted barkentine-rigged clipper ships of yesteryear—the last one had been built 140 years ago. Krafft turned his boyhood dreams into reality in 1991, with the introduction of the tallest of the tall ships in the world, the Belgian-built *Star Flyer*. It has sails hoisted aloft on four masts, the tallest being 226 feet (69 m) high. One year later, the almost identical *Star Clipper* emerged from the same shipyard as *Star Flyer*.

These are no ordinary clipper ships; they are built for passengers, who share in the experience of the trade winds of the Caribbean (and other areas). With accommodations for as many as 180 passengers, the new breed of clipper ships are the only ones that are fully certified under the U.S. Coast Guard regulations. In addition to this, they also carry Lloyd's Register of Ship-

ping's highest rating—a rating that has not been bestowed on any other sailing vessel since 1911.

Star Flyer, the first clipper sailing ship to be built for 140 years, became the first commercial sailing vessel to cross the North Atlantic in 90 years, and one of only a handful of sailing ships ever to be allowed into the Port of Miami under full sail. It is no exaggeration to say that to be aboard Star Clippers is to seem to have died and gone to the yachtsman's heaven.

While the rigging and sails above decks are totally traditional, accommodations below decks are extremely well equipped, though not as lavish as those on the Club Meds and Windstars. Spacious cabins are each equipped with twin beds that convert into a double bed, individually controlled air-conditioning, two-channel audio, color television (they didn't have those in 1840),

This is the 170-passenger Star Flyer *(Star Clipper) under full sail. She is a true clipper ship, but with all modern amenities.*

personal safe, and private bathroom with shower, toilet, sink, and even a hairdryer (the deluxe cabins also have a bathtub and a refrigerator).

Take minimal clothing, for these ships are the ultimate in casual dress. No jacket and tie are needed in the dining room, which can accommodate all the passengers at once in an open seating. Short-sleeved shirts and shorts for the men, very casual shorts and tops for the ladies, are the order of the day (and night). The deck crew are real sailors, brought up with yachts and tall ships—and most wouldn't set foot on a cruise ship.

Passengers gather each morning for "captain's story-time." The captain also explains the sailing maneuvers when changing the rigging or directing the ship as it sails into port. Passengers are encouraged to lend a hand, pulling on thick ropes to haul up the main sail. And they love it. At the end of the cruise, tipping (at a suggested $8 per passenger per day) is pooled and is distributed to all members of the crew.

Passengers are provided with many of the amenities of large modern cruise vessels, such as air-conditioning, cashless cruising, occasional live music, a small shop, and a pool to swim in. There is no dress code, so you can be as relaxed as you wish. At 9 a.m. each day the captain, sometimes in two or three languages, gives a daily briefing of the important events of the day, such as what time he expects to enter port, the wind and the sea conditions, and when passengers can help furl or unfurl the sails if they so wish.

The Star Clippers also carry a fine range of watersports craft for the use of passengers—at no extra charge (except scuba diving). The equipment includes a water-ski boat, sailfish, scuba diving, and snorkeling gear.

While cuisine aboard the Star Clippers is perhaps less than the advertised excellence (as far as presentation and choice are concerned), one has to take into account the tiny galley and preparation space provided. Seating in the dining room is awkward for "correct"

A typical cabin aboard the three 148-passenger Windstar Cruises ships. Each has a twin or queen-size bed; stocked minibar; multi-channel television and videocassette player; CD-player; direct-dial telephone; private bathroom with shower.

service, and consists of six-seat tables set along the sides of the room. However, this *is* supposed to be a casual experience.

The above comments also apply in general to the beautiful, elegant *Sea Cloud*, which is an authentic 1930s three-masted barkentine whose masts are as high as a 20-story building. She was the largest private yacht ever built, when she was constructed in 1931 by E. F. Hutton for his wife, Marjorie Merriweather Post. Built for $1 million in the Krupp shipyard in Kiel, Germany, this steel-hulled yacht is immensely impressive. The cuisine is quite superb, although the choices are limited. This ship has some beautiful cabins, including two lavish owner's suites (both of them with fireplaces and a French canopy bed) left over from her private yacht days, and gorgeous hand-crafted interiors.

In addition to retained and refurbished original suites and cabins, with their paneling, antiques and dressers, some newer, smaller cabins were also added when a consortium of German yachtsmen purchased the ship. Recent owners spent $7.5 million refurbishing her. Many original oil paintings adorn her inner walls. Now owned and operated under charter, *Sea Cloud* sails in both the Caribbean and the Mediterranean waters and is a tribute to elegant times past. The wood-paneled dining room is splendid.

Another new three-masted barkentine, owned and operated by German entrepreneur Peter Deilmann, *Lili Marleen* is the culmination of a lifelong dream. Built in 1994, this vessel cruises the Caribbean during the winter and the Mediterranean during the summer, and caters specifically to the German-speaking market.

Another vintage vessel, *Sir Francis Drake*, also offers you a real working tall ship experience. With carpeted cabins that each have a private bathroom, the ship caters to a more casual clientele than the two Star Clipper ships or *Sea Cloud*. The cuisine is very simple fare, with no frills, though not as basic as that found on the ships of Windjammer Barefoot Cruises or the Maine Windjammer Association.

CONTEMPORARY SAIL-CRUISE SHIPS

At the other extreme, if you like sailing but want all your needs taken care of automatically (no energy needed), look no further than *Club Med I* and *Club Med II* (Club Méditerranée)—with five masts the world's largest sail-cruise ships—and *Wind Song*, *Wind Spirit*, and *Wind Star* (Windstar Cruises), each with four masts. How so? Nary a hand touches the sails. It's all controlled by computer from an ultra-high-tech bridge. These ships are the contemporary ocean-going robots.

Club Med ships are first and foremost cruise vessels with very impressive sails and tall aluminum masts, while Windstar Cruises' ships carry less than half the number of passengers of the Club Med ships (and fewer than the Star Clippers). From a yachtsman's point of view, the sail-to-power ratio is laughable. And that's why these cruise ships with sails have engine power to get them into and out of port. (The Star Clippers, by contrast, do it by sail alone, except when there isn't any wind—which isn't often.) The Windstar ships were built first. On some itineraries, when there's little wind, you could well be under motor power for most of the cruise, with only a few hours spent under sail. Windstar and Club Med ships would probably be under sail for no more than 40 per cent of the time they were at sea.

It was a Norwegian living in New York, Karl Andren, who first turned the concept of a cruise vessel with sails into reality. "Boyhood dream stuff," he said. The shipyard he chose to build his ships, the Société Nouvelle des Ateliers et Chantiers du Havre (ACH, as it is known in Le Havre), enjoyed the challenge of building these most unusual vessels. The shipyard had great expertise in the design and construction of cable-laying ships using the hydraulic power of servomechanisms—a concept that was adopted for the Windstar computer-controlled sail rig. Gilbert Fournier, the president of the shipyard, and an expert computer programmer, was fascinated with this ship project. Three Windstar ships were delivered (a fourth was planned but never built). These ships carry mainly North American passengers, whereas the Club Med ships are geared to cater principally to French-speaking passengers.

The Windstar and Club Med ships offer quite luxurious accommodations, excellent full-service meals, and a fine-tuned service. These ships have several public rooms, all with contemporary decor. Entertainment is also provided, though the standard is amateurish on Club Med ships.

Another, slightly smaller but very chic new entrant is the ultra-sleek *Le Ponant*. This three-masted ship caters to just 64 French-speaking passengers in elegant, yet casual, high-tech surroundings, developing the original Windstar concept to a very advanced state of 1990s technology.

Aboard the Club Meds, Star Clippers, Windstars and *Le Ponant*, watersports take over in the Caribbean when you're not ashore sampling the delights of smaller islands like St. Barthelemy, St. Eustatius, or Les Isles du Saintes, where the huge "white-whale" cruise ships can't go. The Club Meds, Windstars and *Le Ponant* feature an aft, fold-down watersports platform. On-board equipment includes scuba diving gear (with full certification course), snorkeling equipment, water-ski boat, windsail boats and rubber Zodiacs to take you to private, unspoiled beaches.

A separate section in Part Three compares these beautiful ships (see pages 450–460).

World Cruises

THE WORLD CRUISE

The ultimate classic voyage for any experienced traveler is a world cruise. This is usually defined as the complete circumnavigation of the earth in a continuous one-way voyage. The ports of call are planned for their interest and their diversity, and the entire trip can go on for as long as six months.

Voyages that go from cold to warm climates—almost always during January, February, and March, when the weather in the Orient is at its best—give you the experience of crisp, clear days, sparkling nights, delicious food, tasteful entertainment, superb accommodations, delightful company, and unforgettable memories. It is for some the cultural, social, and travel experience of a lifetime, and for the few who can afford it, an annual event!

The concept of the world sea cruise first became popular in the 1920s, although it has existed since the 1880s. The first round-the-world voyage was made by the Portuguese navigator Ferdinand Magellan in 1539.

In 1909, for example, the German company Hapag's steamer *Cleveland* left from New York on a complete world cruise, a journey that was to last a whole year, visit 21 ports, and end in San Francisco in February 1910.

A world cruise on today's modern ships means experiencing stabilized,

The superb 600-passenger Europa (Hapag Lloyd Cruises)*operates one world cruise and several long cruises each year. .*

air-conditioned comfort in luxury cabins, and splendid sightseeing and excursions on shore and overland. On some ships, every passenger will get to dine with the captain at least once.

A world cruise gives you the chance to indulge yourself. Although the idea may sound extravagant, it need not be, and fares can be as low as $100 per day, up to more than $3,000 per day. Alternatively, you can book a segment of the cruise if that fits your pocket.

The cost of a world cruise depends on your choice of ship and accommodations. For 1997, a double occupancy cruise fare will vary from about $8,000 to more than $100,000 per person. *QE2*'s split-level penthouse suites, for example, command in excess of $300,000 each (based on two persons occupying a suite). Gratuities alone would be more than $2,000 for the full voyage! At the other end of the scale, a Russian/Ukrainian-registered vessel is the least expensive way of going round the world by ship. It almost pays not to stay at home; the trip will cost less than $100 per person per day—and that includes gratuities!

PLANNING AND PREPARATION

Few enterprises can match the complexity of planning and preparing for a world cruise. More than 675,000 main meals will be prepared in the ship's galleys during a *QE2* world cruise, for example. Several hundred professional entertainers, specialist lecturers, bands, and musicians must all be booked about a year in advance of the trip. Crew changeovers during the cruise must be organized. A ship the size of Cunard's *QE2* requires two major crew changes during the three-month-long voyage. This normally involves chartering a jumbo jet to and from the relevant port of call. Airline tickets must be arranged for personnel flying in to join the ship—in the right port, and at the right time.

Because a modern world cruise ship has to be totally self-contained, a warehouse-full of spare parts (electrical, plumbing and engineering supplies, for example) must be planned for, ordered, loaded, and stored somewhere aboard ship prior to sailing. For just

DID YOU KNOW ...?

...that the first floating eclipse expedition was led by U.S. astronomer Ted Pedas in 1972, when 800 passengers sailed to a spectacular rendezvous with totality in the North Atlantic?

...that a whole county in Iowa raises all its beef cattle for Carnival Cruise Lines?

P&O Cruises' 1,399-passenger Canberra *is one example of a low-budget ship that operates a world cruise each year. It's better, and probably cheaper, than staying home!*

about every shipboard department, the same basic consideration will apply: once at sea, it will be impossible to pick up a replacement projector bulb, air-conditioning belt, table tennis ball, saxophone reed, or anything else that the ship might run out of.

The cruise director will have his or her hands full planning entertainment and social events for such a long voyage—not like the "old days," when an occasional game of bingo, or the horse racing, or the daily tote would satisfy passengers.

Another preparation will include reserving fuel at various ports on the itinerary. How much fuel does a cruise ship use? Well, that depends on the size of the ship. On *Canberra*'s round-the-world cruise, the 44,807-grt liner would steam 53 feet (16 m) per gallon of fuel, at a cruising speed of 20 knots.

A cruise line must give advance notice of the date and time that pilots will be needed, together with requirements for tugs, docking services, customs and immigration authorities, or

meetings with local dignitaries and the press. Then there's the organization of dockside labor and stevedoring services at each port of call, plus planning and contracting of bus or transportation services for shore excursions.

The complexity of the preparations requires the concerted efforts of many departments and people on every continent to bring about, with precise timing, this ultimate cruising experience for travelers.

DOING A WORLD CRUISE SEGMENT

Cruises to exotic destinations—China, the Orient, the South Pacific, around Africa and in the Indian Ocean, and around South America—offer all the delights that are associated with a world cruise. The cruise can be shorter and hence less expensive, yet offer the same elegance and comfort, splendid food, delightful ambiance and interesting, well-traveled fellow passengers.

An exotic voyage can be a totally self-contained cruise to a specific destination, lasting anywhere from 30 days to more than 100. Or you can book a segment of a world cruise to begin at one of its ports of call, getting off at another port. "Segmenting" is ideal for those who wish to be a part of a world cruise but have neither the time nor the money for the prolonged extravagance of a three- to six-month cruise vacation.

The segment cruising idea involves flying either to or from your cruise, or both. You can travel to join your exotic cruise at principal ports such as Genoa, Rio de Janeiro, Acapulco, Honolulu, Sydney, Hong Kong, Singapore, Bangkok, Colombo, Bombay, Mombasa, or Athens, depending on the ship and itinerary.

Ships that already cruise worldwide during the year offer the most experienced world cruises or segments. Many of the world cruise ships often operate at about 75 per cent capacity, thus providing their passengers with considerably more space to move around in than they would normally have.

WORLD CRUISE FLEET

The following list includes ships that are presently scheduled to operate a world cruise in 1997.

Albatros (Phoenix Seereisen)
Asuka (NYK Cruises)
Canberra (P&O Cruises)
Crystal Symphony (Crystal Cruises)
Delphin (Delphin Seereisen)
Europa (Hapag Lloyd Cruises)
Maxim Gorki (Phoenix Seereisen)
Oriana (P&O Cruises)
QE2 (Cunard)
Rotterdam (Holland America Line)
Royal Viking Sun (Cunard)

GOING P.O.S.H.

This colloquialism for "grand" or "first rate" has its origin in the days of ocean steamship travel between England and India. Wealthy passengers would, at some considerable extra cost, book their round trip passage as "Port Outward, Starboard Home." In this way they would secure cabins on what was thought to be the cooler side of the ship while crossing the unbearably hot Indian Ocean under the sun. Subsequently abbreviated to P.O.S.H., the expression soon came to be applied to first-class passengers who could afford that luxury (*Brewers Dictionary of Phrase & Fable*, Cassell).

However, the reality is that the monsoon winds that blow in and out of the Asian area shift between winter and summer, so that the sheltered side of a ship would change according to the season. Further, in looking at deck plans of ships of the period, it appears that most cabins were located *centrally*, with indoor promenades or corridors along each side, so the actual definition of the origin of P.O.S.H. could be said to be taken as artistic license.

Crossings

By "crossings," I mean crossings of the North Atlantic, that is, 3,000 miles (4,828 km) or so of it, from the Old World to the New World—or vice versa, although crossings might also include any other major ocean, such as the Pacific or the Indian Ocean.

Crossing the North Atlantic by ship is an adventure, when time seems to be suspended—the most delicious way of enjoying life aboard ship. It actually takes little more than a long weekend. After the embarkation procedures have been completed, you will be shown to the gangway. Cross the gangway from pier to ship and you are in another world—a world that provides a complete antidote to the pressures of contemporary life ashore, and allows you to engage in the fine art of doing nothing, if you so wish. After the exhilaration of a North Atlantic crossing, the anticipation of landfall among passengers throughout any ship is nothing short of electric.

ATLANTIC OCEAN

Hemmed in by the polar ice caps, the Atlantic Ocean divides Europe and Africa from the Americas. It is three times the size of North America, and contains the world's longest mountain range, which extends (undersea) over 7,000 miles (11,265 km) and rises to more than 6,000 feet (1,829 m) above the ocean floor. The only points of this ridge that rise to the surface are at St.

Helena (Ascension), St. Paul's Rocks (in the Azores), and Tristan da Cunha. The ocean's average width is 2,500 miles (4,023 km).

Although half the size of the Pacific Ocean, the Atlantic receives more than half of the water drainage of the world (four times that of the Pacific Ocean). Its average depth is 18,900 feet (5,761 m) and its greatest depth, which is known as the Milwaukee Depth, goes beyond 30,240 feet (9,217 m).

Crossing the North Atlantic by passenger vessel should be considered an art form. I have done it myself more than 135 times, and always enjoy it immensely. As a former professional musician, I often consider crossings as rests, in musical parlance, for both are described as "passages." Indeed, musicians do often "hear" rests in between notes. So if ports of call are the musical notes of a voyage, then the rests are the days at sea—a temporary interlude, when the indulgence of the person and psyche are of paramount importance.

Experienced mariners will tell you that a ship only behaves like a ship when it is on a crossing, as that's what a real ship is built for. Yet the days when ships were built specifically for crossings are almost gone. The only ship left offering a regularly scheduled transatlantic service (a "crossing") is Cunard's QE2, the 70,267-grt ship designed to hold well against the worst weather the Atlantic has to offer. Indeed, captains work harder on an Atlantic crossing than on regular cruising schedules.

The most unpredictable weather in the world, together with fog off the Grand Banks of Newfoundland, can mean that the ship's captain will spend tortuous hours on the bridge, with little time for socializing. When it's foggy, the crew of *QE2* is frequently pestered by passengers eager to know if the ship has yet approached latitude 41°46' north, longitude 50°14' west—which is where *Titanic* struck an Arctic iceberg on that fateful April night in 1912.

There is something that is magical in "doing a crossing." It takes you back to the days when hordes of passengers turned up at the piers of the ports of New York, Southampton, Cherbourg, or Hamburg, accompanied by chauffeurs and steamer trunks, jewels and finery ablaze in a show of what they thought was the finest in life. Movie stars of the 1920s, 1930s and 1940s often traveled abroad on the largest liners of the day, to arrive refreshed and ready to dazzle their European public.

There is also the excitement and anticipation that precedes a crossing—the hubbub and bustle of check-in, of crossing the threshold of the gangway before being welcomed into the calmness aboard and then escorted to one's accommodations for the next several days. Once the umbilical cord of the gangway is severed, bow and stern mooring lines are cast off, and with three long blasts on its deep whistle *QE2* is pried gently from her berth. She sails silently down the waterway, away from the world, as pretty as a picture, as serene as a Rolls-Royce, and as sure as the Bank of England. The passengers on deck observe the foolhardy yachtsmen dangerously cutting under *QE2*'s raked bows, while numerous motorboats try to keep up with the giant liner as she edges down the

The one and only Queen Elizabeth 2 *(or* QE2 *as she is affectionately known), with her greyhound-like, sleek profile, long foredeck and massive funnel. She is the last of the great transatlantic superliners.*

Hudson River, past Battery Park City, the Statue of Liberty, the restored Ellis Island, and then out toward the Verrazano-Narrows Bridge and out to the open sea. Coming the other way, arriving in New York by ship is one of the world's most thrilling travel experiences. Following a five-day westbound crossing on *QE2*, where days are 25 hours long (they are 23 hours long on an eastbound crossing), everything else is an anticlimax.

QE2 can accommodate up to 40 cars per crossing—just in case you really don't want to be separated from your wheels. It also provides kennels, so that you can even take your pet, although when crossing eastbound to Southampton, do remember that pets will have to be quarantined for up to six months. *QE2* is a distillation of over 150 years of transatlantic traditions, an oasis of creature comforts offered by no other ship.

Apart from *QE2*'s regular crossings, there are a number of cruise lines today that feature transatlantic crossings. Although little more than repositioning of cruises—a way of moving ships that cruise the Mediterranean in summer to the Caribbean in winter, and vice versa—they do offer more chances to experience the romance and adventure of a crossing, usually in the spring and in the fall. Perhaps the most unusual transatlantic crossings—made twice a year—are aboard the sail-cruise vessel *Star Flyer*—a four-masted barkentine vessel that can carry 180 passengers, totally under sail.

Most cruise ships performing repositioning crossings actually cross the Atlantic by using the "sunny southern route"—that is, they set sail from southern ports such as Ft. Lauderdale, San Juan, or Barbados, and end the journey in Lisbon, Genoa, or Copenhagen via the Azores or the Canary Islands off the coast of northern Africa. In this way they avoid the more difficult weather that is often encountered in the North Atlantic. The crossings take longer, however, and last between eight and 12 days.

QUEEN ELIZABETH 2 (QE2): MILESTONES OVER THE YEARS

Queen Elizabeth 2 is a very special ship—part liner, part cruise ship—a real legend in her own lifetime, and the only ship offering regularly scheduled crossings all year. I worked aboard her in two roles: from December 1968 to October 1969 as leader of a jazz group; and then from 1977 to 1980 as the shore excursion manager/deputy cruise director.

Instead of allowing the ship to deteriorate, Cunard has spent a vast sum of money on refurbishments over time, the most recent being a $60 million refit in November/December 1994 that greatly improved the flow of passengers on and off the ship, and further enhanced her already considerable facilities and amenities.

During the ship's initial planning stages, the naval architect Dan Wallace and the director of engineering Tom Kameen were responsible for the ship's design, which was to be for a high-speed, twin-screw ship capable of carrying out safely a five-day transatlantic crossing. Cunard's chairman, Sir Basil Smallpiece, invited James Gardner and

Dennis Lennon, well known industrial designers, to be general design co-ordinators. Gardner concentrated on the exterior aesthetics, while Lennon, in addition to designing the restaurant interiors—the basic shape of which had already been determined by constructional and operational requirements—was also involved with the introduction of a design signature that would be immediately apparent anywhere on the ship; for example, in staircases and corridors. The aim was that the interior design of QE2 would emphasize the "classless" ship concept.

1955

Preparation work for a large liner such as QE2 had already been underway for some time by 1955. It had involved introducing an intensive weight-saving exercise in the design of Cunard's Sylvania, which was then under construction at Glasgow's famous Clydebank shipyards. By agreement with the ship builder, John Brown's, various experimental features were built into this ship. Most of these were successful and provided many weight-saving devices which were to be adopted some 10 years later for QE2. These included lightweight furniture, fiberglass shower units, new types of deck coverings, as well as new construction and joinery methods.

In conjunction with British Steel's research section, a new type of girder was developed and tested. This girder had large holes for the various services (piping, wiring, etc.) cut in during fabrication, with the depth of the girder being slightly increased in order to compensate for the reduced tension. The result was a girder that was much

lighter than the standard ones of the time, and which was used experimentally in Sylvania—a ship which was pioneering the way ships were built in terms of advanced construction techniques and materials usage.

October 1963

Construction plans and financing were announced by Cunard in England.

December 30, 1964

The contract to build was signed by Sir John Brocklebank, then chairman of Cunard, and Lord Aberconway, then chairman of Upper Clyde Shipbuilders (formerly John Brown's), a consortium of five major shipyards on the upper reaches of the River Clyde in Scotland. Some 300 British workers contributed to the building and furnishing of the ship. The contract price was £25.5 million, but this inevitably escalated as a result of increases in wage rates and costs of material during the building period. On completion, the total cost was approximately £30 million.

Coincidental with the building of QE2 was the financial improvement of the Cunard Group, which meant that in 1968 the company was able to forgo part of a loan negotiated with the Board of Trade. This was in addition to the loan of £17.6 million obtained in 1964 under the British government's shipbuilding credit scheme. There was never any question of a direct construction subsidy from the government; Cunard was entirely responsible for meeting the full cost of QE2. A condition of the loan was that the proceeds of the sale of the liner Queen Elizabeth would be paid to the finance company who provided the loan.

July 4, 1965

America's Independence Day—which also happened to be the 125th anniversary of the maiden voyage of Cunard's first ship, *Britannia*, in 1840—was the day the first prefabricated section of the keel for hull number 736 of *QE2* was laid in the shipyard.

September 20, 1967

"I name this ship *Queen Elizabeth the Second*. May God bless her and all who sail in her." With these historic words, Queen Elizabeth II named the new liner—not after herself, as some had claimed, but simply because this was the second ship to bear that name (the first *Queen Elizabeth* was still in operation at that time). Apparently it was an impulse on the part of the queen to add "second" to the name, which no one, not even at Cunard headquarters, had expected, as it had been secretly agreed to name the ship simply *Queen Elizabeth*. Ahead of her lay a year of fitting out; the new ship was to fill two roles—those of transatlantic express liner and leisure cruise ship.

On the transatlantic run, she was to be a two-class ship. It was decided that class distinction would be completely absent in the naming of public spaces, rooms and decks. The passengers occupying the best accommodations would simply have certain spaces and rooms reserved expressly for their use.

In addition, there was to be single-sitting dining in the Grill Room and Columbia Restaurants, but two sittings would be held in the Britannia Restaurant. However, the greater part of the accommodations would be open to all on board without restrictions. The passengers would then be allotted a restaurant according to the accommodations that had been chosen.

December 1968

Queen Elizabeth 2 (or just *QE2* as she became affectionately known) sailed gracefully out of Gourock, Scotland, with 600 John Brown men aboard, still doing the final fitting-out work. A brochure had advertised a Christmas Cruise, but those who had booked were informed that this had been canceled when Cunard refused to take delivery of the ship because she was not completed. Instead, the workmen had a good Christmas (the beer flowed freely). *QE2*'s captain was Commodore William ("Bill") Warwick and its cruise director was Bryan Vickers. I was aboard.

April 18, 1969

QE2 was commissioned.

April 22, 1969

In a demonstration of local support, coat hangers for the crew were donated by the District Spastics Association of Southampton, England—*QE2*'s home port. Cunard finally accepted delivery of the new ship from the builders and embarked on a "Preview Cruise" to the ports of Las Palmas, Tenerife, and Lisbon. I was aboard with my own jazz trio, which performed each night in what was then the ship's most elegant nightclub (for first-class passengers only)—the Q4 Room (no longer in existence, although it was the "in" place to be in those days).

I remember well that the featured film was *2001: A Space Odyssey*, and that an English rock band called The Applejacks was playing. The ship also had four "go-go" dancers, and they worked in the 736 Room (the discotheque of the day, but which is now the exclusive Queens' Grill—according to many, the finest restaurant afloat). Twice each day, passengers gathered for a classical concert staged in the Upper Deck Library.

May 2, 1969, Maiden Voyage

QE2 sailed from the port of Southampton on her maiden voyage. Her Majesty Queen Elizabeth II and her husband, the Duke of Edinburgh, paid an official visit to the ship prior to sailing. Five days later the ship arrived in New York harbor to a tumultuous local welcome. She was greeted to the city by Mayor John Lindsay. I was aboard.

June 1970

QE2 crosses from Southampton to New York in 3 days, 20 hours and 42 minutes, at an average speed of 30.36 knots. A casino is also added as U.S. gaming laws are relaxed.

October 1970

QE2's inaugural long cruise gets underway—a 37-day voyage around North America, South America, and Africa.

January 9, 1971

In a dramatic rescue in the Grenadines, QE2 takes on board 501 passengers and crew from the burning wreck of the 19,828-grt French Line cruise ship Antilles, and lands them at Barbados.

January 1975, World Cruise

QE2's first world cruise sets off. It is to be a successful voyage, and the ship is welcomed enthusiastically with celebrations and parties in all her ports of call. She proves herself eminently newsworthy.

May 1975

QE2 meets "Operation Tall Ships" in Tenerife, Canary Islands.

1977, Refit

The Britannia Restaurant is converted into Tables of the World (later nicknamed "Stables of the World")—the largest of the ship's four restaurants. America also made a contribution to the changing face of QE2, and in Bethlehem Steel Shipyard in Bayonne, New Jersey, two ultra-deluxe suites, appropriately called Queen Mary and Queen Elizabeth, were added.

The Grill Room was renamed the Princess Grill and the 736 Club (formerly a discotheque) was transformed into the Queens Grill. At the same time, the under-used 24-hour Coffee Shop was divided up and reworked into the galley (kitchen) space and the Queens Grill Lounge/Bar.

The forward Lookout Bar on Upper Deck was, sadly, changed into an enlarged galley for the Tables of the World. The London Gallery, an experimental art gallery with paintings for sale, was converted into the Reading Room—a restful space for the first-class passengers.

On Upper Deck amidships, the Portside Promenade and Library were transformed into a full casino and re-christened The Players Club. Meanwhile, the Theatre Bar was converted into a discotheque for the younger passengers, although this change never really became a success.

As the brochures often state (and this picture shows) you can do all, or almost nothing, aboard a cruise ship.

1978

The National Geographic organization made a feature film about the great liners, featuring *QE2*.

January 1979

Included in the itinerary of *QE2*'s world cruise was a maiden transit of the Suez Canal, which was experienced by the greatest number of passengers ever.

May 1982, the Falklands

QE2 was requisitioned by the British government for service as a troop ship in the Falkland Islands. The requisition came just as she was crossing from New York to Southampton after her inaugural visit to Philadelphia. I was aboard.

When she arrived in Southampton, it took only seven days to convert *QE2* into a troop ship, complete with heli-copter landing pads. All the furniture, artworks, slot machines, pianos and plants were off-loaded and placed into storage at the Pickford's warehouse in Southampton.

August 1982

QE2 sails for engine trials following a nine-week-long refit to reconvert her to passenger service following her service as a troop ship in the Falklands. The Golden Door Spa at Sea was added. The Q4 Room was converted into the Club Lido.

The ship's hull was painted pebble grey—not a pretty sight! *QE2* sailed on a transatlantic crossing for the first time since her Falklands service.

April 1983

For the first time, *QE2* was paired for holiday packages with British Airways' supersonic aircraft, Concorde.

May 1983

QE2 honors New York's leading ladies with an afternoon tea and a British fashion show as part of the "Britain Salutes New York" festivities. Guests of honor included city council woman Carol Bellamy.

October 1983, Marathon

QE2 enters a five-man team in the New York City Marathon. A collection is made by the ship for the National Lifeboat Association and Guide Dogs for the Blind charities. As a result, a guide dog, whose picture is hung on a wall aboard the ship, was subsequently christened "Marathon."

January 1984

A "magrodome" sliding glass roof was fitted on to the Club Lido indoor/outdoor leisure center (this later proved to be only moderately successful). As a sign of the times, the Reading Room was changed into a Computer Center, which fast became an extremely popular facility. Later in the year, Cunard signed a $40 million contract with British Airways. Nowadays more than 10,000 passengers take a round-trip in completely unique style—one leisurely crossing on QE2, the other at supersonic speed on the Concorde, between London and New York.

June 1984

The first seagoing branch of Harrods was opened on board by the film and stage actress Hermione Gingold.

December 1984

The refurbishment of the Columbia Restaurant, with its decor being transformed by softer colors and lighting.

January 1985

American Express opened the first seagoing finance center aboard ship. It was located in the 2-Deck lobby.

July 1985

Captain Robert ("Bob") Arnott, QE2's longest serving captain, retires.

January 1986

The first regular television programming at sea began operating, courtesy of NBC-TV. Passengers watched the Superbowl live in Lima, Peru, while on the ship's annual world cruise.

March 1986

The prestigious International Herald Tribune became the first newspaper to be printed on board ship, by means of its transmission to QE2 via satellite.

May 1986

A royal touch is provided by Queen Elizabeth, the Queen Mother, who visits QE2 in Southampton for the Cunarder Queen Mary's 50th anniversary celebrations.

October 1986, Refit

QE2 makes her last voyage as a steam ship, prior to entering the Lloyd Werft shipyard in Bremerhaven in Germany for a huge, six-month-long, $160 million refit. Her steam engines and three boilers were exchanged for a nine-unit, diesel-electric propulsion system, and her two fixed-pitch six-bladed propellers were replaced by two skew-backed, controllable-pitch, five-bladed propellers weighing 42 tons each. A new and fatter funnel was constructed, designed to prevent any soot from falling on to her expansive open decks.

The refit took 179 days and a work-force of men from 34 different countries was involved.

April 29, 1987

QE2 undertakes her inaugural crossing from Southampton to New York under diesel-electric power. A flotilla of small craft led by millionaire publisher Malcolm Forbes' famed yacht, *Highlander*, escort the "new" QE2 past the Statue of Liberty.

May 8, 1994

QE2 slides gracefully away from her berth at Southampton Docks. There were no outward celebrations on the deck: no champagne, no streamers, no cruise staff—in fact nothing to show that this was the silver anniversary of her maiden voyage from Southampton to New York some 25 years earlier. On the bridge for the historic moment were the ship's first master, Commodore William Warwick (now retired, but then commodore of the Cunard fleet and captain of QE2 on her maiden crossing in May 1969), his son, Ron Warwick, a Cunard captain, and the ship's present master, Captain John Burton-Hall. There were five passengers aboard who had been on the original crossing, of whom I was one.

The only commemoration of this special occasion was a large banner draped over a section of the Ocean Terminal, which conveyed the simple message, "Congratulations from ABP" (Associated British Ports). There was a celebration of another kind, however, with jazz music giants George Shearing, Gerry Mulligan, Ronnie Scott and others playing their way across the North Atlantic.

November 1994, Refit

QE2 was placed into drydock at the Blohm & Voss shipyard in Hamburg, Germany, for one month for an extensive refit. She underwent a dramatic $45 million interior refurbishment, including numerous structural changes designed to facilitate better passenger flow and even more dining (and other facility) choices. All cabin bathrooms were replaced (a mammoth task), and several new suites were added, as well as an enlarged library, a new shop with books and memorabilia, a multimedia center, and a florist shop. The Club Lido magrodome-covered pool was replaced with a new, informal al fresco buffet dining area, called The Lido, complete with its own separate preparation galley and bar. The Mauretania Restaurant was re-named the Caronia Restaurant, together with a superb new Crystal Bar (which includes a long model of *Caronia*, the former Cunard world cruise ship). In addition, the Columbia Restaurant became the Mauretania Restaurant (a magnificent 16-foot-long/5-m model of *Mauretania* of 1907 is displayed proudly at the head of the "D" stairway outside the restaurant), and a new Captain's Dining Area was added. The three Grill Rooms remain (but Queens' Grill was refurbished, and banquette seating was replaced by individual seating). The original Princess Grill has survived, while the second Princess Grill had its name changed to Britannia Grill.

The shops are still located on the upper level of the showlounge, but the horseshoe-shaped stairway behind the stage has been blocked off, thus creating a dedicated showlounge. A new

Golden Lion Pub now occupies the former Theatre Bar location.

The Midships Bar was completely refurbished, expanded, and rechristened the Chart Room, with charts of many ports of call in three stages (current chart, chart from the turn of the century, and one from over a hundred years ago). The Yacht Club is greatly enlarged into a new nightclub created from the space that was gained from an extension of the aft deck.

Unfortunately, the German shipyard where she underwent the refit didn't deliver the ship to Cunard in a completed state and, as a result, the company received bad press for having an unfinished ship and a great many unhappy passengers. All was resolved in the weeks following the refit, however, and she is now the stunning, majestic ship that one would expect.

THE FUTURE

During the past 25 years, *QE2* has become one of the most popular and successful liners ever built. She has sailed more than three-and-a-half million nautical miles, catering to more than 1.5 million passengers on over 1,000 voyages. Her interiors have been changed into those reminiscent of the ocean liners of yesteryear, which is what passengers have always expected of this ship. Until now, however, the interiors have been disappointing, built as she was in the late 1960s, when contemporary design favored the extensive use of plastic laminates (some 2 million sq. ft./185,800 m^2 of Formica laminates were used in her original interiors). Now completed, the new enhancements provide space, grace, and pace.

Perhaps in her next refit the Midships Lobby could be made into a two-deck-high affair, with all ship's passenger services, such as the purser's office, bank, and housekeeping office, located on the upper level of the expanded lobby, with passengers embarking into the lower level.

Will *QE2* survive into the 21st century? All the signs indicate that she will, if only to provide a regularly scheduled transatlantic service (many of her regular passengers do not fly). In the face of stiff competition from all the new ships, with their high-tech toys and playgrounds, this superliner simply cannot compete for cruise business. The exception, however, is when she operates her annual round-the-world cruise, when her speed helps her cross the world's vast oceans faster than any other cruise ship afloat, and provides her passengers with more time in ports of call.

PART THREE

How a Ship is Evaluated

I have been evaluating and rating cruise ships and the cruise product professionally since 1980, and have continually refined the rating and evaluation system, in particular taking into account more of the passenger "software" and actual cruise product experienced. Two other ship evaluation and rating staff also assist in this task.

This section includes 208 ocean-going cruise ships, expedition ships and tall ships that were in service when this book was completed in July 1996. All except 11 new ships have been carefully evaluated, taking into account more than 300 separate inspection points based on personal sailings and visits to ships. For the sake of clarity, the inspections are channeled into 15 sections. With a possible 10 points per section, the maximum possible score for any ship is thus 150 points.

Expedition cruise vessels and tall sail-cruise ships cannot be judged by the same criteria as "normal" cruise ships because they are purpose-built, and many have unique features that reflect the type of expeditions or sailing experiences they offer. I have thus adopted a weighting system for any exceptional cases.

I have also taken into consideration the fact that passengers of different nationalities expect different things from their cruise experiences. For example, the passenger expectations on ships operating in the Mediterranean with European passengers (particularly older vessels) vary considerably from those of North American passengers, who often want the latest in high-tech interiors, facilities, and features, while their European counterparts enjoy older ships with more traditional fittings and fixtures, and less razzle-dazzle entertainment.

The stars beside the name of the ship at the top of each page relate directly to the Overall Rating. The highest number of stars awarded is five (★★★★★), the lowest is one (★). A plus (+) indicates that a ship deserves just that little bit more than the number of stars attained. However, it is the number of points achieved, rather than the number of stars, that is perhaps more useful.

Overall Rating	Number of Stars
135.1-150.0	★★★★★+
125.1-135.0	★★★★★
115.1-125.0	★★★★+
105.1-115.0	★★★★
100.1-105.0	★★★+
90.1-100.0	★★★
85.1-90.0	★★+
80.1-85.0	★★
80.1 or less	★

Cruise lines are in the business of creating and selling cruise products and vacation packages of (marketed and perceived) excellence. The common factor of all cruise ships is quality.

Therefore, in appraising the cruise industry, *it is inevitable that scores will be on the high side, and the difference in score from one ship to another may be very slight.*

COMMENTS

The smaller details and my personal comments on each ship may help you determine what is best for you. These have been separated into four parts:

+ (positive comments)
– (negative comments)
Dining (comments on cuisine, service, and the dining room experience), and
Other Comments (comments about the ship or product).

Needless to say, there is no such thing as a "standard" cruise ship. They come in all sizes and shapes, and a wide variety of internal layouts, facilities, appointments, and levels of service. The one thing all ships do have in common is gross registered tonnage, which is often abbreviated to grt. This is an international measurement used for ship classification and insurance purposes.

Since the size of the ship plays an important part in the kind of facilities, level of comfort, and, of course, number of passengers on board, the ships are divided into five categories, according to the number of passengers carried (based on two per cabin, plus or minus any single occupancy cabins):

a) Ships carrying under 250 passengers.
b) Ships carrying between 250 and 500 passengers.

c) Ships carrying between 500 and 1,000 passengers.
d) Ships carrying between 1,000 and 2,000 passengers.
e) Ships carrying more than 2,000 passengers.

The evaluating and rating system takes into account the onboard level of service from, and the attitude of, the crew (hospitality). The rating of expedition cruise vessels also includes garbage compacting and incineration, waste disposal, as well as compliance with the most recent environmental and safety regulations (MARPOL V).

The results, comments, and ratings are strictly personal, and are intended to guide you in formulating your own opinions and cruise plans. They are also intended to help travel agents to differentiate between the many cruise ships and cruise products in today's marketplace.

CHANGES IN THE RATINGS

Cruise lines, ship owners, and operators should note that ratings, like stocks and shares, *can go down as well as up*, even when things have supposedly been improved aboard their ships. This is explained by increased competition, the introduction of newer ships that have better custom-designed facilities, and other market- or passenger-driven factors. With an increasing number of ships in the marketplace, and the building of ships for niche operations, tougher evaluations have become increasingly important.

When discounting was introduced in order to stimulate the demand for cruises in certain markets, so too were greater cost-cutting measures. As a result, cruise cuisine and service standards have suffered cut-backs in the past few years. The ratings reflect this trend accurately.

Ratings and evaluations cover four principal areas:
1) The Ship
2) Accommodations
3) Cuisine/Service
4) Cruise Product

1) THE SHIP

Ship: Hardware/Maintenance

This score reflects: the general profile and condition of the ship, both internally and externally. It takes into account the following factors: the ship's age and maintenance requirements; the condition of the hull, exterior paintwork, decking materials, caulking, swimming pool surrounds, deck furniture, lifeboats, life rafts, and life-preserving equipment; interior cleanliness with regard to the public restrooms, elevators, floor coverings, carpeting, wall coverings, stairways, passageways, doorways, other access points, crew stairways, alleyways, accommodations and galleys; food preparation, food storage rooms, and refrigeration units; and garbage handling, compacting, incineration, and waste disposal facilities.

Cleanliness and hygiene standards have become increasingly important factors in all aspects of everyday life, and even more so aboard cruise ships, which may really be considered as a microcosm of modern society.

Ship: Space/Flow/Comfort

This score reflects: the use of common passenger spaces, including: outside deck areas; sunbathing and sheltered deck space; swimming pools; outdoor and indoor promenades; interior spaces—density and passenger flow, and ceiling height; lobby areas, stairways and passageways, and public restrooms and facilities; lighting, direction signs, air-conditioning, smoke extraction and ventilation flow; the degree of comfort or crowding (passenger space ratio), density, and crew to passenger ratio.

Ship: Decor/Furnishings

This score reflects: the overall interior design and decor, including appearance and condition; color combinations and visual appeal; hard and soft furnishings (including suitability and practicality); wood (and imitation wood) paneling, veneers, and use of glass and plastics; carpet material, tuft density, color and pattern practicality, and fit and finish (including seams and edging); chair design and comfort; ceiling treatments, bulkheads and treatments; reflective surfaces; artwork quality, suitability and aesthetic appeal; and color definition and lighting.

Ship: Fitness Facilities

This score reflects: the health spa, its location and its accessibility; the gymnasium, exercise room, and fitness, sports, and games facilities; spa treatments and rejuvenation programs; swimming pools, whirlpools, grand baths, saunas, steam rooms, and massage rooms (size and cleanliness); and running, jogging, and walking tracks.

2) ACCOMMODATIONS

Cabins: Comfort/Facilities

This score reflects: the design and layout of cabins, balconies, beds and berths, furniture (its placement and practicality), and other fittings; closets and other hanging space, drawer space, and bedside tables; vanity unit, bathroom facilities, washbasin, cabinets, and toiletries storage; lighting, air-conditioning and ventilation; audiovisual facilities; quality and degree of luxuriousness; and bulkhead insulation, noise, and vibration levels.

Cabins: Software

This score reflects: the soft furnishings and details in cabins, including: the information manual (list of services), paper and postcards (including personalized stationery); telephone directory; laundry lists; tea- and coffee-making equipment; fresh flowers (if any), fruit (if any); and bathroom amenities kits, bathrobes, slippers, and the size, thickness, quality, and material content of towels.

3) CUISINE

This section is perhaps the most important, as food is often the main feature of today's cruise package. Cruise lines put maximum emphasis on telling passengers how good their food is, often to the point of being unable to deliver what is promised. Generally, however, the standard of food is good.

The rule of thumb is: if you were to eat out in a good restaurant, what would you expect? Does the ship meet your expectations? Would you come back again for the food?

There are perhaps as many different tastes as there are passengers. The "standard" market cruise lines cater for a wide range of tastes. Upscale cruise lines can offer food cooked individually to your taste. Generally, as in any good restaurant, you get what you pay for. Over the past two years, many cruise lines have been cutting back on their food (as well as the service), and this has had more effect on the ratings for 1997.

Food: Dining Room/Cuisine

This score reflects: the main dining room's physical structure, window treatments, seating (alcoves and individual chairs, with or without armrests), lighting and ambiance, table set-ups, the quality and condition of linen, china, and cutlery, and table centerpieces (flowers); menus, food quality, presentation, food combinations, culinary creativity, variety, appeal, taste, palatability, freshness, color, balance, garnishes, and decorations; appetizers, soups, pastas, flambeaus, and so on; fresh fruit and cakes; the wine list; and the price range.

Food: Buffets/Informal Dining

This score reflects: the hardware (including the provision of sneeze guards, tongs, ice containers and ladles, and serving utensils); buffet displays, appeal and presentation, trays and set-ups, correct food temperatures; breakfast, luncheon, deck buffets, midnight buffets, and late-night snacks; decorative elements such as ice carvings; and staff attitude, service, and communication skills.

Food: Quality of Ingredients

This score reflects: the overall quality of ingredients used, including: consistency and portion size; grades of meat, fish and fowl; and the price paid by the cruise company for its food product per passenger per day. It is the quality of ingredients that most dictates the eventual presentation, aesthetic appeal and quality of the finished product—as well as its taste.

SERVICE

Service: Dining Room

This score reflects: the professionalism of all restaurant staff: maître d'hôtel, dining room managers, head section waiters, and waiters and assistant waiters (busboys). It includes correct place settings and service, communication skills, attitude, flair, and finesse.

Service: Bars/Lounges

This score reflects: lighting and ambiance; service in bars and lounges; noise levels; communication skills (between bartenders and bar staff and passengers in particular); staff attitude, personality, flair and finesse; and the correct use of glasses.

Service: Cabins

This score reflects: the cleaning and housekeeping staff, butlers, cabin stewards and stewardesses, and supervisory staff; efficiency and professionalism; visibility and availability; attention to cleanliness and extra attention to detail; in-cabin food service; promptness, speed and accuracy; linen provision and changes; and language and communication skills.

4) CRUISE PRODUCT

Cruise: Entertainment

This score reflects: the overall entertainment program and content as designed and targeted to specific passenger demographics. Cruise ship entertainment has to appeal to passengers who are of widely varying ages, types, and tastes.

The rating includes: the physical plant (stage/bandstand); proficiency of technical support, lighting, follow spotlight operation, and set and backdrop design; sound and light systems, recorded click-tracks and cues, and special effects; the variety, quality and timing of large-scale production shows, including content, story and plot, cohesion, set design, creativeness of costumes, relevancy, quality, choreography, and vocal content; cabaret; variety shows; singers; visual acts; bands and solo musicians.

Cruise: Activities Program

This score reflects: the variety, quality and quantity of daytime activities and events. The rating includes: the cruise director and cruise staff (including their visibility, availability, ability, and professionalism); sports and exercise programs; participation games; special-interest programs; mind-enrichment lectures and demonstrations; variety, content, and timing of activities; and staff attitude and competence in running activities.

Cruise: Overall Hospitality

This score reflects: the level of hospitality of the crew and their attention to detail and personal satisfaction. It includes: the professionalism of senior officers, middle management, supervisors, cruise staff, and general crew; social contact, appearance and dress codes; atmosphere and ambiance; motivation; communication skills (of crucial importance); and the general ambiance and impression created.

Watersports Facilities

This score reflects: the watersports equipment that is carried (including banana boat, jet skis, scuba tanks, and snorkeling equipment); the waterski boat; windsurfers; watersports instruction programs, overall staff supervision; the marina (usually located aft) or side-retractable watersports platforms; and the enclosed swimming area (if applicable).

NOTES

Expedition Cruise Ships/ Tall Ships/Wind-Sail Ships

These are highly specialized vessels that offer a particular kind of cruise experience. Consequently, they do not feature the same facilities as the majority of "standard" cruise ships, and their ratings are calculated in a different manner. The total score awarded is based on the cruise experience offered, the range and quality of onboard facilities, the product itself, and the extent to which the company is concerned for the environment.

Expedition Ships

These vessels are constructed for in-depth expedition cruising, with special ice-hardened hulls and the classification to operate legally in ecologically and environmentally sensitive areas.

They are given a rating and a total score based on a number of relevant extra criteria. These include: classification of service; suitability for expeditions; overall cleanliness, hygiene, and sanitation; wet and dry garbage treatment and handling; concern for the environment; itineraries; shore expeditions; lecture facilities and lecturers; expedition leaders; medical facilities; evacuation provisions; operation of the inflatable Zodiac landing craft; helicopter; air and ground transportation; ticketing and documentation; and the experience and reputation of the expedition company concerned.

Tall Ships/ Sail-Cruise Experience

These ships are either specially constructed so as to provide a genuine sail-powered experience (*Lili Marleen, Sea Cloud, Sir Francis Drake, Star Clipper, Star Flyer*), or they are contemporary vessels that have been built to emulate sail-powered vessels but are really sail-assisted (*Club Med I, Club Med II, Le Ponant, Wind Song, Wind Spirit, Wind Star*).

They provide another dimension to the cruise experience, and, as with true expedition ships, cannot be evaluated in precisely the same way as other oceangoing cruise ships.

Their rating also includes a number of extra, relevant criteria. These include the following: on-board sail-cruise experience; relaxation facilities; provision of in-cabin entertainment facilities; existence or otherwise of open bridge policy; watersports facilities; expert lecturers and instructors; privacy and quiet spaces; destinations; and environmental policy.

WHAT MAKES A FIVE-STARS-PLUS (★★★★★+) CRUISE SHIP

Ship owners and cruise marketing directors often proudly describe their products as "luxury" and of a "five-star-plus" or "five-star" standard. However, in reality, very few ships deserve this designation. To merit it requires a combination of discreet sophistication and impeccable service; almost every individual need must be anticipated, and every amenity within the structural provisions of today's passenger ships must be provided. The cruise product should allow for a completely relaxed and hassle-free vacation.

The items listed are just some of the things required of any ship that is aiming for the highest rating of Five-Stars-Plus. Ships that do not meet any of the following criteria will have points deducted accordingly. This is the reason that cruise ship and cruise product ratings vary so enormously (from five-stars-plus down to one star), and hence the value of this book.

The training of crew to the highest levels of service is the responsibility of any ship owner who is competing for passengers willing to pay between $500 and $3,000 per person per day. Passengers want and demand what they perceive as "value for money"— no matter what amount is paid. Crew members that cannot communicate with passengers well, in their own language, will inevitably fail to provide the same level of contact or service to those passengers.

While the introduction of rampant discounting has lowered the expectation level of many passengers, the level and quality of service demanded by those paying the topmost rates is quite justified.

Hardware (The Ship Itself)

- The Passenger Space Ratio must be 35.0 or better (based on two per suite/cabin and obtained by dividing the gross registered tonnage (grt) by the number of passenger beds).
- The ship must be kept in pristine condition, with no visible signs of rusting steel work.
- Safety must be of the utmost importance, with thoroughly trained fire crews, constant drills, and single-language communications for all emergency procedures.
- All lifeboat davits and safety equipment must be fully functional, and inspected by senior shipboard management once each week.
- Paintwork must be immaculate at all times (ships must be constantly painted, and a five-stars-plus rating will not be considered for any ship that defers painting and minor maintenance items to drydock time only).
- All exterior fittings, gangway mechanisms, lighting, to be in pristine condition. Any faulty equipment must be replaced, and no wear and tear will be tolerated.
- All gangways are to be in immaculate condition, with non-slip stair treads and wood or rubber-grip or similar handrails.
- No light bulbs to be missing (not working) from the "string of lights" between the bow, mast, funnel, and stern.
- Shuttle buses to be provided in ports of call where a city or town center is

more than a few minutes away from the ship.

SOFTWARE (DECOR, HOSPITALITY AND SERVICE STANDARDS)

Accommodations

- Accommodations designated as "suites" *must* have a day (lounge) area and a completely separate bedroom with a closing (and lockable) door. Cabins should certainly not be described as "suites" if there is simply a curtain separating the sleeping area from the lounge area.
- The minimum cabin size must be 200 sq. ft. (18.5 m²).
- Cabin placement and insulation to be of such thickness that a telephone ringing in an adjacent cabin cannot be heard.
- Privacy curtains to be installed between cabin entrance and sleeping or lounge area.
- Fresh flowers are to be placed in all cabins.
- Personalized stationery in all suites (and in all cabins on any ship with fewer than 300 passengers).
- Leather-bound stationery/cabin service folder should be provided.
- 100 per cent cotton (or 100 per cent cotton loop) towels (to include hand towel, face towel, shower towel, large bath towel). Bath towels should be a minimum size of 48 inches by 30 inches (122 cm by 76 cm).
- 100 per cent cotton bed linen, including pillowcases, should be provided (points are deducted for cotton/polyester mix). It should ideally feature the cruise line's logo.

- Thick 100 per cent cotton ankle-length bathrobe, which must be changed daily, should be provided.
- Special pillows for those passengers who are "allergy-sensitive" are to be available.
- Minimum of six storage drawers per passenger.
- Walk-in closets for all top-grade accommodations, and for "suites."
- Illuminated closets for all other cabins, with wooden (not plastic) hangers, tie rail, and shoe horn.
- Full or half-tiled bathroom with bathtub and shower (bidet in all suites).
- Refrigerator or mini-bar (fully stocked), with appropriate glassware, paper napkins, coasters, and cocktail stirrers.
- Separate make-up desk with mirror (could serve as a writing desk).
- Hairdryer (built-in or free standing).
- Enclosed toiletries cabinet and storage space.
- Audio-visual entertainment center to include color television and VCR player (preferably also a CD player), and enclosed cabinet where possible. One remote control for all units.
- Three channels of audio including one classical channel.
- Lunch and dinner menus delivered daily to all suites and upper-grade cabins.
- Direct-dial satellite-linked telephone.
- Lockable personal safe (must be easy to operate, either with a key, or digitally, but not with a credit card).
- No sharp edges on furniture (rounded edges and corners only).
- Electrical sockets must be labeled with the correct voltage.

- Course-by-course in-suite or in-cabin meal service, with individual chairs and adjustable-height dining table.
- Amenities kits to contain (minimum): shampoo, conditioner, body lotion, quality soap, sewing kit and emery board.
- Wood (fire-retardant treated) rather than metal cabinetry and drawers.
- World news to be delivered to all cabins each day.
- In each port of call, newspapers should be made available (where possible).
- "Butler Service" should include pressing of clothes on embarkation, if needed, and canapés each evening, correctly presented on a silver or other display tray.
- Balcony furniture to have cushions or pads for seating areas, wiped down daily.
- Canvas (not plastic) laundry bags for personal self-service launderette use.
- Bottled water is to be provided without charge and replaced daily.
- Umbrellas for all passengers (ships of up to 300 passengers), and for all passengers in "suites" on ships of over 300 passengers.
- Service pantries located opposite passenger cabins to have "silent closing" device fitted.

Dining/Cuisine

- Waiters should be able to recognize whether a passenger is right- or left-handed and set or change tableware accordingly.
- Place settings must include proper fish knives and forks.
- There must be no "spotting" on cutlery.

- The finest quality plateware, with different patterns for dining room, informal dining and cabin service items, should be used.
- Finger bowls must be provided for courses that include the use of fingers (mussels in shells, for example).
- Dining room meals to be placed on linen tablecloth with linen napkins, and changed for each meal.
- Finest quality glassware, and correct wine glasses, must be used.
- Special (off-menu) orders must be possible at any time in the dining room (by giving reasonable notice).
- Tableside cooking and presentation of whole fish, carved meats, poultry, pasta and flambeau dessert items.
- Dessert trolley and cheese trolley (both with cover) should be used when possible. A minimum of four types of biscuits/crackers should be offered.
- Beluga or Sevruga caviar in unlimited quantities, and at any time, served with the correct style of mother-of-pearl or bone (not metal) caviar spoons.
- Meals individually cooked to order on ships of under 250 passengers.
- All sauces must be presented in the correct sauce boats, and never in bottles.
- Bottled water must be provided, without charge, in all dining areas. Silver pitchers should be towel-wrapped to prevent condensation from dripping.
- Afternoon tea to have a minimum of six different types of premium teas available, plus herbal teas. No "supermarket" blended varieties.
- Paper doilies should be placed under all teacups for afternoon tea service.

- Cappuccino/espresso coffees should be available without charge in the dining room and at least two bars/lounges. A crystallized sugar stick should be provided.
- No packeted sugar to be used in the dining room. All sugars should be presented in porcelain or stainless steel bowls (with attached lid, and spoon). No sugar should be on the table during meals; only when tea or coffee is served.
- Course-by-course in-cabin dining at any time (in all cabins for ships of under 300 passengers; in "penthouse" or "suite" categories for ships of over 300 passengers).
- The wine list and stock should equal that of a one-star Michelin restaurant ashore, with a minimum of: three types of champagne; 30 white wines; 30 red wines; and 5 rosé or "blush" wines. Non- and low-alcoholic and organic wines should also be offered.
- Wine sommelier service with appropriate decanters, correct-sized glassware, and leather-bound wine list.
- Bartenders that know your correct name and remember your favorite drinks.
- Dress codes must be enforced at all times in the dining room.
- Senior officers and social staff to host passenger tables each evening (preferably on a rotation basis).
- Nutritional information (to include approximate calorie, fat, protein content) should be available to passengers requesting same, perhaps in an alternative menu.
- Waiters are to wear name badges (on the same side) at all times, and should provide efficient service

without touching passengers at any time. In a fixed (not open) seating arrangement, they should ideally learn and use passengers' surnames when addressing them. The language of a formal dining room should be used whenever possible ("would you like coffee, sir/madam?" and not "coffee sir?"). Hands should be properly manicured and nails should not be overly long nor in poor trim.
- Waiters should not offer "recommended" dishes, except when asked to do so by the executive chef or maître d'. Instead, they should merely describe accurately how each dish is prepared and presented.
- Waiters must always serve to the correct side of the passenger. Likewise, they (or their assistants/busboys) must always take finished plates away from the correct side of the passenger. There should be no leaning over tables except when absolutely necessary (large alcove tables, for example).
- Waiters (or assistant waiters/busboys) should not, at any time, take away a finished plate from any table while other passengers at the same table are still eating the same course.

General
- Meet and greet staff should be at the airport to offer "refreshment packs" for passengers arriving on long-haul flights.
- All luggage must be transported as "seamlessly" as possible without being handled by the passenger.
- White-gloved staff members must escort passengers to their suites or cabins upon embarkation.

- "No" should not be heard as an answer to any reasonable request.
- Ticket documentation box must include leather ticket/document wallet, and leather key card or boarding pass holder.
- Camera to be positioned on the bridge, facing forward, for in-cabin television system.
- Newspapers to be provided in ports of call whenever possible.
- Room service for simple items such as coffee, tea, croissants, etc., must take no more than five minutes.
- Room service for complete meals and complex orders must take no longer than 15 minutes.
- Full book and video library access 24 hours per day without charges of any kind (except on unreturned items).
- Complimentary self-service launderette.
- Concierge or similar to attend to personal comfort details, arrangement of private cocktail parties, etc.
- Tender service that is continuous when in port, and not at designated times. Tenders must have clean cushioned seating areas, and tender stations ashore must have first-aid kits.
- Tour operators ashore must be told that each unit of transportation must have a practical first-aid kit suitable for most emergencies.
- Fresh flowers or pot pourri should be provided in all cabin bathrooms.
- Fresh flowers (not plastic) should be provided in shore tenders.
- Oriental rugs in lobby areas and public restrooms.
- Pot pourri baskets or flower baskets should be provided in all public restrooms.

- Separate gangway for crew members (tidal conditions permitting).
- Cushions placed on seats and backs of all outdoor chairs (at the poolside, indoor/outdoor cafés, for example).
- The highest level of security, which should include combination passenger ID/charge cards.
- Baggage to be placed outside cabins upon retiring on the last night of the cruise (and not at any time specified before 3 a.m. on the morning of arrival).
- All port taxes and gratuities must be included.
- The crew must communicate in a single language (maritime tradition states "English") for all safety procedures.
- Crew alleyways to have individual steel garbage cans (not plastic) with separation of paper and plastic.

Outdoor Decks/Leisure Areas

- Deck chaise longue chairs must be wood, aluminum or stainless steel (not plastic).
- Thick cushioned pads must be provided on all outdoor deck lounge chairs. Towels must be rolled up and placed on them each morning (weather permitting).
- A supply of 100 per cent cotton towels must be available at all times.
- Swimming pools and whirlpools available 24 hours, except in the event of cleaning, refilling, or other maintenance.
- Shower stalls should have wall-mounted dispensers for shampoo, soap, etc.
- Deck beverage service available on all open decks with seating areas, not just the principal deck.

The Ratings and Evaluations

Ship Profiles

Technical and specific information on each ship is given, followed by a point by point evaluation and a summary including positive and negative points, comments on the dining experience as well as other general comments.

Prefixes

The prefixes on the name of a ship are used to denote the type of propulsion system that is being used:

cs = "club ship" concept
ib = ice-breaker (diesel or nuclear)
ms = motor ship (diesel)
mts = motor twin screw (diesel) or motor turbine ship (steam)
mv = motor vessel (diesel)
msy = motor sailing yacht
RMS = Royal Mail Ship
ss = steam ship
ssc = semi-submersible craft (swath)
sts = sail training ship
tes = turbo-electric ship (steam)
ts = turbine steamer (steam) or twin screw vessel
tsmv = twin screw motor vessel
ys = yacht ship

Operates

Main cruising areas (e.g. Caribbean).

Length

The cruise length is given only for ships operating year-round cruises to destinations such as the Bahamas, Caribbean or South-East Asia, for example.

Cruise Line

It should be noted here that the cruise line and operator will be different if the company that owns the vessel does not market and operate it.

First Entered Service

Where two dates are given, the first is the date of the ship's maiden passenger voyage when new, the second is the date that the ship began service for the present operator.

Christened By

Where two names are given, the first is the name of the person who christened the ship when it was first built, while the second is the name of the person who christened the ship for its present owner/operator.

Interior Design

The name of the principal coordinating architect is given, but it should be noted that the interior design of most new ships is often the result of a complex partnership of a number of designers. Older ships (which were smaller than today's vessels) often had only a single interior designer.

Propulsion

The number of main engines is given, together with the output (at 100 per cent), expressed either as:

bhp = brake horsepower
kW = kilowatts generated
shp = shaft horsepower.

Propellers

Included is the type of propeller, where known.

CP = controllable (variable) pitch
FP = fixed (direct) pitch

Passenger Capacity

The number of passengers is based on:
a) Two beds/berths per cabin, plus all single cabins;
b) All available beds/berths filled.

Passenger Space Ratio

Achieved by dividing the gross registered tonnage (grt) by the number of passengers.

Cabin Size Range

From the smallest cabin to the largest suite, in square feet and square meters, rounded up to the nearest number.

Wheelchair Cabins

Cabins designed to accommodate passengers with mobility problems.

NOTE

In the **Other Comments** section at the bottom of each page, all gratuities are usually at extra cost unless included in the price and extra gratuities are strictly prohibited. Likewise, insurance and port taxes are also at extra cost unless specifically stated as included.

mv Aegean Dolphin ★★★

OPERATES

3, 4 AND 7-DAY MEDITERRANEAN CRUISES

Cruise Line			Dolphin Hellas Shipping
Former Names			Narcis/Alkyon
Gross Tonnage			11,563
Builder			Santierul N. Galatz (Romania)
Reconstruction:			Perama Shipyards (Greece)
Original Cost			n/a
Christened By			Captain A. Angelopoulos
Entered Service			1974/May 1988
Interior Design			A&M Katzourakis
Country of Registry			Greece
Tel No	113-0627	Fax No	113-0627
Length (ft/m)			460.9/140.50
Beam (ft/m)	67.2/20.50	Draft (ft/m)	20.3/6.20
Propulsion			diesel-mech (10,296kW)
Propellers			2 (CP)
Decks	8	Crew	190
Pass. Capacity (basis 2) 576		(all berths) 670	
Pass. Space Ratio (basis 2) 20.0		(all berths) 17.2	
Officers			Greek
Total Cabins			288
Size Range (sq ft/m)			135-290/12.5-27.0
Outside Cabins	202	Inside Cabins	86
Single Cabins			0
Balcony Cabins			0
Wheelchair Cabins			Yes
Cabin Current	220 AC	Refrigerator	Yes
Cabin TV	Yes	VCR	No
Dining Rooms	1	Sittings	2

Elevators			2
Casino	Yes	Slot Machines	Yes
Swimming Pools (outside) 1		(inside)	0
Whirlpools	0	Gymnasium	Yes
Sauna/Steam Room	Yes/No	Massage	Yes
Self-Service Launderette			Yes
Movie Theater/Seats			Yes/176
Library	Yes	Children's Facilities	No
Watersports Facilities			None
Classification Society			Lloyd's Register

RATINGS	SCORE
Ship: Condition/Cleanliness	6.7
Ship: Space/Flow/Comfort	6.7
Ship: Decor/Furnishings	6.9
Ship: Fitness Facilities	6.1
Cabins: Comfort/Facilities	6.7
Cabins: Software	7.0
Food: Dining Room/Cuisine	6.3
Food: Buffets/Informal Dining	5.9
Food: Quality of Ingredients	5.8
Service: Dining Room	6.4
Service: Bars	6.3
Service: Cabins	6.6
Cruise: Entertainment	5.7
Cruise: Activities Program	5.7
Cruise: Hospitality Standard	6.1
OVERALL RATING	94.8

+ The public rooms are tastefully decorated in contemporary colors, but with much use of mirrored surfaces. There's a good showroom, laid out amphitheater-style. The Belvedere Lounge, set high atop ship and forward, features a smart piano bar and good views. The mostly outside cabins are reasonably spacious for ship size and have picture windows. Bathrobes provided. Dialysis station is a bonus. Service is quite attentive.

— Open decks are crowded and there's limited sunning space when the ship is full. Cabins do not have enough drawer or closet space for two. The cabin bathrooms themselves are small, but just adequate. Too many loud announcements, in several languages, are irritating. Has a steep, narrow gangway in some ports.

Dining The dining room, set low down, is bright and cheerful, but rather cramped, and has mostly large tables (no tables for two). Features a mixed Continental cuisine, with limited choice, particularly of breads, cheeses and fresh fruits. Buffets are minimal.

Other Comments This ship's profile looks quite smart, following an extensive $26 million conversion/stretch in 1988, but is somewhat angular. This ship is for Europeans, and will cruise you in comfortable but densely populated surroundings, and at a fairly decent price, but don't expect much finesse.

cs Aida ★★★★+

OPERATES

BALTIC, CARIBBEAN AND MEDITERRANEAN CRUISES

Cruise Line	Deutsche Seetouristik		
Former Names	-		
Gross Tonnage	38,600		
Builder	Kvaerner Masa Yards (Finland)		
Original Cost	DM300 million		
Christened By	n/a		
Entered Service	June 1996		
Interior Design	Partner Ship Design		
Country of Registry	Germany		
Tel No	n/a	Fax No	n/a
Length (ft/m)		634.1/193.3	
Beam (ft/m)	90.5/27.6	Draft (ft/m)	20.3/6.2
Propulsion		diesel (21,720kW)	
Propellers		2 (CP)	
Decks	9	Crew	370
Pass. Capacity (basis 2) 1,186		(all berths) 1,230	
Pass. Space Ratio (basis 2) 32.5		(all berths) 31.3	
Officers		German	
Total Cabins		593	
Size Range (sq ft/m)	145.3-387.5/13.5-36.0		
Outside Cabins	391	Inside Cabins	202
Single Cabins	0	Balcony Cabins	4
Wheelchair Cabins		4	
Cabin Current		220 AC	
Refrigerator	No (suites have minibar)		
Cabin TV	Yes	VCR	No
Dining Rooms	1	Sittings	2
Elevators		5	

Casino	No	Slot Machines	No
Swimming Pools (outside)	1	(inside)	0
Whirlpools	3	Gymnasium	Yes
Sauna/Steam Room	Yes/Yes	Massage	Yes
Self-Service Launderette			Yes
Movie Theater/Seats			No
Library			Yes
Children's Facilities			Yes
Watersports Facilities			None
Classification Society		Germanischer Lloyd	

RATINGS	SCORE
Ship: Condition/Cleanliness	9.3
Ship: Space/Flow/Comfort	9.0
Ship: Decor/Furnishings	9.1
Ship: Fitness Facilities	8.6
Cabins: Comfort/Facilities	8.2
Cabins: Software	8.6
Food: Dining Room/Cuisine	7.7
Food: Buffets/Informal Dining	8.2
Food: Quality of Ingredients	7.8
Service: Dining Room	7.7
Service: Bars	7.4
Service: Cabins	7.7
Cruise: Entertainment	7.3
Cruise: Activities Program	7.7
Cruise: Hospitality Standard	8.3
OVERALL RATING	122.6

+ This new ship has a sleek contemporary profile, and is well proportioned, with a swept-back funnel and wedge-shaped stern. There is an outdoor teakwood wrap-around promenade deck, good for strolling or for sitting in a deck lounge chair and just taking in the sea air. Outside on deck, the area surrounding the swimming pool has several tiered levels for deck chairs and sun lounging. There's also a fine "Wellness Center" located aft, which measures 11,840 sq ft (1,100 m²) and contains a sauna, massage and other treatment rooms, and large lounging area.

Inside, there's no wasted space, signage is good and easy to read, and finding one's way around is a simple matter. The decor is really upbeat and trendy, and should appeal to younger passengers, particularly those who have never cruised before. A large observation lounge is set high atop the ship overlooking the bow. There is a wide array of intimate public rooms and spaces from which to choose.

The accommodations feature contemporary decor with a bright, youthful, somewhat contemporary Italian look. Cabins feature multi-patterned fabrics, wood-trimmed cabinetry, and rattan furniture. There are outside de luxe cabins, and "club class" cabins (a mix of outside and inside standards, many with one bed and convertible daytime sofa bed). Four suites also have forward-facing private balconies and more luxurious furnishings and fittings.

236

Seating in the small cabin lounge areas is in contemporary rattan chairs. All cabin bathrooms, which are compact though well designed and practical, feature wall-mounted soap/shampoo dispensers, so there's no wastage of throwaway plastic bottles.

One lounge features novel "fish on a stick" decoration of drinks tables. The feel is youthful, colorful, unpretentious, casual, and very relaxed. This is really a "family-friendly" ship, with lots of activities for younger family members, from 9:00 a.m. to 6:00 p.m. every day. There are several children's and youth programs, although the product should appeal more to young couples and singles.

— The cabins have a somewhat limited amount of drawer space, but you won't need many clothes anyway, so it's not really a drawback. Cabin bathrooms do not feature a hairdryer, which would be a useful addition, nor is there a toiletries cabinet. The crew to passenger ratio is poor, although, to be fair, not many waiters are needed as so many informal buffet meals are featured.

Dining There certainly are plenty of dining options aboard this ship, and food really is available 24 hours a day. The main dining room (262 seats) is very attractive, and has tables for four, six or eight. There are also two buffet restaurants, one à la carte restaurant (74 seats), and one specialty restaurant (44 seats). As on Deutsche Seetouristik's other ship, *Arkona* (presently under long-term charter), the standard of food is quite good, with good general presentation and decent service, and a fine selection of breads, cheeses and cold cuts.

Other Comments This ship, built specifically for the Arkona Group, is the company's first newbuild. Deutsche Seetouristik, which is part of the Arkona Group, also has its own private island, KIRR, situated in the national park of Mecklenburg-Vorpommern off the coast of northern Germany, as well as hotels in five cities in Germany.

The ship caters exclusively to youthful German-speaking couples using the "Club Ship" idea, which comes from the company's own land-based resorts and which features the "animateur" or "participation" concept. Alternating seven-day itineraries can be combined for a 14-day cruise vacation. In addition, packages created by other German tour operators also add land stays for an even longer cruise and resort holiday experience. This presents a good amount of flexibility. All port taxes and insurance are included. The airlines used in the various fly-cruise programs are Condor and Hapag-Lloyd.

ts Albatros ★★★

OPERATES
7-DAY EUROPE CRUISES

Cruise Line	Phoenix Seereisen	Casino	Yes	Slot Machines	Yes
Former Names	Dawn Princess/FairWind/Sylvania	Swimming Pools (outside) 3		(inside)	0
Gross Tonnage	24,803	Whirlpools	0	Gymnasium	Yes
Builder	John Brown & Co. (UK)	Sauna/Steam Room Yes/No		Massage	Yes
Original Cost	n/a	Self-Service Launderette			No
Christened By	n/a	Movie Theater/Seats			No
Entered Service	Jun 1957/Aug 1993	Library			No
Interior Design	Barbara Dorn	Children's Facilities			No
Country of Registry	Bahamas	Watersports Facilities			None
Tel No 130-6132 Fax No 130-6133		Classification Society			Lloyd's Register
Length (ft/m)	608.2/185.40				
Beam (ft/m) 80.3/24.49 Draft (ft/m) 29.3/8.94		**RATINGS**			**SCORE**
Propulsion	steam turbine (18,300kW)	Ship: Condition/Cleanliness			6.3
Propellers	2 (FP)	Ship: Space/Flow/Comfort			6.1
Decks 11 Crew 330		Ship: Decor/Furnishings			6.6
Pass. Capacity (basis 2) 940 (all berths) 1,100		Ship: Fitness Facilities			5.0
Pass. Space Ratio (basis 2) 26.3 (all berths) 22.5		Cabins: Comfort/Facilities			6.4
Officers	German	Cabins: Software			6.7
Total Cabins	470	Food: Dining Room/Cuisine			6.8
Size Range (sq ft/m)	90-241/8.3-22.3	Food: Buffets/Informal Dining			6.6
Outside Cabins 239 Inside Cabins 231		Food: Quality of Ingredients			6.7
Single Cabins	0	Service: Dining Room			6.8
Balcony Cabins 0 Wheelchair Cabins 0		Service: Bars			7.0
Cabin Current	110 AC	Service: Cabins			7.2
Refrigerator	Category A only	Cruise: Entertainment			7.3
Cabin TV No VCR No		Cruise: Activities Program			6.6
Dining Rooms 2 Sittings 1		Cruise: Hospitality Standard			7.0
Elevators	3	OVERALL RATING			99.1

+   This is a sturdily constructed ship, stable at sea, and is quite well maintained. A second swimming pool, fitted into a former cargo hold, is for children. There is plenty of dark wood paneling and trim, with solid brass accents used throughout. Has a good-sized library. Wide range of cabin sizes and configurations, all with heavy-duty furniture. Features excellent and extensive itineraries that provide much of interest to those seeking to cruise in an older style of ship in very casual surroundings. Young, willing Phoenix Seereisen staff.

—   There's not much open deck and sunning space, especially when full. Public rooms are few, always crowded, and full of cigarette smoke.

Dining The two dining rooms are really quite charming, but the tables are close together. The menu is not very creative, and there is limited choice. Service is friendly and attentive, in true European style.

Other Comments This all-white ship was built in true vintage ocean liner style, and has a large centrally placed funnel. Furnishings consist of heavy, patterned fabrics that are very comfortable. This unpretentious ship does have an interesting old-world ambiance and charm that somehow help to make up for the lack of finesse associated with more upscale and expensive products. Operated specifically for German-speaking passengers.

ms Alla Tarasova ★★+

Cruise Line	Murmansk Shipping		
Former Names	-		
Gross Tonnage	3,985		
Builder	Brodgradiliste Uljanik (Yugoslavia)		
Original Cost	n/a	Christened By	n/a
Entered Service	1976		
Interior Design	n/a		
Country of Registry	Russia		
Tel No	n/a	Fax No	n/a
Length (ft/m)	328.1/100.01		
Beam (ft/m) 53.2/16.24	Draft (ft/m)	15.2/4.65	
Propulsion	diesel (3,884kW)		
Propellers	1 (FP)		
Decks	3	Crew	80
Pass. Capacity (basis 2) 100	(all berths) 118		
Pass. Space Ratio (basis 2) 39.8	(all berths) 33.7		
Officers	Russian		
Total Cabins	50		
Size Range (sq ft/m)	n/a		
Outside Cabins	50	Inside Cabins	0
Single Cabins	0		
Balcony Cabins	0	Wheelchair Cabins	0
Cabin Current	220 AC		
Refrigerator	No		
Cabin TV	No	VCR	No
Dining Rooms	1	Sittings	1
Elevators	0		
Casino	No	Slot Machines	No

Swimming Pools (outside)			No
(inside)			No
Whirlpools	No	Gymnasium	No
Sauna/Steam Room	No/No	Massage	No
Self-Service Launderette			No
Movie Theater/Seats			No
Library			Yes
Children's Facilities			No
Watersports Facilities			No
Classification Society			RS

RATINGS	SCORE
Ship: Condition/Cleanliness	7.9
Ship: Space/Flow/Comfort	5.5
Ship: Decor/Furnishings	6.8
Ship: Fitness Facilities	3.0
Cabins: Comfort/Facilities	5.8
Cabins: Software	6.2
Food: Dining Room/Cuisine	6.5
Food: Buffets/Informal Dining	5.9
Food: Quality of Ingredients	6.0
Service: Dining Room	6.4
Service: Bars	6.5
Service: Cabins	6.8
Cruise: Entertainment	4.2
Cruise: Activities Program	4.7
Cruise: Hospitality Standard	6.9
OVERALL RATING	89.1

+ This ship has an ice-strengthened royal blue hull. Nicely refurbished in 1992, this little ship now specializes in close-in destination cruising. Tidy, neat and clean throughout, with fairly attractive, though rather plain, decor that is comfortable. All cabins are outside and have lower beds, with private bathroom, shower and toilet. Many cabins can be used by single cruisegoers. Two larger cabins (called suites, which they are not) are quite well equipped. The dress code is very informal. Has a small number of Zodiac rubber landing craft for shore exploring and tendering.

— Has very limited public spaces. Cabins have tiny bathrooms (of the "me first, you next" variety). Poor library needs better selection of books. There's no forward observation lounge.

Dining Pleasant, though somewhat dark dining room seats everyone at one sitting. The catering is often done by a European company. There are limited menu choices, but the food is quite wholesome, although fresh produce is rarely used. Limited selection of breads, cheeses and fruits.

Other Comments This ship is not glamorous, but she is very cozy and caters to travelers rather than cruisegoers. Often chartered to special interest packagers, such as Noble Caledonia, Marine Expeditions or Quark Expeditions for "soft" exploration cruises.

mv Americana ★★★★

Cruise Line	Ivaran Lines	Casino Yes	Slot Machines Yes
Former Names	-	Swimming Pools (outside) 1	(inside) 0
Gross Tonnage	19,203	Whirlpools 1	Gymnasium Yes
Builder	Hyundai Heavy Industries (S.Korea)	Sauna/Steam Room Yes/No	Massage Yes
Original Cost	$85 million	Self-Service Launderette	Yes
Christened By	Mrs Kari Holter-Sorensen	Movie Theater/Seats	No
Entered Service	Mar 1988	Library	Yes
Interior Design	Platou Design	Children's Facilities	No
Country of Registry	Norway	Watersports Facilities	None
Tel No 131-1131	Fax No 131-2714	Classification Society	Det Norske Veritas
Length (ft/m)	579.7/176.70		
Beam (ft/m) 85.3/26.00	Draft (ft/m) 28.8/8.80	**RATINGS**	**SCORE**
Propulsion	diesel (18,564bhp)	Ship: Condition/Cleanliness	8.6
Propellers	1 (CP)	Ship: Space/Flow/Comfort	7.4
Decks 6	Crew 44	Ship: Decor/Furnishings	8.1
Pass. Capacity (basis 2) 88	(all berths) 108	Ship: Fitness Facilities	7.3
Pass. Space Ratio (basis 2) 218.2	(all berths) 177.8	Cabins: Comfort/Facilities	8.0
Officers	Norwegian	Cabins: Software	8.1
Total Cabins	52	Food: Dining Room/Cuisine	7.8
Size Range (sq ft/m)	134-500/12.5-46.5	Food: Buffets/Informal Dining	7.2
Outside Cabins 40	Inside Cabins 12	Food: Quality of Ingredients	7.7
Single Cabins	20	Service: Dining Room	7.8
Balcony Cabins 4	Wheelchair Cabins 0	Service: Bars	7.6
Cabin Current	110/220 AC	Service: Cabins	7.4
Refrigerator	No	Cruise: Entertainment	6.0
Cabin TV No	VCR No	Cruise: Activities Program	6.2
Dining Rooms 1	Sittings 1	Cruise: Hospitality Standard	7.7
Elevators	2	OVERALL RATING	112.9

+ The incredible space ratio is because this is a well-designed freighter-cruise ship with excellent passenger facilities placed astern of a 1,120-capacity container section. Elegant and beautifully finished interior. Plenty of live tropical plants, soft leather chairs and space are appreciated. Has a neat double-spiral staircase. Two owners' suites are lavish, with separate bedroom and living room, and big picture windows. Other cabins are lovely, well equipped, with restful decor and excellent soft furnishings. Several single cabins. Generous sheltered and open sunning space. Well-stocked library. Gentlemen "hosts" carried on all voyages.

— No wrap-around promenade deck, no room service (except on doctor's orders), and no cushioned pads for outdoor deck lounge chairs. Has a steep gangway in ports of call.

Dining Elegant dining room has beautiful table settings and china, and overlooks the sea. Cuisine, while not elaborate, is appealing, well prepared, and features Norwegian and Continental fare. Breakfast and lunch are buffet-style.

Other Comments A minimum of 50 passengers assures priority berths in ports. For the older passenger with time to spare, who enjoys privacy and quiet, as well as the chance to explore places alone. This is the ultimate in contemporary freighter-cruise travel, with a fine itinerary. Passengers are mostly experienced cruisegoers of age 60 and up. Port taxes are included.

mv Andaman Princess ★★+

OPERATES

*7-DAY ANDAMAN SEA/GULF OF
THAILAND CRUISES*

Cruise Line			Siam Cruise
Former Names			Apollo III/Svea Jarl
Gross Tonnage			5,097
Builder			Finnboda (Sweden)
Original Cost			$8 million
Christened By			Countess Estelle Bernadotte/
			Mrs Prani Yasasindhu
Entered Service			Apr 1962/1990
Interior Design			Kitti Sindhusek/
			Chulalonggkorn University
Country of Registry			Thailand
Tel No	-	Fax No	-
Length (ft/m)			332.8/101.45
Beam (ft/m)	56.5/17.25	Draft (ft/m)	15.6/4.76
Propulsion			diesel (3,603kW)
Propellers			1 (FP)
Decks	6	Crew	200
Pass. Capacity (basis 2) 276		(all berths) 350	
Pass. Space Ratio (basis 2) 18.4		(all berths) 14.5	
Officers			Thai
Total Cabins			138
Size Range (sq ft/m)			54-344/5.0-32.0
Outside Cabins	86	Inside Cabins	52
Single Cabins			0
Balcony Cabins	0	Wheelchair Cabins	0
Cabin Current	220 AC	Refrigerator	No
Cabin TV	No	VCR	No
Dining Rooms	2	Sittings	1

Elevators			2
Casino	Yes	Slot Machines	Yes
Swimming Pools (outside) 0		(inside)	0
Whirlpools 1 (large, indoor)		Gymnasium	Yes
Sauna/Steam Room Yes/No		Massage	Yes
Self-Service Launderette			No
Movie Theater/Seats			No
Library	No	Children's Facilities	Yes
Watersports Facilities			None
Classification Society			Lloyd's Register

RATINGS	SCORE
Ship: Condition/Cleanliness	5.6
Ship: Space/Flow/Comfort	5.8
Ship: Decor/Furnishings	6.0
Ship: Fitness Facilities	3.7
Cabins: Comfort/Facilities	6.0
Cabins: Software	6.1
Food: Dining Room/Cuisine	6.1
Food: Buffets/Informal Dining	5.8
Food: Quality of Ingredients	6.0
Service: Dining Room	6.6
Service: Bars	6.3
Service: Cabins	6.4
Cruise: Entertainment	5.4
Cruise: Activities Program	5.6
Cruise: Hospitality Standard	6.8
OVERALL RATING	88.2

+ Her original steam engines were exchanged for diesel propulsion in 1981. Lovely brass staircase. Lots of original wood paneling throughout. Snorkels and masks provided free, while underwater cameras can be rented. Has a Fuji express photo lab for instant service. Good children's learning center teaches three alphabets. Except for 12 suites, most of which have lifeboat views, most cabins are small, cleanly appointed, and quite comfortable. All have been refurbished. Closet and storage space is limited.

— There's no outdoor deck space at all, but then Asian passengers seldom like sunbathing. Passageways are narrow and cramped.

Dining The two dining rooms are quite charming and have acres of lovely original wood paneling. The food is typically good quality Thai and Chinese, with attentive service from a very willing staff. There is also a 24-hour coffee shop for casual snacks.

Other Comments Charming ex-Swedish night ferry with aft-placed funnel has seen many internal changes. An extensive refurbishment has equipped the ship for specialized cruising. This is the first attempt at operating a full-service cruise ship by Thai owners for Asian passengers, but it is not the luxury experience it claims to be yet. It is, however, an excellent way to experience cruising in Thai waters at modest rates.

ms Antonina Nezhdanova ★★

OPERATES
VARIOUS CRUISES

Cruise Line	Far East Shipping		
Former Names	-		
Gross Tonnage	3,941		
Builder	Brodgradiliste Uljanik (Yugoslavia)		
Original Cost	n/a		
Christened By	n/a		
Entered Service	1978		
Interior Design	n/a		
Country of Registry	Russia		
Tel No	140-0371	Fax No	140-0371
Length (ft/m)	328.1/100.01		
Beam (ft/m) 53.2/16.24		Draft (ft/m)	15.2/4.65
Propulsion	diesel (3,884kW)		
Propellers	1 (FP)		
Decks	6	Crew	100
Pass. Capacity (basis 2) 96		(all berths)	188
Pass. Space Ratio (basis 2) 41.0		(all berths)	20.9
Officers	Russian		
Total Cabins	48		
Size Range (sq ft/m)	n/a		
Outside Cabins	48	Inside Cabins	0
Single Cabins	0		
Balcony Cabins	0	Wheelchair Cabins	0
Cabin Current	220 AC		
Refrigerator	No		
Cabin TV	No	VCR	No
Dining Rooms	1	Sittings	1
Elevators	0		

Casino	No	Slot Machines	No
Swimming Pools (outside)	1	(inside)	No
Whirlpools	No	Gymnasium	No
Sauna/Steam Room	Yes/No	Massage	No
Self-Service Launderette			No
Movie Theater/Seats			Yes/75
Library			Yes
Children's Facilities			No
Watersports Facilities			None
Classification Society			RS

RATINGS	SCORE
Ship: Condition/Cleanliness	5.3
Ship: Space/Flow/Comfort	5.5
Ship: Decor/Furnishings	6.1
Ship: Fitness Facilities	3.0
Cabins: Comfort/Facilities	5.7
Cabins: Software	6.0
Food: Dining Room/Cuisine	6.0
Food: Buffets/Informal Dining	5.4
Food: Quality of Ingredients	6.0
Service: Dining Room	6.2
Service: Bars	6.4
Service: Cabins	6.5
Cruise: Entertainment	4.2
Cruise: Activities Program	4.6
Cruise: Hospitality Standard	6.1
OVERALL RATING	83.0

+ Intimate, small ship with well-balanced profile is one of a series of eight identical sisters. Some have now been sold while others are sometimes chartered to European operators. Has an ice-hardened hull suitable for some "soft" expedition cruising. Good open deck space for the size of the vessel. Has an outdoor observation deck plus an enclosed promenade deck for inclement weather. Charming forward music lounge has wooden dance floor. Rich, highly polished wood paneling throughout. Lovely winding brass-railed main staircase. Cabins are compact and spartan, but most can accommodate four persons, and stewardess service is basically sound.

— There's no indoor observation lounge. Poor lecture room with non-existent ventilation. Poor accounting system (no cashless cruising). Announcements are too loud and rather military in style. This is simply too small a ship for much open water cruising.

Dining The dining room is dark and unappealing, even though it has portholes. The food is an eclectic mixture, and certainly not memorable, with its heavy sauces and salt in everything. Very limited menu choice. Poor selection of cheeses and fruits. Willing waitress service.

Other Comments This ship is small, yet comfortable, and has plenty of character. Often chartered to Western operators for "soft" expedition-style cruises.

ms Arkona ★★★★

OPERATES

VARIOUS CRUISES WORLDWIDE

Cruise Line	Deutsche Seetouristik	Casino	No	Slot Machines	No
Former Names	Astor (I)	Swimming Pools (outside) 1	(inside)	1
Gross Tonnage	18,591	Whirlpools	0	Gymnasium	Yes
Builder	Howaldtswerke Deutsche Werft	Sauna/Steam Room Yes/No	Massage	Yes
	(Germany)	Self-Service Launderette	No
Original Cost	$55 million	Movie Theater/Seats	No
Christened By	Ms Lisa Wiethucter	Library	Yes
Entered Service	Dec 1981/Oct 1985	Children's Facilities	No
Interior Design	Hans Sabert	Watersports Facilities	None
Country of Registry	Germany	Classification Society	Germanischer Lloyd

Tel No	112-1511	Fax No	112-1512
Length (ft/m)			539.2/164.35
Beam (ft/m) 74.1/22.60		Draft (ft/m)	20.0/6.11
Propulsion/Propellers		diesel (13,200kW)/2 (CP)
Decks	8	Crew	243
Pass. Capacity (basis 2) 516		(all berths) 618
Pass. Space Ratio (basis 2) 36.0		(all berths) 30.1
Officers			German
Total Cabins			258
Size Range (sq ft/m)			n/a
Outside Cabins	176	Inside Cabins	82
Single Cabins			0
Balcony Cabins	0	Wheelchair Cabins	0
Cabin Current			220 AC
Refrigerator		No (suites have minibar)
Cabin TV	Yes	VCR	No
Dining Rooms	1	Sittings	2
Elevators			3

RATINGS	SCORE
Ship: Condition/Cleanliness	8.1
Ship: Space/Flow/Comfort	8.0
Ship: Decor/Furnishings	7.9
Ship: Fitness Facilities	6.7
Cabins: Comfort/Facilities	7.8
Cabins: Software	7.8
Food: Dining Room/Cuisine	7.7
Food: Buffets/Informal Dining	7.6
Food: Quality of Ingredients	7.7
Service: Dining Room	6.8
Service: Bars	6.7
Service: Cabins	6.8
Cruise: Entertainment	6.6
Cruise: Activities Program	6.5
Cruise: Hospitality Standard	7.3
OVERALL RATING	110.0

+ Well-constructed ship has a handsome profile. Good open deck and sunning space, with gorgeous teakwood decking and rails. Beautifully appointed interior fittings and decor, with much rosewood paneling and trim. Subdued lighting and soothing ambiance, highlighted by fine artwork throughout. Has good meetings facilities, a fine library, and, more important, an excellent pub with draught German beer. Excellent indoor spa and fitness center. Boat Deck suite rooms are simply lovely. Other cabins are well equipped and decorated. Bathrooms are compact but fully tiled, with good toiletry cabinet. Good traditional European hotel service.

— No wrap-around promenade deck. Atmosphere a little starchy. Many smokers.

Dining The Arkona Restaurant, located high in the ship, has big picture windows and is quite elegant, with dark wood paneling and restful decor. The food is adequate to very good, though choice is somewhat limited. The occasional formal candlelight dinners are romantic. Limited cabin service menu.

Other Comments This ship cruises under long-term charter to German operators, and features good value-for-money cruising in contemporary comfort with German-speaking passengers who appreciate quality, fine surroundings, good food, and excellent destination-intensive itineraries. Port taxes are included.

ms Astor ★★★★+

OPERATES
VARIOUS CRUISES WORLDWIDE

Cruise Line	AquaMarin Cruises		
Former Names	Fedor Dostoyevsky/Astor (II)		
Gross Tonnage	20,158		
Builder Howaldtswerke Deutsche Werft (Germany)			
Original Cost	$65 million		
Christened By	Inta Gleich/Marie Louise Marjan		
Entered Service	Feb 1987/Dec 1995		
Interior Design	Hans Sabert		
Country of Registry	Bahamas		
Tel No 140-2771/140-2772	Fax No 140-0125		
Length (ft/m)	579.0/176.50		
Beam (ft/m) 74.1/22.61	Draft (ft/m) 20.0/6.10		
Propulsion	diesel (15,400kW)		
Propellers	2 (CP)		
Decks	7	Crew	295
Pass. Capacity (basis 2) 590		(all berths) 650	
Pass. Space Ratio (basis 2) 34.1		(all berths) 31.0	
Officers	Russian/Ukrainian		
Total Cabins	295		
Size Range (sq ft/m)	140.0-280.0/13.0-26.0		
Outside Cabins	199	Inside Cabins	96
Single Cabins	0		
Balcony Cabins	0	Wheelchair Cabins	0
Cabin Current	220 AC		
Refrigerator	Yes		
Cabin TV	Yes	VCR	No
Dining Rooms	1	Sittings	2
Elevators	3		

Casino	No	Slot Machines	No
Swimming Pools (outside) 1	(inside)	1
Whirlpools	0	Gymnasium	Yes
Sauna/Steam Room Yes/No	Massage	Yes
Self-Service Launderette	no (has ironing room)
Movie Theater/Seats	No
Library	Yes
Children's Facilities	Yes
Watersports Facilities	None
Classification Society	Germanischer Lloyd

RATINGS	SCORE
Ship: Condition/Cleanliness	8.2
Ship: Space/Flow/Comfort	8.2
Ship: Decor/Furnishings	8.3
Ship: Fitness Facilities	7.6
Cabins: Comfort/Facilities	8.0
Cabins: Software	8.1
Food: Dining Room/Cuisine	7.8
Food: Buffets/Informal Dining	7.7
Food: Quality of Ingredients	7.5
Service: Dining Room	7.7
Service: Bars	7.7
Service: Cabins	7.9
Cruise: Entertainment	7.7
Cruise: Activities Program	7.6
Cruise: Hospitality Standard	8.7
OVERALL RATING	118.7

+ Very attractive ship with raked, squarish funnel. Finest ship in the Russian/Ukrainian-owned fleet. Built in the best German tradition. Almost everything is absolutely top quality. Fine teakwood decking and rails and polished wood everywhere. Excellent worldwide itineraries. Basketball court. Supremely comfortable and varied public rooms and conference facilities. Wood-paneled tavern with German beer on draught is a fine retreat. Fine mix of traditional and contemporary styling. Well-designed interior fitness center and pool. Dark-wood-accented cabins are superbly equipped and tastefully decorated in fresh pastel colors. There is plenty of closet and drawer space. Good bathrooms, with toiletries cabinet, bathrobes for all.

— The cabin service menu needs upgrading. Charge for sauna is absurd.

Dining Exquisite dining room is elegant. Service is friendly, although food quality needs more attention, with presentation and choice below the standard of the rest of the product. Buffets are well presented.

Other Comments Nice continental atmosphere. Operated specifically for German-speaking passengers following extensive refurbishment in late 1995. This ship provides style, comfort, and elegance, and a fine leisurely cruise experience. Port taxes, insurance, and gratuities are included.

ms Astra ★★

OPERATES
VARIOUS MEDITERRANEAN
CRUISES

Cruise Line	Caravella Shipping	Casino	No
Former Names	Istra	Swimming Pools (outside)	1
Gross Tonnage	5,635	Whirlpools	0
Builder	Brodgradiliste (Yugoslavia)	Sauna/Steam Room	No/No
Original Cost	n/a	Self-Service Launderette	
Christened By	n/a	Movie Theater/Seats	
Entered Service	1965/May 1993	Library	
Interior Design	n/a	Children's Facilities	
Country of Registry	Russia	Watersports Facilities	
Tel No	140-3475	Classification Society	

Casino	No	Slot Machines	No
Swimming Pools (outside)	1	(inside)	0
Whirlpools	0	Gymnasium	No
Sauna/Steam Room	No/No	Massage	No
Self-Service Launderette			No
Movie Theater/Seats			No
Library			Yes
Children's Facilities			No
Watersports Facilities			None
Classification Society			Russian Survey

Tel No	140-3475	Fax No	140-3475
Length (ft/m)			383.8/116.8m
Beam (ft/m)	54.1/16.5m	Draft (ft/m)	18.3/5.6m
Propulsion			diesel (11,030kW)
Propellers			2 (FP)
Decks	5	Crew	120
Pass. Capacity (basis 2)	282	(all berths)	282
Pass. Space Ratio (basis 2)	19.9	(all berths)	19.9
Officers			Russian
Total Cabins			141
Size Range (sq ft/m)			n/a
Outside Cabins	83	Inside Cabins	58
Single Cabins			0
Balcony Cabins	0	Wheelchair Cabins	0
Cabin Current			220 AC
Refrigerator			No
Cabin TV	No	VCR	No
Dining Rooms	1	Sittings	1
Elevators			0

RATINGS	SCORE
Ship: Condition/Cleanliness	5.6
Ship: Space/Flow/Comfort	5.0
Ship: Decor/Furnishings	6.0
Ship: Fitness Facilities	4.0
Cabins: Comfort/Facilities	5.1
Cabins: Software	5.4
Food: Dining Room/Cuisine	6.2
Food: Buffets/Informal Dining	5.7
Food: Quality of Ingredients	5.7
Service: Dining Room	6.3
Service: Bars	6.4
Service: Cabins	6.5
Cruise: Entertainment	5.0
Cruise: Activities Program	5.8
Cruise: Hospitality Standard	6.0
OVERALL RATING	84.7

+ This small ship is quite attractive, and is particularly good for "nooks and crannies" ports of call. Has an enclosed teak promenade deck. Interior decor is attractive in general. Features interesting itineraries. A two-deck-high Lido Bar is attractive. Very casual dress code and unpretentious relaxed ambiance. The service staff are very friendly and most attentive.

— Few public rooms, and little open deck space. Maintenance and cleanliness need a lot more attention. Teakwood decking is in poor condition. Upper berths in cabins do not have sufficient grab ("anti-fall-out") protection. Public rooms are always busy and it's hard to get away from the cigarette smokers. The crew tend to put themselves first, passengers second.

Dining Although the dining room is quite warm and attractive, and features decent place settings, there are no tables for two, and tables are close together. The food itself is limited in choice and variety. The selection of vegetables, fresh fruits and breads could be better. Ukrainian waitresses are quite charming, but, although friendly and attentive, there's no finesse.

Other Comments This small ship has a typical low-built early sixties profile. At present the ship is cruising for the German-speaking and Russian markets, with passengers cruising on a price-sensitive budget.

ms Astra II ★★★

OPERATES
BALTIC AND
MEDITERRANEAN CRUISES

Cruise Line		Neckermann Seereisen
Former Names		Golden Odyssey
Gross Tonnage		10,563
Builder		Helsingor Skibsvog (Denmark)
Original Cost		$22 million
Christened By		-
Entered Service		Sept 1974/Oct 1995
Interior Design		John Terzoglou
Country of Registry		Bahamas (C6115)
Tel No 110-4672	Fax No	110-3461
Length (ft/m)		426.8/130.10
Beam (ft/m) 62.9/19.20	Draft (ft/m)	17.0/5.20
Propulsion		diesel (11,033kW)
Propellers		2 (CP)
Decks 7	Crew	215
Pass. Capacity (basis 2) 460	(all berths)	489
Pass. Space Ratio (basis 2) 22.9	(all berths)	21.6
Officers		East European
Total Cabins		227
Size (sq ft./m.):		121-262 sq ft.
Outside Cabins 181	Inside Cabins	46
Single Cabins		0
Balcony Cabins		0
Wheelchair Cabins		0
Cabin Current 110 AC	Refrigerator	No
Cabin TV No	VCR	No
Dining Rooms		1
Sittings		1

Elevators			2
Casino	No	Slot Machines	No
Swimming Pools (outside) 1		(inside)	0
Whirlpools	0	Gymnasium	Yes
Sauna/Steam Room Yes/No		Massage	Yes
Self-Service Launderette			No
Movie Theater/Seats			Yes/154
Library			Yes
Children's Facilities/Playroom:			No
Classification Society			Lloyd's Register

RATINGS	SCORE
Ship: Condition/Cleanliness	6.3
Ship: Space/Flow/Comfort	6.1
Ship: Decor/Furnishings	6.0
Ship: Fitness Facilities	4.0
Cabins: Comfort/Facilities	6.1
Cabins: Software	6.5
Food: Dining Room/Cuisine	6.2
Food: Buffets/Informal Dining	5.8
Food: Quality of Ingredients	5.6
Service: Dining Room	6.7
Service: Bars	6.8
Service: Cabins	7.1
Cruise: Entertainment	6.2
Cruise: Activities Program	5.7
Cruise: Hospitality Standard	6.6
OVERALL RATING	91.7

+ Sleek-looking small ship has a well-balanced, compact, almost contemporary profile. Well maintained, although now 20 years old. Elegant, intimate ship with a loyal following, for good reason. The ship is very clean and tidy throughout. Outdoor promenade deck. Good selection of public rooms for ship size. Cabins, although not large, are tastefully furnished and decorated, with a fair amount of closet and drawer space, and pleasant artwork. Attentive staff offer fine-tuned personal service that is personable without being condescending.

— The cabins are small, as are the bathrooms, and towels also are small. Has a steep, narrow gangway in many ports. The plumbing is tired and troublesome at times.

Dining Very comfortable dining room, with good quality Continental food that is well presented. The menu choice is good, and the food is geared specifically to German tastes.

Other Comments This ship, now owned by Caravella Shipping, offers comfortable surroundings, at a moderate price, to a well-chosen palette of destinations. Ideally suited to passengers who want a small ship atmosphere and who don't like big ships. Under charter to Neckermann Seereisen for 225 days each year until the year 2002.

ms Asuka ★★★★★

OPERATES
ASIA/CIRCLE JAPAN/
SOUTH PACIFIC CRUISES

Cruise Line			NYK Cruises
Former Names			-
Gross Tonnage			28,717
Builder	Mitsubishi Heavy Industries (Japan)		
Original Cost			$86 million
Christened By			Mr Jiro Nemoto
Entered Service			Dec 1991
Interior Design	Kenmochi Design/Robert Tillberg		
Country of Registry			Japan
Tel No 120-4654/-4660	Fax No		120-4662
Length (ft/m)			632.5/192.81
Beam (ft/m) 81.0/24.70	Draft (ft/m)		20.3/6.20
Propulsion/Propellers	diesel (17,300kW)/2 (CP)		
Decks	8	Crew	243
Pass. Capacity (basis 2) 584		(all berths) 604	
Pass. Space Ratio (basis 2) 49.1		(all berths) 47.5	
Officers			Japanese
Total Cabins			292
Size Range (sq ft/m)		182-650/17.0-60.3	
Outside Cabins	292	Inside Cabins	0
Single Cabins			0
Balcony Cabins	100 (all have binoculars)		
Wheelchair Cabins			2
Cabin Current			110 AC
Refrigerator			All cabins
Cabin TV	Yes	VCR	No
Dining Rooms		1 (+ sushi restaurant)	
Sittings			2

Elevators			5
Casino	Yes	Slot Machines	Yes
Swimming Pools (outside) 1		(inside)	0
Whirlpools	3	Gymnasium	Yes
Sauna/Steam Room Yes/Yes		Massage	Yes
Self-Service Launderette			Yes
Movie Theater/Seats			Yes/97
Library	Yes	Children's Facilities	No
Watersports Facilities			None
Classification Society		Nippon Kaiji Kyokai	

RATINGS	SCORE
Ship: Condition/Cleanliness	9.1
Ship: Space/Flow/Comfort	8.3
Ship: Decor/Furnishings	8.8
Ship: Fitness Facilities	8.6
Cabins: Comfort/Facilities	8.7
Cabins: Software	8.6
Food: Dining Room/Cuisine	8.8
Food: Buffets/Informal Dining	8.1
Food: Quality of Ingredients	8.7
Service: Dining Room	8.7
Service: Bars	8.6
Service: Cabins	8.4
Cruise: Entertainment	8.6
Cruise: Activities Program	7.4
Cruise: Hospitality Standard	9.3
OVERALL RATING	128.7

+ Handsome exterior styling, with good open deck space. Good meetings facilities with high-tech equipment. Wrap-around outdoor promenade deck. Excellent and spacious true Japanese grand bath. Many intimate public rooms. Elegant interior decor and pleasing colors. Superb "club" suites. Excellent insulation between cabins. Good closet and drawer space. Tea-making units and bathtubs in all cabins. Traditional "Watushi" tatami room. Features sushi-making classes. Cellular pay telephones. Good entertainment.

— "Cake-layer" stacking of public rooms hampers passenger flow. Standard cabin bathrooms are rather small. No butler service in the "club" suites. Balcony door handles are awkward in the suites. Massage room is located away from the grand bath area and should be integrated.

Dining The dining room has good space around tables, but there are not enough tables for two. Japanese and Western food. Features traditional Japanese breakfast and luncheon, and Western-style dinners. Excellent Hotel Okura chain menus and food. Chinaware is Wedgwood. The sushi bar features fresh seafood, beautifully presented. Traditional Washitsu tatami room for tea ceremonies.

Other Comments This is the first all-new large ship specially designed for the Japanese cruise market. Children under 10 not allowed. Gratuities are neither expected, nor permitted.

ms Atalante ★★+

Cruise Line			Paradise Cruises
Former Names			Tahitien
Gross Tonnage			13,113
Builder		Arsenal de la Marine Nationale	
			Française (France)
Original Cost			n/a
Christened By			n/a
Entered Service			May 1953/Dec 1992
Interior Design			n/a
Country of Registry			Cyprus
Tel No 357-9-545600		Fax No	357-9-370298
Length (ft/m)			548.5/167.20
Beam (ft/m) 67.9/20.70		Draft (ft/m)	25.5/7.80
Propulsion			diesel (7,700kW)
Propellers			2 (FP)
Decks	5	Crew	160
Pass. Capacity (basis 2) 484		(all berths)	635
Pass. Space Ratio (basis 2) 27.0		(all berths)	20.6
Officers			Greek
Total Cabins			242
Size Range (sq ft/m)		129.1-247.5/12.0-23.0	
Outside Cabins	188	Inside Cabins	54
Single Cabins			2
Balcony Cabins	0	Wheelchair Cabins	18
Cabin Current			220 AC/200 DC
Refrigerator		Top grade cabins only	
Cabin TV	Yes	VCR	No
Dining Rooms	1	Sittings	2

Elevators			0
Casino	Yes	Slot Machines	Yes
Swimming Pools (outside) 2		(inside)	0
Whirlpools	0	Gymnasium	No
Sauna/Steam Room No/No		Massage	No
Self-Service Launderette			No
Movie Theater/Seats	No	Library	No
Children's Facilities			No
Watersports Facilities			None
Classification Society			Bureau Veritas

RATINGS	SCORE
Ship: Condition/Cleanliness	5.8
Ship: Space/Flow/Comfort	6.0
Ship: Decor/Furnishings	6.0
Ship: Fitness Facilities	4.1
Cabins: Comfort/Facilities	6.2
Cabins: Software	6.2
Food: Dining Room/Cuisine	5.8
Food: Buffets/Informal Dining	5.6
Food: Quality of Ingredients	5.4
Service: Dining Room	6.1
Service: Bars	6.1
Service: Cabins	6.3
Cruise: Entertainment	5.0
Cruise: Activities Program	5.2
Cruise: Hospitality Standard	6.0
OVERALL RATING	85.8

+ This former passenger-car liner has a small, squat funnel amidships and a long foredeck. She is a very stable ship at sea, with a deep draft, and rides well. There is a generous amount of open deck and sunning space, but the outdoor decking is worn in several places. The interior decor is also dated and worn, yet adequate and comfortable for those who do not want the glitz of newer ships. Cabins are small and rather spartan, although most have been recently redecorated in pastel shades. There is limited closet space, but you don't need much clothing for this casual cruise environment.

— The vessel has a very awkward layout. The nightlife is disco-loud. There's no finesse anywhere, although the staff are reasonably enthusiastic. New cabins installed in 1993 are subject to extreme squeaks and are noisy (difficult to sleep in). Few public rooms.

Dining The dining room is low down in the ship and musty. The food is quite basic, that's all— with little choice. Poor selection of breads, fruits and cheeses. Buffets are minimal and could be more attractive.

Other Comments This ship is for the young, budget-minded cruiser wanting to party and travel with just the basics and without much service.

ts Ausonia ★★★

OPERATES

6-11 DAY EUROPE CRUISES

Cruise Line	Grimaldi Cruises	Casino	No	Slot Machines	No

Cruise Line	Grimaldi Cruises
Former Names	-
Gross Tonnage	12,609
Builder	Cantieri Riuniti dell' Adriatico (Italy)
Original Cost	n/a
Christened By	n/a
Entered Service	Sep 1957
Interior Design	n/a
Country of Registry	Italy
Tel No 115-0673 Fax No	115-0673
Length (ft/m)	522.5/159.26
Beam (ft/m) 69.8/21.29 Draft (ft/m)	21.4/6.54
Propulsion	steam turbine (12,799kW)
Propellers	2 (FP)
Decks 8 Crew	210
Pass. Capacity (basis 2) 506 (all berths)	808
Pass. Space Ratio (basis 2) 24.9 (all berths)	15.6
Officers	Italian
Total Cabins	253
Size Range (sq ft/m)	69.9-269.1/6.5-25.0
Outside Cabins 154 Inside Cabins	99
Single Cabins	8
Balcony Cabins 0 Wheelchair Cabins	0
Cabin Current 220 AC Refrigerator	No
Cabin TV	Yes (upper grade cabins only)
VCR	No
Dining Rooms 2 Sittings	2
Elevators	1

Casino No Slot Machines	No
Swimming Pools (outside) 1 (inside)	0
Whirlpools 1 Gymnasium	No
Sauna/Steam Room Yes/No Massage	Yes
Self-Service Launderette	No
Movie Theater/Seats	Yes/125
Library	No
Children's Facilities	No
Watersports Facilities	None
Classification Society	Lloyd's Register

RATINGS	SCORE
Ship: Condition/Cleanliness	7.5
Ship: Space/Flow/Comfort	7.2
Ship: Decor/Furnishings	7.0
Ship: Fitness Facilities	4.7
Cabins: Comfort/Facilities	6.1
Cabins: Software	6.2
Food: Dining Room/Cuisine	6.4
Food: Buffets/Informal Dining	5.7
Food: Quality of Ingredients	6.0
Service: Dining Room	6.1
Service: Bars	6.1
Service: Cabins	6.3
Cruise: Entertainment	5.5
Cruise: Activities Program	5.7
Cruise: Hospitality Standard	6.0
OVERALL RATING	92.5

+ Well-maintained ship with classic, swept-back lines and profile. Quite clean and tidy. Good open deck and sunning space. Ship underwent much mechanical and galley upgrading in late 1990. Also, the upgraded public areas are light and spacious. Ballroom is pleasantly decorated in blues and creams. Small, compact, yet reasonably comfortable cabins were refurbished in 1989–90. All have private facilities; uppermost cabin grades have full bathtub, others have showers, while two new suites feature whirlpool baths. There are several family cabins.

— Passengers are very heavy smokers and it's almost impossible to get away from it. Has a steep gangway in most ports.

Dining The dining rooms are set high up, and have good ocean views, but are extremely noisy. Friendly, efficient and bubbly Italian service throughout. Good Continental food, with some excellent pasta, although sauces are very heavy. Midnight pizza parties very popular. Poor selection of fruits and cheeses.

Other Comments This ship operates in four languages (announcements are long, loud and constant) and offers regular Mediterranean cruise service in very comfortable surroundings, with Italian flair, but no finesse in either food or service.

ms Azerbaydzhan ★★★

OPERATES
VARIOUS CRUISES

Cruise Line	CTC Cruise Lines		
Former Names	-		
Gross Tonnage	15,065		
Builder	Wartsila (Finland)		
Original Cost	$25 million		
Christened By	n/a		
Entered Service	Jan 1976		
Interior Design	Lloyd Werft		
Country of Registry	Ukraine		
Tel No	140-0740	Fax No	140-0740
Length (ft/m)			512.5/156.24
Beam (ft/m) 72.3/22.05	Draft (ft/m)		19.4/5.92
Propulsion		diesel (13,430kW)	
Propellers			2 (CP)
Decks	8	Crew	240
Pass. Capacity (basis 2) 460		(all berths) 635	
Pass. Space Ratio (basis 2) 32.7		(all berths) 23.7	
Officers			Ukrainian
Total Cabins			230
Size Range (sq ft/m)		150-428/14.0-39.7	
Outside Cabins	112	Inside Cabins	118
Single Cabins			0
Balcony Cabins	0	Wheelchair Cabins	0
Cabin Current			220 AC
Refrigerator		Boat deck cabins only	
Cabin TV Boat Deck cabins only		VCR	No
Dining Rooms	2	Sittings	1
Elevators			1

Casino	Yes	Slot Machines	Yes
Swimming Pools (outside) 1		(inside)	0
Whirlpools	0	Gymnasium	Yes
Sauna/Steam Room Yes/No		Massage	Yes
Self-Service Launderette			Yes
Movie Theater/Seats			Yes/145
Library			Yes
Children's Facilities			Yes
Watersports Facilities			None
Classification Society Ukraine Register of Shipping			

RATINGS	SCORE
Ship: Condition/Cleanliness	6.2
Ship: Space/Flow/Comfort	6.1
Ship: Decor/Furnishings	6.0
Ship: Fitness Facilities	4.7
Cabins: Comfort/Facilities	6.1
Cabins: Software	6.3
Food: Dining Room/Cuisine	5.8
Food: Buffets/Informal Dining	5.2
Food: Quality of Ingredients	5.4
Service: Dining Room	6.5
Service: Bars	7.1
Service: Cabins	7.2
Cruise: Entertainment	5.2
Cruise: Activities Program	5.7
Cruise: Hospitality Standard	6.7
OVERALL RATING	90.2

+ This smart-looking ship has a squared funnel housing. Suites and deluxe cabins are large and very nicely furnished, and have wood-paneled walls and cabinetry. Other cabins are small, have clean lines and are simply furnished, without much closet and drawer space, but they are quite adequate and comfortable. Smart, but quite basic, the ship provides a civilized way to get to and from Australia (once each way each year). Good for price-sensitive travelers. Good European itineraries.

— There are really too many inside cabins. The cabin insulation in general is poor. Has a steep, narrow gangway in most ports. Inflexible staff need more hospitality training.

Dining Has two rather plain, but cozy dining rooms; one is for smokers, the other for non-smokers. Attentive and friendly waitress service, but there's no real finesse. The cuisine is so-so, with limited choice, yet is presented nicely, and service comes with a smile.

Other Comments This ship has an informal, unpretentious ambiance. This ship, and CTC Cruises, will provide a good cruise experience for a modest price, principally for British and other European passengers. Has British (low-budget) entertainment, and Ukrainian crew show. Port taxes are included.

mv Bali Sea Dancer ★★★

OPERATES

3- AND 4-DAY INDONESIA CRUISES

Cruise Line	P&O Spice Island Cruises		
Former Names	Illiria		
Gross Tonnage	3,852		
Builder	Cantieri Navale Pellegrino (Italy)		
Original Cost	n/a		
Christened By	n/a		
Entered Service	1962		
Interior Design	n/a		
Country of Registry	Liberia		
Tel No	124-1440	Fax No	124-1441
Length (ft/m)			332.6/101.40
Beam (ft/m) 48.0/14.66		Draft (ft/m)	16.4/5.02
Propulsion			diesel (4,281kW)
Propellers			2 (FP)
Decks	4	Crew	90
Pass. Capacity (basis 2) 143		(all berths)	148
Pass. Space Ratio (basis 2) 26.9		(all berths)	26.0
Officers			British
Total Cabins			74
Size Range (sq ft/m)			n/a
Outside Cabins	64	Inside Cabins	10
Single Cabins			9
Balcony Cabins	0	Wheelchair Cabins	0
Cabin Current			220 AC
Refrigerator			No
Cabin TV	No	VCR	No
Dining Rooms	1	Sittings	Open
Elevators			0

Casino	No	Slot Machines	No
Swimming Pools (outside) 1		(inside)	0
Whirlpools	0	Gymnasium	No
Sauna/Steam Room No/No		Massage	No
Self-Service Launderette			No
Movie Theater/Seats:			No
Library	Yes	Children's Facilities	No
Watersports Facilities			None
Classification Society		American Bureau	
		of Shipping	

RATINGS	SCORE
Ship: Condition/Cleanliness	7.0
Ship: Space/Flow/Comfort	7.0
Ship: Decor/Furnishings	7.4
Ship: Fitness Facilities	3.6
Cabins: Comfort/Facilities	7.0
Cabins: Software	7.1
Food: Dining Room/Cuisine	7.0
Food: Buffets/Informal Dining	6.7
Food: Quality of Ingredients	7.0
Service: Dining Room	7.1
Service: Bars	7.0
Service: Cabins	7.3
Cruise: Lecturers	6.3
Cruise: Activities Program	4.6
Cruise: Hospitality Standard	7.1
OVERALL RATING	99.2

+ A real gem of a ship, used for cruises for nature-lovers. Quite small and compact, and ideal for her present operating area. The ship is very clean throughout and quite well maintained despite her age. Well equipped, and the limited number of public rooms have pleasing decor and fabrics, all recently refurbished. The main lounge has fluted columns, and there is a well-stocked reference library. There are some interesting works of art throughout. The cabins are reasonably spacious for the size of the ship, and have wood trim. All have private bathroom with shower, except two deluxe cabins, which have full bathtub. Fine, attentive, yet unobtrusive service from the all-Greek crew.

— The cabins have little closet and drawer space, and bathrooms are small.

Dining Has a charming dining room. The cuisine is centred on the Asian region, with some Indonesian specialities. Features open seating dining (you may sit where and with whom you like).

Other Comments This small ship will provide a very comfortable destination-oriented cruise experience for those seeking to get close to the natural, ecologically interesting world in the Indonesian islands.

mv Berlin ★★★★+

OPERATES

VARIOUS CRUISES WORLDWIDE

Cruise Line	Deilmann Reederei	Casino	No	Slot Machines	No
Former Names	Princess Mahsuri	Swimming Pools (outside) 1	(inside)	1
Gross Tonnage	9,570	Whirlpools	0	Gymnasium	Yes
Builder	Hawaldtswerke Deutsche	Sauna/Steam Room Yes/No	Massage	Yes
	Werft (Germany)	Self-Service Launderette	No
Original Cost n/a Christened By n/a	Movie Theater/Seats	Yes/330
Entered Service	Jun 1980	Library	Yes
Interior Design	HDW/Nobiskrug shipyard	Children's Facilities	On request
Country of Registry	Germany	Watersports Facilities	None
Tel No 112-0251 Fax No 112-0264	Classification Society	Germanischer Lloyd

Length (ft/m)	457.0/139.30
Beam (ft/m) 57.5/17.52 Draft (ft/m) 15.7/4.80

RATINGS	SCORE
Ship: Condition/Cleanliness	8.1
Ship: Space/Flow/Comfort	7.9
Ship: Decor/Furnishings	7.9
Ship: Fitness Facilities	6.8
Cabins: Comfort/Facilities	7.8
Cabins: Software	7.8
Food: Dining Room/Cuisine	8.0
Food: Buffets/Informal Dining	8.1
Food: Quality of Ingredients	7.8
Service: Dining Room	7.9
Service: Bars	7.8
Service: Cabins	7.7
Cruise: Entertainment	7.9
Cruise: Activities Program	7.8
Cruise: Hospitality Standard	8.0
OVERALL RATING	117.3

Propulsion	diesel (7,060kW)
Propellers	2 (CP)
Decks	8	Crew	180
Pass. Capacity (basis 2) 420	(all berths) 446
Pass. Space Ratio (basis 2) 22.6	(all berths) 21.3
Officers	German
Total Cabins	210
Size Range (sq ft/m)	93-192/8.6-17.8
Outside Cabins 157 Inside Cabins 53
Single Cabins	0
Balcony Cabins 0 Wheelchair Cabins 0
Cabin Current	220 AC
Refrigerator Promenade/Main Deck cabins only
Cabin TV Yes VCR No
Dining Rooms 2 Sittings 2
Elevators	2

+ Handsome contemporary ship, with crisp, clean all-white lines and well-balanced profile. Has an ice-strengthened hull. Star of the long-running German television show *Traumschiff* (Dream Ship). Very tidy throughout, this is a well-appointed ship with elegant, tasteful, though somewhat dark European decor. Beautiful collection of original oil paintings from the owner's personal collection. Cabins are small, but very comfortable and well equipped. Bathrooms have shower units, no bathtubs. Intimate, highly personable atmosphere.

— No forward observation lounge. Has a small swimming pool. Interior passageways are quite narrow.

Dining Lovely dining room has big picture windows, and several tables for two. Attentive, professional and correct European service with a smile. The food caters strictly to German tastes, with cream sauces accompanying entrees. Good selection of breads and cheeses.

Other Comments Stretched in 1986. This charming ship will provide a rather exclusive destination-intensive cruise experience in elegant, intimate, and contemporary surroundings for the discerning German-speaking passenger who doesn't need constant entertainment. Insurance and gratuities are included.

ms Black Prince ★★★+

Cruise Line	Fred Olsen Cruise Lines	Casino	Yes	Slot Machines No
Former Names	-	Swimming Pools (outside) 1		(inside) 1
Gross Tonnage	11,209	Whirlpools	2	Gymnasium Yes
Builder	Fender Werft (Germany)	Sauna/Steam Room Yes/No		Massage Yes
Original Cost	$20 million	Self-Service Launderette		No
Christened By	Lady Doris Denny	Movie Theater/Seats No		Library Yes
Entered Service	1966	Children's Facilities		Yes
Interior Design	Platou Design	Watersports Facilities		Zodiacs, windsurfers,
Country of Registry	Norway			waterski, banana boat
Tel No 131-3217	Fax No 131-3217	Classification Society		Det Norske Veritas
Length (ft/m)	470.4/143.40			
Beam (ft/m) 66.6/20.30	Draft (ft/m) 20.0/6.10	**RATINGS**		**SCORE**
Propulsion	diesel (12,310kW)	Ship: Condition/Cleanliness		7.2
Propellers	2 (CP)	Ship: Space/Flow/Comfort		7.2
Decks 7	Crew 200	Ship: Decor/Furnishings		7.3
Pass. Capacity (basis 2) 446	(all berths) 517	Ship: Fitness Facilities		6.1
Pass. Space Ratio (basis 2) 25.1	(all berths) 21.6	Cabins: Comfort/Facilities		6.6
Officers	European	Cabins: Software		6.8
Total Cabins	238	Food: Dining Room/Cuisine		7.2
Size Range (sq ft/m)	80-226/7.5-21.0	Food: Buffets/Informal Dining		6.6
Outside Cabins 168	Inside Cabins 70	Food: Quality of Ingredients		6.8
Single Cabins	30	Service: Dining Room		7.2
Balcony Cabins 0	Wheelchair Cabins 2	Service: Bars		6.9
Cabin Current	230 AC	Service: Cabins		7.2
Refrigerator	Upper grade cabins only	Cruise: Entertainment		7.4
Cabin TV Yes	VCR No	Cruise: Activities Program		6.4
Dining Rooms 2	Sittings 1	Cruise: Hospitality Standard		7.7
Elevators	2	**OVERALL RATING**		**104.6**

+ Well-maintained ship, and run with family pride. Good indoor fitness leisure center. Features a fine indoor swimming pool (unusual for a small ship). Life-size chess game is fun. Restrained decor and ambiance, with much of the soft furnishings hand tailored on board. Good wooden stairways. Outside suites are good (particularly Gran Canaria and Lanzarote, with their wood paneled walls). Other cabins are small, but well equipped and tastefully decorated. An ironing room is provided. Large number of single cabins. The two-level showlounge is quite pleasant.

— Often difficult to get away from smokers. Sadly, there is a charge for room service. Many cabins have poor air-conditioning. Entertainment is a low-cost, tightly budgeted affair.

Dining The two main dining rooms (both non-smoking) have big picture windows. First- and second-sitting diners sometimes exchange sittings, a good arrangement. Food is generally of high quality, but there should be more menu choice, particularly at buffet lunches.

Other Comments Solidly built white ship, converted to a full cruise ship in 1986, has a somewhat ungainly profile. Lots of repeat passengers who wouldn't dream of trying another vessel. Well suited to the informal British market, particularly for passengers of senior years. Currency aboard: UK Sterling (£). Recommended gratuities: UK£4.00 per passenger per day.

ms Black Watch

OPERATES

VARIOUS CRUISES WORLDWIDE

Cruise Line	Fred Olsen Cruise Lines		
Former Names	Star Odyssey/Westward/		
	Royal Viking Star		
Gross Tonnage	28,492		
Builder	Wartsila (Finland)		
Original Cost	$22.5 million		
Christened By	Mrs Thor Heyerdahl		
Entered Service	Jun 1972/Nov 1996		
Interior Design	Njal Eide		
Country of Registry	Bahamas		
Tel No 110-4507	Fax No	110-4554	
Length (ft/m)	674.1/205.47		
Beam (ft/m) 82.6/25.20	Draft (ft/m)	24.7/7.55	
Propulsion/Propellers	diesel (13,400kW)/2 (CP)		
Decks 8	Crew	325	
Pass. Capacity (basis 2) 832	(all berths) 927		
Pass. Space Ratio (basis 2) 34.2	(all berths) 30.7		
Officers	European		
Total Cabins	438		
Size Range (sq ft/m)	136-580/12.6-53.8		
Outside Cabins 390	Inside Cabins	48	
Single Cabins	44		
Balcony Cabins 9	Wheelchair Cabins	0	
Cabin Current	110/220 AC		
Refrigerator	Suites only		
Cabin TV Yes	VCR	No	
Dining Rooms 1	Sittings	1	
Elevators	5		

Casino	Yes	Slot Machines	Yes
Swimming Pools (outside) 2		(inside)	0
Whirlpools	2	Gymnasium	Yes
Sauna/Steam Room Yes/Yes		Massage	Yes
Self-Service Launderette			Yes
Movie Theater/Seats			Yes/156
Library			No
Children's Facilities			Yes
Watersports Facilities			None
Classification Society		Det Norske Veritas	

RATINGS	SCORE
Ship: Condition/Cleanliness	NYR
Ship: Space/Flow/Comfort	NYR
Ship: Decor/Furnishings	NYR
Ship: Fitness Facilities	NYR
Cabins: Comfort/Facilities	NYR
Cabins: Software	NYR
Food: Dining Room/Cuisine	NYR
Food: Buffets/Informal Dining	NYR
Food: Quality of Ingredients	NYR
Service: Dining Room	NYR
Service: Bars	NYR
Service: Cabins	NYR
Cruise: Entertainment	NYR
Cruise: Activities Program	NYR
Cruise: Hospitality Standard	NYR
OVERALL RATING	

+ This handsome ship has a sharply raked bow and distinctive lines. Has excellent open deck and sunning space, and a fine health-fitness spa high atop the ship. The interior decor is restful, having been made more attractive in a recent refit. Good materials, fabrics and soft furnishings, including the use of the Black Watch tartan, create a pleasant, warm ambiance. Spacious public rooms have high ceilings. Good cinema with a steeply tiered floor. The observation lounge high atop ship has commanding views and is very comfortable. Wide range of cabins, from spacious suites to small inside cabins. All are nicely equipped, and have good closet, drawer and storage space. Non-smoking cabins are also available.

— Some cabin bathrooms have awkward access, and the cabin drawers are tinny and noisy. The insulation between cabins is also poor.

Dining The dining room has a high ceiling and provides plenty of space at each table. Good cuisine, attractively presented, with an emphasis on seafood. Food quality is good, though menu choice is somewhat limited, particularly at the buffet lunches. Good range of wines. Communication with the Filipino waiters can occasionally prove frustrating.

Other Comments Stretched in 1981. Acquired by Fred Olsen Cruise Lines in late 1996, this ship will provide a good cruise experience, at a modest price. Not rated at press time.

ms Bolero ★★★+

OPERATES

7-DAY MEDITERRANEAN CRUISES

Cruise Line	Festival Cruises		
Former Names	Starward		
Gross Tonnage	16,107		
Builder	A.G. Weser (Germany)		
Original Cost	n/a		
Christened By	Ms Olga Mowinckel		
Entered Service	Dec 1968/Dec 1995		
Interior Design	Tage Wandborg/Michael		
	Katzourakis		
Country of Registry	Panama		
Tel No 135-4502	Fax No 135-4502		
Length (ft/m)	525.3/160.13		
Beam (ft/m) 74.9/22.84	Draft (ft/m) 20.4/6.22		
Propulsion/Propellers	diesel (12,950kW)/2 (CP)		
Decks 7	Crew 338		
Pass. Capacity (basis 2) 802	(all berths) 954		
Pass. Space Ratio (basis 2) 20.1	(all berths) 16.3		
Officers	Greek		
Total Cabins	401		
Size Range (sq ft/m)	111.9-324.0/10.4-30.1		
Outside Cabins 237	Inside Cabins 164		
Single Cabins	0		
Balcony Cabins 0	Wheelchair Cabins 2		
Cabin Current	110/220 AC		
Refrigerator	No		
Cabin TV No	VCR No		
Dining Rooms 1	Sittings 2		
Elevators	4		

Casino Yes	Slot Machines Yes
Swimming Pools (outside) 2	(inside) 0
Whirlpools 0	Gymnasium Yes
Sauna/Steam Room Yes/No	Massage Yes
Self-Service Launderette	No
Movie Theater/Seats	Yes/210
Library	Yes
Children's Facilities	No
Watersports Facilities	None
Classification Society	Det Norske Veritas

RATINGS	SCORE
Ship: Condition/Cleanliness	7.8
Ship: Space/Flow/Comfort	6.7
Ship: Decor/Furnishings	7.3
Ship: Fitness Facilities	5.9
Cabins: Comfort/Facilities	7.0
Cabins: Software	7.1
Food: Dining Room/Cuisine	7.6
Food: Buffets/Informal Dining	6.9
Food: Quality of Ingredients	6.2
Service: Dining Room	7.4
Service: Bars	7.2
Service: Cabins	7.2
Cruise: Entertainment	6.7
Cruise: Activities Program	6.3
Cruise: Hospitality Standard	7.5
OVERALL RATING	104.8

+ This ship has a modern, smart-looking upper profile with dual swept-back funnels. Good choice of public rooms with clean, modern furnishings and upbeat, cheerful decor throughout. Good balconied theater. Except for five good-sized suites, the cabins are quite compact units that are moderately comfortable, with bright, contemporary colors, and quite adequate for a one-week cruise.

— Has a less than handsome duck-tailed sponson stern. Reasonable open deck and sunning space, but this high-density vessel feels crowded when full. Noisy diesels are noticeable in some parts of the vessel. Cabin closet and drawer space are poor and metal drawers are tinny.

Dining Has a charming dining room, with some tables overlooking the stern. Reasonably good cruise food and menu choice, as on sister ship *The Azur*. Service comes with a smile. Has a limited selection of breads, fruits and cheeses.

Other Comments Formerly owned by Norwegian Cruise Line and acquired in 1995 by Festival Cruises (known in the USA as Azur-Bolero Cruises), the ship has a warm, friendly ambiance. Though not large, she is a good sized vessel for Mediterranean cruises, and is operated specifically for European passengers. Festival Cruises provides a well-tuned cruise experience in comfortable, though not elegant, surroundings, at a modest price.

ms Bremen ★★★★+

OPERATES

WORLDWIDE EXPEDITION CRUISES
(INCLUDING ANTARCTICA)

Cruise Line	Hapag-Lloyd Tours
Former Names	Frontier Spirit
Gross Tonnage	6,752
Builder	Mitsubishi Heavy Industries (Japan)
Original Cost	$42 million
Christened By	Mrs Kaoru Kanetaka/
	Mrs Wedemeier
Entered Service	Nov 1990/Nov 1993
Interior Design	Wilfried Kohnemann
Country of Registry	Bahamas
Tel No	110-3404	Fax No	110-3405
Length (ft/m)	365.8/111.51
Beam (ft/m) 55.7/17.00	Draft (ft/m)	15.7/4.80
Propulsion	diesel (4,855kW)
Propellers	2 (CP)
Decks	6	Crew	94
Pass. Capacity (basis 2) 164	(all berths) 184
Pass. Space Ratio (basis 2) 41.1	(all berths) 36.6
Officers	European
Total Cabins	82
Size Range (sq ft/m)	175-322/16.2-30.0
Outside Cabins	82	Inside Cabins	0
Single Cabins	0
Balcony Cabins	18	Wheelchair Cabins	2
Cabin Current	110 AC	Refrigerator	No
Cabin TV	Yes	VCR	Yes
Dining Rooms	1 (open seating)
Elevators	2

Casino	No	Slot Machines	No
Swimming Pools (outside) 1	(inside)	0
Whirlpools	0	Gymnasium	Yes
Sauna/Steam Room Yes/No	Massage	No
Self-Service Launderette			Yes
Lecture/Film Room:		Yes (seats 164)
Library	Yes	Zodiacs	12
Helicopter Pad			Yes
Watersports Facilities			None
Classification Society		Lloyd's Register

RATINGS	SCORE
Ship: Condition/Cleanliness	8.6
Ship: Space/Flow/Comfort	8.2
Ship: Expedition Equipment	8.5
Ship: Decor/Furnishings	8.3
Cabins: Comfort/Facilities	8.2
Cabins: Software	8.1
Food: Dining Room/Cuisine	8.1
Food: Buffets/Informal Dining	7.8
Food: Quality of Ingredients	8.0
Service: Dining Room	8.0
Service: Bars	8.2
Service: Cabins	8.0
Cruise: Itineraries/Operations	8.5
Cruise: Lecture Program	8.4
Cruise: Hospitality Standard	8.2
OVERALL RATING	123.1

+ This purpose-built expedition cruise vessel (ex-*Frontier Spirit*) has a handsome contemporary profile and the latest equipment. Its wide beam provides great stability, and long cruising range and ice-hardened hull give access to the most remote destinations. Zero-discharge waste handling and the highest ice classification make her usable anywhere. All equipment for in-depth marine and shore excursions provided. The all-outside cabins are spacious and well equipped. Some cabins also have a small balcony, a first on an expedition cruise vessel. Fine, well-planned destination-intensive itineraries, good documentation and port information. Soft drinks in refrigerators are replenished daily, at no charge.

— Has a steep gangway. The sauna is tiny. Cabins don't have much drawer space.

Dining Dining room is quite charming. Food is excellent, with high-quality ingredients, although it is highly salted. Good breads, pastries, cheeses and fruits. Service is very good, with bilingual (German- and English-speaking) waiters and waitresses immaculately dressed.

Other Comments This ship will provide you with an outstanding learning and expedition experience. Well-chosen itineraries and thoughtful passenger care are combined with a high degree of comfort. The ship's interiors were upgraded in late 1993. Caters principally to German-speaking passengers. Insurance, port taxes and gratuities are included.

mv Caledonian Star ★★★+

OPERATES

WORLDWIDE EXPEDITION CRUISES

Cruise Line	Noble Caledonia		
Former Names	North Star/Marburg/Lindmar		
Gross Tonnage	3,095		
Builder	A.G. Weser Seebeckwerft (Germany)		
Original Cost	n/a		
Christened By	Ms Barbro Svensson		
Entered Service	1966/1984		
Interior Design	Robert Tillberg		
Country of Registry	Bahamas		
Tel No	110-4706	Fax No	110-4766
Length (ft/m)	292.6/89.20		
Beam (ft/m) 45.9/14.00	Draft (ft/m) 20.3/6.20		
Propulsion	diesel (3,236kW)		
Propellers	1 (FP)		
Decks 6	Crew 60		
Pass. Capacity (basis 2) 120	(all berths) 150		
Pass. Space Ratio (basis 2) 25.7	(all berths) 20.6		
Officers	Scandinavian		
Total Cabins	61		
Size Range (sq ft/m)	192-269/17.8-25.0		
Outside Cabins 68	Inside Cabins 0		
Single Cabins	2		
Balcony Cabins	0		
Wheelchair Cabins	0		
Cabin Current	110/220 AC		
Refrigerator	All cabins		
Cabin TV Yes	VCR Yes		
Dining Rooms	1 (open sitting)		

Elevators			0
Casino	Yes	Slot Machines	Yes
Swimming Pools (outside)			1
Whirlpools	0	Gymnasium	No
Sauna/Steam Room	No/No	Massage	No
Self-Service Launderette			No
Lecture/Film Room	No	Library	Yes
Zodiacs	4	Helicopter Pad	No
Watersports Facilities			None
Classification Society		Det Norske Veritas	

RATINGS	SCORE
Ship: Condition/Cleanliness	7.2
Ship: Space/Flow/Comfort	5.6
Ship: Expedition Equipment	7.1
Ship: Decor/Furnishings	7.0
Cabins: Comfort/Facilities	5.8
Cabins: Software	6.0
Food: Dining Room/Cuisine	7.4
Food: Buffets/Informal Dining	6.7
Food: Quality of Ingredients	7.0
Service: Dining Room	7.4
Service: Bars	7.5
Service: Cabins	7.6
Cruise: Itineraries/Operations	7.5
Cruise: Lecture Program	7.6
Cruise: Hospitality Standard	7.5
OVERALL RATING	104.9

+ Reasonably handsome ship is extremely well maintained. Has an open-bridge policy. Warm, intimate ambiance. Good range of public rooms. The all-outside cabins are compact but comfortable, and decorated in warm, muted tones. All have minibar-refrigerator, VCR, and good closet and drawer space. Comfortable and unpretentious, with a casual dress code. Carries Zodiac landing craft for in-depth excursions, and an enclosed, contemporary shore tender. Fine lecture room/library also has videos for in-cabin use. Excellent lecturers on every cruise make this a real life-enrichment and learning experience for an intellectual clientele.

— Interior stairways are a little steep. Exterior stairway to Zodiac embarkation point is steep. Ceilings are plain. Noise from the diesel engines (generators) is irksome. Communication can sometimes prove frustrating.

Dining The dining room is small but charming, and chairs are quite small. European cuisine is slanted toward British tastes, with high-quality, very fresh ingredients, but not a lot of menu choice. Attentive and friendly service.

Other Comments This comfortable ship provides a well-tuned destination-intensive, soft expedition cruise experience, at a very reasonable price, and attracts many loyal repeat passengers, most of whom are British.

mv Calypso ★★★

OPERATES
VARIOUS CRUISES WORLDWIDE

Cruise Line	Transocean Tours		
Former Names	Sun Fiesta/Canguro Verde, Durr		
Gross Tonnage	8,000		
Builder	Fincantieri (Italy)		
Original Cost	n/a	Christened By	n/a
Entered Service	1968/Jun 1994		
Interior Design	A&M Katzourakis		
Country of Registry	Bahamas		
Tel No	130-6564	Fax No	130-6565
Length (ft/m)	425.0 ft/129.5		
Beam (ft/m)	63.0/19.2	Draft (ft/m)	17.7/5.4
Propulsion	diesel (7,790kW)		
Propellers	2 (CP)		
Decks	8	Crew	240
Pass. Capacity (basis 2) 502	(all berths) 618		
Pass. Space Ratio (basis 2) 15.9	(all berths) 12.9		
Officers	Greek/European		
Total Cabins	251		
Size Range (sq ft/m)	135-244/12.5-22.6		
Outside Cabins	158	Inside Cabins	93
Single Cabins	0		
Balcony Cabins	0		
Wheelchair Cabins	2		
Cabin Current	110 AC		
Refrigerator	No		
Cabin TV	Yes	VCR	No
Dining Rooms	1	Sittings	2
Elevators	2		

Casino	Yes	Slot Machines	Yes
Swimming Pools (outside) 1	(inside)		0
Whirlpools	1	Gymnasium	Yes
Sauna/Steam Room	No/No	Massage	Yes
Self-Service Launderette			No
Movie Theater/Seats			No
Library			Yes
Children's Facilities			No
Watersports Facilities			None
Classification Society		Lloyd's Register	

RATINGS	SCORE
Ship: Condition/Cleanliness	6.4
Ship: Space/Flow/Comfort	6.2
Ship: Decor/Furnishings	6.9
Ship: Fitness Facilities	5.5
Cabins: Comfort/Facilities	6.8
Cabins: Software	7.2
Food: Dining Room/Cuisine	7.3
Food: Buffets/Informal Dining	6.6
Food: Quality of Ingredients	6.8
Service: Dining Room	6.7
Service: Bars	6.4
Service: Cabins	6.9
Cruise: Entertainment	6.1
Cruise: Activities Program	5.8
Cruise: Hospitality Standard	6.4
OVERALL RATING	98.0

+ This ship was recently reconstructed, and features an enclosed promenade deck. Has a good number and range of public rooms for the size of the ship. The mostly outside cabins are quite attractive, with pastel colors, but the fabrics and soft furnishings could be of better quality. Cabin bathrooms have showers. No cabins have bathtubs. Some 66 cabins have double beds, while others are twins, with many featuring third and fourth berths.

— This high-density ship means it's really crowded when it's full, so expect long lines for embarkation, disembarkation, shore excursions and buffets. Expect a large number of smokers. Cabins are small, and barely adequate. Has steep, narrow outdoor deck stairways.

Dining The dining room, located aft, is attractive and well decorated. Good general standard of cuisine and service. Attractive buffets feature plenty of cheeses and cold cuts of meat. Has a limited room service menu and selection of fruits.

Other Comments This former Strintzis Line ferry was reconstructed in Greece, but her profile is not an attractive one. Regency Cruises has such a diverse fleet that it's hard to find consistency. This ship is under a five-year bareboat charter to Transocean Cruise Lines, so it carries a predominantly German-speaking clientele who strictly seek to travel to interesting and somewhat off-beat destinations in modest surroundings, at a low price.

tes Canberra ★★★

OPERATES
14-DAY EUROPE CRUISES

Cruise Line	P&O Cruises	Elevators	6
Former Names	-	Casino	Yes	Slot Machines	Yes
Gross Tonnage	44,807	Swimming Pools (outside) 3	(inside)	0
Builder	Harland & Wolff (UK)	Whirlpools	0	Gymnasium	Yes
Original Cost	UK£17,021,000	Sauna/Steam Room	No/No	Massage	Yes
Christened By	Dame Pattie Menzies, GBE	Self-Service Launderette		Yes
Entered Service	Jun 1961	Movie Theater/Seats		Yes/460
Interior Design	Sir High Casson/	Library	Yes	Children's Facilities Yes
	John Wright/Barbara Oakley	Watersports Facilities		None
Country of Registry	Great Britain	Classification Society		Lloyd's Register

Cruise Line		P&O Cruises
Former Names		-
Gross Tonnage		44,807
Builder		Harland & Wolff (UK)
Original Cost		UK£17,021,000
Christened By		Dame Pattie Menzies, GBE
Entered Service		Jun 1961
Interior Design		Sir High Casson/ John Wright/Barbara Oakley
Country of Registry		Great Britain
Tel No 144-0205	Fax No	144-0205
Length (ft/m)		818.5/249.49
Beam (ft/m) 102.5/31.25	Draft (ft/m)	32.2/9.84
Propulsion		turbo-electric (64,876kW)
Propellers		2 (FP)
Decks 10	Crew	860
Pass. Capacity (basis 2) 1,399	(all berths)	1,641
Pass. Space Ratio (basis 2) 32.0	(all berths)	27.3
Officers		British
Total Cabins		780 (236 without facilities)
Size Range (sq ft/m)		63-525/5.8-48.7
Outside Cabins 462	Inside Cabins	318
Single Cabins		161
Balcony Cabins 0	Wheelchair Cabins	0
Cabin Current		230 AC
Refrigerator	Categories AA/AB/AC/AD only	
Cabin TV Yes (upper grade cabins only)	VCR	No
Dining Rooms 2	Sittings	2

Elevators			6
Casino	Yes	Slot Machines	Yes
Swimming Pools (outside) 3	(inside)		0
Whirlpools	0	Gymnasium	Yes
Sauna/Steam Room	No/No	Massage	Yes
Self-Service Launderette			Yes
Movie Theater/Seats			Yes/460
Library	Yes	Children's Facilities	Yes
Watersports Facilities			None
Classification Society			Lloyd's Register

RATINGS	SCORE
Ship: Condition/Cleanliness	6.6
Ship: Space/Flow/Comfort	7.0
Ship: Decor/Furnishings	6.7
Ship: Fitness Facilities	6.1
Cabins: Comfort/Facilities	6.3
Cabins: Software	6.4
Food: Dining Room/Cuisine	6.1
Food: Buffets/Informal Dining	5.6
Food: Quality of Ingredients	6.0
Service: Dining Room	7.1
Service: Bars	7.2
Service: Cabins	7.3
Cruise: Entertainment	7.3
Cruise: Activities Program	6.6
Cruise: Hospitality Standard	7.1
OVERALL RATING	99.4

+ White ship has good open deck and sunning space, and British-style canvas deck chairs. Constant upgrading has changed some public rooms, added new features and decor. Popular favorites are the Crow's Nest Bar and Cricketer's Club. Lots of good wood paneling. Luxury suites are good, with heavy-duty wood furniture. Wide range and variety of other cabins to choose from. This is an excellent ship for families with children, who will discover all the nooks and crannies. Efficient, courteous service from Goanese stewards.

— Expect long lines for shore tenders, buffets and disembarkation. Some cabins share nearby bathroom facilities. Cabins on "B" Deck have obstructed views. There are simply too many repetitive announcements. Smokers seem to be everywhere.

Dining Atlantic (large) and Pacific (smaller) restaurants feature British and "colonial" cuisine. Good curries, plentiful meat, fish and desserts, but lacks lobster, shrimp and pasta dishes. Poor bread selection. Senior officers host tables nightly.

Other Comments Often dubbed the "great white whale," this ship is probably due for retirement soon. She will provide you with a cruise vacation package in very comfortable, though not elegant, surroundings, at an affordable price. All port taxes and insurance are included for British passengers. Allow about UK£3.00 per person, per day for gratuities.

ms Carina ★★

OPERATES
CARIBBEAN AND MEDITERRANEAN
CRUISES

Cruise Line			Phoenix Seereisen
Former Names			Ayvasovskiy
Gross Tonnage			7,127
Builder			Alsthom Atlantique
Original Cost			n/a
Christened By			n/a
Entered Service			1976/Apr 1996
Interior Design			n/a
Country of Registry			Ukraine
Tel No	140-1204	Fax No	140-1204
Length (ft/m)			398.6/121.50
Beam (ft/m)	57.4/17.50	Draft (ft/m)	14.7/4.50
Propulsion			diesel (7,650kW)
Propellers			2 (CP)
Decks	5	Crew	90
Pass. Capacity (basis 2) 168		(all berths) 300	
Pass. Space Ratio (basis 2) 42.4		(all berths) 23.7	
Officers			Ukrainian
Total Cabins			84
Size Range (sq ft/m)			n/a
Outside Cabins	84	Inside Cabins	0
Single Cabins			0
Balcony Cabins	0	Wheelchair Cabins	0
Cabin Current	220 AC	Refrigerator	No
Cabin TV	Yes	VCR	No
Dining Rooms	1	Sittings	1
Elevators			0
Casino	No	Slot Machines	Yes

Swimming Pools (outside)			1 (dip pool)
(inside)			1
Whirlpools	0	Gymnasium	No
Sauna/Steam Room Yes/No		Massage	No
Self-Service Launderette			No
Movie Theater/Seats			No
Library			No
Children's Facilities			No
Watersports Facilities			None
Classification Society			CIS

RATINGS	SCORE
Ship: Condition/Cleanliness	6.4
Ship: Space/Flow/Comfort	5.3
Ship: Decor/Furnishings	6.1
Ship: Fitness Facilities	4.0
Cabins: Comfort/Facilities	5.6
Cabins: Software	5.2
Food: Dining Room/Cuisine	6.2
Food: Buffets/Informal Dining	5.7
Food: Quality of Ingredients	5.6
Service: Dining Room	6.2
Service: Bars	6.3
Service: Cabins	6.1
Cruise: Entertainment	4.6
Cruise: Activities Program	4.6
Cruise: Hospitality Standard	6.4
OVERALL RATING	84.3

+ This attractive and well-proportioned small ship is now under charter to Phoenix Seereisen, the German cruise operator. A forward outdoor observation area overlooks the bridge. There is a small indoor saltwater pool, most unusual for a ship of this small size. The cabins are all outside, and are quite basic, although they all now have a television.

— Poor open deck space. No wrap-around outdoor promenade deck. Has only a limited amount of public rooms. Steep, narrow gangway in most ports. Cabins (except for four "suites") are small and spartan, with little closet and drawer space for a one-week cruise, and tiny bathrooms.

Dining Comfortable, almost attractive dining room has large picture windows and there are mostly tables for four. The food is adequate, but there's not much choice and it's highly salted. Limited bread, cheese, and fruit selection. The service, by Ukrainian waitresses, is pleasant, but it comes without any finesse.

Other Comments This ship provides German-speaking passengers with a casual cruise experience in friendly, unstuffy surroundings. If you don't expect much elegance and finesse from this cruise product, you might enjoy it. Refreshingly, tipping is not expected.

ms Carnival Destiny

OPERATES

7-DAY CARIBBEAN CRUISES

Cruise Line		Carnival Cruise Lines
Former Names		-
Gross Tonnage		100,000
Builder		Fincantieri (Italy)
Original Cost		$400 million
Christened By		n/a
Entered Service		Nov 1996
Interior Design		Joe Farcus
Country of Registry		Panama
Tel No	n/a	Fax No	n/a
Length (ft/m)		892.3/272.0
Beam (ft/m)	116.0/35.3	Draft (ft/m)	27.0/8.2
Propulsion		diesel-electric (63,400kW)
Propellers		2 (CP)
Decks	12	Crew	1,000
Pass. Capacity (basis 2) 2,642		(all berths) 3,350
Pass. Space Ratio (basis 2) 37.8		(all berths) 29.8
Officers		Italian
Total Cabins		1,321
Size Range (sq ft/m)		180-483/16.7-44.8
Outside Cabins	740	Inside Cabins	519
Single Cabins		0
Balcony Cabins	418	Wheelchair Cabins	25
Cabin Current	110 AC	Refrigerator Suites only
Cabin TV	Yes	VCR	No
Dining Rooms	2	Sittings	2
Elevators		13
Casino	Yes	Slot Machines	Yes

Swimming Pools (outside)		3 (1 with magrodome)
(inside)			1
Whirlpools	7	Gymnasium	Yes
Sauna/Steam Room Yes/Yes		Massage	Yes
Self-service Launderette			No
Movie Theater/Seats		1/1,040 (showlounge)
Library			Yes
Children's Facilities/Playroom:			Yes
Watersports Facilities			None
Classification Society		Lloyd's Register

RATINGS	SCORE
Ship: Condition/Cleanliness	NYR
Ship: Space/Flow/Comfort	NYR
Ship: Decor/Furnishings	NYR
Ship: Fitness Facilities	NYR
Cabins: Comfort/Facilities	NYR
Cabins: Software	NYR
Food: Dining Room/Cuisine	NYR
Food: Buffets/Informal Dining	NYR
Food: Quality of Ingredients	NYR
Service: Dining Room	NYR
Service: Bars	NYR
Service: Cabins	NYR
Cruise: Entertainment	NYR
Cruise: Activities Program	NYR
Cruise: Hospitality Standard	NYR
OVERALL RATING	NYR

+ This stunning new ship has the most balanced profile of all the ships in the Carnival fleet, even though the bow is extremely short. A retractable glass dome in three sections (magrodome) covers an aft swimming pool (one of four) and provides shelter in inclement weather conditions. Amidships is the longest water slide at sea (200ft in length), as well as tiered sunbathing decks between two pools and several hot tubs.

Inside the ship, Joe Farcus, the interior designer, has outdone himself. It is wonderfully grand, and a fantasy land for the senses. Like its smaller predecessors, this ship features a double-wide indoor promenade, a nine-deck-high glass-domed rotunda atrium lobby and an extensive Nautica Spa. The three-level showlounge is quite stunning, and features a revolving stage, hydraulic orchestra pit, and seating on three levels, with the upper levels tiered through two decks, as well as a proscenium over the stage that acts as a scenery loft. For those that like to gamble, the Millionaire's Club Casino is certainly the largest at sea.

Children are provided with good facilities, including their own outdoor pool, and are well cared for with "Camp Carnival", the line's extensive children's program.

Spread over four decks, over half of all outside cabins (which are, at 225 sq.ft./21m^2 the largest in the market) have private balconies, with glass rather than steel balustrades, for better, unobstructed ocean views. Balconies extend from the ship's side and feature bright fluorescent lighting. The standard cabins are a good size, and come equipped with all the basics, although the furniture is rather square and angular, with no rounded edges. Three decks of cabins (eight on each deck, each with private balcony) overlook the stern (with three days at sea on each of two alternating itineraries, vibration should be kept to a minimum).

From the viewpoint of safety, passengers will be able to embark directly into the lifeboats from their secured position without having to wait for them to be lowered, thus saving time in the event of a real emergency. Well done.

— This certainly is a big ship, with lots of people, and that means lines, particularly for shore excursions, buffets, embarkation and disembarkation (even though the Port of Miami has greatly improved terminal facilities specifically for this ship, with some 90 check-in desks). It also means a very impersonal cruise experience. For such as large ship, there really is not much open deck space per passenger, so on the three sea days, you can expect extreme crowding, and no privacy whatsoever. There are no cushioned deck chair pads.

In cabins with balconies, the partition between each balcony is open at top and bottom, so you will be able to hear noise from neighbors, or smell their smoke. In the mid-nineties, it is disappointing to see three categories of cabins (both outside and inside) which still have upper as well as lower bunk beds.

Dining The ship's two dining rooms (the Galaxy, forward, has 706 seats; the Universe, aft, has 1,090 seats) each span two decks (a first for any Carnival ship), and incorporate a dozen pyramid-shaped domes and chandeliers. The Universe dining room features a two-deck-high wall of glass overlooking the stern. There are tables for four, six and eight (and even a few tables for two). Dining room entrances have comfortable drinking areas for pre-dinner cocktails. The menus, which have been recently upgraded, feature a better selection than before, with more choices, and improved quality entree items.

There are also many casual dining options, particularly during the daytime. The two-deck-high Sun and Sea Restaurant, the ship's informal eatery, is adjacent to the aft pool and can be covered by a magrodome glass cover in inclement weather. Other places to eat include a trattoria (Italian cuisine), Happy Valley (Chinese cuisine), a 24-hour pizzeria, a patisserie and a grill (for fast food).

Other Comments Besides the shipyard, some 700 sub-contractors were involved in building *Carnival Destiny*. Presently the world's largest cruise ship, and Carnival's 11th new ship in the past 15 years, she is the first ship to be built that cannot transit the Panama Canal due to her size. She is destined to become the ultimate floating playground for young adults, for those that enjoy constant stimulation and close contact with others—a live board game with every move executed in typically grand, colorful Carnival style. Potential passengers should note that this is definitely an all-American experience and product, with all its attendant glitz.

ms Carousel ★★★+

OPERATES
7-DAY MEDITERRANEAN CRUISES

Cruise Line	Airtours Cruises	Casino	Yes	Slot Machines	Yes
Former Names	Nordic Prince	Swimming Pools (outside) 1	(inside)	0
Gross Tonnage	23,200	Whirlpools	0	Gymnasium	Yes
Builder	Wartsila (Finland)	Sauna/Steam Room Yes/No	Massage	Yes
Original Cost	$13.5 million	Self-Service Launderette	No
Christened By	Ms Ingrid Bergman	Movie Theater/Seats	No
Entered Service	Jul 1971/May 1995	Library	No
Interior Design	Njal Eide	Children's Facilities	No
Country of Registry	Norway	Watersports Facilities	None
Tel No 131-0547 Fax No	131-0547	Classification Society	Det Norske Veritas
Length (ft/m)	637.5/194.32		

Beam (ft/m) 78.8/24.03 Draft (ft/m)	21.9/6.70
Propulsion	diesel (13,400kW)
Propellers	2 (CP)
Decks 7 Crew	434
Pass. Capacity (basis 2) 1,062 (all berths)	1,200
Pass. Space Ratio (basis 2) 21.8 (all berths)	19.3
Officers	European
Total Cabins	531
Size Range (sq ft/m)	120-483/11.1-44.8
Outside Cabins 345 Inside Cabins	186
Single Cabins	0
Balcony Cabins 0 Wheelchair Cabins	0
Cabin Current	110 AC
Refrigerator	Owner's suite only
Cabin TV No VCR	No
Dining Rooms 1 Sittings	2
Elevators	4

RATINGS	SCORE
Ship: Condition/Cleanliness	7.5
Ship: Space/Flow/Comfort	6.6
Ship: Decor/Furnishings	7.0
Ship: Fitness Facilities	6.6
Cabins: Comfort/Facilities	5.8
Cabins: Software	7.7
Food: Dining Room/Cuisine	6.6
Food: Buffets/Informal Dining	6.3
Food: Quality of Ingredients	6.8
Service: Dining Room	6.6
Service: Bars	6.5
Service: Cabins	6.1
Cruise: Entertainment	7.6
Cruise: Activities Program	7.6
Cruise: Hospitality Standard	7.6
OVERALL RATING	102.9

+ Fairly smart, modish look with nicely raked bow. Polished outdoor wrap-around promenade deck and wooden railings. Good interior layout and passenger flow, with clean, bright decor. Good wooden paneling and trim. Casual dress code for unstuffy cruising. Very affordable for families with children. Good pre- and post-cruise hotel programs.

— Cabins are not assigned until you arrive at the ship. Expect lines for embarkation, disembarkation, buffets, and shore tenders. Open deck space for sunning is crowded and noisy. Passageways are narrow. Cabins are very small, with mediocre closets, and almost no storage space. Too many announcements. "Blue coat" social staff provide the entertainment.

Dining Good general dining room operation, although food all seems to taste the same. No tables for two. Limited selection of breads and fruits. Attentive, friendly but rather hurried dining room service that means you eat rather than dine.

Other Comments The ship, acquired by Airtours Cruises in 1995, will provide you with an activity-filled cruise product in comfortable, but noisy, surroundings. Airtours packages things well, and this ship is ideal for families on a limited budget. Currency is UK£ Sterling. Note that cabin voltage is 110 volts, so bring adapters. Tipping is recommended at UK£5.00 per day. Insurance is included (but you are charged for it unless you decline coverage).

ms Celebration ★★★★

OPERATES

7-DAY CARIBBEAN CRUISES
(YEAR-ROUND)

Cruise Line	Carnival Cruise Lines
Former Names	-
Gross Tonnage	47,262
Builder	Kockums (Sweden)
Original Cost	$135 million
Christened By	Ms Kathie Lee Gifford
Entered Service	Mar 1987
Interior Design	Joe Farcus
Country of Registry	Liberia (ELQX6)
Tel No 124-0526 Fax No	124-0526
Length (ft/m)	732.6/223.30
Beam (ft/m) 92.5/28.20 Draft (ft/m)	25.5/7.80
Propulsion	diesel (23,520kW)
Propellers	2 (CP)
Decks 10 Crew	670
Pass. Capacity (basis 2) 1,486 (all berths)	1,896
Pass. Space Ratio (basis 2) 31.8 (all berths)	24.9
Officers	Italian
Total Cabins	743
Size Range (sq ft/m)	185/17.1
Outside Cabins 453 Inside Cabins	290
Single Cabins	0
Balcony Cabins	10
Wheelchair Cabins	14
Cabin Current	110 AC
Refrigerator	Category 12 only
Cabin TV Yes VCR	No
Dining Rooms 2 Sittings	2

Elevators			8
Casino Yes	Slot Machines		Yes
Swimming Pools (outside) 3	(inside)		0
Whirlpools 2	Gymnasium		Yes
Sauna/Steam Room Yes/No	Massage		Yes
Self-Service Launderette			Yes
Movie Theater/Seats No	Library		Yes
Children's Facilities			Yes
Watersports Facilities			None
Classification Society		Lloyd's Register	

RATINGS	SCORE
Ship: Condition/Cleanliness	7.8
Ship: Space/Flow/Comfort	7.6
Ship: Decor/Furnishings	6.7
Ship: Fitness Facilities	7.8
Cabins: Comfort/Facilities	7.6
Cabins: Software	7.4
Food: Dining Room/Cuisine	6.7
Food: Buffets/Informal Dining	6.5
Food: Quality of Ingredients	5.3
Service: Dining Room	7.1
Service: Bars	7.2
Service: Cabins	6.4
Cruise: Entertainment	8.0
Cruise: Activities Program	7.8
Cruise: Hospitality Standard	6.7
OVERALL RATING	106.6

+ Double-width indoor promenades and good selection of public rooms. Colorful artwork. Nautically themed decor in Wheelhouse Bar-Grill. Features New Orleans-themed decor throughout the public rooms. Cabins, most of which are identical, are generously sized, very comfortable and well equipped. Especially good are ten suites with private balconies. Huge, very active, noisy casino. Party atmosphere good for anyone wanting a stimulating cruise experience. Wide range of entertainment and activities. Excellent for families with children.

— Swimming pools are small, but open deck space is quite good. Expect long lines for embarkation, disembarkation, buffets and shore tenders. Dining rooms cramped and noisy. Disappointing buffets. Nowhere to go for privacy and quiet. Too many announcements.

Dining The two dining rooms are cramped when full, and extremely noisy (both, however, are non-smoking). Quantity, not quality, prevails, and not much is spent on the food product.

Other Comments Flamboyant interior decor in public rooms is stimulating, not restful, except for the beautiful, and unused, Admiral's Library, the only quiet room aboard. This ship offers dazzle and sizzle for the whole family and provides a good choice for a first cruise, if you like lots of people, lots of noise, and lively action around you.

ms Century ★★★★+

OPERATES
7-DAY CARIBBEAN CRUISES

Cruise Line	Celebrity Cruises		
Former Names	-		
Gross Tonnage	70,606		
Builder	Meyer Werft (Germany)		
Original Cost	$320 million		
Christened By	Ms Christina Chandris		
Entered Service	Dec 1995		
Interior Design	Katzourakis/McNeece		
Country of Registry	Liberia (ELQX6)		
Tel No	36363-3911	Fax No	36363-3920
Length (ft/m)		807.1/246.00	
Beam (ft/m) 105.6/32.20	Draft (ft/m)	24.6/7.50	
Propulsion/Propellers	diesel (29,250kW)/2 (CP)		
Decks	10	Crew	843
Pass. Capacity (basis 2) 1,750	(all berths) 2,150		
Pass. Space Ratio (basis 2) 40.3	(all berths) 32.8		
Officers			Greek
Total Cabins			875
Size Range (sq ft/m)	172-1,515/15.7-140.7		
Outside Cabins	571	Inside Cabins	304
Single Cabins			0
Balcony Cabins	61	Wheelchair Cabins	8
Cabin Current		110/220 AC	
Refrigerator			Yes
Cabin TV	Yes	VCR Upper grades only	
Dining Rooms	2	Sittings	2
Elevators			9
Casino	Yes	Slot Machines	Yes

Swimming Pools (outside)			2
Swimming Pools (inside)		1 hydropool	
Whirlpools	4	Gymnasium	Yes
Sauna/Steam Room Yes/Yes	Massage	Yes	
Self-service Launderette			No
Movie Theater/Seats		Yes/190	
Library			Yes
Children's Facilities/Playroom:			Yes
Watersports Facilities			None
Classification Society		Lloyd's Register	

RATINGS	SCORE
Ship: Condition/Cleanliness	9.1
Ship: Space/Flow/Comfort	8.8
Ship: Decor/Furnishings	9.0
Ship: Fitness Facilities	9.1
Cabins: Comfort/Facilities	8.5
Cabins: Software	8.5
Food: Dining Room/Cuisine	8.2
Food: Buffets/Informal Dining	7.7
Food: Quality of Ingredients	7.9
Service: Dining Room	8.1
Service: Bars	8.0
Service: Cabins	7.8
Cruise: Entertainment	8.3
Cruise: Activities Program	7.9
Cruise: Hospitality Standard	7.9
OVERALL RATING	124.8

+ A well balanced, contemporary ship, despite its squarish stern with the distinctive Celebrity Cruises "X" funnel ("X" being the Greek letter "C," which stands for Chandris, the owning company). With a high passenger space ratio for such a large ship, there is no real sense of crowding, and passenger flow has been well thought out. There are 4.5 acres of open deck space. A high crew/passenger ratio of 1:9 provides excellent passenger service.

There is a three-quarter, bi-level teakwood promenade deck and for joggers, a wrap-around jogging track at the top of the ship. A two-level, 1,000 seat showlounge/theater with side balconies features a huge stage, a split hydraulic orchestra pit, and the latest in high-tech lighting and sound equipment. Many of the stunning public rooms have television or video screens, all connected to Sony electronics. The walls of the three-deck-high main foyer (atrium) are covered with nine large television screens which provide constantly changing scenery. An outstanding AquaSpa (9,340 sq ft/867.6m^2), set forward and high, has huge panoramic windows and the latest high-tech equipment, all set in a Japanese environment, complete with shoji screens and Japanese rock garden.

Wide passageways provide plenty of indoor space for strolling, and passenger flow is excellent. There is also a dedicated movie theater, which doubles as a conference and meeting center with all the latest audio-visual technology, as well as simultaneous translation in three languages, and headsets for the hearing-impaired. Michael's Club is a special triangular-shaped room that has become a favorite watering place for those who smoke, with decor reminiscent of a real English gentlemen's club. Several sizes of Cuban cigars are hand-rolled each day by a cigar maker.

Outstanding are the 500 pieces of art that adorn the ship. It is a $3.8 million art collection that includes many Warhol favorites and some fascinating contemporary sculptures. In fact, the *Century* collection includes a comprehensive survey of the most important artists and the major developments in art since the 1960s. It embraces Abstract Expressionism, Pop, Conceptualism, Minimalism and Neo-Expressionism.

A wide variety of cabin types includes 18 family cabins, each with two lower beds, two fold-away beds and one upper berth. All cabins have interactive television and entertainment systems (you can even go shopping interactively), as well as hairdryers in the bathrooms, and 100% cotton towels. All cabins also have a personal safe, mini-bar refrigerator and hairdryer and are nicely decorated, with warm wood-finish furniture and none of the "boxy" feel of cabins on many ships due to the placement of vanity and audio-video consoles at an angle. In addition, all suites (deck 10) feature butler service and in-cabin dining facilities.

The ultimate in accommodations aboard this ship are two beautifully decorated Presidential Suites of 1,173 sq ft (109m^2), located mid-ships in the most desirable position (can be combined with adjacent mini-suite to provide a total of 1,515 sq ft (140.7m^2) of living space). Each has a marble-floored foyer, living room with mahogany wood floor and hand-woven rug; separate dining area with six-seat dining table; butler's pantry with wet bar, wine bar with private label stock, refrigerator and microwave; huge private balcony with dining table for two, chaise lounge chairs with cushioned pads, hot tub and dimmer-controlled lighting; master bedroom with fine fabrics and draperies, Egyptian cotton bed linens, king-sized bed; all-marble bathroom with jet-spray shower and whirlpool bath; walk-in closet with abundant storage space. Interactive Sony audio and video facilities for booking shore excursions, ordering room service and purchasing goods from the ship's boutiques, so you don't have to leave your quarters if you don't wish to. Electrically operated blinds and other goodies are standard, with everything controlled from a special unit. Excellent medical facilities.

— Expect some lines for embarkation, disembarkation, shore excursions, and informal buffet meals, although the staff do their best to minimize any discomfort, and embarkation is staggered. Disembarkation is the one weak link in the Celebrity operation. The dining room chairs should, but do not, have armrests. The suites have three remotes for television/audio equipment, where one would be better. There are no cabins for singles.

Dining A grand staircase connects the upper and lower levels of the two-level dining room, each level with its own finishing galley. The design of the two galleys is excellent, and is such that food that should be hot *does* arrive hot at the table. Three different decorative panels, changed according to theme nights, adorn the huge aft windows.

There is also a huge indoor/outdoor lido café, called "Islands", with four well-designed serving stations, as well as two grill serving stations located adjacent to the swimming pools.

An in-suite dining alternative is featured for the two Presidential and 48 Century suites. Celebrity Cruises has established an enviable reputation for fine dining aboard its ships, and this tradition is being continued on this ship. Michel Roux, whose design of Celebrity Cruises' menus and tight control over their correct cooking and delivery, will assure consistency of product. All meals are made from scratch, with nothing pre-cooked or pre-packaged ashore. However, the standard 24-hour cabin menu is very disappointing and extremely limited.

Other Comments This new large ship for Celebrity Cruises (almost 50% larger than *Horizon/Zenith*) provides a fine mix of contemporary features. Her interior is really stunning, not only from a passenger facilities point of view, but also from the standpoint of technical and engineering excellence, and the over-indulgence of fire and safety equipment. Overall, she is a fine ship for a big-ship cruise vacation.

ss Constitution ★★★

OPERATES

*7-DAY HAWAII CRUISES
(YEAR-ROUND)*

Cruise Line	American Hawaii Cruises		
Former Names	Oceanic Constitution		
Gross Tonnage	30,090		
Builder	Bethlehem Shipbuilders (USA)		
Original Cost	$20 million		
Christened By	Mrs Charles Bey		
Entered Service	Jun 1951/Jun 1982		
Interior Design	Henry Dreyfuss		
Country of Registry	USA		
Tel No	-	Fax No	-
Length (ft/m)			681.7/207.80
Beam (ft/m) 88.9/27.10	Draft (ft/m)		30.1/9.20
Propulsion	steam turbine (40,456kW)		
Propellers			2 (FP)
Decks	9	Crew	315
Pass. Capacity (basis 2) 796	(all berths) 1,004		
Pass. Space Ratio (basis 2) 37.8	(all berths) 29.9		
Officers	American		
Total Cabins	398		
Size Range (sq ft/m)	75-410/7.0-38.0		
Outside Cabins	179	Inside Cabins	219
Single Cabins			9
Balcony Cabins	0	Wheelchair Cabins	0
Cabin Current			110 AC
Refrigerator	Category 0/AA/A only		
Cabin TV	No	VCR	No
Dining Rooms	2	Sittings	2
Elevators			4

Casino	No	Slot Machines	No
Swimming Pools (outside) 2	(inside)		0
Whirlpools	0	Gymnasium	Yes
Sauna/Steam Room Yes/No	Massage		Yes
Self-Service Launderette			Yes
Movie Theater/Seats			Yes/144
Library	Yes	Children's Facilities	Yes
Watersports Facilities			None
Classification Society	American Bureau		
	of Shipping		

RATINGS	SCORE
Ship: Condition/Cleanliness	6.2
Ship: Space/Flow/Comfort	6.8
Ship: Decor/Furnishings	6.1
Ship: Fitness Facilities	5.8
Cabins: Comfort/Facilities	6.2
Cabins: Software	7.0
Food: Dining Room/Cuisine	6.3
Food: Buffets/Informal Dining	6.1
Food: Quality of Ingredients	6.4
Service: Dining Room	6.6
Service: Bars	6.7
Service: Cabins	6.4
Cruise: Entertainment	6.0
Cruise: Activities Program	6.2
Cruise: Hospitality Standard	6.4
OVERALL RATING	95.2

+ American-built, registered and crewed, this ship has expansive open deck space and two freshwater swimming pools. Wrap-around outdoor promenade deck. Public areas are spacious, with high ceilings. Varied range of cabin types and configurations, most of which offer ample room, decent closet and drawer space, and bright decor. Heavy-duty furniture and fittings are designed for unkind oceans. Some outside cabins have windows that open.

— Solidly constructed vessel is now over 40 years old and needs more than a facelift. Poor air-conditioning in several places. Awkward interior layout, with numerous dead-end passageways. Room service is slow. Showlounge is too small and always crowded. Drinks prices excessive. No stabilizers, so the ship rolls…and rolls. Public bathrooms are old.

Dining Two dining rooms are quite spacious, with well-spaced tables. Typically American-Polynesian food, but presentation and menu choice could be better. Poor bread selection. Good self-service buffet. Very expensive wine list (most are Californian). Service comes with a smile, but is slow and lacks finesse. First evening's dinner is buffet-style.

Other Comments Families with children cruise during the summer and other school holidays, otherwise passengers are 50+. Scheduled to return to service in April 1997 following an extended lay-up and refit, but this was canceled. The ship has now been withdrawn from service.

mv CostaAllegra ★★★+

OPERATES
7-13 DAY CARIBBEAN AND
MEDITERRANEAN CRUISES

Cruise Line			Costa Cruises
Former Names			Annie Johnson
Gross Tonnage			28,430
Builder		Mariotti Shipyards (Italy)	
Original Cost			$175 million
Christened By	Adrienne Greene, Cheryl Myerson,		
Dorothy Maitland, Bernice Rosmarin, Nancy Lian			
Entered Service			Dec 1992
Interior Design			Guido Canali
Country of Registry			Liberia (ELRB7)
Tel No	125-2216	Fax No	125-2217
Length (ft/m)			616.7/187.94
Beam (ft/m) 84.6/25.75		Draft (ft/m)	27.1/8.22
Propulsion/Propellers		diesel (19,200kW)/2 (CP)	
Decks	8	Crew	405
Pass. Capacity (basis 2) 810		(all berths) 1,066	
Pass. Space Ratio (basis 2) 35.1		(all berths) 26.6	
Officers			Italian
Total Cabins			405
Size Range (sq ft/m)			105-266/9.8-24.7
Outside Cabins	218	Inside Cabins	187
Single Cabins			0
Balcony Cabins			10
Wheelchair Cabins			8 (inside)
Cabin Current			110 AC
Refrigerator			Grand suites only
Cabin TV	Yes	VCR	No
Dining Rooms	1	Sittings	2

Elevators			4
Casino	Yes	Slot Machines	Yes
Swimming Pools (outside) 1		(inside)	0
Whirlpools	3	Gymnasium	Yes
Sauna/Steam Room Yes/Yes		Massage	No
Self-Service Launderette			No
Movie Theater/Seats			Yes/370
Library	Yes	Children's Facilities	Yes
Watersports Facilities			None
Classification Society			RINA

RATINGS	SCORE
Ship: Condition/Cleanliness	7.8
Ship: Space/Flow/Comfort	7.6
Ship: Decor/Furnishings	7.7
Ship: Fitness Facilities	6.6
Cabins: Comfort/Facilities	6.7
Cabins: Software	7.2
Food: Dining Room/Cuisine	6.8
Food: Buffets/Informal Dining	6.6
Food: Quality of Ingredients	6.6
Service: Dining Room	7.3
Service: Bars	7.2
Service: Cabins	6.8
Cruise: Entertainment	6.6
Cruise: Activities Program	6.5
Cruise: Hospitality Standard	6.5
OVERALL RATING	104.5

+ Slightly longer and larger than her sister ship *CostaMarina*, this ship enjoys better quality interior fit and finish. Has a high glass-to-steel ratio, with numerous glass domes and walls admitting light. Good outdoor deck and sunning space. Cushioned pads provided for outdoor lounge chairs. Interesting glass-enclosed stern. Surprisingly fine interior decor with restful colors and soft furnishings. Decks are named after famous Italian painters.

— Angular-looking ship. Upright funnel takes getting used to. No forward observation lounge. Nice domed decorative ceilings. There are many small inside cabins, and all cabins suffer from poor soundproofing. Expect long lines at buffets. Many pillars obstruct sightlines in showroom. Pompous attitude of officers should be addressed.

Dining The dining room is quite spacious and has window views on three sides, but there are no tables for two. Dinner is later when the ship operates in Europe. The cuisine is mostly Continental with many Italian dishes featured, and generally excellent service from a bubbly staff. Good fresh pasta dishes served daily. Fruit and cheese selection is poor.

Other Comments This ship will provide a good first cruise experience for young adults who enjoy European service and a real upbeat, elegant atmosphere with an Italian accent.

mv CostaClassica ★★★★

OPERATES

*7-DAY CARIBBEAN AND
EUROPE CRUISES*

Cruise Line	Costa Cruises	Elevators		8
Former Names	-	Casino	Yes	Slot Machines	Yes
Gross Tonnage	52,950	Swimming Pools (outside) 2	(inside)	0
Builder	Fincantieri (Italy)	Whirlpools	4	Gymnasium	Yes
Original Cost	$325 million	Sauna/Steam Room Yes/Yes	Massage	Yes
Christened By	Emilia Costa Viganego/	Self-Service Launderette		No
	Angie Dickenson	Movie Theater/Seats		Yes/577
Entered Service	Jan 1992	Library	Yes	Children's Facilities	Yes
Interior Design	Gregotti Associates	Watersports Facilities		None
Country of Registry	Liberia (ELRB9)	Classification Society		RINA
Tel No 125-2234 Fax No 125-2244				
Length (ft/m)	718.5/220.61	**RATINGS**		**SCORE**
Beam (ft/m) 98.4/30.8 Draft (ft/m) 25.0/7.60		Ship: Condition/Cleanliness		8.0
Propulsion	diesel (22,800kW)	Ship: Space/Flow/Comfort		8.0
Propellers	2 (CP)	Ship: Decor/Furnishings		8.1
Decks 10 Crew 590		Ship: Fitness Facilities		8.2
Pass. Capacity (basis 2) 1,308 (all berths) 1,766		Cabins: Comfort/Facilities		8.0
Pass. Space Ratio (basis 2) 40.4 (all berths) 29.9		Cabins: Software		8.0
Officers	Italian	Food: Dining Room/Cuisine		7.2
Total Cabins	654	Food: Buffets/Informal Dining		6.4
Size Range (sq ft/m) 185-430/17.2-40.0		Food: Quality of Ingredients		6.5
Outside Cabins 438 Inside Cabins 216		Service: Dining Room		7.7
Single Cabins	0	Service: Bars		7.6
Balcony Cabins	10	Service: Cabins		7.8
Wheelchair Cabins	6 (inside)	Cruise: Entertainment		6.7
Cabin Current 110 AC Refrigerator Suites only		Cruise: Activities Program		7.1
Cabin TV Yes VCR No		Cruise: Hospitality Standard		7.2
Dining Rooms 1 Sittings 2		**OVERALL RATING**		**112.5**

+ Contemporary, innovative Italian design. Good business and conference facilities. Has fascinating artwork, including six hermaphrodite statues in one lounge. Fine multi-tiered amphitheater-style showroom. Cabins are generously sized and have cherrywood veneered cabinetry, useful sliding doors to bathroom and closets, and good cabin soundproofing.

— The interior is best described as an innovative design project that almost works. Forward observation lounge/nightclub sits atop ship like a lump of cheese, and fails as a nightclub. Multi-level atrium is stark, angular and cold. Poor informal buffet area. Indifferent service. Uncarpeted, marble-covered staircases are institutional. Long lines for embarkation, disembarkation shore tenders, and buffets.

Dining Dining room has a lovely, indented white ceiling, but is noisy. Good number of tables for two. Changeable wall panels create a European Renaissance atmosphere, albeit at the expense of blocking windows. Dinner on European cruises is late. Reasonable Continental cuisine, with many Italian (salty) dishes, but presentation, quality, and service are poor. Alfresco Café (outdoors) is good. Steep charge for lounge afternoon tea should stop. Breakfast and luncheon buffets are poor, and long lines mean crowding. Poor bread rolls and fruit.

Other Comments This ship has brought Costa into the mainstream—Italian-style.

mv CostaMarina ★★★+

Cruise Line	Costa Cruises	Casino	Yes	Slot Machines	Yes
Former Names	Axel Johnson	Swimming Pools (outside) 1	(inside)	0
Gross Tonnage	25,441	Whirlpools	3	Gymnasium	Yes
Builder	Marriotti Shipyards (Italy)	Sauna/Steam Room Yes/Yes	Massage	Yes
Original Cost	$130 million	Self-Service Launderette	No
Christened By	Ersiliaa Bracaloni Pitorri/	Movie Theater/Seats	Yes/442
	Annette Funicello	Library	Yes
Entered Service	Jul 1990	Children's Facilities	Yes
Interior Design	Guido Canali	Watersports Facilities	None
Country of Registry	Liberia (ELRB2)	Classification Society	RINA

Tel No	125-2245	Fax No	125-2246
Length (ft/m)			571.8/174.25
Beam (ft/m) 84.6/25.75	Draft (ft/m)	26.1/8.20
Propulsion		diesel (19,152kW)
Propellers		2 (CP)
Decks	8	Crew	390
Pass. Capacity (basis 2) 772	(all berths) 1,025
Pass. Space Ratio (basis 2) 31.8	(all berths) 24.0
Officers		Italian
Total Cabins		386
Size Range (sq ft/m)	104-258/9.7-24.6
Outside Cabins	183	Inside Cabins	203
Single Cabins			14
Balcony Cabins 0	Wheelchair Cabins 8 (inside)
Cabin Current 110 AC	Refrigerator	No
Cabin TV	Yes	VCR	No
Dining Rooms	1	Sittings	2
Elevators			4

RATINGS	SCORE
Ship: Condition/Cleanliness	7.8
Ship: Space/Flow/Comfort	7.6
Ship: Decor/Furnishings	7.7
Ship: Fitness Facilities	6.6
Cabins: Comfort/Facilities	6.7
Cabins: Software	7.2
Food: Dining Room/Cuisine	6.8
Food: Buffets/Informal Dining	6.6
Food: Quality of Ingredients	6.6
Service: Dining Room	7.3
Service: Bars	7.2
Service: Cabins	6.8
Cruise: Entertainment	6.6
Cruise: Activities Program	6.5
Cruise: Hospitality Standard	6.5
OVERALL RATING	104.5

+ High glass-to-steel ratio, with numerous glass domes and walls. Good passenger flow throughout her public room spaces. There are some well-stocked boutiques for shopping. The outside cabins are quite comfortable, yet plain. The illuminated cabin numbers are novel.

— Fit and finish is below the standard of competing ships in same price category. Very limited open deck and sunning space. There's no forward observation lounge. Has tiny swimming pool. Simply too many inside cabins. Poor sightlines in showroom with too many (14) pillars. Poor library.

Dining The dining room, located aft, has ocean views on three sides, is reasonably spacious, and reached by escalator. Awful lime green (institutional) color. There are only two tables for two. Table candle lights are poor quality. Good pasta, Continental cuisine, and bubbly service.

Other Comments Interesting, angular looking mid-sized ship. Has a cutaway stern replaced virtually by glass wall, and stark upright funnel cluster. Most public rooms located above accommodation decks. This very Italian ship will provide a good first cruise experience for young adults, but is much better suited to European passengers.

ms CostaPlaya ★★★+

OPERATES
7-DAY CARIBBEAN
(INCLUDING CUBA) CRUISES

Cruise Line			Costa Cruises
Former Names			Pearl/Ocean Pearl/
		Pearl of Scandinavia/Finnstar
Gross Tonnage			12,475
Builder			Wartsila (Finland)
Original Cost			n/a
Christened By		HRH Princess Galyani Vadhana
Entered Service			May 1967/Nov 1995
Interior Design			A&M Katzourakis
Country of Registry			Bahamas
Tel No	110-5351	Fax No	130-5352
Length (ft/m)			517.4/157.7
Beam (ft/m)	65.9/20.10	Draft (ft/m)	19.0/5.80
Propulsion			diesel (12,060kW)
Propellers			2 (CP)
Decks	9	Crew	232
Pass. Capacity (basis 2) 489			(all berths) 739
Pass. Space Ratio (basis 2) 25.5			(all berths) 16.8
Officers			British
Total Cabins			250
Size Range (sq ft/m)			n/a
Outside Cabins	188	Inside Cabins	62
Single Cabins			11
Balcony Cabins	0	Wheelchair Cabins	6
Cabin Current			110/220 AC
Refrigerator			No
Cabin TV	No	VCR	No
Dining Rooms	1	Sittings	2

Elevators			2
Casino	Yes	Slot Machines	Yes
Swimming Pools (outside) 1		(inside)	1
Whirlpools	0	Gymnasium	Yes
Sauna/Steam Room	Yes/No	Massage	Yes
Self-Service Launderette			No
Movie Theater/Seats			Yes/62
Library	Yes	Children's Facilities	No
Watersports Facilities			None
Classification Society			Bureau Veritas

RATINGS	SCORE
Ship: Condition/Cleanliness	6.7
Ship: Space/Flow/Comfort	5.9
Ship: Decor/Furnishings	7.1
Ship: Fitness Facilities	5.7
Cabins: Comfort/Facilities	7.0
Cabins: Software	7.2
Food: Dining Room/Cuisine	7.0
Food: Buffets/Informal Dining	6.6
Food: Quality of Ingredients	6.6
Service: Dining Room	7.4
Service: Bars	7.1
Service: Cabins	7.1
Cruise: Entertainment	6.6
Cruise: Activities Program	6.4
Cruise: Hospitality Standard	7.3
OVERALL RATING	101.7

+ Mildly attractive profile. Tasteful decor includes many earth tones, and some interesting artwork. Lovely refinished woods give much warmth. Indonesian and Filipino hotel staff provide personal service with a smile, although standards have declined. Explorer Deck cabins (called "suites" by the line) are quite spacious, with lots of wood paneling and portholes that open. Other cabins are quite roomy and well equipped, with lots of closet, drawer and storage space. Top-price accommodations have bathtubs, others have showers.

— Awkward layout with some dead-end passageways. Too many announcements. Ship could be cleaner. Cabin soft furnishings worn, and air-conditioning controls not clearly calibrated.

Dining The dining room is very attractive, set high in the ship and located forward, with excellent ocean views. The food is quite creative, but presentation is uninspiring. Breads and pastry items are poor, and there's a limited selection of cheeses and fruits.

Other Comments Originally built as a ferry, this ship was reconstructed in 1988 as a cruise vessel. After sailing for 12 years in the Far East, the ship was repositioned to the Caribbean area in September 1995, operating seven-day cruises. This ship provides a low-cost way for European passengers (mainly German and Italian) to experience the Caribbean and Cuba.

ss CostaRiviera ★★★★

OPERATES
7-DAY CARIBBEAN AND
MEDITERRANEAN CRUISES

Cruise Line	Costa Cruises
Former Names	American Adventure/
	CostaRiviera/Guglielmo Marconi
Gross Tonnage	31,500
Builder	Cantieri Riuniti dell' Adriatico (Italy)
Original Cost	$33.7 million (reconstruction)
Christened By	Ms Connie Stevens/4 children
Entered Service	Nov 1963/Dec 1993
Interior Design	Jeffrey Howard
Country of Registry	Liberia (ELRB6)

Tel No	125-2212	Fax No	125-2215
Length (ft/m)			700.9/213.65
Beam (ft/m)	94.1/28.71	Draft (ft/m)	28.3/8.65
Propulsion		steam turbine (32,800kW)
Propellers			2 (FP)
Decks	8	Crew	654
Pass. Capacity (basis 2) 924		(all berths) 1,500
Pass. Space Ratio (basis 2) 34.0		(all berths) 21.0
Officers			Italian
Total Cabins			462
Size Range (sq ft/m)			150-210/14.0-19.5
Outside Cabins	286	Inside Cabins	176
Single Cabins			0
Balcony Cabins	0	Wheelchair Cabins	0
Cabin Current			110/220 AC
Refrigerator			No
Cabin TV	No	VCR	No
Dining Rooms	1	Sittings	2

Elevators			7
Casino	Yes	Slot Machines	Yes
Swimming Pools (outside) 3		(inside)	0
Whirlpools		3	Gymnasium Yes
Sauna/Steam Room Yes/No		Massage	Yes
Self-Service Launderette			Yes
Movie Theater/Seats			Yes/186
Library	Yes	Children's Facilities	No
Watersports Facilities			None
Classification Society			RINA

RATINGS	SCORE
Ship: Condition/Cleanliness	8.0
Ship: Space/Flow/Comfort	7.4
Ship: Decor/Furnishings	7.6
Ship: Fitness Facilities	6.2
Cabins: Comfort/Facilities	7.2
Cabins: Software	7.3
Food: Dining Room/Cuisine	7.2
Food: Buffets/Informal Dining	6.6
Food: Quality of Ingredients	6.7
Service: Dining Room	7.4
Service: Bars	7.5
Service: Cabins	7.4
Cruise: Entertainment	7.4
Cruise: Activities Program	7.3
Cruise: Hospitality Standard	7.5
OVERALL RATING	108.7

+ Solidly built ship is stable at sea and rides well, owing to her deep draft. Built-up fore and aft decks provide a good amount of open deck and sunning space. The interior styling, colors, appointments, and everything else is geared to families. Good array of public rooms. The cabins are for cozy families. Many cabins are for families of five or six, and many others will accommodate four. Has a very casual, bubbly ambiance and relaxed dress code.

— The ship lacks a forward observation lounge. Cabin insulation is not good, and bathrooms are very small. Expect lines for embarkation, disembarkation, buffets, and shore excursions. Too many announcements.

Dining Dining room is large and bubbly, but quite plain and unattractive, especially the ceiling. Good Continental food, with plentiful pasta, pizza, buffets. Good service from an international staff comes with a smile, but this is not for those who like quiet dining.

Other Comments Reconstructed former three-class ocean liner completely refurbished in 1993 in theme-park style for families, then refurbished again for Italian family cruising in 1994. This ship will cruise you in comfortable family-filled surroundings for a modest price, and is lots of fun. Think of this as a colorful, activity-filled ship, particularly catering to an Italian family clientele.

mv CostaRomantica ★★★★+

Cruise Line			Costa Cruises
Former Names			-
Gross Tonnage			53,049
Builder			Fincantieri (Italy)
Original Cost			$325 million
Christened By		Maria Alessandra Fantoni Costa	
Entered Service			Nov 1993
Interior Design			Gregotti Associates
Country of Registry			Liberia (ELRB8)
Tel No	115-2232	Fax No	115-2231
Length (ft/m)			718.5/220.61
Beam (ft/m)	98.4/30.89	Draft (ft/m)	25.0/7.60
Propulsion			diesel (22,800kW)
Propellers			2 (CP)
Decks	10	Crew	600
Pass. Capacity (basis 2) 1,356		(all berths) 1,782	
Pass. Space Ratio (basis 2) 39.1		(all berths) 29.7	
Officers			Italian
Total Cabins			678
Size Range (sq ft/m)			185-430/17.2-40.0
Outside Cabins	462	Inside Cabins	216
Single Cabins			0
Balcony Cabins			10
Wheelchair Cabins			6 (inside)
Cabin Current			110 AC
Refrigerator			Suites/Mini-suites only
Cabin TV	Yes	VCR	No
Dining Rooms	1	Sittings	2

Elevators			8
Casino	Yes	Slot Machines	Yes
Swimming Pools (outside) 2		(inside)	0
Whirlpools		4	Gymnasium Yes
Sauna/Steam Room Yes/No		Massage	Yes
Self-Service Launderette			No
Movie Theater/Seats			Yes/626
Library	Yes	Children's Facilities	Yes
Watersports Facilities			None
Classification Society			RINA

RATINGS	SCORE
Ship: Condition/Cleanliness	8.4
Ship: Space/Flow/Comfort	8.4
Ship: Decor/Furnishings	8.6
Ship: Fitness Facilities	8.2
Cabins: Comfort/Facilities	8.2
Cabins: Software	8.0
Food: Dining Room/Cuisine	7.5
Food: Buffets/Informal Dining	6.6
Food: Quality of Ingredients	6.6
Service: Dining Room	7.6
Service: Bars	7.3
Service: Cabins	7.6
Cruise: Entertainment	7.9
Cruise: Activities Program	7.6
Cruise: Hospitality Standard	7.6
OVERALL RATING	116.1

+ Sister ship to *CostaClassica*, but with better interior design. Excellent business and conference facilities. Decor is tasteful, and will appeal to both Europeans and sophisticated North Americans. Multi-level atrium is open and spacious, with a revolving mobile sculpture. Good amphitheater-style two-deck-high, multi-tiered showroom, and has interesting artwork. Also has a small chapel (in a different location to that on her sister ship). Apart from 16 suites and 18 mini-suites, which are superb, almost all cabins are of a generous size, with nicely finished cherrywood cabinetry. Good number of triple and quad cabins, ideal for families.

— Layout and flow somewhat disjointed. Showroom has stark upright seating, and sightlines are interrupted by 10 large pillars. Cabin bathrooms and showers are small. Expect long lines for embarkation, disembarkation, shore tenders, and buffets.

Dining Dining room is better designed and a little less noisy than on *CostaClassica*, with many tables for two. Reasonable Continental cuisine, but presentation, quality, and service need more attention. Poor selection of bread rolls and fruits. However, pastas are fine. Much improved and more practical buffet layout than on her sister ship.

Other Comments Bold, contemporary ship has upright funnel cluster typical of Italian styling today. Well established in Europe, Costa goes cruising Italian-style, something it does well.

ms CostaVictoria

Cruise Line	Costa Cruises		
Former Names	-		
Gross Tonnage	74,000		
Builder	Bremer Vulkan (Germany)		
Original Cost	$350 million		
Christened By	n/a		
Entered Service	July 1996		
Interior Design	Gregotti Associates/Robert Tillberg		
Country of Registry	Liberia		
Tel No	n/a	Fax No	n/a
Length (ft/m)	823.0/251.0		
Beam (ft/m) 105.5/32.25	Draft (ft/m) 25.6/7.80		
Propulsion/Propellers	diesel (30,000kW)/2 (CP)		
Decks	14	Crew	780
Pass. Capacity (basis 2) 1,950	(all berths) 2,250		
Pass. Space Ratio (basis 2) 37.9	(all berths) 32.8		
Officers	Italian		
Total Cabins	965		
Size Range (sq ft/m)	150-721/15.0-67.0		
Outside Cabins	625	Inside Cabins	340
Single Cabins	0		
Balcony Cabins	6		
Wheelchair Cabins	6		
Cabin Current	110/220 AC		
Refrigerator	Yes		
Cabin TV	Yes	VCR	No
Dining Rooms	2	Sittings	2
Elevators	12		

Casino	Yes	Slot Machines	Yes
Swimming Pools (outside) 2	(inside)		1
Whirlpools	8	Gymnasium	Yes
Sauna/Steam Room Yes/No	Massage		Yes
Self-Service Launderette			Yes
Movie Theater/Seats			Yes/950
Library			Yes
Children's Facilities/Playroom			Yes
Watersports Facilities			None
Classification Society			RINA

RATINGS	SCORE
Ship: Condition/Cleanliness	NYR
Ship: Space/Flow/Comfort	NYR
Ship: Decor/Furnishings	NYR
Ship: Fitness Facilities	NYR
Cabins: Comfort/Facilities	NYR
Cabins: Software	NYR
Food: Dining Room/Cuisine	NYR
Food: Buffets/Informal Dining	NYR
Food: Quality of Ingredients	NYR
Service: Dining Room	NYR
Service: Bars	NYR
Service: Cabins	NYR
Cruise: Entertainment	NYR
Cruise: Activities Program	NYR
Cruise: Hospitality Standard	NYR
OVERALL RATING	

+ Where this ship differs from most of the 70,000+ grt ships is in her unusual European interior decor. It's modern without being too glitzy, and bold without being brash. The bridge, as is normal on this size ship today, is fully enclosed. There is an outdoor teakwood wrap-around promenade deck and jogging track.

Inside the ship is a multi-level forward-facing observation lounge; on one side of it is a small waterfall, while balconies open forward of the lounge. Altogether, it is a very stunning space.

A seven-deck-high atrium has four glass elevators that go right up to a crystal dome, set on the deck where two outside swimming pools, four blocks of showers, and an ice cream bar and grille are located. There is a large forward shopping gallery with ocean-view walls, set around one level of the atrium.

Most unusual for a new ship (and very welcome by European standards) is an indoor swimming pool, sauna, Turkish bath, and large gymnasium, as well as an adjacent indoor jogging track. There is also a tennis court and a solarium.

Accommodations consist of six large suites and 14 mini-suites, while some 65 per cent of all cabins are outside. Only 16 of the inside cabins accommodate four, while all other cabins are for two or three persons. There are six cabins for the physically challenged; all are well located, and are adjacent to the elevators in the center of the ship. Cabins feature wood cabinetry, with ample closet and drawer space. Six suites feature Laura Ashley fabrics.

The ship's bubbly staff will help passengers enjoy life Italian-style, which means the emphasis is very much on informality.

— None known at press time, although, as with any large ship, there will be lines for embarkation, disembarkation, and shore excursions.

Dining The two main dining rooms (Fantasia and Sinfonia) are expansive. There are very few tables for two, and most are for four, six or eight and feature marble and pine walls. The cuisine is good, basic fare. The presentation is also good, although garnishes to dress the plates are somewhat lacking. As you'd expect, there's always plenty of pasta.

The ship also features a two-deck-high al fresco-style café with indoor-outdoor seating (under sail-cloth canvas for the outdoor section). However, the buffet displays and variety of foods could be much more creative.

Other Comments The ship's exterior profile is similar to that of an enlarged version of the popular and very successful *CostaClassica* and *CostaRomantica*, and is one of a pair, the second (to be named *CostaOlympia*) being due for delivery in 1998. Costa Cruises now has a (mostly) contemporary fleet, operating in the Caribbean, Mediterranean, and South America, having replaced most of its older tonnage in the past five years. An additional informal dining area is available, and of course, there's the obligatory pizzeria.

mv Crown Princess ★★★★+

OPERATES

7-DAY ALASKA AND CARIBBEAN CRUISES

Cruise Line	Princess Cruises
Former Names	-
Gross Tonnage	70,000
Builder	Fincantieri Navali (Italy)
Original Cost	$276.8 million
Christened By	Ms Sophia Loren
Entered Service	Jul 1990
Interior Design	H. Chambers Company
Country of Registry	Italy
Tel No 115-0543 Fax No	115-0544
Length (ft/m)	804.7/245.30
Beam (ft/m) 105.8/32.26 Draft (ft/m)	26.5/8.10
Propulsion	diesel-electric (24,000kW)
Propellers	2 (CP)
Decks 11 Crew	696
Pass. Capacity (basis 2) 1,590 (all berths)	1,910
Pass. Space Ratio (basis 2) 44.0 (all berths)	36.6
Officers	Italian
Total Cabins	795
Size Range (sq ft/m)	190-575/17.6-53.4
Outside Cabins 624 Inside Cabins	171
Single Cabins	0
Balcony Cabins 184 Wheelchair Cabins	10
Cabin Current	110/220 AC
Refrigerator	All cabins
Cabin TV Yes VCR	No
Dining Rooms 1 Sittings	2
Elevators	9

Casino	Yes	Slot Machines	Yes
Swimming Pools (outside) 2		(inside)	0
Whirlpools	4	Gymnasium	Yes
Sauna/Steam Room Yes/No		Massage	Yes
Self-Service Launderette			Yes
Movie Theater/Seats			Yes/169
Library			Yes
Children's Facilities			No
Watersports Facilities			None
Classification Society			Lloyd's Register

RATINGS	SCORE
Ship: Condition/Cleanliness	8.0
Ship: Space/Flow/Comfort	7.8
Ship: Decor/Furnishings	7.9
Ship: Fitness Facilities	8.0
Cabins: Comfort/Facilities	8.1
Cabins: Software	8.2
Food: Dining Room/Cuisine	7.2
Food: Buffets/Informal Dining	7.0
Food: Quality of Ingredients	7.3
Service: Dining Room	7.4
Service: Bars	7.7
Service: Cabins	7.8
Cruise: Entertainment	8.1
Cruise: Activities Program	7.8
Cruise: Hospitality Standard	7.6
OVERALL RATING	115.9

+ Innovative styling mixed with traditional features, and spacious interior layout. Good swimming pool deck. An observation dome features large casino, dance floor and live music. Good health spa facilities. Strikingly elegant three-deck-high atrium features grand staircase with fountain sculpture (real, stand-up cocktail parties are held here). Understated pastel decor is highlighted by colorful artwork. Well-designed cabins have large bathrooms, good soundproofing, walk-in closets, refrigerator, safe, and interactive video system.

— No wrap-around outdoor promenade deck (the only walking space is along the sides of the ship). When full, there is not enough outdoor space, and little connection with outside. No non-enclosed forward viewing space. Too many pillars in public rooms obstruct sightlines. Internal layout somewhat disjointed. Cabins for the physically challenged have obstructed views. Expect lines for embarkation, disembarkation, buffets, shore excursions, and tenders.

Dining Large dining room lacks tables for two. Some interesting tables overlook the stern. Disappointing, stodgy cuisine, with poor creativity and presentation. Pasta dishes are good. Service is reasonable, but perfunctory. There is an excellent, but small, pizzeria.

Other Comments This ship provides a decent cruise environment in elegant and comfortable surroundings, with service by a lukewarm staff.

276

mv Crystal Harmony ★★★★★+

OPERATES
VARIOUS CRUISES WORLDWIDE

Cruise Line		Crystal Cruises
Former Names	-	Gross Tonnage 48,621
Builder	Mitsubishi Heavy Industries (Japan)
Original Cost		$240 million
Christened By		Ms Mary Tyler Moore
Entered Service		Jul 1990
Interior Design		Robert Tillberg
Country of Registry		Bahamas
Tel No	110-3237	Fax No	110-3234
Length (ft/m)		790.5/240.96
Beam (ft/m) 97.1/29.60	Draft (ft/m) 24.6/7.50
Propulsion		diesel-electric (32,800kW)
Propellers		2 (CP)
Decks 8	Crew 545	Total Cabins 480
Pass. Capacity (basis 2) 960	(all berths) 1,010
Pass. Space Ratio (basis 2) 50.6	(all berths) 48.9
Officers		Scandinavian/Japanese
Size Range (sq ft/m)		183-948/17.0-88.0
Outside Cabins 461	Inside Cabins 19
Single Cabins		0
Balcony Cabins		260
Wheelchair Cabins		4
Cabin Current		115/220 AC
Refrigerator		All cabins
Cabin TV Yes	VCR	Yes
Dining Rooms	3 (2 alternative restaurants)
Sittings	2 (dinner only, main restaurant)
Elevators		8

Casino	Yes	Slot Machines	Yes
Swimming Pools (outside)	2 (1 with magrodome)
(inside)			0
Whirlpools	2	Gymnasium	Yes
Sauna/Steam Room Yes/Yes	Massage	Yes
Self-Service Launderette		Yes
Movie Theater/Seats		Yes/270
Library	Yes	Children's Facilities Yes
Classification Society		Lloyd's Register/
		Nippon Kaiji Kyokai

RATINGS	SCORE
Ship: Condition/Cleanliness	9.1
Ship: Space/Flow/Comfort	9.5
Ship: Decor/Furnishings	9.2
Ship: Fitness Facilities	9.0
Cabins: Comfort/Facilities	8.7
Cabins: Software	9.0
Food: Dining Room/Cuisine	8.8
Food: Buffets/Informal Dining	8.8
Food: Quality of Ingredients	8.6
Service: Dining Room	9.1
Service: Bars	9.0
Service: Cabins	9.0
Cruise: Entertainment	9.1
Cruise: Activities Program	8.7
Cruise: Hospitality Standard	9.5
OVERALL RATING	135.1

+ Handsome contemporary ship with raked clipper bow and well-balanced, sleek flowing lines. Excellent open deck, sunning space, and sports facilities which include a paddle tennis court. One of two outdoor swimming pools has a swim-up bar and can be covered by a magrodome. There's almost no sense of crowding anywhere, a superb example of comfort by design, quality construction and engineering. Has wrap-around teakwood deck for walking. Fine assortment of public entertainment lounges and small intimate rooms. Outstanding are the Vista (observation) Lounge and the supremely tranquil, elegant Palm Court, one of the nicest rooms afloat. A Business Center features laptop computer, printer, satellite fax, phone.

Has an excellent book and video library. Theater features high-definition video projection, and special headsets for the hearing-impaired. Useful self-service launderette on each deck. Fine quality fabrics and soft furnishings, china, flatware and silver are used. Fine in-cabin television programming, and close-captioned videos for the hearing-impaired.
Spacious, well-designed accommodations, including four spectacular Crystal penthouses that feature a huge private balcony and lounge, bedroom with queen-sized bed and electric curtains, and stunning ocean-view bathroom. Five butlers feature the best in personal service in the top category suites (Penthouse Deck 10 with a total of 132 beds), where all room service food arrives on sterling silver trays. More than 50% of all cabins have private

balconies, and are supremely comfortable. Even in standard cabins, there's plenty of drawer space, some recently added to lower-grade cabins, although closet hanging space is somewhat limited for long voyages. Excellent cabin soundproofing. Generously sized Nutrogena personal bathroom amenities. Smokers will enjoy the fine range of cigars available in the Vista Lounge. Very friendly, well-trained, highly professional staff and excellent teamwork, under the direction of an all-European middle management. The decorations on the Christmas cruise are simply stunning. It is the extra attention to detail that makes a cruise on this ship so special, such as few announcements, and no background music.

— The main dining room features two sittings for dinner (the earlier sitting is too rushed). There should be separate entrances for the two alternative restaurants (at present one entrance serves both). Except for the penthouse suites, cabin bathrooms are somewhat compact, and closet space is quite limited, particularly on longer voyages. Some cabins (grades G and I), but no public rooms, have obstructed views.

Dining The dining room is elegant, with plenty of space around each table, well-placed waiter service stations, and a good number of tables for two. Food is attractively presented and well served in a correct but friendly manner. It is of a very high standard, with fine quality ingredients used throughout. Features a mixture of European specialties and North American favorites. The menus are extremely varied, and special orders are available, as is caviar and many other niceties. All in all, the food is most acceptable and, with the choice of the two alternative dining spots, provides consistently high ratings from passengers.

Dinner in the main dining room is in two sittings, but with two alternative restaurants, off-menu choices and a fine hand-picked European staff and impeccable service, dining is memorable.

Pasta specialties are made each day on request to the head waiters. For those who enjoy caviar, it is available, but is Sevruga (Malossol) and not Beluga. The wine list is superb. Afternoon Tea (and coffee) in the Palm Court is delightful, and refreshed constantly. Superlative choice of sandwiches, cakes and pastries. Needless to say, service is generally excellent.

Two alternative restaurants—Prego (superb pasta dishes), and Kyoto, with pseudo-Japanese specialties (there's no extra charge, other than a recommended $5 waiter gratuity per meal that should be included in the cruise fare)—are intimate, have great views and fine food.

Other Comments This ship has just about everything for the discerning, seasoned traveler that wants and is prepared to pay for good style, space, and the comfort and the facilities of a large vessel capable of longer voyages. It is without doubt an outstanding example of the latest style in contemporary grand hotels afloat and provides abundant choices and flexibility. Following a refit in 1995, some of the public rooms have been expanded (most notably the casino). You'll be surrounded by a cocoon of creative comfort and pampering to the highest degree. Insurance and gratuities are extra, but should be included.

ms Crystal Symphony ★★★★★+

OPERATES

ALASKA/AUSTRALASIA/SOUTHEAST
ASIA CRUISES

Cruise Line	Crystal Cruises
Gross Tonnage	50,202
Builder	Masa-Yards (Finland)
Original Cost	$300 million
Christened By	Ms Angela Lansbury
Entered Service	May 1995
Interior Design	Robert Tillberg
Country of Registry	Bahamas
Tel No	630-916820/30/40/50/60
Fax No	130-6716
Length (ft/m)	777.8/237.10
Beam (ft/m) 98.0/30.20	Draft (ft/m) 24.9/7.60
Propulsion	diesel-electric (33,880kW)
Propellers	2 (CP)
Decks 8	Crew 530
Pass. Capacity (basis 2) 960	(all berths) 1,010
Pass. Space Ratio (basis 2) 52.2	(all berths) 49.7
Officers	Scandinavian
Total Cabins	480
Size Range (sq ft/m)	202-982/18.7-91.2
Outside Cabins 480	Inside Cabins 0
Single Cabins	0
Balcony Cabins 276	Wheelchair Cabins 7
Cabin Current	110/220 AC
Refrigerator	All cabins
Cabin TV Yes	VCR Yes
Dining Rooms	3
Sittings	2 (dinner only, main dining room)

Elevators			8
Casino	Yes	Slot Machines	Yes
Swimming Pools (outside)		2 (1 with magrodome)
(inside)			0
Whirlpools	2	Gymnasium	Yes
Sauna/Steam Room Yes/Yes		Massage	Yes
Self-Service Launderette			Yes
Movie Theater/Seats			Yes/143
Library	Yes	Children's Facilities	Yes
Classification Society		Lloyd's Register

RATINGS	SCORE
Ship: Condition/Cleanliness	9.3
Ship: Space/Flow/Comfort	9.5
Ship: Decor/Furnishings	9.3
Ship: Fitness Facilities	9.1
Cabins: Comfort/Facilities	8.7
Cabins: Software	9.0
Food: Dining Room/Cuisine	8.8
Food: Buffets/Informal Dining	8.6
Food: Quality of Ingredients	8.6
Service: Dining Room	9.1
Service: Bars	9.0
Service: Cabins	9.0
Cruise: Entertainment	9.1
Cruise: Activities Program	8.7
Cruise: Hospitality Standard	9.5
OVERALL RATING	135.3

+ This is a contemporary ship that has nicely raked clipper bow and well-balanced lines. Excellent open deck, sunning space, and sports facilities. The aft of two outdoor pools can be covered by a magrodome in inclement weather. No sense of crowding anywhere, a superb example of comfort by design, high-quality construction and engineering. Has a wide wrap-around teakwood deck, uncluttered by lounge chairs. Interior decor is restful, with color combinations that don't jar the senses. Good mixture of public entertainment lounges and small intimate rooms. Outstanding is the Palm Court, a forward observation lounge that is tranquil, and one of the nicest rooms afloat (it is larger than on the sister ship). There's an excellent book, video and CD-ROM library (combined with a Business Center). The theater (smaller than on the sister ship) features high-definition video projection, and headsets for the hearing-impaired. Useful self-service launderette on each deck. Fine quality fabrics and soft furnishings, china, flatware and silver are used. Excellent in-cabin television programming (including CNN and ESPN), and close-captioned videos for the hearing-impaired.

Spacious, well-designed accommodations include two spectacular 982 sq ft (91.2m^2) Crystal penthouses with a huge balcony and lounge, bedroom with queen-sized bed, and stunning ocean-view bathroom with large whirlpool bath. Butlers feature the best in personal service in the top category suites on Penthouse Deck 10, where all room service food arrives on sterling silver trays, and lots of extra goodies are provided for occupants. All other cabins (called "penthouses" by Crystal Cruises) on Deck 10 are worth the asking price, being extremely spacious, supremely comfortable and quiet units equipped with everything necessary for refined, private living at sea.

More than 50% of all cabins have private balconies, are very well equipped and extremely comfortable, with excellent sound insulation. Even in the lowest category of standard cabins, there's plenty of drawer space, but the 7.25 ft (2.2m) of closet hanging space may prove somewhat limited for long voyages. Has generously sized personal bathroom amenities, duvets and down pillows. European stewardesses provide excellent service and attention. Highly professional and attentive staff. It is the extra attention to detail that make a cruise on this ship so special, such as very few announcements.

— Some might not like the "apartment block" look of the ship's exterior, it's the look of the future, as balconies become the norm. Balcony partitions are not floor to ceiling (so you can hear your neighbors). The main dining room features two sittings for dinner (the earlier sitting is too rushed). Some cabins (grades G and I), but no public rooms, have obstructed views. Except for the penthouse suites, cabin bathrooms are somewhat compact. There's no wrap-around passageway on Deck 6 as there is on the sister ship (dead-ends lead to the two alternative restaurants). A privacy curtain should be placed between entrance and sleeping area in all non-Penthouse Deck cabins.

Dining The main dining room is quite elegant, with crisp design and plenty of space around each table, well-placed waiter service stations, and ample tables for two. It is somewhat noisy at times, and not conducive to a fine dining experience. It is well laid out, and features a raised, circular central section. There are tables for two (many of them positioned adjacent to large windows), four, six or eight.

Food is attractively presented and well served (mix of plate and silver service). It is of a high standard, with fine quality ingredients used. Features mainly European dishes. Menus are extremely varied, and feature a good selection of meat, fish and vegetarian dishes. Special (off-menu) orders are available, as is caviar and other culinary niceties. Overall, the food is most acceptable for a large ship and, with the choice of the two alternative dining spots, receives high passenger praise. Dinner in the main dining room is in two sittings, but with two alternative restaurants, off-menu choices, a fine European staff and excellent service, dining can be quite memorable. Fresh pasta and dessert flambeau specialties are made each day by the head waiters at tableside. The wine list is excellent. Afternoon Tea in the Palm Court is a delightful daily event. The Lido provides breakfast and luncheon buffets that are fairly standard fare.

Two alternative dining rooms, the 75-seat "Prego" (serving Italian cuisine), and the 84-seat "Jade Garden" (serving contemporary Chinese dishes), are appreciably larger and set on a lower deck (Deck 6) than on the sister ship, and each restaurant has a separate entrance and themed decor. They both provide an excellent standard of culinary fare, with food individually cooked to order, at no extra charge (but the recommended $5 waiter gratuity per meal should be included in the cruise fare). In addition, The Bistro provides a fine array of snacks, cakes, coffees, and teas throughout the day, with unusual, Crystal-logo china.

Other Comments Besides abundant space, it's the staff that makes this cruise experience really special. They are a fine-tuned, well-trained group whose middle name is hospitality. With few design defects, *Crystal Symphony* is a refined ship in today's contemporary cruise industry, and a fine sea-going resort for those that want the newest in furnishings and surroundings. There are subtle differences between this and sister ship *Crystal Harmony*, notably in the repositioning of the two alternative restaurants, to a lower deck; the doubling in size of the popular Crystal Cove and the Lido Cafe. Gratuities should be included on a ship so highly rated (they can be pre-paid, however). Port taxes and insurance are extra.

mv Cunard Countess ★★★+

OPERATES

7- AND 14-DAY CARIBBEAN CRUISES (YEAR-ROUND)

Cruise Line			Cunard
Former Names			-
Gross Tonnage			17,593
Builder		Burmeister & Wein (Denmark)	
Original Cost			UK£12 million
Christened By		Mrs Janet Armstrong	
Entered Service			Aug 1976
Interior Design			McNeece Design
Country of Registry			Bahamas
Tel No	110-4676	Fax No	110-4676
Length (ft/m)			536.6/163.56
Beam (ft/m)	74.9/22.84	Draft (ft/m)	19.0/5.82
Propulsion			diesel (15,670kW)
Propellers			2 (CP)
Decks	8	Crew	360
Pass. Capacity (basis 2) 812		(all berths) 959	
Pass. Space Ratio (basis 2) 21.6		(all berths) 18.3	
Officers			British
Total Cabins			406
Size Range (sq ft/m)			88-265/8.1-24.6
Outside Cabins	249	Inside Cabins	149
Single Cabins			0
Balcony Cabins	0	Wheelchair Cabins	0
Cabin Current			110/220 AC
Refrigerator			Grades 1, 2 only
Cabin TV	No	VCR	No
Dining Rooms	1	Sittings	2
Elevators			2

Casino	Yes	Slot Machines	Yes
Swimming Pools (outside) 1		(inside)	0
Whirlpools	2	Gymnasium	Yes
Sauna/Steam Room Yes/No		Massage	No
Self-Service Launderette			No
Movie Theater/Seats			Yes/126
Library			Yes
Children's Facilities			No
Watersports Facilities			None
Classification Society			Lloyd's Register

RATINGS	SCORE
Ship: Condition/Cleanliness	6.1
Ship: Space/Flow/Comfort	6.3
Ship: Decor/Furnishings	6.6
Ship: Fitness Facilities	6.7
Cabins: Comfort/Facilities	5.8
Cabins: Software	7.7
Food: Dining Room/Cuisine	6.6
Food: Buffets/Informal Dining	6.1
Food: Quality of Ingredients	6.2
Service: Dining Room	7.0
Service: Bars	6.8
Service: Cabins	7.2
Cruise: Entertainment	7.3
Cruise: Activities Program	7.1
Cruise: Hospitality Standard	7.6
OVERALL RATING	101.1

+ Has a modern profile, with clean lines and a distinctive swept-back red funnel. Good selection of public rooms have attractive, light colors and decor. Good indoor-outdoor entertainment nightclub incorporates an aft open deck area. The cabins, mostly of a standard (small) size, are furnished with much lighter colors and better combinations, are small, space-efficient units with metal fixtures and thin walls.

— High-density vessel. Poor cabin insulation, which means you hear your neighbors brushing their hair. Cabins on the lowest deck (2 Deck) suffer from vibration and the odor of fuel. Outside decks need attention. The cabin service snack menu should be upgraded. Cramped charter flights are a turn-off, but then, the price is right.

Dining Pleasant dining room has large picture windows. Reasonable banquet food standard, tailored for UK passengers. Out of the ordinary requests difficult. Poor fruit and cheese selection. Good, cheerful service from an attentive staff, but it lacks the finesse that made Cunard famous.

Other Comments Passengers seeking a casual, destination-intensive cruise will probably like this, and come back for more. Good mainly for a destination-oriented and informal first Caribbean cruise experience. Gratuities included for UK passengers only.

ms Cunard Dynasty ★★★★

OPERATES

7-DAY ALASKA AND CARIBBEAN CRUISES

Cruise Line	Cunard
Former Names	-
Gross Tonnage	19,089
Builder	Union Navale de Levante (Spain)
Original Cost	$100 million
Christened By	Mrs Betty Ford
Entered Service	Jul 17, 1993
Interior Design	Yran & Storbraaten
Country of Registry	Panama
Tel No	133-7757 Fax No 133-7761
Length (ft/m)	537.4/163.81
Beam (ft/m) 73.8/22.5	Draft (ft/m) 17.7/5.40
Propulsion diesel (13,200kW)	Propellers 2 (CP)
Decks 7	Crew 330
Pass. Capacity (basis 2) 800	(all berths) 916
Pass. Space Ratio (basis 2) 23.8	(all berths) 20.8
Officers	European/Scandinavian
Total Cabins	401
Size Range (sq ft/m)	140-350/13.0-32.5
Outside Cabins 277	Inside Cabins 124
Single Cabins	0
Balcony Cabins	10
Wheelchair Cabins	4
Cabin Current	110/220 AC
Refrigerator	Category 1 only
Cabin TV Yes	VCR No
Dining Rooms	1
Sittings	2 (open seating breakfast/lunch)

Elevators			4
Casino Yes		Slot Machines	Yes
Swimming Pools (outside) 1		(inside)	0
Whirlpools 3		Gymnasium	Yes
Sauna/Steam Room Yes/No		Massage	Yes
Self-Service Launderette			No
Movie Theater/Seats No		Library	No
Children's Facilities			No
Watersports Facilities			None
Classification Society		Det Norske Veritas	

RATINGS	SCORE
Ship: Condition/Cleanliness	8.3
Ship: Space/Flow/Comfort	7.8
Ship: Decor/Furnishings	8.1
Ship: Fitness Facilities	8.0
Cabins: Comfort/Facilities	7.8
Cabins: Software	8.0
Food: Dining Room/Cuisine	7.6
Food: Buffets/Informal Dining	6.8
Food: Quality of Ingredients	6.5
Service: Dining Room	7.8
Service: Bars	7.5
Service: Cabins	7.1
Cruise: Entertainment	7.8
Cruise: Activities Program	4.8
Cruise: Hospitality Standard	7.2
OVERALL RATING	111.1

+ Handsome exterior styling. Good open deck and sunning space. Well-designed five-deck-high glass-walled atrium and off-center stairways add a sense of spaciousness. Clever interior design connects passengers with sea and light. Pleasant artwork. Interior decor in public spaces is warm and inviting, with contemporary, but not brash, art deco color combinations. Nicely furnished, wood-trimmed cabins feature large picture windows and come well equipped, complete with vanity desk unit, a good amount of drawer space, curtained windows, and personal safe. Bathrooms are somewhat compact, but are nicely fitted out and have an excellent shower stall.

— Cabins have poor soundproofing. Tiny health spa. Poorly designed showlounge is liable to congestion. Long lines for buffets and tenders. Passengers in cabins on Deck 4 are disturbed by anyone running or jogging on the open deck above, as insulation is poor.

Dining Attractive dining room is cramped, and there are no tables for two, but ambiance is warm. Cuisine is disappointing, and lacks presentation. A varied menu is provided but food arrives invariably overcooked (a problem of distance from the galley).

Other Comments This sleek mid-sized ship is handsome, and is a refreshing change for those that don't want to cruise on larger ships. Gratuities are included for UK passengers.

mts Daphne ★★★+

OPERATES

12-DAY EUROPE/
MEDITERRANEAN CRUISES

Cruise Line	Costa Cruises		
Former Names	Therisos Express/Port Sydney		
Gross Tonnage	9,436		
Builder	Swan, Hunter (UK)		
Original Cost	n/a		
Christened By	n/a		
Entered Service	Mar 1955/Jul 1975		
Interior Design	A&M Katzourakis		
Country of Registry	Liberia		
Tel No	124-6505	Fax No	124-3127
Length (ft/m)	532.7/162.39		
Beam (ft/m)	70.2/21.42	Draft (ft/m)	28.4/8.66
Propulsion	diesel (9,850kW)		
Propellers	2 (FP)		
Decks	7	Crew	260
Pass. Capacity (basis 2) 412	(all berths) 508		
Pass. Space Ratio (basis 2) 22.9	(all berths) 18.5		
Officers	Italian		
Total Cabins	206		
Size Range (sq ft/m)	150-349/14.0-32.5		
Outside Cabins	189	Inside Cabins	17
Single Cabins	0		
Balcony Cabins	6		
Wheelchair Cabins	0		
Cabin Current	220 DC	Refrigerator	Suites only
Cabin TV	Suites only	VCR	No
Dining Rooms	1	Sittings	1
Elevators	2		

Casino	Yes	Slot Machines	Yes
Swimming Pools (outside) 1	(inside)		0
Whirlpools	2	Gymnasium	Yes
Sauna/Steam Room Yes/No	Massage		Yes
Self-Service Launderette			Yes
Movie Theater/Seats			Yes/200
Library			Yes
Children's Facilities			No
Watersports Facilities			None
Classification Society			RINA

RATINGS	SCORE
Ship: Condition/Cleanliness	7.1
Ship: Space/Flow/Comfort	7.2
Ship: Decor/Furnishings	7.1
Ship: Fitness Facilities	5.7
Cabins: Comfort/Facilities	7.0
Cabins: Software	7.2
Food: Dining Room/Cuisine	7.2
Food: Buffets/Informal Dining	6.6
Food: Quality of Ingredients	6.7
Service: Dining Room	7.1
Service: Bars	7.0
Service: Cabins	7.1
Cruise: Entertainment	5.7
Cruise: Activities Program	6.0
Cruise: Hospitality Standard	7.0
OVERALL RATING	101.7

+ This ship has an expansive outdoor deck and plenty of sunning space. Well-maintained vessel. Features bright, contemporary decor in the public rooms. Has a large, fine theater, which is especially good for meetings and groups. Other public rooms have fairly high ceilings. Has very spacious cabins with good, solid fittings and heavy-duty doors. There's plenty of closet and drawer space, and very good insulation between each cabin. The cabin bathrooms are of a generous size.

— There's no forward-looking observation lounge, and no wrap-around promenade deck.

Dining The dining room is quite charming, and has uncluttered seating. Has friendly, attentive and quite bubbly European service with many Italian waiters, but there's little finesse. The food is generally good, especially the pasta, of which there is plenty.

Other Comments Identical in outward appearance to sister *Princess Danae*. Originally constructed as a general cargo vessel, she was well reconstructed as a cruise ship. This is a very comfortable ship, built to a high standard. This ship maintains an air of intimacy, has a fine range of public rooms, and represents good value when cruising on itineraries longer than a week.

ms Dawn Princess

OPERATES

*7-DAY ALASKA AND
CARIBBEAN CRUISES*

Cruise Line	Princess Cruises		Casino	Yes	Slot Machines	Yes
Former Names	-		Swimming Pools (outside) 3	(inside)	0
Gross Tonnage	77,000		Whirlpools	5	Gymnasium	Yes
Builder	Fincantieri (Italy)		Sauna/Steam Room Yes	Massage	Yes
Original Cost	$300 million		Self-Service Launderette		Yes
Christened By	n/a		Movie Theater		Yes
Entered Service	Apr 1997		Library		Yes
Interior Design	Njal R. Eide/Giacomo Mortola		Children's Facilities		Yes
Country of Registry	Liberia		Watersports Facilities		None
Tel No n/a Fax No	n/a		Classification Society	Lloyd's Register

Length (ft/m)	856.2/261.0		**RATINGS**	**SCORE**
Beam (ft/m) 105.8/32.25 Draft (ft/m)	26.0/7.95		Ship: Condition/Cleanliness	NYR
Propulsion/Propellers diesel-electric/2 (FP)			Ship: Space/Flow/Comfort	NYR
Decks 14 Crew	900		Ship: Decor/Furnishings	NYR
Pass. Capacity (basis 2) 1,950 (all berths) 2,250			Ship: Fitness Facilities	NYR
Pass. Space Ratio (basis 2) 39.4 (all berths) 34.2			Cabins: Comfort/Facilities	NYR
Officers Italian			Cabins: Software	NYR
Total Cabins	1,050		Food: Dining Room/Cuisine	NYR
Size Range (sq ft/m) 159-611/14.7-56.7			Food: Buffets/Informal Dining	NYR
Outside Cabins 652 Inside Cabins 398			Food: Quality of Ingredients	NYR
Single Cabins	0		Service: Dining Room	NYR
Balcony Cabins 446 Wheelchair Cabins 20			Service: Bars	NYR
Cabin Current	110/220 AC		Service: Cabins	NYR
Refrigerator	Yes		Cruise: Entertainment	NYR
Cabin TV Yes VCR Suites only			Cruise: Activities Program	NYR
Dining Rooms 2 main/3 others			Cruise: Hospitality Standard	NYR
Sittings 2 (main dining rooms)			OVERALL RATING	
Elevators	11			

+ For such a large ship, she has a strong, bold profile. Features a wide wrap-around teakwood promenade deck. There are many public rooms to choose from, including several with a cosy atmosphere. Lots of glass area on the upper decks. There's plenty of space, and passenger flow is generally good. The health spa complex surrounds a swimming pool suspended between two decks. There are two other pools. Has a conference center for up to 300. An excellent collection of art work has been chosen. The cabins are extremely functional; 70% of outside cabins have private balconies. Has an intimate feel inside, despite her size, due to clever design and decor.

— No wrap-around outdoor promenade deck, and only two main stairways. Standard cabins are small. There are a lot of inside cabins. As on any large ship, expect long lines for embarkation, disembarkation, buffets, shore tenders and shore excursions.

Dining There are two main dining rooms; each has its own galley and is split into multi-tier sections. Apart from these, there are several other informal dining areas including a Patisserie, a Wine/Caviar bar and a Pizzeria.

Other Comments The design is quite handsome for this size of ship. The rating is expected to be similar to its sister ship *Sun Princess* (see that entry for more in-depth comments).

mv Dimitriy Shostakovich ★★

OPERATES
14-DAY EUROPE CRUISES

Cruise Line	Black Sea Shipping		
Former Names	-		
Gross Tonnage	10,303		
Builder	A. Warski (Poland)		
Original Cost	n/a	Christened By	n/a
Entered Service	1980		
Interior Design	n/a		
Country of Registry	Ukraine		
Tel No	140-1336	Fax No	140-1336
Length (ft/m)	450.0/137.15		
Beam (ft/m) 68.8/21.00	Draft (ft/m)	17.3/5.28	
Propulsion	diesel (12,800kW)		
Propellers	2 (CP)		
Decks	7	Crew	150
Pass. Capacity (basis 2) 278	(all berths) 494		
Pass. Space Ratio (basis 2) 37.0	(all berths) 20.8		
Officers	Russian/Ukrainian		
Total Cabins	139		
Size Range (sq ft/m)	100-320/9.3-29.7		
Outside Cabins	66	Inside Cabins	73
Single Cabins	0		
Balcony Cabins	0		
Wheelchair Cabins	0		
Cabin Current	220 AC		
Refrigerator	No		
Cabin TV	No	VCR	No
Dining Rooms	1	Sittings	1
Elevators	1		

Casino	No	Slot Machines	No
Swimming Pools (outside) 1	(inside)	0	
Whirlpools	0	Gymnasium	Yes
Sauna/Steam Room Yes/No	Massage	Yes	
Self-Service Launderette	No		
Movie Theater/Seats	No		
Library	Yes		
Children's Facilities	No		
Watersports Facilities	None		
Classification Society	RS		

RATINGS	SCORE
Ship: Condition/Cleanliness	6.6
Ship: Space/Flow/Comfort	6.2
Ship: Decor/Furnishings	6.0
Ship: Fitness Facilities	5.6
Cabins: Comfort/Facilities	5.5
Cabins: Software	6.1
Food: Dining Room/Cuisine	5.3
Food: Buffets/Informal Dining	5.1
Food: Quality of Ingredients	5.1
Service: Dining Room	6.1
Service: Bars	6.2
Service: Cabins	6.2
Cruise: Entertainment	4.3
Cruise: Activities Program	4.7
Cruise: Hospitality Standard	5.8
OVERALL RATING	84.8

+ Has a fully enclosed bridge, as well as an ice-hardened hull, good for cold-weather cruise areas. One of a series of five Polish-built vessels intended for all-weather line voyages.

— Lacks a forward observation lounge. Limited open deck and sunning space and tiny swimming pool. Limited choice of public rooms.

Dining The dining room is reasonably comfortable, and everyone dines in one sitting, with food served family style. The food is pretty basic, no more, and menu choice is very limited, as is the selection of breads, cheeses, and fruits.

Other Comments This ship has a square, angular profile with upright stern, stubby bow and fat funnel. Interior decor is rather spartan, yet the ambiance is comfortable, made better by tropical plants. Cabins, some with upper pullman berths, are small and utilitarian in fittings and furnishings, but adequate. Bathrooms are small, however. This ship features a regular 14-day itinerary that provides a destination-oriented, basic cruise experience for an international clientele, at modest rates, nothing more.

ms Disney Magic

OPERATES

*3- AND 4-DAY BAHAMAS
CRUISES (YEAR-ROUND)*

Cruise Line	Disney Cruise Line	Casino	No
Former Names	-	Swimming Pools (outside) 3	
Gross Tonnage	85,000	Whirlpools	6
Builder	Fincantieri (Italy)	Sauna/Steam Room Yes/Yes	
Original Cost	$350 million	Self-Service Launderette	
Christened By	n/a	Movie Theater/Seats	
Entered Service	Jan 1998	Library	
Interior Design	Yran & Storbraaten/R. Tillberg	Children's Facilities	
Country of Registry	Bahamas	Watersports Facilities	
Tel No	n/a Fax No n/a	Classification Society	
Length (ft/m)	964.5/294.00		

Casino	No
Swimming Pools (outside) 3	(inside) 0
Whirlpools 6	Gymnasium Yes
Sauna/Steam Room Yes/Yes	Massage Yes
Self-Service Launderette	Yes (3)
Movie Theater/Seats	Yes/270
Library	Yes
Children's Facilities	Yes
Watersports Facilities	None
Classification Society	Lloyd's Register

Beam (ft/m) 105.7/32.22 Draft (ft/m) 26.2/8.0		
Propulsion	diesel-electric (38,000kW)	
Propellers	2 (FP)	
Decks n/a Crew	945	
Pass. Capacity (basis 2) 1,760 (all berths) 2,800		
Pass. Space Ratio (basis 2) 48.2 (all berths) 30.3		
Officers	European/Norwegian	
Total Cabins	880	
Size Range (sq ft/m) 180.8-968.7/16.8-90.0		
Outside Cabins 640 Inside Cabins 240		
Family Cabins	80	
Balcony Cabins 280 Wheelchair Cabins 20		
Cabin Current 110 AC Refrigerator Yes		
Cabin TV Yes VCR Suites only		
Dining Rooms 3 main (+ 1 alternative, 1 café)		
Sittings	2	
Elevators	12	

RATINGS	SCORE
Ship: Condition/Cleanliness	NYR
Ship: Space/Flow/Comfort	NYR
Ship: Decor/Furnishings	NYR
Ship: Fitness Facilities	NYR
Cabins: Comfort/Facilities	NYR
Cabins: Software	NYR
Food: Dining Room/Cuisine	NYR
Food: Buffets/Informal Dining	NYR
Food: Quality of Ingredients	NYR
Service: Dining Room	NYR
Service: Bars	NYR
Service: Cabins	NYR
Cruise: Entertainment	NYR
Cruise: Activities Program	NYR
Cruise: Hospitality Standard	NYR
OVERALL RATING	

+ This is the first ship built with two funnels since the 1950s, and provides the vessel with an ocean liner profile that fits in with the Disney image of Main Street, USA.

There is a separate swimming pool and sunbathing area for adults only. You can expect some incredible children's programming and entertainment. Disney's private island (fully owned by Disney) promises to be an outstanding facility.

— It's costly for a short cruise.

Dining There are three main dining rooms (Lumière, Islands, Animator's Palette), each with a unique theme. On the three-night cruise, passengers move to each dining room in turn (together with their waiter, so gratuities go only to that person), which provides a different dining experience for each night. There's also Paolo, an elegant 140-seat alternative Italian restaurant for adults only; an indoor-outdoor café serving breakfast, lunch, snacks and a buffet dinner for children; an ice cream and frozen yoghurt bar; and a pool bar for hamburgers, hot dogs, pizza, and sandwiches.

Other Comments This brand new ship's profile is quite streamlined, yet it is also nostalgic, with its two funnels (one of which is really a dummy, but contains a variety of public spaces, including a sports bar and a broadcast center).

There is a 5,500 sq ft (510.9 m^2) shopping area with Disney Cruise Line-themed clothing, collectibles, and specialty items. There's also a spectacular 1,040-seat Walt Disney Theater (spread over four decks), piano bar, adults-only nightclub/disco, family lounge (330 seats), dedicated cinema (where classic Disney films will be shown, as well as first-run movies), a sports deck with paddle tennis court, table tennis, basketball court and shuffleboard, and a golf driving range. The ship also has a 6,700 sq ft (622.4 m^2) ocean-view fitness spa.

The children's area measures a huge 13,000 sq ft (1,207.7 m^2), and there will be more than 30 counselors on any given cruise. There is also a separate family/children's pool, designated teen club and video game arcade. There is a children's drop-off service in the evenings. Private babysitting services are available, as are character "tuck-ins" for children, and character breakfast and lunch. Strollers (pushchairs) are also available, at no charge. Those who thought that Disney would add ostentatious decoration on the ship's exterior were wrong. Only from the air, flying over the ship, you might just make out Mickey's ears painted onto the bottom of the aft swimming pool, otherwise there's little to let you know that this is a Disney ship, from the outside. Inside, it's a different story.

The first of two sister ships for Disney Cruise Lines, this ship will appeal to couples, single parents, and families, and the vacation package combines a three- or four-day cruise with a stay at Walt Disney World, all encapsulated in one well-controlled, crime-free environment. The ship's home port is Port Canaveral, Florida, and the starting date is January 1998.

ss Dolphin IV ★★+

OPERATES
2-DAY BAHAMAS CRUISES (YEAR-ROUND)

Cruise Line	Canaveral Cruise Line
Former Names	Ithaca/Amelia De Melo/Zion
Gross Tonnage	13,000
Builder	Howaldtswerke Deutsche
	Werft (Germany)
Original Cost	n/a
Christened By	n/a
Entered Service	Mar 1956/Jan 1979
Interior Design	n/a
Country of Registry	Bahamas
Tel No	-	Fax No	-
Length (ft/m)	501.2/152.77
Beam (ft/m) 65.1/19.87	Draft (ft/m) 27.5/8.40
Propulsion	steam turbine (7,723kW)
Propellers	1 (FP)
Decks	7	Crew	290
Pass. Capacity (basis 2) 588	(all berths) 684
Pass. Space Ratio (basis 2) 22.1	(all berths) 19.0
Officers	Greek
Total Cabins	281
Size Range (sq ft/m)	73-258/6.7-24.0
Outside Cabins	206	Inside Cabins	75
Single Cabins	0
Balcony Cabins	0	Wheelchair Cabins	0
Cabin Current	110/220 AC
Refrigerator	No
Cabin TV	No	VCR	No
Dining Rooms	1	Sittings	2

Elevators			1
Casino	Yes	Slot Machines	Yes
Swimming Pools (outside) 1	(inside)	0
Whirlpools	1	Gymnasium	Yes
Sauna/Steam Room No/No	Massage	No
Self-Service Launderette		No
Movie Theater/Seats	No	Library	No
Children's Facilities			Yes
Watersports Facilities			None
Classification Society		Lloyd's Register

RATINGS	SCORE
Ship: Condition/Cleanliness	6.0
Ship: Space/Flow/Comfort	5.3
Ship: Decor/Furnishings	6.0
Ship: Fitness Facilities	4.2
Cabins: Comfort/Facilities	6.2
Cabins: Software	6.1
Food: Dining Room/Cuisine	6.6
Food: Buffets/Informal Dining	5.8
Food: Quality of Ingredients	6.1
Service: Dining Room	6.2
Service: Bars	6.4
Service: Cabins	6.6
Cruise: Entertainment	6.0
Cruise: Activities Program	6.0
Cruise: Hospitality Standard	6.1
OVERALL RATING	89.6

+ Attractive-looking older ship with pleasing lines, even with its now very noticeable center-sag. The ship's public rooms are well decorated in clean, crisp, contemporary colors, with much use of reflective surfaces. There is a good shopping area. The showroom is reasonable, but the stage would be better at the opposite end, and seating is uncomfortable for long periods. The cabins are small, yet comfortable and quite adequate for short cruises. Friendly staff and ambiance.

— The open deck and sunning area are cramped owing to the ship's high passenger density. Has a very claustrophobic discotheque. The cabins on lower decks suffer from noise (and the smell of diesel) from the engine-room. Entertainment is rather weak and low budget.

Dining Charming dining room has warm ambiance, but is narrow and has a low ceiling. The food is reasonably good, even creative, but ingredients aren't the best. Service is moderately good, but is hurried and lacking in finesse, although the staff are friendly and try to please. Good buffet displays.

Other Comments This ship has a good, friendly, and lively ambiance and is recommended for short, fun cruises for the young, active set, but I wonder how much longer this ship can compete with the bright new ships that offer more facilities, and indeed more of everything.

mv Don Juan ★★★

OPERATES
7-DAY MEDITERRANEAN CRUISES

Cruise Line	Royal Hispania Cruises
Former Names	Crown del Mar/
	Las Palmas de Gran Canarias
Gross Tonnage	10,000
Builder	Union Navale de Levante (Spain)
Original Cost	n/a
Christened By	n/a
Entered Service	1967/Jul 1994
Interior Design	G.M.O. Design
Country of Registry	Panama
Tel No 135-1264 Fax No	135-1264
Length (ft/m)	428.8/130.70
Beam (ft/m) 62.9/19.20 Draft (ft/m)	18.0/5.50
Propulsion	diesel-electric (11,769kW)
Propellers	2 (CP)
Decks 6 Crew	195
Pass. Capacity (basis 2) 448 (all berths)	469
Pass. Space Ratio (basis 2) 22.3 (all berths)	21.3
Officers	Spanish
Total Cabins 209 Size Range (sq ft/m)	n/a
Outside Cabins 130 Inside Cabins	79
Single Cabins	0
Balcony Cabins 0 Wheelchair Cabins	1
Cabin Current	110/220 AC
Refrigerator	No
Cabin TV	Yes
Dining Rooms 1 Sittings	2
Elevators	1

Casino	Yes	Slot Machines	Yes
Swimming Pools (outside) 1	(inside)		0
Whirlpools	2	Gymnasium	No
Sauna/Steam Room Yes/No		Massage	Yes
Self-Service Launderette			No
Movie Theater/Seats			No
Library			No
Children's Facilities/Playroom			Yes
Watersports Facilities			None
Classification Society		Lloyd's Register	

RATINGS	SCORE
Ship: Condition/Cleanliness	7.0
Ship: Space/Flow/Comfort	6.6
Ship: Decor/Furnishings	7.6
Ship: Fitness Facilities	4.3
Cabins: Comfort/Facilities	6.9
Cabins: Software	7.1
Food: Dining Room/Cuisine	6.0
Food: Buffets/Informal Dining	5.8
Food: Quality of Ingredients	6.0
Service: Dining Room	7.0
Service: Bars	7.1
Service: Cabins	7.2
Cruise: Entertainment	5.7
Cruise: Activities Program	6.0
Cruise: Hospitality Standard	6.7
OVERALL RATING	97.0

+ Has a good amount of open deck space. Inside, soft earth tones are used. Has a three-deck high atrium. Five suites, located just below the navigation bridge, command forward views, are well furnished, and have full bathtubs (most other cabins have showers), but no balconies. Standard cabins are adequate at best.

— Most public rooms are set below accommodation decks, except for one forward observation lounge. The showroom is set between accommodation decks, which makes it noisy at night for some passengers. Standard cabins have almost no drawer space, little closet space, and small bathrooms. There are no cushioned pads for deck lounge chairs. The ship seems to have a permanent list.

Dining The dining room is set low down, and has ocean views, but it's a little dark and somber. There are no tables for two. Cuisine is barely adequate, and menu choice is very limited. Reasonably attentive service staff throughout, but there's no finesse, and it's hard to communicate.

Other Comments Refurbished in 1994, this former Spanish ferry sports a new, though somewhat angular look. This ship will provide a comfortable cruise experience, but forget the word "luxury," for this is quite basic.

ms Dreamward ★★★★

OPERATES

7-DAY BERMUDA AND
CARIBBEAN CRUISES

Cruise Line			Norwegian Cruise Line
Former Names			-
Gross Tonnage			39,217
Builder		Chantiers de l'Atlantique (France)	
Original Cost			$240 million
Christened By			Ms Diana Ross
Entered Service			Dec 1992
Interior Design			Yran & Storbraaten
Country of Registry			Bahamas
Tel No	130-5510	Fax No	130-5507
Length (ft/m)			623.3/190.00
Beam (ft/m)	93.5/28.50	Draft (ft/m)	22.3/6.80
Propulsion			diesel (18,480kW)
Propellers			2 (CP)
Decks	11	Crew	483
Pass. Capacity (basis 2) 1,246		(all berths) 1,450	
Pass. Space Ratio (basis 2) 32.9		(all berths) 28.2	
Officers			Norwegian
Total Cabins			623
Size Range (sq ft/m)		140-350/13.0-32.5	
Outside Cabins	530	Inside Cabins	93
Single Cabins			0
Balcony Cabins			48
Wheelchair Cabins		6 (+ 30 for hearing-impaired)	
Cabin Current			110 AC
Refrigerator			Category 1/2/3 only
Cabin TV	Yes	VCR	No
Dining Rooms	4	Sittings	2

Elevators			7
Casino	Yes	Slot Machines	Yes
Swimming Pools (outside) 2		(inside)	0
Whirlpools		2	Gymnasium	Yes
Sauna/Steam Room Yes/No		Massage	Yes
Self-Service Launderette			No
Movie Theater/Seats	No	Library	Yes
Children's Facilities			Yes
Watersports Facilities			None
Classification Society			Det Norske Veritas

RATINGS	SCORE
Ship: Condition/Cleanliness	8.6
Ship: Space/Flow/Comfort	7.9
Ship: Decor/Furnishings	8.1
Ship: Fitness Facilities	8.0
Cabins: Comfort/Facilities	7.8
Cabins: Software	8.0
Food: Dining Room/Cuisine	7.2
Food: Buffets/Informal Dining	6.3
Food: Quality of Ingredients	6.4
Service: Dining Room	7.6
Service: Bars	7.5
Service: Cabins	7.5
Cruise: Entertainment	8.2
Cruise: Activities Program	7.8
Cruise: Hospitality Standard	7.7
OVERALL RATING	114.6

+ Built first, this sister to *Windward* has a handsome, well-balanced profile, despite its large, square funnel. Has inboard lifeboats and red rubber-covered promenade deck. Much innovative design incorporated, with good passenger flow. Inside, the ship absorbs passengers well even when full. The tiered pool deck is innovative, and the aft sun terraces are a plus. Pastel interior color scheme is soothing. Cabins feature wood-trimmed cabinetry, and warm decor, but there's almost no drawer space (closets have shelves), so take minimal clothing. All cabins have a sitting area, but this takes away free space, making movement tight. Bathrooms are small. Special cabins for hearing impaired are innovative.

— Entrance lobby is uninviting. Carpeted stairwell steps are tinny. Room service menu poor. The casino is intimate, but cramped.

Dining There are three main Dining Rooms: The Sun Terrace, The Terraces, The Four Seasons (all have the same menu and food), plus The Bistro (for casual dining) and Sports Bar for breakfast, luncheon and teatime buffets (poor). The food is adequate, but not memorable. Service is perfunctory, at best. The wine list is good, with very moderate prices.

Other Comments This ship is proving to be highly successful for NCL's sports-minded passengers. Provides a good alternative to the mega-ships and mega-crowds.

ms Ecstasy ★★★★

Cruise Line		Carnival Cruise Lines
Former Names		-
Gross Tonnage		70,367
Builder		Kvaerner Masa-Yards (Finland)
Original Cost		$275 million
Christened By		Ms Kathie Lee Gifford
Entered Service		Jun 1991
Interior Design		Joe Farcus
Country of Registry		Liberia
Tel No 124-4233	Fax No	124-4234
Length (ft/m)		855.8/260.60
Beam (ft/m) 104.0/31.40	Draft (ft/m)	25.9/7.89
Propulsion		diesel-electric (42,240kW)
Propellers		2 (CP)
Decks	10 Crew	920
Pass. Capacity (basis 2) 2,040	(all berths) 2,594	
Pass. Space Ratio (basis 2) 34.4	(all berths) 27.1	
Officers		Italian
Total Cabins		1,020
Size Range (sq ft/m)		185-421/17.0-39.0
Outside Cabins	618 Inside Cabins	402
Single Cabins		0
Balcony Cabins		54
Wheelchair Cabins		20
Cabin Current		110 AC
Refrigerator		Category 11/12 only
Cabin TV	Yes VCR	No
Dining Rooms	2 Sittings	2

Elevators			14
Casino	Yes	Slot Machines	Yes
Swimming Pools (outside) 3		(inside)	0
Whirlpools	6	Gymnasium	Yes
Sauna/Steam Room	Yes/Yes	Massage	Yes
Self-Service Launderette			Yes
Movie Theater/Seats	No	Library	Yes
Children's Facilities			Yes
Watersports Facilities			None
Classification Society			Lloyd's Register

RATINGS	SCORE
Ship: Condition/Cleanliness	8.1
Ship: Space/Flow/Comfort	7.8
Ship: Decor/Furnishings	7.2
Ship: Fitness Facilities	7.8
Cabins: Comfort/Facilities	7.6
Cabins: Software	7.4
Food: Dining Room/Cuisine	6.8
Food: Buffets/Informal Dining	6.5
Food: Quality of Ingredients	5.6
Service: Dining Room	7.1
Service: Bars	7.2
Service: Cabins	6.4
Cruise: Entertainment	7.9
Cruise: Activities Program	7.8
Cruise: Hospitality Standard	6.6
OVERALL RATING	107.8

+ This big ship has good passenger flow, and clever interior design. Vintage Rolls Royce on indoor promenade. Fine health spa. Stunning 10-ton sculpture graces marble and glass atrium that spans seven decks. Lovely library, but few books. Plain, but comfortable cabins are quite roomy and practical, with good storage space and practical bathrooms. Suites are attractive. Chinatown Lounge has hanging lanterns and smoking dragon. This ship will provide a great introduction to cruising for the novice passenger seeking an action-packed, dare I say, orgasmic, short cruise experience in contemporary surroundings, with the minimum of fuss and finesse, lots of enthusiasm and a real swinging party atmosphere. You'll have a fine time if you like nightlife and silly games, even if the line does emphasize the "fun" theme constantly.

— Neon lighting in the interior decor. Color combinations are too vivid. Too many people, too many annoying announcements, and too much hustling for drinks. Long lines for embarkation, disembarkation, and buffets.

Dining The two dining rooms have attractive decor and colors, but are large, crowded, and very noisy. The food is adequate, no more (despite being upgraded). Service is robotic.

Other Comments Life in the fast lane, this is cruising in theme-park fantasy land. An enthusiastic staff will make sure you have fun, and that's what Carnival does best.

ss Enchanted Isle ★★★

OPERATES

*7-DAY MEXICO CRUISES
(YEAR-ROUND)*

Cruise Line	Commodore Cruise Line	Casino Yes	Slot Machines Yes
Former Names Commodore Hotel/Enchanted Isle/		Swimming Pools (outside) 1	(inside) 0
Bermuda Star/Veendam/Monarch Star/Argentina		Whirlpools 0	Gymnasium Yes
Gross Tonnage	23,395	Sauna/Steam Room Yes/No	Massage Yes
Builder	Ingalls Shipbuilding (USA)	Self-Service Launderette	No
Original Cost	$26 million	Movie Theater/Seats	Yes/200
Christened By	n/a	Library	No
Entered Service	Dec 1958/Feb 1995	Children's Facilities	Yes
Interior Design	VFD Interiors	Watersports Facilities	None
Country of Registry	Panama	Classification Society	Lloyd's Register
Tel No 133-3171 Fax No	133-3201		

RATINGS	SCORE

Length (ft/m)	617.5/188.22	Ship: Condition/Cleanliness	6.4
Beam (ft/m) 88.1/26.88 Draft (ft/m)	27.2/8.30	Ship: Space/Flow/Comfort	6.2
Propulsion	steam turbine (19,000kW)	Ship: Decor/Furnishings	6.6
Propellers	2 (FP)	Ship: Fitness Facilities	4.5
Decks 9 Crew	350	Cabins: Comfort/Facilities	6.3
Pass. Capacity (basis 2) 729	(all berths) 729	Cabins: Software	6.6
Pass. Space Ratio (basis 2) 32.0	(all berths) 32.0	Food: Dining Room/Cuisine	6.3
Officers	European	Food: Buffets/Informal Dining	5.8
Total Cabins	366	Food: Quality of Ingredients	6.0
Size Range (sq ft/m)	104-293/9.6-27.2	Service: Dining Room	6.0
Outside Cabins 290 Inside Cabins	76	Service: Bars	6.2
Single Cabins	3	Service: Cabins	6.4
Balcony Cabins 0 Wheelchair Cabins	0	Cruise: Entertainment	6.0
Cabin Current	110 AC	Cruise: Activities Program	5.6
Refrigerator No Cabin TV	No	Cruise: Hospitality Standard	6.1
Dining Rooms 1 Sittings	2	OVERALL RATING	91.0
Elevators	3		

+ Nice ocean liner profile with big, but false, funnel. Stable sea ship that has been quite well maintained. The ship has a rather homely, matronly look and ambiance. Good exterior teakwood decking. Good choice of public rooms and open deck areas. The cabins are quite spacious, with solid, heavy-duty furniture and fittings.

— The interior is by no means glamorous, though it is quite pleasant, but becoming rather dated and worn. Poor sightlines in showlounge.

Dining The dining room is located on a lower deck and needs more light. Buffets are really limited. The dining room food is decent, but menu choice is limited. Service is attentive and friendly, but there's no finesse.

Other Comments Large casino is not at all inviting. This ship will provide a decent first-time cruise experience, in a fun atmosphere, at a down to earth price, providing you don't expect too much.

ms Enchantment of the Seas

Cruise Line	Royal Caribbean Cruises		
Former Names	-		
Gross Tonnage	73,600		
Builder	Kvaerner Masa Yards (Finland)		
Original Cost	$300 million		
Christened By	n/a		
Entered Service	Sep 1997		
Interior Design	Njal Eide, Howard Snoweiss, Per Hoydahl, Lars Iwdal, Tom Graboski, SMC Design		
Country of Registry	Liberia		
Tel No	n/a	Fax No	n/a
Length (ft/m)			915.8/279.1
Beam (ft/m)	105.6/32.2	Draft (ft/m)	25.0/7.62
Propulsion	diesel-electric (50,400kW)		
Propellers			2 (FP)
Decks	11	Crew	760
Pass. Capacity (basis 2) 1,954		(all berths) 2,440	
Pass. Space Ratio (basis 2) 37.6		(all berths) 30.1	
Officers			International
Total Cabins			977
Size Range (sq ft/m)		158-1,033/14.7-96.0	
Outside Cabins	578	Inside Cabins	399
Single Cabins			0
Balcony Cabins	212	Wheelchair Cabins	14
Cabin Current			110/220 AC
Refrigerator			Category A/B/C/D
Cabin TV	Yes	VCR	Category A/B
Dining Rooms	1	Sittings	2

Elevators			9
Casino	Yes	Slot Machines	Yes
Swimming Pools (outside)			1
(inside)	1 (indoor-outdoor w/glass roof		
Whirlpools	6	Gymnasium	Yes
Sauna/Steam Room Yes/Yes		Massage	Yes
Self-Service Launderette			No
Movie Theater/Seats	No	Library	Yes
Children's Facilities			Yes
Classification Society		Det Norske Veritas	

RATINGS	SCORE
Ship: Condition/Cleanliness	NYR
Ship: Space/Flow/Comfort	NYR
Ship: Decor/Furnishings	NYR
Ship: Fitness Facilities	NYR
Cabins: Comfort/Facilities	NYR
Cabins: Software	NYR
Food: Dining Room/Cuisine	NYR
Food: Buffets/Informal Dining	NYR
Food: Quality of Ingredients	NYR
Service: Dining Room	NYR
Service: Bars	NYR
Service: Cabins	NYR
Cruise: Entertainment	NYR
Cruise: Activities Program	NYR
Cruise: Hospitality Standard	NYR
OVERALL RATING	

+ This ship looks long, with the funnel well aft. Has a well-rounded stern (as on *Sovereign of the Seas*-class ships), and a Viking Crown Lounge in the center. This, together with the forward mast, provides three distinct focal points in her exterior profile. There is a wrap-around outdoor promenade deck, while inside is a seven-deck-high atrium. A delightful champagne terrace bar sits forward of the lower level of the two-deck-high dining room. The ship has two showrooms—one (875 seats) for big production shows, the other (575 seats) for smaller shows and cabarets. The children's and teens' facilities are good. All standard cabins have twin beds that convert to a double bed. Ample closet space for a one-week cruise.

— As with any large ship, expect long lines to form for embarkation, disembarkation, shore excursions, and buffets. No cushioned pads for the deck lounge chairs.

Dining The 1,195-seat dining room is two decks high, with a grand staircase connecting the two levels. General comments about the food operation aboard the company's now well-established *Legend of the Seas* and *Splendour of the Seas* apply, but some innovative options have evolved. There's an intimate champagne bar and the popular Windjammer Café.

Other Comments This is one of a pair of the latest breed of ships for this very popular cruise line (her sister ship being *Grandeur of the Seas*), introduced in December 1996.

ts EugenioCosta ★★★+

Cruise Line	Costa Cruises	Casino Yes	Slot Machines Yes
Former Names	Eugenio C	Swimming Pools (outside) 2	(inside) 0
Gross Tonnage	32,753	Whirlpools 1	Gymnasium Yes
Builder	Cantieri Riuniti dell' Adriatico (Italy)	Sauna/Steam Room Yes/No	Massage Yes
Original Cost	$24.5 million	Self-Service Launderette	Yes
Christened By	Pinuccia Costa Musso	Movie Theater/Seats	Yes/230
Entered Service	Aug 1966/Dec 1994	Library	Yes
Interior Design	Architects Zoncada/De Jorio	Children's Facilities	Yes
Country of Registry	Liberia (ELRN2)	Watersports Facilities	None
Tel No 125-2247 Fax No 125-2247		Classification Society	RINA
Length (ft/m)	713.2/217.39		

Beam (ft/m) 96.1/29.39 Draft (ft/m) 28.3/8.63	**RATINGS** **SCORE**
Propulsion steam turbine (40,456kW)	Ship: Condition/Cleanliness 7.1
Propellers 2 (FP)	Ship: Space/Flow/Comfort 7.3
Decks 10 Crew 480	Ship: Decor/Furnishings 7.6
Pass. Capacity (basis 2) 1,012 (all berths) 1,418	Ship: Fitness Facilities 6.3
Pass. Space Ratio (basis 2) 32.3 (all berths) 23.0	Cabins: Comfort/Facilities 7.3
Officers Italian	Cabins: Software 7.4
Total Cabins 506 (8 without facilities)	Food: Dining Room/Cuisine 6.7
Size Range (sq ft/m) 93-236/8.7-22.0	Food: Buffets/Informal Dining 6.3
Outside Cabins 271 Inside Cabins 235	Food: Quality of Ingredients 6.7
Single Cabins 0	Service: Dining Room 7.3
Balcony Cabins 0	Service: Bars 7.3
Wheelchair Cabins 0	Service: Cabins 7.6
Cabin Current 127 AC Refrigerator No	Cruise: Entertainment 6.1
Cabin TV No VCR No	Cruise: Activities Program 6.4
Dining Rooms 1 Sittings 2	Cruise: Hospitality Standard 7.1
Elevators 5	OVERALL RATING 104.5

✚ She has good teakwood decking outdoors and good open deck and sunning space. Spacious array of public rooms feature new, theme-park decor and colors. There's a good range of accommodations, with many different styles, sizes, and configurations of cabins. This ship is comfortable throughout, and provides good value cruising for families in a no-ties required setting that is unashamedly an ultra-casual, high-density, floating all-year-round summer camp.

— Long lines for embarkation, disembarkation, buffets, and shore tenders. Many passengers smoke heavily, and it's almost impossible to get away from them. Non-smokers should choose another ship.

Dining Pasta dishes are excellent, but other dishes can only be described as adequate, and certainly not memorable. Poor selection of breads, cheeses, and fruits.

Other Comments This well-proportioned ex-ocean liner has the graceful flowing lines of a sixties ocean liner and twin slender funnels aft. Provides good value cruises for its mainly Italian-speaking clientele.

ms Europa ★★★★★+

OPERATES

VARIOUS CRUISES WORLDWIDE

Cruise Line		Hapag-Lloyd Cruises
Former Names	-	Gross Tonnage 37,012
Builder		Bremer Vulkan (Germany)
Original Cost		$120 million
Christened By		Mrs Simone Veil
Entered Service		Jan 1982
Interior Design		Wilfried Kohnemann
Country of Registry		Germany
Tel No 112-0756	Fax No	112-0756
Length (ft/m)		654.9/199.63
Beam (ft/m) 93.8/28.60	Draft (ft/m)	27.6/8.42
Propulsion		diesel (21,270kW)
Propellers		2 (CP)
Decks	10	Crew 300
Pass. Capacity (basis 2) 600		(all berths) 600
Pass. Space Ratio (basis 2) 61.6		(all berths) 61.6
Officers		German
Total Cabins		316
Size Range (sq ft/m)		150-420/14.0-39.0
Outside Cabins	260	Inside Cabins 56
Single Cabins		32
Balcony Cabins		0
Wheelchair Cabins		1
Cabin Current		110/220 AC
Refrigerator		All cabins
Cabin TV Yes	VCR	Yes
Dining Rooms 1	Sittings	1
Elevators		4

Casino No	Slot Machines	No
Swimming Pools (outside)		2 (1 magdrodome)
Swimming Pools (inside)		1 (fresh water)
Whirlpools	0	Gymnasium Yes
Sauna/Steam Room Yes/No	Massage	Yes
Self-Service Launderette		Yes
Movie Theater/Seats		Yes/238
Library Yes	Children's Facilities	No
Watersports Facilities		None
Classification Society		Germanischer Lloyd

RATINGS	SCORE
Ship: Condition/Cleanliness	9.3
Ship: Space/Flow/Comfort	9.5
Ship: Decor/Furnishings	9.4
Ship: Fitness Facilities	9.6
Cabins: Comfort/Facilities	9.3
Cabins: Software	9.2
Food: Dining Room/Cuisine	9.2
Food: Buffets/Informal Dining	9.0
Food: Quality of Ingredients	8.9
Service: Dining Room	8.8
Service: Bars	8.8
Service: Cabins	9.0
Cruise: Entertainment	8.7
Cruise: Activities Program	8.6
Cruise: Hospitality Standard	9.2
OVERALL RATING	136.5

+ This well-designed, handsome, contemporary ship presents a really well-balanced profile. She is a superb, stable, and well-behaved ship at sea and *looks* like a ship, not a floating hotel. Although now fifteen years old, she still has the appearance of a three year old vessel and is aging very gracefully. Immaculate maintenance and care are evident throughout. Has outstanding outdoor deck and sunning space, including a private (FKK) nudist deck just aft of the funnel. The indoor swimming pool is bigger than most outdoor pools on new, much larger ships and is well used by her passengers.

There is an incredible amount of space per passenger, even when the ship is full. Dark restful colors are applied in most public rooms and subtle, hidden lighting is used throughout. The Belvedere Lounge, the ship's forward observation lounge, is still one of the most elegant rooms afloat.

Some fine artwork and sculptures are featured. There is also an outstanding health spa with many rejuvenation facilities and treatments not available on any other ship, and arguably the most professional and dedicated spa staff to be found anywhere. It is run by Polly's Vital Center (Polly Hillbrunner), from Kitzbühel in Austria, one of the world's most famous personal health and bodycare clinics.

Every cabin on this ship is excellent, and all were completely refurbished in 1995. All feature lighted closets, dark wood cabinetry with rounded edges, several full-length mirrors, television and VCR, mini-bar refrigerator with complimentary soft drinks, beer, personal safe, hairdryer and excellent cabin insulation. The bathrooms have really deep bathtubs (some cabins have shower only), a three-head shower unit, a large toiletries cabinet and handsome-sized amenities.

Refreshingly, there's not a trace of horse racing, gambling tables or slot machines. The entertainment is quite varied, with many classical and chamber concerts, some light opera, as well as lighter show fare, and often a "conferencière" (a special type of German master of ceremonies).

An impeccable, friendly European staff provide classic service that ranges from formal to informal. There are virtually no announcements. This ship deserves praise for providing a most elegant cruise experience in supremely luxurious and quiet, spacious surroundings. The qualities of elegance, space, and grace abound everywhere. This company offers fascinating itineraries that are well planned, with several overnight stays, and late night departures as standard.

— There is no wrap-around outdoor promenade deck (only a half-length port and starboard promenade). There are no cabins with private balconies. The bath towels are a little small.

Dining The dining room is extremely spacious, and with a single sitting for all meals, dining is quite unhurried. Fine, traditional silver service and plenty of space between tables help to provide an elegant dining experience. There is also a large, extremely varied cold table for breakfast and luncheon. A "gala night" buffet is held in the dining room once each cruise, always a favorite with *Europa* passengers.

The menus are not repeated, even on long voyages and excellent quality fresh food ingredients are used (all meats are American). Caviar (both Russian and Iranian) is always available, as are special orders and tableside flambé items. The food and cuisine are of course geared to German (including Austrian and Swiss-German) tastes, which means a wide variety of meat and fish dishes, as well as many breads and cheeses.

Other Comments Although there are no balcony cabins and there is no wrap-around promenade deck, the food, service and quiet, refined ambiance are really outstanding. If you are seeking a restful, restorative cruise, with fine quality European entertainment, excellent, seldom repeated worldwide itineraries, superb food and first class service, then this German-language ship is probably unbeatable. Port taxes and insurance are included. Passengers are almost entirely German-speaking, though many staff speak English. It's just about the ultimate totally relaxing cruise experience, to be enjoyed particularly on long cruises with plenty of days at sea. Repeat passengers will know that there is nothing finer for the German market at present. In 1997, the company will celebrate its 150th anniversary; perhaps there will be a new ship on the horizon for the millenium.

mv Explorer ★★★

OPERATES

*WORLDWIDE EXPEDITION CRUISES
(INCLUDING ANTARCTICA)*

Cruise Line	Abercrombie & Kent
Former Names	Society Explorer/
	Lindblad Explorer/World Explorer
Gross Tonnage	2,398
Builder	Nystad Varv Shipyard (Finland)
Original Cost	$2.5 million
Christened By	Mrs Sonja Lindblad
Entered Service	1969/Mar 1993
Interior Design	n/a
Country of Registry	Liberia
Tel No 124-1223	Fax No 124-1223
Length (ft/m)	239.1/72.88
Beam (ft/m) 46.0/14.03	Draft (ft/m) 13.7/4.20
Propulsion	diesel (2,795kW)
Propellers	1 (FP)
Decks 6	Crew 71
Pass. Capacity (basis 2) 100	(all berths) 114
Pass. Space Ratio (basis 2) 23.9	(all berths) 21.0
Officers	European
Total Cabins	50
Size Range (sq ft/m)	68.9-162.0/6.41-15.05
Outside Cabins 50	Inside Cabins 0
Single Cabins	8
Balcony Cabins	0
Wheelchair Cabins	0
Cabin Current 220 AC	Refrigerator No
Cabin TV No	VCR No
Dining Rooms	1 (open seating)

Elevators			0
Casino No		Slot Machines	No
Swimming Pools (outside)			1
Whirlpools 0		Exercise Room	Yes
Sauna/Steam Room Yes/No		Massage	Yes
Self-Service Launderette			No
Lecture/Film Room Yes		Library	Yes
Zodiacs Yes		Helicopter Pad	No
Watersports Facilities			None
Classification Society		Det Norske Veritas	

RATINGS	SCORE
Ship: Condition/Cleanliness	6.0
Ship: Space/Flow/Comfort	5.6
Ship: Expedition Equipment	6.7
Ship: Decor/Furnishings	6.2
Cabins: Comfort/Facilities	5.5
Cabins: Software	5.4
Food: Dining Room/Cuisine	6.4
Food: Buffets/Informal Dining	6.1
Food: Quality of Ingredients	6.0
Service: Dining Room	7.0
Service: Bars	6.6
Service: Cabins	7.0
Cruise: Itineraries/Operations	7.8
Cruise: Lecture Program	7.6
Cruise: Hospitality Standard	7.6
OVERALL RATING	97.5

+ Well fitted out with all necessary equipment, including Zodiac rubber landing craft. Now ageing and showing signs of wear and tear. National Geographic maps presented in all cabins. Tasteful interior decor in public rooms. Large reference library. Outstanding lecturers and nature specialists placed on board by Abercrombie & Kent.

— The cabins are extremely small and utilitarian, with little closet, drawer, and storage space. Even so, they are just about adequate for an expedition; bathrooms are really tiny, however, and don't have much room even for toiletries.

Dining Intimate dining room is cheerful, though noisy, but seats all passengers at one sitting. Good, creatively presented food (but there's little choice) and wine list. Smiling, attentive, and genuinely friendly service, but it's quite casual.

Other Comments This specialist, unpretentious expedition cruise vessel with ice-hardened hull has a well-balanced profile and is extremely maneuverable, although she is now looking tired, and maintenance could be improved. This is cruising for the serious adventurer who wants to explore the world, yet have some of the basic creature comforts of home within reach. All shore excursions, and gratuities, are included.

tss Fairstar ★★★

OPERATES

14-DAY ASIA/SOUTH PACIFIC CRUISES

Cruise Line	P&O Holidays	Casino Yes	Slot Machines Yes
Former Names	Oxfordshire	Swimming Pools (outside) 1	(inside) 0
Gross Tonnage	23,764	Whirlpools 0	Gymnasium Yes
Builder	Fairfield Shipbuilding (UK)	Sauna/Steam Room No/No	Massage No
Original Cost	n/a	Self-Service Launderette	No
Christened By	Lady Dorothea Head	Movie Theater/Seats	Yes/360
Entered Service	Feb 1957/Aug 1973	Library	No
Interior Design	n/a	Children's Facilities	Yes
Country of Registry	Liberia	Watersports Facilities	None
Tel No 124-0245 Fax No	124-0245	Classification Society	Lloyd's Register
Length (ft/m)	609.4/185.76		

Beam (ft/m) 78.2/23.86 Draft (ft/m) 27.5/8.41	
Propulsion steam turbine (13,400kW)	
Propellers 2 (FP)	
Decks 10 Crew 460	
Pass. Capacity (basis 2) 976 (all berths) 1,598	
Pass. Space Ratio (basis 2) 24.3 (all berths) 14.8	
Officers Italian	
Total Cabins 488 (68 without facilities)	
Size Range (sq ft/m) 86-301/8.0-28.0	
Outside Cabins 169 Inside Cabins 319	
Single Cabins 0	
Balcony Cabins 0	
Wheelchair Cabins 0	
Cabin Current 115 AC Refrigerator No	
Cabin TV No VCR No	
Dining Rooms 2 Sittings 2	
Elevators 4	

RATINGS	SCORE
Ship: Condition/Cleanliness	6.0
Ship: Space/Flow/Comfort	5.1
Ship: Decor/Furnishings	6.6
Ship: Fitness Facilities	4.7
Cabins: Comfort/Facilities	5.3
Cabins: Software	6.2
Food: Dining Room/Cuisine	6.5
Food: Buffets/Informal Dining	6.2
Food: Quality of Ingredients	5.7
Service: Dining Room	7.7
Service: Bars	6.7
Service: Cabins	6.6
Cruise: Entertainment	6.1
Cruise: Activities Program	6.1
Cruise: Hospitality Standard	6.0
OVERALL RATING	91.5

+ Well-constructed older ship has classic lines and profile has new dolphin logo on her funnel. Well maintained. New late-night Brasserie Delfino is popular. Sail-cloth awning around swimming pool provides shade. Has a recently added arcade shopping area. Good for families with children, with plenty of noisy activities. Other cabins fine for two, crowded with more. There is a curfew for children at night.

— Limited open deck and sunning space. Expect lines for embarkation, disembarkation, shore tenders, and buffets. No sophistication. Public rooms are barely adequate for the number of passengers, and it's difficult to get away from smokers. Too many duty-free shops, and lines. Take books to read (there's no library). Has really small cabin bathrooms, most with exposed plumbing. There are too many irritating announcements, like at summer camp.

Dining The dining rooms, although crowded and noisy, have plenty of tables for two. The cuisine is low-budget banquet food, and is strictly quantity, not quality, although it's adequate, and there's always plenty of good pasta. There is an excellent pizzeria.

Other Comments Lacks any sort of glamor, but makes up for it in spirit and boisterous cruise atmosphere. Good value for money cruise product for younger "down-under" passengers who want a lively, active, noisy, fun-filled cruise.

ms Fantasy ★★★★

OPERATES

3- AND 4-DAY BAHAMAS CRUISES
(YEAR-ROUND)

Cruise Line		Carnival Cruise Lines	
Former Names			-
Gross Tonnage			70,367
Builder		Kvaerner Masa-Yards (Finland)	
Original Cost			$225 million
Christened By		Mrs Tellervo Koivisto	
Entered Service			Mar 1990
Interior Design			Joe Farcus
Country of Registry			Liberia
Tel No	124-2660	Fax No	124-2661
Length (ft/m)			855.8/263.60
Beam (ft/m) 104.0/31.40		Draft (ft/m)	25.9/7.90
Propulsion		diesel-electric (42,240kW)	
Propellers			2 (CP)
Decks	10	Crew	920
Pass. Capacity (basis 2) 2,044		(all berths) 2,634	
Pass. Space Ratio (basis 2) 34.4		(all berths) 26.7	
Officers			Italian
Total Cabins			1,022
Size Range (sq ft/m)		185-421/17.0-39.0	
Outside Cabins	620	Inside Cabins	402
Single Cabins			0
Balcony Cabins			54
Wheelchair Cabins			20
Cabin Current			110 AC
Refrigerator		Category 11/12 only	
Cabin TV	Yes	VCR	No
Dining Rooms	2	Sittings	2

Elevators			14
Casino	Yes	Slot Machines	Yes
Swimming Pools (outside) 3		(inside)	0
Whirlpools	6	Gymnasium	Yes
Sauna/Steam Room Yes/Yes		Massage	Yes
Self-Service Launderette			Yes
Movie Theater/Seats	No	Library	Yes
Children's Facilities			Yes
Watersports Facilities			None
Classification Society		Lloyd's Register	

RATINGS	SCORE
Ship: Condition/Cleanliness	8.0
Ship: Space/Flow/Comfort	7.8
Ship: Decor/Furnishings	6.8
Ship: Fitness Facilities	7.8
Cabins: Comfort/Facilities	7.6
Cabins: Software	7.4
Food: Dining Room/Cuisine	6.7
Food: Buffets/Informal Dining	6.5
Food: Quality of Ingredients	5.3
Service: Dining Room	7.0
Service: Bars	7.2
Service: Cabins	6.4
Cruise: Entertainment	7.9
Cruise: Activities Program	7.8
Cruise: Hospitality Standard	6.3
OVERALL RATING	106.5

+ Although externally angular and not handsome, this is one of eight identical megaships for Carnival. Features vibrant colors and extensive use of neon lighting for sensory stimulation. Six-deck-high atrium features spectacular artistic centerpiece. Expansive open deck areas. Public entertainment lounges, bars, and clubs galore, with something for everyone. Delightful library and quiet reading room, but few books. Dazzling colors and 21st-century-themed designs in handsome public rooms connected by wide indoor boulevards. Lavish multi-tiered showroom. Three-deck-high glass enclosed health spa. Banked jogging track. Gigantic casino has non-stop action.

— Expect long lines for embarkation, disembarkation, shore excursions, and buffets. Too many annoying announcements and hustling for drinks. Large shop, poor merchandise.

Dining The two large dining rooms are noisy, but the decor is attractive. The food is very disappointing (despite being upgraded). The service is basic, and pushy, with no finesse.

Other Comments First of a series of eight sister ships. Although the cuisine is so-so, the real fun begins at sundown, when Carnival excels in sound, lights, and razzle-dazzle shows. From the futuristic Electricity Disco to the ancient Cleopatra's Bar, this ship will entertain you well.

ms Fascination ★★★★

OPERATES
*7-DAY CARIBBEAN CRUISES
(YEAR-ROUND)*

Cruise Line		Carnival Cruise Lines
Former Names		-
Gross Tonnage		70,367
Builder		Kvaerner Masa-Yards (Finland)
Original Cost		$315 million
Christened By		Mrs Jean Farcus
Entered Service		Jul 1994
Interior Design		Joe Farcus
Country of Registry		Liberia
Tel No 134-6374	Fax No	134-6375
Length (ft/m)		855.0/260.60
Beam (ft/m) 104.9/31.69	Draft (ft/m)	25.7/7.86
Propulsion		diesel-electric (42,240kW)
Propellers		2 (CP)
Decks 10	Crew	920
Pass. Capacity (basis 2) 2,040	(all berths) 2,594	
Pass. Space Ratio (basis 2) 34.4	(all berths) 26.7	
Officers		Italian
Total Cabins		1,020
Size Range (sq ft/m)		185-421/17.0-39.0
Outside Cabins 618	Inside Cabins	402
Single Cabins		20
Balcony Cabins		26
Wheelchair Cabins		0
Cabin Current		110 AC
Refrigerator		Category 11/12 only
Cabin TV Yes	VCR	No
Dining Rooms 2	Sittings	2

Elevators			14
Casino	Yes	Slot Machines	Yes
Swimming Pools (outside) 3		(inside)	0
Whirlpools	6	Gymnasium	Yes
Sauna/Steam Room Yes/Yes		Massage	Yes
Self-Service Launderette			Yes
Movie Theater/Seats	No	Library	Yes
Children's Facilities			Yes
Watersports Facilities			None
Classification Society			Lloyd's Register

RATINGS	SCORE
Ship: Condition/Cleanliness	8.5
Ship: Space/Flow/Comfort	7.8
Ship: Decor/Furnishings	8.7
Ship: Fitness Facilities	7.8
Cabins: Comfort/Facilities	7.6
Cabins: Software	7.4
Food: Dining Room/Cuisine	6.7
Food: Buffets/Informal Dining	6.5
Food: Quality of Ingredients	5.3
Service: Dining Room	7.1
Service: Bars	7.2
Service: Cabins	6.5
Cruise: Entertainment	8.2
Cruise: Activities Program	7.8
Cruise: Hospitality Standard	6.4
OVERALL RATING	109.5

+ One of a series of eight identical megaships for Carnival reflects the fine creative interior design work of Joe Farcus. Almost vibration-free service from diesel electric propulsion system. The atrium lobby is six decks high, with cool marble and hot neon, topped by large glass dome, and a spectacular artistic centerpiece. Expansive open deck areas, but never enough when the ship is full. 28 outside suites have whirlpool tubs and elegant decor. Public entertainment lounges, bars, and clubs galore, with something for everyone. Sophisticated Hollywood design theme in handsome public rooms connected by wide indoor boulevards crave your indulgence, as will the photo opportunities with life-like figures from the movies. Lavish multi-tiered showroom and fine razzle-dazzle shows. Has a three-deck-high glass-enclosed health spa and gymnasium. Gigantic casino has non-stop action.

— As with all large ships, expect long lines for embarkation, disembarkation, shore excursions, and buffets.

Dining Two huge, noisy dining rooms (both are non-smoking) with the usual efficient, assertive service. Improved cuisine so-so, but first-time passengers seem to accept it.

Other Comments The real fun begins at sundown, when Carnival excels in decibels. This ship will entertain you in timely fashion.

mv Fuji Maru ★★★★

OPERATES
JAPAN/SOUTH EAST ASIA CRUISES

Cruise Line	Mitsui OSK Passenger Line	Swimming Pools (outside) 1	(inside)	0
Former Names	- Gross Tonnage 23,340	Whirlpools	0 (4 Japanese Baths)	
Builder	Mitsubishi (Japan)	Gymnasium		Yes
Original Cost	$55 million	Sauna/Steam Room Yes/No	Massage	Yes*
Christened By	Mr Shintaro Ishiwara	Self-Service Launderette		Yes
Entered Service	Apr 1989	Movie Theater/Seats Yes/142	Library	Yes
Interior Design Osamu Higuchi/Mikiya Murakami		Children's Facilities		Yes*
Country of Registry	Japan	Watersports Facilities		None
Tel No 120-0467 Fax No 120-0470		Classification Society	Nippon Kaiji Kyokai	
Length (ft/m)	547.9/167.00		* = on leisure cruises only	
Beam (ft/m) 78.7/24.00 Draft (ft/m) 21.4/6.55				
Propulsion	diesel (15,740kW)	**RATINGS**		**SCORE**
Propellers	2 (CP)	Ship: Condition/Cleanliness		7.5
Decks	8 Crew 190	Ship: Space/Flow/Comfort		7.8
Pass. Capacity (basis 2) 328	(all berths) 603	Ship: Decor/Furnishings		7.6
Pass. Space Ratio (basis 2) 71.1	(all berths) 38.7	Ship: Fitness Facilities		6.4
Officers	Japanese	Cabins: Comfort/Facilities		6.7
Total Cabins	164	Cabins: Software		7.1
Size Range (sq ft/m)	182-376/17.0-35.0	Food: Dining Room/Cuisine		7.3
Outside Cabins	164 Inside Cabins 0	Food: Buffets/Informal Dining		6.6
Single Cabins	0	Food: Quality of Ingredients		7.0
Balcony Cabins	0 Wheelchair Cabins 2	Service: Dining Room		7.3
Cabin Current	100 AC	Service: Bars		7.4
Refrigerator	Suites, Deluxe cabins only	Service: Cabins		6.9
Cabin TV Yes VCR No		Cruise: Entertainment		6.7
Dining Rooms 1 Sittings 1		Cruise: Activities Program		6.7
Elevators	5	Cruise: Hospitality Standard		8.3
Casino Yes* Slot Machines No		OVERALL RATING		107.3

+ Well thought out and flexible multi-functional design, principally for incentives, conventions, as a seminar and training ship and individual passengers. Extensive lecture and conference rooms, the largest of which is two decks high, seats 600, and converts into a sports stadium or hall for industrial product introductions. Elegant lobby and two-level atrium. Classic wood-paneled library. Has two Japanese-style grand baths, and traditional "Washitsu" tatami mat room. "Hanaguruma" owner's room is elegant for small formal functions. Sakura Salon is soothing, with Western and traditional Japanese design. High-tech media and television system throughout (bilingual multiplex televisions in crew cabins). Two suites are lovely, and deluxe cabins are of a high standard, with full bathtubs. Other simply furnished cabins are ideal for seminar and school usage. Folded blankets are lovely.

— Indoor areas clean and tidy, but some outdoor upper decks need attention.

Dining The dining room is attractive, has a high ceiling, but bright lighting. Japanese or Western cuisine for all meals. The food is of a good standard, with simple, but colorful, presentation. There are several beverage machines.

Other Comments Good exhibition, training, and educational charter cruise ship with up to date facilities, although not ideally designed for individual passengers. No tipping is allowed.

ms Funchal ★★+

Cruise Line			Arcalia Shipping
Former Names			-
Gross Tonnage			9,563
Builder		Helsingor Skibsvog (Denmark)	
Original Cost	n/a	Christened By	n/a
Entered Service			Oct 1961/May 1986
Interior Design			George Potamianos
Country of Registry			Panama
Tel No	133-0320	Fax No	133-6716
Length (ft/m)			503.6/153.1
Beam (ft/m)	62.5/19.08	Draft (ft/m)	20.3/6.20
Propulsion			diesel (7,356kW)
Propellers			2 (FP)
Decks	6	Crew	155
Pass. Capacity (basis 2) 439		(all berths) 548	
Pass. Space Ratio (basis 2) 21.4		(all berths) 17.4	
Officers			European
Total Cabins			236
Size Range (sq ft/m)		102.2-252.9/9.5-23.5	
Outside Cabins	149	Inside Cabins	87
Single Cabins			33
Balcony Cabins	0	Wheelchair Cabins	0
Cabin Current	220 AC	Refrigerator	No
Cabin TV	No	VCR	No
Dining Rooms	1	Sittings	1
Elevators			2
Casino	Yes	Slot Machines	Yes

Swimming Pools (outside) 1		(inside)	0
Whirlpools	0	Gymnasium	Yes
Sauna/Steam Room Yes/No		Massage	No
Self-Service Launderette			No
Movie Theater/Seats			No
Library			Yes
Children's Facilities			No
Watersports Facilities			None
Classification Society			Rinave Portuguesa

RATINGS	SCORE
Ship: Hardware/Maintenance	5.6
Ship: Space/Flow/Comfort	6.1
Ship: Decor/Furnishings	6.4
Ship: Fitness Facilities	3.5
Cabins: Comfort/Facilities	6.1
Cabins: Software	6.1
Food: Dining Room/Cuisine	6.0
Food: Buffets/Informal Dining	5.4
Food: Quality of Ingredients	6.0
Service: Dining Room	6.2
Service: Bars	6.6
Service: Cabins	6.7
Cruise: Entertainment	6.0
Cruise: Activities Program	5.6
Cruise: Hospitality Standard	7.0
OVERALL RATING	89.3

+ This small ship has a classic, well-balanced, but now dated profile. Has a very warm, charming and attentive Portuguese staff, and a loyal passenger following. Although showing her age, she has twin sheltered promenade decks for those who enjoy strolling. The refurbished public rooms are well laid out, with plenty of wood paneling and wood trim. The cabins are very compact, yet quite well appointed, with just enough closet and drawer space. They are decorated in pleasing colors.

— Cabin bathrooms are very small and utilitarian. Some back-to-back cabins share bathrooms (a red light goes on in the opposing cabin when the bathroom is in use). There are too many cabin categories. Has sloppy paintwork everywhere.

Dining The dining rooms are quite tastefully decorated, and have a real cozy, old-world atmosphere. The food, which is European in style (that means plenty of fish and meats) is surprisingly good, and the service is friendly from the Portuguese waiters. There is a limited selection of cheeses and fruits.

Other Comments Very popular with northern Europeans in the summer, and Brazilians in the winter, this ship offers a destination-oriented cruise experience in comfortable, old world surroundings, ideally suited to singles and couples seeking good value for money, but North Americans may find the ship to be too eclectic. Good if you like small, older ships with their accompanying eccentricities. Often operates under charter to various tour operators.

ms Galaxy

Cruise Line			Celebrity Cruises
Former Names			-
Gross Tonnage			73,850
Builder			Meyer Werft (Germany)
Original Cost			$320 million
Christened By			n/a
Entered Service			Dec 1996
Interior Design			Katzourakis/McNeece
Country of Registry			Liberia
Tel No	n/a	Fax No	n/a
Length (ft/m)			852.0/259.70
Beam (ft/m) 105.6/32.20		Draft (ft/m)	24.2/7.40
Propulsion/Propellers		diesel (29,250kW)/2 (CP)	
Decks	10	Crew	770
Pass. Capacity (basis 2) 1,908		(all berths) 2,262	
Pass. Space Ratio (basis 2) 38.7		(all berths) 32.6	
Officers			Greek
Total Cabins			954
Size Range (sq ft/m)		172-1,515/15.7-140.7	
Outside Cabins	650	Inside Cabins	304
Single Cabins			0
Balcony Cabins	220	Wheelchair Cabins	8
Cabin Current			110/220 AC
Refrigerator	Yes	Cabin TV	Yes
VCR		Deck 10 suites only	
Dining Rooms	2	Sittings	2
Elevators			9
Casino	Yes	Slot Machines	Yes

Swimming Pools (outside)		2
Swimming Pools (inside)	1 (under magrodome)	
Whirlpools	3	Gymnasium Yes
Sauna/Steam Room Yes/No	Massage	Yes
Self-Service Launderette		No
Movie Theater/Seats		No
Library		Yes
Children's Facilities/Playroom		Yes
Watersports Facilities		None
Classification Society		Lloyd's Register

RATINGS	SCORE
Ship: Condition/Cleanliness	NYR
Ship: Space/Flow/Comfort	NYR
Ship: Decor/Furnishings	NYR
Ship: Fitness Facilities	NYR
Cabins: Comfort/Facilities	NYR
Cabins: Software	NYR
Food: Dining Room/Cuisine	NYR
Food: Buffets/Informal Dining	NYR
Food: Quality of Ingredients	NYR
Service: Dining Room	NYR
Service: Bars	NYR
Service: Cabins	NYR
Cruise: Entertainment	NYR
Cruise: Activities Program	NYR
Cruise: Hospitality Standard	NYR
OVERALL RATING	

+ Slightly longer than sister ship *Century*, the extra length provides room for a third swimming pool, covered by a large glass magrodome. Inside are a four-deck-high main foyer and a three-deck-high atrium. There's a 1,000-seat showlounge with large side balconies, and good sightlines from just about every seat. The Aquaspa contains 9,040 sq. ft. (839.8 m²) of space. The largest suites are the Presidential Suites, located amidships; each is a 1,173 sq ft (109 m²) penthouse with an interconnecting door. When joined with the next-door suite the apartment suite measures a whopping 1,515 sq ft (140.7 m²).

— Despite over 4.5 acres (1.8 ha) of open deck space, it seems small on days at sea when the ship is full. No cabins for singles. Though improved, shore excursions are still a weak point.

Dining Huge two-level dining room, with a grand staircase. Each level has its own galley, and the noise level in both sections is quite acceptable. There's also a bi-level lido café, with four serving lines, and a small café for coffee and pastries. In-cabin dining is an option for passengers in the Presidential and 12 Century suites.

Other Comments Celebrity Cruises is known for its excellent cuisine and presentation, although it is more difficult to deliver on the new, larger ships. *Galaxy* is a stunning new ship, with some outstanding facilities.

ms Grand Princess

OPERATES
7-DAY CARIBBEAN
CRUISES (YEAR-ROUND)

Cruise Line			Princess Cruises
Former Names			-
Gross Tonnage			104,000
Builder			Fincantieri (Italy)
Original Cost			$385 million
Entered Service			Oct 1997
Interior Design			Teresa Anderson/
			Giacomo Mortola
Country of Registry			Italy
Tel No	n/a	Fax No	n/a
Length (ft/m)			935.0/285.0
Beam (ft/m)	n/a	Draft (ft/m)	n/a
Propulsion			n/a
Propellers			2 (FP)
Decks	n/a	Crew	1,100
Pass. Capacity (basis 2) 2,600		(all berths) n/a	
Pass. Space Ratio (basis 2) 38.4		(all berths) n/a	
Officers			n/a
Total Cabins			1,300
Size Range (sq ft/m)			n/a
Outside Cabins	n/a	Inside Cabins	n/a
Single Cabins			n/a
Balcony Cabins	n/a	Wheelchair Cabins	n/a
Cabin Current			110/220 AC
Refrigerator			n/a
Cabin TV	Yes	VCR	n/a
Dining Rooms	3	Sittings	2
Elevators			16

Casino	Yes	Slot Machines	Yes
Swimming Pools (outside and inside)			n/a
Whirlpools	n/a	Gymnasium	Yes
Sauna/Steam Room	Yes/Yes	Massage	Yes
Self-Service Launderette			Yes
Movie Theater/Seats			Yes/n/a
Library			Yes
Children's Facilities			Yes
Watersports Facilities			None
Classification Society			Lloyd's Register

RATINGS	SCORE
Ship: Condition/Cleanliness	NYR
Ship: Space/Flow/Comfort	NYR
Ship: Decor/Furnishings	NYR
Ship: Fitness Facilities	NYR
Cabins: Comfort/Facilities	NYR
Cabins: Software	NYR
Food: Dining Room/Cuisine	NYR
Food: Buffets/Informal Dining	NYR
Food: Quality of Ingredients	NYR
Service: Dining Room	NYR
Service: Bars	NYR
Service: Cabins	NYR
Cruise: Entertainment	NYR
Cruise: Activities Program	NYR
Cruise: Hospitality Standard	NYR
OVERALL RATING	

+ This is a very large ship, and presents a surprisingly bold, forthright profile. Inside the ship, passengers can choose from a wide range of public rooms, and there are also many intimate rooms. There's plenty of space, and passenger flow is expected to be good. The health spa complex surrounds a swimming pool suspended between two decks. An excellent collection of artwork has been chosen. I expect the cabins to be extremely functional; some 750 cabins (70 per cent of outside cabins) have private balconies.

— None known at press time. As on any large ship, you should expect long lines for embarkation, disembarkation, buffets, shore tenders, and shore excursions.

Dining There are three main dining rooms, each one split into multi-tier sections. Each dining room also has its own galley. Apart from these, three other dining areas offer indoor-outdoor dining, and there's also a large and spectacular pizzeria. A pâtisserie and wine/caviar bar/pizzeria are additional informal dining areas.

Other Comments The striking, innovative design for this huge ship, now the world's largest (though not the longest), is indicative of what's to come in the future for the big players in this industry.

ms Grandeur of the Seas

OPERATES

CARIBBEAN CRUISES

Cruise Line		Royal Caribbean Cruises
Former Names		-
Gross Tonnage		73,600
Builder		Kvaerner Masa Yards (Finland)
Original Cost		$300 million
Christened By		n/a
Entered Service		Nov 1996
Interior Design		Njal Eide
Country of Registry		n/a
Tel No	n/a Fax No	n/a
Length (ft/m)		915.6/279.1
Beam (ft/m) 105.6/32.2	Draft (ft/m)	25.0/7.62
Propulsion		diesel-electric (50,400kW)
Propellers		2 (FP)
Decks	11 Crew	768
Pass. Capacity (basis 2) 1,950	(all berths) 2,432	
Pass. Space Ratio (basis 2) 37.7	(all berths) 30.2	
Officers		Norwegian
Total Cabins		977
Size Range (sq ft/m)	137-1,147/12.8-106.6	
Outside Cabins	578 Inside Cabins	399
Single Cabins		0
Balcony Cabins	212 Wheelchair Cabins	14
Cabin Current		110/220 AC
Refrigerator		Some cabins
Cabin TV	Yes VCR	Some cabins
Dining Rooms	1 Sittings	2
Elevators		9

Casino	Yes	Slot Machines	Yes
Swimming Pools (outside)			1
(inside)	1 (indoor-outdoor w/glass roof)		
Whirlpools	6	Gymnasium	Yes
Sauna/Steam Room Yes/Yes		Massage	Yes
Self-Service Launderette			No
Movie Theater/Seats	No	Library	Yes
Children's Facilities/Playroom			Yes
Watersports Facilities			None
Classification Society		Det Norske Veritas	

RATINGS	SCORE
Ship: Condition/Cleanliness	NYR
Ship: Space/Flow/Comfort	NYR
Ship: Decor/Furnishings	NYR
Ship: Fitness Facilities	NYR
Cabins: Comfort/Facilities	NYR
Cabins: Software	NYR
Food: Dining Room/Cuisine	NYR
Food: Buffets/Informal Dining	NYR
Food: Quality of Ingredients	NYR
Service: Dining Room	NYR
Service: Bars	NYR
Service: Cabins	NYR
Cruise: Entertainment	NYR
Cruise: Activities Program	NYR
Cruise: Hospitality Standard	NYR
OVERALL RATING	

+ This ship has a lengthy design profile, with a funnel placed well aft, a well-rounded stern (as on *Sovereign of the Seas*-class ships), and a Viking Crown Lounge in the center. This, together with the forward mast, provides three distinct focal points in profile. The Viking Crown Lounge sits between funnel and mast and overlooks the forward section of the swimming pool deck. There is a wrap-around outdoor promenade deck and, inside, a seven-deck-high atrium. Good children's and teens' facilities. All standard cabins have twin beds that convert to a double bed. There's ample closet space for a one-week cruise.

— None known at press time, though you should expect long lines, as on any large vessel. No cushioned pads are provided for deck lounge chairs.

Dining Huge, two-deck-high dining room seats 1,195. General comments about the food operation aboard *Legend of the Seas* and *Splendour of the Seas* apply, but there are some innovative options. There's an intimate champagne bar and the popular Windjammer Café.

Other Comments This is another new ship design for Royal Caribbean Cruises (her sister ship is *Enchantment of the Seas*), with what should prove to be an excellent passenger flow. The ship will be good for first-time cruisegoers who want very comfortable surroundings and all the latest facilities in one neat, well-packaged and, predictably, fine-tuned cruise vacation.

mv Gripsholm ★★★

OPERATES
VARIOUS CRUISES WORLDWIDE

Cruise Line		Transocean Tours
Former Names	Regent Sea/Samantha/San Paolo/
		Navarino/Gripsholm
Gross Tonnage		22,785
Builder	Ansaldo Sestri-Ponente (Italy)
Original Cost		UK£7,000,000
Christened By	Princess Margarethe/Robert Stack
Entered Service		May 1957/Nov 1985
Interior Design	Patricia Hayes & Associates
Country of Registry		Bahamas
Tel No	110-3126	Fax No	110-3257
Length (ft/m)		631.2/192.41
Beam (ft/m) 81.8/24.95	Draft (ft/m)	27.8/8.49
Propulsion		diesel (11,916kW)
Propellers		2
Decks	8	Crew	365
Pass. Capacity (basis 2) 714	(all berths) 760
Pass. Space Ratio (basis 2) 31.9	(all berths) 29.9
Officers		European
Total Cabins		357
Size Range (sq ft/m)	172-280/16.0-26.0
Outside Cabins	337	Inside Cabins	20
Single Cabins		0
Balcony Cabins	0	Wheelchair Cabins	3
Cabin Current	110 AC	Refrigerator Suites only
Cabin TV	No	VCR	No
Dining Rooms	2 (1 smoking, 1 non-smoking)
Sittings		2

Elevators			4
Casino	Yes	Slot Machines	Yes
Swimming Pools (outside) 1	(inside)	0
Whirlpools	2	Gymnasium	Yes
Sauna/Steam Room Yes/No	Massage	Yes
Self-Service Launderette		No
Movie Theater/Seats		Yes/218
Library	Yes	Children's Facilities No
Watersports Facilities		None
Classification Society	Lloyd's Register

RATINGS	SCORE
Ship: Condition/Cleanliness	6.0
Ship: Space/Flow/Comfort	7.1
Ship: Decor/Furnishings	6.4
Ship: Fitness Facilities	5.3
Cabins: Comfort/Facilities	5.8
Cabins: Software	6.7
Food: Dining Room/Cuisine	7.4
Food: Buffets/Informal Dining	6.8
Food: Quality of Ingredients	6.9
Service: Dining Room	7.0
Service: Bars	7.1
Service: Cabins	6.4
Cruise: Entertainment	5.6
Cruise: Activities Program	6.0
Cruise: Hospitality Standard	6.2
OVERALL RATING	96.7

+ Well-constructed former ocean liner has classic lines and styling, and is one of only a handful of two-funnel ships. Generous open deck and sunning space, with good teakwood decking. Has a glass-enclosed promenade deck. Wide array of public rooms, which are quite spacious and well appointed, with high ceilings and lots of wood accents. The ship has indoor whirlpools and adjacent spa facilities. Distinct European flair is evident in the decor, furnishings, and colors. Richly paneled library. The mostly outside cabins, in wide variety of configurations, are of generous proportions, with spacious closets and ample drawer space; most beds parallel the ship's axis. Friendly, comfortable ambiance throughout.

— The ship looks well worn and tired and is in need of more investment in maintenance. Awkward layout and flow, due to conversion from former two-class liner. Stale cigarette smoke odor everywhere, particularly in soft furnishings. Most Sun Deck cabins have lifeboat-obstructed views. Poor book selection in the library. Long lines for buffets and shore tenders.

Dining Bright, cheerful dining room is split into three sections. Open seating for breakfast and lunch. The company only provides a low budget for food, and it shows.

Other Comments Go for the destinations and this ship will provide cruising in a good style reminiscent of bygone days, and at a modest price, for German-speaking passengers.

ms Hanseatic ★★★★★+

OPERATES

*WORLDWIDE EXPEDITION CRUISES
(INCLUDING ANTARCTICA)*

Cruise Line	Hanseatic Tours		Swimming Pools (outside)		1
Former Names	-		Whirlpools		1
Gross Tonnage	8,378		Exercise Room		Yes
Builder	Rauma Yards (Finland)		Sauna/Steam Room Yes/No	Massage	Yes
Original Cost	$68 million		Self-Service Launderette		No
Christened By	Ms Dagmar Berghoff		Lecture/Film Room		Yes (seats 160)
Entered Service	Mar 1993		Library Yes	Zodiacs	14
Interior Design	Wilfried Koehnemann		Helicopter Pad		Yes
Country of Registry	Bahamas		Watersports Facilities		banana boat
Tel No 110-3730 Fax No	110-3726		Classification Society	Det Norske Veritas	
Length (ft/m)	402.9/122.80				
Beam (ft/m) 59.1/18.00 Draft (ft/m)	15.5/4.71		**RATINGS**		**SCORE**
Propulsion	diesel (5,880kW)		Ship: Condition/Cleanliness		9.2
Propellers	2 (CP)		Ship: Space/Flow/Comfort		9.1
Decks 6 Crew	122		Ship: Expedition Equipment		9.3
Pass. Capacity (basis 2) 184	(all berths) 194		Ship: Decor/Furnishings		9.1
Pass. Space Ratio (basis 2) 45.5	(all berths) 43.1		Cabins: Comfort/Facilities		9.1
Officers	German		Cabins: Software		9.1
Total Cabins	92		Food: Dining Room/Cuisine		8.8
Size Range (sq ft/m)	231.4-470.3/21.5-43.7		Food: Buffets/Informal Dining		8.6
Outside Cabins 92 Inside Cabins	0		Food: Quality of Ingredients		8.7
Single Cabins	0		Service: Dining Room		8.7
Balcony Cabins	0		Service: Bars		8.7
Wheelchair Cabins	2		Service: Cabins		8.8
Cabin Current 220 AC Refrigerator	Yes		Cruise: Itineraries/Operations		9.5
Cabin TV Yes VCR	Yes		Cruise: Lecture Program		9.2
Dining Rooms 1 Sittings	1		Cruise: Hospitality Standard		9.2
Elevators	2		OVERALL RATING		135.1

+ Fine luxury ship, fittings and furnishings, under long-term charter to Hanseatic Tours. Has fully enclosed bridge, ice-hardened hull with highest classification, the latest high-tech navigation equipment, and an open bridge policy. Staff are very helpful. Special boot-washing room provided. The all-outside cabins, located forward, are large and well appointed, and include separate lounge area, mini-bar, television. Bathrooms have bathtub and bathrobe. There are only two types of cabins; 34 have double beds, others have twin beds. Bridge Deck suites and cabins have butler service and full in-cabin dining privileges. Outstanding, well-planned itineraries. Informal ambiance. Has outstanding lecturers and naturalists.

— No cabins have private balconies.

Dining The dining room is elegant, warm, and welcoming, and features fine Rosenthal china and silverware. The cuisine and service are first rate, with high-quality ingredients used. Very creative and nicely presented. Excellent selection of breads, cheeses, and fruits. An alternative à la carte dining room has been added.

Other Comments Provides destination-intensive, nature and life-enrichment expedition cruises in elegant surroundings to fascinating places. Port taxes, insurance, gratuities and most shore excursions are included.

mv Hebridean Princess ★★★★★

OPERATES
7-DAY SCOTTISH COAST CRUISES

Cruise Line	Hebridean Island Cruises		
Former Names	Columba		
Gross Tonnage	2,112		
Builder	Hall Russell (Scotland)		
Original Cost	n/a		
Christened By	HRH the Duchess of York		
Entered Service	1964/Apr 1989		
Interior Design	Susan Binns		
Country of Registry	Scotland		
Tel No	144-0772	Fax No	144-0772
Length (ft/m)			235.0/71.6
Beam (ft/m)	46.0/14.0	Draft (ft/m)	10.0/3.0
Propulsion			diesel (1,790kW)
Propellers			2 (FP)
Decks	5	Crew	35
Pass. Capacity (basis 2) 48		(all berths) 55	
Pass. Space Ratio (basis 2) 44.0		(all berths) 38.4	
Officers			British
Total Cabins			29
Size Range (sq ft/m)		112-367/10.4-34.0	
Outside Cabins	4	Inside Cabins	0
Single Cabins			10
Balcony Cabins	4	Wheelchair Cabins	0
Cabin Current			240 AC
Refrigerator			Yes
Cabin TV	Yes	VCR	Yes (some cabins)
Dining Rooms	1	Sittings	1
Elevators			0

Casino	No	Slot Machines	No
Swimming Pools (outside) 0		(inside)	0
Whirlpools	0	Gymnasium	Yes
Sauna/Steam Room No/No		Massage	No
Self-Service Launderette			No
Movie Theater/Seats			No
Library			Yes
Children's Facilities			No
Watersports Facilities			None
Classification Society			Lloyd's Register

RATINGS	SCORE
Ship: Condition/Cleanliness	8.6
Ship: Space/Flow/Comfort	8.4
Ship: Facilities	9.0
Ship: Expedition Equipment	8.0
Ship: Fitness/Watersports Facilities	6.0
Cabins: Comfort/Facilities	8.3
Cabins: Software	9.0
Food: Dining Room/Cuisine	9.1
Food: Buffets/Informal Dining	8.8
Food: Quality of Ingredients	8.5
Service: Dining Room	8.6
Service: Bars	8.5
Service: Cabins	8.4
Cruise: Entertainment/Lecture Program	7.7
Cruise: Hospitality Standard	9.3
OVERALL RATING	126.2

+ Charming little ship that combines stately home service with a warm country cottage ambience. Tiree Lounge features a real brick-walled fireplace. All cabins have different color schemes and names (there are no numbers, and, refreshingly, no door locks). All are individually designed and created (with sweeping Laura Ashley-style drapes), and come in a range of configurations: double-bed, twin-bed, or single-bed. All except three have a private bathroom with bath or shower with real Victorian bathroom fittings (some are gold-plated). The brass cabin portholes actually open. Use of the ship's small boats, speedboat, bicycles, and fishing gear is included in the price, as are entrance fees to gardens, castles, and other attractions. Specialist guides accompany all cruises.

— This vessel is strong, but does have structural limitations and noisy engines that cause some vibration (however, the engines don't run at night, and the ship anchors before bedtime). It's often cold (and very wet) in the Scottish islands, so take plenty of warm clothing for layering.

Dining Non-smoking dining room. Outstanding cuisine is the same quality and presentation as the Sea Goddess ships. Fresh produce is purchased locally—a welcome change from the mass catering of most cruise ships. Although there are no flambé items (the galley has electric, not gas, cookers), what is created is beautifully presented and of the very highest standard.

Breakfast menus alternate every two days and feature special dishes in addition to the traditional Scottish fare. Although there's waiter service for most things, there's also a delightful buffet table display for breakfast and luncheon. Freshly squeezed orange juice (difficult to obtain on most cruise ships) is always available. Superb wine list, with moderate prices. Many wonderful whiskies and vintage cognacs (try the 50-year-old Remy Martin Louis XIII). Highly personal and attentive service.

Other Comments Inspector Hercules Poirot would be at home here. It is a sheer pleasure to cruise on this ship—a superb Scottish Island Fling. Direct bookings are accepted. Now the only cruise vessel in the world with an all-British crew, she is one of the world's best kept travel secrets.

ms Holiday ★★★★

OPERATES

3- AND 4-DAY BAJA CALIFORNIA CRUISES (YEAR-ROUND)

Cruise Line		Carnival Cruise Lines	
Former Names		-	
Gross Tonnage		46,052	
Builder		Aalborg Vaerft (Denmark)	
Original Cost		$170 million	
Christened By		Mrs Lin Arison	
Entered Service		Jul 1985	
Interior Design		Joe Farcus	
Country of Registry		Bahamas	
Tel No	110-3216	Fax No	110-3216
Length (ft/m)		726.9/221.57	
Beam (ft/m)	92.4/28.17	Draft (ft/m)	25.5/7.77
Propulsion		diesel (22,360kW)	
Propellers		2 (CP)	
Decks	9	Crew	660
Pass. Capacity (basis 2) 1,452		(all berths) 1,800	
Pass. Space Ratio (basis 2) 31.7		(all berths) 25.5	
Officers		Italian	
Total Cabins		726	
Size Range (sq ft/m)		185-190/17.0-17.6	
Outside Cabins	447	Inside Cabins	279
Single Cabins		0	
Balcony Cabins		10	
Wheelchair Cabins		15	
Cabin Current		110 AC	
Refrigerator		Category 12 only	
Cabin TV	Yes	VCR	No
Dining Rooms	2	Sittings	2

Elevators			8
Casino	Yes	Slot Machines	Yes
Swimming Pools (outside) 3		(inside)	0
Whirlpools	2	Gymnasium	Yes
Sauna/Steam Room Yes/No		Massage	Yes
Self-Service Launderette			Yes
Movie Theater/Seats	No	Library	Yes
Children's Facilities			Yes
Watersports Facilities			None
Classification Society		Lloyd's Register	

RATINGS	SCORE
Ship: Condition/Cleanliness	7.8
Ship: Space/Flow/Comfort	7.6
Ship: Decor/Furnishings	6.6
Ship: Fitness Facilities	7.8
Cabins: Comfort/Facilities	7.6
Cabins: Software	7.4
Food: Dining Room/Cuisine	6.7
Food: Buffets/Informal Dining	6.4
Food: Quality of Ingredients	5.6
Service: Dining Room	7.0
Service: Bars	7.2
Service: Cabins	6.5
Cruise: Entertainment	8.0
Cruise: Activities Program	7.6
Cruise: Hospitality Standard	6.5
OVERALL RATING	106.3

+ Distinctive swept-back wing-tipped funnel. Numerous public rooms on two entertainment decks, with Broadway-themed interior decor. Bright decor in all public rooms except for the elegant Carnegie Library. Double-wide indoor promenade, with real red and cream bus (used as a snack cafe). Stunning multi-tiered showroom. Excellent casino with round-the-clock action. Plenty of dazzle and sizzle entertainment. "Camp Carnival" takes care of junior cruisers; facilities include virtual reality machines. Cabins are quite spacious and attractive.

— Bold, slab-sided contemporary ship with short, rakish bow and stubby stern—typical of new buildings today. Expect long lines for embarkation, disembarkation, shore tenders, and buffets. Constant hustling for drinks, but at least it's done with a knowing smile. Noisy.

Dining The two dining rooms (both are non-smoking) have low ceilings, making the raised center sections seem rather crowded, and very noisy. Food is quantity, not quality. Service is average, and hurried. Buffets are very basic, as is the selection of breads, rolls, and fruit.

Other Comments This ship, now over 10 years old, is ideal for a first cruise experience in glitzy, lively surroundings, and for those who enjoy constant stimulation, loud music and a fun-filled atmosphere, without much finesse, at an attractive price. There's no doubt that

ms Hong Kong Dragon Star ★★★★

OPERATES

SOUTH-EAST ASIA CRUISES

Cruise Line	Topnew Cruises	Whirlpools	1	Gymnasium	No

Cruise Line	Topnew Cruises		
Former Names	Columbus Caravelle/		
	Sally Caravelle/Delfin Caravelle		
Gross Tonnage	7,560		
Builder	Rauma Yards (Finland)		
Original Cost	$60 million		
Christened By	Mrs Leena Matomaki		
Entered Service	Jul 1990/Jan 1996		
Interior Design	Arto Kukkasiemi		
Country of Registry	Bahamas		
Tel/Fax No	130-5133		
Length (ft/m)	381.8/116.40		
Beam (ft/m) 55.7/17.00	Draft (ft/m)	14.4/4.40	
Propulsion/Propellers	diesel (6,000kW)/2 (CP)		
Decks 5	Crew	120	
Pass. Capacity (basis 2) 250	(all berths) 303		
Pass. Space Ratio (basis 2) 29.0	(all berths) 25.0		
Officers Ukrainian	Total Cabins	178	
Size Range (sq ft/m)	78-243/7.2-22.5		
Outside Cabins 98	Inside Cabins	80	
Single Cabins 78	Balcony Cabins	8	
Wheelchair Cabins		2	
Cabin Current 220 AC	Refrigerator All cabins		
Cabin TV Yes	VCR	Yes	
Dining Rooms 1	Sittings	1	
Elevators		2	
Casino No	Slot Machines	No	
Swimming Pools (outside) 1	(inside)	0	

Whirlpools 1	Gymnasium	No
Sauna/Steam Room	Yes (2)/No	
Massage	Yes	
Self-Service Launderette	No	
Lecture Room/Theater/Seats	Yes/156	
Library	Yes	
Children's Facilities	No	
Watersports Facilities	None	
Classification Society	American Bureau	
	of Shipping	

RATINGS	SCORE
Ship: Condition/Cleanliness	7.9
Ship: Space/Flow/Comfort	7.7
Ship: Decor/Furnishings	8.8
Ship: Fitness Facilities	6.2
Cabins: Comfort/Facilities	7.9
Cabins: Software	7.9
Food: Dining Room/Cuisine	7.7
Food: Buffets/Informal Dining	7.1
Food: Quality of Ingredients	7.3
Service: Dining Room	7.6
Service: Bars	7.7
Service: Cabins	8.8
Cruise: Entertainment	7.0
Cruise: Activities Program	6.0
Cruise: Hospitality Standard	7.7
OVERALL RATING	113.3

+ Twin swept-back outboard funnels highlight the smart exterior design of this small cruise ship, with its ice-hardened hull and shallow draft. Carries rubber landing craft for flexible, in-depth destination-oriented soft expedition cruise itineraries. All cabins are quiet, as they are located forward, with public rooms aft. Has an attractive wintergarden area and forward observation bar. Good outdoor observation decks. Well-designed lecture facilities.

Contemporary interior design uses pleasing colors and complementary fabrics. Cabins are furnished to a high standard. Eight suites feature private balcony and whirlpool bathtub. Bathrobes for all. Large number of single cabins makes this a good vessel for solo cruising.

— Soundproofing between cabins is poor. Cabin bathrooms have small towels.

Dining Spacious dining room has light decor and good ambiance, and accommodates all passengers at one sitting. Service is by Russian and Ukrainian waitresses. The food quality is good, but menu choice is rather limited.

Other Comments This ship cruises from Hong Kong and caters to a sophisticated local market.

mv Horizon ★★★★+

OPERATES
7-DAY ALASKA AND 10/11-DAY CARIBBEAN CRUISES

Cruise Line			Celebrity Cruises
Former Names			-
Gross Tonnage			46,811
Builder			Meyer Werft (Germany)
Original Cost			$185 million
Christened By			Mrs D. J. Chandris
Entered Service			May 1990
Interior Design			Katzourakis/McNeece
Country of Registry			Liberia
Tel No	124-3527	Fax No	124-3532
Length (ft/m)			680.7/207.49
Beam (ft/m)	95.1/29.00	Draft (ft/m)	23.6/7.20
Propulsion			diesel (19,960kW)
Propellers			2 (CP)
Decks	9	Crew	645
Pass. Capacity (basis 2) 1,354		(all berths) 1,660	
Pass. Space Ratio (basis 2) 34.5		(all berths) 28.1	
Officers			Greek
Total Cabins			677
Size Range (sq ft/m)			185-334/17.0-31.0
Outside Cabins	529	Inside Cabins	148
Single Cabins			0
Balcony Cabins	0	Wheelchair Cabins	4
Cabin Current			110 AC
Refrigerator			No
Cabin TV	Yes	VCR	No
Dining Rooms	1	Sittings	2
Elevators			7

Casino	Yes	Slot Machines	Yes
Swimming Pools (outside) 2		(inside)	0
Whirlpools	3	Gymnasium	Yes
Sauna/Steam Room	Yes/No	Massage	Yes
Self-Service Launderette			No
Movie Theater/Seats			Yes/850
Library			Yes
Children's Facilities			Yes
Watersports Facilities			None
Classification Society			Lloyd's Register

RATINGS	SCORE
Ship: Condition/Cleanliness	9.0
Ship: Space/Flow/Comfort	8.7
Ship: Decor/Furnishings	8.6
Ship: Fitness Facilities	8.1
Cabins: Comfort/Facilities	8.2
Cabins: Software	8.1
Food: Dining Room/Cuisine	8.4
Food: Buffets/Informal Dining	8.0
Food: Quality of Ingredients	8.0
Service: Dining Room	8.2
Service: Bars	8.1
Service: Cabins	8.1
Cruise: Entertainment	8.5
Cruise: Activities Program	8.3
Cruise: Hospitality Standard	8.3
OVERALL RATING	124.6

+ Handsome contemporary ship. Spacious public rooms, with good passenger flow. Elegant furnishings and appointments. Soothing pastel colors. Wood-paneled casino has a stately home look. Two-level showroom has excellent sightlines. The lobby is unusual, with its peachy Miami Beach Art Deco look. Cabins have fine quality fittings, tastefully decorated and above average size, with excellent closet and drawer space and good insulation. Suites have butler service. Good entertainment and cruise staff, although standards have fallen slightly.

— No self-service launderette, nor cabins with balconies. Too many announcements at times. No cushioned pads for the deck lounge chairs. Bathroom towels are small and too skimpy.

Dining Celebrity Cruises has achieved an enviable reputation for providing fine quality food, presentation, and service. The menu is excellent, with a wide variety of dishes. The dining room is large, yet feels small and elegant, with several tables for two. Informal cafe features good breakfast and lunch buffets, and an outdoor grill serves fast food items. Separate menu for vegetarians and children. Caviar (at extra charge) is available in the America's Cup Club.

Other Comments This ship delivers a well-defined North American cruise experience at a most modest price. It represents outstanding value for money.

ms Imagination ★★★★

OPERATES

7-DAY WESTERN CARIBBEAN CRUISES (YEAR-ROUND)

Cruise Line	Carnival Cruise Lines		
Former Names	-		
Gross Tonnage	70,367		
Builder	Kvaerner Masa-Yards (Finland)		
Original Cost	$330 million		
Christened By	Jodi Dickinson		
Entered Service	July 1995		
Interior Design	Joe Farcus		
Country of Registry	Panama (3F2W4)		
Tel No 134-7673	Fax No 134-7674		
Length (ft/m)	855.0/260.60		
Beam (ft/m) 104.0/31.40	Draft (ft/m) 25.9/7.90		
Propulsion	diesel-electric (42,240kW)		
Propellers	2 (CP)		
Decks 10	Crew	920	
Pass. Capacity (basis 2) 2,040	(all berths) 2,594		
Pass. Space Ratio (basis 2) 34.4	(all berths) 26.7		
Officers	Italian		
Total Cabins	1,020		
Size Range (sq ft/m)	185-421/17.0-39.0		
Outside Cabins 620	Inside Cabins	402	
Single Cabins	0		
Balcony Cabins	54		
Wheelchair Cabins	20		
Cabin Current	110 AC		
Refrigerator	Category 11/12 only		
Cabin TV Yes	VCR	No	
Dining Rooms 2	Sittings	2	

Elevators			14
Casino Yes	Slot Machines		Yes
Swimming Pools (outside) 3	(inside)		0
Whirlpools 6	Gymnasium		Yes
Sauna/Steam Room Yes/Yes	Massage		Yes
Self-Service Launderette			Yes
Movie Theater/Seats No	Library		Yes
Children's Facilities			Yes
Watersports Facilities			None
Classification Society		Lloyd's Register	

RATINGS	SCORE
Ship: Condition/Cleanliness	9.2
Ship: Space/Flow/Comfort	8.1
Ship: Decor/Furnishings	8.4
Ship: Fitness Facilities	8.0
Cabins: Comfort/Facilities	7.6
Cabins: Software	7.4
Food: Dining Room/Cuisine	6.7
Food: Buffets/Informal Dining	7.0
Food: Quality of Ingredients	5.3
Service: Dining Room	7.0
Service: Bars	7.2
Service: Cabins	6.4
Cruise: Entertainment	8.6
Cruise: Activities Program	7.8
Cruise: Hospitality Standard	6.5
OVERALL RATING	111.2

+ Fifth in a series of eight Carnival megaships that reflects the creative talents of interior designer Joe Farcus, whose philosophy is that the cruise ship environment provides an escape from routine. Ethereal decor in public rooms connected by wide indoor boulevards. Fine artistic centerpiece in the atrium. Expansive open deck areas and an excellent health spa. There's also a $1 million living art collection. Ship buffs will like the six Stephen Card paintings of clipper ships in the Grand Bar. The Victorian-era-style library is a curious room, with intentionally mismatched furnishings, fine oriental rugs, and even some books. Lavish yet elegant multi-tiered showroom and fine, frenetic razzle-dazzle shows.

— Some would say that the sensory and auditory indulgence is a little over the top. There are too many announcements. Expect lines for embarkation, disembarkation, buffets, shore tenders, and excursions, and no quiet spaces aboard to get away from crowds. Aggressive hustling for drinks. Cabin bathroom amenities are minimal.

Dining Two large, noisy dining rooms have the usual efficient, programmed, assertive service. The improved cuisine is fair. One plus is a 24-hour pizzeria.

Other Comments Has a forthright, angular appearance typical of today's space-creative designs. This ship will entertain those who are young at heart in fine fashion.

ss Independence ★★★

Cruise Line	American Hawaii Cruises			
Former Names	Oceanic Independence/Sea Luck I			
Gross Tonnage	30,090			
Builder	Bethlehem Shipbuilders (USA)			
Original Cost	$25 million			
Christened By	Mrs John Slater			
Entered Service	Feb 1951/Jun 1980			
Interior Design	Henry Dreyfuss/			
	Dian Cleve/Henry Beer			
Country of Registry	USA			
Tel No 808-847-3172	Fax No 808-848-0406			
Length (ft/m)	682.4/208.01			
Beam (ft/m) 89.1/27.18	Draft (ft/m) 30.1/9.19			
Propulsion	steam turbine (40,456kW)			
Propellers	2 (FP)			
Decks	9 Crew	315		
Pass. Capacity (basis 2) 809	(all berths) 1,025			
Pass. Space Ratio (basis 2) 37.1	(all berths) 29.3			
Officers	American			
Total Cabins	414			
Size Range (sq ft/m)	70-375/6.5-34.8			
Outside Cabins 203	Inside Cabins 211			
Single Cabins	19			
Balcony Cabins 0	Wheelchair Cabins 3			
Cabin Current	110 AC			
Refrigerator	Category O/AA/A only			
Cabin TV No VCR	No			
Dining Rooms 1 Sittings	2			

Elevators			4
Casino	No	Slot Machines	No
Swimming Pools (outside) 2		(inside)	0
Whirlpools	0	Gymnasium	Yes
Sauna/Steam Room	Yes/No	Massage	Yes
Self-Service Launderette			Yes
Movie Theater/Seats			Yes/144
Library	Yes	Children's Facilities	Yes
Classification Society		American Bureau	
		of Shipping	

RATINGS	SCORE
Ship: Condition/Cleanliness	6.2
Ship: Space/Flow/Comfort	6.8
Ship: Decor/Furnishings	6.1
Ship: Fitness Facilities	5.8
Cabins: Comfort/Facilities	6.2
Cabins: Software	7.0
Food: Dining Room/Cuisine	6.3
Food: Buffets/Informal Dining	6.1
Food: Quality of Ingredients	6.4
Service: Dining Room	6.6
Service: Bars	6.7
Service: Cabins	6.4
Cruise: Entertainment	6.0
Cruise: Activities Program	6.2
Cruise: Hospitality Standard	6.4
OVERALL RATING	95.2

+ American-built, crewed, and registered, this ship has spacious public rooms with high ceilings (not as attractive as on sister ship *Constitution*). Has good facilities for meetings. Expansive open deck space for sun-worshippers. Wrap-around outdoor promenade deck. New Hawaii-themed decor is an improvement. Wide range of cabin types and configurations, all of which offer ample room to move in, plus decent closet and drawer space and fairly bright decor. Has heavy-duty furniture and fittings, designed for unkind oceans. Local Hawaiian artists have their artwork featured on board. Dress is very casual.

— Now over 40 years old. Slow room service. Showlounge is not large enough and is always crowded. Cabin bathrooms are small. Drinks prices are high. There are no stabilizers, so the ship rolls in any inclement weather, which is often.

Dining Dining room is set low down, and without an ocean view (bi-level forward section is more elegant), but it's fairly cheerful, and has tables for two, four, and six. The cuisine is American, with quantity, not quality. Good self-service buffet area.

Other Comments Laid-back atmosphere prevails, with Aloha smiles. This is a destination-intensive cruise on a ship that is still tired, despite a $30 million refurbishment in 1994.

ms Inspiration ★★★★

OPERATES
7-DAY CARIBBEAN CRUISES
(YEAR-ROUND)

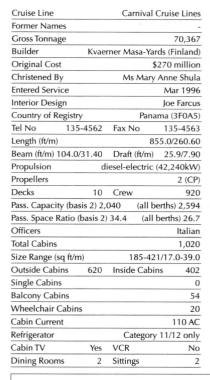

Cruise Line	Carnival Cruise Lines		
Former Names	-		
Gross Tonnage	70,367		
Builder	Kvaerner Masa-Yards (Finland)		
Original Cost	$270 million		
Christened By	Ms Mary Anne Shula		
Entered Service	Mar 1996		
Interior Design	Joe Farcus		
Country of Registry	Panama (3FOA5)		
Tel No	135-4562	Fax No	135-4563
Length (ft/m)			855.0/260.60
Beam (ft/m) 104.0/31.40	Draft (ft/m)		25.9/7.90
Propulsion	diesel-electric (42,240kW)		
Propellers			2 (CP)
Decks	10	Crew	920
Pass. Capacity (basis 2) 2,040	(all berths) 2,594		
Pass. Space Ratio (basis 2) 34.4	(all berths) 26.7		
Officers			Italian
Total Cabins			1,020
Size Range (sq ft/m)	185-421/17.0-39.0		
Outside Cabins	620	Inside Cabins	402
Single Cabins			0
Balcony Cabins			54
Wheelchair Cabins			20
Cabin Current			110 AC
Refrigerator	Category 11/12 only		
Cabin TV	Yes	VCR	No
Dining Rooms	2	Sittings	2

Elevators			14
Casino	Yes	Slot Machines	Yes
Swimming Pools (outside) 3	(inside)		0
Whirlpools	6	Gymnasium	Yes
Sauna/Steam Room Yes/Yes	Massage		Yes
Self-Service Launderette			Yes
Movie Theater/Seats	No	Library	Yes
Children's Facilities			Yes
Watersports Facilities			None
Classification Society			Lloyd's Register

RATINGS	SCORE
Ship: Hardware/Maintenance	9.2
Ship: Space/Flow/Comfort	8.1
Ship: Decor/Furnishings	8.6
Ship: Fitness Facilities	8.0
Cabins: Comfort/Facilities	7.6
Cabins: Software	7.4
Food: Dining Room/Cuisine	6.8
Food: Buffets/Informal Dining	7.0
Food: Quality of Ingredients	5.6
Service: Dining Room	7.1
Service: Bars	7.2
Service: Cabins	6.4
Cruise: Entertainment	8.7
Cruise: Activities Program	7.8
Cruise: Hospitality Standard	6.7
OVERALL RATING	112.2

✚ Like her sister ships in the same size and class (*Ecstasy, Fantasy, Imagination* and *Sensation*), this ship also has a seven-deck-high atrium, which is topped by a glass dome, and features scrolled shapes resembling the necks and heads of violins, and a marble staircase. There are expansive open deck areas and an excellent, three-deck-high glass enclosed health spa. There are public entertainment lounges, bars and clubs galore, with something for just about everyone. The public rooms are all connected by wide indoor boulevards, and beg your attention and indulgence.

A wide palette of colors and design themes have been used throughout, although the ship does feature somewhat softer decor than on some of Carnival's ships. Includes a $1 million art collection. The decor itself is themed after the arts (in an art nouveau style) and literature. Particularly fascinating is the avant garde rendition of the famed Mona Lisa, in Pablo's Lounge.

The Shakespeare library is a stunning, stately room (25 of his quotations adorn the oak veneer. Another dazzling room is the Rock and Roll Discotheque, with its guitar-shaped dance floor and video dance club feature, with dozens of video monitors around the room. The ship also features a lavish, multi-tiered showroom and high energy razzle-dazzle shows. The casino is large, but always humming with hopeful action.

The outside suites are decorated in a jazzy style, and have whirlpool tubs, although they are not large. The standard cabins are a good size, but quite plainly decorated, although they provide a comfortable home away from home.

— There are no cushioned pads for the deck lounge chairs, which are plastic, and hard to sit on with just a towel. Expect lines for embarkation, disembarkation, shore tenders and buffets. There is constant, aggressive hustling for drinks. There are many announcements. There's too much use of plastic on board, particularly in the informal food service areas.

Dining There are two large (rather noisy, or perhaps that should be translated better as "lively") dining rooms. The cuisine *has* been improved somewhat by this cruise line during the past two years, but it's not definitely not Carnival's strong point (it is, for example, difficult to ask for anything remotely unusual or off menu). Service is attentive, but highly programmed, is really too fast and assertive, and doesn't have any finesse. The wine list is definitely not for lovers of fine wines.

What has improved also is the quality of food available at the informal food outlets such as in the Brasserie Bar and Grill, which also includes a pizzeria (open 24 hours).

Other Comments The company's brochure tells it like it is, and provides a good look at the unpretentious lifestyle of its passengers. This ship provides a fine adult playground for those that like to party. It will entertain you well, but don't go for the food, go for the fun, the almost non-stop, all-too predictable action and participation activities, and for a way to visit the Caribbean in a well packaged manner that would best be described as a "compact Las Vegas afloat".

ss IslandBreeze ★★★+

OPERATES

*7-DAY CARIBBEAN (WINTER), 2/5-DAY
NEW ENGLAND (SUMMER) CRUISES*

Cruise Line	Dolphin Cruise Line	Casino	Yes
Former Names	Festivale/TransVaal Castle/		

Cruise Line	Dolphin Cruise Line
Former Names	Festivale/TransVaal Castle/
	S.A. Vaal
Gross Tonnage	38,175
Builder	John Brown & Co. (UK)
Original Cost	n/a
Christened By	Mrs Clara Zonis
Entered Service	Jan 1962/Oct 1978
Interior Design	Joe Farcus
Country of Registry	Bahamas
Tel No 110-3150	Fax No 110-3150
Length (ft/m)	760.1/231.70
Beam (ft/m) 90.1/27.49	Draft (ft/m) 31.9/9.75
Propulsion	steam turbine (32,800kW)
Propellers	2 (FP)
Decks 9	Crew 580
Pass. Capacity (basis 2) 1,146	(all berths) 1,400
Pass. Space Ratio (basis 2) 33.3	(all berths) 27.2
Officers	Italian
Total Cabins	580
Size Range (sq ft/m)	50-167/4.6-15.5
Outside Cabins 272	Inside Cabins 308
Single Cabins	14
Balcony Cabins 10	Wheelchair Cabins 0
Cabin Current 110 AC	Refrigerator No
Cabin TV No	VCR No
Dining Rooms 1	Sittings 2
Elevators	4

Casino	Yes	Slot Machines	Yes
Swimming Pools (outside)	3	(inside)	0
Whirlpools	0	Gymnasium	Yes
Sauna/Steam Room Yes/No		Massage	Yes
Self-Service Launderette		No (has ironing room)	
Movie Theater/Seats			Yes/202
Library			Yes
Children's Facilities			Yes
Watersports Facilities			None
Classification Society			Lloyd's Register

RATINGS	SCORE
Ship: Condition/Cleanliness	7.2
Ship: Space/Flow/Comfort	7.5
Ship: Decor/Furnishings	6.2
Ship: Fitness Facilities	6.9
Cabins: Comfort/Facilities	7.5
Cabins: Software	7.2
Food: Dining Room/Cuisine	6.2
Food: Buffets/Informal Dining	6.2
Food: Quality of Ingredients	5.3
Service: Dining Room	6.7
Service: Bars	6.5
Service: Cabins	6.4
Cruise: Entertainment	8.0
Cruise: Activities Program	7.1
Cruise: Hospitality Standard	6.1
OVERALL RATING	101.0

+ Classic former ocean liner with well-balanced profile and long, tiered foredeck. She looks like a real ship, and has a good amount of open deck space. Very well maintained. Her interiors retain much of the original wood and brass fittings intact from her former days as a Union Castle liner. Has a good array of public rooms. Fascinating steel art deco staircase. Cabins are spacious, with plenty of closet and drawer space, and heavy-duty fittings. Some large cabins are especially good for families.

— Contemporary colors blend well, but are perhaps too bold. Outside cabins on Veranda deck have obstructed views. The staff are not overly friendly, hustle for drinks, and English is a problem for some. Expect long lines for embarkation, disembarkation, shore tenders, and buffets. There are too many repetitive announcements.

Dining Dining room, located low down, is bright, cheerful, and noisy. There are no tables for two. The food, and its quality, are mediocre. Service is fair, but is hurried and lacks polish.

Other Comments Now under long-term charter to Dolphin Cruise Line. Good older ship experience, with lively casino action, for the young at heart who want a low budget cruise in comfortable surroundings and little panache.

ms Island Princess ★★★★

OPERATES
EUROPE/ORIENT/SOUTH PACIFIC
CRUISES

Cruise Line		Princess Cruises		Casino	Yes	Slot Machines	Yes
Former Names		Island Venture		Swimming Pools (outside) 2		(inside)	0
Gross Tonnage		19,907		Whirlpools	0	Gymnasium	Yes
Builder	Rheinstahl Nordseewerke (Germany)			Sauna/Steam Room Yes/No		Massage	Yes
Original Cost		$25 million		Self-Service Launderette			No
Christened By		n/a		Movie Theater/Seats			Yes/250
Entered Service		Feb 1972/1974		Library			Yes
Interior Design		Robert Tillberg		Children's Facilities			No
Country of Registry		Great Britain		Watersports Facilities			None
Tel No 144-0214	Fax No	144-0214		Classification Society		Lloyd's Register

Cruise Line		Princess Cruises
Former Names		Island Venture
Gross Tonnage		19,907
Builder	Rheinstahl Nordseewerke (Germany)	
Original Cost		$25 million
Christened By		n/a
Entered Service		Feb 1972/1974
Interior Design		Robert Tillberg
Country of Registry		Great Britain
Tel No 144-0214	Fax No	144-0214
Length (ft/m)		553.6/168.74
Beam (ft/m) 80.8/24.64	Draft (ft/m)	24.5/7.49
Propulsion		diesel (13,400kW)
Propellers		2 (CP)
Decks 7	Crew	350
Pass. Capacity (basis 2) 610	(all berths) 717	
Pass. Space Ratio (basis 2) 32.6	(all berths) 27.7	
Officers		British
Total Cabins		305
Size Range (sq ft/m)		126-443/11.7-41.0
Outside Cabins 238	Inside Cabins	67
Single Cabins		2
Balcony Cabins 0	Wheelchair Cabins	2
Cabin Current		110/220 AC
Refrigerator	Category A/B/C/D/DD only	
Cabin TV Yes	VCR	No
Dining Rooms 1	Sittings	2
Elevators		4

Casino Yes	Slot Machines Yes
Swimming Pools (outside) 2	(inside) 0
Whirlpools 0	Gymnasium Yes
Sauna/Steam Room Yes/No	Massage Yes
Self-Service Launderette	No
Movie Theater/Seats	Yes/250
Library	Yes
Children's Facilities	No
Watersports Facilities	None
Classification Society	Lloyd's Register

RATINGS	SCORE
Ship: Condition/Cleanliness	7.7
Ship: Space/Flow/Comfort	7.6
Ship: Decor/Furnishings	8.0
Ship: Fitness Facilities	6.2
Cabins: Comfort/Facilities	7.5
Cabins: Software	7.6
Food: Dining Room/Cuisine	7.3
Food: Buffets/Informal Dining	7.0
Food: Quality of Ingredients	6.7
Service: Dining Room	7.9
Service: Bars	8.0
Service: Cabins	7.8
Cruise: Entertainment	8.1
Cruise: Activities Program	7.8
Cruise: Hospitality Standard	8.0
OVERALL RATING	113.2

+ Very attractive profile and exterior styling for this 24-year-old ship. Has very pleasing lines, and recently underwent a dramatic facelift and refurbishment program. Sharply dressed officers and crew. Extremely spacious public areas, with wide passageways and high ceilings in public rooms. Pleasant two-deck-high lobby. Tasteful decor, with pastel colors and pleasing artwork. Forward observation lounge also acts as an indoor buffet dining area. The suites are quite large and well designed. Other cabins have ample room, are well equipped, with plenty of closet and drawer space. Bathrobes and upgraded amenities provided in all cabins.

— There is no wrap-around outdoor promenade deck.

Dining Features a lovely dining room (non-smoking), with decent service from an attentive staff. Food quality is basically good, if uncreative, and standards that had slipped for a couple of years are now improving again. Good pasta dishes. Poor bread rolls, pastry items, and fruits.

Other Comments Quality prevails aboard. This mid-sized ship is ageing well, is quite elegant, and will provide a good cruise experience from start to finish, in very comfortable surroundings, for the older passenger that wants plenty of space and doesn't want to be part of the larger, more impersonal ships.

mv Italia Prima ★★★★

OPERATES

VARIOUS CRUISES WORLDWIDE

Cruise Line	Nina Cruise Line/Neckermann Seereisen		
Former Names	Volkerfreundschaft/ Stockholm/Fridtjof Nansen		
Gross Tonnage	15,000		
Builder	Varco Chiapella (Italy)		
Original Cost	$150 million (reconstruction)		
Christened By	Dr. Margarita Tasi		
Entered Service	Feb 1948/May 1994		
Interior Design	Giuseppe De Jorio		
Country of Registry	Italy		
Tel No 115-2210/-2214	Fax No115-2211/-2215		
Length (ft/m)	525.2/160.10		
Beam (ft/m) 68.8/21.04	Draft (ft/m)	24.6/7.5	
Propulsion/Propellers	diesel (11,200kW)/2 (CP)		
Decks	7	Crew	260
Pass. Capacity (basis 2) 540		(all berths) 600	
Pass. Space Ratio (basis 2) 27.7		(all berths) 25.0	
Officers	Italian		
Total Cabins	260		
Size Range (sq ft/m)	129-376/12.0-35.0		
Outside Cabins	221	Inside Cabins	39
Single Cabins			0
Balcony Cabins	0	Wheelchair Cabins	0
Cabin Current	110/220 AC		
Refrigerator			Yes
Cabin TV	Yes	VCR	No
Dining Rooms	1	Sittings	1

Elevators			2
Casino	Yes	Slot Machines	Yes
Swimming Pools (outside) 1		(inside)	0
Whirlpools		1	Gymnasium	Yes
Sauna/Steam Room	Yes/Yes (Turkish Bath)		
Massage			Yes
Self-Service Launderette			No
Movie Theater/Seats			Yes/400
Library	Yes	Children's Facilities	No
Classification Society			RINA

RATINGS	SCORE
Ship: Condition/Cleanliness	8.1
Ship: Space/Flow/Comfort	8.0
Ship: Decor/Furnishings	8.5
Ship: Fitness Facilities	6.6
Cabins: Comfort/Facilities	8.2
Cabins: Software	8.4
Food: Dining Room/Cuisine	7.4
Food: Buffets/Informal Dining	6.1
Food: Quality of Ingredients	6.4
Service: Dining Room	7.3
Service: Bars	7.0
Service: Cabins	7.6
Cruise: Entertainment	7.2
Cruise: Activities Program	6.1
Cruise: Hospitality Standard	7.6
OVERALL RATING	110.5

+ Has a wrap-around outdoor promenade deck and wooden "steamer" chairs. Fine selection of public rooms to choose from, including a good 400-seat auditorium for meetings. Lovely interiors with excellent fit and finish, and fine quality materials. Contemporary decor, with good selection of artwork. All cabins have bathtubs and mini-bars. 38 suites feature Jacuzzi bathtubs. Also has a Turkish bath, which is quite unusual on today's ships.

— No forward observation lounge. Small swimming pool is really a "dip" pool. Movie theater seats are not staggered. The cabins on Sole Deck forward have lifeboat-obstructed views. No cushioned pads for deck chairs. Steep gangway designed for European, not Caribbean, ports.

Dining The large dining room, set low down, is attractive and has tables for two, four, six, and eight. Features distinctive Italian cuisine, with excellent pasta. There is a good selection of Italian wines (house wines are included for lunch and dinner). Also has a pizzeria. There is a limited selection of breads, fruits, and cheeses, and the cabin service menu is poor.

Other Comments This ex-ocean liner made history when she rammed and sank the *Andrea Doria* in 1956. Reconstructed as a cruise ship in 1994. She is under charter for most of each year to Neckermann Seereisen, and thus caters mainly to a German-speaking clientele (for the rest of the year she caters to other Europeans).

ms Ivan Franko ★★+

OPERATES
EUROPE CRUISES

Cruise Line	Black Sea Shipping	Casino	No	Slot Machines	No
Former Names	-	Swimming Pools (outside)	1	(inside)	1
Gross Tonnage	. 20,064	Whirlpools	0	Gymnasium	Yes
Builder	VEB Mathias Thesen (Germany)	Sauna/Steam Room	Yes/No	Massage	Yes
Original Cost	n/a Christened By	n/a	Self-Service Launderette	No
Entered Service	Nov 1964	Movie Theater/Seats	Yes/130
Interior Design	Shipyard	Library	Yes
Country of Registry	Ukraine	Children's Facilities	No
Tel No	140-0233 Fax No 140-0233	Watersports Facilities	None
Length (ft/m)	577.4/176.00	Classification Society	RS

Beam (ft/m) 77.4/23.60	Draft (ft/m) 26.8/8.17
Propulsion	diesel (15,700kW)

RATINGS	SCORE
Propellers	2 (CP)	Ship: Condition/Cleanliness	6.0
Decks	8 Crew 340	Ship: Space/Flow/Comfort	6.2
Pass. Capacity (basis 2) 580	(all berths) 714	Ship: Decor/Furnishings	6.0
Pass. Space Ratio (basis 2) 34.5	(all berths) 28.1	Ship: Fitness Facilities	5.0
Officers	Russian	Cabins: Comfort/Facilities	5.9
Total Cabins	290	Cabins: Software	6.1
Size Range (sq ft/m)	n/a	Food: Dining Room/Cuisine	5.3
Outside Cabins	287 Inside Cabins 3	Food: Buffets/Informal Dining	5.1
Single Cabins	0	Food: Quality of Ingredients	5.2
Balcony Cabins	3	Service: Dining Room	6.2
Wheelchair Cabins	0	Service: Bars	6.7
Cabin Current	220 AC	Service: Cabins	7.1
Refrigerator	No	Cruise: Entertainment	5.1
Cabin TV No VCR	No	Cruise: Activities Program	5.4
Dining Rooms 2 Sittings	2	Cruise: Hospitality Standard	5.7
Elevators	3	OVERALL RATING	87.0

+ Classic lines and traditional profile with strong ice-hardened hull, which means that this ship is very stable at sea, even in unkind weather conditions. There is a good selection of public rooms to choose from, and most have fairly high ceilings. The interior decor also looks tired and worn, but the wood paneling does add a degree of warmth and coziness.

— Black hull with white superstructure now looks tired and worn. The ship needs better maintenance and cleaning. The stairwells are uncarpeted and quite institutional. The cabins are almost all outside, but are simply and skimpily furnished, and some have no private facilities. There is little closet and drawer space, and bathrooms are small.

Dining The dining room is operated more like a cafeteria than a restaurant. Food is heavy, salty, poorly presented and choice is limited. Poor selection of breads, cheeses, and fruits. The service is unrefined, and there is much room for improvement. The staff are willing, however, but need more direction from management.

Other Comments This ship is in need of a major refurbishment and upgrading. Good for families on a low budget, but there's no finesse anywhere, and the operation is not up to international standards.

ms Jubilee ★★★★

OPERATES

*7-DAY MEXICAN RIVIERA CRUISES
(YEAR-ROUND)*

Cruise Line			Carnival Cruise Lines
Former Names			-
Gross Tonnage			47,262
Builder			Kockums (Sweden)
Original Cost			$135 million
Christened By			Mrs Yvonne Ryding
Entered Service			Jul 1986
Interior Design			Joe Farcus
Country of Registry			Liberia
Tel No	124-0503	Fax No	124-0503
Length (ft/m)			733.0/223.40
Beam (ft/m)	92.5/28.20	Draft (ft/m)	24.9/7.60
Propulsion			diesel (23,520kW)
Propellers			2 (CP)
Decks	10	Crew	670
Pass. Capacity (basis 2) 1,486		(all berths)	1,896
Pass. Space Ratio (basis 2) 31.8		(all berths)	24.9
Officers			Italian
Total Cabins			743
Size Range (sq ft/m)			185-420/17.0-39.0
Outside Cabins	453	Inside Cabins	290
Single Cabins			0
Balcony Cabins			10
Wheelchair Cabins			14
Cabin Current			110 AC
Refrigerator			Category 12 only
Cabin TV	Yes	VCR	No
Dining Rooms	2	Sittings	2

Elevators			8
Casino	Yes	Slot Machines	Yes
Swimming Pools (outside) 3		. (inside)	0
Whirlpools	2	Gymnasium	Yes
Sauna/Steam Room Yes/No		Massage	Yes
Self-Service Launderette			Yes
Movie Theater/Seats	No	Library	Yes
Children's Facilities			Yes
Watersports Facilities			None
Classification Society			Lloyd's Register

RATINGS	SCORE
Ship: Condition/Cleanliness	7.6
Ship: Space/Flow/Comfort	7.6
Ship: Decor/Furnishings	6.7
Ship: Fitness Facilities	7.8
Cabins: Comfort/Facilities	7.6
Cabins: Software	7.4
Food: Dining Room/Cuisine	6.7
Food: Buffets/Informal Dining	6.4
Food: Quality of Ingredients	5.6
Service: Dining Room	7.0
Service: Bars	7.2
Service: Cabins	6.5
Cruise: Entertainment	8.0
Cruise: Activities Program	7.6
Cruise: Hospitality Standard	6.7
OVERALL RATING	106.4

+ This large ship has a short, rakish bow. Distinctive swept-back funnel. Flamboyant, vivid colors in all public rooms except for the elegant Churchill's Library, which has few books. Huge casino has round-the-clock action. Cabins are quite spacious, neatly equipped, and have attractive decor. Especially nice are ten large suites. Outside cabins feature large picture windows. Numerous public rooms spread throughout two entertainment decks. Excellent double-wide promenade deck features a white gazebo. Stimulating multi-tiered Atlantis Lounge showroom has huge theater stage. Constant entertainment and activities.

— Has rather glitzy decor that is designed to stimulate, not relax you. Expect long lines for embarkation, disembarkation, shore tenders, and buffets. There are simply too many annoying and unnecessary announcements. Constant hustling for drinks.

Dining The two dining rooms (both non-smoking) are attractive, but have low ceilings, and a raised center section is cramped. The food, though upgraded, is still very much a low-budget Americana affair. Poor selection of breads, rolls, and fruit. Service is hurried and lacks finesse.

Other Comments This ship provides novice cruisers with an excellent, action-filled and noisy first cruise experience in crowded surroundings. Fun-filled and stimulating for party-goers. Good for singles who want lots of life and constant action. Provides very good value.

mv Kapitan Dranitsyn ★★★

OPERATES
ARCTIC/ANTARCTICA EXPEDITION
CRUISES

Cruise Line	Murmansk Shipping		
Former Names	-		
Gross Tonnage	12,288		
Builder	Wartsila (Finland)		
Original Cost	n/a		
Christened By	L.I. Sobolev		
Entered Service	Dec 1980		
Interior Design	n/a		
Country of Registry	Russia		
Tel No 140-5675	Fax No 140-5660		
Length (ft/m)	434.6/132.49		
Beam (ft/m) 86.9/26.50	Draft (ft/m) 27.8/8.50		
Propulsion	diesel-electric (22,000hp)		
Propellers	3 (CP)		
Decks 4	Crew 90		
Pass. Capacity (basis 2) 112	(all berths) 112		
Pass. Space Ratio (basis 2) 109.7	(all berths) 109.7		
Officers	Russian		
Total Cabins	50		
Size Range (sq ft/m)	150.6-269/14.0-25.0		
Outside Cabins 50	Inside Cabins 0		
Single Cabins	0		
Balcony Cabins	0		
Wheelchair Cabins	0		
Cabin Current 220 AC	Refrigerator No		
Cabin TV No	VCR No		
Dining Rooms	1		
Sittings	1		

Elevators			0
Casino	No	Slot Machines	No
Swimming Pools (outside)	0	(inside)	1
Whirlpools	0	Gymnasium	Yes
Sauna/Steam Room	Yes/No	Massage	No
Lecture/Film Room	No	Library	Yes
Zodiacs			4
Helicopter Pad		Yes (1 helicopter)	
Watersports Facilities			None
Classification Society			RS

RATINGS	SCORE
Ship: Condition/Cleanliness	7.0
Ship: Space/Flow/Comfort	6.0
Ship: Expedition Equipment	8.7
Ship: Decor/Furnishings	5.4
Cabins: Comfort/Facilities	5.6
Cabins: Software	5.8
Food: Dining Room/Cuisine	6.7
Food: Buffets/Informal Dining	6.1
Food: Quality of Ingredients	6.5
Service: Dining Room	6.4
Service: Bars	6.3
Service: Cabins	6.6
Cruise: Itineraries/Operations	7.7
Cruise: Lecture Program	7.6
Cruise: Hospitality Standard	7.4
OVERALL RATING	99.8

+ This real, working icebreaker, one of a fleet of 10, has an incredibly thick hull, forthright profile and a bow like an inverted whale head. Diesel-electric engines allow her to plough through ice several feet thick. Plenty of open deck and observation space. Cabins are spread over four decks and all have private facilities, and plenty of storage space. There is always a team of excellent naturalists and lecturers aboard. Heavy parka and boots are provided for passengers, who become participants in this kind of hands-on expedition cruising.

— Basic cruise amenities and spartan decor. Tremendous roaring noise when the vessel ploughs through pack ice.

Dining Hearty food, and generous portions, with an emphasis on fish, is served by hearty waitresses in a dining room that is comfortable and practical without being the slightest bit pretentious. The food production and presentation is supervised by Scandinavian advisors, who import Western foods specifically for these chartered voyages.

Other Comments The funnel is placed amidships and the accommodation block is placed forwards. This vessel is particularly good for tough expedition cruising, and will provide practical surroundings, a friendly, experienced, and dedicated crew, and excellent value for money in true expeditionary style. Another vessel of the same type is *Kapitan Khlebnikov*.

ms Kareliya ★★★

OPERATES
7-DAY EUROPE CRUISES

Cruise Line	CTC Cruise Lines
Former Names	Leonid Brezhnev
Gross Tonnage	15,065
Builder	Wartsila (Finland)
Original Cost	$25 million
Christened By	Mrs Landeman
Entered Service	Dec 1976/Mar 1981
Interior Design	Wartsila/Lloyd Werft
Country of Registry	Ukraine (ELSF7)
Tel No	140-0261	Fax No	140-0261
Length (ft/m)			512.6/156.27
Beam (ft/m) 71.8/21.90	Draft (ft/m)	19.4/5.92
Propulsion		diesel (13,430kW)
Propellers			2 (CP)
Decks	8	Crew	250
Pass. Capacity (basis 2) 472		(all berths) 644
Pass. Space Ratio (basis 2) 31.1		(all berths) 23.3
Officers			Ukrainian
Total Cabins			236
Size Range (sq ft/m)		90-428/8.4-38.0
Outside Cabins	110	Inside Cabins	126
Single Cabins			0
Balcony Cabins	0	Wheelchair Cabins	0
Cabin Current			220 AC
Refrigerator		Boat Deck cabins only
Cabin TV		Boat Deck cabins only
VCR			No
Dining Rooms	2	Sittings	1

Elevators			2
Casino	Yes	Slot Machines	Yes
Swimming Pools (outside) 1		(inside)	0
Whirlpools	0	Gymnasium	Yes
Sauna/Steam Room Yes/No		Massage	Yes
Self-Service Launderette			Yes
Movie Theater/Seats			Yes/140
Library	Yes	Children's Facilities	Yes
Watersports Facilities			None
Classification Society Ukraine Register of Shipping

RATINGS	SCORE
Ship: Condition/Cleanliness	6.3
Ship: Space/Flow/Comfort	6.2
Ship: Decor/Furnishings	6.1
Ship: Fitness Facilities	4.7
Cabins: Comfort/Facilities	6.1
Cabins: Software	6.3
Food: Dining Room/Cuisine	5.9
Food: Buffets/Informal Dining	5.2
Food: Quality of Ingredients	5.4
Service: Dining Room	6.5
Service: Bars	7.0
Service: Cabins	7.3
Cruise: Entertainment	4.7
Cruise: Activities Program	5.6
Cruise: Hospitality Standard	6.8
OVERALL RATING	90.1

+ Smart-looking vessel sports a large square funnel. Has pleasing interior, but the decor is uncoordinated. Her newer facilities provide more public rooms. The library and book selection have improved. Boat Deck suites are large and well equipped. Other cabins are on the small side, but adequate, with reasonable closet space. Features a wide range of interesting and popular itineraries.

— Some inner cabins share bathrooms. There's little drawer space in most cabins – hard for long voyages. Cabin bathrooms are small and utilitarian, with little space for toiletries. Has a steep gangway in many ports. No cabin service menu. Sadly, no fresh flowers anywhere.

Dining The two dining rooms (one for smokers, one for non-smokers) are quite attractive, but noisy, with service by Ukrainian waitresses who try hard, although there's no finesse, and more direction is needed. The menu choice is very limited, and quality needs improving. Poor selection of breads, fruits, and cheeses.

Other Comments This ship provides comfortable, reasonably warm and friendly surroundings. Caters primarily to British passengers seeking a destination-intensive cruise in comfortable surroundings, at a modest price. Port taxes are included. Gratuities are not compulsory, but expected.

ms Kazakhstan II ★★★+

OPERATES
VARIOUS CRUISES WORLDWIDE

Cruise Line	Delphin Seereisen	Casino	No	Slot Machines	No

Cruise Line		Delphin Seereisen	Casino	No	Slot Machines	No
Former Names		Belorussiya	Swimming Pools (outside) 1		(inside)	0
Gross Tonnage		16,214	Whirlpools	0	Gymnasium	Yes
Builder		Wartsila (Finland)	Sauna/Steam Room	Yes/No	Massage	Yes
Original Cost		$25 million	Self-Service Launderette			Yes
Christened By		Mrs Stepanova	Movie Theater/Seats			No
Entered Service		Jan 1975/Dec 1993	Library			Yes
Interior Design		Lloyd Werft	Children's Facilities			No
Country of Registry		Cyprus (P3RG5)	Watersports Facilities			None
Tel No 112-5275	Fax No	112-5276	Classification Society		Germanischer Lloyd	
Length (ft/m)		512.5/156.24				
Beam (ft/m) 71.8/21.90	Draft (ft/(m):	20.3/6.2	**RATINGS**			**SCORE**
Propulsion		diesel (13,430kW)	Ship: Condition/Cleanliness			7.7
Propellers		2 (CP)	Ship: Space/Flow/Comfort			6.6
Decks 8	Crew	234	Ship: Decor/Furnishings			7.4
Pass. Capacity (basis 2) 466		(all berths) 536	Ship: Fitness Facilities			6.5
Pass. Space Ratio (basis 2) 34.7		(all berths) 30.2	Cabins: Comfort/Facilities			6.7
Officers		European	Cabins: Software			7.2
Total Cabins		237	Food: Dining Room/Cuisine			6.2
Size Range (sq ft/m)		150-492/14.0-45.7	Food: Buffets/Informal Dining			6.1
Outside Cabins 128	Inside Cabins	105	Food: Quality of Ingredients			6.0
Single Cabins		0	Service: Dining Room			7.3
Balcony Cabins 0	Wheelchair Cabins	0	Service: Bars			7.4
Cabin Current		220 AC	Service: Cabins			7.3
Refrigerator		Boat deck cabins only	Cruise: Entertainment			6.4
Cabin TV Yes		VCR No	Cruise: Activities Program			6.2
Dining Rooms 2	Sittings	1	Cruise: Hospitality Standard			6.7
Elevators		2	OVERALL RATING			101.7

+ Has good outdoor promenade decks. New facilities added following an extensive refit and refurbishment program that improved almost all public areas and added new fitness facilities and much better outdoor pool/lido deck. The suites on Boat Deck are extremely large and well equipped. Other cabins are compact, and adequate, although bathrooms are small. The ship has smart interior decor and furnishings.

— Has poor cabin insulation and little drawer space. Service, while quite friendly, shows little finesse, and communication is sometimes frustrating.

Dining Has two dining rooms, one each for smokers and non-smokers. The food, while attractively presented, and quite reasonable, is of a limited choice and quality, although the catering is improving slowly. Limited selection of breads, cheeses, and fruits, and buffets are very simple.

Other Comments This smart-looking modern ship has a square, contemporary funnel, and has been smartly refurbished throughout following a shipyard roll-over incident. This ship will provide a comfortable cruise experience for an international, but mostly German-speaking, clientele at an extremely attractive price, but there's little finesse, and it's not a luxury product, nor does it pretend to be. Port taxes, insurance, and gratuities are included.

ms Klaudia Yelanskaya ★

OPERATES
KOLA PENINSULA CRUISES

Cruise Line			Murmansk Shipping
Former Names			-
Gross Tonnage			3,941
Builder		Brodgradiliste Uljanik (Yugoslavia)	
Original Cost			n/a
Christened By			n/a
Entered Service			1976
Interior Design			n/a
Country of Registry			Russia
Tel No	140-1764	Fax No	140-1764
Length (ft/m)			328.1/100.01
Beam (ft/m)	53.2/16.24	Draft (ft/m)	15.2/4.65
Propulsion			diesel (3,884kW)
Propellers			1 (FP)
Decks	6	Crew	80
Pass. Capacity (basis 2) 104		(all berths) 186	
Pass. Space Ratio (basis 2) 37.8		(all berths) 21.1	
Officers			Russian
Total Cabins			52
Size Range (sq ft/m)			n/a
Outside Cabins	52	Inside Cabins	0
Single Cabins			0
Balcony Cabins			0
Wheelchair Cabins			0
Cabin Current	220 AC	Refrigerator	No
Cabin TV	No	VCR	No
Dining Rooms	1	Sittings	1
Elevators			0

Casino	No	Slot Machines	No
Swimming Pools (outside) 1		(inside)	No
Whirlpools	No	Gymnasium	No
Sauna/Steam Room Yes/No		Massage	No
Self-Service Launderette			No
Movie Theater/Seats			Yes/75
Library			Yes
Children's Facilities			No
Watersports Facilities			None
Classification Society			RS

RATINGS	SCORE
Ship: Condition/Cleanliness	5.6
Ship: Space/Flow/Comfort	4.8
Ship: Decor/Furnishings	6.0
Ship: Fitness Facilities	3.0
Cabins: Comfort/Facilities	5.5
Cabins: Software	5.7
Food: Dining Room/Cuisine	5.3
Food: Buffets/Informal Dining	5.0
Food: Quality of Ingredients	4.6
Service: Dining Room	6.0
Service: Bars	6.2
Service: Cabins	6.4
Cruise: Entertainment	5.0
Cruise: Activities Program	4.4
Cruise: Hospitality Standard	5.7
OVERALL RATING	79.2

+ Intimate, small ship with well-balanced profile is one of a series of eight identical sisters often chartered by European operators. Has an ice-hardened hull suitable for "soft" expedition cruising. Good open deck spaces for ship size. Recently underwent extensive refurbishment. Outdoor observation deck and enclosed promenade deck for inclement weather. Charming forward music lounge has wooden dance floor. Rich, highly polished wood paneling throughout and winding brass-railed main staircase. Good movie theater-lecture room.

— Cabins are compact and spartan, and most can accommodate four persons, but space really is tight, and there's little closet and drawer space.

Dining Comfortable dining room has ocean views, but no tables for two. Limited choice of food, which is hearty, but service is friendly and quite attentive. Poor selection of breads, fruits, and cheeses.

Other Comments Although small, and not glamorous at all, this is a comfortable ship that has plenty of character. Presently cruising with Russian passengers only.

mv Konstantin Simonov ★★

OPERATES

3-DAY BALTIC CRUISES

Cruise Line	Baltic Line	Casino	No	Slot Machines	Yes

Cruise Line			Baltic Line	Casino	No	Slot Machines	Yes
Former Names			-	Swimming Pools (outside) 1		(inside)	0
Gross Tonnage			9,885	Whirlpools	0	Gymnasium	No
Builder			Szszecin (Poland)	Sauna/Steam Room Yes/No		Massage	Yes
Original Cost			n/a	Self-Service Launderette			No
Christened By			n/a	Movie Theater/Seats			No
Entered Service			1982	Library			Yes
Interior Design			n/a	Children's Facilities			No
Country of Registry			Russia	Watersports Facilities			None
Tel No	-	Fax No	-	Classification Society			RS
Length (ft/m)			441.2/134.50				
Beam (ft/m) 68.8/21.00		Draft (ft/m)	17.3/5.28	**RATINGS**			**SCORE**
Propulsion			diesel (12,800kW)	Ship: Condition/Cleanliness			6.6
Propellers			2 (CP)	Ship: Space/Flow/Comfort			6.2
Decks	6	Crew	160	Ship: Decor/Furnishings			6.0
Pass. Capacity (basis 2) 278		(all berths) 492		Ship: Fitness Facilities			5.6
Pass. Space Ratio (basis 2) 35.5		(all berths) 20.0		Cabins: Comfort/Facilities			5.5
Officers			Russian	Cabins: Software			6.1
Total Cabins			139	Food: Dining Room/Cuisine			5.3
Size Range (sq ft/m)			100-320/9.2-29.7	Food: Buffets/Informal Dining			5.1
Outside Cabins	50	Inside Cabins	89	Food: Quality of Ingredients			5.1
Single Cabins			0	Service: Dining Room			6.1
Balcony Cabins	0	Wheelchair Cabins	0	Service: Bars			6.2
Cabin Current			220 AC	Service: Cabins			6.2
Refrigerator		Suites and deluxe cabins only		Cruise: Entertainment			4.3
Cabin TV	Suites only	VCR	No	Cruise: Activities Program			4.7
Dining Rooms	2	Sittings	1	Cruise: Hospitality Standard			5.8
Elevators			1	OVERALL RATING			84.8

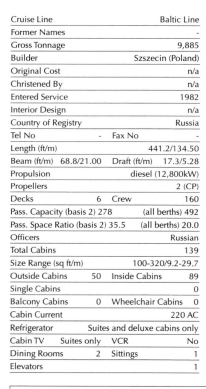

+ Has a fully enclosed bridge for all-weather operation. One of a series of five vessels intended for line voyages and short cruises. The interior decor is rather spartan and totally void of glitz. The ambiance is reasonably friendly. The suites are large and well equipped. Standard cabins are small and some are fitted with upper pullman berths. Most are utilitarian in fittings and furnishings, but quite adequate.

— Lacks a forward observation lounge. Has very limited open deck and sunning space and tiny swimming pool. Both public room and cabin soft furnishings could be better.

Dining There are several dining rooms and cafeterias to choose from. The food quality varies depending on dining area chosen, but is quite adequate, no more, and menu choice is very limited.

Other Comments This ship has a square, angular profile with square stern, stubby bow and a fat, squat funnel. Wide choice of cabins. Choice of several bars. Service lacks training and finesse. Has Finnish cruise staff. Provides a basic low-cost cruise experience for an international clientele wanting to visit St. Petersburg, at modest rates, nothing more.

ms Kristina Regina ★★★

OPERATES

BALTIC CRUISES

Cruise Line	Kristina Cruises		
Former Names	Borea/Bore		
Gross Tonnage	3,878		
Builder	Oskarshamn Shipyard (Sweden)		
Original Cost	n/a		
Christened By	n/a		
Entered Service	1960/1987		
Interior Design	n/a		
Country of Registry	Finland		
Tel/Fax No	162-3154		
Length (ft/m)	327.4/99.80		
Beam (ft/m) 50.1/15.30	Draft (ft/m)	17.3/5.30	
Propulsion/Propellers	diesel (3,223kW)/2		
Decks 6	Crew	55	
Pass. Capacity (basis 2) 276	(all berths) 350		
Pass. Space Ratio (basis 2) 14.0	(all berths) 11.0		
Officers	Finnish		
Total Cabins	141		
Size Range (sq ft/m)	65-125/6-11.6		
Outside Cabins 108	Inside Cabins	33	
Single Cabins 0	Balcony Cabins	0	
Wheelchair Cabins	0		
Cabin Current 220 AC	Refrigerator	No	
Cabin TV	Deluxe cabins only		
VCR	No		
Dining Rooms	2 (1 for buffets, 1 for à la carte)		
Sittings	1		
Elevators	0		

Casino	No	Slot Machines	No
Swimming Pools (outside) 0		(inside)	0
Whirlpools	0	Gymnasium	No
Sauna/Steam Room Yes/No		Massage	No
Self-Service Launderette			No
Movie Theater/Seats			No
Library			Yes
Children's Facilities			Yes
Watersports Facilities			None
Classification Society		Lloyd's Register	

RATINGS	SCORE
Ship: Condition/Cleanliness	6.6
Ship: Space/Flow/Comfort	5.4
Ship: Decor/Furnishings	6.7
Ship: Fitness Facilities	3.7
Cabins: Comfort/Facilities	5.7
Cabins: Software	6.3
Food: Dining Room/Cuisine	6.4
Food: Buffets/Informal Dining	6.0
Food: Quality of Ingredients	6.3
Service: Dining Room	7.1
Service: Bars	7.4
Service: Cabins	7.3
Cruise: Entertainment	3.5
Cruise: Activities Program	4.8
Cruise: Hospitality Standard	7.8
OVERALL RATING	91.0

+ Has a wrap-around wooden promenade deck. Features beautiful hardwoods and lots of brass throughout her interior decor. The Scandinavian artwork is quite fascinating. The ship exudes old-world charm. Has a well-designed auditorium that doubles as a movie theater. All cabins have shower and toilet, radio and telephone, but not much else, and they are really tiny, as are the bathrooms. There are also five allergy-free cabins.

— This is a high-density ship, so there's little room to move about inside when the ship is full. The cabins have very little closet and drawer space, so take only what's necessary.

Dining The dining room is charming, and features Continental (European) cuisine, with a distinct accent on fish, seafood, and fresh berries. The breads and cheeses are also good. Fine, hearty and friendly service comes with a smile.

Other Comments This lovely old-world ship was built specifically for close-in northern European coastal and archipelago cruises, and was extensively refurbished in 1990. She is one of the very few ships left today that has two funnels, and is owned by a single family concern. Currency: U.S. dollars/Finnish marks.

ms La Palma ★★+

OPERATES
7/11-DAY EUROPE CRUISES

Cruise Line	Intercruise	Elevators	0
Former Names	Delphi/La Perla/	Casino	Yes	Slot Machines	Yes
	Ferdinand De Lesseps	Swimming Pools (outside) 1	(inside)	0
Gross Tonnage	11,608	Whirlpools	0	Gymnasium	No
Builder Forges et Chantiers de la Gironde (France)	Sauna/Steam Room No/No	Massage	No
Original Cost	n/a	Self-Service Launderette	No
Christened By	George D. Louris	Movie Theater/Seats No	Library	Yes
Entered Service	Oct 1952/Apr 1978	Children's Facilities	No
Interior Design	George D. Louris	Watersports Facilities	None
Country of Registry	Greece	Classification Society	Grecian Lloyd
Tel No 113-0506 Fax No 113-0506		
Length (ft/m)	492.4/150.09	**RATINGS**	**SCORE**
Beam (ft/m) 62.6/19.10 Draft (ft/m) 22.0/6.72	Ship: Condition/Cleanliness	6.1
Propulsion	diesel (9,100kW)	Ship: Space/Flow/Comfort	6.3
Propellers	2 (FP)	Ship: Decor/Furnishings	6.5
Decks 7 Crew 230	Ship: Fitness Facilities	4.0
Pass. Capacity (basis 2) 648 (all berths) 832	Cabins: Comfort/Facilities	6.2
Pass. Space Ratio (basis 2) 17.9 (all berths) 13.9	Cabins: Software	6.3
Officers	Greek	Food: Dining Room/Cuisine	6.2
Total Cabins	324	Food: Buffets/Informal Dining	5.8
Size Range (sq ft/m)	105-215/9.7-20.0	Food: Quality of Ingredients	6.0
Outside Cabins 176 Inside Cabins 148	Service: Dining Room	6.4
Single Cabins	5	Service: Bars	6.2
Balcony Cabins 0 Wheelchair Cabins 0	Service: Cabins	6.5
Cabin Current	110/220 AC	Cruise: Entertainment	5.4
Refrigerator	Category AS/A only	Cruise: Activities Program	5.6
Cabin TV Yes (DeLuxe cabins only) VCR No	Cruise: Hospitality Standard	6.3
Dining Rooms 1 Sittings 2	OVERALL RATING	89.8

+ Basically a well-maintained vessel. Plenty of open deck and sunning space except when ship is full. Water slide into swimming pool for children. This is one of only two ships to feature an isolated nudist sunbathing deck (the other being Hapag-Lloyd's *Europa*). Has a popular Bavarian beer garden on deck. Cheerful interior decor, with plenty of wood and wood trim throughout. Ten suites are very spacious and nicely furnished, while other cabins are moderately so. All have private facilities and all have been refurbished.

— Has steep gangway in most ports of call. Beverages are extremely expensive.

Dining Dining room is set low down, but is quite cozy. The continental cuisine is adequate, but there is little choice, especially for non-meat eaters. Poor selection of breads, cheeses, and fruits. Service comes with a smile, but without any finesse.

Other Comments Traditional older styling, with low funnel profile. Passageways have floor-to-ceiling carpeting which is difficult to keep clean, but provides good insulation. This is a high-density ship that caters best to young couples, families, and active singles on a very modest budget. Flexible scheduling means passengers can embark and disembark at almost every port and take a full cruise, or segment. Mostly multinational European passengers, and multilingual staff. Cruise rate is moderate.

mv Langkapuri Star Aquarius ★★★★+

OPERATES

*2/3-DAY SOUTH-EAST ASIA CRUISES
(YEAR-ROUND)*

Cruise Line		Star Cruise
Former Names	Athena	Gross Tonnage	40,022
Builder		Wartsila (Finland)
Original Cost		SEK650 million
Christened By		Ms Marianne Myrsten
Entered Service		Apr 1989/Dec 1993
Interior Design		Robert Tillberg/PM design
Country of Registry		Panama
Tel No		02-011-719543
Fax No		02-011-719514
Length (ft/m)		579.3/176.6
Beam (ft/m)	97.1/29.6	Draft (ft/m)	20.3/6.2
Propulsion		diesel (23,760kW)
Propellers		2 (CP)
Decks	12	Crew	750
Pass. Capacity (basis 2) 1,530		(all berths) 1,900
Pass. Space Ratio (basis 2) 26.1		(all berths) 21.0
Officers		Scandinavian
Total Cabins		718
Size Range (sq ft/m)		67-145/6.3-13.5
Outside Cabins	303	Inside Cabins	415
Single Cabins			42
Balcony Cabins	0	Wheelchair Cabins	6
Cabin Current	220 AC	Refrigerator	No
Cabin TV	Yes	VCR	No
Dining Rooms		4 (+3 cafes)
Sittings			1
Elevators			5

Casino	Yes	Slot Machines	Yes
Swimming Pools (outside) 1		(inside)	1
Whirlpools	6	Gymnasium	Yes
Sauna/Steam Room	Yes/Yes	Massage	Yes
Self-Service Launderette			No
Movie Theater/Seats		Yes (2)/210 each
Library			Yes
Children's Facilities			Yes
Watersports Facilities			None
Classification Society		Det Norske Veritas

RATINGS	SCORE
Ship: Condition/Cleanliness	8.4
Ship: Space/Flow/Comfort	7.7
Ship: Decor/Furnishings	8.4
Ship: Fitness Facilities	8.3
Cabins: Comfort/Facilities	6.0
Cabins: Software	7.6
Food: Dining Room/Cuisine	8.3
Food: Buffets/Informal Dining	7.8
Food: Quality of Ingredients	8.1
Service: Dining Room	7.8
Service: Bars	7.3
Service: Cabins	7.2
Cruise: Entertainment	7.5
Cruise: Activities Program	7.0
Cruise: Hospitality Standard	8.7
OVERALL RATING	116.1

+ This ex-Viking Line ferry has been skillfully converted into a cruise vessel specifically for the Asian family market, with a reduction in berths to 1,900 (from 2,200). The ship sports a deep blue hull, and a blue band around the funnel base. Scandinavian design combined with a touch of the Orient, this ship even has a helipad. Features a large duty-free shopping center and supermarket. There is very imperial casino for VIPs, which is large and has a 13-feet-high, finely detailed ceiling and regal decor (there's also a second casino for general passenger use). Has a karaoke lounge and eight private karaoke rooms.

Except for some very large suites for top-paying passengers, the cabins are very small, and come with just basic facilities (some are for families, with quad occupancy). The top suites, each of which is decorated in luxurious materials, feature two bathrooms, butler service, and a private club meeting room, private sundeck, and spa.

Besides a general Universe Fitness and Health Bar (with juice bar and low-calorie items), there is a superb health club for men (King Neptune), with an extensive range of facilities, including a gymnasium, indoor pool, two whirlpools, massage, steam, and sauna facilities.

There are 11 meeting rooms (all have audio-visual facilities), two conference auditoriums and a business center, with full secretarial support, computers, fax, telex, and copy machines. Has outstanding family facilities for children and teens, with a wide assortment of computers and video game machines in the huge children's entertainment and play center. There's also free ice cream for kids.

— Such a high-density ship means crowded public rooms, and long lines for shore visits, buffets, embarkation, and disembarkation. The standard cabin bathrooms really are very small indeed. The amount of open deck space is quite limited, but is possibly sufficient for the Asian market.

Dining With seven restaurants to choose from, there's a wide choice of cuisine and dining styles. This ship has a real Chinese Restaurant called Ocean Palace (Cantonese and Sichuan cuisine) with a Hong Kong chef, and live fish tanks from which to select your seafood, as well as private dining rooms; Kamogawa Japanese restaurant, including sushi bar and waitresses in kimonos, as well as private tatami rooms; Marco Polo Italian restaurant (featuring candlelight dining); Spice Island buffet restaurant for laksa, satay, and hawker delights; Mariner buffet, with food to choose from large open-concept kitchen stalls, and children's buffet; Castaway Cafe, which features afternoon teas and coffees; Blue Lagoon, for fast food snacks (open 24 hours a day). There are more choices on this ship than just about any other ship, particularly for families with children.

Other Comments With a low, very attractive ticket price, everything on board (including food, except for the buffet restaurant) costs extra, so a cruise for the family can end up being quite expensive. The ship does, however, offer a tremendous number of choices for the whole family, and the service and hospitality is superb (better than any ship out of Miami, for example), and really fine-tuned. Gratuities are strictly forbidden. Star Cruise is without doubt the Carnival Cruise Lines of East Asia.

ms Leeward ★★★★

OPERATES

*3- AND 4-DAY BAHAMAS/MEXICO
CRUISES (YEAR-ROUND)*

Cruise Line		Norwegian Cruise Line
Former Names		Sally Albatros/Viking Saga
Gross Tonnage		25,000
Builder		Wartsila (Finland)
Original Cost	n/a	Christened By n/a
Entered Service		1980/Oct 1995
Interior Design		L. Heikkinen/Yran & Storbraaten
Country of Registry		Liberia
Tel No	554-7010	Fax No 554-7011
Length (ft/m)		492.1/150.0
Beam (ft/m)	82.6/25.2	Draft (ft/m) 18.0/5.5
Propulsion		diesel (19,120kW)
Propellers		2 (CP)
Decks	7	Crew 400
Pass. Capacity (basis 2) 950		(all berths) 1,150
Pass. Space Ratio (basis 2) 26.3		(all berths) 21.7
Officers		Norwegian
Total Cabins		475 (548)
Size Range (sq ft/m)		53-387/5.0-36.0
Outside Cabins	219	Inside Cabins 256
Single Cabins		0
Balcony Cabins		10
Wheelchair Cabins		6
Cabin Current		110/220 AC
Refrigerator		No
Cabin TV	Yes	VCR No
Dining Rooms	2	Sittings 2
Elevators		4

Casino	Yes	Slot Machines	Yes
Swimming Pools (outside) 1		(inside)	0
Whirlpools	1	Gymnasium	Yes
Sauna/Steam Room Yes/No		Massage	Yes
Self-Service Launderette			No
Movie Theater/Seats			No
Library			No
Children's Facilities/Playroom			Yes
Watersports Facilities			None
Classification Society		Bureau Veritas	

RATINGS	SCORE
Ship: Condition/Cleanliness	8.2
Ship: Space/Flow/Comfort	7.7
Ship: Decor/Furnishings	8.0
Ship: Fitness Facilities	7.9
Cabins: Comfort/Facilities	7.8
Cabins: Software	7.4
Food: Dining Room/Cuisine	7.5
Food: Buffets/Informal Dining	7.2
Food: Quality of Ingredients	6.6
Service: Dining Room	7.3
Service: Bars	7.3
Service: Cabins	7.6
Cruise: Entertainment	8.1
Cruise: Activities Program	7.4
Cruise: Hospitality Standard	7.6
OVERALL RATING	113.2

+ Sleek, swept-back wedge-shaped design with steeply tiered aft decks. Has a teakwood wrap-around outdoor promenade deck for joggers and strollers, large aft deck and recreation center. Glitzy but pleasant lobby. Features contemporary, bright decor, with modern artworks. Good showlounge, with tiered seating. Pleasing ambiance. Some top-grade cabins have angled private balconies. Six cabins specially designed for allergy sufferers. Sports fans will like the Sports Bar and Grill, an informal television-filled long bar and adjacent fast food joint.

— There's hardly any bow to this ship. No forward observation lounge. Poor pool deck. This is a high-density ship with many low ceilings. Cabins are very small and bathrooms are *tiny*. Many outside cabins on Deck 6 have obstructed views.

Dining Besides the two principal dining rooms, located aft, there's also Le Bistro, an 80-seat informal and alternative dining area for pasta and other lighter fare. Service is generally good, but hurried. Menu choice is good, and presentation is reasonable, but no finesse. Limited selection of breads, cheeses, and fruits.

Other Comments A 1995 refit cost $60 million. Has a flat, squared-off stern, with car deck ramps (ideal for the Miami–Cuba run). Also has a fully unclosed bridge. Presently under a four-year charter to Norwegian Cruise Line for short cruises, for which the ship is well suited.

ms Legend of the Seas ★★★★+

OPERATES

*7-10 DAY ALASKA, HAWAII AND
PANAMA CANAL CRUISES*

Cruise Line	Royal Caribbean Cruises		
Former Names	-		
Gross Tonnage	70,950		
Builder	Chantiers de l'Atlantique (France)		
Original Cost	$325 million		
Christened By	Mrs Cindy Pritzker		
Entered Service	May 1995		
Interior Design	Njal Eide		
Country of Registry	Norway (LAV04)		
Tel No	363-600710	Fax No	363-600712
Length (ft/m)	867.0/264.20		
Beam (ft/m) 105.0/32.00	Draft (ft/m)	24.5/7.46	
Propulsion	diesel (40,200kW)		
Propellers	2 (CP)		
Decks	11	Crew	732
Pass. Capacity (basis 2) 1,804	(all berths) 2,064		
Pass. Space Ratio (basis 2) 39.3	(all berths) 34.3		
Officers	Norwegian		
Total Cabins	902		
Size Range (sq ft/m)	138-1,148/12.8-106.6		
Outside Cabins	575	Inside Cabins	327
Single Cabins	0		
Balcony Cabins	231	Wheelchair Cabins	17
Cabin Current	110/220 AC		
Refrigerator	Upper grades only		
Cabin TV	Yes	VCR	Suites only
Dining Rooms	1	Sittings	2
Elevators	11		

Casino	Yes	Slot Machines	Yes
Swimming Pools (outside)		2 (1 with sliding roof)	
Swimming Pools (inside)			0
Whirlpools	4	Gymnasium	Yes
Sauna/Steam Room	Yes/Yes	Massage	Yes
Self-Service Launderette			No
Movie Theater/Seats	No	Library	Yes
Children's Facilities			Yes
Watersports Facilities			None
Classification Society		Det Norske Veritas	

RATINGS	SCORE
Ship: Condition/Cleanliness	9.3
Ship: Space/Flow/Comfort	9.1
Ship: Decor/Furnishings	9.1
Ship: Fitness Facilities	9.0
Cabins: Comfort/Facilities	8.6
Cabins: Software	8.7
Food: Dining Room/Cuisine	8.1
Food: Buffets/Informal Dining	7.7
Food: Quality of Ingredients	7.1
Service: Dining Room	7.9
Service: Bars	7.6
Service: Cabins	7.6
Cruise: Entertainment	8.5
Cruise: Activities Program	7.9
Cruise: Hospitality Standard	8.2
OVERALL RATING	124.4

+ This ship's contemporary profile looks somewhat unbalanced (though it soon grows on you), but she does have a nicely tiered stern. The pool deck amidships overhangs the hull to provide an extremely wide deck, while still allowing the ship to navigate the Panama Canal. With engines placed midships, there is little noise and no noticeable vibration, and the ship has an operating speed capability of 24 knots. Inside the ship, the interior decor is quite stunning and colorful (it's too glitzy for European tastes). The outside light is brought inside in many places, with an extensive amount of glass area that provides extensive contact with sea and air (there is, in fact, over two acres of glass). Features an innovative single-level sliding glass roof (not a magrodome) over the more formal setting of one of two swimming pools, thus providing a multi-activity, all-weather indoor-outdoor area, called The Solarium. The glass roof provides shelter for the Roman-style pool and adjacent health and fitness facilities (which are superb) and slides aft to cover the miniature golf course when required (both can't be covered at the same time, however).

There are two full entertainment decks to play on, sandwiched between five decks full of cabins. The tiered and balconied showlounge, which covers two decks, is expansive and has excellent sightlines, very comfortable seats; several large-scale production shows are provided here, and there's an orchestra "pit" that can be raised or lowered as required. A multi-tiered seven-deck-high atrium lobby, complete with a huge stainless steel sculpture, connects with the impressive Viking Crown Lounge via glass-walled elevators. The casino is really expansive, overly glitzy and packed absolutely full to the gills. The Library, which has a bust of Shakespeare outside, is a fine facility, with over 2,000 books.

Golfers will (hopefully) enjoy the 18-hole, 6,000 sq ft (557.5m^2) miniature golf course, aptly named "Legend of the Links" (it's the first of its kind on any cruise ship). It has the topography of a real championship course, complete with trees, foliage, grass, bridges, water hazards, and lighting for play at night. The holes themselves are 155-230 sq ft.

Royal Caribbean Cruises has thankfully realized that small cabins do not happy passengers make. The company has therefore set about designing a ship with much larger standard cabins than any of its previous vessels. Some cabins on Deck 8 also have a larger door for wheelchair access in addition to the 17 cabins for the physically handicapped, and the ship is very accessible, with lots of ramped areas and sloping decks. All cabins have sitting area, and beds that convert to double configuration, and there's ample closet and drawer space, although there's not much space around the bed, and the showers could have been better.

Cabins with balconies have glass railings rather than steel/wood to provide less intrusive sightlines. The largest accommodations, named The Royal Suite, is beautifully designed; there's even a baby grand piano, whirlpool, and all the comfort toys; it is finely decorated, and is a superb living space for those that can afford the best. Adjacent to the best cabins are several quiet sitting areas amidships.

— There is, sadly, no separate movie theater on this large ship. The casino could be somewhat disorienting, with its mirrored walls and lights flashing everywhere, although it's no different to those found in Las Vegas fantasy gaming halls. As with any large ship, you can expect to find yourself standing in lines for embarkation, disembarkation, buffets, and shore excursions, although the company does its best to minimize such lines. Seventeen cabin categories is really too many. Sadly, there are no cabins for singles.

Dining The two-deck-high dining room has dramatic two-deck-high glass side walls, so many passengers both upstairs and downstairs can see both the ocean and each other in reflection (it would, perhaps, have been even better located at the stern), but it is quite noisy when full (call it atmosphere). There is also a cavernous indoor-outdoor cafe, located towards the bow and above the bridge, as well as a good-sized snack area, which provide more informal dining choices. Menus and food choices were much improved in 1995, and presentation has also been improved. In addition, full vegetarian menus were also introduced. Royal Caribbean Cruises delivers consistently good, programmed food and service, with waiters that are smartly dressed and very attentive. Special orders are seldom possible, however, there's no decent caviar, and tableside carving and flambeau items are not possible.

Overall Comments A natural evolution, this ship is an outstanding new cruise vessel for the many repeat passengers who appreciate Royal Caribbean's consistent delivery of a well-integrated, fine-tuned, very comfortable and well-liked product. With larger cabins, and a ship of excellent decor and contemporary style, *Legend of the Seas* has taken Royal Caribbean passengers, most of whom are typically from middle-America, into a much upgraded cruise experience from that of the company's other ships. The ship provides an excellent value for money cruise experience for all ages. Similar comments apply to identical sister ship *Splendour of the Seas*.

ms Leisure World ★★★

CRUISE AREA
*1-4 DAY SOUTH-EAST ASIA CRUISES
(YEAR-ROUND)*

Cruise Line			New Century Tours
Former Names			Fantasy World/Asean World/
			Shangri-La World/Skyward
Gross Tonnage			16,254
Builder			Seebeckwerft (Germany)
Original Cost			n/a
Christened By			Lin Arison
Entered Service			Dec 1969/1990
Interior Design			Tage Wandborg
Country of Registry			BVI
Tel No	110-4164	Fax No	110-4164
Length (ft/m)			525.3/160.13
Beam (ft/m)	74.9/22.84	Draft (ft/m)	20.6/6.29
Propulsion			diesel (12,950kW)
Propellers			2 (CP)
Decks	8	Crew	250
Pass. Capacity (basis 2) 730		(all berths) 1,071	
Pass. Space Ratio (basis 2) 22.2		(all berths) 15.1	
Officers			International
Total Cabins			365
Size Range (sq ft/m)			90-330/8.3-30.5
Outside Cabins	219	Inside Cabins	145
Single Cabins			0
Balcony Cabins	0	Wheelchair Cabins	0
Cabin Current			110/220 AC
Refrigerator			No
Cabin TV	No	VCR	No
Dining Rooms	1	Sittings	2

Elevators			4
Casino	Yes	Slot Machines	Yes
Swimming Pools (outside) 1		(inside)	0
Whirlpools	0	Gymnasium	Yes
Sauna/Steam Room	Yes/No	Massage	Yes
Self-Service Launderette			No
Movie Theater/Seats			Yes/180
Library	Yes	Children's Facilities	Yes
Watersports Facilities			None
Classification Society			Det Norske Veritas

RATINGS	SCORE
Ship: Condition/Cleanliness	6.1
Ship: Space/Flow/Comfort	6.2
Ship: Decor/Furnishings	6.3
Ship: Fitness Facilities	5.7
Cabins: Comfort/Facilities	6.0
Cabins: Software	6.5
Food: Dining Room/Cuisine	6.2
Food: Buffets/Informal Dining	5.7
Food: Quality of Ingredients	5.6
Service: Dining Room	6.1
Service: Bars	6.0
Service: Cabins	6.2
Cruise: Entertainment	5.7
Cruise: Activities Program	5.9
Cruise: Hospitality Standard	6.1
OVERALL RATING	90.3

+ Attractive but somewhat dated, seventies-looking ship has a distinctive daytime sun lounge set high and forward against the ship's mast. Refurbished interior features light, airy decor in clean, crisp colors. Lounge and bar atop ship has plenty of light. Pleasant balconied theater. Good karaoke lounge for sing-alongs, and the casino action is constant and noisy.

— Very high-density ship means crowded public areas and long lines for buffets and elevators. Except for 10 suites, the cabins are small and have very limited closet and drawer space and tinny metal furniture, as well as poor cabin soundproofing. The staff lack finesse. Despite what the brochures proclaim, this is not a luxury ship. Attracts many gamblers.

Dining The dining room, although attractive, is cramped and extremely noisy, and food service is fast and without finesse. Choice of à la carte menu or Asian/Western buffet. There's a mixture of Asian and Western dishes. The food quality is so-so, but then the price is reasonably low. Cheerful, but rather hurried service from a staff that lacks finesse, and wine service that is quite poor.

Other Comments Adequate for short cruises. This ship is fine for active passengers wanting an upbeat cruise experience at a fair price, in comfortable, friendly, but not elegant, surroundings.

ms Maasdam ★★★★+

OPERATES
*7-DAY ALASKA AND
CARIBBEAN CRUISES*

Cruise Line	Holland America Line	Elevators	12
Former Names	-	Casino Yes	Slot Machines Yes
Gross Tonnage	55,451	Swimming Pools (outside)	1
Builder	Fincantieri (Italy)	Swimming Pools (inside)	1 (magrodome)
Original Cost	$215 million	Whirlpools 2	Gymnasium Yes
Christened By	Ms June Allyson	Sauna/Steam Room Yes/No	Massage Yes
Entered Service	Dec 1993	Self-Service Launderette	Yes
Interior Design	VFD Interiors/Joe Farcus	Movie Theater/Seats	Yes/249
Country of Registry	Netherlands (PFRO)	Library Yes	Children's Facilities No
Tel No 624-295813 Fax No	130-2514	Classification Society	Lloyd's Register
Length (ft/m)	719.3/219.30		
Beam (ft/m) 101.0/30.80 Draft (ft/m)	24.6/7.50	**RATINGS**	**SCORE**
Propulsion	diesel-electric (34,560kW)	Ship: Condition/Cleanliness	8.7
Propellers	2 (CP)	Ship: Space/Flow/Comfort	8.4
Decks 10 Crew	588	Ship: Decor/Furnishings	8.5
Pass. Capacity (basis 2) 1,264 (all berths) 1,627		Ship: Fitness Facilities	7.7
Pass. Space Ratio (basis 2) 43.8 (all berths) 34.0		Cabins: Comfort/Facilities	8.1
Officers	Dutch	Cabins: Software	8.1
Total Cabins	632	Food: Dining Room/Cuisine	7.2
Size Range (sq ft/m) 187-1,126/17.3-104.5		Food: Buffets/Informal Dining	6.8
Outside Cabins 501 Inside Cabins	131	Food: Quality of Ingredients	6.7
Single Cabins	0	Service: Dining Room	6.5
Balcony Cabins	150	Service: Bars	7.2
Wheelchair Cabins	6	Service: Cabins	8.0
Cabin Current	110/220 AC	Cruise: Entertainment	7.5
Refrigerator	Category PS/S/A/B only	Cruise: Activities Program	7.7
Cabin TV Yes VCR	No	Cruise: Hospitality Standard	8.3
Dining Rooms 1 Sittings	2	OVERALL RATING	115.4

+ The decor is softer, more sophisticated, and far less eclectic than on sister ship *Statendam*. Antiques and artwork are stunning, and beautifully displayed. Fine flower arrangements in public areas. Has good passenger flow. Three-deck-high atrium foyer. A "magrodome" roof covers the large indoor-outdoor swimming pool/whirlpools and central lido area. Two-deck-high showroom is well thought out, but the ceiling is low and balcony sightlines are not good. Relaxing reference (no fiction) library. 28 suites, each able to accommodate four, feature an in-suite dining alternative. Other cabins are spacious, tastefully decorated and well laid out.

— Expect lines for embarkation, disembarkation, buffets, shore tenders, and shore excursions. Cabin closet space is tight. Communication with staff is often frustrating. No division of smoking and no-smoking areas at the outdoor Lido Cafe. No bell-push outside suites. Extra charge for self-service launderette machines.

Dining The two-level dining room, located at the stern (upper level for smokers, lower level for non-smokers) is dramatic, with panoramic views on three sides. Open seating breakfast and lunch, two sittings for dinner. Food and service standards are going down.

Other Comments This is a well-built, quality ship, but the cruise product itself needs some fine-tuning in the food, service, and communication departments.

ms Majesty of the Seas ★★★★+

OPERATES

7-DAY CARIBBEAN CRUISES
(YEAR-ROUND)

Cruise Line	Royal Caribbean Cruises	Casino	Yes	Slot Machines	Yes
Former Names	-	Swimming Pools (outside) 2	(inside)	0
Gross Tonnage	73,941	Whirlpools	2	Gymnasium	Yes
Builder	Chantiers de l'Atlantique	Sauna/Steam Room	Yes/No	Massage	Yes
Original Cost	$300 million	Self-Service Launderette	No
Christened By	H.M. Queen Sonja of Norway	Movie Theater/Seats	Yes/200
Entered Service	Apr 1992	Library	Yes
Interior Design	Njal Eide	Children's Facilities	Yes
Country of Registry	Norway	Watersports Facilities	None
Tel No 131-3370	Fax No	131-3370	Classification Society	Det Norske Veritas
Length (ft/m)	873.6/266.30		

Beam (ft/m) 105.9/32.30	Draft (ft/m) 24.9/7.60
Propulsion	diesel (21,844kW)
Propellers	2 (CP)
Decks	12	Crew	822
Pass. Capacity (basis 2) 2,354	(all berths) 2,744
Pass. Space Ratio (basis 2) 31.4	(all berths) 26.9
Officers	Norwegian
Total Cabins	1,177
Size Range (sq ft/m)	120-446/11.0-41.5
Outside Cabins 732	Inside Cabins 445
Single Cabins	0
Balcony Cabins 62	Wheelchair Cabins 4
Cabin Current	110 AC
Refrigerator	Category R/A only
Cabin TV Yes	VCR No
Dining Rooms 2	Sittings 2
Elevators	18

RATINGS	SCORE
Ship: Condition/Cleanliness	8.0
Ship: Space/Flow/Comfort	8.0
Ship: Decor/Furnishings	7.9
Ship: Fitness Facilities	7.6
Cabins: Comfort/Facilities	7.6
Cabins: Software	7.7
Food: Dining Room/Cuisine	7.9
Food: Buffets/Informal Dining	7.6
Food: Quality of Ingredients	7.1
Service: Dining Room	7.7
Service: Bars	7.6
Service: Cabins	7.6
Cruise: Entertainment	8.2
Cruise: Activities Program	7.9
Cruise: Hospitality Standard	8.0
OVERALL RATING	116.4

+ Spacious, well-designed interior, with excellent signage. RCCL's trademark Viking Crown lounge and bar surrounds funnel and provides stunning view. Beautiful, well-stocked library adds class. Five-deck-high Centrum is a focal point. While suites are more spacious, most cabins are small, but attractively decorated. Special "family suites," located amidships, sleep four. Excellent headline name cabaret and extensive general entertainment program.

— Deck space cramped when full. Cabins are small. Too many announcements. Expect long lines for embarkation, disembarkation, buffets, and shore tenders.

Dining Two musical-themed dining rooms are large, attractive, and colorful. Dining operation is well orchestrated, with emphasis on highly programmed service that is hurried.
Food is consistently good, but not memorable. Features French, Oriental, Italian, Caribbean, and American theme nights, with waiters/busboys in appropriate costumes. Extensive wine list. Staff are overly friendly, even intrusive.

Other Comments You'll be overwhelmed by the public spaces, and underwhelmed by the size of the cabins. Well-run, fine-tuned, highly programmed cruise product geared particularly to those passengers seeking an action-packed cruise vacation in seven days, at a moderately good price, with around 2,500 fellow passengers.

mv Marco Polo ★★★★

OPERATES

EAST EUROPEAN, ORIENT, PACIFIC
AND INDIAN OCEAN CRUISES

Cruise Line			Orient Lines
Former Names			Aleksandr Pushkin
Gross Tonnage			20,502
Builder		VEB Mathias Thesen (Germany)	
Original Cost			n/a
Christened By			Patricia Herrod
Entered Service			Apr 1966/Oct 1993
Interior Design			A&M Katzourakis
Country of Registry			Bahamas
Tel No	630-869310	Fax No	130-6216
Length (ft/m)			578.4/176.28
Beam (ft/m)	77.4/23.60	Draft (ft/m)	26.8/8.17
Propulsion			diesel (14,444kW)
Propellers			2 (CP)
Decks	8	Crew	356
Pass. Capacity (basis 2) 848		(all berths) 915	
Pass. Space Ratio (basis 2) 24.1		(all berths) 22.4	
Officers			European
Total Cabins			425
Size Range (sq ft/m)			120-480/11.0-44.5
Outside Cabins	294	Inside Cabins	131
Single Cabins (doubles sold for single occupancy)			
Balcony Cabins			0
Wheelchair Cabins			2
Cabin Current			110/220 AC
Refrigerator			Suites/Jr. suites only
Cabin TV	Yes	VCR	No
Dining Rooms	2	Sittings	2

Elevators			4
Casino	Yes	Slot Machines	Yes
Swimming Pools (outside) 1		(inside)	0
Whirlpools		3	Gymnasium	Yes
Sauna/Steam Room Yes/No		Massage	Yes
Self-Service Launderette			No
Movie Theater/Seats	No	Library	Yes
Children's Facilities	No	Zodiacs	10
Helipad:			Yes
Classification Society			Bureau Veritas

RATINGS	SCORE
Ship: Condition/Cleanliness	8.0
Ship: Space/Flow/Comfort	7.7
Ship: Decor/Furnishings	8.0
Ship: Fitness Facilities	7.6
Cabins: Comfort/Facilities	7.7
Cabins: Software	7.7
Food: Dining Room/Cuisine	8.3
Food: Buffets/Informal Dining	8.1
Food: Quality of Ingredients	7.8
Service: Dining Room	7.7
Service: Bars	7.5
Service: Cabins	7.7
Cruise: Entertainment	5.8
Cruise: Activities Program	6.8
Cruise: Hospitality Standard	7.7
OVERALL RATING	114.1

+ Has a good profile, a strong ice-strengthened hull, and huge storage spaces for long voyages. Completely refitted and refurbished, she now features destination-intensive cruises at very realistic prices. Fitted with the latest navigational aids and biological waste treatment center. There's even a helicopter landing pad. Tasteful interior decor, with careful use of mirrored surfaces, and colors that do not clash. She is a comfortable vessel throughout and rides well. Cabins are adequate, no more.

— Some Upper Deck and Sky Deck cabins have lifeboat-obstructed views. Cabin software and detail is not the high point of this ship. There are not enough elevators. Expect long lines for Zodiac shore tenders.

Dining The main dining room is nicely decorated, practical in design, and functions well, but it's noisy and tables are very close together. There are tables for two to ten. Fine place settings and china. The food itself is of a very high standard, with good presentation. The wine list is limited, but reasonably priced.

Other Comments Specialist expedition lecturers lead some cruises, while others will have a program of fine lecturers and specialists. Excellent and well-planned destination-intensive itineraries. Gratuities are not included. Port taxes are included for E.U. passengers only.

ts Maxim Gorki ★★★★

OPERATES
EUROPE CRUISES

Cruise Line	Phoenix Seereisen	Elevators	4
Former Names	Hanseatic/Hamburg	Casino No	Slot Machines No
Gross Tonnage	24,981	Swimming Pools (outside) 1	(inside) 1
Builder	Howaldtswerke Deutsche	Whirlpools 0	Gymnasium Yes
	Werft (Germany)	Sauna/Steam Room Yes/No	Massage Yes
Original Cost	UK£5.6 million	Self-Service Launderette	Yes
Christened By	n/a	Movie Theater/Seats	Yes/290
Entered Service	Mar 1969/Jan 1974	Library	Yes
Interior Design	n/a	Children's Facilities	No
Country of Registry	Bahamas	Classification Society	Det Norske Veritas
Tel No	130-5670/140-2204		
Fax No	130-5671/140-2205	**RATINGS**	**SCORE**
Length (ft/m)	638.8/194.72	Ship: Condition/Cleanliness	7.8
Beam (ft/m) 87.3/26.62 Draft (ft/m) 27.0/8.25		Ship: Space/Flow/Comfort	8.0
Propulsion	steam turbine (16,900kW)	Ship: Decor/Furnishings	7.9
Propellers	2 (FP)	Ship: Fitness Facilities	6.8
Decks 10 Crew	340	Cabins: Comfort/Facilities	6.5
Pass. Capacity (basis 2) 650	(all berths) 788	Cabins: Software	6.9
Pass. Space Ratio (basis 2) 38.4	(all berths) 31.7	Food: Dining Room/Cuisine	7.1
Officers	Russian/Ukrainian	Food: Buffets/Informal Dining	6.7
Total Cabins	326	Food: Quality of Ingredients	6.8
Size Range (sq ft/m)	145.3-296.0/13.5-27.0	Service: Dining Room	7.4
Outside Cabins 210 Inside Cabins	116	Service: Bars	7.5
Single Cabins 2 Balcony Cabins	0	Service: Cabins	7.6
Wheelchair Cabins	0	Cruise: Entertainment	7.4
Cabin Current 220 AC Refrigerator Suites only		Cruise: Activities Program	6.8
Cabin TV Yes VCR	No	Cruise: Hospitality Standard	7.2
Dining Rooms 3 Sittings	1	OVERALL RATING	108.4

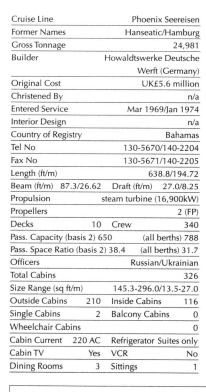

+ This all-white ship has long, pleasing lines and outer styling, easily identified by its odd-looking, platform-topped funnel. Generally well maintained, with more facilities added during her last refurbishment. Has good open deck and sunning space. Well-designed public rooms. Good wood paneling throughout. Fine Russian crew show. The cabins are spacious, and many have wood paneling and trim; large bathrooms feature a full bathtub in all except 20 cabins. Superb deluxe cabins are fully equipped, and have huge picture windows, while others have portholes. In-cabin Russian and German satellite TV programs.

— Now 25 years old, the ship needs refurbishing extensively, particularly the wood paneling. Old-fashioned entertainment facilities. The decor, while restful, is dark and dull.

Dining The three nicely decorated restaurants are set low down, but are cheerfully decorated. Excellent lager on draught, and water fountains on all accommodation decks. Moderately good food, and wine at lunch and dinner is included, but more choice, and better presentation, would be welcome. Attentive, courteous service from a well-meaning staff.

Other Comments This ship provides an excellent cruise experience in very comfortable, almost elegant, surroundings, at a modest price. Particularly targeted to German-speaking passengers who appreciate good value. Port taxes, insurance and gratuities are included.

ms Megastar Aries ★★★★+

OPERATES
7-DAY SOUTH-EAST ASIA CRUISES
(YEAR-ROUND)

Cruise Line	Star Cruise	Casino	No	Slot Machines No
Former Names	Aurora I/Lady Diana	Swimming Pools (outside) 1	(inside) 0	
Gross Tonnage	3,300	Whirlpools 0	Gymnasium No	
Builder	Flender Werft (Germany)	Sauna/Steam Room No/No	Massage No	
Original Cost	$35 million	Self-Service Launderette	No	
Christened By	Ms Carol Theodore	Movie Theater/Seats	No	
Entered Service	Jan 1992/Nov 1994	Library	Yes	
Interior Design	Giorgio Vafiadis	Children's Facilities	No	
Country of Registry	Bahamas	Watersports Facilities	None	
Tel No 130-5141 Fax No	130-5144	Classification Society	Germanischer Lloyd	
Length (ft/m)	269.6/82.2			

RATINGS	SCORE
Ship: Condition/Cleanliness	8.8
Ship: Space/Flow/Comfort	7.7
Ship: Facilities	8.4
Ship: Decor/Furnishings	8.8
Ship: Fitness/Watersports Facilities	7.2
Cabins: Comfort/Facilities	8.1
Cabins: Software	8.4
Food: Dining Room/Cuisine	8.2
Food: Buffets/Informal Dining	7.7
Food: Quality of Ingredients	8.2
Service: Dining Room	7.7
Service: Bars	7.7
Service: Cabins	7.9
Cruise: Entertainment/Lecture Program	8.1
Cruise: Hospitality Standard	8.7
OVERALL RATING	121.6

Beam (ft/m) 45.9/14.0	Draft (ft/m)	10.9/3.3	
Propulsion	diesel (3,356kW)		
Propellers	2 (CP)		
Decks 4	Crew	59	
Pass. Capacity (basis 2) 80	(all berths) 80		
Pass. Space Ratio (basis 2) 41.2	(all berths) 41.2		
Officers	Scandinavian		
Total Cabins	44		
Size Range (sq ft/m)	250-430/23.0-40.0		
Outside Cabins 44	Inside Cabins	0	
Single Cabins	6		
Balcony Cabins 0	Wheelchair Cabins	0	
Cabin Current	110/220 AC		
Refrigerator	All cabins		
Cabin TV Yes	VCR	Yes	
Dining Rooms 1	Sittings	Open	
Elevators	0		

+ Features teakwood decks for strolling, and real wooden "steamer" deck chairs. Warm friendly ambiance. Features wood-accented trim and fine soft furnishings, plush chairs and couches, and always fresh flowers. Has a good library. Personal fax machine in each cabin. Has large cabins for ship size, and most are very comfortable, with big picture windows. The bathrooms, which are enormous for the size of the ship, have clean, crisp colors. All cabins have unobstructed views. This is strictly a private club at sea, for VIPs.

— No wrap-around outdoor promenade deck. The swimming pool is tiny – it's really a "dip" pool. Public room space is limited. The ship, being small, rolls in heavy seas.

Dining The dining room is charming, intimate and very comfortable, with smart contemporary decor. The cuisine is Asian and International in style, and food is well prepared and nicely presented, although there is not a great deal of menu choice. Fine china and flatware.

Other Comments Rather like having the privileges of a private yacht, without the burden of ownership, this ship travels off the beaten path to take you in style and comfort. Port taxes are included. An ideal ship for small corporate charters.

ms Megastar Taurus ★★★★+

OPERATES

7-DAY SOUTH-EAST ASIA CRUISES (YEAR-ROUND)

Cruise Line			Star Cruise
Former Names			Aurora II/Lady Sarah
Gross Tonnage			3,300
Builder			Flender Werft (Germany)
Original Cost			$35 million
Christened By			Ms Jeanne Buiter
Entered Service			Feb 1992/Jan 1995
Interior Design			Giorgio Vafiadis
Country of Registry			Bahamas
Tel No	130-5151	Fax No	130-5154
Length (ft/m)			269.6/82.2
Beam (ft/m)	45.9/14.0	Draft (ft/m)	10.9/3.3
Propulsion			diesel (3,356kW)
Propellers			2 (CP)
Decks	4	Crew	59
Pass. Capacity (basis 2) 80		(all berths) 80	
Pass. Space Ratio (basis 2) 41.2		(all berths) 41.2	
Officers			Scandinavian
Total Cabins			44
Size Range (sq ft/m)			250-430/23.0-40.0
Outside Cabins	44	Inside Cabins	0
Single Cabins			6
Balcony Cabins	0	Wheelchair Cabins	0
Cabin Current			110/220 AC
Refrigerator			All cabins
Cabin TV	Yes	VCR	Yes
Dining Rooms	1	Sittings	Open
Elevators			0

Casino	No	Slot Machines	No
Swimming Pools (outside) 1		(inside)	0
Whirlpools	0	Gymnasium	No
Sauna/Steam Room No/No		Massage	No
Self-Service Launderette			No
Movie Theater/Seats			No
Library			Yes
Children's Facilities			No
Watersports Facilities			None
Classification Society			Germanischer Lloyd

RATINGS	SCORE
Ship: Condition/Cleanliness	8.8
Ship: Space/Flow/Comfort	7.7
Ship: Facilities	8.4
Ship: Decor/Furnishings	8.8
Ship: Fitness/Watersports Facilities	7.2
Cabins: Comfort/Facilities	8.1
Cabins: Software	8.4
Food: Dining Room/Cuisine	8.2
Food:·Buffets/Informal Dining	7.7
Food: Quality of Ingredients	8.2
Service: Dining Room	7.7
Service: Bars	7.7
Service: Cabins	7.9
Cruise: Entertainment/Lecture Program	8.1
Cruise: Hospitality Standard	8.7
OVERALL RATING	121.6

+ Smart-looking ship has a low, sleek profile and royal blue hull. Designed for highly personal cruising. Features teakwood outdoor decks and real wooden "steamer" chairs. Cabins are large, have big picture windows, and are superbly equipped with fine woods, writing desk, and fax machine. All cabins have unobstructed views, and bathrooms are large. Limited public spaces, yet these are good for those VIPs seeking a private club ambiance in new and highly sophisticated surroundings, with a small number of fellow travelers.

— There is no wrap-around outdoor promenade deck. The swimming pool is tiny—it's really a "dip" pool. Public room space is limited. The ship, being small, rolls in heavy seas.

Dining The dining room is charming, intimate and very comfortable, with smart contemporary decor. The cuisine is Asian and International in style, and food is well prepared and nicely presented, although there is not a great deal of menu choice. Features fine china and flatware.

Other Comments One of a pair of identical ships originally created for the defunct Windsor Line, but sold before delivery. Great style and fine personal service. Rather like having the privileges of a private yacht, without the burden of ownership. Ideal for small corporate charters. Port taxes are included.

ms Mercury

OPERATES
7-DAY CARIBBEAN CRUISES

Cruise Line			Celebrity Cruises
Former Names			-
Gross Tonnage			73,850
Builder			Meyer Werft (Germany)
Original Cost			$320 million
Christened By			n/a
Entered Service			Nov 1997
Interior Design			Katzourakis/McNeece
Country of Registry			Liberia
Tel No	n/a	Fax No	n/a
Length (ft/m)			852.0/259.70
Beam (ft/m) 105.6/32.20		Draft (ft/m)	24.2/7.40
Propulsion/Propellers		diesel (29,250kW/2 (CP)
Decks	10	Crew	770
Pass. Capacity (basis 2) 1,908		(all berths) 2,262
Pass. Space Ratio (basis 2) 38.7		(all berths) 32.6
Officers			Greek
Total Cabins			954
Size Range (sq ft/m)		172-1,515/15.7-140.7
Outside Cabins	650	Inside Cabins	304
Single Cabins			0
Balcony Cabins	220	Wheelchair Cabins	8
Cabin Current			110/220 AC
Refrigerator	Yes	Cabin TV	Yes
VCR		Deck 10 suites only
Dining Rooms	2	Sittings	2
Elevators			9
Casino	Yes	Slot Machines	Yes

Swimming Pools (outside)			2
(inside)		1 (under magrodome)
Whirlpools	3	Gymnasium	Yes
Sauna/Steam Room Yes/Yes		Massage	Yes
Self-Service Launderette			No
Movie Theater/Seats			No
Library			Yes
Children's Facilities			Yes
Watersports Facilities			None
Classification Society		Lloyd's Register

RATINGS	SCORE
Ship: Condition/Cleanliness	NYR
Ship: Space/Flow/Comfort	NYR
Ship: Decor/Furnishings	NYR
Ship: Fitness Facilities	NYR
Cabins: Comfort/Facilities	NYR
Cabins: Software	NYR
Food: Dining Room/Cuisine	NYR
Food: Buffets/Informal Dining	NYR
Food: Quality of Ingredients	NYR
Service: Dining Room	NYR
Service: Bars	NYR
Service: Cabins	NYR
Cruise: Entertainment	NYR
Cruise: Activities Program	NYR
Cruise: Hospitality Standard	NYR
OVERALL RATING	

+ As on her identical sister, *Galaxy*, there will be a two-level, 1,000-seat showlounge, a three-deck-high main foyer with a marble-floored lobby, over 4.5 acres of open deck space, a magrodome-covered indoor/outdoor pool, an AquaSpa, a cinema, a grand two-deck-high dining room and extended children's facilities. The decor will include plenty of wood detailing throughout. Refinements have been made to the three-ship series that Celebrity Cruises has introduced over the past two years.

The accommodations will be very comfortable throughout. The two Presidential suites, located amidships, promise to be at least as spectacular as those aboard *Century* and *Galaxy*.

— None known at time of going to press (see comments for *Galaxy*).

Dining In-suite dining for the two Presidential and 12 Century suites. Has a two-level dining room, each with its own galley, and a grand staircase, as well as bi-level lido café. Expect the same, excellent cuisine, overseen by Michel Roux, that has made Celebrity Cruises the shining star of the contemporary cruise industry.

Other Comments This ship is identical in size to her sister ship *Galaxy*, and the same general comments will apply.

ss Meridian ★★★★

OPERATES
BERMUDA/SOUTH AMERICA CRUISES

Cruise Line	Celebrity Cruises
Former Names	Galileo/Galileo Galilei
Gross Tonnage	30,440
Builder	Cantieri Riuniti dell' Adriatico (Italy)
Original Cost	n/a
Christened By	Mrs Jeanne Chandris
Entered Service	Apr 1963/Feb 1990
Interior Design	A&M Katzourakis
Country of Registry	Panama
Tel No	110-3143	Fax No	110-3145
Length (ft/m)			700.9/213.65
Beam (ft/m) 94.1/28.71	Draft (ft/m)	28.3/8.64
Propulsion	steam turbine (32,800kW)
Propellers			2 (FP)
Decks	8	Crew	580
Pass. Capacity (basis 2) 1,106	(all berths) 1,398
Pass. Space Ratio (basis 2) 27.5	(all berths 21.7
Officers			Greek
Total Cabins			553
Size Range (sq ft/m)			n/a
Outside Cabins	295	Inside Cabins	258
Single Cabins			0
Balcony Cabins	0	Wheelchair Cabins	2
Cabin Current			110/220 AC
Refrigerator			Suites only
Cabin TV	No	VCR	No
Dining Rooms	1	Sittings	2
Elevators			3

Casino	Yes	Slot Machines	Yes
Swimming Pools (outside) 1	(inside)	0
Whirlpools	3	Gymnasium	Yes
Sauna/Steam Room Yes/No	Massage	Yes
Self-Service Launderette		No
Movie Theater/Seats		Yes/218
Library		Yes
Children's Facilities		Yes
Watersports Facilities		None
Classification Society		Lloyd's Register

RATINGS	SCORE
Ship: Condition/Cleanliness	7.6
Ship: Space/Flow/Comfort	7.1
Ship: Decor/Furnishings	7.6
Ship: Fitness Facilities	7.0
Cabins: Comfort/Facilities	7.2
Cabins: Software	8.0
Food: Dining Room/Cuisine	8.3
Food: Buffets/Informal Dining	7.9
Food: Quality of Ingredients	8.0
Service: Dining Room	8.0
Service: Bars	7.5
Service: Cabins	7.8
Cruise: Entertainment	7.6
Cruise: Activities Program	7.4
Cruise: Hospitality Standard	7.6
OVERALL RATING	114.6

+ Well-balanced classic ship profile, with rakish bow, rounded stern and new funnel. Expansive sheltered deck areas and open deck sunning space. Wide selection of cabin sizes and configurations, and all are well equipped. Captain's Deck suites have skylights, are large, comfortable, and well equipped. Public rooms have high ceilings and soft, very elegant pastel decor and color tones throughout, with good use of mirrored surfaces. Large casino. Charming twin garden lounges for quiet reading.

— No forward observation lounge. Expect lines for embarkation, disembarkation, shore tenders, and buffets, especially during the summer Bermuda season when the ship is often under charter. Cabin bathrooms are small. No cushioned pads for deck lounge chairs.

Dining The dining room is warm and inviting. Fine, French-influenced cuisine with varied menus created by three-star Michelin master chef Michel Roux. Good selection of pastries and dessert items. The service, by a mainly European staff, is friendly, attentive, and polished. Very attractive and well-presented buffets.

Other Comments This ship delivers an excellent, friendly cruise experience, with fine service and outstanding value for money at very realistic rates. Very highly recommended and especially suited to the longer 10- and 11-day cruise itineraries, which are outstanding.

ms Mermoz ★★★

OPERATES

14-DAY CARIBBEAN AND
EUROPE CRUISES

Cruise Line			Paquet Cruises
Former Names			Jean Mermoz
Gross Tonnage			13,691
Builder		Chantiers de l'Atlantique (France)	
Original Cost	n/a	Christened By	n/a
Entered Service			May 1957/Sep 1970
Interior Design			Marc Held
Country of Registry			Bahamas
Tel No	110-4216	Fax No	110-4216
Length (ft/m)			531.5/162.01
Beam (ft/m)	65.0/19.82	Draft (ft/m)	20.9/6.40
Propulsion			diesel (8,000kW)
Propellers			2 (FP)
Decks	9	Crew	320
Pass. Capacity (basis 2) 533		(all berths) 662	
Pass. Space Ratio (basis 2) 25.6		(all berths) 20.6	
Officers			French
Total Cabins			275
Size Range (sq ft/m)			n/a
Outside Cabins	217	Inside Cabins	58
Single Cabins			17
Balcony Cabins			0
Wheelchair Cabins			0
Cabin Current			110/220 AC
Refrigerator			No
Cabin TV	No	VCR	No
Dining Rooms	2	Sittings	1
Elevators			2

Casino	Yes	Slot Machines	Yes
Swimming Pools (outside) 2		(inside)	0
Whirlpools	Yes	Gymnasium	No
Sauna/Steam Room	Yes/No	Massage	Yes
Self-Service Launderette			No
Movie Theater/Seats			Yes/240
Library			Yes
Children's Facilities			No
Watersports Facilities			None
Classification Society			Bureau Veritas

RATINGS	SCORE
Ship: Condition/Cleanliness	5.5
Ship: Space/Flow/Comfort	5.7
Ship: Decor/Furnishings	6.0
Ship: Fitness Facilities	4.7
Cabins: Comfort/Facilities	4.8
Cabins: Software	5.8
Food: Dining Room/Cuisine	7.6
Food: Buffets/Informal Dining	6.9
Food: Quality of Ingredients	7.5
Service: Dining Room	7.3
Service: Bars	7.3
Service: Cabins	7.4
Cruise: Entertainment	6.3
Cruise: Activities Program	5.6
Cruise: Hospitality Standard	6.6
OVERALL RATING	95.0

+ Delightful chic art deco interior decor, with earth tone color scheme throughout and a real "colonial" ambiance feel. Quaint and typically French in ambiance and service. Spa and solarium are good, with emphasis on hydrotherapy. The annual Classical Music Festival cruise is a real cultural delight. Much artwork and models are of interest to ship lovers. Cabins are not large, and only basically equipped, but they are tastefully furnished, cozy, and comfortable, with solid fixtures and lots of wood everywhere. Good closet and drawer space. Bathrobes provided for everyone.

— There is no forward observation lounge. The cabin bathrooms are very small. There is a steep, narrow gangway in some ports.

Dining Outstanding cuisine that is extremely creative, especially during special theme cruises. Fine grill room and food. There is also a 65,000-bottle wine cellar, and wine is complementary with dinner.

Other Comments Traditional older ship with good lines and a rather dated profile. Eclectic interiors. This ship has a wonderful, idiosyncratic French character, flair, ambiance, and is for those who enjoy being with French-speaking passengers wishing to cruise at a moderate price. It is, however, time for a more contemporary replacement.

ms Mikhail Sholokhov ★★

OPERATES
INDONESIA/SOUTH PACIFIC CRUISES

Cruise Line		Far Eastern Shipping
Former Names		-
Gross Tonnage		9,878
Builder		Adolf Warski Werft (Poland)
Original Cost		n/a
Christened By		n/a
Entered Service		1986
Interior Design		n/a
Country of Registry		Russia
Tel No 140-0360	Fax No	140-0360
Length (ft/m)		441.0/134.40
Beam (ft/m) 68.8/21.00	Draft (ft/m)	18.3/5.60
Propulsion		diesel (12,800kW)
Propellers		2 (CP)
Decks 7	Crew	168
Pass. Capacity (basis 2) 234	(all berths)	412
Pass. Space Ratio (basis 2) 42.2	(all berths)	23.9
Officers		Russian/Ukrainian
Total Cabins		117
Size Range (sq ft/m)		100-320/9.2-29.7
Outside Cabins 71	Inside Cabins	46
Single Cabins		0
Balcony Cabins		0
Wheelchair Cabins		0
Cabin Current		220 AC
Refrigerator		No
Cabin TV No	VCR	No
Dining Rooms 1	Sittings	1

Elevators			1
Casino	No	Slot Machines	No
Swimming Pools (outside) 1		(inside)	0
Whirlpools	0	Gymnasium	Yes
Sauna/Steam Room Yes/No		Massage	Yes
Self-Service Launderette			No
Movie Theater/Seats	No	Library	Yes
Children's Facilities			No
Watersports Facilities			None
Classification Society			RS

RATINGS	SCORE
Ship: Condition/Cleanliness	6.6
Ship: Space/Flow/Comfort	6.2
Ship: Decor/Furnishings	6.0
Ship: Fitness Facilities	5.6
Cabins: Comfort/Facilities	5.5
Cabins: Software	6.1
Food: Dining Room/Cuisine	5.3
Food: Buffets/Informal Dining	5.1
Food: Quality of Ingredients	5.1
Service: Dining Room	6.1
Service: Bars	6.2
Service: Cabins	6.2
Cruise: Entertainment	4.3
Cruise: Activities Program	4.7
Cruise: Hospitality Standard	5.8
OVERALL RATING	84.8

+ This ship has an ice-hardened hull and fully enclosed bridge for all-weather operations. One of a series of five built in Poland. Attractive, though dated decor in the limited number of public rooms.

— This is a somewhat boxy looking vessel with a stubby bow and huge square funnel. Has reasonably good open deck and sunning space, but the swimming pool is very small. Limited number of public rooms. There's no cashless cruising here.

Dining The dining room is cheerful, and dining is family style. Food and menu choice are reasonable, no more. Service is perfunctory, but the female waitress staff do try.

Other Comments Interior decor is reasonably pleasant, but somewhat spartan. Cabins are small, space-efficient units that have little warmth. Operates mainly in the Indonesian islands and the South Pacific. This ship provides a reasonable cruise experience that is definitely for the budget-conscious. Don't expect any finesse.

mv Minerva ★★★★+

OPERATES

WORLDWIDE
LIFE-ENRICHMENT CRUISES

Cruise Line	Swan Hellenic Cruises			
Former Names	Okean			
Gross Tonnage	12,000			
Builder	Marriotti (Italy)			
Original Cost	n/a			
Christened By	n/a			
Entered Service	Apr 1996			
Interior Design	RFW Design			
Country of Registry	Bermuda			
Tel No	n/a	Fax No	n/a	
Length (ft/m)			436.3/133.0	
Beam (ft/m) 65.6/20.0	Draft (ft/m)		19.6/6.0	
Propulsion			2 x diesels	
Propellers			2 (CP)	
Decks	6	Crew	157	
Pass. Capacity (basis 2) 392		(all berths) 456		
Pass. Space Ratio (basis 2) 30.6		(all berths) 26.3		
Officers			European	
Total Cabins			194	
Size Range (sq ft/m)	140.1-277.0/13.02-25.74			
Outside Cabins	142	Inside Cabins	52	
Single Cabins			4	
Balcony Cabins	12	Wheelchair Cabins	4	
Cabin Current			220 AC	
Refrigerator			No	
Cabin TV	Yes	VCR	No	
Dining Rooms	1	Sittings	Open seating	
Elevators			2	

Casino	No	Slot Machines	No
Swimming Pools (outside) 1		(inside)	0
Whirlpools	0	Gymnasium	Yes
Sauna/Steam Room Yes/No		Massage	Yes
Self-Service Launderette			Yes
Movie Theater/Seats			Yes/300
Library			Yes
Children's Facilities			No
Watersports Facilities			None
Classification Society			Lloyd's Register

RATINGS	SCORE
Ship: Condition/Cleanliness	9.0
Ship: Space/Flow/Comfort	8.7
Ship: Decor/Furnishings	9.1
Ship: Fitness Facilities	8.5
Cabins: Comfort/Facilities	8.6
Cabins: Software	8.7
Food: Dining Room/Cuisine	8.0
Food: Buffets/Informal Dining	7.2
Food: Quality of Ingredients	7.5
Service: Dining Room	8.4
Service: Bars	8.3
Service: Cabins	8.3
Cruise: Entertainment	8.5
Cruise: Activities Program	8.3
Cruise: Hospitality Standard	8.6
OVERALL RATING	124.7

+ This ship has a well-balanced profile, with a single, central funnel. There is ample open and shaded deck space for this size ship, and a teakwood wrap-around promenade deck. There is an excellent selection of public rooms, including a well-stocked library with a classical theme decor. The decor generally is contemporary yet restrained. Cigar smokers will appreciate the special smoking room and humidor service. The range of accommodations is well thought out, and all have excellent closet and storage space. Features well-planned in-depth itineraries and shore excursions (the majority of which are included in the cruise fare), accompanied by the finest lecturers.

— None known at press time.

Dining Features open-seating dining (dine with whomever you wish) in both the main restaurant and the informal indoor-outdoor café.

Other Comments This ship was constructed specifically for Swan Hellenic Cruises in 1996 by V-Ships, the owner, to replace *Orpheus*, which Swan Hellenic had chartered for the previous 21 years. This really is cruising for the intelligent passenger who yearns to learn more about life and times in civilizations past and present, albeit in a refined, comfortable setting.

ms Monarch of the Seas ★★★★+

OPERATES

7-DAY CARIBBEAN CRUISES
(YEAR-ROUND)

Cruise Line	Royal Caribbean Cruises
Former Names	-
Gross Tonnage	73,941
Builder	Chantiers de l'Atlantique
Original Cost	$300 million
Christened By	Ms Lauren Bacall
Entered Service	Nov 1991
Interior Design	Njal Eide
Country of Registry	Norway
Tel No 131-2764 Fax No	131-2764
Length (ft/m)	873.6/266.30
Beam (ft/m) 105.9/32.30 Draft (ft/m)	24.9/7.60
Propulsion	diesel (21,844kW)
Propellers	2 (CP)
Decks 12 Crew	822
Pass. Capacity (basis 2) 2,354 (all berths)	2,744
Pass. Space Ratio (basis 2) 31.0 (all berths)	26.9
Officers	Norwegian
Total Cabins	1,177
Size Range (sq ft/m)	120-441/11.1-41.5
Outside Cabins 732 Inside Cabins	445
Single Cabins	0
Balcony Cabins 62 Wheelchair Cabins	4
Cabin Current	110 AC
Refrigerator	Category R/A only
Cabin TV Yes VCR	No
Dining Rooms 2 Sittings	2
Elevators	18

Casino	Yes	Slot Machines	Yes
Swimming Pools (outside) 2		(inside)	0
Whirlpools	2	Gymnasium	Yes
Sauna/Steam Room Yes/No		Massage	Yes
Self-Service Launderette			No
Movie Theater/Seats		Yes (2)/146 each	
Library			Yes
Children's Facilities			Yes
Watersports Facilities			None
Classification Society		Det Norske Veritas	

RATINGS	SCORE
Ship: Condition/Cleanliness	8.0
Ship: Space/Flow/Comfort	8.0
Ship: Decor/Furnishings	7.9
Ship: Fitness Facilities	7.6
Cabins: Comfort/Facilities	7.6
Cabins: Software	7.7
Food: Dining Room/Cuisine	7.9
Food: Buffets/Informal Dining	7.6
Food: Quality of Ingredients	7.1
Service: Dining Room	7.7
Service: Bars	7.6
Service: Cabins	7.8
Cruise: Entertainment	8.2
Cruise: Activities Program	7.9
Cruise: Hospitality Standard	8.0
OVERALL RATING	116.6

+ Almost identical in size and appearance to sister *Sovereign of the Seas*, but with improved internal layout, public room features, passenger flow and signage. Surprisingly stable and smooth sailing. Many public rooms, from large to small. RCCL's trademark Viking Crown lounge and bar surrounds funnel and provides a stunning view. Five-deck-high atrium is the interior focal point, and glass-walled elevators. Exceptionally fine library. While suites are more spacious, most cabins are small, but comfortable, and attractively decorated. Special "family suites," located amidships, sleep four. Has good childrens' and teens' programs.

— This ship has small cabins, but the line's philosophy is that you won't spend much time in your cabin. Poor room service menu. Too many announcements. Expect long lines for disembarkation, buffets, and shore tenders.

Dining The two musical-themed dining rooms are large (no tables for two), but have good service and food. Most nights are themed (French, Oriental, Italian, Caribbean, American), with waiters and busboys in appropriate costumes. Good wine list.

Other Comments Provides excellent facilities, with consistently good, well-operated but highly programmed service from an attentive, though robotic, staff. This translates to a rather impersonal but activity-filled cruise experience as one of over 2,000 passengers each week.

ss Monterey ★★★

Cruise Line			Mediterranean Shipping Cruises
Former Names			Free State Mariner
Gross Tonnage			21,051
Builder			Bethlehem Steel Corp. (USA)
Original Cost	n/a	Christened By	n/a
Entered Service			Dec 1952/Aug 1988
Interior Design			Platou Design
Country of Registry			Liberia
Tel No	133-3517	Fax No	133-3517
Length (ft/m)			563.6/171.81
Beam (ft/m)	76.3/23.27	Draft (ft/m)	29.3/8.95
Propulsion			steam turbine (14,400kW)
Propellers			1 (FP)
Decks	4	Crew	280
Pass. Capacity (basis 2) 600			(all berths) 638
Pass. Space Ratio (basis 2) 35.0			(all berths) 32.9
Officers			Italian
Total Cabins			300
Size Range (sq ft/m)			64.5-344.4/6.5-32
Outside Cabins	171	Inside Cabins	129
Single Cabins			0
Balcony Cabins	0	Wheelchair Cabins	0
Cabin Current			110 AC
Refrigerator			Category 13, 14 only
Cabin TV			Category 13, 14 only
VCR			No
Dining Rooms	1	Sittings	2
Elevators			2

Casino	Yes	Slot Machines	Yes
Swimming Pools (outside)	1	(inside)	0
Whirlpools	2	Gymnasium	Yes
Sauna/Steam Room	Yes/No	Massage	Yes
Self-Service Launderette			No
Movie Theater/Seats			Yes/107
Library	Yes	Children's Facilities	No
Watersports Facilities			None
Classification Society			American Bureau of Shipping

RATINGS	SCORE
Ship: Condition/Cleanliness	6.3
Ship: Space/Flow/Comfort	6.4
Ship: Decor/Furnishings	6.4
Ship: Fitness Facilities	5.3
Cabins: Comfort/Facilities	6.8
Cabins: Software	7.1
Food: Dining Room/Cuisine	6.7
Food: Buffets/Informal Dining	6.2
Food: Quality of Ingredients	6.6
Service: Dining Room	7.7
Service: Bars	7.0
Service: Cabins	7.4
Cruise: Entertainment	6.4
Cruise: Activities Program	6.0
Cruise: Hospitality Standard	7.3
OVERALL RATING	99.6

+ This ship has a traditional fifties liner profile. This is a very stable sea ship with an almost vertical bow and an overhanging aircraft-carrier-like stern that is not at all handsome. She was refurbished in moderate art deco style, when a new sports deck was added. Good sheltered and open deck space. Very friendly, bubbly Italian crew and atmosphere. There is a wide choice of cabin sizes and configurations – but only the top three categories have full bathtubs. Has extremely spacious suites; other cabins are very roomy, well-equipped units. Bathrobes are provided.

— Lacks a forward observation lounge. There is too much cold steel, and not enough warmth in the interior decoration. Cabins forward on Boat Deck have lifeboat-obstructed views.

Dining The charming two-tier dining room is set low down, and decorated in soft earth tones, so the ambiance is quite charming, but it is noisy when full. Features Continental cuisine, with some excellent pasta dishes. Poor selection of breads, cheeses, and fruits. Service is friendly and attentive, in typical Italian style, but somewhat hurried.

Other Comments This ship will cruise you in reasonably elegant style and surroundings, with mainly European, and particularly Italian-speaking passengers. Currency aboard: Lire. Port taxes are included.

mv Nantucket Clipper ★★★

OPERATES
7- TO 14-DAY US/CANADA COAST
AND VIRGIN ISLANDS CRUISES

Cruise Line			Clipper Cruise Line
Former Names			-
Gross Tonnage			1,471
Builder			Jeffboat (USA)
Original Cost			$9 million
Christened By			Ms Christiane Ebsworth
Entered Service			Dec 1984
Interior Design			n/a
Country of Registry			USA
Tel No	none	Fax No	none
Length (ft/m)			207.0/63.00
Beam (ft/m)	37.0/11.20	Draft (ft/m)	8.0/2.40
Propulsion			diesel (700kW)
Propellers			2 (FP)
Decks	4	Crew	37
Pass. Capacity (basis 2)	102	(all berths)	102
Pass. Space Ratio (basis 2)	14.4	(all berths)	14.4
Officers			American
Total Cabins			51
Size Range (sq ft/m)			121-138/11.2-12.8
Outside Cabins	51	Inside Cabins	0
Single Cabins			0
Balcony Cabins			0
Wheelchair Cabins			0
Cabin Current	110 AC	Refrigerator	No
Cabin TV	No	VCR	No
Dining Rooms	1	Sittings	1
Elevators			0

Casino	No	Slot Machines	No
Swimming Pools (outside)	0	(inside)	0
Whirlpools	0	Gymnasium	No
Sauna/Steam Room	No/No	Massage	No
Self-Service Launderette			No
Movie Theater/Seats			No
Library	Yes	Children's Facilities	No
Watersports Facilities			None
Classification Society		American Bureau of Shipping	

RATINGS	SCORE
Ship: Condition/Cleanliness	6.4
Ship: Space/Flow/Comfort	4.0
Ship: Decor/Furnishings	6.8
Ship: Fitness Facilities	3.0
Cabins: Comfort/Facilities	6.1
Cabins: Software	6.5
Food: Dining Room/Cuisine	7.1
Food: Buffets/Informal Dining	6.2
Food: Quality of Ingredients	7.0
Service: Dining Room	7.1
Service: Bars	7.0
Service: Cabins	7.3
Cruise: Entertainment	4.0
Cruise: Activities Program	5.6
Cruise: Hospitality Standard	7.3
OVERALL RATING	91.4

+ This small, shallow draft vessel is specially built for coastal and inland cruises and is very maneuverable. Well maintained. Extremely high-density ship has only two public rooms – the dining room and an observation lounge. Wrap-around open teakwood walking deck. Passengers can visit the bridge at any time. The all-outside cabins (in four categories) are very small, but somehow comfortable and tastefully furnished, with wood-accented trim, and good sound insulation.

— Has very small cabins. High engine noise level when under way. The per diem price is high for what you get, and air fare is extra.

Dining The dining room is warm and inviting, and has large picture windows. There are table assignments only for dinner, which is at a single sitting. There are no tables for two. Features simple and plain cuisine, with limited menu choice and small portions.

Other Comments Service is by young, friendly all-American college-age types. This is most definitely an "Americana" experience for those seeking particularly to learn more about the coastal ports around the USA. Casual and unstructured lifestyle, rather like a small, but not luxurious, country club afloat, with much attention to detail. Not to be compared with big ship ocean cruising. No mindless activities or corny games.

ms Nautican ★★★★

OPERATES

3-, 5- AND 7-DAY SOUTH EAST ASIA CRUISES (YEAR-ROUND)

Cruise Line		Cruise Lines International	
Former Names		Crown Monarch	
Gross Tonnage		15,271	
Builder		Union Navale de Levante (Spain)	
Original Cost		$95 million	
Christened By		Mrs Gunvar "Gigi" Grundstad	
Entered Service		Dec 1990/Oct 1994	
Interior Design		Oliver Design	
Country of Registry		Panama	
Tel No	133-3627	Fax No	133-3630
Length (ft/m)		494.4/150.72	
Beam (ft/m)	67.6/20.62	Draft (ft/m)	17.7/5.40
Propulsion		diesel (13,680kW)	
Propellers		2 (CP)	
Decks	7	Crew	215
Pass. Capacity (basis 2) 510		(all berths) 556	
Pass. Space Ratio (basis 2) 29.9		(all berths) 27.4	
Officers		International	
Total Cabins		255	
Size Range (sq ft/m)		145-398/13.5-37.0	
Outside Cabins	225	Inside Cabins	30
Single Cabins		0	
Balcony Cabins		10	
Wheelchair Cabins		5	
Cabin Current		110 AC	
Refrigerator		Category 1 only	
Cabin TV	Yes	VCR	No
Dining Rooms	1	Sittings	2

Elevators			4
Casino	Yes	Slot Machines	Yes
Swimming Pools (outside) 1		(inside)	0
Whirlpools	2	Gymnasium	Yes
Sauna/Steam Room Yes/No		Massage	Yes
Self-Service Launderette			No
Movie Theater/Seats	No	Library	Yes
Children's Facilities			No
Watersports Facilities			None
Classification Society		Det Norske Veritas	

RATINGS	SCORE
Ship: Condition/Cleanliness	7.4
Ship: Space/Flow/Comfort	7.7
Ship: Decor/Furnishings	8.6
Ship: Fitness Facilities	7.1
Cabins: Comfort/Facilities	7.7
Cabins: Software	7.9
Food: Dining Room/Cuisine	7.5
Food: Buffets/Informal Dining	6.8
Food: Quality of Ingredients	6.6
Service: Dining Room	7.4
Service: Bars	7.2
Service: Cabins	7.5
Cruise: Entertainment	7.1
Cruise: Activities Program	6.0
Cruise: Hospitality Standard	7.5
OVERALL RATING	110.0

+ This is a handsome, highly maneuverable small ship with swept-back funnel and fine, well-balanced profile. Has reasonably good open deck and sunning space. Lifeboats are well located to avoid obstructed views. Numerous public rooms to choose from, all tastefully decorated and very comfortable. Well-designed interior has an excellent layout and good passenger flow. Suites with private balconies are excellent. All other cabins are nicely appointed and have elegant, pleasing decor and wood accents, and double-to-twin convertible beds, with floral-patterned bedspreads. Most cabins are large for the ship size.

— The indoor/outdoor cafe is poorly designed and has very limited seating and traffic flow. Poor cabin soundproofing. Disappointing cuisine needs attention and some upgrading, as does the service.

Dining The dining room is quite charming, elegantly appointed, and has real wood chairs with arm rests, warm decor, and an informal atmosphere. The food is generally good, with generous portions, but choice is limited. Service is good to excellent, from a friendly and attentive staff.

Other Comments This ship, under charter from Effjohn, will provide Asian passengers with a pleasant cruise experience in comfortable, contemporary surroundings, at a modest price.

ms Nieuw Amsterdam ★★★★

OPERATES

7-DAY ALASKA AND CARIBBEAN
CRUISES

Cruise Line		Holland America Line
Former Names		-
Gross Tonnage		33,930
Builder	Chantiers de l'Atlantique (France)	
Original Cost		$150 million
Christened By		HRH Princess Margriet
Entered Service		Jul 1983
Interior Design		VFD Interiors
Country of Registry		Netherlands (PGCH)
Tel No	130-2552	Fax No	130-2553
Length (ft/m)		704.2/214.66
Beam (ft/m) 89.4/27.26	Draft (ft/m)	24.6/7.52
Propulsion		diesel (21,600kW)
Propellers		2 (CP)
Decks	10	Crew	542
Pass. Capacity (basis 2) 1,210	(all berths) 1,350
Pass. Space Ratio (basis 2) 28.0	(all berths) 25.1
Officers		Dutch
Total Cabins		605
Size Range (sq ft/m)		152-295/14.0-27.5
Outside Cabins	411	Inside Cabins	194
Single Cabins		0
Balcony Cabins		0
Wheelchair Cabins		4
Cabin Current		110/220 AC
Refrigerator		Category A only
Cabin TV	Yes	VCR	No
Dining Rooms	1	Sittings	2

Elevators			7
Casino	Yes	Slot Machines	Yes
Swimming Pools (outside) 2	(inside)	0
Whirlpools	1	Gymnasium	Yes
Sauna/Steam Room Yes/No	Massage	Yes
Self-Service Launderette			Yes
Movie Theater/Seats			Yes/230
Library	Yes	Children's Facilities	No
Watersports Facilities			None
Classification Society		Lloyd's Register

RATINGS	SCORE
Ship: Condition/Cleanliness	8.0
Ship: Space/Flow/Comfort	8.2
Ship: Decor/Furnishings	8.0
Ship: Fitness Facilities	6.7
Cabins: Comfort/Facilities	8.0
Cabins: Software	7.6
Food: Dining Room/Cuisine	6.1
Food: Buffets/Informal Dining	6.0
Food: Quality of Ingredients	6.0
Service: Dining Room	6.6
Service: Bars	7.3
Service: Cabins	8.1
Cruise: Entertainment	6.7
Cruise: Activities Program	7.1
Cruise: Hospitality Standard	7.8
OVERALL RATING	108.2

+ Has nicely raked bow. Plenty of open deck space. Traditional teakwood outdoor decks, including wrap-around promenade deck. Spacious interior design and layout, with soothing color combinations. Much polished teak and rosewood paneling. Stunning antiques and artwork. Explorers' Lounge is relaxing for after-meal coffee and live chamber music. Balconied main lounge reminiscent of former ocean liner era. Spacious and well-equipped cabins have quality furniture and fittings, wood paneling, good counter and storage space, and good-sized bathrooms. Top three categories have full bathtubs. Several cabins have king- or queen-sized beds, and cabin insulation is good.

— Suffers from vibration at stern. Indonesian waiters try hard, but communication is at times frustrating. Some cabins on Boat and Navigation Decks have obstructed views. Expect long lines for buffets and shore tenders. Has poor entertainment.

Dining The dining room is large and attractive, with ample space. Open seating for breakfast and lunch, two sittings for dinner. Food is attractively presented, but not adventurous, and the quality has deteriorated lately. Poor choice of breads, bread rolls, and fruits.

Other Comments Recommended for seasoned, senior-age travelers wanting a quality, traditional cruise experience, in elegant surroundings, at a realistic and moderate price level.

ms Nippon Maru ★★★★

OPERATES
JAPAN/SOUTH EAST ASIA CRUISES

Cruise Line		Mitsui OSK Passenger Line
Former Names		-
Gross Tonnage		21,903
Builder	Mitsubishi Heavy Industries (Japan)	
Original Cost		$59.4 million
Christened By		Mr Susumi Temporin
Entered Service		Sep 1990
Interior Design	Osamu Higuchi/Mikiya Murakami	
Country of Registry		Japan
Tel No	120-0462	Fax No	120-0462
Length (ft/m)		546.7/166.65
Beam (ft/m) 78.7/24.00	Draft (ft/m)	21.4/6.55
Propulsion		diesel (15,740kW)
Propellers		2 (CP)
Decks	7	Crew	160
Pass. Capacity (basis 2) 408	(all berths) 607
Pass. Space Ratio (basis 2) 53.6	(all berths) 36.0
Officers		Japanese
Total Cabins		204
Size Range (sq ft/m)	150-430/14.0-40.0
Outside Cabins	189	Inside Cabins	15
Single Cabins		0
Balcony Cabins 0	Wheelchair Cabins	2
Cabin Current 100 AC	Refrigerator	Yes
Cabin TV	Yes	VCR	No
Dining Rooms	1	Sittings	1
Elevators		5
Casino	Yes*	Slot Machines	No

Swimming Pools (outside) 1 (inside)	0
Whirlpools	4 (Japanese baths)
Gymnasium	Yes
Sauna/Steam Room Yes/No Massage	Yes*
Self-Service Launderette	Yes
Movie Theater/Seats	Yes/135
Library	Yes
Children's Facilities	Yes*
Classification Society	Nippon Kaiji Kyokai
	* = On leisure cruises only

RATINGS	SCORE
Ship: Condition/Cleanliness	8.0
Ship: Space/Flow/Comfort	7.7
Ship: Decor/Furnishings	8.2
Ship: Fitness Facilities	6.6
Cabins: Comfort/Facilities	7.3
Cabins: Software	7.2
Food: Dining Room/Cuisine	7.5
Food: Buffets/Informal Dining	6.7
Food: Quality of Ingredients	7.1
Service: Dining Room	7.5
Service: Bars	7.4
Service: Cabins	7.0
Cruise: Entertainment	6.8
Cruise: Activities Program	6.8
Cruise: Hospitality Standard	8.3
OVERALL RATING	110.1

+ Traditional profile and single funnel aft of midships. Public rooms have high ceilings. The ship has an elegant, dramatic six-deck-high atrium. Specifically built and outfitted for the domestic Japanese seminar/lecture marketplace and individual passengers. Excellent teakwood decking. Well-designed public rooms have high-quality furnishings and soothing color combinations. Features true Japanese baths, as well as a "Washitsu" tatami room. Most cabins located forward, public rooms aft. Nicely decorated suites and deluxe cabins.

— Interior decor is plain and unexciting. The showlounge could be improved somewhat.

Dining The dining room is quite basic, and features both traditional Japanese cuisine and some Western dishes. One sitting for leisure cruises and two sittings for ship charter cruises. The food presentation standard is good but simplistic, and menu choice is limited.

Other Comments Has a small outdoor swimming pool with magrodome sliding glass roof. Balconied main lounge. Tastefully decorated suites and deluxe cabins with good storage space. While suites and deluxe cabins are quite elegant and well equipped, the standard cabins, which form the majority, are quite small and spartan, though adequate. This ship is principally for Japanese individual passengers who want to cruise at moderate rates without the extra luxury touches one might expect in a top hotel. No tipping is allowed.

ms Noordam ★★★★

Cruise Line	Holland America Line			
Former Names	-			
Gross Tonnage	33,930			
Builder	Chantiers de l'Atlantique (France)			
Original Cost	$160 million			
Christened By	Mrs Beatrijs van De Wallbake			
Entered Service	Apr 1984			
Interior Design	VFD Interiors			
Country of Registry	Netherlands (PGHT)			
Tel No	130-2541	Fax No	130-2537	
Length (ft/m)			704.2/214.66	
Beam (ft/m)	89.4/27.26	Draft (ft/m)	24.2/7.40	
Propulsion			diesel (21,600kW)	
Propellers			2 (CP)	
Decks	10	Crew	530	
Pass. Capacity (basis 2) 1,210		(all berths) 1,350		
Pass. Space Ratio (basis 2) 28.0		(all berths) 25.1		
Officers			Dutch	
Total Cabins			605	
Size Range (sq ft/m)		152-295/14..0-27.5		
Outside Cabins	411	Inside Cabins	194	
Single Cabins			0	
Balcony Cabins			0	
Wheelchair Cabins			4	
Cabin Current			110/220 AC	
Refrigerator			Category A only	
Cabin TV	Yes	VCR	No	
Dining Rooms	1	Sittings	2	

Elevators			7
Casino	Yes	Slot Machines	Yes
Swimming Pools (outside) 2		(inside)	0
Whirlpools	1	Gymnasium	Yes
Sauna/Steam Room Yes/No		Massage	Yes
Self-Service Launderette			Yes
Movie Theater/Seats			Yes/230
Library	Yes	Children's Facilities No	
Watersports Facilities			None
Classification Society		Lloyd's Register	

RATINGS	SCORE
Ship: Condition/Cleanliness	8.0
Ship: Space/Flow/Comfort	8.2
Ship: Decor/Furnishings	8.0
Ship: Fitness Facilities	6.7
Cabins: Comfort/Facilities	8.0
Cabins: Software	7.6
Food: Dining Room/Cuisine	6.1
Food: Buffets/Informal Dining	6.0
Food: Quality of Ingredients	6.0
Service: Dining Room	6.6
Service: Bars	7.3
Service: Cabins	8.1
Cruise: Entertainment	6.7
Cruise: Activities Program	7.1
Cruise: Hospitality Standard	7.8
OVERALL RATING	108.2

+ Traditional teakwood outdoor decks, including wrap-around promenade. Outstanding 17th- and 18th-century artwork and Dutch artifacts, well displayed. Flower bouquets are lovely. Crow's Nest observation lounge is a good retreat. Explorers' Lounge is fine for after-dinner coffees with live chamber music. Good indoor/outdoor dining area. Spacious and practical cabins have plenty of storage space, good closets and decent bathrooms (top three categories have full bathtubs). All cabins are well equipped, and have good insulation.

— Some cabins on Boat and Navigation Decks have obstructed views. Expect lines for buffets. Has poor entertainment. Frustrating trying to communicate with newer staff.

Dining Charming and spacious dining room. Open seating for breakfast and lunch, two sittings for dinner. Generally good service from Indonesian staff—always with a smile. Features international cuisine with an American flavor, but ingredients are not the best in quality, and entrees are tasteless. Poor choice of breads, rolls, and fruits.

Other Comments Identical squarish exterior to *Nieuw Amsterdam* with same squat, angular design, but different interior colors and decor. This ship will cruise you (leave the children at home, please, for they'll be out of place here) for a week in an elegant style, but at an affordable, realistic price.

ms Nordic Empress ★★★★

OPERATES

*3- AND 4-DAY BAHAMAS CRUISES
(YEAR-ROUND)*

Cruise Line	Royal Caribbean Cruises		
Former Names	-		
Gross Tonnage	48,563		
Builder	Chantiers de l'Atlantique (France)		
Original Cost	$170 million		
Christened By	Ms Gloria Estefan		
Entered Service	Jun 1990		
Interior Design	Njal Eide		
Country of Registry	Liberia		
Tel No 124-3540	Fax No	124-3547	
Length (ft/m)	692.2/211.00		
Beam (ft/m) 100.7/30.70	Draft (ft/m)	23.2/7.10	
Propulsion	diesel (16,200kW)		
Propellers	2 (CP)		
Decks 12	Crew	671	
Pass. Capacity (basis 2) 1,600	(all berths) 2,020		
Pass. Space Ratio (basis 2) 30.2	(all berths) 24.0		
Officers	Scandinavian		
Total Cabins	800		
Size Range (sq ft/m)	117-269/10.8-25.0		
Outside Cabins 471	Inside Cabins	329	
Single Cabins	0		
Balcony Cabins 69	Wheelchair Cabins	4	
Cabin Current	110 AC		
Refrigerator	Category R/A only		
Cabin TV Yes	VCR	No	
Dining Rooms 1	Sittings	2	
Elevators	7		

Casino			Yes
Slot Machines			Yes-220
Swimming Pools (outside) 2	(inside)		0
Whirlpools	4	Gymnasium	Yes
Sauna/Steam Room Yes/No	Massage		Yes
Self-Service Launderette			No
Movie Theater/Seats No	Library		No
Children's Facilities			Yes
Watersports Facilities			None
Classification Society		Det Norske Veritas	

RATINGS	SCORE
Ship: Condition/Cleanliness	8.0
Ship: Space/Flow/Comfort	7.6
Ship: Decor/Furnishings	7.6
Ship: Fitness Facilities	7.3
Cabins: Comfort/Facilities	7.2
Cabins: Software	7.7
Food: Dining Room/Cuisine	7.8
Food: Buffets/Informal Dining	7.6
Food: Quality of Ingredients	7.1
Service: Dining Room	7.7
Service: Bars	7.6
Service: Cabins	7.6
Cruise: Entertainment	8.2
Cruise: Activities Program	7.9
Cruise: Hospitality Standard	7.8
OVERALL RATING	114.7

+ Contemporary ship with short bow and squared stern looks quite stunning. Designed specifically for the short cruise market, for which the ship is well suited. Has outdoor polished wood wrap-around promenade deck. Dramatic use of glass-enclosed viewing spaces. Stunning nine-deck-high atrium is focal point. Lots of crystal and brass to reflect light. Ingenious use of lighting effects in interiors. Tri-level casino has sailcloth ceiling. Superb outdoor pool deck designed for evenings under the stars. Viking Crown Lounge, aft of the funnel, is a bi-level nightclub-disco. Nine cabins have private balconies overlooking the stern. All cabins convert to double bed configuration and are very small, though comfortable.

— Expect lines for embarkation, disembarkation, and buffets. Two-level showroom has poor sightlines in balcony. Constant repetitive announcements are irritating.

Dining Two-level musical-themed dining room is delightful, though noisy, and has huge windows overlooking the stern. The dining room operation is well orchestrated, with emphasis on highly programmed service with some finesse. The food is consistently good, but not memorable. Menu choices are varied. Wine list is quite extensive.

Other Comments This is a glamorous, well-designed ship for short party atmosphere cruises, with high passenger density, and lots of activities designed for the whole family.

ss Norway ★★★★

OPERATES

*7-DAY BAHAMAS/CARIBBEAN
CRUISES (YEAR-ROUND)*

Cruise Line	Norwegian Cruise Line	Swimming Pools (outside)		2
Former Names	France	Swimming Pools (inside)	1 (plus Aquacize pool)	
Gross Tonnage	76,049	Whirlpools	2 Gymnasium	Yes
Builder	Chantiers de l'Atlantique (France)	Sauna/Steam Room Yes/No	Massage	Yes
Original Cost	$80 million	Self-Service Launderette		Yes
Christened By	Madame Charles de Gaulle	Movie Theater/Seats		Yes/840
Entered Service	Feb 1962/Jun 1980	Library		Yes
Interior Design	Tage Wandborg/Angelo Donghia	Children's Facilities		Yes
Country of Registry	Bahamas	Watersports Facilities		None
Tel No 110-4603 Fax No	110-4604	Classification Society		Bureau Veritas
Length (ft/m)	1035.1/315.50			

Beam (ft/m) 109.9/33.50 Draft (ft/m)	35.4/10.80	**RATINGS**	**SCORE**
Propulsion	steam turbine (29,850kW)	Ship: Condition/Cleanliness	7.6
Propellers	4 (FP)	Ship: Space/Flow/Comfort	7.5
Decks 12 Crew	875	Ship: Decor/Furnishings	7.3
Pass. Capacity (basis 2) 2,044 (all berths) 2,370		Ship: Fitness Facilities	8.0
Pass. Space Ratio (basis 2) 37.2 (all berths) 32.8		Cabins: Comfort/Facilities	7.8
Officers Norwegian Total Cabins	1,013	Cabins: Software	6.7
Size Range (sq ft/m)	100-957/9.2-89.0	Food: Dining Room/Cuisine	7.5
Outside Cabins 647 Inside Cabins	366	Food: Buffets/Informal Dining	7.2
Single Cabins 20 Balcony Cabins	56	Food: Quality of Ingredients	6.4
Wheelchair Cabins	11	Service: Dining Room	7.2
Cabin Current	110 AC	Service: Bars	7.1
Refrigerator Category 1/2/3/4/5/owner's suite only		Service: Cabins	7.5
Cabin TV Yes VCR	No	Cruise: Entertainment	8.2
Dining Rooms 2 Sittings	2	Cruise: Activities Program	7.6
Elevators	13	Cruise: Hospitality Standard	7.3
Casino Yes Slot Machines	Yes	OVERALL RATING	110.9

+ She is still a majestic-looking ship, with two large funnels, despite major structural alterations that added two completely new glass-enclosed decks atop the ship a couple of years ago. The new decks provide 135 outside suites and junior suites, and lower the profile of the two wing-tip funnels considerably, but the balconies are not very private. Two large landing craft provide fast, efficient transportation ashore.

A 1993 refurbishment also refreshed her interiors, and some rooms now feature art deco touches reminiscent of the former ocean liner she once was. There are two different color schemes in the forward and aft sections, which help first-time passengers to find their way around.

The public rooms are, for the most part, quite pleasing, and many have high ceilings. Soft furnishings and much marble freshened the ship's interior recently. The ship has well-varnished outdoor decks, but the astroturf on the ship's top deck just isn't right. Features a good indoor Roman Spa, set low down in the ship, and a range of spa programs. There is an extensive jogging track (but it can't be used before 8:00 a.m. as it's located above some of the most expensive cabins). Club International is an elegant carryover from the ship's former days, and is still the perfect meeting place for cocktails and sophisticated evenings. Excellent proscenium theater for dazzle and sizzle production shows. Large active casino invites you to spend your money, and it's noisy.

Outstanding owner's suites are extremely lavish, and new suites on two decks atop the ship are very comfortable (however, all suite occupants should really have a private dining room). There are many cabins suitable for families of four or five, even six.

Take the family, as children and teens will have a fine time aboard this ship—she's so large, there are plenty of places to play.

— Expect long lines everywhere: for embarkation, disembarkation, shore excursions, shore tenders, and particularly for breakfast and lunch buffets. The open deck and sunning space is quite poor, particularly when the ship is full. Doesn't dock anywhere because of its size and deep draft (a problem for the non-ambulatory). Roman Spa fitness facilities incur hefty extra charge, plus an added 12 per cent tip. There are still too many announcements, making for too much of a holiday camp atmosphere.

Dining There are two large dining rooms—nicest is the Windward, with its fine domed ceiling and wall murals retained from her former days as the first-class dining room, while the Leeward (the former tourist-class restaurant) has a fine balcony. There are few tables for two, however, and tables are close together. The food is not memorable, and, for the most part, menus are uninspiring and quite disappointing. The selection of bread rolls and fruit is poor. The standard of the cuisine in general can be said to be no more than reasonable American hotel banquet food, though it has become better in the last year or so. Good, moderately priced wine list, but there's almost nothing for lovers of good wine. The service ranges from poor to very good.

Le Bistro is an informal alternative dining spot for a change from the two restaurants (and the attendant noise), and offers a taste of Italy in a contemporary South Miami Beach style, at no extra charge (it always seems difficult to get a table, however).

The casual, outdoor buffet area is useful for those out on deck, but it is always crowded, with long lines to get to what can best be described as food as it should *not* be presented—it never looks good, despite staff efforts to restock the display.

Other Comments This ship, formerly the grand classic transatlantic ocean liner *France*, was for many years the world's largest cruise ship (she's still the longest). Like Cunard's legendary *QE2*, *Norway* is a floating contemporary city. This ship should prove fascinating for active passengers and families with children of all ages. *Norway* will provide an action-packed, sun-filled cruise in comfortable rather than overpopulated surroundings, at a decent price.

ms Norwegian Crown ★★★★

OPERATES

ALASKA AND CARIBBEAN CRUISES

Cruise Line	Norwegian Cruise Line		
Former Names	Crown Odyssey		
Gross Tonnage	34,242		
Builder	Meyer Werft (Germany)		
Original Cost	$178 million		
Christened By	Ms Irene Panagopoulos		
Entered Service	Jun 1988/Mar 1996		
Interior Design	Katzourakis/Terzoglou		
Country of Registry	Bahamas		
Tel No 110-4673	Fax No	110-4674	
Length (ft/m)	615.9/187.75		
Beam (ft/m) 92.5/28.20	Draft (ft/m)	23.8/7.26	
Propulsion	diesel (21,330kW)		
Propellers	2 (CP)		
Decks 10	Crew	470	
Pass. Capacity (basis 2) 1,052	(all berths) 1,221		
Pass. Space Ratio (basis 2) 32.5	(all berths) 28.0		
Officers	Norwegian		
Total Cabins	526		
Size Range (sq ft/m)	154-615/14.3-57.0		
Outside Cabins 412	Inside Cabins	114	
Single Cabins	0		
Balcony Cabins 16	Wheelchair Cabins	4	
Cabin Current	110 AC		
Refrigerator	Categories AA/AB only		
Cabin TV No	VCR	No	
Dining Rooms 1	Sittings	2	
Elevators	4		

Casino Yes	Slot Machines	Yes
Swimming Pools (outside) 1	(inside)	1
Whirlpools 4	Gymnasium	Yes
Sauna/Steam Room Yes/No	Massage	Yes
Self-Service Launderette		Yes
Movie Theater/Seats		Yes/215
Library		Yes
Children's Facilities		No
Watersports Facilities		None
Classification Society	Lloyd's Register	

RATINGS	SCORE
Ship: Condition/Cleanliness	8.4
Ship: Space/Flow/Comfort	8.2
Ship: Decor/Furnishings	8.2
Ship: Fitness Facilities	7.8
Cabins: Comfort/Facilities	8.2
Cabins: Software	8.1
Food: Dining Room/Cuisine	7.6
Food: Buffets/Informal Dining	6.9
Food: Quality of Ingredients	6.4
Service: Dining Room	7.4
Service: Bars	7.5
Service: Cabins	7.3
Cruise: Entertainment	8.0
Cruise: Activities Program	7.1
Cruise: Hospitality Standard	7.6
OVERALL RATING	114.7

+ This well-designed and built ship has a handsome profile with generally good passenger flow, ample space, and fine quality interiors. Spacious layout and good array of public rooms. Generous warm woods and marble used. Has a teakwood wrap-around outdoor promenade deck. Excellent Roman-style indoor spa, pool and facilities. Good theater-style showroom, but sightlines could be better. Suites are spacious; each is decorated in a different style. Most other cabins have good closet and drawer space, and come well equipped. Cabin soundproofing is good. Non-smoking cabins are available. Friendly staff.

— There are lots of mirrored surfaces. Expect long lines for tenders, embarkation, disembarkation (especially), elevators, and buffets. There are no padded mattresses for the deck lounge chairs.

Dining Large, noisy, dining room features a stained-glass ceiling and comfortable seating. The cuisine is not gourmet either in quality or presentation, but is more than adequate. Service is generally good and attentive. Decent, well-priced wine list.

Other Comments For many years a favorite of passengers of the now defunct Riyal Cruise Line, this ship is excellent for the young-at-heart, and exudes style and charm at a really moderate price.

ss OceanBreeze ★★★

OPERATES

3- AND 4-DAY BAHAMAS
CRUISES (YEAR-ROUND)

Cruise Line		Dolphin Cruise Line	
Former Names		Azure Seas/Calypso/	
		Monarch Star/Southern Cross	
Gross Tonnage			21,486
Builder		Harland & Wolff (UK)	
Original Cost			n/a
Christened By		HRH Queen Elizabeth II	
Entered Service		Mar 1955/May 1992	
Interior Design		A&M Katzourakis	
Country of Registry			Panama
Tel No	124-6254	Fax No	124-6254
Length (ft/m)			603.8/184.06
Beam (ft/m)	80.0/24.41	Draft (ft/m)	26.1/7.97
Propulsion		steam turbine (14,900kW)	
Propellers			2 (FP)
Decks	9	Crew	380
Pass. Capacity (basis 2) 782		(all berths) 946	
Pass. Space Ratio (basis 2) 27.4		(all berths) 22.7	
Officers			International
Total Cabins			391
Size Range (sq ft/m)		99-400/90.0-37.0	
Outside Cabins	241	Inside Cabins	150
Single Cabins			0
Balcony Cabins	0	Wheelchair Cabins	0
Cabin Current			110/220 AC
Refrigerator			No
Cabin TV	No	VCR	No
Dining Rooms	1	Sittings	2

Elevators			2
Casino	Yes	Slot Machines	Yes
Swimming Pools (outside) 1		(inside)	0
Whirlpools		1	Gymnasium	Yes
Sauna/Steam Room	Yes/No	Massage	No
Self-Service Launderette			No
Movie Theater/Seats			Yes/55
Library	Yes	Children's Facilities	No
Watersports Facilities			None
Classification Society			Bureau Veritas

RATINGS	SCORE
Ship: Condition/Cleanliness	6.5
Ship: Space/Flow/Comfort	5.9
Ship: Decor/Furnishings	6.5
Ship: Fitness Facilities	4.5
Cabins: Comfort/Facilities	6.3
Cabins: Software	6.5
Food: Dining Room/Cuisine	7.0
Food: Buffets/Informal Dining	6.8
Food: Quality of Ingredients	6.6
Service: Dining Room	6.8
Service: Bars	6.9
Service: Cabins	7.1
Cruise: Entertainment	6.8
Cruise: Activities Program	6.6
Cruise: Hospitality Standard	6.8
OVERALL RATING	97.6

+ Older ship has long, low profile and single funnel astern. Well maintained, although showing her age in places. Good open deck and sunning space. Two-level casino is beautifully decorated, in art deco style, and action-packed, in what used to be the movie theater. Cabins are reasonably comfortable and nicely decorated in earth tones, and, though not large, they are well equipped, and have heavy-duty fittings. Has a good children's program for families.

— Expect lines for embarkation, disembarkation, shore excursions, and buffets. There are lots of smokers among passenger carry. Many crew members do not speak English well.

Dining The dining room is located low down in the ship, but has a warm and very cheerful ambiance, though the chairs do not have armrests. The food is generally quite good, and there's plenty of it, but it isn't gourmet food at all, despite what the brochure claims. Service is quite reasonable and attentive, but there's no finesse. Limited choice of cheeses and fruits.

Other Comments This is a good ship for those wanting a decent cruise experience for a modest price, in casual surroundings, to the southern Caribbean and Panama Canal (on alternating itineraries). At the start and end of the cruise you have to deal with the awful, crowded Aruba airport, so be prepared.

ms Ocean Majesty ★★★+

OPERATES

7-DAY AEGEAN/
MEDITERRANEAN CRUISES

Cruise Line	Majestic International Cruises	Casino	Yes	Slot Machines	Yes
Former Names	Homeric/Olympic/Ocean Majesty/	Swimming Pools (outside) 1	(inside)	0

Left column	
Cruise Line	Majestic International Cruises
Former Names	Homeric/Olympic/Ocean Majesty/ Kypros Star/Juan March
Gross Tonnage	10,417
Builder	Union de Levante (Spain)
Original Cost	$65 million
Christened By	Chios Breeze Marine
Entered Service	1966/Apr 1994
Interior Design	D. Androutsopoulos & Assoc.
Country of Registry	Greece
Tel No 113-2141	Fax No 113-2142
Length (ft/m)	443.8/135.30
Beam (ft/m) 62.9/19.20	Draft (ft/m) 19.5/5.95
Propulsion/Propellers	diesel (12,200kW)/2 (CP)
Decks 8	Crew 235
Pass. Capacity (basis 2) 535	(all berths) 621
Pass. Space Ratio (basis 2) 19.4	(all berths) 16.7
Officers	Greek
Total Cabins	273
Size Range (sq ft/m)	96-182/9.0-17.0
Outside Cabins 186	Inside Cabins 87
Single Cabins	11
Balcony Cabins 8	Wheelchair Cabins 2
Cabin Current	110/220 AC
Refrigerator	Suites only
Cabin TV Suites only	VCR No
Dining Rooms 1	Sittings 2
Elevators	3

Right column			
Casino	Yes	Slot Machines	Yes
Swimming Pools (outside)	1	(inside)	0
Whirlpools	1	Gymnasium	Yes
Sauna/Steam Room	Yes/No	Massage	Yes
Self-Service Launderette			No
Movie Theater/Seats	No	Library	Yes
Children's Facilities			Yes
Watersports Facilities			None
Classification Society		American Bureau	
		of Shipping	

RATINGS	SCORE
Ship: Condition/Cleanliness	7.5
Ship: Space/Flow/Comfort	6.7
Ship: Decor/Furnishings	7.7
Ship: Fitness Facilities	4.4
Cabins: Comfort/Facilities	6.9
Cabins: Software	7.1
Food: Dining Room/Cuisine	6.6
Food: Buffets/Informal Dining	6.4
Food: Quality of Ingredients	6.0
Service: Dining Room	7.3
Service: Bars	7.2
Service: Cabins	7.3
Cruise: Entertainment	5.9
Cruise: Activities Program	6.1
Cruise: Hospitality Standard	7.1
OVERALL RATING	100.2

+ This ship has a pleasing, balanced, almost handsome profile with an aft funnel. Has several good, practical public rooms, bars and lounges, furnished with fine quality materials and fabrics. The decor includes an abundance of highly polished mirrored surfaces. Cabins are small and functional, but with little closet and drawer space.

— This is a high-density vessel, so expect lines for embarkation, disembarkation, shore excursions, and buffets. Open deck and sunning space is limited. Cabin bathrooms are extremely small. Rather awkward interior layout and steep interior stairways with short steps.

Dining The dining room is set low down, and, although quite attractive, it is also extremely noisy (particularly at the tables adjacent to the waiter stations). No tables for two. The cuisine is Continental, with the emphasis on Greek preparation and presentation. Limited selection of breads, fruits, and cheeses, and buffets are generally simple and unimaginative affairs.

Other Comments A former Spanish ro-ro vessel (sister vessel to the present *Don Juan*), this ship has undergone an extensive transformation into a cruise vessel, with the exception of hull, shaft, and propellers, all completed in 1994. The conversion was good, but her built-up stern is not really handsome. Cruising aboard this ship will provide a busy, destination-oriented experience in surroundings that are quite comfortable, often operates under various charters.

ms Oceanic Grace ★★★★

OPERATES
JAPAN/SOUTH EAST ASIA CRUISES

Cruise Line	Oceanic Cruises	Casino	No	Slot Machines	No

Cruise Line	Oceanic Cruises
Former Names	-
Gross Tonnage	5,218
Builder	NKK Tsu Shipyard (Japan)
Original Cost	$40 million
Christened By	Ms Mineko Takamine
Entered Service	Apr 1989
Interior Design	Studio Acht
Country of Registry	Japan
Tel No 120-1634 Fax No	120-6134
Length (ft/m)	337.5/102.90
Beam (ft/m) 50.5/15.40 Draft (ft/m)	14.1/4.30
Propulsion	diesel (5,192kW)
Propellers	2 (CP)
Decks 4 Crew	70
Pass. Capacity (basis 2) 120 (all berths) 120	
Pass. Space Ratio (basis 2) 43.4 (all berths) 43.4	
Officers	Japanese
Total Cabins	60
Size Range (sq ft/m)	196-260/18.2-24.0
Outside Cabins 60 Inside Cabins	0
Single Cabins	0
Balcony Cabins	8
Wheelchair Cabins	1
Cabin Current 115 AC Refrigerator All cabins	
Cabin TV Yes VCR	Yes
Dining Rooms 1 Sittings	1
Elevators	1

Casino	No	Slot Machines	No
Swimming Pools (outside) 1		(inside)	0
Whirlpools	1	Gymnasium	Yes
Sauna/Steam Room Yes/Yes		Massage	Yes
Self-Service Launderette			No
Movie Theater/Seats	No	Library	Yes
Children's Facilities			No
Watersports Facilities		Aft platform, scuba,	
		snorkel, water-ski, Zodiacs	
Classification Society		Nippon Kaiji Kyokai	

RATINGS	SCORE
Ship: Condition/Cleanliness	8.7
Ship: Space/Flow/Comfort	8.3
Ship: Decor/Furnishings	8.5
Ship: Fitness/Watersports	8.6
Cabins: Comfort/Facilities	8.5
Cabins: Software	8.3
Food: Dining Room/Cuisine	8.7
Food: Buffets/Informal Dining	8.6
Food: Quality of Ingredients	8.7
Service: Dining Room	8.3
Service: Bars	8.4
Service: Cabins	8.1
Cruise: Entertainment	7.4
Cruise: Activities Program	7.3
Cruise: Hospitality Standard	8.8
OVERALL RATING	125.2

+ Has impressive contemporary looks and twin outboard funnels. Has a decompression chamber for scuba divers. Plenty of open deck and sunning space. Teakwood jogging track. Integrated, balanced East-West interior design concept, decor and color combinations. Clean, sophisticated decor throughout. Can be used as a two-class ship for "membership club" cruising. Tastefully furnished all-outside cabins feature blond wood cabinetry, three-sided mirrors, personal safe, mini-bar/refrigerator, safe, tea-making unit, cotton bathrobes, slippers, shoe horn, clothes brush and deep, full-sized bathtub.

— The small swimming pool is really a "dip" pool. Cabins with balconies have awkward balcony door handles. Bathroom toilet seats are too high, particularly for Japanese passengers. Watersports equipment is not used on the short cruises around the Japan coast. Room service items are at extra charge.

Dining Warm and inviting dining room features the freshest of foods from local ports of call. Features Japanese cuisine. Chefs and hotel staff are provided by the superb Palace Hotel in Tokyo.

Other Comments This is an excellent ship for watersports aficionados. Scuba equipment rental is extra. Port taxes are included. Gratuities are neither expected nor allowed.

mts Odysseus ★★★

OPERATES

MEDITERRANEAN/RED SEA CRUISES

Cruise Line	Royal Olympic Cruises	Casino	Yes	Slot Machines	Yes
Former Names	Aquamarine/Marco Polo/	Swimming Pools (outside)	1	(inside)	0
	Princesa Isabel	Whirlpools	4	Gymnasium	Yes
Gross Tonnage	12,000	Sauna/Steam Room Yes/No	Massage	Yes
Builder	Society Espanola Shipyard (Spain)	Self-Service Launderette			No
Original Cost	n/a	Movie Theater/Seats			Yes/145
Christened By	n/a	Library			Yes
Entered Service	1962/Spring 1987	Children's Facilities			No
Interior Design	Arminio Lozzi	Watersports Facilities			None
Country of Registry	Greece	Classification Society		Lloyd's Register

Tel No 113-0652	Fax No 113-0252		
Length (ft/m)	483.1/147.30		
Beam (ft/m) 61.2/18.67	Draft (ft/m) 24.1/7.35		
Propulsion	diesel (6,766kW)		
Propellers	2 (CP)		
Decks 7	Crew 194		
Pass. Capacity (basis 2) 454	(all berths) 484		
Pass. Space Ratio (basis 2) 26.4	(all berths) 24.7		
Officers	Greek		
Total Cabins	226		
Size Range (sq ft/m)	102-280/9.5-26.0		
Outside Cabins 183	Inside Cabins 43		
Single Cabins	0		
Balcony Cabins 0	Wheelchair Cabins 0		
Cabin Current 110 AC	Refrigerator No		
Cabin TV No	VCR No		
Dining Rooms 2	Sittings 2		
Elevators	1		

RATINGS	SCORE
Ship: Condition/Cleanliness	6.9
Ship: Space/Flow/Comfort	6.5
Ship: Decor/Furnishings	6.8
Ship: Fitness Facilities	3.7
Cabins: Comfort/Facilities	6.4
Cabins: Software	6.9
Food: Dining Room/Cuisine	6.6
Food: Buffets/Informal Dining	6.3
Food: Quality of Ingredients	6.0
Service: Dining Room	7.3
Service: Bars	7.2
Service: Cabins	7.3
Cruise: Entertainment	5.4
Cruise: Activities Program	5.7
Cruise: Hospitality Standard	7.2
OVERALL RATING	96.2

+ This attractive-looking vessel has a balanced profile, and was acquired and completely reconstructed in 1987 by Epirotiki Cruise Line (now part of Royal Olympic Cruises). There is ample open deck and sunning space. Has twin teak-decked sheltered promenades. There is a good range of public rooms featuring pleasing Mediterranean decor, and some decent artwork throughout. The Taverna is especially popular with the younger set. Attractive, quite roomy, mostly outside cabins have convertible sofa-bed (a few have double beds), good closet and drawer space, and tasteful wood trim.

— Has steep gangway in most ports. Cabin bathrooms and shower stalls are small, with little space to store toiletry items.

Dining The dining room is quite charming, though it tends to be noisy. Food is typically continental, and features several Greek dishes (extensive use of oil). Warm, attentive service, but the menu choice is rather limited. The quality and selection of breads, cheeses, and fruits could be better.

Other Comments This ship is for those who want to cruise at modest cost, in warm surroundings, on a very comfortable vessel, in the Aegean and Mediterranean areas. Often chartered by learning enrichment tour operators.

ms Olga Sadovskaya ★★

OPERATES
VARIOUS SOUTHEAST ASIA CRUISES

Cruise Line	Pacific Cruise Company	Casino	No	Slot Machines	No
Former Names	Orient Star/Olga Sadovskaya	Swimming Pools (outside) 1	(inside)	No
Gross Tonnage	3,941	Whirlpools	No	Gymnasium	No
Builder	Brodgradiliste Uljanik (Yugoslavia)	Sauna/Steam Room Yes/No	Massage	No
Original Cost	n/a	Self-Service Launderette	No
Christened By	n/a	Movie Theater/Seats	Yes/75
Entered Service	1977/1994	Library	Yes
Interior Design	n/a	Children's Facilities	No
Country of Registry	Russia	Watersports Facilities	None
Tel No 140-0371 Fax No	140-0371	Classification Society	RS

Length (ft/m)	328.1/100.01
Beam (ft/m) 53.2/16.24 Draft (ft/m)	15.2/4.65
Propulsion	diesel (3,884kW)
Propellers	1 (FP)
Decks 6 Crew	100
Pass. Capacity (basis 2) 96	(all berths) 188
Pass. Space Ratio (basis 2) 41.0	(all berths) 20.9
Officers	Russian
Total Cabins	48
Size Range (sq ft/m)	n/a
Outside Cabins 48 Inside Cabins	0
Single Cabins	0
Balcony Cabins	0
Wheelchair Cabins	0
Cabin Current 220 AC Refrigerator	No
Cabin TV No VCR	No
Dining Rooms 1 Sittings	1
Elevators	0

RATINGS	SCORE
Ship: Condition/Cleanliness	5.3
Ship: Space/Flow/Comfort	5.5
Ship: Decor/Furnishings	6.1
Ship: Fitness Facilities	3.0
Cabins: Comfort/Facilities	5.7
Cabins: Software	6.0
Food: Dining Room/Cuisine	5.8
Food: Buffets/Informal Dining	5.3
Food: Quality of Ingredients	5.6
Service: Dining Room	6.2
Service: Bars	6.4
Service: Cabins	6.5
Cruise: Entertainment	4.2
Cruise: Activities Program	4.6
Cruise: Hospitality Standard	6.1
OVERALL RATING	82.3

+ Intimate small ship has a well-balanced profile. Has an ice-hardened hull suitable for soft expedition cruising. Reasonable open deck space for ship size. Recently underwent extensive refurbishment. Outdoor observation deck and enclosed promenade deck for inclement weather. Charming forward music lounge has wooden dance floor. Rich, highly polished wood paneling throughout. Lovely winding brass-railed main staircase. Good cinema/lecture room.

— The cabins are very compact and spartan, but most can accommodate four persons. Has a steep, narrow gangway in ports of call. The cabin insulation is rather poor.

Dining Comfortable dining room has ocean views. Limited choice of food, but service is friendly and quite attentive. Poor selection of breads, fruits, and cheeses.

Other Comments This ship is very small, yet reasonably comfortable, and has plenty of character, but don't expect much finesse from the service aspects of the cruise.

tts Olympic ★★★+

OPERATES
7-DAY AEGEAN/
MEDITERRANEAN CRUISES

Cruise Line	Royal Olympic Cruises	Elevators	4
Former Names	FiestaMarina/Carnivale/	Casino Yes	Slot Machines Yes
	Empress of Britain/Queen Anna Maria	Swimming Pools (outside) 2	(inside) 1
Gross Tonnage	31,500	Whirlpools 1	Gymnasium Yes
Builder	Fairfield Shipbuilding (UK)	Sauna/Steam Room Yes/No	Massage Yes
Original Cost	UK£7,500,000	Self-Service Launderette	No (has ironing room)
Christened By	H.M. Queen Elizabeth II/	Movie Theater/Seats	Yes/180
	Ms Dayanara Torres	Library No	Children's Facilities Yes
Entered Service	Apr 1956/1994	Watersports Facilities	None
Interior Design	Joe Farcus	Classification Society	Lloyd's Register
Country of Registry	Bahamas (C6KD)		

Tel No 113-2333 Fax No 113-2334	**RATINGS**	**SCORE**
Length (ft/m) 640.0/195.08	Ship: Condition/Cleanliness	6.7
Beam (ft/m) 87.0/26.51 Draft (ft/m) 29.0/8.84	Ship: Space/Flow/Comfort	6.3
Propulsion steam turbine (22,400kW)	Ship: Decor/Furnishings	7.3
Propellers 2 (FP)	Ship: Fitness Facilities	5.3
Decks 9 Crew 550	Cabins: Comfort/Facilities	6.2
Pass. Capacity (basis 2) 976 (all berths) 1,386	Cabins: Software	6.5
Pass. Space Ratio (basis 2) 32.2 (all berths) 22.7	Food: Dining Room/Cuisine	7.1
Officers Greek	Food: Buffets/Informal Dining	6.6
Total Cabins 488	Food: Quality of Ingredients	6.2
Size Range (sq ft/m) 101.7-301.3/9.36-28.0	Service: Dining Room	7.1
Outside Cabins 221 Inside Cabins 267	Service: Bars	7.2
Single Cabins 0	Service: Cabins	7.3
Balcony Cabins 0 Wheelchair Cabins 0	Cruise: Entertainment	7.5
Cabin Current 110 AC Refrigerator No	Cruise: Activities Program	6.5
Cabin TV No VCR No	Cruise: Hospitality Standard	7.5
Dining Rooms 1 Sittings 2	OVERALL RATING	101.3

+ This solidly built former ocean liner has a midships funnel, while teak outdoor and glass-enclosed indoor promenade decks encircle the ship. Has had an extensive recent refurbishment. The interior colors are quite stimulating, and the public rooms have rather jazzy decor. The casino is large for a Europe-based ship. Has some delightful original woods and polished brass throughout her public spaces. Large whirlpool added, and new colorful tiled outdoor deck. There is a wide range of cabins, most of them large, some with rich wood furniture, all of them redecorated recently. Many cabins have third and fourth berths.

— She's an old ship, and the cabin bathrooms are small. Constant multilingual announcements are irritating. Expect lines for embarkation, disembarkation, buffets, and shore excursions.

Dining The dining room is crowded, and noisy, but nicely redecorated. The food, be aware, is not for gourmets.

Other Comments Royal Olympic Cruises provides good family cruising in an unsophisticated and very casual setting, for a first cruise at a decent price, to some fascinating destinations.

ms Oriana ★★★★+

OPERATES

*12- TO 90-DAY VARIOUS CRUISES
WORLDWIDE*

Cruise Line/Operator:		P&O Cruises
Former Names		-
Gross Tonnage		69,153
Builder		Meyer Werft (Germany)
Original Cost		UK£200 million
Christened By		H.R.H. Queen Elizabeth II
Entered Service		Apr 1995
Interior Design		Tillberg/McNeece/Yran
Country of Registry		Great Britain
Tel No 145-3403	Fax No	145-3404
Length (ft/m)		853.0/260.0
Beam (ft/m) 105.6/32.2	Draft (ft/m)	25.9/7.9
Propulsion		diesel (47,750kW)
Propellers		2 (CP)
Decks 10	Crew	760
Pass. Capacity (basis 2) 1,828	(all berths)	1,975
Pass. Space Ratio (basis 2) 37.8	(all berths)	35.0
Officers		British
Total Cabins		914
Size Range (sq ft/m)		151-501/14.0-46.5
Outside Cabins 594	Inside Cabins	320
Single Cabins		112
Balcony Cabins 118	Wheelchair Cabins	8
Cabin Current		110/220 AC
Refrigerator		Yes
Cabin TV Yes	VCR	Suites only
Dining Rooms 2	Sittings	2
Elevators		10

Casino	Yes	Slot Machines	Yes
Swimming Pools (outside)	3	(inside)	0
Whirlpools	5	Gymnasium	Yes
Sauna/Steam Room	Yes/Yes	Massage	Yes
Self-Service Launderette			Yes
Movie Theater/Seats			Yes/189
Library			Yes
Children's Facilities			Yes
Watersports Facilities			None
Classification Society		Lloyd's Register	

RATINGS	SCORE
Ship: Condition/Cleanliness	9.2
Ship: Space/Flow/Comfort	9.0
Ship: Decor/Furnishings	9.2
Ship: Fitness Facilities	8.7
Cabins: Comfort/Facilities	8.7
Cabins: Software	9.0
Food: Dining Room/Cuisine	7.7
Food: Buffets/Informal Dining	7.1
Food: Quality of Ingredients	7.5
Service: Dining Room	8.2
Service: Bars	8.1
Service: Cabins	8.2
Cruise: Entertainment	8.7
Cruise: Activities Program	7.0
Cruise: Hospitality Standard	8.1
OVERALL RATING	124.4

+ This ship is, thankfully, quite conventional, and is evolutionary rather than revolutionary. Capable of speedy long distance cruising. Has the largest stabilizers of any ship, covering an area of 231 sq ft (21.5m²). She is a ship that takes Canberra's traditional appointments and public rooms and adds more up-to-date touches, together with better facilities and passenger flow, and a feeling of timeless elegance.

Her interiors are welcoming, relaxing and restrained. Splendid amount of open deck and sunning space, important for her outdoors-loving British passengers. Has an extra-wide wrap-around outdoor promenade deck. Features inboard lifeboats as do so many ships today. The stern superstructure is nicely rounded and has several tiers that overlook an aft deck, pool and children's outdoor facilities. Inside, the well laid-out design provides good horizontal passenger flow and wide passageways. Fine detailed ceiling treatments. Specific areas have been designed to attract different age groups and lifestyles.

There is a four-deck-high atrium and waterfall; it is elegant but not glitzy, topped by a dome of Tiffany glass. Large number of public entertainment rooms. The Theatre Royal, designed by John Wyckham, is decorated in rich reds and has individually air-conditioned seats, an orchestra pit, revolving stage and excellent acoustics. Anderson's Lounge (named after the founder members of the Peninsular Steam Navigation Company in the 1830s) features a series of 19th century marine paintings, and is decorated in the manner of a British gentleman's club. Although there's no fireplace, it's the most popular lounge.

The fine, restful library has a well-chosen selection of hardback books (a librarian would be a useful addition), skillfully crafted tables and some extremely comfortable chairs. Lord's Tavern is, without doubt, the most sporting place to pitch a beverage or two, decorated as it is in cricket memorabilia (indeed the ship's interior designer, John McNeece's own house stands on the site of the original Lord's cricket ground in London). Thackeray's (writing room) is named after William Makepeace Thackeray, a former P&O passenger. Carpeting throughout the ship is of excellent quality, much of it custom designed and made (100% wool). There are some outstanding pieces of sculpture that provide a living museum afloat, and original artwork by all-British artists that include tapestries and sculptures.

The health spa, run by Champney's, is located forward and atop ship, is quite large, and provides all the latest alternative therapy treatments. The co-ed sauna is a large facility (most ships have separate saunas for men and women).

Wide range of well-equipped cabin configurations and categories, including family cabins with extra beds (110 cabins can accommodate four persons). Some suites and cabins with balconies have an inter-connecting door, and include a trouser press, ironing board and iron, neatly tucked into a cupboard, binoculars, umbrella, a large atlas, and a second television. Bathrooms, however, are disappointing, with an ordinary sink; I expected a marble unit. The whirlpool bathtubs are good, however, although they have high sides to step over.

There is much use of rich, warm limed oak or cherrywood in the cabins, which makes even the least expensive four-berth cabin seem inviting. There's also a good number of cabins for single passengers. Bathrooms are compact, and feature art deco-style cabinets and lighting.

The most expensive suites are pleasant, but not at all impressive when compared to suites on other contemporary ships; they do, however, have a trouser press, ironing board and iron, as well as sliding glazed panels between bedroom and sitting room, and private balcony.

Children and teens have their own "Club Oriana" programs with their own rooms ("Peter Pan" and "Decibels"), and outdoor pool for the children. There's also a special "night nursery" for small children (ages 2 to 5). The cabins also have a baby listening facility.

— Suite bathrooms are inferior to those on other like-sized ships. The theater seats would provide better stage sightlines if they had been staggered. The Pacific Lounge has too many pillars that obstruct sightlines. The aerobic exercise room and health spa are not connected (you first must go out of the spa, into a foyer, and then into the exercise room). Expect lines for embarkation, disembarkation, buffets, the Reception Desk, and shore tenders.

Dining The two restaurants, Peninsular and Oriental, allocated according to the cabin grade and cabin chosen, are midships and aft. Both are quite handsome (each has tables for two, four, six, or eight) and have interesting ceilings, chandeliers and decor. Oriental Restaurant has windows on three sides, including the stern. Has Anton Mosimann-designed signature dishes. The time allotted for meals is quite short; thus, "eat and run" instead of "dining" tends to be the norm. Meals are fairly non-memorable, standard fare, and presentation is rather lacking, although I expect this to improve.

The light and airy indoor/outdoor Conservatory buffet café offers alternative light breakfast and luncheon buffets, and 24-hour self-service beverage stands. For the British market, an alternative restaurant featuring Indian food would have been a useful addition.

Other Comments Oriana is the first cruise ship specifically designed for the growing British market. This is a ship and not a hotel, however, something that will please the P&O traditionalists, and provide a fine cruise experience principally for British passengers who don't want to fly to get to their cruise ship. Finally, port taxes and insurance are included for British passengers. For gratuities, allow about UK£3.00 per person, per day.

mv Orient Venus ★★★★

OPERATES

VARIOUS JAPAN/SOUTH EAST
ASIA CRUISES

Cruise Line	Japan Cruise Line
	(Nippon Cruise Kyakusen)
Former Names	-
Gross Tonnage	21,884
Builder	Ishikawajima Heavy Industries (Japan)
Original Cost	$150 million
Christened By	Mr Yasuo Iritani
Entered Service	Jul 1990
Interior Design	Daimaru Design & Engineering
Country of Registry	Japan
Tel No 120-1731 Fax No	120-1731
Length (ft/m)	570.8/174.00
Beam (ft/m) 78.7/24.00 Draft (ft/m)	21.3/6.52
Propulsion	diesel (18,540bhp)
Propellers	2 (CP)
Decks 8 Crew	120
Pass. Capacity (basis 2) 390 (all berths)	606
Pass. Space Ratio (basis 2) 56.1 (all berths)	36.1
Officers	Japanese
Total Cabins	195
Size Range (sq ft/m)	183-592/17.0-55.0
Outside Cabins 195 Inside Cabins	0
Single Cabins	0
Balcony Cabins	2
Wheelchair Cabins	0
Cabin Current 110 AC Refrigerator	All cabins
Cabin TV Yes VCR	No
Dining Rooms 2 Sittings	1

Elevators	3
Casino No Slot Machines	No
Swimming Pools (outside) 1 (inside)	0
Whirlpools 0 Gymnasium	Yes
Sauna/Steam Room No/No Massage	No
Self-Service Launderette	Yes
Movie Theater/Seats	Yes/606
Library Yes Children's Facilities	No
Watersports Facilities	None
Classification Society	Nippon Kaiji Kyokai

RATINGS	SCORE
Ship: Condition/Cleanliness	8.1
Ship: Space/Flow/Comfort	8.0
Ship: Decor/Furnishings	8.0
Ship: Fitness Facilities	7.8
Cabins: Comfort/Facilities	7.8
Cabins: Software	7.5
Food: Dining Room/Cuisine	7.4
Food: Buffets/Informal Dining	7.2
Food: Quality of Ingredients	7.0
Service: Dining Room	7.7
Service: Bars	7.8
Service: Cabins	7.6
Cruise: Entertainment	7.0
Cruise: Activities Program	7.2
Cruise: Hospitality Standard	7.9
OVERALL RATING	114.0

+ New conventional-shaped ship has a graceful profile. Night and Day lounge set at funnel base looking forward over swimming pool. Expansive open deck and sunning space. Windows of the Orient is a small attractive, peaceful forward observation lounge. Superb conference facilities with small conference room and main lecture room with 620 moveable seats. Fine array of public rooms with tasteful and very inviting decor throughout. Horseshoe-shaped main lounge has fine sightlines to platform stage. Expansive open sunning deck aft of funnel. Four cabin grades provide variety of well-equipped, all-outside, Western-style cabins. Two suites are huge and have private balconies.

— Does not really cater to individual passengers well. The decor is rather plain in many public rooms.

Dining Very attractive main dining room. Romanesque Grill is unusual, with classic period decor and high, elegant ceiling. Features reasonably good, but rather commercial Japanese cuisine exclusively.

Other Comments This Western-style ship will provide its mostly Japanese corporate passengers with extremely comfortable surroundings, and a superb cruise and seminar/learning environment and experience.

mts Orpheus ★★★

OPERATES

14-DAY SOUTHERN EUROPE CRUISES

Cruise Line	Royal Olympic Cruises		
Former Names	Thesus/Munster I/Munster		
Gross Tonnage	5,092		
Builder	Harland & Wolff (UK)		
Original Cost	n/a		
Christened By	n/a		
Entered Service	1952/1969		
Interior Design	Arminio Lozzi		
Country of Registry	Greece		
Tel No 113-3165	Fax No	113-1336	
Length (ft/m)	374.8/114.26		
Beam (ft/m) 50.1/15.30	Draft (ft/m)	16.0/4.88	
Propulsion	diesel (4,119kW)		
Propellers	2 (FP)		
Decks 6	Crew	140	
Pass. Capacity (basis 2) 304	(all berths) 310		
Pass. Space Ratio (basis 2) 16.7	(all berths) 16.4		
Officers	Greek		
Total Cabins	152		
Size Range (sq ft/m)	99.8-226.0/9.28-21.00		
Outside Cabins 117	Inside Cabins	35	
Single Cabins	7		
Balcony Cabins 0	Wheelchair Cabins	0	
Cabin Current	220 AC		
Refrigerator	No		
Cabin TV No	VCR	No	
Dining Rooms 1	Sittings	Open	
Elevators	0		

Casino	No	Slot Machines	No
Swimming Pools (outside) 1		(inside)	0
Whirlpools	0	Gymnasium	No
Sauna/Steam Room No/No		Massage	No
Self-Service Launderette			No
Movie Theater/Seats			No
Library			Yes
Children's Facilities			No
Watersports Facilities			None
Classification Society			Lloyd's Register

RATINGS	SCORE
Ship: Condition/Cleanliness	6.6
Ship: Space/Flow/Comfort	6.4
Ship: Decor/Furnishings	6.7
Ship: Fitness Facilities	3.9
Cabins: Comfort/Facilities	6.0
Cabins: Software	6.7
Food: Dining Room/Cuisine	6.7
Food: Buffets/Informal Dining	6.2
Food: Quality of Ingredients	6.0
Service: Dining Room	7.5
Service: Bars	7.2
Service: Cabins	7.4
Cruise: Entertainment	7.2
Cruise: Activities Program	7.0
Cruise: Hospitality Standard	7.9
OVERALL RATING	99.4

+ Traditional ship profile, with small, squat funnel. Charming and very well maintained. Ample open deck and sunning space for a ship of this size, including a wrap-around outdoor promenade deck. Comfortable public rooms with Mediterranean decor, good fabrics, and fine artwork. Cabins are compact but nicely appointed and quite adequate. Informality is the order of the day. The ship itself is secondary but has a very homely ambiance, and operates on a long-term charter to Swan Hellenic for a program of outstanding, in-depth life-enrichment cruises. Repeat passengers are known, rather proudly, as "Swans."

— High density means that public rooms are always crowded when the ship is full. There is a limited amount of closet, drawer, and storage space.

Dining The dining room is quite attractive and features an open seating policy. Attentive, friendly service from single-nationality crew. The food itself is quite reasonable, but certainly not memorable, and the selection of breads, cheeses, and fruits is limited.

Other Comments The company features a cast of excellent guest lecturers who provide informed, yet informal presentations aboard all cruises. Insurance, gratuities and all shore excursions are included for the ship's mainly British passengers.

mv Pacific Princess ★★★★

OPERATES
VARIOUS CRUISES WORLDWIDE

Cruise Line	Princess Cruises	Casino Yes	Slot Machines Yes
Former Names	Sea Venture	Swimming Pools (outside) 2	(inside) 0
Gross Tonnage	20,636	Whirlpools 0	Gymnasium Yes
Builder	Rheinstahl Nordseewerke (Germany)	Sauna/Steam Room Yes/No	Massage Yes
Original Cost	$25 million	Self-Service Launderette	No
Christened By	n/a	Movie Theater/Seats	Yes/250
Entered Service	May 1971/Apr 1975	Library	Yes
Interior Design	Robert Tillberg	Children's Facilities	No
Country of Registry	Great Britain	Watersports Facilities	None
Tel No 144-0212	Fax No 144-0212	Classification Society	Lloyd's Register
Length (ft/m)	553.6/168.74		
Beam (ft/m) 80.8/24.64	Draft (ft/m) 25.2/7.70	**RATINGS**	**SCORE**
Propulsion	diesel (13,240kW)	Ship: Condition/Cleanliness	7.7
Propellers	2 (CP)	Ship: Space/Flow/Comfort	7.6
Decks 7	Crew 350	Ship: Decor/Furnishings	8.0
Pass. Capacity (basis 2) 610	(all berths) 717	Ship: Fitness Facilities	6.2
Pass. Space Ratio (basis 2) 33.8	(all berths) 28.7	Cabins: Comfort/Facilities	7.5
Officers	British	Cabins: Software	7.6
Total Cabins	305	Food: Dining Room/Cuisine	7.3
Size Range (sq ft/m)	126-443/11.7-41.0	Food: Buffets/Informal Dining	7.0
Outside Cabins 238	Inside Cabins 67	Food: Quality of Ingredients	6.7
Single Cabins	2	Service: Dining Room	7.9
Balcony Cabins 0	Wheelchair Cabins 2	Service: Bars	8.0
Cabin Current	110/220 AC	Service: Cabins	7.8
Refrigerator	Category A/B/C/D/DD only	Cruise: Entertainment	8.1
Cabin TV Yes	VCR No	Cruise: Activities Program	7.8
Dining Rooms 1	Sittings 2	Cruise: Hospitality Standard	8.0
Elevators	4	OVERALL RATING	113.2

+ This is a well-proportioned, handsome ship with high superstructure and quite graceful lines. Has been recently upgraded and is well maintained. Has plenty of good open deck space and decent sunning areas. Spacious public areas have wide passageways. One swimming pool has magrodome roof for use in inclement weather. Tasteful earth-toned decor throughout, with complementary artwork. Good movie theater. Suites and all other cabins are quite roomy and well appointed. Excellent production shows and general entertainment. Very smartly dressed officers and crew. Bathrobes for all passengers

— No wrap-around outdoor promenade deck, and the present teak decking is badly worn in many places. The outdoor lido deck's buffet area is untidy.

Dining The dining room (non-smoking) is located on a lower deck, but has nice, light decor and feels comfortable and spacious. Good service and fairly good food, although standards have been slipping, as a result of discounted fares.

Other Comments This ship is definitely for the older passenger, is quite elegant and moderately expensive, but will cruise you in very comfortable, elegant surroundings, in style. However, it is small compared to Princess Cruises' newer ships and cannot offer the same range of facilities and services.

ms Polaris ★★★★

OPERATES
WORLDWIDE EXPEDITION CRUISES

Cruise Line		Special Expeditions
Former Names		Lindblad Polaris/Oresund
Gross Tonnage		2,214
Builder		Aalborg Vaerft (Denmark)
Original Cost		n/a
Christened By		n/a
Entered Service		1960/May 1987
Interior Design		G. Unnar Svensson
Country of Registry		Bahamas
Tel No	110-4424	Fax No	110-3276
Length (ft/m)		236.6/72.12
Beam (ft/m)	42.7/13.03	Draft (ft/m)	13.7/4.30
Propulsion		diesel (2,354kW)
Propellers		2 (CP)
Decks	4	Crew	43
Pass. Capacity (basis 2) 82		(all berths) 84
Pass. Space Ratio (basis 2) 27.0		(all berths) 26.3
Officers		Swedish
Total Cabins		41
Size Range (sq ft/m)		100-230/9.2-21.3
Outside Cabins	41	Inside Cabins	0
Single Cabins		0
Balcony Cabins	0	Wheelchair Cabins	0
Cabin Current	220 AC	Refrigerator	No
Cabin TV	No	VCR	No
Dining Rooms		1 (open seating)
Elevators		0
Casino	No	Slot Machines	No

Swimming Pools (outside)			0
Whirlpools	0	Exercise Room	No
Sauna/Steam Room	Yes/No	Massage	No
Self-Service Launderette			No
Lecture/Film Room			No
Library			Yes
Zodiacs			8
Helicopter Pad			No
Watersports Facilities			None
Classification Society			Bureau Veritas

RATINGS	SCORE
Ship: Condition/Cleanliness	7.3
Ship: Space/Flow/Comfort	5.7
Ship: Expedition Equipment	7.6
Ship: Decor/Furnishings	7.4
Cabins: Comfort/Facilities	5.6
Cabins: Software	6.4
Food: Dining Room/Cuisine	7.6
Food: Buffets/Informal Dining	7.3
Food: Quality of Ingredients	6.9
Service: Dining Room	7.7
Service: Bars	7.5
Service: Cabins	7.6
Cruise: Itineraries/Operations	8.0
Cruise: Lecture Program	7.8
Cruise: Hospitality Standard	8.1
OVERALL RATING	108.5

+ This "soft" expedition cruise vessel, of modest proportions, sports a dark blue hull and white superstructure. Well maintained. Sports a fantail and improved aft outdoor lounge area. Carries Zodiacs and a glass-bottom boat. Tidy Scandinavian interior furnishings and decor, with lots of wood trim. The cabins are quite roomy and nicely appointed, but there's little drawer space. Some have been refurbished, and feature large (lower) beds with wooden headboards. Each has a hairdryer. Cabin keys are not used. Friendly, very intimate atmosphere on board. Excellent lecturers and nature observers, and a restful, well-stocked library.

— There are few public rooms. There is no cabin service menu. Cabin bathrooms are really tiny.

Dining Dining room has big picture windows. Seating is now at individual tables for improved access. Has very good food, with major emphasis on fish and seafood dishes. There is also a fine wine list. Breakfast and lunch are buffet-style. Friendly service from a caring, attentive staff.

Other Comments There is no formal entertainment, and no one needs it, but there are always specialist lecturers accompanying all cruises. This is a delightful vessel to choose for your next destination- and learning-intensive "soft" expedition cruise experience.

mts Princesa Amorosa ★★+

OPERATES
7-DAY MEDITERRANEAN CRUISES

Cruise Line	Louis Cruise Lines	Casino	Yes
Former Names	Galaxias/Galaxy/Scottish Coast	Swimming Pools (outside) 1	
Gross Tonnage	5,026	Whirlpools	0
Builder	Harland & Wolff (UK)	Sauna/Steam Room No/No	
Original Cost	n/a	Self-Service Launderette	
Christened By	Mr Costakis Loizou	Movie Theater/Seats	
Entered Service	1957/July 1990	Library	
Interior Design	P. Yapanis	Children's Facilities	
Country of Registry	Cyprus	Watersports Facilities	
Tel No none	Fax No none	Classification Society	

Casino	Yes	Slot Machines	Yes
Swimming Pools (outside)	1	(inside)	0
Whirlpools	0	Gymnasium	No
Sauna/Steam Room	No/No	Massage	No
Self-Service Launderette			No
Movie Theater/Seats			No
Library			Yes
Children's Facilities			No
Watersports Facilities			None
Classification Society			Lloyd's Register

Length (ft/m)			342.2/104.32
Beam (ft/m) 52.6/16.06	Draft (ft/m)		15.7/4.81
Propulsion			diesel 4,781kW
Propellers			2 (FP)
Decks	6	Crew	130
Pass. Capacity (basis 2) 284		(all berths) 327	
Pass. Space Ratio (basis 2) 17.6		(all berths) 15.3	
Officers			Cypriot/Greek
Total Cabins			142
Size Range (sq ft/m)		107.6-172.2/10.0-16.0	
Outside Cabins	115	Inside Cabins	27
Single Cabins			0
Balcony Cabins			0
Wheelchair Cabins			0
Cabin Current 220 AC		Refrigerator	No
Cabin TV No		VCR	No
Dining Rooms	1	Sittings	2
Elevators			0

RATINGS	SCORE
Ship: Condition/Cleanliness	5.6
Ship: Space/Flow/Comfort	5.2
Ship: Decor/Furnishings	6.0
Ship: Fitness Facilities	4.0
Cabins: Comfort/Facilities	5.8
Cabins: Software	6.1
Food: Dining Room/Cuisine	6.1
Food: Buffets/Informal Dining	5.9
Food: Quality of Ingredients	5.8
Service: Dining Room	6.6
Service: Bars	6.2
Service: Cabins	6.3
Cruise: Entertainment	5.0
Cruise: Activities Program	5.1
Cruise: Hospitality Standard	6.6
OVERALL RATING	86.3

+ This older vessel has fairly spacious open decks for her size. Interesting maroon wrought iron staircase balustrades show her former British heritage. Public rooms have been refurbished. Earth-tone colors used to good effect, creating a mild sense of spaciousness. Most cabins are outside and are quite comfortable, with crisp Mediterranean colors and some wood trim, but they are small, and bathrooms do show their age. Pleasant lounge and bar for socializing, with comfortable seating and warm decor. The ambiance aboard is delightfully warm and friendly.

— Limited number of public rooms and facilities. Has a steep, narrow gangway in some ports. The swimming pool is really only a "dip" pool. Cabins above the disco are noisy.

Dining The dining room has portholes and is quite cheery. Food is decidedly Mediterranean, with reasonable choice, and excellent presentation. Full vegetarian menu available. Service is quite cheerful, and the staff try hard. Both à la carte and buffet meals are featured.

Other Comments This small white ship is quite old, but still in good shape (seeing the bridge is like stepping back in time), and she is a hardy, stable ship at sea. She was purchased by her present owners in 1989. This ship is crowded when full, but offers a reasonably pleasant cruise experience if your expectations are not too high.

mv Princesa Marissa ★★★

OPERATES

2 AND 3-DAY EGYPT/ISRAEL CRUISES (YEAR-ROUND)

Cruise Line	Louis Cruise Lines		
Former Names	Finnhansa/Princessan		
Gross Tonnage	10,487		
Builder	Wartsila (Finland)		
Original Cost	n/a		
Christened By	Mr Costakis Loizou		
Entered Service	1966/June, 1987		
Interior Design	G. Petrides/P. Yapanis		
Country of Registry	Cyprus		
Tel No	none	Fax No	none
Length (ft/m)		440.6/134.30	
Beam (ft/m) 65.2/19.90	Draft (ft/m)	18.7/5.70	
Propulsion		diesel (10,300kW)	
Propellers		2 (CP)	
Decks	9	Crew	185
Pass. Capacity (basis 2) 628		(all berths) 839	
Pass. Space Ratio (basis 2) 16.6		(all berths) 12.4	
Officers		Cypriot/Greek	
Total Cabins		314	
Size Range (sq ft/m)	75.3-226.0/7.0-21.0		
Outside Cabins	148	Inside Cabins	166
Single Cabins		0	
Balcony Cabins		0	
Wheelchair Cabins		0	
Cabin Current		220 AC	
Refrigerator		No	
Cabin TV	No	VCR	No
Dining Rooms	2	Sittings	2

Elevators			1
Casino	Yes	Slot Machines	Yes
Swimming Pools (outside) 0		(inside)	0
Whirlpools	0	Gymnasium	No
Sauna/Steam Room Yes/No		Massage	No
Self-Service Launderette			No
Movie Theater/Seats	No	Library	No
Children's Facilities			Yes
Watersports Facilities			None
Classification Society		Det Norske Veritas	

RATINGS	SCORE
Ship: Condition/Cleanliness	6.1
Ship: Space/Flow/Comfort	6.0
Ship: Decor/Furnishings	5.8
Ship: Fitness Facilities	5.6
Cabins: Comfort/Facilities	6.7
Cabins: Software	7.0
Food: Dining Room/Cuisine	5.8
Food: Buffets/Informal Dining	5.8
Food: Quality of Ingredients	5.3
Service: Dining Room	6.0
Service: Bars	5.8
Service: Cabins	6.1
Cruise: Entertainment	5.1
Cruise: Activities Program	5.3
Cruise: Hospitality Standard	6.0
OVERALL RATING	91.4

+ Her interiors are very smart and tidy, and the ship is quite well maintained. The public room decor is very attractive, with warm colors and with well-designed fabrics and soft furnishings. Has small conference facilities. Standard cabins are quite smart and functional. A whole section of new cabins, added in 1995, are of a good size, have picture windows, and decor is bright and cheerful. They also have excellent bathrooms.

— High passenger density. Also has low ceilings, typical of ferry construction. Limited open deck and sunning space. Few crew for so many passengers. Passengers must board through the aft car deck, but it all works and is no real hardship.

Dining The two dining rooms are quite attractive (the forward one is more intimate). Both à la carte and buffet-style meals are featured, and the menu includes three entrees. There is also a full vegetarian menu. Comfortable dining chairs. Good breads and ice cream sundaes.

Other Comments This former passenger-car ferry has a square stern, twin funnels and a short, somewhat stubby bow. This high-density vessel offers transportation, low fares, and food that is attractively presented. She is quite popular with Swedish passengers, who simply want an unsophisticated cruise in unstuffy surroundings. This ship provides year-round short cruises that represent very good value for money, and include all shore excursions in Egypt and Israel.

mv Princesa Victoria ★★★

OPERATES

2 AND 3-DAY EGYPT/ISRAEL CRUISES

Cruise Line	Louis Cruise Lines
Former Names	The Victoria/Victoria/
	Dunottar Castle
Gross Tonnage	14,583
Builder	Harland & Wolff (UK)
Original Cost	n/a
Christened By	Mr Costakis Loizou
Entered Service	Jul 1936/Jan 1993
Interior Design	A&M Katzourakis
Country of Registry	Cyprus
Tel No 110-1627 Fax No 110-1630	
Length (ft/m)	572.8/174.60
Beam (ft/m) 71.9/21.92 Draft (ft/m) 27.8/8.50	
Propulsion	diesel (10,450kW)
Propellers	2 (FP)
Decks 7 Crew	230
Pass. Capacity (basis 2) 566 (all berths) 750	
Pass. Space Ratio (basis 2) 25.7 (all berths) 19.4	
Officers	Cypriot/Greek
Total Cabins	287
Size Range (sq ft/m)	156.0-258.3/14.5-24.0
Outside Cabins 216 Inside Cabins	71
Single Cabins	8
Balcony Cabins 0 Wheelchair Cabins	0
Cabin Current 115 AC Refrigerator Suites only	
Cabin TV Yes VCR	No
Dining Rooms 1 Sittings	2
Elevators	3

Casino	Yes	Slot Machines	Yes
Swimming Pools (outside) 2		(inside)	0
Whirlpools	0	Gymnasium	Yes
Sauna/Steam Room Yes/No		Massage	No
Self-Service Launderette			No
Movie Theater/Seats			Yes/250
Library			Yes
Children's Facilities			Yes
Watersports Facilities			None
Classification Society		Lloyd's Register	

RATINGS	SCORE
Ship: Condition/Cleanliness	6.5
Ship: Space/Flow/Comfort	6.0
Ship: Decor/Furnishings	6.1
Ship: Fitness Facilities	5.3
Cabins: Comfort/Facilities	6.8
Cabins: Software	7.0
Food: Dining Room/Cuisine	6.6
Food: Buffets/Informal Dining	6.1
Food: Quality of Ingredients	5.7
Service: Dining Room	6.3
Service: Bars	6.0
Service: Cabins	6.3
Cruise: Entertainment	5.6
Cruise: Activities Program	5.5
Cruise: Hospitality Standard	6.7
OVERALL RATING	92.5

+ This ship has been well maintained, despite her age. The center stairway is real art deco-style. Good amount of open deck space. Friendly ambiance aboard. Cabins are quite spacious, with heavy-duty furniture and fittings. Suite rooms are cavernous, and large bathrooms come with deep, full bathtubs.

— The Riviera Club is a contemporary room that's totally out of keeping with the rest of ship. Repetitive announcements are irritating. Poor separation of smokers and non-smokers. You'll find lines for buffets. There are no showers at the twin swimming pools.

Dining The dining room is set low down, but is comfortable, and has a fine two-deck-high center section with barrel-shaped ceiling, and with music balcony and lots of wood paneling. The standard of cuisine is good, particularly for the price you pay. There are three entrees, as well as a complete vegetarian menu. Salads, bakery items, and fruits are reasonable.

Other Comments This is a solidly constructed ship of vintage years that has a classic liner profile. Provides a good cruise experience for first-time cruisers, in pleasant surroundings, and at a most realistic price. Represents outstanding value for money, particularly for those seeking an add-on to their hotel vacation in Cyprus.

mts Princess Danae ★★★+

OPERATES

CARIBBEAN AND BRAZIL CRUISES

Cruise Line			Arcalia Shipping
Former Names		Baltica/Danae/Therisos Express/	
			Port Melbourne
Gross Tonnage			17,074
Builder			Swan, Hunter (UK)
Original Cost			n/a
Christened By			n/a
Entered Service			Jul 1955/1994
Interior Design			n/a
Country of Registry			Panama
Tel No	134-6425	Fax No	134-6425
Length (ft/m)			532.7/162.39
Beam (ft/m)	70.0/21.34	Draft (ft/m)	41.9/12.8
Propulsion			diesel (9,850kW)
Propellers			2 (FP)
Decks	7	Crew	240
Pass. Capacity (basis 2) 544		(all berths) 657	
Pass. Space Ratio (basis 2) 31.3		(all berths) 25.9	
Officers			European
Total Cabins			272
Size (sq ft/m):		200.0-270.0/18.5-25.0	
Outside Cabins	226	Inside Cabins	46
Single Cabins			0
Balcony Cabins			6
Wheelchair Cabins			0
Cabin Current			220 AC
Refrigerator			No
Dining Rooms	1	Sittings	2

Elevators			2
Casino	Yes	Slot Machines	Yes
Swimming Pools (outside) 1		(inside)	0
Whirlpools	2	Gymnasium	Yes
Sauna:	Yes	Massage	Yes
Movie Theater/Seats:			Yes/275
Cabin TV	No	Library	Yes
Children's Facilities/Playroom:			No
Classification Society			American Bureau
			of Shipping

RATINGS	SCORE
Ship: Condition/Cleanliness	7.1
Ship: Space/Flow/Comfort	7.1
Ship: Decor/Furnishings	7.2
Ship: Fitness Facilities	5.7
Cabins: Comfort/Facilities	6.8
Cabins: Software	7.1
Food: Dining Room/Cuisine	6.3
Food: Buffets/Informal Dining	6.2
Food: Quality of Ingredients	6.2
Service: Dining Room	7.1
Service: Bars	7.1
Service: Cabins	7.2
Cruise: Entertainment	5.9
Cruise: Activities Program	6.1
Cruise: Hospitality Standard	7.2
OVERALL RATING	100.3

+ Solidly built ship with good lines. Has a good amount of open deck space for sunning. Pleasant old-world ambiance. Features high-quality interior appointments that are solidly made. Spacious public rooms, although the decor is somewhat conservative. A new bar amidships was recently added. Roomy, traditional theater with three audio channels for simultaneous translation for international conventions. Good-sized cabins have heavy-duty furniture and fittings and lots of closet and drawer space.

— There is no forward observation lounge. Cabins located under the disco can suffer from thumping noise late at night. The lower-grade cabins are very spartan.

Dining The dining room is decorated quite nicely and has a high ceiling. Features Continental/European cuisine and service that is quite attentive.

Other Comments Having undergone refurbishment early in 1996, this ship will provide a comfortable, though by no means glamorous, cruise for its passengers, many of whom are from South America. Provides Caribbean cruises from Santo Domingo (winter) and cruises from Brazil during the summer.

mv Professor Khromov ★★+

OPERATES

EXPEDITION CRUISES TO ANTARCTICA

Cruise Line			Quark Expeditions
Former Names			-
Gross Tonnage			2,142
Builder			(Finland)
Original Cost			n/a
Christened By			n/a
Entered Service			1983
Interior Design			n/a
Country of Registry			Russia
Tel No	n/a	Fax No	n/a
Length (ft/m)			234.9/71.6
Beam (ft/m)	42/12.8	Draft (ft/m)	15.0/4.6
Propulsion			diesel (3,120shp)
Propellers			2 (CP)
Decks	3	Crew	25
Pass. Capacity (basis 2) 36		(all berths)	36
Pass. Space Ratio (basis 2) 59.5		(all berths)	59.5
Officers			Russian
Total Cabins			19
Size Range (sq ft/m)			
Outside Cabins	18	Inside Cabins	0
Single Cabins			0
Balcony Cabins	0	Wheelchair Cabins	3
Cabin Current			220 V
Refrigerator			No
Cabin TV	No	VCR	No
Dining Rooms	1	Sittings	1
Elevators			0

Casino	No	Slot Machines	0
Swimming Pools (outside) 0		(inside)	0
Whirlpools	0	Gymnasium	No
Sauna/Steam Room Yes/No		Massage	No
Self-Service Launderette			No
Movie Theater/Seats			No
Library			Yes
Children's Facilities			No
Watersports Facilities			None
Classification Society			Russian KMLi

RATINGS	SCORE
Ship: Condition/Cleanliness	7.0
Ship: Space/Flow/Comfort	5.2
Ship: Decor/Furnishings	5.6
Ship: Fitness Facilities	4.0
Cabins: Comfort/Facilities	5.4
Cabins: Software	6.1
Food: Dining Room/Cuisine	6.2
Food: Buffets/Informal Dining	5.6
Food: Quality of Ingredients	5.7
Service: Dining Room	6.0
Service: Bars	6.2
Service: Cabins	6.4
Cruise: Entertainment	6.0
Cruise: Activities Program	6.3
Cruise: Hospitality Standard	7.1
OVERALL RATING	88.8

+ This vessel was specially constructed for polar and oceanographic research, and is not to be taken as a cruise ship, although it was refurbished and converted to carry passengers in 1991. Has an ice-hardened hull, good for Arctic and Antarctic cruising. All passengers have access to the navigation bridge. Has several Zodiac landing craft. Public rooms consist of a library and lounge/bar. The dining room, which accommodates all passengers at one sitting, also serves as a lecture room. Has good medical facilities.

— With the exception of a single "suite", almost all other cabins are quite small and those lowest on deck share a bathroom. Has a steep, narrow gangway.

Dining There is one dining room. The cuisine is hearty fare, with no frills. When under charter to Quark Expedition/Noble Caledonia, a Western chef oversees the food operation.

Other Comments This is cruising, expedition-style. It provides a somewhat primitive but genuine adventure experience to places others can only dream about. The bigger ships can't get this close to Antarctica. The same comments apply to sister ship *Professor Molchanov*.

mts Queen Elini ★

Cruise Line		Vergina Cruises
Former Names	City of Rhodos/33 Orientales	
Gross Tonnage		6,497
Builder		Society Espanola de
		Construciones Navale (Spain)
Original Cost		n/a
Christened By		n/a
Entered Service		1966/1995
Interior Design		n/a
Country of Registry		Greece
Tel No	113-3131 Fax No	113-3131
Length (ft/m)		427.5/130.31
Beam (ft/m)	56.7/17.30 Draft (ft/m)	13.8/4.21
Propulsion		diesel (5,737kW)
Propellers		2 (FP)
Decks	5 Crew	160
Pass. Capacity (basis 2) 416	(all berths)	503
Pass. Space Ratio (basis 2) 15.6	(all berths)	12.9
Officers		Greek
Total Cabins		208
Size Range (sq ft/m)		n/a
Outside Cabins	144 Inside Cabins	64
Single Cabins		0
Balcony Cabins	0 Wheelchair Cabins	0
Cabin Current	220 AC Refrigerator	No
Cabin TV	No VCR	No
Dining Rooms	1 Sittings	2
Elevators		0

Casino	No	Slot Machines	No
Swimming Pools (outside)	1	(inside)	0
Whirlpools	0	Gymnasium	No
Sauna/Steam Room	No/No	Massage	No
Self-Service Launderette			No
Movie Theater/Seats			No
Library	No	Children's Facilities	No
Watersports Facilities			None
Classification Society		American Bureau	
		of Shipping	

RATINGS	SCORE
Ship: Condition/Cleanliness	5.4
Ship: Space/Flow/Comfort	4.4
Ship: Decor/Furnishings	5.6
Ship: Fitness Facilities	3.0
Cabins: Comfort/Facilities	5.3
Cabins: Software	5.5
Food: Dining Room/Cuisine	5.2
Food: Buffets/Informal Dining	5.0
Food: Quality of Ingredients	4.9
Service: Dining Room	6.0
Service: Bars	5.8
Service: Cabins	6.0
Cruise: Entertainment	4.6
Cruise: Activities Program	4.8
Cruise: Hospitality Standard	5.0
OVERALL RATING	76.5

+ The public rooms are aft, away from cabins, so noise in them is minimized. Has a long, unattractive profile (this ship was rebuilt from a former Argentinean coastal ferry), but it's alright for the passenger who wants a low-grade cruise experience. Except for some "suites," the cabins are small and barely adequate.

— This very high-density vessel is cramped even when not full. Has only two main public rooms plus a dining room. Has a small swimming pool, and not much open deck space for sunning. Cabin bathrooms are *tiny*, and spartan. The ship's decor is well worn, unclean, and needs some refurbishment. There are too many announcements. Steep gangway in most ports.

Dining The dining room is mildly attractive, but has a low ceiling and is very noisy. The cuisine, in a word, is basic, low-budget food that is unattractively presented and quite mediocre. Limited selection of breads, cheeses and fruits. The service is adequate, but there's not even a flicker of finesse.

Other Comments This ship, now getting a little long in the tooth, caters to those who need to cruise on a very limited budget, don't mind noise, or crowded places. Recently acquired by Vergina Cruises, a division of Vergina Lines, the Piraeus-based ferry company. Operates seasonally to Egypt and Israel.

tsmv Queen Elizabeth 2 ★★★★★ *to* ★★★★

OPERATES

5-DAY SCHEDULED TRANSATLANTIC SERVICE AND CARIBBEAN/ EUROPE/WORLD CRUISES

Cruise Line	Cunard	Casino	Yes	Slot Machines Yes
Former Names	-	Swimming Pools (outside) 1		(inside) 2
Gross Tonnage	70,327	Whirlpools	4	Gymnasium Yes
Builder	Upper Clyde Shipbuilders (UK)	Sauna/Steam Room Yes/Yes		Massage Yes
Original Cost	UK£29,091,000	Self-Service Launderette		Yes (12 machines)
Christened By	H.M. Queen Elizabeth II	Movie Theater/Seats		Yes/531
Entered Service	May 1969	Library	Yes	Children's Facilities Yes
Interior Design	Dennis Lennon & Partners	Watersports Facilities		None
Country of Registry	Great Britain	Classification Society		Lloyd's Register

Tel No 144-0412 Fax No 144-1331	
Length (ft/m) 963.0/293.50	
Beam (ft/m) 105.1/32.03 Draft (ft/m) 32.4/9.87	
Propulsion diesel-electric (99,900kW)	
Propellers 2 (CP)	
Decks 13 Crew 1,015	
Pass. Capacity (basis 2) 1,756 (all berths) 1,892	
Pass. Space Ratio (basis 2) 40.0 (all berths) 37.1	
Officers British	
Total Cabins 936	
Size Range (sq ft/m) 107-785/10.0-73.0	
Outside Cabins 665 Inside Cabins 271	
Single Cabins 116	
Balcony Cabins 33 Wheelchair Cabins 4	
Cabin Current 110/220 AC	
Refrigerator All Grill-Class cabins	
Cabin TV All cabins VCR All Grill-Class cabins	
Dining Rooms 5 Sittings 1 (2 in Mauretania)	
Elevators 13	

Ratings:
(a) Grill Class; (b) Caronia Class; (c) Mauretania Class

RATINGS SCORE	(a)	(b)	(c)
Ship: Condition/Cleanliness	9.1	8.6	7.7
Ship: Space/Flow/Comfort	9.1	8.4	7.6
Ship: Decor/Furnishings	9.1	8.5	7.8
Ship: Fitness Facilities	9.0	9.0	9.0
Cabins: Comfort/Facilities	9.2	8.5	7.7
Cabins: Software	9.1	8.6	7.8
Food: Dining Room/Cuisine	9.3	7.6	6.6
Food: Buffets/Informal Dining	8.3	8.3	8.3
Food: Quality of Ingredients	9.3	8.2	7.0
Service: Dining Room	9.1	7.2	6.6
Service: Bars	8.8	8.5	8.0
Service: Cabins	9.1	8.5	7.0
Cruise: Entertainment	8.4	8.4	8.5
Cruise: Activities Program	8.6	8.4	8.6
Cruise: Hospitality Standard	9.2	8.1	6.6
OVERALL RATING	134.7	124.8	114.8

+ QE2 is the only regularly scheduled transatlantic liner still in service, and the fastest, as well as the most integrated cruise ship in the world. Excellent range of joint travel programs.

— Expect lines for embarkation, disembarkation, shore tenders, and, at peak times, buffets. Has two sittings in the Mauretania Restaurant. Baggage delivery could be improved. There is no forward observation lounge. Following the latest refurbishment, there are no small, intimate hideaway bars. Sadly, there is no forward lookout bar. Passenger flow from 4 Deck and 5 Deck cabins to the Caronia Restaurant is awkward. One cannot have just a sauna without paying a $10 charge for a "Spa Experience" package; this is absurd.

Dining There are five restaurants (which include many tables for two), assigned according to the grade of suite or cabin booked. The menus are always varied and well balanced.

Other Comments She is a world-renowned dual-purpose superliner that performs a regular schedule of two dozen or so transatlantic crossings as well as several cruises each year, together with an annual round-the-world cruise from January to April.

Originally constructed as a steam turbine ship, she underwent a $160 million refit in Bremen, Germany, in 1986. Her old steam turbines were extracted and exchanged for a diesel-electric propulsion system, resulting in greater speed, better economy and more reliability. A new, fatter funnel was constructed, designed to better keep any soot off her expansive open decks.

In Nov/Dec 1994, the ship underwent a dramatic $45 million interior refurbishment which included numerous structural changes, designed to improve passenger flow and offer more dining. A coordinated color scheme was chosen, with the use of beautiful wood paneling and more traditional furnishings reminiscent of the ocean liners of yesteryear.

All cabin bathrooms were entirely replaced. They now sport marble fixtures and bright new art deco-style toiletries cabinets. Several new suites were added, as well as an enlarged library, with multimedia CD-Rom center and a fine new, enlarged memorabilia/bookshop and dedicated florist. The Club Lido magrodome-covered pool was replaced with a new informal buffet bistro-like dining area (The Lido) with its own galley and bar.

The present Mauretania (Premium Class) was moved from Upper Deck to where the Columbia Restaurant was formerly located on Quarter Deck, and a new Captain's Dining Area was added. The Columbia Restaurant (Deluxe Class) was moved upstairs to become the Caronia Restaurant. The three Grill Rooms remain, with the former Princess Grill Starboard now renamed Britannia Grill. The balcony of the showlounge (formerly the Grand Lounge) was blocked off, and the room became a more dedicated showlounge. The shops themselves remain in their present position, as does the Theatre. A new Golden Lion Pub now occupies replaced the former Theatre Bar. The former Midships Bar was expanded and renamed The Chart Room. The Yacht Club was greatly enlarged and a new night club created from space from an aft deck extension. The new enhancements have provided grace, pace and space.

Other Comments: *Transatlantic Crossings* She is the fastest cruise ship presently in service, but even at speeds over 30 knots there's almost no vibration at the stern. Features the most extensive facilities of any passenger ship afloat. Also carries up to 40 cars.

There are three distinct classes: Grill Class (424 beds), Caronia Class (558 beds) and Mauretania Class (910 beds). Grill Class accommodations consist of penthouse suites (with butler service) and "luxury" outside cabins, with dining in one of three grill rooms: Queens Grill, Britannia Grill and Princess Grill (5-stars). Caronia Class accommodations consist of outside double cabins, and inside and outside single cabins, with dining in the Caronia Restaurant (4-stars). Mauretania Class accommodations feature lower-priced cabin grades, with two-sitting dining in the Mauretania Restaurant (3-stars). All other restaurants feature one sitting dining with flexible dining hours.

All passengers enjoy the use of all public rooms, except the Queens Grill Lounge, reserved exclusively for Grill Class passengers. The Queens Grill has its own separate galley, the best waiters and service, a formal atmosphere, and food that is extremely good when ordered off-menu. The Britannia Grill, Princess Grill and Caronia Restaurant share the same galley, but service in the intimate Britannia Grill and Princess Grill is superior. The Mauretania Restaurant has a fine menu but food is served by the least experienced waiters. Grill Class and Caronia Class passengers have a separate deck space and assigned chairs (for an extra fee), but sit with all other passengers for shows, other entertainment events, and social functions.

Grill Class is an elegant way to cross the Atlantic; Caronia Class (formerly first class) isn't quite what it used to be; Mauretania Class (formerly transatlantic class) is mass transportation, albeit in a fine, price-sensitive setting. This is the last of the transatlantic liners and a wonderful experience, and there are still many people who do not like to fly who enjoy the grace of this ship, and the enormous amount of personal luggage one is allowed—good for relocating between continents.

Other Comments: *Cruises* The extensive refit in December 1994 improved the interior of the ship immeasurably. The Penthouse Suites are truly superb. Heritage Trail, a ship-wide display of ocean liner history that ship buffs everywhere will find fascinating, includes wonderful ship models of former Cunarders (including a stunning 16-foot illuminated model of the 1907

Mauretania outside the restaurant of the same name), and a great abundance of memorabilia items (some of which are for sale in the fine new memorabilia bookshop/library).

The Grand Lounge is now a dedicated showlounge with thrust stage, has three seating tiers and a new high-tech sound system. A new Tour and Travel Center was added. Shopping concourse features brand name merchandise at European prices. The extended, expansive, aft-facing Yacht Club is a delightfully nautical, practical and popular room that becomes a good nightclub (afternoon classical concerts here are a delight). Extensive safety deposit center and passenger accounts office, and an automated telephone system.

The Queens Room, now used as a ballroom, is more stately than before, with comfortable chairs. The Midships Lobby, the ship's embarkation point, has a distinctive, true ocean liner feel, with its fine birds-eye maple woodwork and wrap-around murals of the former and present Cunard Queens. Beauty Salons, and all five restaurants remain, but two restaurants have been repositioned, three have been renamed and one redecorated. The large computer center is a real bonus. There is a dedicated florist and greenery (flower dispensary). Has a large self-service launderette (no charge). The Lido, a large, informal bistro dining area (with 24-hour hot beverage dispense stations), is a real bonus on cruises. The elegant Chart Room Bar (formerly the Midships Bar) is better than before. There's also a large balconied theater.

The Golden Lion Pub is a roaring success, with its Victorian decor, and selection of 20 beers (both bottled and draught). Superb Library (houses over 6,000 books in five languages, together with the video library and memorabilia bookshop) has been doubled in size, and features two professional librarians (the only ship to do so). Player's Club Casino features fitting art deco and blond wood decor. The health spa is extensive, and its treatment programs (at extra cost) are varied. Synagogue. British officers and seamanship, but hotel staff has changed to an international mix, quite attentive and service-oriented, though many don't speak English well. Consistently good quality entertainment and outstanding lecture programs. One class only for cruises. Dining room assigned according to accommodations chosen. Open or one sitting in all dining rooms except Mauretania. Luncheon and midnight buffets are improved. Cashless cruising. Excellent laundry and dry-cleaning facilities. English nannies and childrens' facilities.

Offers refined living at sea for those in upper-grade accommodations, otherwise it's just a big ship, albeit with some superb facilities. *QE2* is certainly the most perfectly integrated ship afloat, and she's fast. Tender ports should be avoided whenever possible, although the new double deck shore tenders are superb.

MORE ABOUT *QE2* Physically challenged passengers will appreciate four new cabins specially equipped for wheelchair-bound passengers. They were created using the newly introduced guidelines of the American Disabled Association (ADA). The cabin door is wide enough for a wheelchair to pass through easily (no "lip"). The bathroom door slides open electronically at the touch of a button (located at wheelchair height), and there is no "lip" into the bathroom. The full bath has special assist handles, and the toilet has grab bars in the right places. Closets have hanging rails that have a hydraulically balanced long lever that lowers the rail towards the outside of the closet, down to the height you need. There's an intercom, alarm, and remote-control of lighting, curtains, and doors. These cabins are also good for the hearing-impaired, as there are three brightly colored lighted signs on the cabin bulkhead, as well as a telephone system for the deaf.

While these cabins are specially designed for the physically challenged, their ingenious design would not upset a regular passenger. The Cunard/British Airways Concorde program is most definitely worth saving for. Combining a *QE2* transatlantic crossing with a one-way British Airways Concorde flight is, without doubt, the ultimate way to go. Five days one way, and three hours, fifteen minutes the other is one of the great travel experiences available today. And, with the special, Cunard-subsidized fares, there's no excuse for not indulging, at least once in your life. All gratuities are now included.

ssc Radisson Diamond ★★★★★

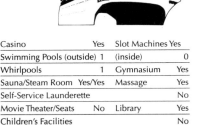

OPERATES

*4, 5 AND 7-DAY CARIBBEAN AND
MEDITERRANEAN CRUISES*

Cruise Line		Radisson Seven Seas Cruises	Casino	Yes	Slot Machines Yes
Gross Tonnage		20,295	Swimming Pools (outside) 1	(inside)	0
Builder		Rauma Yards (Finland)	Whirlpools	1	Gymnasium	Yes
Original Cost		$125 million	Sauna/Steam Room Yes/Yes	Massage	Yes
Christened By		Dame Kiri Te Kanawa	Self-Service Launderette		No
Entered Service		May 1992	Movie Theater/Seats	No	Library	Yes
Interior Design		Vincent Kwok Interiors	Children's Facilities		No
Country of Registry		Finland	Watersports Facilities	Retractable aft marina,
Tel No 162-3243	Fax No	162-3252		jet-ski, water-ski
Length (ft/m)		423.2/129.00	Classification Society	Det Norske Veritas

Beam (ft/m) 104.9/32.00	Draft (ft/m)	26.2/8.00			
Propulsion		diesel (11,340kW)	**RATINGS**		**SCORE**
Propellers		2 nozzles	Ship: Condition/Cleanliness		9.0
Decks	6	Crew	192	Ship: Space/Flow/Comfort		8.6
Pass. Capacity (basis 2) 354		(all berths) 354	Ship: Decor/Furnishings		8.4
Pass. Space Ratio (basis 2) 57.3		(all berths) 57.3	Ship: Fitness Facilities		6.8
Officers		Finnish/American	Cabins: Comfort/Facilities		9.2
Total Cabins		177	Cabins: Software		8.7
Size Range (sq ft/m)		220/20.5	Food: Dining Room/Cuisine		9.1
Outside Cabins	177	Inside Cabins	0	Food: Buffets/Informal Dining		9.0
Single Cabins		0	Food: Quality of Ingredients		9.0
Balcony Cabins		123	Service: Dining Room		8.7
Wheelchair Cabins		2	Service: Bars		8.2
Cabin Current		110/220 AC	Service: Cabins		9.2
Refrigerator		All cabins	Cruise: Entertainment		7.3
Cabin TV	Yes	VCR	Yes	Cruise: Activities Program		6.7
Dining Rooms		1 (+1 Grill Restaurant)	Cruise: Hospitality Standard		8.2
Sittings	Open	Elevators	3	OVERALL RATING		126.1

+ This ship features an innovative design. She is stable, with four stabilizing fins (two on the inner side of each pontoon) so motion is really minimal when compared to conventional (monohull) vessels. The wide beam design provides outstanding passenger space, although the public rooms are stacked vertically. Casino has gaming tables on one side of the passageway, slot machines on the other.

A five-deck-high atrium has glass-enclosed elevators. There is also a little-used underwater viewing area (actually two portholes). There is a good outdoor jogging track.

Nicely designed, spacious and well-equipped all-outside cabins, most with private balconies (they even have lights), are all furnished in blond woods, with marble bathroom vanities and tiny bathtub. There are bay windows in 47 suites.

All cabins are the same size, with the exception of two VIP master suites with private balconies. Each cabin is an outside, with oversized window or floor-to-ceiling balcony windows or door, and features a spacious sitting area with sofa and chairs, dressing table with hairdryer, minibar and refrigerator, telephone, color remote-control TV with integral VCR player, twin beds which convert to a queen sized unit, two good strong, adjustable reading lamps that are bright, a personal safe (somewhat hidden and difficult for older passengers to reach and operate), full-length mirror, and excellent, usable drawer space. Closet space, however, is very small, but adequate for short cruises. It is, however, tight for two even on a 7-day cruise, worse for longer cruises.

Each cabin has a mini-bar which is stocked with beer and soft drinks; half-liter bottles of four liquors are provided. Bottled mineral water carries the name and logo of the ship. The only glasses provided are two champagne flutes and two small glasses for mixed cocktails.

Has a sophisticated business center and facilities that are ideal for small groups and conventions. For groups and meetings, the high-tech audio and video conference facilities, and a high-tech security system that uses approximately 50 cameras to monitor just about everywhere, provide a good feeling of exclusivity.

— The design means that many public rooms are inside, with little or no connection with the sea. Flowers, and more flowers, would help a lot. Has a maximum speed of 12.5 knots, which means leisurely cruising, but slow going on longer itineraries. Awkward one-way (contra-flow) interior staircase is frustrating. The spaciousness of the ship, while providing flexibility of the several individual public rooms, actually detracts from the overall flow. Also awkward is the multi-level entertainment room. Has excellent health spa facilities, but they can't be reached by elevator. Still has some uncomfortable chairs in the main dining room. The meet and greet service is inconsistent and the subject of passenger complaints. Cabin bathrooms have tiny tubs (they are not bathtubs, but shower tubs).

Dining The two-deck-high dining room is quite elegant, and has a 270 degree view over the stern, and open seating (you can dine when and where you wish). Cuisine quality and food presentation are European in style, and quite outstanding in quality, choice and presentation. Also features health foods and dietary specials. The waitresses (there are no waiters) are quite charming, supervised superbly by experienced Italian headwaiters. Although basic whites and reds are included for lunch and dinner, a wine list is available for those who appreciate better wines (at extra cost).

The "Grill" is an alternative casual indoor/outdoor dining spot (at no extra charge). Run like a real restaurant ashore (make reservations early), this informal dining spot features superb home-made pasta dishes daily, fine menu, cream sauces and exotic garnishes. Each day is different, and food is presented, in small portions, course by course. It is lovingly prepared and exquisite to taste, although somewhat rich. Seating is at sturdy, practical glass-topped wooden tables for two, four, or six. Table-side dessert flambeaus are often featured. Dining is a pleasure on this ship, and it is the vessel's strongest point.

Other Comments This semi-submersible twin hulled cruise vessel, which looks like a white-caped "Batman" from the stern, certainly has distinctive looks, although its design has not been as successful as hoped. This ship will appeal to those seeking extremely high standards of service in sophisticated and personable, "hotel-style" surroundings, with unstructured day activities. Gratuities are included.

ms Regal Empress ★★+

OPERATES

2- TO 7-DAY BERMUDA AND
CARIBBEAN CRUISES

Cruise Line	Regal Cruises	Casino	Yes
Former Names	Caribe I/Olympia	Swimming Pools (outside) 1	(inside) 0
Gross Tonnage	22,979	Whirlpools 2	Gymnasium Yes
Builder	Alex Stephen & Son (UK)	Sauna/Steam Room No/No	Massage No
Original Cost	n/a	Self-Service Launderette	No
Christened By	HRH Queen Frederica	Movie Theater/Seats	Yes/166
Entered Service	Oct 1953/May 1993	Library	Yes
Interior Design	n/a	Children's Facilities	Yes
Country of Registry	Bahamas	Watersports Facilities	None
Tel No -	Fax No -	Classification Society	Lloyd's Register
Length (ft/m)	611.8/186.50		

Casino	Yes	Slot Machines	Yes
Swimming Pools (outside)	1	(inside)	0
Whirlpools	2	Gymnasium	Yes
Sauna/Steam Room	No/No	Massage	No
Self-Service Launderette			No
Movie Theater/Seats			Yes/166
Library			Yes
Children's Facilities			Yes
Watersports Facilities			None
Classification Society		Lloyd's Register	

Beam (ft/m) 79.0/24.10	Draft (ft/m) 28.2/8.60
Propulsion	diesel (14,400bhp)
Propellers	2 (FP)
Decks 8	Crew 345
Pass. Capacity (basis 2) 875	(all berths) 1,160
Pass. Space Ratio (basis 2) 26.2	(all berths) 19.8
Officers	European
Total Cabins	451
Size Range (sq ft/m)	105-295/9.7-27.5
Outside Cabins 226	Inside Cabins 225
Single Cabins	9
Balcony Cabins 0	Wheelchair Cabins 1
Cabin Current	110 AC
Refrigerator	No
Cabin TV No	VCR No
Dining Rooms 1	Sittings 2
Elevators	3

RATINGS	SCORE
Ship: Condition/Cleanliness	5.7
Ship: Space/Flow/Comfort	5.9
Ship: Decor/Furnishings	6.3
Ship: Fitness Facilities	5.0
Cabins: Comfort/Facilities	6.5
Cabins: Software	6.3
Food: Dining Room/Cuisine	6.1
Food: Buffets/Informal Dining	5.6
Food: Quality of Ingredients	5.4
Service: Dining Room	6.0
Service: Bars	6.1
Service: Cabins	6.4
Cruise: Entertainment	6.0
Cruise: Activities Program	5.8
Cruise: Hospitality Standard	6.4
OVERALL RATING	89.5

+ This 40-year-old ship has a traditional ocean liner profile. Good open deck space for sun-lovers, although very crowded when the ship is full. Polished teak decking. Enclosed promenade decks are popular with strollers. Satin woods and brass on staircases. Superb library with original paneling. There is a wide range of cabin sizes and configurations. Most are quite roomy, with good closet and reasonable drawer space, and heavy-duty fittings.

— Steep, narrow gangway in some ports. Expect lines for embarkation, disembarkation and buffets. Has an awkward layout; many passageways are dead ends.

Dining Lovely old-world dining room is a step back in time, with its original oil paintings on burnished wood paneling, ornate lighting fixtures, etched glass panels, and original murals depicting New York and Rio. Most tables are for six or more, with a few tables for four. Smoking and non-smoking sections are provided on the starboard and port sides respectively. Food is plentiful, but the buffets are awful.

Other Comments Large casino sees lively, noisy action. This ship will provide you with a cruise in adequate surroundings, at a modest price, but the ship is old and service is perfunctory, at best.

mv Regal Princess ★★★★+

OPERATES

7-DAY ALASKA AND CARIBBEAN CRUISES

Cruise Line	Princess Cruises	Casino	Yes	Slot Machines	Yes
Former Names	-	Swimming Pools (outside) 2	(inside)	0
Gross Tonnage	70,000	Whirlpools	4	Gymnasium	Yes
Builder	Fincantieri Navali (Italy)	Sauna/Steam Room Yes/No	Massage	Yes
Original Cost	$276.8 million	Self-Service Launderette	Yes
Christened By	Mrs Margaret Thatcher	Movie Theater/Seats	Yes/169
Entered Service	Aug 1991	Library	Yes
Interior Design	H. Chambers Company	Children's Facilities	No
Country of Registry	Liberia	Watersports Facilities	None
Tel No 124-5712 Fax No 124-5712	Classification Society	Lloyd's Register
Length (ft/m)	803.8/245.00		

Beam (ft/m) 105.6/32.20 Draft (ft/m) 25.5/7.80	

RATINGS	SCORE
Propulsion diesel (24,000kW)	Ship: Condition/Cleanliness	8.0
Propellers 2 (CP)	Ship: Space/Flow/Comfort	7.8
Decks 12 Crew 696	Ship: Decor/Furnishings	8.1
Pass. Capacity (basis 2) 1,590 (all berths) 1,910	Ship: Fitness Facilities	8.0
Pass. Space Ratio (basis 2) 44.0 (all berths) 36.6	Cabins: Comfort/Facilities	8.1
Officers Italian	Cabins: Software	8.2
Total Cabins 795	Food: Dining Room/Cuisine	7.4
Size Range (sq ft/m) 190-587/17.6-54.5	Food: Buffets/Informal Dining	7.2
Outside Cabins 624 Inside Cabins 171	Food: Quality of Ingredients	7.0
Single Cabins 0	Service: Dining Room	7.5
Balcony Cabins 184 Wheelchair Cabins 10	Service: Bars	7.7
Cabin Current 110/220 AC	Service: Cabins	7.9
Refrigerator All cabins	Cruise: Entertainment	8.1
Cabin TV Yes VCR No	Cruise: Activities Program	7.8
Dining Rooms 1 Sittings 2	Cruise: Hospitality Standard	7.6
Elevators 9	OVERALL RATING	116.4

+ Innovative styling mixed with traditional features. Has twin pools. Dolphin-shaped observation dome is huge, and houses the casino, but it doesn't work as a nightclub. Elegant three-deck-high atrium is spacious and well designed. Well-coordinated colors and carpeting. Flowers and lovely artwork help create a more intimate atmosphere. Plenty of public rooms, but most have pillars obstructing flow and sightlines. Excellent drinks from extensive list in Characters Bar. Well-designed accommodations, with ample drawer and hanging space, and spacious, marble-walled bathrooms. Prompt, attentive room service.

— Crowded outdoor sunning space when the ship is full. Disjointed layout. No wrap-around outdoor promenade deck. Galley fumes seem to waft constantly over the aft open decks. Suites and mini-suites suffer from poor ceiling insulation and noise from lido deck above. Expect lines for embarkation, disembarkation, shore tenders, and buffets.

Dining Has a quieter dining hall than on the *Crown*, but it's still noisy (though non-smoking), and there are no tables for two. Unfortunately, the food quality not as good as one would expect from this company, although it is improving. Poor bread and fruits.

Other Comments This is the sister ship to the *Crown Princess*. Ideal for those who want a big ship around them, with well-proven service, but there's little contact with the outside.

mts Regina Maris ★★★

OPERATES

7-DAY RED SEA CRUISES

Cruise Line	Phoenix Seereisen	Casino	No	Slot Machines	No

Cruise Line	Phoenix Seereisen
Former Names	Argonaut/Orion/Vixen
Gross Tonnage	4,500
Builder	Frieder, Krupp Germaniawerft (Germany)
Original Cost	n/a
Christened By	n/a
Entered Service	Sep 1929/1995
Interior Design	Maurice Bailey
Country of Registry	Malta
Tel No 113-0507	Fax No 113-0507
Length (ft/m)	339.2/103.4
Beam (ft/m) 45.2/13.8	Draft (ft/m) 19.0/5.8
Propulsion/Propellers	diesel (2,684kW)/2 (DP)
Decks	4
Crew	100
Pass. Capacity (basis 2) 168	(all berths) 170
Pass. Space Ratio (basis 2) 26.7	(all berths) 26.4
Officers	European
Total Cabins	84
Size Range (sq ft/m)	102.2-150.0/9.5-14.0
Outside Cabins 82	Inside Cabins 2
Single Cabins	0
Balcony Cabins 0	Wheelchair Cabins 0
Cabin Current	110/220 AC
Refrigerator	No
Cabin TV No	VCR No
Dining Rooms 1	Sittings 1
Elevators	1

Casino	No	Slot Machines	No
Swimming Pools (outside) 1		(inside)	0
Whirlpools	0	Gymnasium	No
Sauna/Steam Room No/No		Massage	No
Self-Service Launderette			No
Movie Theater/Seats			No
Library			Yes
Children's Facilities			No
Watersports Facilities			None
Classification Society			Lloyd's Register

RATINGS	SCORE
Ship: Condition/Cleanliness	7.2
Ship: Space/Flow/Comfort	6.6
Ship: Decor/Furnishings	7.2
Ship: Fitness Facilities	3.5
Cabins: Comfort/Facilities	6.3
Cabins: Software	6.6
Food: Dining Room/Cuisine	7.1
Food: Buffets/Informal Dining	6.3
Food: Quality of Ingredients	6.4
Service: Dining Room	6.6
Service: Bars	7.1
Service: Cabins	7.1
Cruise: Entertainment	5.3
Cruise: Activities Program	6.0
Cruise: Hospitality Standard	7.4
OVERALL RATING	96.7

+ Charming vintage ship, has been well maintained (refurbished in 1993), has a warm, intimate and informal atmosphere. Some gorgeous woods and trim are used throughout her public spaces. Homely decor is used in the limited public rooms. The winding center stairway is lovely. Extensive artworks of Classical Greece are featured throughout. This ship always features interesting itineraries, supplemented by guest lecturers and minimal entertainment. Cabins are adequate, no more.

— Does not have an observation lounge. Cabin bathrooms are small. The gangway is steep in most ports.

Dining Large dining room features all passengers in a single sitting. Good Mediterranean-style food, but selection of breads, rolls, cheeses and fruits could be improved. Attentive, friendly service, but without finesse.

Other Comments She was built originally as a private yacht for the American wool magnate Carl Julius Forstmann and is now sailing under charter to Phoenix Seereisen. This ship will provide a comfortable, though basic cruise experience for the traveler who doesn't like large, new ships, crowds and an impersonal environment. However, she is now well into an advanced age and should be retired.

ms Renaissance One/Two/ Three/Four ★★★★

OPERATES
7-DAY CRUISES WORLDWIDE

Cruise Line		Renaissance Cruises	
Former Names	n/a	Gross Tonnage	3,990
Builder		Cantieri Navale Ferrari (Italy)	
Original Cost		$20 million each	
Christened By	Ms C Astrup (1); Mrs G Reggio (2);		
Mrs Papagapitos (3)		Mrs F Paoletti (4)	
Entered Service		Dec 1989 (1) Apr 1990 (2)	
		Aug 1990 (3) Jan 1991 (4)	
Interior Design		Bertelotti/Yran & Storbraaten	
Country of Registry		Liberia	
Tel/Fax No		(1) 115-0510/115-0565;	
(2) 125-0164/125-0165; (3) 125-0166/125-0167;			
(4) 125-0171/125-0172			
Length (ft/m)		289.6/88.30	
Beam (ft/m)	50.1/15.30	Draft (ft/m)	11.9/3.65
Propulsion/Propellers		diesel (3,514kW)/2 (CP)	
Decks	5	Crew	72
Pass. Capacity (basis 2) 100		(all berths) 111	
Pass. Space Ratio (basis 2) 39.9		(all berths) 35.9	
Officers		Italian	
Total Cabins		50	
Size Range (sq ft/m)		231-282/21.5-26.2	
Outside Cabins	50	Inside Cabins	0
Single Cabins		0	
Balcony Cabins	4	Wheelchair Cabins	0
Cabin Current	110 AC	Refrigerator	All cabins
Cabin TV	Yes	VCR	Yes
Dining Rooms	1	Sittings	1

Elevators	1	Children's Facilities	No
Casino	Yes	Slot Machines	Yes
Swimming Pools (outside) 1		(inside)	0
Whirlpools	1	Gymnasium	No
Sauna/Steam Room	Yes/No	Massage	No
Self-Service Launderette			No
Movie Theater/Seats	No	Library	No
Watersports Facilities		Aft platform, sailfish,	
	snorkel equipment, zodiacs		
Classification Society			RINA

RATINGS	SCORE
Ship: Condition/Cleanliness	7.2
Ship: Space/Flow/Comfort	7.3
Ship: Decor/Furnishings	8.0
Ship: Fitness Facilities	7.5
Cabins: Comfort/Facilities	8.0
Cabins: Software	8.0
Food: Dining Room/Cuisine	7.6
Food: Buffets/Informal Dining	7.1
Food: Quality of Ingredients	7.6
Service: Dining Room	8.0
Service: Bars	7.8
Service: Cabins	8.0
Cruise: Entertainment	6.0
Cruise: Activities Program	6.3
Cruise: Hospitality Standard	7.6
OVERALL RATING	112.0

+ Contemporary private yacht look, with twin flared funnels and handsome styling throughout. Redesigned layout (*Renaissance Five–Eight*) makes the second set of four vessels superior to the first four in the series, especially for stability and comfort. All have exquisite all-outside suites, which combine highly polished imitation rosewood paneling with lots of mirrors, handcrafted Italian furniture, wet bar (pre-stocked when you book, at extra cost). Wooden outside promenade deck. Refined and attractive interior decor. Accommodations are located forward, with public rooms aft. Cabins have queen-sized bed, a sitting area, and feature most things you need. Bathrooms have showers with fold-down seat, real teakwood floors and marble vanities.

— *Renaissance One–Four* don't sail well in inclement weather, being smaller and less stable than *Renaissance Five–Eight*. Tiny "dip" pool is not a swimming pool. Open deck and sunning space is quite cramped. Plastic woods instead of real woods everywhere (looks too perfect). Small library is attractive, but book selection is poor. Cabins have small closets. Space for luggage is tight, and there is not much drawer space. Bathrooms are very compact and none have bathtubs.

Dining The dining room, which has open seating, is small and elegant. It is on lowest deck and has portholes (a requirement of the construction regulations), although it is quite cozy

ms Renaissance Five/Six/ Seven/Eight ★★★★

OPERATES
7-DAY CRUISES WORLDWIDE

Cruise Line	Renaissance Cruises		
Former Names	n/a	Gross Tonnage	4,280
Builder	Nuovi Cantieri Apuania (Italy)		
Original Cost	$25 million each		
Christened By	Mrs Lyng-Olsen (5);		
Blessed by shipyard priest (6); n/a (7); n/a (8)			
Entered Service	Mar 1991 (5); Oct 1991 (6);		
	Dec 1991 (7); May 1992 (8)		
Interior Design	Bertelotti/Yran & Storbraaten		
Country of Registry	Liberia		
Tel/Fax No	(5) 125-0135/ 125-0134;		
(6) 125-0142/125-0141;	(7) 115-1322/125-0146;		
	(8) 115-1375/125-0145		
Length (ft/m)	297.2/90.60		
Beam (ft/m) 50.1/15.30	Draft (ft/m)	12.9/3.95	
Propulsion/Propellers	diesel (5,000kW)/2 (CP)		
Decks	5	Crew	72
Pass. Capacity (basis 2) 114	(all berths) 114		
Pass. Space Ratio (basis 2) 37.5	(all berths) 37.5		
Officers	Italian		
Total Cabins	50		
Size Range (sq ft/m)	215-312/20.0-29.0		
Outside Cabins	50	Inside Cabins	0
Single Cabins			0
Balcony Cabins	4	Wheelchair Cabins	0
Cabin Current 110 AC	Refrigerator	All cabins	
Cabin TV	Yes	VCR	Yes
Dining Rooms	1	Sittings	1

Elevators	1	Children's Facilities	No
Casino	Yes	Slot Machines	Yes
Swimming Pools (outside) 1		(inside)	0
Whirlpools	1	Gymnasium	No
Sauna/Steam Room Yes/No		Massage	Yes
Self-Service Launderette			No
Movie Theater/Seats	No	Library	Yes
Watersports Facilities		Aft platform, sailfish,	
		snorkel equipment, Zodiacs	
Classification Society			RINA

RATINGS	SCORE
Ship: Condition/Cleanliness	8.0
Ship: Space/Flow/Comfort	7.8
Ship: Decor/Furnishings	8.2
Ship: Fitness Facilities	7.8
Cabins: Comfort/Facilities	8.1
Cabins: Software	8.0
Food: Dining Room/Cuisine	7.7
Food: Buffets/Informal Dining	7.1
Food: Quality of Ingredients	7.4
Service: Dining Room	7.8
Service: Bars	7.7
Service: Cabins	7.8
Cruise: Entertainment	6.6
Cruise: Activities Program	6.4
Cruise: Hospitality Standard	7.7
OVERALL RATING	114.1

and welcoming, and there are tables for two, four, six, and even eight. Sit where you like, with whom you like, and at what time you like. Meals are self-service buffet-style cold foods for breakfast and lunch, with hot foods chosen from a table menu and served properly. The dining room operation works well. Food quality, choice and presentation are all fairly decent, but not at all memorable. While the food is reasonably presented, it is quite limited in choice, particularly the entrees. An "800 Calorie" menu is good for those wanting small portions. Service is fair to good, depending on ship and crew.

Other Comments This is a fleet of eight small, intimate cruise vessels, out of a fleet of eight (Nos 1 and 2 on Singapore-based charter). Similar in concept to the *Sea Goddess* ships, though less formal, and less expensive. These vessels are comfortable and inviting, but have been poorly maintained since new. Not the equal of other small luxury ships, but neither is the price. These ships will provide a destination-intensive, refined, quiet and very relaxed cruise experience for passengers who don't like crowds, dressing up, scheduled activities, or entertainment. While not up to the standard of *Sea Goddess* or *Seabourn*, these small ships can still provide a pleasant cruise experience, for a moderate sum of money.

mv Rhapsody ★★★+

Cruise Line	Mediterranean Shipping Cruises	Casino	Yes
Former Names	Cunard Princess/Cunard Conquest	Swimming Pools (outside) 1	(inside) 0
Gross Tonnage	17,495	Whirlpools 2	Gymnasium Yes
Builder	Burmeister & Wein (Denmark)	Sauna/Steam Room Yes/No	Massage No
Original Cost	UK£12 million	Self-Service Launderette	No
Christened By	HRH Princess Grace of Monaco	Movie Theater/Seats	Yes/130
Entered Service	Mar 1977/May 1995	Library	Yes
Interior Design	McNeece Design	Children's Facilities	No
Country of Registry	Bahamas	Watersports Facilities	None
Tel No 110-4111 Fax No 110-4111		Classification Society	Lloyd's Register
Length (ft/m)	536.6/163.56		
Beam (ft/m) 74.9/22.84 Draft (ft/m) 19.0/5.82			

Casino		Yes	Slot Machines Yes

RATINGS	SCORE
Propulsion diesel (15,670kW)	
Propellers 2 (CP)	

Propulsion	diesel (15,670kW)
Propellers	2 (CP)
Decks 8 Crew	350
Pass. Capacity (basis 2) 804	(all berths) 959
Pass. Space Ratio (basis 2) 21.7	(all berths) 18.1
Officers	British
Total Cabins	402
Size Range (sq ft/m)	88-265/8.1-24.6
Outside Cabins 266	Inside Cabins 136
Single Cabins	1
Balcony Cabins 0	Wheelchair Cabins 0
Cabin Current	110/220 AC
Refrigerator	Category 1/2 only
Cabin TV No VCR	No
Dining Rooms 1	Sittings 2
Elevators	2

RATINGS	SCORE
Ship: Condition/Cleanliness	6.8
Ship: Space/Flow/Comfort	6.3
Ship: Decor/Furnishings	6.6
Ship: Fitness Facilities	6.7
Cabins: Comfort/Facilities	5.8
Cabins: Software	7.7
Food: Dining Room/Cuisine	6.6
Food: Buffets/Informal Dining	6.1
Food: Quality of Ingredients	6.2
Service: Dining Room	7.0
Service: Bars	6.8
Service: Cabins	7.2
Cruise: Entertainment	7.3
Cruise: Activities Program	7.1
Cruise: Hospitality Standard	7.6
OVERALL RATING	101.8

+ Has a good amount of open deck space for sun-worshippers. Fine selection of public rooms with attractive decor, in light, bright colors, including an observation lounge above the bridge overlooking the bow. Has an excellent indoor-outdoor entertainment nightclub, which incorporates the occasional use of an aft open deck area. The cabins have pleasant soft furnishings, and closet and drawer space is reasonable.

— Cabins are small and compact, with tinny metal fixtures, and very thin walls that provide extremely poor cabin insulation. There's no outdoor wrap-around outdoor promenade deck.

Dining Pleasant dining room has sea views from big picture windows. Reasonable banquet food standard tailored to Italian passengers, with typical Italian food, including lots of pasta dishes. Service is bubbly, cheerful, and attentive, and comes with a smile, but lacks finesse. Limited selection of breads and fruits. Poor cabin service menu.

Other Comments Almost identical sister ship to *Cunard Countess*, with the same contemporary profile and good looks. Acquired in 1995 by StarLauro Cruises (now MSC), as a replacement for *Achille Lauro*. This ship will provide a very comfortable first cruise experience in a pleasing, very informal environment, at an excellent price, to some well-chosen destinations. This ship is now marketed almost exclusively to Italian passengers.

ms Rhapsody of the Seas

OPERATES

Cruise Line	Royal Caribbean Cruises	Casino	Yes	Slot Machines Yes
Former Names	-	Swimming Pools (outside)		1
Gross Tonnage	75,000	Swimming Pools (inside)		1 (outside-inside)
Builder	Chantiers de l'Atlantique (France)	Whirlpools	6	Gymnasium Yes
Original Cost	$275 million	Sauna/Steam Room Yes/Yes	Massage	Yes
Christened By	n/a	Self-Service Launderette		No
Entered Service	Apr 1997	Movie Theater/Seats		No
Interior Design	Njal Eide, Howard Snoweiss,	Library	Yes	Children's Facilities Yes
	Per Hoydahl, Lars Iwdal, Tom Graboski	Watersports Facilities		None
Country of Registry	n/a	Classification Society	Det Norske Veritas	

Tel No	n/a Fax No	n/a
Length (ft/m)		915.3/279.0
Beam (ft/m) 105.6/32.2	Draft (ft/m)	24.9/7.6
Propulsion/Propellers	diesel-electric/2 (FP)	
Decks	11 Crew	765
Pass. Capacity (basis 2) 2,000	(all berths) 2,435	
Pass. Space Ratio (basis 2) 37.5	(all berths) 30.8	
Officers	International	
Total Cabins	1,000	
Size Range (sq ft/m)	148.5-1,059.2/13.8-98.4	
Outside Cabins 593	Inside Cabins	407
Single Cabins		0
Balcony Cabins 229	Wheelchair Cabins 14	
Cabin Current	110/220 AC	
Refrigerator	Category A/B/C/D	
Cabin TV Yes VCR	Category A/B	
Dining Rooms 1	Sittings	2
Elevators		9

RATINGS	SCORE
Ship: Condition/Cleanliness	NYR
Ship: Space/Flow/Comfort	NYR
Ship: Decor/Furnishings	NYR
Ship: Fitness Facilities	NYR
Cabins: Comfort/Facilities	NYR
Cabins: Software	NYR
Food: Dining Room/Cuisine	NYR
Food: Buffets/Informal Dining	NYR
Food: Quality of Ingredients	NYR
Service: Dining Room	NYR
Service: Bars	NYR
Service: Cabins	NYR
Cruise: Entertainment	NYR
Cruise: Activities Program	NYR
Cruise: Hospitality Standard	NYR
OVERALL RATING	

Comments Sister ship to *Vision of the Seas*, which is set to debut in 1998, this ship has similar design features that make all Royal Caribbean ships very identifiable. The company provides a consistently good, well-programmed cruise vacation for those seeking to cruise on a large ship, with a small city of other like-minded passengers.

ss Rotterdam ★★★+

OPERATES
ALASKA AND CARIBBEAN CRUISES

Cruise Line		Holland America Line
Former Names		-
Gross Tonnage		38,645
Builder		Rotterdamsche Dry Dock (Holland)
Original Cost		$30 million
Christened By		HRH Queen Juliana
Entered Service		Sep 1959
Interior Design		Kym Anton/Julie Stanley
Country of Registry		Netherlands (PHEI)
Tel No 630-600610	Fax No	130-2554
Length (ft/m)		748.6/228.20
Beam (ft/m) 94.1/28.71	Draft (ft/m)	29.6/9.04
Propulsion		steam turbine (28,700kW)
Propellers		2 (FP)
Decks 10	Crew	603
Pass. Capacity (basis 2) 1,114	(all berths)	1,250
Pass. Space Ratio (basis 2) 34.6	(all berths)	30.9
Officers		Dutch
Total Cabins		575
Size Range (sq ft/m)		112-370/10.5-34.3
Outside Cabins 307	Inside Cabins	268
Single Cabins		32
Balcony Cabins		0
Wheelchair Cabins		0 (ramps available)
Cabin Current		110 AC
Refrigerator		Category A only
Cabin TV No	VCR	No
Dining Rooms 2	Sittings	2

Elevators			7
Casino	Yes	Slot Machines	Yes
Swimming Pools (outside) 1		(inside)	1
Whirlpools	0	Gymnasium	Yes
Sauna/Steam Room Yes/No		Massage	Yes
Self-Service Launderette			Yes
Movie Theater/Seats			Yes/620
Library			Yes
Children's Facilities			No
Classification Society			Lloyd's Register

RATINGS	SCORE
Ship: Condition/Cleanliness	6.7
Ship: Space/Flow/Comfort	7.0
Ship: Decor/Furnishings	6.6
Ship: Fitness Facilities	6.3
Cabins: Comfort/Facilities	6.1
Cabins: Software	7.5
Food: Dining Room/Cuisine	6.3
Food: Buffets/Informal Dining	6.1
Food: Quality of Ingredients	6.6
Service: Dining Room	6.6
Service: Bars	7.1
Service: Cabins	7.4
Cruise: Entertainment	6.4
Cruise: Activities Program	6.6
Cruise: Hospitality Standard	7.5
OVERALL RATING	100.7

+ Sturdily built ship has handsome rounded lines. This grand dame is lovely—and well loved by her followers. Gracious and graceful, she has been well maintained. Expansive open deck and sunning space, with real wooden deck lounge chairs. Gorgeous flower displays offset otherwise drab interior. Beautiful wood paneling and wood trim. Two-level art deco Ritz Carlton is most elegant. Wide choice of cabin sizes and configurations, all comfortably equipped. Lots of cabins for single cruisers. Lovely balconied theater.

— No wrap-around outdoor promenade deck. Numerous public rooms, but poor color combinations. Smokers and non-smokers are poorly separated. Expensive casino seems out of place. Many cabin bathrooms have exposed plumbing. Has poor entertainment. Expect lines for embarkation, disembarkation, buffets and shore tenders.

Dining Two high-ceilinged dining rooms. Reasonable food, but robotic service. Open sitting for breakfast and lunch; two sittings for dinner. Food is attractively presented, but meals are not memorable, and standards have declined. Limited selection of breads, cheeses, and fruit.

Other Comments A cruise on this stately ship fits comfortably—like a well-worn shoe—and the price is agreeable, too. However, remember that she is an old lady, and cannot compete with the latest high-tech contemporary ships. She will be retired in September 1997.

ms Rotterdam VI

Cruise Line	Holland America Line	Casino	Yes Slot Machines Yes
Former Names	-	Swimming Pools (outside) 1	(inside) 1
Gross Tonnage	62,000	Whirlpools 2	Gymnasium Yes
Builder	Fincantieri (Italy)	Sauna/Steam Room Yes/Yes	Massage Yes
Original Cost	$250 million	Self-Service Launderette	Yes
Christened By	n/a	Movie Theater/Seats	Yes/235
Entered Service	Aug 1997	Library	Yes
Interior Design	VFD Interiors	Children's Facilities	Yes
Country of Registry	n/a	Watersports Facilities	None
Tel No n/a Fax No	n/a	Classification Society	Lloyd's Register
Length (ft/m)	777.5/237.0		
Beam (ft/m) 105.8/32.25 Draft (ft/m)	25.5/7.8	**RATINGS**	**SCORE**
Propulsion	diesel-electric (37,500kW)	Ship: Condition/Cleanliness	NYR
Propellers	2 (CP)	Ship: Space/Flow/Comfort	NYR
Decks 12 Crew	644	Ship: Decor/Furnishings	NYR
Pass. Capacity (basis 2) 1,320 (all berths) 1,668		Ship: Fitness Facilities	NYR
Pass. Space Ratio (basis 2) 46.9 (all berths) 37.1		Cabins: Comfort/Facilities	NYR
Officers	Dutch	Cabins: Software	NYR
Total Cabins	660	Food: Dining Room/Cuisine	NYR
Size Range (sq ft/m) 185-1,126/17.1-104.5		Food: Buffets/Informal Dining	NYR
Outside Cabins 382 Inside Cabins	118	Food: Quality of Ingredients	NYR
Single Cabins	0	Service: Dining Room	NYR
Balcony Cabins 160 Wheelchair Cabins 20		Service: Bars	NYR
Cabin Current	110/220 AC	Service: Cabins	NYR
Refrigerator Cat. PS, S, A only		Cruise: Entertainment	NYR
Cabin TV Yes VCR Cat. PS, S, A only		Cruise: Activities Program	NYR
Dining Rooms 2 Sittings	2	Cruise: Hospitality Standard	NYR
Elevators	16	OVERALL RATING	

+ Constructed to look like a slightly larger and much sleeker version of the *Statendam*-class ships, yet retaining the graceful lines of the former *Rotterdam*. Has a twin funnel feature which will be recognized by previous Holland America Line passengers. She will be capable of a 25-knot speed, useful for longer distance itineraries. There will be a magrodome-covered lido pool deck between the mast and funnels. I expect the decor to be restrained and refined, with much use of wood accenting. One room will feature a glass ceiling.

Passengers in the 36-full verandah suites will have a private Concierge Lounge with a concierge to handle such things as special dining arrangements. Disabled passengers will have 20 cabins to choose from, including two suites.

— None known at time of going to press.

Dining There are two dining rooms, with tables for four, six or eight. The food is expected to be a notch above that presently served on other HAL ships, with better buffets and more attention to detail. An Italian restaurant will be available to all passengers.

Other Comments This new ship will replace the present *Rotterdam* when she is retired in September 1997. All the indications are that *Rotterdam VI* will be the finest ship ever for Holland America Line.

ms Royal Majesty ★★★★

OPERATES

*3- AND 4-DAY BAHAMAS AND
7-DAY BERMUDA CRUISES*

Cruise Line	Majesty Cruise Line		
Former Names	-		
Gross Tonnage	32,396		
Builder	Kvaerner Masa Yards (Finland)		
Original Cost	$229 million		
Christened By	Ms Liza Minelli		
Entered Service	Sep 1992		
Interior Design	A&M Katzourakis		
Country of Registry	Panama		
Tel No 133-6557	Fax No	133-6563	
Length (ft/m)	567.9/173.10		
Beam (ft/m) 90.5/27.60	Draft (ft/m)	20.3/6.20	
Propulsion	diesel (21,120kW)		
Propellers	2 (CP)		
Decks 9	Crew	525	
Pass. Capacity (basis 2) 1,056	(all berths) 1,501		
Pass. Space Ratio (basis 2) 31.3	(all berths) 21.5		
Officers	Greek		
Total Cabins	528 (132 no-smoking)		
Size Range (sq ft/m)	118-375/11.0-34.8		
Outside Cabins 343	Inside Cabins	185	
Single Cabins	0		
Balcony Cabins 0	Wheelchair Cabins	4	
Cabin Current	110/220 AC		
Refrigerator	Suites only		
Cabin TV Yes	VCR	Suites only	
Dining Rooms 1	Sittings	2	
Elevators	4		

Casino	Yes	Slot Machines	Yes
Swimming Pools (outside) 1		(inside)	0
Whirlpools	2	Gymnasium	Yes
Sauna/Steam Room Yes/No		Massage	Yes
Self-Service Launderette			No
Movie Theater/Seats			Yes/100
Library			Yes
Children's Facilities		Yes (also children's pool)	
Watersports Facilities			none
Classification Society		Lloyd's Register	

RATINGS	SCORE
Ship: Condition/Cleanliness	8.7
Ship: Space/Flow/Comfort	8.6
Ship: Decor/Furnishings	8.7
Ship: Fitness Facilities	7.6
Cabins: Comfort/Facilities	8.0
Cabins: Software	8.1
Food: Dining Room/Cuisine	7.7
Food: Buffets/Informal Dining	6.8
Food: Quality of Ingredients	7.0
Service: Dining Room	6.7
Service: Bars	7.0
Service: Cabins	7.4
Cruise: Entertainment	7.6
Cruise: Activities Program	6.7
Cruise: Hospitality Standard	7.2
OVERALL RATING	113.8

+ Smart contemporary ship has a good profile and is a well-conceived vessel. Tastefully appointed, with lots of teak and brass accents, discreet lighting, soothing colors and no glitz. Wide passageways. Circular lobby is bright and classical in appearance. Suites feature butler service, and are well equipped, though not really large. Most other cabins are on the small side, but comfortable, with excellent bathroom showers. There are many cabins designated for non-smokers. All cabins have ironing boards. Bathrobes are provided.

— Open deck and sunning space is cramped. No cushioned pads for deck chairs. Many cabins on Queen's Deck have obstructed views. Showroom is poorly designed, with obstructed sightlines, and production shows are weak. Too many announcements. Expect lines for shore excursions, buffets and pizza.

Dining The dining room is attractive, though very noisy, and the tables are close together. The food, menu, creativity, and service are basically sound, but bread rolls, cheese, and fruits could be better. Service is too fast, consistently poor, and seems to be getting worse, however.

Other Comments In the Royal Observatory, models and plans of 19th-century sailing ships provide a nautical ambiance. This ship will provide you with a very comfortable short cruise experience in warm, elegant surroundings, with a modicum of hospitality.

mv Royal Princess ★★★★+

OPERATES
VARIOUS CRUISES WORLDWIDE

Cruise Line		Princess Cruises
Former Names		-
Gross Tonnage		44,348
Builder		Wartsila (Finland)
Original Cost		$165 million
Christened By	HRH Princess Diana of Wales	
Entered Service		Nov 1984
Interior Design		Njal Eide
Country of Registry		Great Britain
Tel No 144-0211	Fax No	144-0215
Length (ft/m)		754.5/230.00
Beam (ft/m) 95.8/29.20	Draft (ft/m)	25.5/7.80
Propulsion		diesel (29,160kW)
Propellers		2 (CP)
Decks 9	Crew	520
Pass. Capacity (basis 2) 1,200	(all berths)	1,275
Pass. Space Ratio (basis 2) 36.9	(all berths)	34.7
Officers		British
Total Cabins		600
Size Range (sq ft/m)		68-806/6.3-74.8
Outside Cabins 600	Inside Cabins	0
Single Cabins		0
Balcony Cabins 150	Wheelchair Cabins	10
Cabin Current		110/220 AC
Refrigerator		All cabins
Cabin TV Yes	VCR	No
Dining Rooms 1	Sittings	2
Elevators		6

Casino	Yes	Slot Machines	Yes
Swimming Pools (outside)		2 (+2 splash pools)	
Swimming Pools (inside)			0
Whirlpools	2	Gymnasium	Yes
Sauna/Steam Room Yes/No		Massage	Yes
Self-Service Launderette			Yes
Movie Theater/Seats			Yes/150
Library	Yes	Children's Facilities	No
Watersports Facilities			None
Classification Society			Lloyd's Register

RATINGS	SCORE
Ship: Condition/Cleanliness	8.7
Ship: Space/Flow/Comfort	8.8
Ship: Decor/Furnishings	8.8
Ship: Fitness Facilities	7.8
Cabins: Comfort/Facilities	8.6
Cabins: Software	8.2
Food: Dining Room/Cuisine	7.7
Food: Buffets/Informal Dining	7.2
Food: Quality of Ingredients	7.0
Service: Dining Room	7.5
Service: Bars	7.7
Service: Cabins	7.8
Cruise: Entertainment	8.2
Cruise: Activities Program	8.0
Cruise: Hospitality Standard	8.3
OVERALL RATING	120.3

+ Contemporary outer styling, with short, well raked bow. Quality construction. Excellent outdoor deck and sunning space, and wrap-around outdoor promenade deck. Good, though unconventional, interior layout and passenger flow has passenger cabins above public room decks. Spacious passageways and delightful staircases. Contemporary but not garish, the decor reflects the feeling of space, openness, and light. All-outside cabins are well appointed and comfortable. Suites are gorgeous and feature upgraded amenities. All cabins have full bathtub and shower, and three-sided mirrors. Prompt, attentive room service. Large, beautifully appointed public rooms. Bathrobes are provided for all passengers.

— Lacks small, intimate public rooms, although public rooms are spacious. Some cabins on Baja and Caribe decks have lifeboat-obstructed views. Cabin numbering system is illogical. Signs throughout the ship are adequate, but most are hard to read.

Dining The elegant dining room is set low down, adjacent to the lobby. Food and service are moderately good, having been improved recently. There is always a pasta dish on the menu, and table captains are willing to make something special for you. Portions are generous.

Other Comments This ship, will provide a fine cruise experience in spacious, elegant surroundings, at the appropriate price, although attention to the small details is missing.

ms Royal Seas ★★★

OPERATES

CARIBBEAN, MEDITERRANEAN AND
SOUTH AMERICA CRUISES

Cruise Line	Royal Seas Cruise Line
Former Names	Sea Venture/Ukraine/Kazakhstan
Gross Tonnage	15,402
Builder	Wartsila (Finland)
Original Cost	$25 million
Christened By	n/a
Entered Service	Jul 1975/Mar 1996
Interior Design	n/a
Country of Registry	Ukraine
Tel No 140-0772	Fax No 140-0772
Length (ft/m)	512.6/156.27
Beam (ft/m) 72.3/22.05	Draft (ft/m) 19.4/5.92
Propulsion	diesel (13,430kW)
Propellers	2 (CP)
Decks 7	Crew 250
Pass. Capacity (basis 2) 452	(all berths) 640
Pass. Space Ratio (basis 2) 34.0	(all berths) 24.0
Officers	Ukrainian
Total Cabins	235
Size Range (sq ft/m)	90-492/8.4-45.7
Outside Cabins 117	Inside Cabins 118
Single Cabins	0
Balcony Cabins	0
Wheelchair Cabins	0
Cabin Current 220 AC	Refrigerator No
Cabin TV No	VCR No
Dining Rooms 2	Sittings 1
Elevators	1

Casino	Yes	Slot Machines	Yes
Swimming Pools (outside) 1		(inside)	0
Whirlpools	0	Gymnasium	Yes
Sauna/Steam Room Yes/No		Massage	Yes
Self-Service Launderette			Yes
Movie Theater/Seats			Yes/140
Library			Yes
Children's Facilities			No
Watersports Facilities			None
Classification Society	Ukraine Register of Shipping		

RATINGS	SCORE
Ship: Condition/Cleanliness	6.6
Ship: Space/Flow/Comfort	6.4
Ship: Decor/Furnishings	6.4
Ship: Fitness Facilities	4.8
Cabins: Comfort/Facilities	6.0
Cabins: Software	6.4
Food: Dining Room/Cuisine	6.3
Food: Buffets/Informal Dining	5.8
Food: Quality of Ingredients	5.5
Service: Dining Room	6.8
Service: Bars	7.0
Service: Cabins	7.2
Cruise: Entertainment	5.6
Cruise: Activities Program	5.6
Cruise: Hospitality Standard	6.8
OVERALL RATING	93.2

+ Fairly sleek-looking ship with contemporary profile and smart, square funnel. Has a good outdoor promenade area. Recent refurbishment added a movie theater, new nightclub, foyer, Crimea Bar and more cabins. Eight suites on Boat Deck are quite spacious, have full bathtubs, good closet and drawer space and artwork. Other cabins are small and sparingly furnished, but quite adequate.

— Most cabins have little drawer space, and the insulation is poor. Communication with staff is frustrating even though the staff are friendly. There are no cushioned pads for the deck chairs.

Dining There are two dining rooms, both of which are nicely decorated, and are quite comfortable. One is for smokers, the other for non-smokers, but there are no tables for two. One wall features a multi-color, multi-image contemporary glass mural.

Other Comments The service is somewhat perfunctory, but the staff do try hard. The ship itself provides a good cruise experience at a modest price, but there's little finesse.

mv Royal Star ★★★

OPERATES

VARIOUS SOUTH INDIAN OCEAN CRUISES

Cruise Line	Star Line Cruises	Casino Yes	Slot Machines Yes
Former Names	Ocean Islander/San Giorgio/	Swimming Pools (outside) 1	(inside) 0
	City of Andros	Whirlpools 0	Gymnasium Yes
Gross Tonnage	5,360	Sauna/Steam Room Yes/No	Massage Yes
Builder	Cantieri Riuniti dell' Adriatico (Italy)	Self-Service Launderette	No
Original Cost	n/a	Movie Theater/Seats No	Library Yes
Christened By	Mrs Sandra Ruedin	Children's Facilities	No
Entered Service	1956/Dec 1990	Watersports Facilities	None
Interior Design	A&M Katzourakis	Classification Society	American Bureau
Country of Registry	Bahamas		of Shipping

Tel No 110-4407 Fax No 110-3460	
Length (ft/m) 367.4/112.00	
Beam (ft/m) 51.0/15.55 Draft (ft/m) 18.2/5.56	
Propulsion/Propellers diesel (4,817kW)/2 (FP)	
Decks 5 Crew 120	
Pass. Capacity (basis 2) 222 (all berths) 255	
Pass. Space Ratio (basis 2) 24.1 (all berths) 21.0	
Officers Greek	
Total Cabins 111	
Size Range (sq ft/m) 107-398/10.0-37.0	
Outside Cabins 97 Inside Cabins 14	
Single Cabins 0	
Balcony Cabins 1 Wheelchair Cabins 0	
Cabin Current 110/220 AC	
Refrigerator Superior suites only	
Cabin TV No VCR Superior suites only	
Dining Rooms 1 Sittings 2	
Elevators 1	

RATINGS	SCORE
Ship: Condition/Cleanliness	6.7
Ship: Space/Flow/Comfort	6.8
Ship: Decor/Furnishings	7.1
Ship: Fitness Facilities	4.3
Cabins: Comfort/Facilities	6.4
Cabins: Software	6.7
Food: Dining Room/Cuisine	7.0
Food: Buffets/Informal Dining	6.6
Food: Quality of Ingredients	6.8
Service: Dining Room	7.2
Service: Bars	7.3
Service: Cabins	7.4
Cruise: Entertainment	5.2
Cruise: Activities Program	4.8
Cruise: Hospitality Standard	6.7
OVERALL RATING	97.0

+ Charming little vessel, with well-balanced profile. Best suited for cruising in sheltered areas. Clean and tidy throughout. Warm, intimate and highly personable ambiance. Ample open deck space for sunning. Attractive contemporary Scandinavian interior decor. The cabins, although not large, are pleasantly decorated with good-quality furnishings and ample closet and drawer space.

— Has a steep, narrow gangway in some ports. Cabin bathrooms are tiny.

Dining Charming dining room, with good service and international cuisine, although standards are variable. Table wines are included with meals. Limited selection of breads, cheeses and fruits. Limited cabin service menu. Poor afternoon tea.

Other Comments Well packaged and operated by the African Safari Club group of hotels, this ship will provide a most enjoyable cruise and safari experience in very comfortable, small-ship surroundings, at an extremely realistic price.

ms Royal Viking Sun ★★★★★+

OPERATES

VARIOUS CRUISES WORLDWIDE

Cruise Line	Cunard		
Former Names	-		
Gross Tonnage	37,845		
Builder	Wartsila (Finland)		
Original Cost	$125 million		
Christened By	Mr James Stewart		
Entered Service	Dec 1988		
Interior Design	Njal Eide		
Country of Registry	Bahamas		
Tel No	110-4517	Fax No	110-4514
Length (ft/m)		674.2/205.50	
Beam (ft/m) 91.8/28.00	Draft (ft/m)	23.6/7.20	
Propulsion		diesel (21,120kW)	
Propellers		2 (CP)	
Decks	8	Crew	460
Pass. Capacity (basis 2) 740	(all berths) 814		
Pass. Space Ratio (basis 2) 51.1	(all berths) 46.4		
Officers		Norwegian	
Total Cabins		370	
Size Range (sq ft/m)		138-724/12.8-67.2	
Outside Cabins	350	Inside Cabins	20
Single Cabins			2
Balcony Cabins			145
Wheelchair Cabins			4
Cabin Current	110 AC	Refrigerator	All cabins
Cabin TV	Yes	VCR	Yes
Dining Rooms	1	Sittings	1
Elevators			4

Casino	Yes	Slot Machines	Yes
Swimming Pools (outside)	2	(inside)	0
Whirlpools	2	Gymnasium	Yes
Sauna/Steam Room	Yes/Yes	Massage	Yes
Self-Service Launderette			Yes
Movie Theater/Seats			Yes/101
Library			Yes
Children's Facilities			No
Watersports Facilities			None
Classification Society		Det Norske Veritas	

RATINGS	SCORE
Ship: Condition/Cleanliness	9.1
Ship: Space/Flow/Comfort	9.5
Ship: Decor/Furnishings	9.4
Ship: Fitness Facilities	9.2
Cabins: Comfort/Facilities	9.2
Cabins: Software	9.1
Food: Dining Room/Cuisine	9.0
Food: Buffets/Informal Dining	9.0
Food: Quality of Ingredients	8.7
Service: Dining Room	9.2
Service: Bars	9.1
Service: Cabins	9.4
Cruise: Entertainment	8.6
Cruise: Activities Program	8.6
Cruise: Hospitality Standard	9.4
OVERALL RATING	136.5

+ This contemporary, well-designed ship has sleek, flowing lines, a sharply raked bow and well-rounded profile, with lots of floor-to-ceiling glass. The ship's tenders are thoughtfully air-conditioned and even have radar, and a toilet. Maintenance of the ship is excellent. Wide outdoor teakwood decks provide excellent walking areas, including a wrap-around promenade deck (even the ship's bridge has a wooden floor). There are two glass-walled elevators. Separate baggage elevators mean passengers never have to wait for luggage. Has an incredibly spacious interior layout. Impressive public rooms and tasteful decor reign throughout. Two handrails, one wooden, one chrome, are provided on all stairways, a thoughtful extra touch. The Stella Polaris Lounge, the ship's forward observation lounge, is simply lovely, and one of the most elegant lounges at sea. Pebble Beach is the name of the ship's own golf club, complete with wet bar and electronic golf simulator. The Dickens Library is now a well organized center. Distinguished male guest hosts are provided on all cruises. The Owner's Suite, at 723 sq ft (67.2m²), is delightful, and features two bathrooms, one of which has a large whirlpool bathtub with ocean views. Fine penthouse suites have large balconies, and gracious butler service. Most cabins are of generous proportions, and are well appointed, with just about everything you would need. Some 38 percent of all cabins have a private balcony.

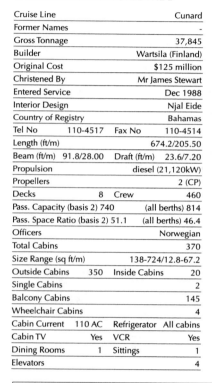

All cabins have walk-in closets, lockable drawers, full-length mirrors, hairdryers, and fluffy cotton bathrobes. Fine Scandinavian stewardesses provide excellent, unobtrusive service. Four well equipped, L-shaped cabins for the handicapped are well designed, quite large, and feature special wheel-in bathroom with shower facilities, and closet. First class air is provided to all passengers on long, exotic voyages. Cunard seems committed to keeping up the standards aboard this ship, and that's good for passengers.

— More maintenance needed on the balconies. There's no way to get from the uppermost pool, which has a swim-up (sit-in) bar, to the second pool, located adjacent to the health spa and gymnasium, without first going inside the vessel. The carpeting quality in some areas is poor, however, with too many strips and joins, typical of shipyard subcontractors. The Oak Room features a marble fireplace, although it can't be used due to United States Coast Guard regulations.

Dining Excellent cuisine and fine European service are provided in an unhurried, caring atmosphere, with a menu that is never repeated, no matter how long the voyage. The food is creative and well presented, with good use of garnishes. There is a delightful, well-chosen wine list from distinguished vintners from around the world. There is also a separate, but somewhat under-used wine bar.

In the dining room, mineral water, which should be included at these prices, should be served for all meals, instead of the chlorinated water provided. There's also an excellent and well utilized indoor-outdoor lido buffet area. A separate à la carte Italian dining room is an elegant alternative dining spot with a great view. Although the wine list is extensive, wine prices are quite high.

Other Comments Presently one of the two highest rated ships in the world, this delightful vessel operates mainly long-distance cruises (including an annual complete world cruise) in great comfort. Her beauty is the result of three designers – Njal R. Eide, ship design); Finn G. Nilsson (accommodations); and Frank Mingis (Owner's Suite and Penthouse Suites, who also assisted in selecting the interior color scheme, china, glass and silverware). There are two outdoor swimming pools. The gymnasium and spa facilities are excellent.

Whether by intention or not, the ship has created a two class feeling, with passengers in "upstairs" penthouse suites and "A" grade staterooms gravitating to the somewhat quieter Stella Polaris lounge, while other passengers (the participants) go to the main entertainment deck.

This ship has a wide range of facilities, including a concierge, self-service launderettes, guest lecture program, 24-hour information office, and true 24-hour cabin service, for the discriminating passenger who demands the very finest in personal surroundings, food and service, regardless of price. Absolutely first class, this Sun is set to shine for a long time.

Committed to the pursuit of gracious living at sea, she is one of the finest breed of grand floating hotels, with a warm ambiance, ably commanded by a well-loved and very proud Captain Ola Harsheim. The ship's direct competitors are the *Crystal Harmony/Crystal Symphony* (arguably more elegant ships, with larger suites, but with two sittings for dinner) and the outstanding *Europa* (principally for German-speaking passengers). While this ship is not perfect (the perfect ship has not yet been delivered), the few design flaws that are evident (for example: poorly designed bar service counters; odd signage in the elevators), she is excellent, she will, without doubt, be maintained and even improved by Cunard, who purchased the vessel along with the brand name Royal Viking in 1994. A long cruise aboard *Royal Viking Sun* is arguably one of the world's most civilised travel experiences. Port taxes and all gratuities are included. Finally, the ship's greatest asset is her outstanding, friendly and personable, mostly European crew.

ms Ryndam ★★★★+

OPERATES
7-DAY CARIBBEAN AND EUROPE CRUISES

Cruise Line	Holland America Line		
Former Names	-		
Gross Tonnage	55,451		
Builder	Fincantieri (Italy)		
Original Cost	$215 million		
Christened By	Mrs Madeleine Arison		
Entered Service	Nov 1994		
Interior Design	VFD Interiors/Joe Farcus		
Country of Registry	Netherlands (PHFV)		
Tel No	624-506613	Fax No	130-6563
Length (ft/m)			719.3/219.30
Beam (ft/m) 101.0/30.80		Draft (ft/m)	24.6/7.50
Propulsion		diesel-electric (34,560kW)	
Propellers			2 (CP)
Decks	10	Crew	588
Pass. Capacity (basis 2) 1,264		(all berths) 1,627	
Pass. Space Ratio (basis 2) 43.8		(all berths) 34.0	
Officers			Dutch
Total Cabins			632
Size Range (sq ft/m)		187-1,126/17.3-104.5	
Outside Cabins	501	Inside Cabins	131
Single Cabins			0
Balcony Cabins	150	Wheelchair Cabins	6
Cabin Current			110/220 AC
Refrigerator		Category PS/S/A/B only	
Cabin TV	Yes	VCR	No
Dining Rooms	1	Sittings	2
Elevators			12

Casino	Yes	Slot Machines	Yes
Swimming Pools (outside)			1
Swimming Pools (inside)			1 (magrodome)
Whirlpools	2	Gymnasium	Yes
Sauna/Steam Room Yes/No		Massage	Yes
Self-Service Launderette			Yes
Movie Theater/Seats			Yes/249
Library	Yes	Children's Facilities	No
Watersports Facilities			None
Classification Society			Lloyd's Register

RATINGS	SCORE
Ship: Condition/Cleanliness	8.8
Ship: Space/Flow/Comfort	8.4
Ship: Decor/Furnishings	8.5
Ship: Fitness Facilities	7.7
Cabins: Comfort/Facilities	8.1
Cabins: Software	8.2
Food: Dining Room/Cuisine	7.2
Food: Buffets/Informal Dining	6.8
Food: Quality of Ingredients	6.7
Service: Dining Room	6.5
Service: Bars	7.2
Service: Cabins	8.0
Cruise: Entertainment	7.5
Cruise: Activities Program	7.7
Cruise: Hospitality Standard	8.3
OVERALL RATING	115.6

+ Sister ship to *Maasdam* and *Statendam*. Excellent teakwood decking. Asymmetrical layout breaks up her interiors and reduces bottlenecks. Stunning three-deck-high atrium foyer. Magrodome roof covers indoor-outdoor pool and central lido area. Fine Dutch antiques and art collection. Subdued and tasteful interior decor. Flowers everywhere. Cabins are spacious, tastefully decorated and well laid out, although some are a little cramped for two.

— Two-deck-high showroom is well thought out, but the ceiling is low and sightlines are not good in the upper level. Expect lines at embarkation, disembarkation, for the buffet, and shore tenders. Communication with staff, particularly at the Purser's Office, is often frustrating. Self-service launderette incurs an extra charge for both washers and dryers. Very noisy waiter stations in dining room. No bell-push outside the suites.

Dining Elegant two-deck-high dining room with dramatic grand staircase at stern. Food and service are of typical HAL standards (disappointing and non-memorable), with much use of fine china. In-suite dining can be done in 28 suites, each of which can accommodate four.

Other Comments Well-built ship, the third in a series of four. The ship continues the company's strong maritime traditions, but the food and service components let the rest of the ship and cruise experience down badly at present.

RMS St. Helena ★★★★

OPERATES

WALES-ST. HELENA/SOUTH AFRICA CRUISES

Cruise Line	Curnow Shipping	Casino	No	Slot Machines	Yes

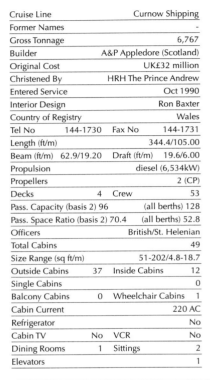

Cruise Line		Curnow Shipping
Former Names		-
Gross Tonnage		6,767
Builder		A&P Appledore (Scotland)
Original Cost		UK£32 million
Christened By		HRH The Prince Andrew
Entered Service		Oct 1990
Interior Design		Ron Baxter
Country of Registry		Wales
Tel No 144-1730	Fax No	144-1731
Length (ft/m)		344.4/105.00
Beam (ft/m) 62.9/19.20	Draft (ft/m)	19.6/6.00
Propulsion		diesel (6,534kW)
Propellers		2 (CP)
Decks 4	Crew	53
Pass. Capacity (basis 2) 96	(all berths)	128
Pass. Space Ratio (basis 2) 70.4	(all berths)	52.8
Officers		British/St. Helenian
Total Cabins		49
Size Range (sq ft/m)		51-202/4.8-18.7
Outside Cabins 37	Inside Cabins	12
Single Cabins		0
Balcony Cabins 0	Wheelchair Cabins	1
Cabin Current		220 AC
Refrigerator		No
Cabin TV No	VCR	No
Dining Rooms 1	Sittings	2
Elevators		1

Casino	No	Slot Machines	Yes
Swimming Pools (outside) 1		(inside)	0
Whirlpools	0	Gymnasium	No
Sauna/Steam Room No/No		Massage	No
Self-Service Launderette			Yes
Movie Theater/Seats			No
Library			Yes
Children's Facilities/Playroom			Yes
Watersports Facilities			none
Classification Society			Lloyd's Register

RATINGS	SCORE
Ship: Condition/Cleanliness	8.4
Ship: Space/Flow/Comfort	7.6
Ship: Decor/Furnishings	8.2
Ship: Fitness Facilities	5.4
Cabins: Comfort/Facilities	7.8
Cabins: Software	8.1
Food: Dining Room/Cuisine	8.2
Food: Buffets/Informal Dining	8.1
Food: Quality of Ingredients	7.7
Service: Dining Room	8.0
Service: Bars	7.9
Service: Cabins	8.0
Cruise: Entertainment	6.4
Cruise: Activities Program	6.4
Cruise: Hospitality Standard	8.1
OVERALL RATING	114.3

+ Has all modern conveniences, including stabilizers and air-conditioning. Passengers can even take their pets. Operates just like a full-size cruise vessel, and has an open bridge policy. Pleasant library/reading lounge. There is a free self-service laundry. Accommodations are in two-, three-, or four-berth cabins, which are simply furnished, yet quite comfortable. The brochure states that landing at Ascension is at times "a hazardous process" owing to slippery and steep wharf steps—now that's telling it like it is. The staff are warm, welcoming, eager to see you enjoying the journey and delightful to sail with.

— Two-sitting dining on such a small ship is rather disruptive. There are nine cabins that do not have private facilities. The swimming pool is really a "dip" pool only, and is tiny.

Dining The dining room is totally non-smoking. The food is very British, with hearty breakfasts and a relatively simple menu, but the food is attractively presented on fine china. Afternoon tea, complete with freshly baked cakes, is a must.

Other Comments This amazing little combination cargo-passenger ship operates a regular Cardiff-Tenerife-St. Helena-Ascension Island-Tristan Da Cunha-Capetown line service which is like a mini-cruise, or long voyage, with lots of days at sea. There are six round-trip sailings each year.

ms Sapphire ★★★+

OPERATES
7-DAY MEDITERRANEAN CRUISES

Cruise Line			Thomson Cruises
Former Names		Sea Prince/Ocean Princess/Italia/	
			Princess Italia
Gross Tonnage			11,125
Builder		Cantieri Navale Felszegi (Italy)	
Original Cost	n/a	Christened By	n/a
Entered Service			Aug 1967/Apr 1995
Interior Design			A&M Katzourakis
Country of Registry			Greece
Tel No	n/a	Fax No	n/a
Length (ft/m)			491.7/149.80
Beam (ft/m)	70.9/21.50	Draft (ft/m)	21.6/6.60
Propulsion			diesel (11,050kW)
Propellers			2 (CP)
Decks	8	Crew	225
Pass. Capacity (basis 2) 500		(all berths) 539	
Pass. Space Ratio (basis 2) 22.5		(all berths) 20.6	
Officers			Greek
Total Cabins			250
Size (sq ft/m.):			75.3-226.0/7-21
Outside Cabins	125	Inside Cabins	125
Single Cabins			0
Balcony Cabins			0
Wheelchair Cabins			0
Cabin Current			110 AC
Refrigerator			No
Cabin TV	No	VCR	No
Dining Rooms	1	Sittings	2

Elevators			5
Casino	Yes	Slot Machines	Yes
Swimming Pools (outside) 1		(inside)	0
Whirlpools	0	Gymnasium	Yes
Sauna/Steam Room	Yes/No	Massage	Yes
Self-service Launderette			No
Cinema/Theatre:			Yes/170
Library			Yes
Children's Facilities/Playroom:			No
Classification Society			RINA

RATINGS	SCORE
Ship: Condition/Cleanliness	7.3
Ship: Space/Flow/Comfort	7.1
Ship: Decor/Furnishings	7.7
Ship: Fitness Facilities	5.9
Cabins: Comfort/Facilities	6.7
Cabins: Software	7.3
Food: Dining Room/Cuisine	6.7
Food: Buffets/Informal Dining	6.3
Food: Quality of Ingredients	6.1
Service: Dining Room	7.0
Service: Bars	6.8
Service: Cabins	7.0
Cruise: Entertainment	6.2
Cruise: Activities Program	6.1
Cruise: Hospitality Standard	7.2
OVERALL RATING	101.3

+ Long, low, handsome lines and swept-back aft-placed funnel provide a very attractive profile for this small ship. Has inboard lifeboats. Has good open deck and sunning space, but the heated outdoor pool is small. Contemporary interior decor with attractive colors add warm decor in public rooms. Reasonable sized cabins have pleasing, though plain, decor, furnishings and fittings. All have tiled bathrooms, but they are small.

— Cabins are not assigned until embarkation. Cabin closet and drawer space is very limited. The sauna is really tiny (big enough for one). Some public rooms have a fairly low ceiling height. Steep gangway in some ports.

Dining Charming dining room has an art deco feel, a raised center ceiling and lovely etched glass dividers, but it is noisy. Reasonably attentive service from willing, friendly staff. Good general standard of international cuisine.

Other Comments Louis Cruise Lines purchased the ship in August 1995, and following extensive refurbishment, entered her into service in April 1996, on behalf of Thomsons, the UK tour operator. This ship will take its mainly British passengers to some decent destinations in good, contemporary surroundings and in a relaxed, casual style. The realistic, inexpensive price of this product is a real bonus.

mv Sea Goddess I ★★★★★+

OPERATES

VARIOUS CARIBBEAN AND
EUROPE CRUISES

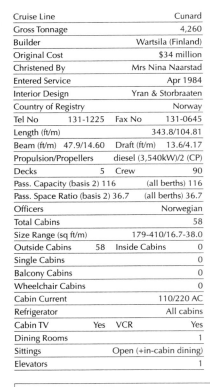

Cruise Line		Cunard
Gross Tonnage		4,260
Builder		Wartsila (Finland)
Original Cost		$34 million
Christened By		Mrs Nina Naarstad
Entered Service		Apr 1984
Interior Design		Yran & Storbraaten
Country of Registry		Norway
Tel No 131-1225	Fax No	131-0645
Length (ft/m)		343.8/104.81
Beam (ft/m) 47.9/14.60	Draft (ft/m)	13.6/4.17
Propulsion/Propellers		diesel (3,540kW)/2 (CP)
Decks 5	Crew	90
Pass. Capacity (basis 2) 116		(all berths) 116
Pass. Space Ratio (basis 2) 36.7		(all berths) 36.7
Officers		Norwegian
Total Cabins		58
Size Range (sq ft/m)		179-410/16.7-38.0
Outside Cabins 58	Inside Cabins	0
Single Cabins		0
Balcony Cabins		0
Wheelchair Cabins		0
Cabin Current		110/220 AC
Refrigerator		All cabins
Cabin TV Yes	VCR	Yes
Dining Rooms		1
Sittings		Open (+in-cabin dining)
Elevators		1

Casino	Yes	Slot Machines	Yes
Swimming Pools (outside) 1		(inside)	0
Whirlpools	1	Gymnasium	Yes
Sauna/Steam Room Yes/No		Massage	Yes
Self-Service Launderette			No
Movie Theater/Seats	No	Library	Yes
Children's Facilities			No
Watersports Facilities Aft platform, scuba, snorkel,			
waterski, windsurf, zodiacs (2)			
Classification Society			Lloyd's Register

RATINGS	SCORE
Ship: Condition/Cleanliness	9.0
Ship: Space/Flow/Comfort	8.8
Ship: Facilities	9.1
Ship: Decor/Furnishings	9.1
Ship: Fitness/Watersports Facilities	9.1
Cabins: Comfort/Facilities	9.0
Cabins: Software	9.0
Food: Dining Room/Cuisine	9.5
Food: Buffets/Informal Dining	9.3
Food: Quality of Ingredients	9.2
Service: Dining Room	9.2
Service: Bars	9.2
Service: Cabins	9.1
Cruise: Entertainment/Lecture Program	8.6
Cruise: Hospitality Standard	9.3
OVERALL RATING	136.5

+ *Sea Goddess I* and *Sea Goddess II* are two lovely vessels that have a sleek, contemporary, handsome profile and private club ambiance. Shallow draft allows access to small ports that mainstream ships cannot enter. Meticulously maintained. They have an aft platform with watersports facilities at no extra charge. Elegant, chic public rooms and decor. Beautiful flower displays and green plants everywhere, giving the ships a warm connection with nature. Cute gymnasium and spa (classes are by Golden Door of California). Oriental rugs in lobby. Fine quality furnishings and fabrics throughout, with marble and blond wood accents. Charming all-outside cabins, although small, come fully equipped with everything you'll need. The bedroom is next to the window, unlike on the *Seabourn* ships, so you can entertain in the living area without going past the sleeping area, as one must on the Seabourns. Everything, including all beverages, wines, and caviar, is included. Hospitality and anticipation are art forms practiced to the highest degree by staff.

— Bathroom doors open inward. Pleasant waterfall at outdoor café, but it doesn't belong on a ship.

Dining Dining is what the *Sea Goddess* experience is all about—the height of *haute cuisine* at sea. Elegant, warm, cozy, inviting dining salons have leather-bound menus, beautiful crystalware and supremely attentive, impeccable personalized European service. Plenty of

mv Sea Goddess II ★★★★★+

OPERATES

VARIOUS EUROPE AND ORIENT CRUISES

Cruise Line			Cunard
Former Names	-	Gross Tonnage	4,260
Builder			Wartsila (Finland)
Original Cost			$34 million
Christened By	HRH Princess Caroline of Monaco		
Entered Service			May 1985
Interior Design			Yran & Storbraaten
Country of Registry			Norway
Tel No	131-1235	Fax No	131-0644
Length (ft/m)			343.8/104.81
Beam (ft/m)	47.9/14.60	Draft (ft/m)	13.6/4.17
Propulsion/Propellers		diesel (3,540kW)/2 (CP)	
Decks	5	Crew	90
Pass. Capacity (basis 2) 115		(all berths) 115	
Pass. Space Ratio (basis 2) 36.7		(all berths) 36.7	
Officers			Norwegian
Total Cabins			58
Size Range (sq ft/m)			179-410/16.7-38.0
Outside Cabins	58	Inside Cabins	0
Single Cabins			1
Balcony Cabins			0
Wheelchair Cabins			0
Cabin Current			110/220 AC
Refrigerator			All cabins
Cabin TV	Yes	VCR	Yes
Dining Rooms			1
Sittings		Open (+in-cabin dining)	
Elevators			1

Casino	Yes	Slot Machines	Yes
Swimming Pools (outside) 1		(inside)	0
Whirlpools		1	Gymnasium	Yes
Sauna/Steam Room Yes/No		Massage	Yes
Self-Service Launderette			No
Movie Theater/Seats	No	Library	Yes
Children's Facilities			No
Watersports Facilities	Aft platform, banana boat,		
scuba, snorkel, waterski, windsurf, zodiacs (2)			
Classification Society			Lloyd's Register

RATINGS	SCORE
Ship: Condition/Cleanliness	9.0
Ship: Space/Flow/Comfort	8.8
Ship: Facilities	9.1
Ship: Decor/Furnishings	9.1
Ship: Fitness/Watersports Facilities	9.1
Cabins: Comfort/Facilities	9.0
Cabins: Software	9.0
Food: Dining Room/Cuisine	9.5
Food: Buffets/Informal Dining	9.3
Food: Quality of Ingredients	9.2
Service: Dining Room	9.2
Service: Bars	9.2
Service: Cabins	9.1
Cruise: Entertainment/Lecture Program	8.6
Cruise: Hospitality Standard	9.3
OVERALL RATING	136.5

space around each table for fine service, and a floating culinary celebration. Tables for two, four, six, or eight are immaculately laid with settings of real silver base plates, pristine white table linen, and always fresh flowers. Hutschenreuther, Villeroy and Boch, and Tiffany are the appointments. Open seating means you dine wherever, whenever, and with whomever you want. Exquisite cuisine, and everything is prepared individually to order. Only the freshest and finest ingredients are used. You can, naturally, dine in-suite at any time, course by course. You can also eat à la carte 24 hours a day if you wish. Has excellent outdoor buffets, and you never have to get your own food. There's plenty of caviar, at any time of the day or night. And never a hint of baked Alaska! A selection of fine wines accompanies each meal, while connoisseurs will appreciate the availability of an extra-cost wine list, of special vintages and premier crus.

Other Comments For the discriminating person requiring a very private environment in which to be pampered in an unstructured setting. Highly recommended for those who do not like cruise ships (particularly the large ships with their platoons of people). Daytime dress code is resort casual, dressy at night. The staff is simply wonderful, and it's hard for them to say "no" to any request. Port taxes and insurance are extra, but all shore excursions and gratuities are included, and no further tipping is allowed. The ship was well refurbished in 1995.

ms Seabourn Legend ★★★★★+

Cruise Line	Seabourn Cruise Line	Swimming Pools (outside) 1 (inside)	0
Former Names	Queen Odyssey/	Whirlpools 3 Gymnasium	Yes
	Royal Viking Queen	Sauna/Steam Room Yes/Yes Massage	Yes
Gross Tonnage	9,975	Self-Service Launderette	Yes
Builder	Schichau Seebeckwerft (Germany)	Movie Theater/Seats	No
Original Cost	$87 million	Library	Yes
Christened By	Mrs Inger Kloster	Children's Facilities	No
Entered Service	Mar 1992/Jul 1996	Watersports Facilities Aft platform with marina	
Interior Design	Yran & Storbraaten	pool, windsurfers, waterski, 2 Zodiacs	
Country of Registry	Norway	Classification Society Det Norske Veritas	
Tel No n/a Fax No	n/a		
Length (ft/m)	439.9/134.10	**RATINGS**	**SCORE**
Beam (ft/m) 62.9/19.20 Draft (ft/m)	16.7/5.10	Ship: Condition/Cleanliness	9.3
Propulsion/Propellers	diesel (7,280kW)/2 (CP)	Ship: Space/Flow/Comfort	9.3
Decks 6 Crew	145	Ship: Facilities	9.0
Pass. Capacity (basis 2) 212 (all berths) 212		Ship: Decor/Furnishings	9.1
Pass. Space Ratio (basis 2) 47.0 (all berths) 47.0		Ship: Fitness/Watersports Facilities	9.2
Officers Norwegian Total Cabins	106	Cabins: Comfort/Facilities	9.4
Size Range (sq ft/m) 277-590/25.7-54.8		Cabins: Software	9.0
Outside Cabins 106 Inside Cabins	0	Food: Dining Room/Cuisine	9.0
Single Cabins 0 Balcony Cabins	6	Food: Buffets/Informal Dining	9.0
Wheelchair Cabins	4	Food: Quality of Ingredients	9.2
Cabin Current	110/220 AC	Service: Dining Room	8.7
Refrigerator	All cabins	Service: Bars	9.0
Cabin TV Yes VCR	Yes	Service: Cabins	9.2
Dining Rooms 1 Sittings	Open	Cruise: Entertainment/Lecture Program	9.0
Elevators	3	Cruise: Hospitality Standard	9.1
Casino Yes Slot Machines	Yes	OVERALL RATING	136.5

✚ She is a strikingly sleek ship with a handsome profile, almost identical in looks to *Seabourn Pride* and *Seabourn Spirit*, but built to an even higher standard, and with streamline bars along the upper superstructure side. The ship features two fine mahogany water taxis. Also features an aft watersports platform and marina, which is used in suitably calm warm water areas.

There is a wide central passageway throughout the accommodation areas. The finest quality interior fixtures, fittings, and fabrics have been combined in her sumptuous public areas to produce an outstandingly elegant decor, with warm color combinations and some fine artwork. Wonderful 360° mural in the reception lobby (a portrait of the ship's interior designer is painted into the mural). Relaxed by day, a more formal dress code applies at night.

All the suites are comfortably large, and beautifully equipped with everything one could need, including large walk-in closet, 100 per cent cotton towels and bathrobes, personalized stationery, and leather ticket wallet, which arrives nicely boxed and packaged. Non-smoking cabins are available.

For the ultimate in privacy, the two Owner's Suites (001/002), located forward on Deck 6, offer a superbly private living environment at sea. Each has a walk-in closet, second closet, one full bathroom and a second room with toilet and washbasin (for guests). There's also a forward-facing balcony, complete with sun lounge chairs and wooden drinks table. These are secluded, and good for nude sunbathing. The living area has ample bookshelf space (included is a complete edition of *Encyclopedia Britannica*), a large refrigerator and drinks cabinet, television and VCR (plus a second television in the bedroom). All windows as well as the door to the balcony have electric blinds, and a complete blackout is possible in both bedroom and living room. On the Christmas cruise, each Owner's Suite has its own decorated and illuminated Christmas tree—a nice touch.

— There is no wrap-around outdoor promenade deck, and few cabins have private balconies. All beverages should ideally be included in the cruise fare, as on the Sea Goddess and Silversea Cruises ships, but then the cruise fare would have to be raised accordingly. Plastic chairs on deck are quite incorrect for this type of ship and should be changed.

Dining In-suite, course-by-course dining is available at any time. Elegant decor prevails in the formal dining room, which has a mixture of marble and carpeted floor. Seabourn's fine, extremely creative cuisine is artfully presented, with almost all items cooked to order. The menu is not repeated, no matter how long the voyage. Special orders are available whenever you want them, and caviar is always available on request. There is always a good selection of exotic fruits and cheeses. The wine list is quite extensive, although prices are rather high. Hand-picked European dining room staff provide impeccable service.

In addition, breakfast and lunch buffets, and informal alternative candlelit dinners, can be taken in the popular café adjacent to the swimming pool.

Other Comments A welcome addition to the Seabourn Cruise Line fleet, this ship will provide discerning passengers with an outstanding level of personal service and a superb, utterly civilized cruise experience. For a grand, small-ship cruise in the finest surroundings, with only just over 100 other couples as neighbors, this ship is very difficult to beat. All gratuities are included, and no further tipping is allowed (the hotel staff receive 15 per cent of all fares paid gross by passengers).

ms Seabourn Pride ★★★★★+

OPERATES

*7- AND 14-DAY EUROPE AND
SOUTH PACIFIC CRUISES*

Cruise Line	Seabourn Cruise Line	Swimming Pools (outside)	1 (+ 1 aft marina-pool)
Gross Tonnage	9,975	(inside)	0
Builder	Seebeckwerft (Germany)	Whirlpools 3	Gymnasium Yes
Original Cost	$50 million	Sauna/Steam Room Yes/Yes	Massage Yes
Christened By	Mrs Shirley Temple Black	Self-Service Launderette	Yes
Entered Service	Dec 1988	Movie Theater/Seats No	Library Yes
Interior Design	Yran & Storbraaten	Watersports Facilities	Aft platform, enclosed
Country of Registry	Norway		marina pool, banana boat, pedalos,
Tel No 131-1351 Fax No	131-1352		scuba, snorkel, windsurf, waterski
Length (ft/m)	439.9/134.10	Classification Society	Det Norske Veritas

Beam (ft/m) 62.9/19.20	Draft (ft/m) 16.8/5.15	
Propulsion/Propellers	diesel (5,355kW)/2 (CP)	

RATINGS	SCORE
Ship: Condition/Cleanliness	9.2
Ship: Space/Flow/Comfort	9.3
Ship: Facilities	9.0
Ship: Decor/Furnishings	8.9
Ship: Fitness/Watersports Facilities	9.2
Cabins: Comfort/Facilities	9.4
Cabins: Software	9.0
Food: Dining Room/Cuisine	9.0
Food: Buffets/Informal Dining	9.0
Food: Quality of Ingredients	9.2
Service: Dining Room	8.7
Service: Bars	9.0
Service: Cabins	9.2
Cruise: Entertainment/Lecture Program	9.0
Cruise: Hospitality Standard	9.1
OVERALL RATING	136.2

Decks 6	Crew	140
Pass. Capacity (basis 2) 204	(all berths) 204
Pass. Space Ratio (basis 2) 48.8	(all berths) 48.8
Officers	Norwegian
Total Cabins	106
Size Range (sq ft/m)	277-575/25.7-53.4
Outside Cabins 106	Inside Cabins 0
Single Cabins	0
Balcony Cabins 6	Wheelchair Cabins 4
Cabin Current	110/220 AC
Refrigerator	All cabins
Cabin TV Yes VCR	Yes
Dining Rooms	1
Sittings	Open (+in-cabin dining)
Elevators	3
Casino Yes Slot Machines	Yes

+ *Seabourn Pride* and *Seabourn Spirit* are strikingly sleek ships with a handsome profile and swept-back, rounded lines. They each have two fine mahogany water taxis. They also feature an aft watersports platform and marina, used in suitably calm warm water areas. There is a wide central passageway throughout the accommodation areas. Inviting, sumptuous public areas have warm colors. Fine quality interior fixtures, fittings and fabrics combine to present an outstanding, elegant decor, color combinations and artwork. All-outside cabins (Seabourn calls them suites) are comfortably large, and beautifully equipped with everything, including refrigerator, personal safe, personalized stationery, and large walk-in illuminated closet with wooden hangers. Beautiful blond wood cabinetry has softly rounded edges. Cabin doors are neatly angled away from passageway. Large, marble bathrooms have two washbasins, decent-sized bathtub, plenty of storage areas, 100% cotton towels and bathrobe.

For ultimate privacy the two Owner's Suites (001/002) offer a superbly private living environment. Each has a walk-in closet plus a second closet, one full bathroom and a second room with toilet and washbasin (for guests), and butler service. There's also a forward-facing balcony, complete with sun lounge chairs and wooden drinks table. These are secluded (good for nude sunbathing). The living area has ample bookshelf space (included is a complete edition of *Encyclopedia Britannica*), refrigerator and drinks cabinet, television and VCR

ms Seabourn Spirit ★★★★★+

OPERATES

VARIOUS 7- AND 14-DAY EUROPE
AND ORIENT CRUISES

Cruise Line		Seabourn Cruise Line
Gross Tonnage		9,975
Builder		Seebeckwerft (Germany)
Original Cost		$50 million
Christened By		Mrs Audun Brynestad
Entered Service		Nov 1989
Interior Design		Yran & Storbraaten
Country of Registry		Norway
Tel No	131-0464	Fax No	131-0527
Length (ft/m)		439.9/134.10
Beam (ft/m)	62.9/19.20	Draft (ft/m)	16.8/5.15
Propulsion/Propellers		diesel (5,355kW)/2 (CP)
Decks	6	Crew	140
Pass. Capacity (basis 2) 204		(all berths) 204
Pass. Space Ratio (basis 2) 48.8		(all berths) 48.8
Officers		Norwegian
Total Cabins		106
Size Range (sq ft/m)		277-575/25.7-53.4
Outside Cabins	106	Inside Cabins	0
Single Cabins		0
Balcony Cabins	6	Wheelchair Cabins	4
Cabin Current		110/220 AC
Refrigerator		All cabins
Cabin TV	Yes	VCR	Yes
Dining Rooms		1
Sittings		Open (+in-cabin dining)
Elevators		3
Casino	Yes	Slot Machines	Yes

Swimming Pools (outside)		1 (+ aft marina-pool)
(inside)			0
Whirlpools	3	Gymnasium	Yes
Sauna/Steam Room Yes/Yes		Massage	Yes
Self-Service Launderette			Yes
Movie Theater/Seats	No	Library	Yes
Watersports Facilities		Aft platform, enclosed
	marina pool, banana boat, pedalos,
	cuba, snorkel, windsurf, waterski
Classification Society		Det Norske Veritas

RATINGS	SCORE
Ship: Condition/Cleanliness	9.2
Ship: Space/Flow/Comfort	9.3
Ship: Facilities	9.0
Ship: Decor/Furnishings	8.9
Ship: Fitness/Watersports Facilities	9.2
Cabins: Comfort/Facilities	9.4
Cabins: Software	9.0
Food: Dining Room/Cuisine	9.0
Food: Buffets/Informal Dining	9.0
Food: Quality of Ingredients	9.2
Service: Dining Room	8.7
Service: Bars	9.0
Service: Cabins	9.2
Cruise: Entertainment/Lecture Program	9.0
Cruise: Hospitality Standard	9.1
OVERALL RATING	136.2

(there's a second television in the bedroom), four-person dining table, and large circular glass coffee table. All windows as well as the door to the balcony have electric blinds, and a complete blackout is possible in both bedroom and living room. However, the telephone system to call the butler is archaic and difficult to master.

— No wrap-around outdoor promenade deck. Deck lounge chairs are plastic. Deck beverage service is spotty (obtaining champagne for the Jacuzzi, for example, has proved an impossible task in the past). No seat cushions on the wooden chairs at the indoor/outdoor café. There's only one dryer in the self-service launderette. Ceilings are very plain. Drinks are extra (except at beginning of the cruise, when your refrigerator is stocked gratis), but they are low-priced.

Dining Marble and carpet dining room features portholes and elegant decor, but is not as intimate as on the Sea Goddesses. Culinary excellence prevails, however, and both food quality and presentation are outstanding. Menus are not repeated, even on long cruises. Special orders are most welcome, and caviar is always available. Service is near impeccable.

Other Comments Not for the budget-minded, these ships are for those desiring the utmost in supremely elegant, stylish, small-ship surroundings (they are too small for long voyages in open waters, however). Utterly civilized cruising. Gratuities are included, and no further tipping is allowed.

ss SeaBreeze I ★★★

OPERATES
7-DAY CARIBBEAN CRUISES
(YEAR-ROUND)

Cruise Line	Dolphin Cruise Line	Casino Yes	Slot Machines Yes
Former Names	Federico "C"/Royale	Swimming Pools (outside) 1	(inside) 0
Gross Tonnage	21,900	Whirlpools 3	Gymnasium Yes
Builder	Ansaldo Sestri-Ponente (Italy)	Sauna/Steam Room No/No	Massage Yes
Original Cost	n/a	Self-Service Launderette	No
Christened By	n/a	Movie Theater/Seats	Yes/110
Entered Service	Mar 1958/Mar 1989	Library	No
Interior Design	A&M Katzourakis	Children's Facilities	Yes
Country of Registry	Bahamas	Watersports Facilities	None
Tel No 133-6354 Fax No	133-6354	Classification Society	Lloyd's Register
Length (ft/m)	605.6/184.61		
Beam (ft/m) 78.9/24.06 Draft (ft/m)	29.0/8.84	**RATINGS**	**SCORE**
Propulsion	steam turbine (21,350kW)	Ship: Condition/Cleanliness	6.1
Propellers	2 (FP)	Ship: Space/Flow/Comfort	5.8
Decks 8 Crew	410	Ship: Decor/Furnishings	6.3
Pass. Capacity (basis 2) 842 (all berths)	1,250	Ship: Fitness Facilities	4.3
Pass. Space Ratio (basis 2) 26.0 (all berths)	17.5	Cabins: Comfort/Facilities	6.3
Officers	Greek	Cabins: Software	6.5
Total Cabins	421	Food: Dining Room/Cuisine	7.1
Size Range (sq ft/m)	65-258/6.0-24.0	Food: Buffets/Informal Dining	6.7
Outside Cabins 263 Inside Cabins	158	Food: Quality of Ingredients	6.5
Single Cabins	2	Service: Dining Room	6.8
Balcony Cabins 0 Wheelchair Cabins	0	Service: Bars	6.9
Cabin Current	110/220 AC	Service: Cabins	7.1
Refrigerator	No	Cruise: Entertainment	6.2
Cabin TV No VCR	No	Cruise: Activities Program	6.6
Dining Rooms 1 Sittings	2	Cruise: Hospitality Standard	6.7
Elevators	4	OVERALL RATING	95.9

+ Classic old former ocean liner styling still looks decent, and has a forthright white profile and sea-wave stripes in the center of her hull. Sports a neat sail-cloth canopy over aft outdoor area. The public rooms are bright and cheerful, and tastefully decorated, although there are lots of mirrored and chromed surfaces. There is a wide variety of cabins and many different configurations to choose from. Many cabins can accommodate five—ideal for families with children. Drawer space is limited but closet space is good. There's no real finesse, but the staff are very willing to please, and they're quite attentive, for a budget operation.

— Open deck and sunning space on this high density ship is quite limited, and thus extremely crowded when full. Has an awkward layout, a carry-over from her former three-class ocean liner nights, hinders passenger flow. Steep passenger gangway in some ports. She's getting too old and should be retired.

Dining The dining room has bright decor, but tables are much too close together for serving comfort. There are, however, several tables for two. Both food and service are very good for the price paid.

Other Comments This ship has plenty of life and atmosphere, is quite comfortable, caters well to families and remains very good value for a first cruise experience, but she is getting old.

ms Seaward ★★★★

OPERATES

7-DAY CARIBBEAN CRUISES
(YEAR-ROUND)

Cruise Line	Norwegian Cruise Line		
Former Names	-		
Gross Tonnage	42,276		
Builder	Wartsila (Finland)		
Original Cost	$120 million		
Christened By	Ms Greta Weiss		
Entered Service	Jun 1988		
Interior Design	Robert Tillberg		
Country of Registry	Bahamas		
Tel No 110-4601	Fax No	110-4602	
Length (ft/m)	708.6/216.00		
Beam (ft/m) 95.1/29.00	Draft (ft/m)	22.9/7.00	
Propulsion	diesel (21,120kW)		
Propellers	2 (CP)		
Decks 9	Crew	630	
Pass. Capacity (basis 2) 1,534	(all berths) 1,798		
Pass. Space Ratio (basis 2) 27.5	(all berths) 23.5		
Officers	Norwegian		
Total Cabins	767		
Size Range (sq ft/m)	110-270/10.2-25.0		
Outside Cabins 486	Inside Cabins	281	
Single Cabins	0		
Balcony Cabins 0	Wheelchair Cabins	4	
Cabin Current	110 AC		
Refrigerator	Category 1/2/3 only		
Cabin TV Yes	VCR	No	
Dining Rooms 2	Sittings	2	
Elevators	6		

Casino	Yes	Slot Machines	Yes
Swimming Pools (outside) 2		(inside)	0
Whirlpools	2	Gymnasium	Yes
Sauna/Steam Room Yes/No		Massage	Yes
Self-Service Launderette			No
Movie Theater/Seats			No
Library			No
Children's Facilities			No
Watersports Facilities			None
Classification Society		Det Norske Veritas	

RATINGS	SCORE
Ship: Condition/Cleanliness	8.0
Ship: Space/Flow/Comfort	7.9
Ship: Decor/Furnishings	7.8
Ship: Fitness Facilities	7.8
Cabins: Comfort/Facilities	7.6
Cabins: Software	6.2
Food: Dining Room/Cuisine	7.5
Food: Buffets/Informal Dining	7.1
Food: Quality of Ingredients	6.3
Service: Dining Room	7.4
Service: Bars	7.5
Service: Cabins	7.2
Cruise: Entertainment	8.0
Cruise: Activities Program	7.1
Cruise: Hospitality Standard	7.5
OVERALL RATING	110.9

+ Fine teakwood outdoor wrap-around promenade deck. The interior decor is designed to remind you of sea and sky: coral, blue and mauve are the predominant colors. There is an excellent gymnasium/fitness center. Striking two-deck-high lobby has a crystal and water sculpture. Has two glass-walled stairways. Lovely Crystal Court two-deck-high lobby. Fine theater-showroom provides large-scale dazzle shows. The most intimate place is the mahogany-paneled Oscar's Lounge. The cabins are of an average size for a 7-day cruise ship, tastefully appointed, and quite comfortable. Hairdryers are included in bathroom.

— Has tinny steps on stairways. There are too many unnecessary announcements.

Dining The two main dining rooms are quite homely, with pastel decor. The cuisine, for a mass-market ship, ranges from adequate to quite good, no more, although it has been improved. The emphasis is on meat dishes, with heavy sauces, and overcooked vegetables. However, fish and fowl are good. Nothing arrives hot at tableside. The service is, on the whole, adequate. The selection of wines is good, but breakfast and luncheon buffets are not.

Other Comments This angular, yet attractive ship with contemporary European cruise-ferry profile has a well-raked bow, and sleek mast and funnel. This ship is well designed, with good passenger flow. It provides a good first-cruise experience, but there's little finesse.

tss Seawind Crown ★★★+

Cruise Line	Seawind Cruise Line	Casino	Yes	Slot Machines Yes
Former Names	Vasco da Gama/	Swimming Pools (outside) 2		(inside) 0
	Infante Dom Henrique	Whirlpools	0	Gymnasium Yes
Gross Tonnage	24,568	Sauna/Steam Room Yes/No		Massage Yes
Builder	Cockerill-Ougree (Belgium)	Self-Service Launderette		No
Original Cost	n/a	Movie Theater/Seats		Yes/208
Christened By	n/a	Library		Yes
Entered Service	Sep 1961/Oct 1991	Children's Facilities		Yes
Interior Design	Kohnemann/Schindler	Watersports Facilities		None
Country of Registry	Panama	Classification Society		Lloyd's Register

Tel No 133-1251 Fax No 133-1252	
Length (ft/m)	641.6/195.59
Beam (ft/m) 84.4/25.73 Draft (ft/m) 26.9/8.20	
Propulsion	steam turbine (16,180kW)
Propellers	2 (FP)
Decks 8 Crew	311
Pass. Capacity (basis 2) 728 (all berths) 823	
Pass. Space Ratio (basis 2) 33.4 (all berths) 29.8	
Officers	Greek
Total Cabins	367
Size Range (sq ft/m)	118-560/11.0-52.0
Outside Cabins 246 Inside Cabins	121
Single Cabins	6
Balcony Cabins 2 Wheelchair Cabins	2
Cabin Current 220 AC Refrigerator	Yes
Cabin TV Yes VCR	No
Dining Rooms 2 Sittings	2
Elevators	4

RATINGS	SCORE
Ship: Condition/Cleanliness	6.7
Ship: Space/Flow/Comfort	7.5
Ship: Decor/Furnishings	7.6
Ship: Fitness Facilities	6.2
Cabins: Comfort/Facilities	6.7
Cabins: Software	7.1
Food: Dining Room/Cuisine	7.3
Food: Buffets/Informal Dining	6.2
Food: Quality of Ingredients	6.6
Service: Dining Room	6.6
Service: Bars	6.3
Service: Cabins	6.6
Cruise: Entertainment	6.1
Cruise: Activities Program	5.6
Cruise: Hospitality Standard	7.0
OVERALL RATING	100.1

+ Handsome profile for this former long-distance line. Extensively refurbished. Has a long foredeck, rakish bow, and teak promenade decks (one outdoor, one covered). Surprisingly spacious, classic vessel. Mix of old-world elegance and contemporary features. Host of public rooms feature tasteful decor and pastel tones. Has a chapel and well-equipped hospital. Fine wood paneling and trim. Spacious foyers. Bavarian-style taverna. Wide assortment of cabins; some with queen-, double- or twin beds, some with upper/lower berths. All cabins have excellent closet and drawer space, refrigerator, hairdryer, cotton bathrobes and towels. The suites (they really are suites) are huge. Sports facilities include indoor squash courts.

— Emergency drill conducted in six languages. Smokers are everywhere. Pleasant movie theater, but seats should be staggered. Announcements in several languages are irritating. Very poor library. Disorganised embarkation.

Dining The two dining rooms are quite comfortable, and both food and service are good considering the cruise fare charged. There are few tables for two. Food budget is quite low. Limited selection of breads, cheeses and fruits.

Other Comments There is a multi-national passenger mix on each cruise, with large contigents of Brazilians and North Americans.

ms Seawing ★★★

OPERATES

6 AND 13-DAY MEDITERRANEAN
CRUISES

Cruise Line			Airtours Cruises
Former Names			Southward
Gross Tonnage			16,607
Builder		Cantieri Navale Del Tirreno	
		et Riuniti (Italy)	
Original Cost	n/a	Christened By	n/a
Entered Service		Nov 1971/Mar 1995	
Interior Design			Tage Wandborg
Country of Registry			Bahamas
Tel No	110-4165	Fax No	110-4165
Length (ft/m)			535.7/163.30
Beam (ft/m)	74.7/22.79	Draft (ft/m)	21.3/6.50
Propulsion			diesel (13,400kW)
Propellers			2 (CP)
Decks	7	Crew	320
Pass. Capacity (basis 2) 754		(all berths) 976	
Pass. Space Ratio (basis 2) 22.0		(all berths) 17.0	
Officers			Norwegian
Total Cabins			377
Size Range (sq ft/m)			90-256/8.3-23.7
Outside Cabins	262	Inside Cabins	115
Single Cabins			0
Balcony Cabins	0	Wheelchair Cabins	0
Cabin Current			110 AC
Refrigerator			Category 1/2 only
Cabin TV	No	VCR	No
Dining Rooms	1	Sittings	2
Elevators			4

Casino	Yes	Slot Machines	Yes
Swimming Pools (outside) 1		(inside)	0
Whirlpools	0	Gymnasium	Yes
Sauna/Steam Room Yes/No		Massage	Yes
Self-Service Launderette			No
Movie Theater/Seats			Yes/198
Library			Yes
Children's Facilities			No
Watersports Facilities			None
Classification Society		Det Norske Veritas	

RATINGS	SCORE
Ship: Condition/Cleanliness	6.7
Ship: Space/Flow/Comfort	6.6
Ship: Decor/Furnishings	7.0
Ship: Fitness Facilities	5.6
Cabins: Comfort/Facilities	6.2
Cabins: Software	6.7
Food: Dining Room/Cuisine	6.6
Food: Buffets/Informal Dining	6.2
Food: Quality of Ingredients	6.1
Service: Dining Room	7.1
Service: Bars	7.0
Service: Cabins	7.1
Cruise: Entertainment	6.5
Cruise: Activities Program	6.7
Cruise: Hospitality Standard	6.8
OVERALL RATING	98.9

+ Has a good selection of comfortable public rooms with bright, contemporary decor. Perhaps the favorite is the nightclub, set high atop the forward mast. Also has a balconied theater. Families with children will find lots to do. Ten suites are quite spacious, and well-equipped, and have full bathtubs; other cabins are compact but clean and tidy, with adequate closet space for these one-week cruises, but not for longer. Airtours provides good value for money with these cruises designed for the young at heart.

— Cabins are not assigned until embarkation. High-density ship means crowds and lines for buffets, embarkation, and disembarkation. Open deck and sunning space limited. Sightlines in the showroom are poor. Too many repetitive announcements. Rowdy ship with lots of children running around during holiday sailings. "Blue coats" provide the entertainment.

Dining Dining room is charming, with warm colors. The food is adequate (for the price), but basic fare. Bread and fruit selections are poor. Service and ambiance are both informal. Extra charge for room service menu items. The wine list is decent, and so are the prices.

Other Comments This ship provides all the right ingredients for an active, fun-filled short cruise vacation for sun-loving couples and families at the right price, tailored specifically to the UK family cruise market (on-board currency is UK£ Sterling).

ms Sensation ★★★★

OPERATES
*7-DAY CARIBBEAN CRUISES
(YEAR-ROUND)*

Cruise Line		Carnival Cruise Lines
Former Names	n/a	Gross Tonnage 70,367
Builder		Kvaerner Masa-Yards (Finland)
Original Cost		$300 million
Christened By		Geri Donnelly, Vicki Freed,
		Roberta Jacoby, Cheri Weinstein
Entered Service		Nov 1993
Interior Design		Joe Farcus
Country of Registry		Liberia
Tel No	134-1372	Fax No 134-1373
Length (ft/m)		855.0/260.60
Beam (ft/m) 104.0/31.40	Draft (ft/m)	25.9/7.90
Propulsion		diesel-electric (42,240kW)
Propellers		2 (CP)
Decks	10 Crew	920
Pass. Capacity (basis 2) 2,040		(all berths) 2,594
Pass. Space Ratio (basis 2) 34.4		(all berths) 26.7
Officers		Italian
Total Cabins		1,020
Size Range (sq ft/m)		185-421/17.0-39.0
Outside Cabins	620 Inside Cabins	402
Single Cabins		0
Balcony Cabins		54
Wheelchair Cabins		20
Cabin Current		110 AC
Refrigerator		Category 11/12 only
Cabin TV	Yes VCR	No
Dining Rooms	2 Sittings	2

Elevators			14
Casino	Yes	Slot Machines	Yes
Swimming Pools (outside) 3		(inside)	0
Whirlpools	6	Gymnasium	Yes
Sauna/Steam Room Yes/Yes		Massage	Yes
Self-Service Launderette			Yes
Movie Theater/Seats	No	Library	Yes
Children's Facilities			Yes
Watersports Facilities			None
Classification Society			Lloyd's Register

RATINGS	SCORE
Ship: Condition/Cleanliness	9.0
Ship: Space/Flow/Comfort	8.1
Ship: Decor/Furnishings	8.2
Ship: Fitness Facilities	7.8
Cabins: Comfort/Facilities	7.6
Cabins: Software	7.4
Food: Dining Room/Cuisine	6.8
Food: Buffets/Informal Dining	6.5
Food: Quality of Ingredients	5.6
Service: Dining Room	7.1
Service: Bars	7.2
Service: Cabins	6.5
Cruise: Entertainment	8.2
Cruise: Activities Program	7.7
Cruise: Hospitality Standard	6.3
OVERALL RATING	110.0

+ Has a dramatic six-deck-high atrium, topped by a large colored-glass dome and an artistic centerpiece. Expansive open deck areas and an excellent health spa including a large gymnasium with the latest high-tech muscle machines. Public entertainment lounges, bars and clubs galore, with something for everyone. Dazzling colors and design themes in handsome public rooms connected by wide indoor boulevards. $1 million art collection, much of it bright and vocal. The library is a lovely room, but few books. The Michelangelo Lounge is a creative thinker's delight, while Fingers Lounge is sheer sensory travel. Lavish multi-tiered showroom and high-energy razzle-dazzle shows. Dramatic three-deck-high glass-enclosed health spa. Huge casino has non-stop action. 28 outside suites have whirlpool tubs. Standard cabins are of a decent size and have ample closet and drawer space.

— Sensory overkill. Large shop, poor merchandise. Too many announcements. Expect long lines for embarkation, disembarkation, buffets, and shore tenders. Aggressive hustling for drinks by bar waiters is irritating, as are drinks in plastic glasses.

Dining Two large dining rooms are noisy. Programmed service and so-so food.

Other Comments This ship will entertain you well, with sensory overkill, like a video game parlor. (See also comments for *Imagination* and other Carnival ships.)

ms Shota Rustaveli ★★+

OPERATES
VARIOUS EUROPE CRUISES

Cruise Line	Black Sea Shipping	Casino	No	Slot Machines	No
Former Names	-	Swimming Pools (outside) 2	(inside)	0
Gross Tonnage	20,499	Whirlpools	0	Gymnasium	Yes
Builder	VEB Mathias Thesen (Germany)	Sauna/Steam Room Yes/No	Massage	Yes
Original Cost	n/a	Self-Service Launderette	Yes
Christened By	n/a	Movie Theater/Seats	Yes/130
Entered Service	Jun 1968	Library	Yes
Interior Design	Shipyard	Children's Facilities	Yes
Country of Registry	Ukraine	Watersports Facilities	None
Tel No 140-0253 Fax No 140-0253		Classification Society	RS

Length (ft/m)	576.6/175.77
Beam (ft/m) 77.4/23.60 Draft (ft/m) 26.5/8.09	
Propulsion	diesel (15,700kW)
Propellers	2 (CP)
Decks 8 Crew	350
Pass. Capacity (basis 2) 493 (all berths) 602	
Pass. Space Ratio (basis 2) 41.4 (all berths) 34.0	
Officers	Russian/Ukrainian
Total Cabins	249
Size Range (sq ft/m)	n/a
Outside Cabins 244 Inside Cabins	5
Single Cabins	0
Balcony Cabins	0
Wheelchair Cabins	0
Cabin Current 220 AC Refrigerator	No
Cabin TV No VCR	No
Dining Rooms 3 Sittings	2
Elevators	3

RATINGS	SCORE
Ship: Condition/Cleanliness	6.0
Ship: Space/Flow/Comfort	6.5
Ship: Decor/Furnishings	6.1
Ship: Fitness Facilities	5.1
Cabins: Comfort/Facilities	6.1
Cabins: Software	6.2
Food: Dining Room/Cuisine	5.7
Food: Buffets/Informal Dining	5.4
Food: Quality of Ingredients	5.6
Service: Dining Room	6.1
Service: Bars	6.6
Service: Cabins	7.3
Cruise: Entertainment	5.5
Cruise: Activities Program	5.4
Cruise: Hospitality Standard	6.1
OVERALL RATING	89.7

+ Good-looking, well-built traditional ship styling. Good teakwood decks and wrap-around open promenade. Good open deck space for sunning, with real wooden deck chairs. Nice inside swimming pool. Spacious interior with quite pleasing decor, although colors are a little dour. Lots of wood paneling and trim. Apart from some de-luxe cabins with private balconies, this ship has small but very comfortable all-outside cabins, with attractive wood accents, solid fixtures, and pleasing decor. Many portholes actually open—unusual in today's air-conditioned world of ships.

— Has a steep, narrow gangway in some ports. Spartan, dated decor. Expect lines for embarkation, disembarkation, buffets, and shore tenders.

Dining The dining room is quite comfortable. The food is quite good (though stodgy), but there is little choice. Limited selection of breads and fruits. Free carafes of wine for lunch and dinner. Service is attentive but somewhat inflexible.

Other Comments This ship, one of a group of five, was nicely renovated in 1991, and is often chartered to a European cruise-tour company. European cruise staff cater well to principally French- and Italian-speaking passengers. Good for the passenger on a low budget who doesn't expect any degree of luxury or finesse.

ms Silver Cloud ★★★★★

OPERATES
VARIOUS CRUISES WORLDWIDE

Cruise Line			Silversea Cruises
Former Names	n/a	Gross Tonnage	16,800
Builder			SEC/T. Mariotti (Italy)
Original Cost			$125 million
Christened By		Mrs Eugenia Beck Lefebvre	
Entered Service			Apr 1994
Interior Design			Yran & Storbraaten
Country of Registry			Bahamas
Tel No	130-6601	Fax No	130-6602
Length (ft/m)			514.4/155.80
Beam (ft/m) 70.62/21.40		Draft (ft/m)	17.3/5.30
Propulsion			diesel (11,700kW)
Propellers			2 (CP)
Decks	8	Crew	185
Pass. Capacity (basis 2) 296		(all berths) 315	
Pass. Space Ratio (basis 2) 56.7		(all berths) 53.3	
Officers			Italian
Total Cabins			148
Size Range (sq ft/m)		240-1,314/22.2-122.0	
Outside Cabins	148	Inside Cabins	0
Single Cabins			0
Balcony Cabins	110	Wheelchair Cabins	0
Cabin Current			110/220 AC
Refrigerator			All cabins
Cabin TV	Yes	VCR	Yes
Dining Rooms	1 (open seating+in-cabin dining)		
Elevators			4
Casino	Yes	Slot Machines	Yes

Swimming Pools (outside) 1		(inside)	0
Whirlpools	2	Gymnasium	Yes
Sauna/Steam Room Yes/Yes		Massage	Yes
Self-Service Launderette			Yes
Movie Theater/Seats			Yes/306
Library			Yes
Children's Facilities			No
Watersports Facilities		side platform, kayaks,	
Zodiacs, sailfish, snorkel, windsurf, waterski boats			
Classification Society			RINA

RATINGS	SCORE
Ship: Condition/Cleanliness	9.2
Ship: Space/Flow/Comfort	9.7
Ship: Decor/Furnishings	9.4
Ship: Fitness Facilities	8.6
Cabins: Comfort/Facilities	9.2
Cabins: Software	9.2
Food: Dining Room/Cuisine	8.7
Food: Buffets/Informal Dining	8.6
Food: Quality of Ingredients	8.6
Service: Dining Room	8.7
Service: Bars	8.5
Service: Cabins	9.2
Cruise: Entertainment	8.6
Cruise: Activities Program	8.3
Cruise: Hospitality Standard	8.7
OVERALL RATING	133.2

+ Sleek, handsome profile, rather like a small version of *Crystal Harmony*, or larger version of the Seabourn ships (*Silver Wind* has better fit and finish than *Silver Cloud*). Vertical stacking of public rooms aft and accommodations forward ensures quiet cabins. There is a teakwood wrap-around outdoor promenade deck, and an excellent, spacious outdoor pool deck. The interiors are well planned, with elegant decor and fine quality soft furnishings, accented by a gentle use of brass and fine woods and creative ceilings. Useful business center as well as a CD-ROM and hardback book library. Excellent two-level showroom with tiered seating.

All outside suites (75% of which have private teakwood balconies) have convertible queen-to-twin beds and are beautifully fitted out with just about everything, including huge floor-to-ceiling windows, large walk-in closets, dressing table, writing desk, stocked mini-bar, and fresh flowers. Marble-floored bathrooms have bathtub and plenty of towels. Personalized stationery, bathrobes and good amenities kit in all cabins. Top suites also have CD-players.

Good watersports facilities for use in warm weather areas. There is an outstanding amount of space per passenger, and no hint of a line anywhere. Excellent documentation is provided.

— Walk-in closets don't provide much hanging space (particularly for full-length items), and doors should open outward instead of inward. While cabin insulation above and below each

ms Silver Wind ★★★★★

OPERATES

VARIOUS CRUISES WORLDWIDE

Cruise Line		Silversea Cruises
Former Names	n/a	Gross Tonnage	16,927
Builder		Societa Esercizio Cantieri (Italy)
Original Cost		$125 million
Christened By		Mrs Patricia Lefebvre
Entered Service		Jan 1995
Interior Design		Yran & Storbraaten
Country of Registry		Italy
Tel No	115-2245	Fax No	115-2250
Length (ft/m)		514.4/155.80
Beam (ft/m) 70.62/21.40	Draft (ft/m)	17.3/5.30
Propulsion		diesel (11,700kW)
Propellers		2 (CP)
Decks	6	Crew	185
Pass. Capacity (basis 2) 296		(all berths) 315
Pass. Space Ratio (basis 2) 57.1		(all berths) 53.7
Officers		Italian
Total Cabins		148
Size Range (sq ft/m)		240-1,314/22.2-122.0
Outside Cabins	153	Inside Cabins	0
Single Cabins			0
Balcony Cabins	110	Wheelchair Cabins	2
Cabin Current		110/220 AC
Refrigerator		All cabins
Cabin TV	Yes	VCR	Yes
Dining Rooms	1 (open seating+in-cabin dining)
Elevators			4
Casino	Yes	Slot Machines	Yes

Swimming Pools (outside) 1	(inside)		0
Whirlpools	2	Gymnasium	Yes
Sauna/Steam Room Yes/Yes	Massage		Yes
Self-Service Launderette			Yes
Movie Theater/Seats			Yes/306
Library			Yes
Children's Facilities			No
Watersports Facilities		side platform, kayaks,
Zodiacs, sailfish, snorkel, windsurf, waterski boats
Classification Society			RINA

RATINGS	SCORE
Ship: Condition/Cleanliness	9.4
Ship: Space/Flow/Comfort	9.7
Ship: Decor/Furnishings	9.4
Ship: Fitness Facilities	8.6
Cabins: Comfort/Facilities	9.2
Cabins: Software	9.2
Food: Dining Room/Cuisine	8.7
Food: Buffets/Informal Dining	8.6
Food: Quality of Ingredients	8.6
Service: Dining Room	8.7
Service: Bars	8.5
Service: Cabins	9.2
Cruise: Entertainment	8.6
Cruise: Activities Program	8.3
Cruise: Hospitality Standard	8.7
OVERALL RATING	133.4

cabin is good, insulation between cabins could be improved, and a privacy curtain should be installed. Spa areas need improvement, and the tiled decor is bland and uninviting. The shorter itineraries are too busy, with not enough days at sea. The self-service launderette is poor and simply not large enough for longer cruises.

Dining Lovely dining room has an arched gazebo center ceiling. Set with fine Limoges china and well-balanced flatware, under a stunning, wavy ceiling. Features 24-hour in-suite dining service, but the balcony tables are too low for outdoor dining. Good dining throughout the ship, with choice of formal and informal areas, although the cuisine and presentation are simply not up to the standards of products like *Sea Goddess* or *Seabourn*. Wines are included for lunch and dinner, a special connoisseur's list is available (at extra charge) for those who enjoy good wines. There is also 24-hour in-cabin dining service (full course by course dinners are available).

Other Comments Managed and operated by "V" Ships, the company that created Sitmar Cruises some years ago. With no pressure, no hype, and a good staff to pamper you, it's a pleasure to cruise on these two ships. Port taxes and insurance are extra, but gratuities are included, and, refreshingly, no further tipping, anywhere on board, is allowed.

tss Sky Princess ★★★★+

OPERATES
*7-DAY ALASKA AND CARIBBEAN
CRUISES*

Cruise Line	Princess Cruises	Casino Yes	Slot Machines Yes
Former Names	Fairsky	Swimming Pools (outside) 3	(inside) 0
Gross Tonnage	46,314	Whirlpools 1	Gymnasium Yes
Builder	C.N.I.M. (France)	Sauna/Steam Room Yes/No	Massage Yes
Original Cost	$156 million	Self-Service Launderette	Yes
Christened By	Mrs Jenny Ueberroth	Movie Theater/Seats	Yes/237
Entered Service	May 1984	Library	Yes
Interior Design	Giacomo Mortola	Children's Facilities	Yes
Country of Registry	Great Britain	Watersports Facilities	None
Tel No 144-2264 Fax No 144-2266		Classification Society	Lloyd's Register
Length (ft/m)	788.6/240.39		

RATINGS	SCORE
Beam (ft/m) 91.3/27.84 Draft (ft/m) 26.7/8.15	

Propulsion steam turbine (21,700kW)	Ship: Condition/Cleanliness 8.1
Propellers 2 (CP)	Ship: Space/Flow/Comfort 8.0
Decks 11 Crew 550	Ship: Decor/Furnishings 8.1
Pass. Capacity (basis 2) 1,200 (all berths) 1,350	Ship: Fitness Facilities 7.7
Pass. Space Ratio (basis 2) 38.5 (all berths) 34.3	Cabins: Comfort/Facilities 8.2
Officers British	Cabins: Software 8.2
Total Cabins 600	Food: Dining Room/Cuisine 7.6
Size Range (sq ft/m) 169-520/15.7-48.3	Food: Buffets/Informal Dining 7.2
Outside Cabins 385 Inside Cabins 215	Food: Quality of Ingredients 7.0
Single Cabins 0	Service: Dining Room 7.6
Balcony Cabins 10 Wheelchair Cabins 10	Service: Bars 7.7
Cabin Current 110 AC	Service: Cabins 7.8
Refrigerator Category AA and B only	Cruise: Entertainment 8.1
Cabin TV Yes VCR No	Cruise: Activities Program 7.7
Dining Rooms 2 Sittings 2	Cruise: Hospitality Standard 7.9
Elevators 6	OVERALL RATING 116.9

+ Well-designed contemporary vessel has short, sharply raked bow and swept-back funnel. First cruise ship to have steam turbine machinery since the *QE2* debuted in 1969. Comfortable, easy layout. Has a good enclosed promenade deck. Fine array of public rooms, including expansive shops. Improved showroom. Horizon Lounge restful at night. Popular Pizzeria. Split casino configuration. Good health spa. Has spacious and very comfortable, well-appointed cabins, with all the essentials, and good-sized showers. Outstanding are the large Lido Deck suites. Cabins have bathrobes for all passengers.

— No wrap-around outdoor promenade deck. Clean, bland, clinical minimalist interior decor lacks warmth. Veranda Café, a popular outdoor buffet area, is poorly designed. Long lines for embarkation, disembarkation, buffets, and shore tenders.

Dining Two dining rooms (both non-smoking) are brightly lit, and there are no tables for two, although decor is pleasant. Pasta dishes are good, but other food lacks quality, flair and presentation. The service, while quite attentive, is somewhat impersonal and superficial.

Other Comments This well-designed ship provides a well-balanced, pleasing cruise experience for the mature passenger, with plenty of space and little crowding.

ms Song of America ★★★★

OPERATES
7-DAY BERMUDA AND
CARIBBEAN CRUISES

Cruise Line	Royal Caribbean Cruises		
Former Names	-		
Gross Tonnage	37,584		
Builder	Wartsila (Finland)		
Original Cost	$140 million		
Christened By	Ms Beverly Sills		
Entered Service	Dec 1982		
Interior Design	Njal Eide		
Country of Registry	Norway		
Tel No	131-3507	Fax No	131-3507
Length (ft/m)			705.0/214.88
Beam (ft/m) 93.1/28.40	Draft (ft/m)		22.3/6.80
Propulsion			diesel (16,480kW)
Propellers			2 (CP)
Decks	11	Crew	535
Pass. Capacity (basis 2) 1,402		(all berths) 1,552	
Pass. Space Ratio (basis 2) 26.8		(all berths) 24.2	
Officers			Norwegian
Total Cabins			701
Size Range (sq ft/m)			120-425/11.0-39.5
Outside Cabins	406	Inside Cabins	295
Single Cabins			0
Balcony Cabins			0
Wheelchair Cabins			0
Cabin Current			110 AC
Refrigerator			Owner's suite only
Cabin TV	Yes	VCR	No
Dining Rooms	1	Sittings	2

Elevators			7
Casino	Yes	Slot Machines	Yes
Swimming Pools (outside) 2		(inside)	0
Whirlpools	0	Gymnasium	Yes
Sauna/Steam Room	Yes/No	Massage	Yes
Self-Service Launderette			No
Movie Theater/Seats	No	Library	Yes
Children's Facilities			No
Watersports Facilities			None
Classification Society			Det Norske Veritas

RATINGS	SCORE
Ship: Condition/Cleanliness	8.2
Ship: Space/Flow/Comfort	7.9
Ship: Decor/Furnishings	8.2
Ship: Fitness Facilities	7.8
Cabins: Comfort/Facilities	5.8
Cabins: Software	7.7
Food: Dining Room/Cuisine	6.8
Food: Buffets/Informal Dining	6.6
Food: Quality of Ingredients	7.1
Service: Dining Room	6.7
Service: Bars	6.5
Service: Cabins	6.1
Cruise: Entertainment	7.8
Cruise: Activities Program	7.6
Cruise: Hospitality Standard	7.4
OVERALL RATING	108.2

✛ Contemporary ship has rounded lines and sharply raked bow. Striking Viking Crown Lounge wrapped around funnel is the line's trademark, and incorporates a bar. Good open deck and sunning space. Beautifully polished wooden decks and rails. Has a good array of public rooms with musical-themed decor. Has conference center for meetings and group business. Better shopping center and casino. The Veranda Café has good flow. Attentive, polished service throughout.

— Dining room is large, but the low ceiling creates a high level of ambient noise. The cabins, and particularly the bathrooms, with their wrap-around shower curtains, are very, very small, yet most passengers seem happy with them. There are many irritating announcements.

Dining Madame Butterfly Dining Room has tables for four to eight (no tables for two). Service is consistently good and the dining operation efficient. French, Italian, Oriental, Caribbean or American themes each night. Food is of a generally high quality and portions are reasonable. Bottled water (extra cost) is pushed heavily; drinking water is not provided *unless requested.*

Other Comments In typical Royal Caribbean Cruises fashion, the ship caters superbly to passengers in the public entertainment rooms. Recommended for both first-time and repeat passengers and provides a consistently good product in very comfortable surroundings.

ms Song of Flower ★★★★★

OPERATES
VARIOUS CRUISES WORLDWIDE

Cruise Line		Radisson Seven Seas Cruises
Former Names		Explorer Starship
Gross Tonnage		8,282
Builder		Kmv (Norway)/Lloyd Werft (Germany)
Original Cost		n/a
Christened By		Ms Mamiko Matsunari
Entered Service		1986/Feb 1990
Interior Design		Yran & Storbraaten
Country of Registry		Norway
Tel No	131-0152	Fax No	131-0153
Length (ft/m)		407.4/124.20
Beam (ft/m)	52.4/16.00	Draft (ft/m)	16.0/4.90
Propulsion		diesel (5,500kW)
Propellers		2 (CP)
Decks	6	Crew	144
Pass. Capacity (basis 2) 214		(all berths) 214
Pass. Space Ratio (basis 2) 38.7		(all berths) 38.7
Officers		Norwegian
Total Cabins		107
Size Range (sq ft/m)		183-398/17.0-37.0
Outside Cabins	107	Inside Cabins	0
Single Cabins		0
Balcony Cabins		10
Wheelchair Cabins		0
Cabin Current	220 AC	Refrigerator	All cabins
Cabin TV	Yes	VCR	Yes
Dining Rooms	1	Sittings	Open
Elevators		2

Casino	Yes	Slot Machines	Yes
Swimming Pools (outside) 1		(inside)	0
Whirlpools	1	Gymnasium	Yes
Sauna/Steam Room Yes/No		Massage	Yes
Self-Service Launderette			No
Movie Theater/Seats	No	Library	Yes
Children's Facilities			No
Watersports Facilities		jet skis, snorkel equipment,
		waterski boat, windsurfers
Classification Society		Det Norske Veritas

RATINGS	SCORE
Ship: Condition/Cleanliness	9.0
Ship: Space/Flow/Comfort	9.2
Ship: Facilities	9.0
Ship: Decor/Furnishings	9.0
Ship: Fitness/Watersports Facilities	8.7
Cabins: Comfort/Facilities	9.0
Cabins: Software	9.0
Food: Dining Room/Cuisine	9.1
Food: Buffets/Informal Dining	9.0
Food: Quality of Ingredients	8.6
Service: Dining Room	8.6
Service: Bars	8.8
Service: Cabins	8.8
Cruise: Entertainment/Lecture Program	8.6
Cruise: Hospitality Standard	9.4
OVERALL RATING	133.8

+ Excellent small cruise ship, with tall, twin funnels that give a somewhat squat profile. Well maintained and cared for, and spotlessly clean. Good sheltered open deck and sunning space. Elegant interior, with warm decor and colors. Fine furnishings and fabrics throughout. Has a compact health spa. Excellent tiered showroom is very comfortable, with good sightlines. Ten suites are really elegant; ten are strictly no-smoking cabins; all others are well equipped. Superb closet and drawer space. Many have (very tiny) bathtubs. Passengers with disabilities should choose a cabin with a shower instead of a bath. Has a wonderful, warm, caring staff who really do anticipate your every need. Totally understated.

— The bow should be a little longer to give a sleeker appearance! Sadly, there are no in-cabin dining facilities for dinner.

Dining Charming dining room has warm colors and ambiance. Very creative food and presentation, with small portions. All alcoholic and non-alcoholic beverages included with the exception of some premium wines. Outstanding personal service from a warm, highly attentive staff. There are several tables for two, and plenty of space around each table.

Other Comments Outstanding, destination-intensive, yet relaxing cruise experience, delivered with style. Gratuities included, no further tipping allowed, but port charges extra.

ms Song of Norway ★★★+

OPERATES

*ALASKA AND MEXICAN
RIVIERA CRUISES*

Cruise Line	Royal Caribbean Cruises		
Former Names	-		
Gross Tonnage	23,005		
Builder	Wartsila (Finland)		
Original Cost	$13.5 million		
Christened By	Mrs Magnhild Borten		
Entered Service	Nov 1970		
Interior Design	Njal Eide		
Country of Registry	Norway		
Tel No	131-0562	Fax No	131-0562
Length (ft/m)			637.5/194.32
Beam (ft/m) 78.8/24.03		Draft (ft/m)	21.9/6.70
Propulsion			diesel (13,400kW)
Propellers			2 (CP)
Decks	8	Crew	423
Pass. Capacity (basis 2) 1,004		(all berths) 1,138	
Pass. Space Ratio (basis 2) 22.5		(all berths) 20.2	
Officers			Norwegian
Total Cabins			502
Size Range (sq ft/m)			120-266/11.0-24.7
Outside Cabins	325	Inside Cabins	177
Single Cabins			0
Balcony Cabins	0	Wheelchair Cabins	0
Cabin Current			110 AC
Refrigerator			Owner's suite only
Cabin TV	No	VCR	No
Dining Rooms	1	Sittings	2
Elevators			4

Casino	Yes	Slot Machines	Yes
Swimming Pools (outside) 1		(inside)	0
Whirlpools	0	Gymnasium	Yes
Sauna/Steam Room No/No		Massage	No
Self-Service Launderette			No
Movie Theater/Seats			No
Library			No
Children's Facilities			No
Watersports Facilities			None
Classification Society			Det Norske Veritas

RATINGS	SCORE
Ship: Condition/Cleanliness	7.4
Ship: Space/Flow/Comfort	6.7
Ship: Decor/Furnishings	7.0
Ship: Fitness Facilities	6.6
Cabins: Comfort/Facilities	5.8
Cabins: Software	7.7
Food: Dining Room/Cuisine	6.8
Food: Buffets/Informal Dining	6.6
Food: Quality of Ingredients	7.1
Service: Dining Room	6.7
Service: Bars	6.5
Service: Cabins	6.1
Cruise: Entertainment	7.8
Cruise: Activities Program	7.6
Cruise: Hospitality Standard	7.4
OVERALL RATING	103.8

+ Contemporary, but now dated seventies look with sleek lines, sharply raked bow and distinctive cantilevered Viking Crown Lounge high up around the ship's funnel. Has a polished wrap-around outdoor wood deck. Has a good, but now dated interior layout that has been well maintained. The Scandinavian decor is clean and bright. There is a good amount of open deck space, but it does get crowded when the ship is full, which is always. Good wood trim in passageways.

— This is a high-density ship with expansive open deck and sunning space that becomes cramped when full—OK in the seventies, but not today. Beautifully polished, though slippery, wooden decks. Narrow passageways. The cabins, which need refurbishing, are very small, and have very limited closet and drawer space. There are too many announcements.

Dining Attractive, but very noisy dining room. It is a good operation, but the food, while consistent, is not memorable. Service is generally good, but very robotic.

Other Comments Stretched in 1978. This ship caters to novice and repeat passengers with well-programmed flair, and consistently provides a fine-tuned cruise product in comfortable, but very crowded surroundings. For the same or similar cruise price, perhaps one should consider one of the company's newer megaships, where there is more space.

mv Southern Cross ★★★+

OPERATES

*AUSTRALASIA, EUROPE
AND MEDITERRANEAN CRUISES*

Cruise Line		CTC Cruise Lines
Former Names		Star/Ship Majestic, Sun Princess,
		Spirit of London
Gross Tonnage		17,270
Builder		Cantieri Navale Del Tirreno
		& Riuniti (Italy)
Original Cost		n/a
Christened By		Mrs Beatrice Marriott
Entered Service		Nov 1972/Mar 1995
Interior Design		A&M Katzourakis
Country of Registry		Bahamas
Tel No	110-4553	Fax No	110-4553
Length (ft/m)		536.0/163.40
Beam (ft/m)	81.4/24.82	Draft (ft/m)	21.3/6.52
Propulsion		diesel (13,450kW)
Propellers		2 (CP)
Decks	7	Crew	270
Pass. Capacity (basis 2)	720	(all berths)	982
Pass. Space Ratio (basis 2)	23.9	(all berths)	17.5
Officers		Ukrainian/European
Total Cabins		377
Size Range (sq ft/m)		99-237/9.0-22.0
Outside Cabins	255	Inside Cabins	122
Single Cabins		29
Balcony Cabins	0	Wheelchair Cabins	2
Cabin Current		220/110 AC
Refrigerator		No
Cabin TV	Yes	VCR	No

Dining Rooms	1	Sittings	2
Elevators			4
Casino	Yes	Slot Machines	Yes
Swimming Pools (outside)		1 (+children's pool)
Whirlpools	0	Gymnasium	Yes
Sauna/Steam Room	No/No	Massage	Yes
Self-Service Launderette			No
Movie Theater/Seats			Yes/186
Library	Yes	Children's Facilities	Yes
Classification Society		Lloyd's Register

RATINGS	SCORE
Ship: Condition/Cleanliness	7.1
Ship: Space/Flow/Comfort	6.6
Ship: Decor/Furnishings	7.2
Ship: Fitness Facilities	5.0
Cabins: Comfort/Facilities	6.6
Cabins: Software	7.0
Food: Dining Room/Cuisine	7.6
Food: Buffets/Informal Dining	7.1
Food: Quality of Ingredients	6.8
Service: Dining Room	7.5
Service: Bars	7.4
Service: Cabins	7.4
Cruise: Entertainment	6.7
Cruise: Activities Program	6.5
Cruise: Hospitality Standard	6.8
OVERALL RATING	103.3

+ Reasonable amount of open deck and sunning space for ship size, but is cramped when full. Interior decor features tasteful earth tones mixed with extensive use of reflective surfaces. Has comfortable public rooms, with pleasant, attractive decor and soft furnishings. The deluxe suites are quite spacious; other cabins are on the small side, but quite well equipped. Well-designed itineraries include plenty of sea days on longer voyages.

— Loud announcements are irritating. No cushion pads for deck lounge chairs. Antiquated cabin telephone system. The cabin walls are very thin, and there's little drawer space.

Dining Charming dining room with high ceiling has a light and airy feel, but is extremely noisy and tables are so close together. Better service than on CTC's other ships, due to increased standards of a catering concession. Although it's all done to a price, the quality of food and presentation is reasonably good. Limited choice of breads, cheeses and fruits. Buffets are good and presented well.

Other Comments The ship has a smart contemporary profile with rakish superstructure, and an unmistakable scarlet red hull. She will provide a comfortable cruise experience that's good value for money, in very informal, relaxed surroundings.

ms Sovereign of the Seas ★★★★+

OPERATES

3/4-DAY BAHAMAS CRUISES
(YEAR-ROUND)

Cruise Line	Royal Caribbean Cruises		
Former Names	-		
Gross Tonnage	73,192		
Builder	Chantiers de l'Atlantique (France)		
Original Cost	$183.5 million		
Christened By	Mrs Roslyn Carter		
Entered Service	Jan 1988		
Interior Design	Njal Eide		
Country of Registry	Norway		
Tel No	131-0711	Fax No	131-0711
Length (ft/m)			873.6/266.30
Beam (ft/m) 105.6/32.20	Draft (ft/m)	24.7/7.55	
Propulsion		diesel (21,844kW)	
Propellers			2 (CP)
Decks	12	Crew	808
Pass. Capacity (basis 2) 2,276		(all berths) 2,524	
Pass. Space Ratio (basis 2) 32.1		(all berths) 28.9	
Officers			Norwegian
Total Cabins			1,138
Size Range (sq ft/m)		120-446/11.0-41.5	
Outside Cabins	722	Inside Cabins	416
Single Cabins			0
Balcony Cabins	0	Wheelchair Cabins	10
Cabin Current			110 AC
Refrigerator		Category R/A only	
Cabin TV	Yes	VCR	No
Dining Rooms	2	Sittings	2
Elevators			18

Casino	Yes	Slot Machines	Yes
Swimming Pools (outside) 2		(inside)	0
Whirlpools	1	Gymnasium	Yes
Sauna/Steam Room Yes/No		Massage	Yes
Self-Service Launderette			No
Movie Theater/Seats		Yes-2/146 each	
Library			Yes
Children's Facilities			Yes
Watersports Facilities			None
Classification Society		Det Norske Veritas	

RATINGS	SCORE
Ship: Condition/Cleanliness	8.0
Ship: Space/Flow/Comfort	8.0
Ship: Decor/Furnishings	7.9
Ship: Fitness Facilities	7.6
Cabins: Comfort/Facilities	7.6
Cabins: Software	7.7
Food: Dining Room/Cuisine	7.9
Food: Buffets/Informal Dining	7.6
Food: Quality of Ingredients	7.1
Service: Dining Room	7.7
Service: Bars	7.6
Service: Cabins	7.6
Cruise: Entertainment	8.2
Cruise: Activities Program	7.9
Cruise: Hospitality Standard	8.0
OVERALL RATING	116.4

+ Handsome megaship has well-balanced profile, nicely rounded lines and high superstructure. Viking Crown Lounge wrapped around funnel has superb views. Has wraparound outdoor polished wood deck. Impressive array of spacious and elegant public rooms. Stunning five-deck-high Centrum lobby, with cascading stairways and two glass-walled elevators. Good two-level showroom and fine array of shops. Twelve suites on Bridge Deck are quite large and nicely furnished; other cabins are very small, but an arched window treatment gives illusion of greater space (almost all cabins convert to double-bed configuration). Good childrens' and teens' programs and counselors. The dress code is casual.

— Open deck space is adequate, no more. Awkward layout. Congested passenger flow in some areas. Cabins have little closet and drawer space (you'll need some "luggage engineering"). Too many announcements.

Dining Two dining rooms feature well-presented food and service, but there are no tables for two. Poor breads, rolls and fruit, but a good selection of light meals for the calorie-conscious, and a vegetarian menu is available. Decent wine list and prices. Staff are overly friendly.

Other Comments This floating resort provides a well-tuned yet somewhat impersonal cruise experience for upwards of 2,000 fellow passengers.

ms Splendour of the Seas ★★★★+

Cruise Line		Royal Caribbean Cruises
Former Names		-
Gross Tonnage		69,130
Builder	Chantiers de l'Atlantique (France)	
Original Cost		$325 million
Christened By		Lise Wilhelmsen
Entered Service		Mar 1996
Interior Design		Njal Eide
Country of Registry		Norway
Tel No	n/a Fax No	n/a
Length (ft/m)		867.0/264.20
Beam (ft/m) 105.0/32.00	Draft (ft/m)	24.5/7.46
Propulsion		diesel (40,200kW)
Propellers		2 (CP)
Decks	11 Crew	732
Pass. Capacity (basis 2) 1,804	(all berths) 2,064	
Pass. Space Ratio (basis 2) 38.3	(all berths) 33.4	
Officers		Norwegian
Total Cabins		902
Size Range (sq ft/m)	138-1,148/12.8-106.6	
Outside Cabins	575 Inside Cabins	327
Single Cabins		0
Balcony Cabins	231 Wheelchair Cabins	17
Cabin Current		110/220 AC
Refrigerator		Upper Grades only
Cabin TV	Yes VCR	Suites only
Dining Rooms	1 Sittings	2
Elevators		11

Casino	Yes	Slot Machines	Yes
Swimming Pools (outside)		2 (1 with sliding roof)	
Swimming Pools (inside)			0
Whirlpools	4	Gymnasium	Yes
Sauna/Steam Room Yes/Yes		Massage	Yes
Self-Service Launderette			No
Movie Theater/Seats	No	Library	Yes
Children's Facilities			Yes
Watersports Facilities			None
Classification Society		Det Norske Veritas	

RATINGS	SCORE
Ship: Condition/Cleanliness	9.3
Ship: Space/Flow/Comfort	9.1
Ship: Decor/Furnishings	9.2
Ship: Fitness Facilities	9.0
Cabins: Comfort/Facilities	8.6
Cabins: Software	8.7
Food: Dining Room/Cuisine	8.1
Food: Buffets/Informal Dining	7.7
Food: Quality of Ingredients	7.1
Service: Dining Room	7.9
Service: Bars	7.6
Service: Cabins	7.6
Cruise: Entertainment	8.5
Cruise: Activities Program	7.9
Cruise: Hospitality Standard	8.2
OVERALL RATING	124.5

+ Nicely raked. With engines midships, vibration and noise are kept low, and the ship's maximum 24-knot speed means she is well equipped for long distance itineraries. Expansive use of glass. Golfers should enjoy the 18-hole minature golf course (extra charge).

Stunning, colorful interior decor. Two entertainment decks. Tiered and balconied two-deck-high showlounge has excellent sightlines and comfortable seats; several large-scale shows are provided. Dazzling casino. A seven-deck-high atrium connects with the Viking Crown Lounge via glass-walled elevators. Library has over 2,000 books. Fine collection of artwork.

Standard cabins are a good size. All cabins have sitting area and beds converting to double configuration; ample closet and drawer space, not much space around the bed and bathroom showers are disappointing.

— As with any large ship, you can expect lines for embarkation, disembarkation, buffets, and shore excursions. Seventeen cabin categories are too many. No cabins for singles.

Dining Dramatic glass side walls in dining room. Large outdoor café and sizeable snack area. Menu choices much improved. Full vegetarian options. Good service. No decent caviar.

Other Comments A fine-tuned product. (See comments for sister ship *Legend of the Seas*.)

mv Star Pisces ★★★★+

OPERATES

*2- AND 3-DAY SOUTH-EAST ASIA
CRUISES (YEAR-ROUND)*

Cruise Line	Star Cruise		
Former Names	Kalypso		
Gross Tonnage	40,012		
Builder	Wartsila (Finland)		
Original Cost	SEK650 million		
Christened By	Ms Marianne Myrsten		
Entered Service	May 1990/May 1994		
Interior Design	Robert Tillberg/PM design		
Country of Registry	Panama		
Tel No 635-286122	Fax No	635-286111	
Length (ft/m)	579.3/176.6		
Beam (ft/m) 97.1/29.6	Draft (ft/m)	20.3/6.2	
Propulsion	diesel (23,760kW)		
Propellers	2 (CP)		
Decks 12	Crew	750	
Pass. Capacity (basis 2) 1,530	(all berths) 1,900		
Pass. Space Ratio (basis 2) 26.1	(all berths) 21.0		
Officers	Scandinavian		
Total Cabins	598		
Size Range (sq ft/m)	67-145/6.3-13.5		
Outside Cabins 258	Inside Cabins	340	
Single Cabins	0		
Balcony Cabins 0	Wheelchair Cabins	0	
Cabin Current 220 AC	Refrigerator	No	
Cabin TV Yes	VCR	No	
Dining Rooms	3 (+2 cafes)		
Sittings	1		
Elevators	5		

Casino Yes	Slot Machines	Yes	
Swimming Pools (outside) 1	(inside)	1	
Whirlpools 3	Gymnasium	Yes	
Sauna/Steam Room Yes/Yes	Massage	Yes	
Self-Service Launderette	No		
Movie Theater/Seats	Yes (2)/210 each		
Library	Yes		
Children's Facilities	Yes		
Watersports Facilities	None		
Classification Society	Det Norske Veritas		

RATINGS	SCORE
Ship: Condition/Cleanliness	8.3
Ship: Space/Flow/Comfort	7.7
Ship: Decor/Furnishings	8.4
Ship: Fitness Facilities	8.2
Cabins: Comfort/Facilities	6.0
Cabins: Software	7.6
Food: Dining Room/Cuisine	8.2
Food: Buffets/Informal Dining	7.7
Food: Quality of Ingredients	8.0
Service: Dining Room	7.8
Service: Bars	7.3
Service: Cabins	7.2
Cruise: Entertainment	7.5
Cruise: Activities Program	7.0
Cruise: Hospitality Standard	8.6
OVERALL RATING	115.5

+ Scandinavian design combined with a touch of the Orient. Helipad. Huge duty-free shopping center and supermarket. Large regal casino for VIPs with high, detailed ceiling (a second casino is for general use). Most cabins are very small, with just basic facilities. Superb health club for men. Many meeting rooms, conference auditoria and a business center. Children's facilities are extensive and include computers and educational rooms, play areas and a huge video machine section. Free ice cream for kids. Excellent Asian hospitality.

— High-density ship means crowded public rooms, and long lines for shore visits, buffets, embarkation, and disembarkation. Cabin insulation is poor and bathrooms are very small. Limited amount of open deck space.

Dining Seven restaurants provide a wide choice of cuisine and dining styles, and all feature very attentive service. This ship has a real Chinese Restaurant (Cantonese and Sichuan) with a Hong Kong chef; Japanese, including a sushi bar and private tatami rooms; Italian; Spice Island buffet restaurant for laksa, satay and hawker delights; and three other snack cafés.

Other Comments Skilfully converted into a cruise vessel specifically for the Asian family market. Has a low ticket price, but everything costs extra. Gratuities are prohibited. (See also comments for *Langkapuri Star Aquarius*.)

ARCADIA

ms Star Princess ★★★★+

OPERATES
VARIOUS ALASKA AND
CARIBBEAN CRUISES

Cruise Line	Princess Cruises	Casino Yes	Slot Machines Yes
Former Names	FairMajesty	Swimming Pools (outside) 3	(inside) 0
Gross Tonnage	63,564	Whirlpools 4	Gymnasium Yes
Builder	Chantiers de L'Atlantique (France)	Sauna/Steam Room Yes/No	Massage Yes
Original Cost	$200 million	Self-Service Launderette	Yes
Christened By	Ms Audrey Hepburn	Movie Theater/Seats	Yes/205
Entered Service	Mar 1989	Library	Yes
Interior Design	Ellerbe Becket	Children's Facilities	Yes
Country of Registry	Liberia	Watersports Facilities	None
Tel No 124-0247 Fax No	124-0236	Classification Society	Lloyd's Register
Length (ft/m)	805.7/245.60		
Beam (ft/m) 105.6/32.20 Draft (ft/m)	25.0/7.62	**RATINGS**	**SCORE**
Propulsion	diesel-electric (39,000kW)	Ship: Condition/Cleanliness	8.1
Propellers	2 (CP)	Ship: Space/Flow/Comfort	8.3
Decks 12 Crew	600	Ship: Decor/Furnishings	8.1
Pass. Capacity (basis 2) 1,470 (all berths)	1,620	Ship: Fitness Facilities	7.7
Pass. Space Ratio (basis 2) 43.2 (all berths)	39.2	Cabins: Comfort/Facilities	8.2
Officers	Italian	Cabins: Software	8.2
Total Cabins	735	Food: Dining Room/Cuisine	7.6
Size Range (sq ft/m)	180-530/16.7-49.2	Food: Buffets/Informal Dining	7.2
Outside Cabins 570 Inside Cabins	165	Food: Quality of Ingredients	7.0
Single Cabins	0	Service: Dining Room	7.6
Balcony Cabins 50 Wheelchair Cabins	10	Service: Bars	7.7
Cabin Current	110/220 AC	Service: Cabins	8.0
Refrigerator	All cabins	Cruise: Entertainment	8.1
Cabin TV Yes VCR	No	Cruise: Activities Program	7.7
Dining Rooms 1 Sittings	2	Cruise: Hospitality Standard	7.9
Elevators	9	OVERALL RATING	117.4

+ Innovative styling mixed with traditional shipboard features. Spacious public rooms have tasteful decor, and an excellent selection of artwork provides some warmth to what would otherwise be a clinical interior. Horseshoe-shaped balconied showroom. Three-deck-high foyer highlighted by kinetic sculpture. Neat wine bar and pizzeria. Characters Bar serves colorful drinks in jazzy glasses. In-pool bar. Multi-tiered main restaurant has two-deck-high center ceiling. Spacious, well-equipped cabins have large, modular bathrooms and plenty of closet, drawer and storage space. Bathrobes provided, as well as better amenities kits.

— No wrap-around outdoor promenade deck. Domed observation lounge is out of traffic flow. Poor outdoor promenade area. Expect lines for embarkation, disembarkation, shore tenders, and buffets. Poor sound insulation between cabins.

Dining Multi-tiered dining room has high center ceiling, but is noisy, and there are no tables for two. Food is adequate, but presentation is lacking. Good pasta dishes. Service is so-so, but could be much improved. Indoor-outdoor buffet restaurant is too small.

Other Comments Provides a traditional approach to cruising for repeat passengers who like a large ship, families, and some degree of anonymity.

Star/Ship Atlantic ★★★★

OPERATES

*3- AND 4-DAY BAHAMAS CRUISES
(YEAR-ROUND)*

Cruise Line	Premier Cruise Lines		
Former Names	Atlantic		
Gross Tonnage	35,143		
Builder	C.N.I.M. (France)		
Original Cost	$100 million		
Christened By	n/a		
Entered Service	Apr 1982/Jan 1989		
Interior Design	A&M Katzourakis		
Country of Registry	Liberia		
Tel No	-	Fax No	-
Length (ft/m)		671.9/204.81	
Beam (ft/m) 89.7/27.36	Draft (ft/m)	25.5/7.80	
Propulsion		diesel (22,070kW)	
Propellers		2 (CP)	
Decks	9	Crew	535
Pass. Capacity (basis 2) 972		(all berths) 1,600	
Pass. Space Ratio (basis 2) 36.1		(all berths) 21.9	
Officers		Greek	
Total Cabins		549	
Size Range (sq ft/m)		137-427/12.7-39.5	
Outside Cabins	380	Inside Cabins	169
Single Cabins		0	
Balcony Cabins	0	Wheelchair Cabins	Yes
Cabin Current	110 AC	Refrigerator	No
Cabin TV	No	VCR	No
Dining Rooms	1	Sittings	2
Elevators		4	
Casino	Yes	Slot Machines	Yes

Swimming Pools (outside) 1	(inside)		1
Whirlpools	3	Gymnasium	Yes
Sauna/Steam Room Yes/No	Massage		Yes
Self-Service Launderette			No
Movie Theater/Seats		Yes/251	
Library			Yes
Children's Facilities			Yes
Watersports Facilities			None
Classification Society		American Bureau	
		of Shipping	

RATINGS	SCORE
Ship: Condition/Cleanliness	8.0
Ship: Space/Flow/Comfort	8.0
Ship: Decor/Furnishings	8.1
Ship: Fitness Facilities	7.3
Cabins: Comfort/Facilities	7.8
Cabins: Software	8.0
Food: Dining Room/Cuisine	7.5
Food: Buffets/Informal Dining	6.6
Food: Quality of Ingredients	6.4
Service: Dining Room	7.2
Service: Bars	7.1
Service: Cabins	7.2
Cruise: Entertainment	6.6
Cruise: Activities Program	6.7
Cruise: Hospitality Standard	6.7
OVERALL RATING	109.2

+ This ship has a short, stubby bow and squat funnel, coupled with a distinctive scarlet red hull. Has an excellent amount of outdoor deck space, although when the ship is full, with lots of children, it can be extremely noisy. The interior is quite spacious, with plenty of public rooms and high ceilings. There is a good indoor-outdoor pool area. Good duty-free shopping. Spacious cabins are generously equipped and very comfortable.

— The decor is somewhat garish in places, but there's a generous amount of stainless steel and teak wood trim. Has a good observation lounge. No cushioned pads are provided for deck lounge chairs. The cabin insulation is very poor. Hundreds of kids mean it's difficult to find a quiet place anywhere. There are too many add-on charges in the Orlando cruise-and-stay programs.

Dining The dining room (non-smoking for both sittings), located on a lower deck, is attractive, but the tables are too close together, so noise level is high. The food quality generally is very good. Good basic service provided by an attentive multi-national staff.

Other Comments Plenty of children's and teens' counselors available. This ship will provide a good cruise experience for families with children at the right price, in typical Premier Cruise Lines style.

Star/Ship Oceanic ★★★+

OPERATES

*3- AND 4-DAY BAHAMAS CRUISES
(YEAR-ROUND)*

Cruise Line	Premier Cruise Lines	Swimming Pools (outside) 2	(inside)	0
Former Names	Oceanic	Whirlpools 3	Gymnasium	Yes
Gross Tonnage	38,772	Sauna/Steam Room No/No	Massage	Yes
Builder	Cantieri Riuniti dell' Adriatico (Italy)	Self-Service Launderette		No
Original Cost	$40 million	Movie Theater/Seats		Yes/420
Christened By	Ms Minnie Mouse	Library		No
Entered Service	Apr 1965/Apr 1986	Children's Facilities		Yes
Interior Design	A&M Katzourakis	Watersports Facilities		None
Country of Registry	Bahamas	Classification Society	American Bureau	
Tel No 112-0520 Fax No	112-0520		of Shipping	
Length (ft/m)	782.1/238.40			
Beam (ft/m) 96.5/29.44 Draft (ft/m)	28.2/8.60	**RATINGS**		**SCORE**
Propulsion	steam turbine (45,100kW)	Ship: Condition/Cleanliness		7.7
Propellers	2 (FP)	Ship: Space/Flow/Comfort		7.5
Decks 10 Crew	565	Ship: Decor/Furnishings		7.6
Pass. Capacity (basis 2) 1,180 (all berths) 1,500		Ship: Fitness Facilities		6.5
Pass. Space Ratio (basis 2) 32.8 (all berths) 25.8		Cabins: Comfort/Facilities		6.8
Officers	Greek	Cabins: Software		7.0
Total Cabins	590	Food: Dining Room/Cuisine		7.5
Size Range (sq ft/m)	139-455/13.0-42.2	Food: Buffets/Informal Dining		6.4
Outside Cabins 261 Inside Cabins	329	Food: Quality of Ingredients		6.4
Single Cabins	0	Service: Dining Room		7.1
Balcony Cabins 8 Wheelchair Cabins	0	Service: Bars		7.1
Cabin Current 110 AC Refrigerator	No	Service: Cabins		7.2
Cabin TV No VCR	No	Cruise: Entertainment		6.6
Dining Rooms 1 Sittings	2	Cruise: Activities Program		6.7
Elevators	5	Cruise: Hospitality Standard		6.6
Casino Yes Slot Machines	Yes	OVERALL RATING		104.7

+ Expansive open deck space for sunning. Swimming pool atop ship has magrodome roof for inclement weather. Contemporary interior decor and cheerful, bright colors. Delightful enclosed promenades. Balconied Sun Deck suites are superb and so spacious. Wide choice of other cabin grades, sizes and shapes. All cabins have heavy-duty furniture and are well equipped, although some need refurbishing. Many cabins feature double beds. This ship does a wonderful job for families with children, with well-trained counselors. Cruise-and-stay packages are well designed.

— Long lines for embarkation, disembarkation, buffets, and shore tenders to out-island. Constant repetitive announcements. No cushioned pads are provided for deck lounge chairs. The interiors need more attention to furnishing detail. There are simply too many add-on charges in the Orlando cruise-and-stay programs.

Dining The dining room (non-smoking for both sittings) is cheerful, but noisy when full. Good food and service considering the cruise fare, but a limited selection of breads, cheeses and fruits. First sitting is non-smoking.

Other Comments Distinctive scarlet red hull. An excellent, family-oriented, fun-filled cruise at an attractive price. More like a summer camp at sea.

ms Statendam ★★★★+

OPERATES

*VARIOUS CARIBBEAN AND
EUROPE CRUISES*

Cruise Line		Holland America Line	
Former Names	-	Gross Tonnage 55,451	
Builder		Fincantieri (Italy)	
Original Cost		$215 million	
Christened By		Lin Arison	
Entered Service		Jan 1993	
Interior Design		VFD Interiors/Joe Farcus	
Country of Registry		Netherlands (PHSG)	
Tel No	130-2515	Fax No	130-2516
Length (ft/m)		719.4/219.30	
Beam (ft/m) 101.0/30.80		Draft (ft/m)	24.6/7.50
Propulsion		diesel-electric (34,560kW)	
Propellers			2 (CP)
Decks	10	Crew	588
Pass. Capacity (basis 2) 1,264		(all berths) 1,627	
Pass. Space Ratio (basis 2) 43.8		(all berths) 34.0	
Officers			Dutch
Total Cabins			632
Size Range (sq ft/m)		187-1,126/17.3-104.5	
Outside Cabins	501	Inside Cabins	131
Single Cabins			0
Balcony Cabins	150	Wheelchair Cabins	6
Cabin Current			110/220 AC
Refrigerator		Category PS/S/A/B only	
Cabin TV	Yes	VCR	No
Dining Rooms	1	Sittings	2
Elevators			12
Casino		Yes Slot Machines	Yes

Swimming Pools (outside)			1
Swimming Pools (inside)		1 (magrodome)	
Whirlpools	2	Gymnasium	Yes
Sauna/Steam Room Yes/No		Massage	Yes
Self-Service Launderette			Yes
Movie Theater/Seats			Yes/249
Library			Yes
Children's Facilities			No
Watersports Facilities			None
Classification Society		Lloyd's Register	

RATINGS	SCORE
Ship: Condition/Cleanliness	8.7
Ship: Space/Flow/Comfort	8.4
Ship: Decor/Furnishings	8.3
Ship: Fitness Facilities	7.7
Cabins: Comfort/Facilities	8.1
Cabins: Software	8.2
Food: Dining Room/Cuisine	7.2
Food: Buffets/Informal Dining	6.8
Food: Quality of Ingredients	6.7
Service: Dining Room	6.5
Service: Bars	7.2
Service: Cabins	8.0
Cruise: Entertainment	7.5
Cruise: Activities Program	7.7
Cruise: Hospitality Standard	8.3
OVERALL RATING	115.3

+ Has teakwood outdoor decks and a traditional wrap-around promenade deck. Magrodome roof covers indoor-outdoor pool, whirlpools and central lido area, whose focal point is a huge dolphin sculpture. Elegant, yet eclectic interior design and decor features traditional styling and use of classic materials—woods and ceramics, providing a restrained approach to interior styling, and little glitz. Three-deck-high atrium foyer with statue is lovely, but space is tight. Good reference library and card room. Art collection adds much color. Suites (each of which can accommodate four) feature an in-suite dining alternative, and free laundry/dry-cleaning. Other cabins are spacious, tastefully decorated and well laid out, and most feature daytime sitting area. Excellent large flower displays throughout.

— Expect long lines for embarkation, disembarkation, shore tenders and buffets. Crows Nest lounge has awful decor. Standard cabins have little closet space for long cruises. Showroom has glitzy decor but poor sightlines. Entertainment is poor. Extra charge for use of the self-service launderette is petty.

Dining Two-level dining room has grand staircase and music balcony. Fine china and silverware. Food and service standards declining. Tasteless food (particularly in the Lido).

Other Comments Really unmemorable cruising that could be better.

ms Stella Oceanis ★★★

OPERATES

*3- AND 4-DAY AEGEAN/
MEDITERRANEAN CRUISES*

Cruise Line	Royal Olympic Cruises	Casino No	Slot Machines No
Former Names	Aphrodite	Swimming Pools (outside) 1	(inside) 0
Gross Tonnage	6,000	Whirlpools 0	Gymnasium No
Builder	Cantieri Riuniti dell' Adriatico (Italy)	Sauna/Steam Room No/No	Massage No
Original Cost	n/a	Self-Service Launderette	No
Christened By	Mrs Isabella Kousseoglou	Movie Theater/Seats	No
Entered Service	1965/1967	Library	Yes
Interior Design	Mrs Isabella Kousseoglou	Children's Facilities	No
Country of Registry	Greece	Watersports Facilities	None
Tel No 113-0471	Fax No 113-0471	Classification Society	Lloyd's Register

Length (ft/m)	344.9/105.14
Beam (ft/m) 55.5/16.92	Draft (ft/m) 14.9/4.56
Propulsion	diesel (8,090kW)
Propellers	1 (CP)
Decks 6	Crew 140
Pass. Capacity (basis 2) 300	(all berths) 369
Pass. Space Ratio (basis 2) 20.0	(all berths) 16.2
Officers	Greek
Total Cabins	159
Size Range (sq ft/m)	96-208/9.0-19.3
Outside Cabins 113	Inside Cabins 46
Single Cabins	0
Balcony Cabins 0	Wheelchair Cabins 0
Cabin Current	220 AC
Refrigerator	No
Cabin TV No	VCR No
Dining Rooms 1	Sittings 2
Elevators	1

RATINGS	SCORE
Ship: Condition/Cleanliness	6.5
Ship: Space/Flow/Comfort	6.0
Ship: Decor/Furnishings	6.8
Ship: Fitness Facilities	3.0
Cabins: Comfort/Facilities	6.5
Cabins: Software	7.2
Food: Dining Room/Cuisine	7.2
Food: Buffets/Informal Dining	7.0
Food: Quality of Ingredients	6.3
Service: Dining Room	7.4
Service: Bars	7.4
Service: Cabins	7.6
Cruise: Entertainment	5.2
Cruise: Activities Program	5.5
Cruise: Hospitality Standard	7.5
OVERALL RATING	97.1

+ Tidy-looking, well-maintained ship with clean, rounded lines. Intimate atmosphere. Public rooms limited, but nicely decorated; a favorite is the Plaka Taverna, decorated in rich woods. The cabins (eight categories) are small, and plainer than on the smaller sister, and have limited closet and drawer space, but those on Lido and Stella decks have interconnecting doors. Some have full bathtub, while others have shower only, but all have private bathrooms.

— Has few public rooms and not much open deck and sunning space. Has a narrow, steep gangway.

Dining Tastefully decorated, charming dining room. Good food, but little choice.

Other Comments This ship lacks the sophistication of the other ships in the fleet, but is nonetheless quite charming. Royal Olympic Cruises provides a fine destination-intensive cruise experience, made better by the charming, friendly officers and staff.

ss Stella Solaris ★★★★

OPERATES

CARIBBEAN, EUROPE AND
SOUTH AMERICA CRUISES

Cruise Line	Royal Olympic Cruises
Former Names	Stella V/Camboge
Gross Tonnage	17,832
Builder	Ateliers et Chantiers de France (France)
Original Cost	n/a
Christened By	Mrs Isabella Kousseoglou
Entered Service	Jul 1953/Jun 1973
Interior Design	Mrs Isabella Kousseoglou
Country of Registry	Greece
Tel No 113-0226	Fax No 113-0227
Length (ft/m)	545.1/166.15
Beam (ft/m) 72.4/22.08	Draft (ft/m) 25.8/7.88
Propulsion	steam turbine (17,900kW)
Propellers	2 (FP)
Decks 8	Crew 330
Pass. Capacity (basis 2) 620	(all berths) 700
Pass. Space Ratio (basis 2) 28.7	(all berths) 25.4
Officers	Greek
Total Cabins	329
Size Range (sq ft/m)	96-225/9.0-21.0
Outside Cabins 250	Inside Cabins 79
Single Cabins	0
Balcony Cabins 0	Wheelchair Cabins 0
Cabin Current	110/220 AC
Refrigerator	No
Cabin TV Yes	VCR No
Dining Rooms 1	Sittings 2
Elevators	3

Casino	Yes	Slot Machines	Yes
Swimming Pools (outside)	1	(inside)	0
Whirlpools	0	Gymnasium	Yes
Sauna/Steam Room	No/No	Massage	Yes
Self-Service Launderette			No
Movie Theater/Seats			Yes/275
Library			Yes
Children's Facilities			No
Watersports Facilities			None
Classification Society			Lloyd's Register

RATINGS	SCORE
Ship: Condition/Cleanliness	7.5
Ship: Space/Flow/Comfort	7.0
Ship: Decor/Furnishings	7.7
Ship: Fitness Facilities	5.1
Cabins: Comfort/Facilities	7.1
Cabins: Software	7.8
Food: Dining Room/Cuisine	7.3
Food: Buffets/Informal Dining	6.9
Food: Quality of Ingredients	6.5
Service: Dining Room	7.8
Service: Bars	7.7
Service: Cabins	7.7
Cruise: Entertainment	6.0
Cruise: Activities Program	5.7
Cruise: Hospitality Standard	7.7
OVERALL RATING	105.5

+ Traditional ship profile, with attractive funnel amidships. Clean and well maintained throughout. Well-planned itineraries. Expansive open deck space, including an outdoor wrap-around promenade deck. Attractive twin pools and sunning area. Elegant public rooms have quality furniture and fixtures. Nice feeling of space and grace. Fresh flowers everywhere add warmth. Cabins are spacious and well appointed – many have full bathtub. Lido Deck suites are delightful. The decor has recently been updated, with brighter fabrics and colors. New health spa facilities added.

— There's no forward observation lounge. Cabins located on Sapphire Deck and midships on Emerald Deck are subject to engine noise.

Dining Delightful dining room features good food, some good wines and old-world European service.

Other Comments This ship is for the older passenger who seeks a relaxed, unhurried and gracious cruise experience in fine surroundings, at reasonable cost, with friendly all-Greek service, but without the hype of the more contemporary ships.

ms Sun Princess ★★★★+

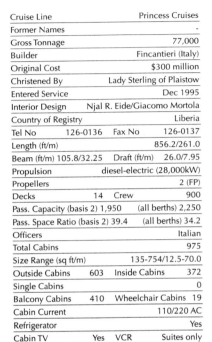

OPERATES

7-DAY ALASKA AND CARIBBEAN CRUISES

Cruise Line		Princess Cruises
Former Names		-
Gross Tonnage		77,000
Builder		Fincantieri (Italy)
Original Cost		$300 million
Christened By		Lady Sterling of Plaistow
Entered Service		Dec 1995
Interior Design		Njal R. Eide/Giacomo Mortola
Country of Registry		Liberia
Tel No 126-0136	Fax No	126-0137
Length (ft/m)		856.2/261.0
Beam (ft/m) 105.8/32.25	Draft (ft/m)	26.0/7.95
Propulsion		diesel-electric (28,000kW)
Propellers		2 (FP)
Decks 14	Crew	900
Pass. Capacity (basis 2) 1,950	(all berths)	2,250
Pass. Space Ratio (basis 2) 39.4	(all berths)	34.2
Officers		Italian
Total Cabins		975
Size Range (sq ft/m)		135-754/12.5-70.0
Outside Cabins 603	Inside Cabins	372
Single Cabins		0
Balcony Cabins 410	Wheelchair Cabins	19
Cabin Current		110/220 AC
Refrigerator		Yes
Cabin TV Yes	VCR	Suites only
Dining Rooms		2 main/3 others
Sittings		2 (main dining rooms)

Elevators			11
Casino	Yes	Slot Machines	Yes
Swimming Pools (outside) 3		(inside)	0
Whirlpools	5	Gymnasium	Yes
Sauna/Steam Room Yes/Yes		Massage	Yes
Self-Service Launderette			Yes
Movie Theater/Seats			Yes/550
Library	Yes	Children's Facilities	Yes
Watersports Facilities			None
Classification Society			Lloyd's Register

RATINGS	SCORE
Ship: Condition/Cleanliness	9.1
Ship: Space/Flow/Comfort	8.7
Ship: Decor/Furnishings	8.9
Ship: Fitness Facilities	8.3
Cabins: Comfort/Facilities	8.4
Cabins: Software	8.6
Food: Dining Room/Cuisine	7.7
Food: Buffets/Informal Dining	7.6
Food: Quality of Ingredients	7.0
Service: Dining Room	7.6
Service: Bars	8.0
Service: Cabins	8.0
Cruise: Entertainment	8.7
Cruise: Activities Program	7.8
Cruise: Hospitality Standard	8.2
OVERALL RATING	122.6

+ Although large, this ship has a good profile, and is well balanced by its large funnel, which contains a deck tennis/basketball/volleyball court in its aft base. There is a wide teakwood outdoor wrap-around promenade deck, teakwood "steamer"-style deck chairs and 93,000 sq ft (8,640m²) of outdoor space. A great amount of glass area on the upper decks provides plenty of light and connection with the outside world.

The ship, while large, has an almost intimate feel to her, which is just what the designers intended. her interiors are very pretty and warm, with attractive colours and welcoming decor that includes some stunning wall murals and other artwork.

There is a wide range of public rooms to choose from, with several intimate rooms and spaces. Tasteful decor throughout, with attractive color combinations. The focal point is a huge four-deck-high atrium lobby, complete with two panoramic glass-walled elevators. The main public entertainment rooms are located under three decks of accommodations. There's plenty of space, the traffic flow is good, and the ship absorbs people well. There are two showrooms, one at each end of the ship: one is a superb 550-seat theater-style showlounge (movies are also shown here); the other is a 480-seat cabaret-style lounge, complete with bar.

The health spa complex, located aft, surrounds a swimming pool, suspended between two decks (there are two other fairly small pools). There is a conference center for up to 300, as well as a business center with computers, copy machine and fax machine. The collection of art work is outstanding, particularly on the stairways, and helps make the ship feel smaller than it is.

The cabins are well designed and functional in layout, if a little on the small side; many outside cabins have private balconies (more than any other Princess ship to date), and all seem to be quite well soundproofed (the balcony partition is not floor-to-ceiling, however, so you can hear your next-door neighbors clearly). Good closet and drawer space in all cabins for a 7-day cruise. The cabin bathrooms are quite practical, and come complete with all the little details one needs. Suites and mini-suites are very well laid out, with larger bathrooms (jacuzzi bathtubs and separate large shower) and a separate bedroom. Real glasses are provided in cabin bathrooms.

— The signage around the ship could be improved. The swimming pools are small for so many passengers and the pool deck is cluttered with plastic deck lounge chairs. Proportionately, there are too many inside cabins. A third, central stairway is needed. There's no escape from the many unnecessary and repetitive announcements that intrude constantly. As on any large ship, you should expect lines and some crowding for embarkation, disembarkation, buffets, shore tenders and shore excursions.

Dining There are two main dining rooms (Marquis and Regency); each has its own galley and is split into multi-tier sections. Breakfast and lunch are open seating; dinner is in two sittings. The dining room food, its presentation and delivery are disappointing and let down this otherwise beautifully decorated ship.

There's also a patisserie (for cappuccino/espresso coffees and pastries), a wine/caviar bar and a pizzeria (complete with cobblestone floors and wrought-iron decorative features). The six different types of pizza are all excellent.

The Horizon Buffet is open almost 24 hours a day and at night, features an informal dinner setting with sit-down waiter service and a small bistro menu (open from 6pm to 2am). Buffet displays are, for the most part, unappetizing and could be improved. The cabin service menu is limited.

Other Comments This ship was, for almost a year, the largest ship (in terms of gross tonnage, but not length) in the cruise industry, superseded in November 1996 by Carnival Cruise line's 100,000-grt *Carnival Destiny*. If you live in the top suites, you'll be well attended; if you don't, you'll be one of a very large number.

ms Sun Viking ★★★+

OPERATES
SOUTHEAST ASIA, CHINA AND JAPAN CRUISES

Cruise Line	Royal Caribbean Cruises		
Former Names	-		
Gross Tonnage	18,556		
Builder	Wartsila (Finland)		
Original Cost	$17.5 million		
Christened By	Mrs Sigurd Skaugen		
Entered Service	Dec 1972		
Interior Design	Njal Eide		
Country of Registry	Norway		
Tel No	131-2151	Fax No	131-2151
Length (ft/m)	563.2/171.69		
Beam (ft/m) 78.8/24.03	Draft (ft/m)	20.6/6.30	
Propulsion	diesel (13,400kW)		
Propellers	2 (CP)		
Decks	8	Crew	341
Pass. Capacity (basis 2) 714	(all berths) 818		
Pass. Space Ratio (basis 2) 25.9	(all berths) 22.6		
Officers	Norwegian		
Total Cabins	357		
Size Range (sq ft/m)	120-237/11.0-22.0		
Outside Cabins	240	Inside Cabins	117
Single Cabins	0		
Balcony Cabins	0		
Wheelchair Cabins	0		
Cabin Current	110 AC		
Refrigerator	Owner's suite only		
Cabin TV	No	VCR	No
Dining Rooms	1	Sittings	2

Elevators			4
Casino	Yes	Slot Machines	Yes
Swimming Pools (outside)	1	(inside)	0
Whirlpools	0	Gymnasium	Yes
Sauna/Steam Room	Yes/No	Massage	Yes
Self-Service Launderette			No
Movie Theater/Seats	No	Library	Yes
Children's Facilities			No
Watersports Facilities			None
Classification Society		Det Norske Veritas	

RATINGS	SCORE
Ship: Condition/Cleanliness	7.4
Ship: Space/Flow/Comfort	6.3
Ship: Decor/Furnishings	6.9
Ship: Fitness Facilities	5.6
Cabins: Comfort/Facilities	5.8
Cabins: Software	7.7
Food: Dining Room/Cuisine	6.8
Food: Buffets/Informal Dining	6.6
Food: Quality of Ingredients	7.1
Service: Dining Room	6.7
Service: Bars	6.5
Service: Cabins	6.1
Cruise: Entertainment	7.2
Cruise: Activities Program	6.7
Cruise: Hospitality Standard	7.4
OVERALL RATING	100.8

+ Well-proportioned ship with contemporary styling. Cantilevered Viking Crown lounge set atop funnel housing provides an impressive view. Smallest and most intimate ship in the Royal Caribbean Cruises fleet, a real gem. Good open deck and sunning space, with wrap-around outdoor polished wood deck. Public rooms decorated in modern Scandinavian style and colors, and named after musicals. Charming, friendly ambiance throughout.

— High-density ship means public rooms are always busy. Long wait for elevator, buffet line, disembarkation. Small and moderately comfortable cabins have little closet, drawer and storage space.

Dining Pleasant, attractive dining room with large picture windows has tables for four, six or eight (no tables for two). Consistently good food and service, although there's little flexibility. Poor breads, rolls and fruit selection. Good wine list but limited vintages.

Other Comments This company wants its passengers out and about the public rooms, not in their small cabins, and caters to passengers wanting a more intimate cruise, with all the Royal Caribbean Cruises trimmings at a fair price.

ms SuperStar Gemini ★★★★

OPERATES

*2- AND 5-DAY SOUTH-EAST ASIA
CRUISES (YEAR-ROUND)*

Cruise Line	Star Cruise	Elevators	4
Former Names	Crown Jewel	Casino	Yes	Slot Machines	Yes
Gross Tonnage	19,046	Swimming Pools (outside) 1	(inside)	0
Builder	Union Navale de Levante (Spain)	Whirlpools 3	Gymnasium	Yes
Original Cost	$100 million	Sauna/Steam Room Yes/Yes	Massage	Yes
Christened By	Isabel Cebrian de Viguerra	Self-Service Launderette	No
Entered Service	Aug 1992/Jul 1995	Movie Theater/Seats No	Library	Yes
Interior Design	Yran & Storbraaten	Children's Facilities	Yes
Country of Registry	Panama (3EW9)	Watersports Facilities	None
Tel No 133-6652 Fax No 133-6653	Classification Society	Det Norske Veritas
Length (ft/m)	537.4/163.81		
Beam (ft/m) 73.8/22.50 Draft (ft/m) 17.7/5.40		

RATINGS	SCORE
Propulsion diesel (13,200kW)	Ship: Condition/Cleanliness	8.0
Propellers 2 (CP)	Ship: Space/Flow/Comfort	7.8
Decks 9 Crew 470	Ship: Decor/Furnishings	8.1
Pass. Capacity (basis 2) 820 (all berths) 900	Ship: Fitness Facilities	8.0
Pass. Space Ratio (basis 2) 23.2 (all berths) 21.1	Cabins: Comfort/Facilities	7.7
Officers European/Scandinavian	Cabins: Software	7.9
Total Cabins 404	Food: Dining Room/Cuisine	7.5
Size Range (sq ft/m) 140-350/13.0-32.5	Food: Buffets/Informal Dining	6.8
Outside Cabins 281 Inside Cabins 123	Food: Quality of Ingredients	6.5
Single Cabins 0	Service: Dining Room	7.6
Balcony Cabins 19 Wheelchair Cabins 4	Service: Bars	7.5
Cabin Current 110/220 AC	Service: Cabins	7.0
Refrigerator Category 1 only	Cruise: Entertainment	7.8
Cabin TV Yes VCR Yes	Cruise: Activities Program	4.8
Dining Rooms 1	Cruise: Hospitality Standard	7.2
Sittings 2 (open seating breakfast/lunch)	OVERALL RATING	110.2

+ Traditional layout with reasonable horizontal passenger flow features picture windows in almost all public rooms, providing a connection with sea and light. Good open deck and sunning space. Attractive decor, with upbeat color combinations. Nicely furnished cabins all feature large picture windows. Although not large, they are very comfortable, with wood-trimmed accents and colorful soft furnishings. Bathrooms are pleasing, and feature a large toiletries cabinet, but they have a small shower area.

— Fit and finish was poor when built. The artwork is not aesthetically pleasing. Poor cabin soundproofing.

Dining Attractive but cramped dining room has charming ambiance, but there are no tables for two. Cuisine is international with an Oriental touch. Food rarely arrives hot.

Other Comments Handsome mid-sized cruise ship with smart exterior styling is the largest ever built in Spain. Features a five-deck-high glass-walled atrium. This ship is a welcome addition and refreshing change for the Asian market. It is a sound product, and, with more tweaking and fine-tuning in the hotel service areas, will prove an admirable success story for Star Cruise.

ts Symphony ★★★

OPERATES

VARIOUS EUROPE CRUISES

Cruise Line	Mediterranean Shipping Cruises	Casino	No	Slot Machines	No
Former Names	EnricoCosta/Enrico "C"/Provence	Swimming Pools (outside) 3	(inside)	0
Gross Tonnage	16,495	Whirlpools	0	Gymnasium	No
Builder	Swan, Hunter (UK)	Sauna/Steam Room No/No	Massage	No
Original Cost	n/a	Self-Service Launderette	Yes
Christened By	n/a	Movie Theater/Seats	Yes/85
Entered Service	Mar 1951/1995	Library	No
Interior Design	Architects Falletti/De Jorio	Children's Facilities	Yes
Country of Registry	Italy	Watersports Facilities	None
Tel No 115-0561 Fax No 115-0561		Classification Society	RINA

Length (ft/m)	579.0/176.49
Beam (ft/m) 73.1/22.31 Draft (ft/m) 24.6/7.52	
Propulsion	diesel (11,768kW)
Propellers	2 (FP)
Decks 7 Crew	330
Pass. Capacity (basis 2) 664 (all berths) 845	
Pass. Space Ratio (basis 2) 24.8 (all berths) 19.5	
Officers	Italian
Total Cabins	332
Size Range (sq ft/m)	86-216/8.0-20.1
Outside Cabins 159 Inside Cabins 173	
Single Cabins	0
Balcony Cabins	0
Wheelchair Cabins	0
Cabin Current 220 DC Refrigerator	No
Cabin TV No VCR	No
Dining Rooms 1 Sittings	2
Elevators	2

RATINGS	SCORE
Ship: Condition/Cleanliness	6.6
Ship: Space/Flow/Comfort	6.1
Ship: Decor/Furnishings	7.3
Ship: Fitness Facilities	4.6
Cabins: Comfort/Facilities	6.4
Cabins: Software	6.8
Food: Dining Room/Cuisine	6.7
Food: Buffets/Informal Dining	6.3
Food: Quality of Ingredients	6.7
Service: Dining Room	7.1
Service: Bars	7.2
Service: Cabins	7.4
Cruise: Entertainment	6.4
Cruise: Activities Program	6.3
Cruise: Hospitality Standard	7.2
OVERALL RATING	99.1

+ This solidly built vessel recently received an extensive refurbishment. Has a deep draft, and so is reasonably stable at sea. Good open deck promenade areas. The newer facilities are fine, while others have been much upgraded. The public rooms feature "Belle Epoque" decor and are very smart, but crowded when full. Cabins are compact but comfortable, with tasteful pastel decor and soft furnishings to match.

— Has steep gangway. Does not have stabilizers. Ceilings are very plain and uninteresting. The entertainment is loud and of very poor quality. There are too many loud, unnecessary and repetitious announcements.

Dining The dining room is comfortable, though rather noisy. Good bubbly Italian service and food, with excellent pasta, but other dishes lack quality.

Other Comments Traditional ocean liner styling, reconstructed from her former life as a cargo-passenger liner, extensively refurbished in 1996. Has a large, single yellow funnel. Beautiful wood paneling and brass trim throughout the ship adds warmth and old-world elegance lacking in many new ships. This ship caters primarily to budget-minded European passengers looking for a Mediterranean cruise without the trimmings, with mainly Italian passengers.

ms Taras Shevchenko ★★+

OPERATES
VARIOUS BLACK SEA AND
MEDITERRANEAN CRUISES

Cruise Line	Primexpress Cruise Lines
Former Names	-
Gross Tonnage	20,027
Builder	VEB Mathias Thesen (Germany)
Original Cost	n/a
Christened By	n/a
Entered Service	Apr 1967/1994
Interior Design	Shipyard team
Country of Registry	Ukraine
Tel No 140-0266 Fax No	140-0266
Length (ft/m)	577.4/176.00
Beam (ft/m) 77.4/23.60 Draft (ft/m)	26.7/8.16
Propulsion	diesel (15,700kW)
Propellers	2 (CP)
Decks 8 Crew	370
Pass. Capacity (basis 2) 574	(all berths) 712
Pass. Space Ratio (basis 2) 34.8	(all berths) 28.1
Officers	Ukrainian
Total Cabins	287
Size Range (sq ft/m)	n/a
Outside Cabins 287 Inside Cabins	0
Single Cabins	0
Balcony Cabins	0
Wheelchair Cabins	0
Cabin Current 220 AC Refrigerator	No
Cabin TV No VCR	No
Dining Rooms 3 Sittings	1
Elevators	3

Casino	Yes	Slot Machines	Yes
Swimming Pools (outside) 2		(inside)	1
Whirlpools	1	Gymnasium	Yes
Sauna/Steam Room Yes/No		Massage	No
Self-Service Launderette			Yes
Movie Theater/Seats			Yes/130
Library			Yes
Children's Facilities			Yes
Watersports Facilities			None
Classification Society			RS

RATINGS	SCORE
Ship: Condition/Cleanliness	5.8
Ship: Space/Flow/Comfort	6.4
Ship: Decor/Furnishings	5.7
Ship: Fitness Facilities	4.8
Cabins: Comfort/Facilities	5.8
Cabins: Software	6.0
Food: Dining Room/Cuisine	6.1
Food: Buffets/Informal Dining	5.4
Food: Quality of Ingredients	5.3
Service: Dining Room	6.1
Service: Bars	6.4
Service: Cabins	6.5
Cruise: Entertainment	5.3
Cruise: Activities Program	5.4
Cruise: Hospitality Standard	5.7
OVERALL RATING	86.7

+ Solidly constructed vessel has nicely rounded lines and a classic profile, with an all-white, ice-hardened hull. Good open deck and sunning space. Has wrap-around outdoor promenade deck. Has pleasant, but very plain interior decor that could do with more tropical greenery to enhance it. Recent substantial refurbishment has upgraded the vessel considerably and added more color. Spacious music salon. Has all-outside cabins that are very comfortable, each with private facilities. 10 suites are very spacious, and tastefully appointed.

— Plain ceilings and spartan decor that is quite dated. Has a narrow, steep gangway in most ports. No cushioned pads on deck chairs. Lower two cabin decks are in poor shape.

Dining Single seating dining room is functional, nothing more, and needs upgrading. The food is adequate, but there's little menu choice. Service is attentively provided by attractive Ukrainian waitresses. Poor selection of bread rolls, cheeses and fruits.

Other Comments While this ship is not yet up to western standards, it was renovated in 1988 and will provide a reasonable cruise experience at a modest rate, for a mostly French and Italian clientele. Often operates under charter, but there's no finesse.

mv The Azur ★★★+

OPERATES

VARIOUS SOUTHERN EUROPE CRUISES

Cruise Line		Festival Cruises
Former Names		Eagle/Azur
Gross Tonnage		14,717
Builder	Dubigeon-Normandie (France)	
Original Cost		n/a
Christened By		n/a
Entered Service		May 1971/Apr1994
Interior Design		A&M Katzourakis
Country of Registry		Panama
Tel No 133-2515	Fax No	133-2515
Length (ft/m)		465.8/142.00
Beam (ft/m) 71.8/21.90	Draft (ft/m)	18.7/5.73
Propulsion		diesel (16,300kW)
Propellers		2 (CP)
Decks 7	Crew	340
Pass. Capacity (basis 2) 665	(all berths) 750	
Pass. Space Ratio (basis 2) 22.1	(all berths) 19.6	
Officers		Greek
Total Cabins		335
Size Range (sq ft/m)	94.7-212.0/8.8-19.7	
Outside Cabins 152	Inside Cabins	183
Single Cabins		10
Balcony Cabins		0
Wheelchair Cabins		2
Cabin Current 220 AC	Refrigerator	No
Cabin TV No	VCR	No
Dining Rooms 1	Sittings	2
Elevators		3

Casino	Yes	Slot Machines	Yes
Swimming Pools (outside) 2		(inside)	0
Whirlpools	0	Gymnasium	Yes
Sauna/Steam Room No/No		Massage	No
Self-Service Launderette			No
Movie Theater/Seats			Yes/175
Library			Yes
Children's Facilities			Yes
Watersports Facilities			none
Classification Society		Bureau Veritas	

RATINGS	SCORE
Ship: Condition/Cleanliness	7.6
Ship: Space/Flow/Comfort	6.6
Ship: Decor/Furnishings	7.5
Ship: Fitness Facilities	7.0
Cabins: Comfort/Facilities	6.5
Cabins: Software	7.0
Food: Dining Room/Cuisine	7.3
Food: Buffets/Informal Dining	6.8
Food: Quality of Ingredients	6.6
Service: Dining Room	7.3
Service: Bars	7.1
Service: Cabins	7.1
Cruise: Entertainment	6.3
Cruise: Activities Program	6.2
Cruise: Hospitality Standard	7.1
OVERALL RATING	104.0

+ Generous open deck space for sunning, but crowded when full. Good selection of public rooms and numerous bars, with light, well-chosen contemporary decor and many mirrored surfaces. Two-level movie theater. Most cabins are plain, but nicely furnished, and decorated in earth tones. Has two outside cabins for the physically challenged. Lively action in the casino. Excellent sports facilities include an indoor squash and volleyball court.

— Small swimming pools. Showroom has poor sightlines and low ceiling (but is good for meetings). Has many inside cabins. Constant announcements in several languages is irritating, but typical of European operations that try to cater for everyone.

Dining Charming low-ceilinged dining room has ocean-view windows on three sides, but uncomfortable chairs. Typically decent food, but presentation lacks flair. Limited selection of breads, fruits and cheeses. Courteous staff and service.

Other Comments Smart though stubby-looking ship has a short bow, and twin tall funnels set well aft. Will appeal to the young and active looking for a good first cruise experience to a host of destinations, at a very reasonable price, as well as to those seeking a venue for meetings and incentive cruises. Operates well in several languages for its multi-national European passengers. Note: Festival Cruises is known in the USA as Azur-Bolero Cruises.

ms Triton ★★★+

OPERATES

3-, 4- AND 7-DAY AEGEAN AND MEDITERRANEAN CRUISES

Cruise Line	Royal Olympic Cruises	Casino	Yes	Slot Machines	Yes
Former Names	Cunard Adventurer/Sunward II	Swimming Pools (outside)	1	(inside)	0

Cruise Line		Royal Olympic Cruises	Casino	Yes	Slot Machines	Yes
Former Names		Cunard Adventurer/Sunward II	Swimming Pools (outside) 1		(inside)	0
Gross Tonnage		14,155	Whirlpools	0	Gymnasium	Yes
Builder		Rotterdamsche Dry Dock (Holland)	Sauna/Steam Room Yes/No		Massage	Yes
Original Cost		n/a	Self-Service Launderette			No
Christened By		n/a	Movie Theater/Seats			Yes/96
Entered Service		Oct 1971/May 1992	Library			Yes
Interior Design		Arminio Lozzi	Children's Facilities			Yes
Country of Registry		Greece	Watersports Facilities			None
Tel No 113-1266	Fax No	113-1266	Classification Society		Lloyd's Register	
Length (ft/m)		491.1/149.70				
Beam (ft/m) 70.5/21.50	Draft (ft/m)	19.22/5.86	**RATINGS**			**SCORE**
Propulsion		diesel (19,860kW)	Ship: Condition/Cleanliness			7.5
Propellers		2 (CP)	Ship: Space/Flow/Comfort			6.5
Decks	7 Crew	265	Ship: Decor/Furnishings			7.4
Pass. Capacity (basis 2) 756		(all berths) 945	Ship: Fitness Facilities			5.2
Pass. Space Ratio (basis 2) 18.7		(all berths) 14.9	Cabins: Comfort/Facilities			6.6
Officers		Greek	Cabins: Software			7.9
Total Cabins		378	Food: Dining Room/Cuisine			7.1
Size Range (sq ft/m)		118-132/11.0-12.2	Food: Buffets/Informal Dining			6.1
Outside Cabins	236 Inside Cabins	142	Food: Quality of Ingredients			6.2
Single Cabins		0	Service: Dining Room			7.2
Balcony Cabins	0 Wheelchair Cabins	0	Service: Bars			6.8
Cabin Current		110/220 AC	Service: Cabins			7.1
Refrigerator		No	Cruise: Entertainment			6.2
Cabin TV	No VCR	No	Cruise: Activities Program			6.1
Dining Rooms	1 Sittings	2	Cruise: Hospitality Standard			7.7
Elevators		2	**OVERALL RATING**			**101.6**

+ Has a handsome, sleek profile and a deep clipper bow. Inside the ship, there is good layout and passenger flow, with ample public rooms and delightful, contemporary interior decor, with some interesting regional artwork. Excellent destination-intensive itineraries are good for those who want to see more places in a short time. Has a wrap-around outdoor promenade deck. Fine nightclub with forward observation views. Good open deck space for sunning. Well-appointed cabins for ship size, even though they are rather small. Friendly staff and ambiance.

— High-density ship means crowded public areas. Small cabins and bathrooms. Long lines for buffets. Too many announcements for tours, when in ports of call. Cabin bathrooms have very small shower units.

Dining While the dining room is quite attractive and has contemporary colors and ambiance, it is also very noisy. The cuisine is Continental in style, which means much use of oils. The choice is adequate, but presentation is inconsistent. Poor bread rolls and fruits. Service is attentive but hurried.

Other Comments Well maintained, although now showing its age. Ideal for short cruises. This ship provides excellent value for money, and features a well delivered product.

ms Tropicale ★★★+

OPERATES

*7-DAY ALASKA AND
CARIBBEAN CRUISES*

Cruise Line			Carnival Cruise Lines
Former Names			-
Gross Tonnage			36,674
Builder			Aalborg Vaerft (Denmark)
Original Cost			$100 million
Christened By			Mrs Madeleine Arison
Entered Service			Jan 1982
Interior Design			Joe Farcus
Country of Registry			Liberia
Tel No	124-0561	Fax No	124-0561
Length (ft/m)			671.7/204.76
Beam (ft/m)	86.7/26.45	Draft (ft/m)	23.3/7.11
Propulsion			diesel (19,566kW)
Propellers			2 (CP)
Decks	10	Crew	550
Pass. Capacity (basis 2) 1,022		(all berths)	1,400
Pass. Space Ratio (basis 2) 35.8		(all berths)	26.1
Officers			Italian
Total Cabins			511
Size Range (sq ft/m)			180/9.2
Outside Cabins	324	Inside Cabins	187
Single Cabins			0
Balcony Cabins			12
Wheelchair Cabins			11
Cabin Current			110 AC
Refrigerator			(Suites only)
Cabin TV	Yes	VCR	No
Dining Rooms	1	Sittings	2

Elevators			8
Casino	Yes	Slot Machines	Yes
Swimming Pools (outside) 3		(inside)	0
Whirlpools	0	Gymnasium	Yes
Sauna/Steam Room Yes/No		Massage	Yes
Self-Service Launderette			Yes
Movie Theater/Seats	No	Library	Yes
Children's Facilities			Yes
Watersports Facilities			None
Classification Society			Lloyd's Register

RATINGS	SCORE
Ship: Condition/Cleanliness	7.7
Ship: Space/Flow/Comfort	7.0
Ship: Decor/Furnishings	6.8
Ship: Fitness Facilities	7.8
Cabins: Comfort/Facilities	7.5
Cabins: Software	7.4
Food: Dining Room/Cuisine	6.7
Food: Buffets/Informal Dining	6.1
Food: Quality of Ingredients	5.3
Service: Dining Room	6.9
Service: Bars	7.0
Service: Cabins	6.4
Cruise: Entertainment	7.5
Cruise: Activities Program	7.6
Cruise: Hospitality Standard	6.6
OVERALL RATING	104.3

+ Distinctive contemporary look, with large, wing-tipped funnel. Well-laid-out interior design, with good passenger flow. Well maintained. Public rooms are decorated in stimulating colors. Always lively casino action. Most cabins are of the standard cookie-cutter variety, with little imaginative decor, and just enough closet and drawer space to manage for a week. Good ship for families with children, as Carnival goes out of its way to entertain young cruisers as well as their parents.

— Noisy, cramped dining room. Long lines for embarkation, disembarkation, shore tenders and buffets. Too many repetitive announcements. Aggressive hustling for drinks.

Dining The dining room is located on a lower deck. It is colorful, cheerful, brightly lit, but noisy, and there are no tables for two. Typical Americana, with quantity, not quality (consistently uninspiring). Poor selection of bread rolls, fresh fruits, cheeses and pastry items. Service is hurried and inflexible, but cheerful. Lunch buffets are poor.

Other Comments This ship will provide novice cruisers with a well-proven product that is attractively packaged, at a reasonable price, but it is not a luxury cruise by any means, nor does it pretend to be. But you'll have fun and lots of hoop-la. This ship will be Carnival's first in the 1996 Alaska summer cruise season.

ss Universe Explorer ★★★

OPERATES

*14-DAY ALASKA AND
CARIBBEAN CRUISES*

Cruise Line	World Explorer Cruises
Former Names	Queen of Bermuda, Canada Star,
Liberte, Island Sun, Volendam, Monarch Sun, Brazil	
Gross Tonnage	23,879
Builder	Ingalls Shipbuilding (USA)
Original Cost	$26 million
Christened By	Mrs Emmett J. McCormack
Entered Service	Sep 1958/Nov 1990
Interior Design	n/a
Country of Registry	Bahamas

Tel No	113-1605	Fax No	133-1605
Length (ft/m)			617.4/188.20
Beam (ft/m) 84.3/25.70		Draft (ft/m)	27.2/8.30
Propulsion		steam turbine (19,000kW)
Propellers			2 (FP)
Decks	8	Crew	365
Pass. Capacity (basis 2) 740		(all berths)	846
Pass. Space Ratio (basis 2) 32.2		(all berths)	28.2
Officers			European
Total Cabins			371
Size Range (sq ft/m)		104-293/9.6-27.2
Outside Cabins	290	Inside Cabins	79
Single Cabins			2
Balcony Cabins	0	Wheelchair Cabins	0
Cabin Current	110 AC	Refrigerator	No
Cabin TV	Yes	VCR	No
Dining Rooms	1	Sittings	2
Elevators			3

Casino	Yes	Slot Machines	Yes
Swimming Pools (outside) 2		(inside)	0
Whirlpools	0	Gymnasium	Yes
Sauna/Steam Room No/No		Massage	Yes
Self-Service Launderette			No
Movie Theater/Seats			Yes/200
Library	Yes	Children's Facilities	Yes
Watersports Facilities			None
Classification Society		American Bureau
			of Shipping

RATINGS	SCORE
Ship: Condition/Cleanliness	6.5
Ship: Space/Flow/Comfort	6.2
Ship: Decor/Furnishings	6.6
Ship: Fitness Facilities	4.5
Cabins: Comfort/Facilities	6.3
Cabins: Software	6.6
Food: Dining Room/Cuisine	6.3
Food: Buffets/Informal Dining	5.8
Food: Quality of Ingredients	6.0
Service: Dining Room	6.0
Service: Bars	6.2
Service: Cabins	6.4
Cruise: Entertainment	6.0
Cruise: Activities Program	6.3
Cruise: Hospitality Standard	6.6
OVERALL RATING	92.3

+ Somewhat traditional ocean liner profile. Extensively refurbished. Beautifully finished outdoor teakwood decks. Being an older ship, there are spacious outdoor promenade areas for walking. The public rooms are quite spacious and well equipped, with high ceilings, and pleasing decor and colors that don't jar the senses. The showroom is quite good, but cannot compare with those on larger, more modern, ships. Has a large casino. There's plenty of sheltered and open sunning space. Two outdoor pools are well used. Cabins are of a generous size, with nice, heavy-duty furniture and fittings.

— Expect long lines for casual buffet meals. Poor sightlines in showlounge.

Dining Charming dining room has large windows which provide more light and a better ambiance. The menu choice is somewhat limited, but service is attentive and comes with a smile, even if it's without finesse. Poor selection of bread rolls, cheeses, and fruits.

Other Comments This ship will provide you with an enjoyable first cruise experience in comfort surroundings reminiscent of old world style, at a very reasonable price. However, with all the discounting, service and product delivery standards have been lowered.

ms Veendam ★★★★+

OPERATES
7-DAY CARIBBEAN AND
EUROPE CRUISES

Cruise Line	Holland America Line
Former Names	-
Gross Tonnage	55,451
Builder	Fincantieri (Italy)
Original Cost	$215 million
Christened By	Ms Debbie Reynolds
Entered Service	May 1996
Interior Design	VFD Interiors/Joe Farcus
Country of Registry	Bahamas (C6NL6)
Tel No 330-943511 Fax No	330-943512
Length (ft/m)	719.3/219.30
Beam (ft/m) 101.0/30.80 Draft (ft/m)	24.6/7.50
Propulsion	diesel-electric (34,560kW)
Propellers	2 (CP)
Decks 10 Crew	588
Pass. Capacity (basis 2) 1,264 (all berths)	1,627
Pass. Space Ratio (basis 2) 43.8 (all berths)	34.0
Officers Dutch Total Cabins	632
Size Range (sq ft/m)	187-1,126/17.3-104.5
Outside Cabins 501 Inside Cabins	131
Single Cabins 0 Balcony Cabins	150
Wheelchair Cabins	6
Cabin Current	110/220 AC
Refrigerator	Category PS/S/A/B only
Cabin TV Yes VCR	No
Dining Rooms 1 Sittings	2
Elevators	12
Casino Yes Slot Machines	Yes

Swimming Pools (outside)	1
Swimming Pools (inside)	1 (magrodome)
Whirlpools 2 Gymnasium	Yes
Sauna/Steam Room Yes/No Massage	Yes
Self-Service Launderette	Yes
Movie Theater/Seats	Yes/249
Library	Yes
Children's Facilities	No
Watersports Facilities	None
Classification Society	Lloyd's Register

RATINGS	SCORE
Ship: Condition/Cleanliness	8.8
Ship: Space/Flow/Comfort	8.4
Ship: Decor/Furnishings	8.5
Ship: Fitness Facilities	7.7
Cabins: Comfort/Facilities	8.1
Cabins: Software	8.2
Food: Dining Room/Cuisine	7.2
Food: Buffets/Informal Dining	6.8
Food: Quality of Ingredients	6.7
Service: Dining Room	6.6
Service: Bars	7.3
Service: Cabins	8.0
Cruise: Entertainment	7.9
Cruise: Activities Program	7.7
Cruise: Hospitality Standard	8.3
OVERALL RATING	116.3

+ This is a well-built ship, and is now the fourth in the *Statendam* class. The ship has a somewhat bold and forthright exterior appearance, but inside, the decor, color coordination and soft furnishings have all evolved somewhat since the first ship in the series (*Statendam*).

It is so good to see that the outside decks have lots of teakwood decking and no sign of astroturf anywhere. A magrodome roof covers an indoor-outdoor pool and central lido area, with a sculpture as the focal point of the whole area.

Inside the ship, there is good passenger flow throughout the main entertainment deck, and plenty of nooks and crannies that are located off a winding passageway. The three-deck high atrium foyer has a sculpture in its center that provides a focal point. The library is quite lovely, and has an extensive range of reference books. What is outstanding and very noticeable is the array of artworks throughout the ship, assembled to represent the Dutch heritage of Holland America Line.

There is a wide range of cabins and suites to choose from, many of which have private balconies (most also have floor to ceiling windows, while other have large picture windows). Most cabins use their space well, are tastefully decorated and also quite well laid out.

However, although drawer space is generally good, closet space is very tight, particularly for long cruises. The bathrooms are good, but bathtubs are small units.

— The two-deck-high showroom is a good room, but the ceiling is low and sightlines are not good from the upper level, although there is some improvement compared to *Maasdam, Ryndam* and *Statendam.* You can expect lines to form for embarkation, disembarkation, for the buffets, and for shore tenders. The cabin service, by Indonesian stewards, is generally good, but is spotty and inconsistent, and communication can prove frustrating sometimes.

Dining The two-deck-high dining room (located at the stern) has dramatic grand staircase (the lower level has windows on three sides) and is an elegant setting. There are tables for two, four, six and eight, but as in most large dining rooms, the noise level can be high at times, particularly for those passengers seated adjacent to the waiter stations. A total of 28 suites feature an in-suite dining alternative for those that want a change from the noise and business of the main dining room.

There is also an extensive, dual serving-line Lido Buffet (one side is smoking, the other non-smoking). The beverage station, however, lets it down, and is typical of those found in family locations ashore in the United States.

The food and service are typical of HAL standards of late, and that means non-memorable, but both presentation and cuisine were seen to be improving last year.

Other Comments The ship continues the company's strong maritime traditions, but the food and dining room service components are still somewhat disappointing, although improvements are being made (one must remember that the cruise prices, however, are very modest). Where Holland America Line scores with passengers is in the friendly attitude and smiling faces of the Filipino and Indonesian service staff.

mv Victoria ★★★★

Cruise Line		P&O Cruises
Former Names		Sea Princess/Kungsholm
Gross Tonnage		28,891
Builder		John Brown & Co. (UK)
Original Cost		$22 million
Christened By		Mrs Dan Axel-Brostron
Entered Service		Apr 1966/Feb 1979
Interior Design		Robert Tillberg
Country of Registry		Great Britain
Tel No 144-0320	Fax No	144-0320
Length (ft/m)		660.2/201.23
Beam (ft/m) 87.1/26.57	Draft (ft/m)	28.0/8.56
Propulsion		diesel (18,800kW)
Propellers		2 (CP)
Decks 8	Crew	380
Pass. Capacity (basis 2) 714	(all berths)	743
Pass. Space Ratio (basis 2) 40.4	(all berths)	38.8
Officers		British
Total Cabins		365
Size Range (sq ft/m)		138-467/12.8-43.3
Outside Cabins 295	Inside Cabins	70
Single Cabins		22
Balcony Cabins 0	Wheelchair Cabins	10
Cabin Current		220 AC
Refrigerator		Category AA/BA/BD only
Cabin TV		Yes (higher grade cabins only)
VCR		No
Dining Rooms 1	Sittings	2

Elevators			4
Casino	Yes	Slot Machines	Yes
Swimming Pools (outside) 2		(inside)	1
Whirlpools	1	Gymnasium	Yes
Sauna/Steam Room Yes/No		Massage	Yes
Self-Service Launderette			Yes
Movie Theater/Seats			Yes/289
Library	Yes	Children's Facilities	Yes
Watersports Facilities			None
Classification Society			Lloyd's Register

RATINGS	SCORE
Ship: Condition/Cleanliness	7.4
Ship: Space/Flow/Comfort	7.6
Ship: Decor/Furnishings	7.5
Ship: Fitness Facilities	6.8
Cabins: Comfort/Facilities	7.4
Cabins: Software	7.6
Food: Dining Room/Cuisine	7.4
Food: Buffets/Informal Dining	6.2
Food: Quality of Ingredients	6.5
Service: Dining Room	7.4
Service: Bars	7.6
Service: Cabins	7.6
Cruise: Entertainment	7.4
Cruise: Activities Program	6.3
Cruise: Hospitality Standard	7.6
OVERALL RATING	107.4

+ Solidly built ex-ocean liner has flowing, rounded lines and well-balanced profile. Nicely refurbished and well maintained. Open deck and sunning space is good. There are numerous spacious public rooms with fine quality furnishings and fabrics, and trimmed with fine woods. Generally good British entertainment. Wide range of cabins to choose from. Most are quite roomy, nicely refurbished, and have excellent closet and drawer space, with fine wood-paneled walls. Generous-sized bathrooms have solid fixtures and storage space for toiletries.

— Some cabins have upper and lower berths. The wine list is quite limited. Plastic chairs at the lido buffet should have cushions. Bathroom towels are small.

Dining Tiered European-style dining room is elegant, with old-world traditions and charm, and display of 18th-century Chinese porcelain. Good general food and selection tailored for British tastes, and excellent service from the Goanese staff. The buffets are very basic, and disappointing in both display and food quality, as is the selection of breads and fruits.

Other Comments You should have an enjoyable cruise experience on this ship, which provides some attention to detail, and European finesse, at an appropriate price. Has mainly British passengers. While an excellent ship for long voyages, at 30 years old, she is now looking a little tired. Port taxes and insurance are included for British passengers.

ms Viking Serenade ★★★★

OPERATES

*3- AND 4-DAY BAJA MEXICO CRUISES
(YEAR-ROUND)*

Cruise Line	Royal Caribbean Cruises
Former Names	Stardancer/Scandinavia
Gross Tonnage	40,132
Builder	Dubigeon-Normandie (France)
Original Cost	$100 million
Christened By	Ms Liv Ullmann/
	Ms Whoopi Goldberg
Entered Service	Oct 1982/Jan 1990
Interior Design	Njal Eide/Petter Yran
Country of Registry	Bahamas
Tel No	110-3132	Fax No	110-3132
Length (ft/m)	623.0/189.89
Beam (ft/m)	88.6/27.01	Draft (ft/m)	22.6/6.90
Propulsion	diesel (19,800kW)
Propellers	2 (CP)
Decks	7	Crew	612
Pass. Capacity (basis 2) 1,512	(all berths) 1,863
Pass. Space Ratio (basis 2) 26.5	(all berths) 21.5
Officers	International
Total Cabins	756
Size Range (sq ft/m)	144-400/13.3-37.0
Outside Cabins	478	Inside Cabins	278
Single Cabins	0
Balcony Cabins	5	Wheelchair Cabins	4
Cabin Current	110 AC
Refrigerator	Category R/A only
Cabin TV	Yes	VCR	No
Dining Rooms	2	Sittings	2

Elevators			5
Casino	Yes	Slot Machines	Yes
Swimming Pools (outside)		1 (magrodome)
(inside)			0
Whirlpools	0	Gymnasium	Yes
Sauna/Steam Room	Yes/No	Massage	Yes
Self-Service Launderette			No
Movie Theater/Seats	No	Library	Yes
Children's Facilities			Yes
Classification Society		Det Norske Veritas

RATINGS	SCORE
Ship: Condition/Cleanliness	7.9
Ship: Space/Flow/Comfort	6.4
Ship: Decor/Furnishings	7.2
Ship: Fitness Facilities	7.5
Cabins: Comfort/Facilities	6.3
Cabins: Software	7.7
Food: Dining Room/Cuisine	6.8
Food: Buffets/Informal Dining	6.6
Food: Quality of Ingredients	7.1
Service: Dining Room	6.7
Service: Bars	6.5
Service: Cabins	6.1
Cruise: Entertainment	7.8
Cruise: Activities Program	7.6
Cruise: Hospitality Standard	7.4
OVERALL RATING	105.6

+ Has good open deck and sunning space, and a magrodome-covered pool for inclement weather. Wide array of public rooms and facilities, including a conference center and Viking Crown lounge cantilevered around the funnel. Public rooms have contemporary decor, tasteful colors and good quality furnishings. Compact cabins are well appointed, and have reasonable closet space for short cruises. Fine health spa facilities. Attentive service from Caribbean staff. Good for families with children.

— So many inside cabins, and drawer space is poor. Tiny cabin bathrooms. Expect lines for embarkation, disembarkation, shore tenders and buffets. Too many announcements.

Dining Two large, attractive dining rooms are well laid out, but there are no tables for two. Typical standard hotel banquet food, perfectly portioned, with robotic presentation, and everything seems to taste the same. Poor bread rolls and fruits.

Other Comments This medium-density ship, which underwent a $75 million reconstruction in 1991, provides a well-programmed cruise experience in upbeat surroundings, at a decent cruise rate.

ms Vistafjord ★★★★★

VARIOUS CRUISES WORLDWIDE

Cruise Line		Cunard
Former Names		-
Gross Tonnage		24,492
Builder		Swan, Hunter (UK)
Original Cost		$35 million
Christened By		Mrs Agnes Cecille Henrikson
Entered Service		May 1973/May 1984
Interior Design		Platou Design
Country of Registry		Bahamas
Tel No	110-4114	Fax No 130-5630
Length (ft/m)		626.9/191.09
Beam (ft/m) 82.1/25.05	Draft (ft/m)	27.0/8.23
Propulsion		diesel (17,900kW)
Propellers		2 (FP)
Decks	9	Crew 379
Pass. Capacity (basis 2) 677		(all berths) 732
Pass. Space Ratio (basis 2) 36.1		(all berths) 33.4
Officers		Norwegian
Total Cabins		376
Size Range (sq ft/m)		67-325/6.2-30.0
Outside Cabins	324	Inside Cabins 52
Single Cabins		73
Balcony Cabins		25
Wheelchair Cabins		4
Cabin Current		110/220 AC
Refrigerator		Category I/II
Cabin TV	Yes	VCR No
Dining Rooms	1	Sittings 1

Elevators			6
Casino	Yes	Slot Machines	Yes
Swimming Pools (outside) 1		(inside)	1
Whirlpools	2	Gymnasium	Yes
Sauna/Steam Room Yes/No		Massage	Yes
Self-Service Launderette			Yes
Movie Theater/Seats			Yes/190
Library	Yes	Children's Facilities	No
Watersports Facilities			None
Classification Society		Lloyd's Register	

RATINGS	SCORE
Ship: Condition/Cleanliness	9.2
Ship: Space/Flow/Comfort	9.1
Ship: Decor/Furnishings	9.1
Ship: Fitness Facilities	8.8
Cabins: Comfort/Facilities	9.0
Cabins: Software	9.2
Food: Dining Room/Cuisine	9.3
Food: Buffets/Informal Dining	8.8
Food: Quality of Ingredients	9.1
Service: Dining Room	9.2
Service: Bars	8.8
Service: Cabins	8.8
Cruise: Entertainment	8.7
Cruise: Activities Program	8.6
Cruise: Hospitality Standard	9.1
OVERALL RATING	134.8

+ Very well maintained and extremely clean. At sea she is stable, smooth and quiet as a swan. Expansive open decks and ample sunning space. Built with the finest quality materials throughout. Teakwood outdoor wrap-around promenade deck, and deck lounge chairs have cushioned pads. Spacious and elegant public rooms with high ceilings. Has tasteful decor throughout, and improved in the latest refit. Thick cotton bathrobes provided for all. Excellent Scandinavian stewardesses. Conservative, sophisticated, classically oriented entertainment. Wide interior stairwells. Suites with balconies are superbly equipped, but all cabins are extremely well appointed and tastefully redecorated (all cabins benefitted from brand new bathrooms, installed in the 1994 refit). All have excellent closet and drawer space and lighted closets. Excellent range of cabins for single travelers.

Really outstanding are two new duplex suites; the lower level contains a bedroom and bathroom with Jacuzzi bathtub; the upper level has an expansive living room, with Bang & Olufsen sound system, treadmill, private bar, another bathroom (with Jacuzzi bathtub), and separate private sauna, while outdoors is a private balcony with whirlpool. Refreshingly few announcements and interruptions.

Few international ships can compete with *Vistafjord* for her relaxing ambiance and service from a well-organized and happy crew.

— Operates in only two languages: English and German (may be negative for some). Some Sun Deck and Promenade Deck suites have obstructed views. Tub chairs in North Cape Bar are uncomfortable.

Dining The dining room is a grand, elegant room, recently expanded, for single-sitting dining. There are many tables for two, four, six or eight. Senior officers host tables for dinner each evening. Single-waiter service in the best European tradition. The tables are a little close together, making it somewhat difficult for waiters to serve in some areas.

Has international cuisine featuring the highest quality and variety of ingredients (outstanding variety of breads and cheeses at every meal, which are particularly appreciated by the ship's 40% German-speaking clientele). At all dining room meals, a cold table is set for such things as breads and cheeses at lunchtime, and passengers can either help themselves (German passengers in particular like to do this), or be served by a waiter. Salad items, salad dressings (10 varieties), juices (9 varieties), and cheeses (a fine selection of more than two dozen international cheeses) are always set on the cold table.

A mixture of silver-service (where entrees and vegetables are brought to the table on large silver platters and served individually), and plate-service (where vegetables and entrees are set artistically on the main course plate) is featured. Extra vegetables can be obtained at any time. Waiters are well trained through a sophisticated management structure on board.

Table-side flambeaus cannot be done at individual tables, but they are done in two or three central locations, and the waiters collect the finished product to take to their respective tables. Although the chef has his favorites, the menus are never repeated, even on the longest voyages. You can also order "off-menu" at any time, and create your own delightful cuisine. Little touches in presentation, such as paper doilies under teacups, soup bowls, and towel-wrapped water jugs, make a difference in product delivery.

Apart from the regular menu (four appetizers, three soups, sorbet, five entrees, two salads, several desserts, and a superb selection of international cheeses at every dinner meal), there is a Golden Door Spa menu, a vegetarian menu, and diabetic dessert every day.

Different color tablecloths and napkins are featured daily for luncheon and dinner. An extensive wine list, with prices ranging from $13 to $400. Cappuccino and espresso coffees are available at any time in the dining room, without charge. Outstanding fruit selection.

Tivoli, a new, completely separate 40-seat Italian à la carte restaurant (an alternative dining spot added in the 1994 refit), is intimate and very elegant, and the food is outstanding, from a varied menu that features many special dishes daily.

The Lido Deck Café is an informal dining area that is extremely popular, but the traffic flow would be improved by a centrally located steam table.

Other Comments This ship has classic liner styling and profile. She is a finely proportioned ship with beautiful, rounded, flowing lines and classic, sleek profile from any angle. Grandly refurbished in late 1994, this ship caters especially well to discerning passengers in an elegant, refined, yet friendly style and supremely comfortable surroundings. Although not shiny and new, but well refurbished, the ship provides one of the world's most pleasant and civilized travel experiences. Gratuities are included.

ms Vistamar ★★★+

Cruise Line	Mar Line		
Former Names	-		
Gross Tonnage	7,478		
Builder	Union Navale de Levante (Spain)		
Original Cost	$45 million		
Christened By	n/a		
Entered Service	Sep 1989		
Interior Design	Oliver Design		
Country of Registry	Liberia		
Tel No 133-2275	Fax No	133-2275	
Length (ft/m)	385.1/117.40		
Beam (ft/m) 55.1/16.82	Draft (ft/m)	14.9/4.55	
Propulsion	diesel (3,900kW)		
Propellers	2 (CP)		
Decks 6	Crew	100	
Pass. Capacity (basis 2) 295	(all berths) 340		
Pass. Space Ratio (basis 2) 25.3	(all berths) 21.9		
Officers	Spanish		
Total Cabins	150		
Size Range (sq ft/m)	n/a		
Outside Cabins 126	Inside Cabins	24	
Single Cabins	5		
Balcony Cabins 0	Wheelchair Cabins	0	
Cabin Current	220 AC		
Refrigerator	No		
Cabin TV Yes	VCR	No	
Dining Rooms 1	Sittings	1	
Elevators	3		

Casino	No	Slot Machines	Yes
Swimming Pools (outside) 1		(inside)	0
Whirlpools	0	Gymnasium	Yes
Sauna/Steam Room Yes/No		Massage	Yes
Self-Service Launderette			No
Movie Theater/Seats			No
Library			Yes
Children's Facilities			No
Watersports Facilities			None
Classification Society		Det Norske Veritas	

RATINGS	SCORE
Ship: Condition/Cleanliness	8.0
Ship: Space/Flow/Comfort	7.8
Ship: Decor/Furnishings	7.6
Ship: Fitness Facilities	5.7
Cabins: Comfort/Facilities	7.6
Cabins: Software	7.7
Food: Dining Room/Cuisine	6.3
Food: Buffets/Informal Dining	6.0
Food: Quality of Ingredients	6.0
Service: Dining Room	6.6
Service: Bars	6.7
Service: Cabins	7.0
Cruise: Entertainment	6.2
Cruise: Activities Program	6.4
Cruise: Hospitality Standard	7.1
OVERALL RATING	102.7

+ Small, rather smart but squat ship profile. Has a single, central staircase. All passenger accommodations are forward, public rooms aft, which means minimal noise in cabins. Wood-trimmed interior decor is attractive and warm, but mirrored ceilings are irritating. Outdoor pool has splash surround and neat water fountain. A very jazzy nightclub/disco, with acres of glass, is set around funnel base. Contemporary four-deck-high atrium with "skydome" has a glass-walled elevator and wrap-around staircase. Cabins are extremely comfortable and come well equipped, although the bathrooms are small.

— Has a narrow, steep gangway in some ports of call. The cabin closet and drawer space is rather limited.

Dining The single sitting dining is attractive, with warm, contemporary colors and decor. The food is moderate, but the selection of breads, cheeses and fruits is limited.

Other Comments Spanish-speaking passengers should enjoy this intimate ship, which features very attractively priced cruises that have comfort, style and flair. Sailings have, however, been somewhat sporadic recently.

ms Westerdam ★★★★

OPERATES

7-DAY CARIBBEAN CRUISES

Cruise Line			Holland America Line
Former Names			Homeric
Gross Tonnage			53,872
Builder			Meyer Werft (Germany)
Original Cost			$150 million
Christened By			n/a
Entered Service			May 1986/Nov 1988
Interior Design			Robert Tillberg/VFD Interiors
Country of Registry			Netherlands (PINW)
Tel No	130-2534	Fax No	130-2532
Length (ft/m)			797.9/243.23
Beam (ft/m)	95.1/29.00	Draft (ft/m)	23.6/7.20
Propulsion			diesel (23,830kW)
Propellers			2 (CP)
Decks	9	Crew	642
Pass. Capacity (basis 2) 1,494		(all berths)	1,773
Pass. Space Ratio (basis 2) 36.0		(all berths)	30.3
Officers			Dutch
Total Cabins			747
Size Range (sq ft/m)			131-425/12.0-39.5
Outside Cabins	495	Inside Cabins	252
Single Cabins			0
Balcony Cabins	0	Wheelchair Cabins	4
Cabin Current	110 AC	Refrigerator	No
Cabin TV	Yes	VCR	No
Dining Rooms	1	Sittings	2
Elevators			7
Casino	Yes	Slot Machines	Yes

Swimming Pools (outside)		2 (1 with magrodome)	
Swimming Pools (inside)			0
Whirlpools	2	Gymnasium	Yes
Sauna/Steam Room Yes/No		Massage	Yes
Self-Service Launderette			Yes-5
Movie Theater/Seats			Yes/237
Library			Yes
Children's Facilities			Yes
Watersports Facilities			None
Classification Society			Lloyd's Register

RATINGS	SCORE
Ship: Condition/Cleanliness	8.0
Ship: Space/Flow/Comfort	8.0
Ship: Decor/Furnishings	7.7
Ship: Fitness Facilities	6.8
Cabins: Comfort/Facilities	7.7
Cabins: Software	7.8
Food: Dining Room/Cuisine	7.2
Food: Buffets/Informal Dining	6.8
Food: Quality of Ingredients	6.7
Service: Dining Room	6.1
Service: Bars	7.2
Service: Cabins	7.9
Cruise: Entertainment	7.0
Cruise: Activities Program	7.4
Cruise: Hospitality Standard	8.0
OVERALL RATING	110.3

+ Has teakwood outdoor decks and a wrap-around promenade deck. Good open deck and sunning space. Elegant, functional interior, with restful public rooms decorated in pastel tones, though some decor looks dated. Absorbs passengers well and has good layout. High-quality furnishings and fabrics throughout. Good open deck space for sunning. Fine health and fitness center. Cabins are generously proportioned, well appointed and equipped with everything, including ample closet, drawer and storage space, and generous-sized bathrooms.

— Too many inside cabins. Long lines for embarkation, disembarkation, buffets, and shore tenders. Magrodome-covered swimming pool deck is too small for number of passengers carried. The entertainment is disappointing.

Dining Traditional dining room has a raised center dome and portholes, highlighted at night by special lighting. The food, while attractively presented, is virtually tasteless. Poor selection of breads, cheeses and fresh fruits. Service is reasonable, though communication is frustrating (smiles can only do so much).

Other Comments This well-built, contemporary ship, which underwent a $84 million stretch in 1990, is fine to cruise on, and provides a fairly refined, comfortable setting, but carries too many passengers, although fortunately, there's never a feeling of being crowded.

ms Windward ★★★★

OPERATES

7-DAY ALASKA AND
CARIBBEAN CRUISES

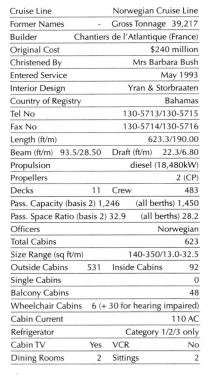

Cruise Line			Norwegian Cruise Line
Former Names		-	Gross Tonnage 39,217
Builder			Chantiers de l'Atlantique (France)
Original Cost			$240 million
Christened By			Mrs Barbara Bush
Entered Service			May 1993
Interior Design			Yran & Storbraaten
Country of Registry			Bahamas
Tel No			130-5713/130-5715
Fax No			130-5714/130-5716
Length (ft/m)			623.3/190.00
Beam (ft/m) 93.5/28.50		Draft (ft/m)	22.3/6.80
Propulsion			diesel (18,480kW)
Propellers			2 (CP)
Decks	11	Crew	483
Pass. Capacity (basis 2) 1,246		(all berths) 1,450	
Pass. Space Ratio (basis 2) 32.9		(all berths) 28.2	
Officers			Norwegian
Total Cabins			623
Size Range (sq ft/m)			140-350/13.0-32.5
Outside Cabins	531	Inside Cabins	92
Single Cabins			0
Balcony Cabins			48
Wheelchair Cabins		6 (+ 30 for hearing impaired)	
Cabin Current			110 AC
Refrigerator			Category 1/2/3 only
Cabin TV	Yes	VCR	No
Dining Rooms	2	Sittings	2

Elevators			7
Casino	Yes	Slot Machines	Yes
Swimming Pools (outside) 2		(inside)	0
Whirlpools		2	Gymnasium Yes
Sauna/Steam Room Yes/No		Massage	Yes
Self-Service Launderette			No
Movie Theater/Seats	No	Library	Yes
Children's Facilities			Yes
Watersports Facilities			None
Classification Society			Det Norske Veritas

RATINGS	SCORE
Ship: Condition/Cleanliness	8.6
Ship: Space/Flow/Comfort	7.9
Ship: Decor/Furnishings	8.2
Ship: Fitness Facilities	8.1
Cabins: Comfort/Facilities	7.8
Cabins: Software	8.0
Food: Dining Room/Cuisine	7.2
Food: Buffets/Informal Dining	6.3
Food: Quality of Ingredients	6.4
Service: Dining Room	7.6
Service: Bars	7.5
Service: Cabins	7.4
Cruise: Entertainment	8.3
Cruise: Activities Program	7.8
Cruise: Hospitality Standard	7.6
OVERALL RATING	114.7

+ Excellent exterior design, protected aft decks and sun terraces overlooking a swimming pool. Good public rooms, and spacious, open lobby area. Soothing interior decor and colors. Good showlounge and colorful, jazzy shows. Cabins are warm and cozy, with soft colors and wood trim. This mid-size ship feels large, and provides plenty of space inside so that crowding shouldn't happen.

— There really is no entrance foyer. Cabins have almost no drawer or storage space. Long lines for buffets. Poor room service.

Dining Three dining rooms: Sun Terrace, The Terraces (which is the nicest), and Four Seasons (all have the same menu and food), plus The Bistro (for casual dining) and ultra-casual Sports Bar. Cuisine is family diner food, with thick sauces. Quantity is present, but not quality. Perfunctory service by waiters whose English is poor. Nice wine list, and well put together. Sports Bar has large selection of beers. Afternoon tea is not served anywhere.

Other Comments Has squat funnel housing, and inboard lifeboats. Upper, tiered outdoor pool deck is always busy, but fun. Fairly good interior layout and passenger flow. Special cabins for the hearing impaired—a first for any large ship. Together with *Dreamward*, she's pricier than NCL's other ships, but worth it for first-time cruisegoers not seeking fine cuisine.

ms World Discoverer ★★★★+

OPERATES

WORLDWIDE EXPEDITION CRUISES
(INCLUDING ANTARCTICA)

Cruise Line		Society Expeditions
Former Names		Bewa Discoverer
Gross Tonnage		3,153
Builder		Schichau Unterweser (Germany)
Original Cost	n/a	Christened By	n/a
Entered Service		Apr 1977
Interior Design		Carleton Varney
Country of Registry		Liberia
Tel No	124-2744	Fax No	124-2744
Length (ft/m)		287.1/87.51
Beam (ft/m)	49.6/15.12	Draft (ft/m)	14.6/4.46
Propulsion/Propellers		diesel (3,530kW)/1 (CP)
Decks	4	Crew	75
Pass. Capacity (basis 2) 138		(all berths) 138
Pass. Space Ratio (basis 2) 22.8		(all berths) 22.8
Officers		European
Total Cabins		71
Size Range (sq ft/m)		89-218/8.2-20.2
Outside Cabins	71	Inside Cabins	0
Single Cabins		0
Balcony Cabins		0
Wheelchair Cabins		0
Cabin Current		110/220 AC
Refrigerator		No
Cabin TV	No	VCR	No
Dining Rooms		1 (open seating)
Elevators		1
Casino	No	Slot Machines	No

Swimming Pools (outside) 1		(inside)	0
Whirlpools	0	Gymnasium	Yes
Sauna/Steam Room No/No		Massage	Yes
Self-Service Launderette			No
Lecture Room/Theater	No	Library	Yes
Zodiacs:		Yes	Helicopter Pad: No
Watersports Facilities		Scuba diving, snorkeling,
		fishing, waterski and windsurf equipment
Classification Society		American Bureau
		of Shipping

RATINGS	SCORE
Ship: Condition/Cleanliness	8.0
Ship: Space/Flow/Comfort	7.7
Ship: Expedition Equipment	7.9
Ship: Decor/Furnishings	7.9
Cabins: Comfort/Facilities	7.7
Cabins: Software	7.8
Food: Dining Room/Cuisine	7.8
Food: Buffets/Informal Dining	7.1
Food: Quality of Ingredients	7.1
Service: Dining Room	7.7
Service: Bars	7.5
Service: Cabins	7.8
Cruise: Itineraries/Operations	8.0
Cruise: Lecture Program	7.6
Cruise: Hospitality Standard	7.6
OVERALL RATING	115.2

+ Features ice-hardened hull and is extremely maneuverable. Well maintained. Well-equipped for in-depth expedition cruising in comfort. Elegant and impressive public rooms and interior decor. Cabins are of good proportions, are comfortable, and very tastefully furnished. Naturalists and expert lecturers and nature specialists escort every expedition. One of the best expedition cruise vessels of its type in service today.

— Has steep passenger gangway. Closet space is limited in cabins.

Dining Has a very attractive, cozy dining room (some tables for two). Big picture windows and comfortable chairs make for an elegant setting. Excellent cuisine and service, although it relies heavily on dairy products. Limited selection of breads and fruits.

Other Comments Sophisticated, small, but very comfortable vessel built expressly for adventure cruising has sleek, well-proportioned profile with contemporary swept-back funnel. This ship provides a fine setting for expedition cruising to some of the most remote destinations in the world. It's quite expensive, but worth it for discerning, well-traveled passengers yearning for a sense of adventure and who enjoy learning about the world around us and its fascinating peoples. Gratuities are not included.

ib Yamal ★★★+

OPERATES
ANTARCTICA/TRANSPOLAR
EXPEDITION CRUISES

Cruise Line		Murmansk Shipping
Former Names	-	Gross Tonnage 20,646
Builder	Baltic Shipyard, Murmansk (Russia)	
Original Cost		$150 million
Christened ByVinogradov Vladimirovna		
Interior Design	n/a	
Entered Service		Nov 1992
Country of Registry		Russia (UPOL)
Tel No 140-5744	Fax No	140-5745
Length (ft/m)		492.1/150.00
Beam (ft/m) 98.4/30.00	Draft (ft/m) 36.0/11.00	
Propulsion	nuclear-powered turbo-elec	
		(75,000shp)
Propellers		3
Decks	4 Crew	130
Pass. Capacity (basis 2) 100		(all berths) 100
Pass. Space Ratio (basis 2) 206.4	(all berths) 206.4	
Officers		Russian/Ukrainian
Total Cabins		50
Size Range (sq ft/m)		130-300/14.3-27.8
Outside Cabins	50 Inside Cabins	0
Single Cabins		0
Balcony Cabins	0 Wheelchair Cabins	0
Cabin Current		220 AC
Refrigerator		All cabins
Cabin TV	Yes VCR	Yes
Dining Rooms	1 Sittings	open seating
Elevators		0

Casino	No	Slot Machines	No
Swimming Pools (inside)			1
Whirlpools	0	Gymnasium	Yes
Sauna/Steam Room			Yes-2/No
Massage			No
Self-Service Launderette			Yes
Lecture/Film Room		Yes (seats 100)	
Library	Yes	Zodiacs	4
Helicopter Pad	2 helicopters for passenger use		
Classification Society			RS

RATINGS	SCORE
Ship: Condition/Cleanliness	7.6
Ship: Space/Flow/Comfort	6.0
Ship: Expedition Equipment	9.0
Ship: Decor/Furnishings	5.8
Cabins: Comfort/Facilities	5.7
Cabins: Software	6.0
Food: Dining Room/Cuisine	6.8
Food: Buffets/Informal Dining	6.4
Food: Quality of Ingredients	7.0
Service: Dining Room	6.6
Service: Bars	6.6
Service: Cabins	6.6
Cruise: Itineraries/Operations	7.8
Cruise: Lecture Program	7.7
Cruise: Hospitality Standard	7.6
OVERALL RATING	103.2

+ The ultimate in technology accompanies this special ship, one of a fleet of the world's most powerful ice-breakers. Has Zodiacs for shore landings, plus two helicopters for reconnaissance and passenger sightseeing use. Rugged, yet surprisingly comfortable surroundings. Tiered lecture theater with stage is the setting for a team of biologists, scientists, geologists and other lecturers. Has two lounges. Heated indoor pool. All cabins are generously sized, and are outside, all with private facilities. Attentive and friendly Russian service. Passengers are allowed on the bridge at all times.

— Limited closet and drawer space in most cabins. Bathrooms are small and utilitarian. Limited number of public rooms.

Dining Nicely appointed dining room. The catering, supervised by a Swedish company (when under charter to Quark Expeditions) is surprisingly hearty, with plenty of meat and potato dishes, but little fruit and cheese. Remember, this is not gourmet cuisine.

Other Comments This is an incredible vessel, with a three-inch-thick reinforced bow for negotiating tough ice conditions. Has enough fuel for four years without refueling! Try the incredible Transpolar voyage via the North Pole. This is one of the most unusual, exciting expedition cruise experiences available today.

mv Yorktown Clipper ★★★

OPERATES
VARIOUS U.S. COAST AND
CARIBBEAN CRUISES

Cruise Line	Clipper Cruise Line		
Former Names	-		
Gross Tonnage	2,354		
Builder	First Coast Shipbuilding (USA)		
Original Cost	$12 million		
Christened By	Mrs Richard Wilson		
Entered Service	Apr 1988		
Interior Design	Christner Partnership		
Country of Registry	USA		
Tel No	none	Fax No	none
Length (ft/m)		257.0/78.30	
Beam (ft/m) 43.0/13.10	Draft (ft/m)	8.0/2.43	
Propulsion	diesel (1,400shp)		
Propellers	2 (FP)		
Decks	4	Crew	37
Pass. Capacity (basis 2) 138		(all berths) 149	
Pass. Space Ratio (basis 2) 17.0		(all berths) 15.7	
Officers	American		
Total Cabins	69		
Size Range (sq ft/m)		121-138/11.2-12.8	
Outside Cabins	69	Inside Cabins	0
Single Cabins	0		
Balcony Cabins	0	Wheelchair Cabins	0
Cabin Current 110 AC		Refrigerator	No
Cabin TV	No	VCR	No
Dining Rooms	1	Sittings	1
Elevators			0
Casino	No	Slot Machines	No

Swimming Pools (outside) 0		(inside)	0
Whirlpools	0	Gymnasium	No
Sauna/Steam Room No/No		Massage	No
Self-Service Launderette			No
Movie Theater/Seats			No
Library			Yes
Children's Facilities			No
Watersports Facilities			None
Classification Society		American Bureau	
		of Shipping	

RATINGS	SCORE
Ship: Condition/Cleanliness	7.3
Ship: Space/Flow/Comfort	4.0
Ship: Decor/Furnishings	7.3
Ship: Fitness Facilities	3.0
Cabins: Comfort/Facilities	6.1
Cabins: Software	6.5
Food: Dining Room/Cuisine	7.2
Food: Buffets/Informal Dining	6.2
Food: Quality of Ingredients	7.0
Service: Dining Room	7.1
Service: Bars	7.0
Service: Cabins	7.3
Cruise: Entertainment	4.0
Cruise: Activities Program	5.6
Cruise: Hospitality Standard	7.5
OVERALL RATING	93.1

+ This small vessel is built for coastal and inland cruises. Has shallow draft and good maneuverability. Well maintained. Teakwood outdoor sun deck. Has rubber Zodiac craft for close-in excursions. Glass-walled observation lounge. The all-outside cabins are small, but, with lots of wood-accented trim and restful colors, are quite comfortable and tastefully furnished. "Americana" experience for those seeking to learn more about the coastal ports around the USA. Casual, unregimented lifestyle, rather like a small, congenial country club.

— This is a high-density ship with only two public rooms: a dining room and a lounge. High engine and generator noise when underway.

Dining Warm, inviting dining room has large picture windows, but no tables for two. Friendly service is provided by young, all-American mid-western college types. The food is of good quality, and made from locally purchased fresh ingredients, although there is little choice. Limited selection of breads and fruits.

Other Comments This ship cannot be compared with big ship ocean cruising. The per diem price is high for what you get, and air fare is extra, but it does appeal to the older American passenger who doesn't want to be on the megaships.

mv Zenith ★★★★+

OPERATES
7-DAY BERMUDA AND
CARIBBEAN CRUISES

Cruise Line		Celebrity Cruises	
Former Names		-	
Gross Tonnage		47,255	
Builder		Meyer Werft (Germany)	
Original Cost		$210 million	
Christened By		Mrs Antony Chandris	
Entered Service		Apr 1992	
Interior Design		Katzourakis/McNeece	
Country of Registry		Liberia	
Tel No	124-5564	Fax No	124-5567
Length (ft/m)		681.0/207.59	
Beam (ft/m)	95.1/29.00	Draft (ft/m)	23.6/7.20
Propulsion		diesel (19,960kW)	
Propellers		2 (CP)	
Decks	9	Crew	628
Pass. Capacity (basis 2) 1,374		(all berths) 1,796	
Pass. Space Ratio (basis 2) 34.3		(all berths) 26.3	
Officers		Greek	
Total Cabins		687	
Size Range (sq ft/m)		185-334/17.0-31.0	
Outside Cabins	541	Inside Cabins	146
Single Cabins			0
Balcony Cabins	0	Wheelchair Cabins	4
Cabin Current			110 AC
Refrigerator			No
Cabin TV	Yes	VCR	No
Dining Rooms	1	Sittings	2
Elevators			7

Casino	Yes	Slot Machines	Yes
Swimming Pools (outside) 2		(inside)	0
Whirlpools	3	Gymnasium	Yes
Sauna/Steam Room Yes/No		Massage	Yes
Self-Service Launderette			No
Movie Theater/Seats			Yes/850
Library			Yes
Children's Facilities			Yes
Watersports Facilities			None
Classification Society		Lloyd's Register	

RATINGS	SCORE
Ship: Condition/Cleanliness	9.1
Ship: Space/Flow/Comfort	8.7
Ship: Decor/Furnishings	8.9
Ship: Fitness Facilities	8.2
Cabins: Comfort/Facilities	8.1
Cabins: Software	8.1
Food: Dining Room/Cuisine	8.5
Food: Buffets/Informal Dining	8.0
Food: Quality of Ingredients	8.0
Service: Dining Room	8.2
Service: Bars	8.1
Service: Cabins	8.1
Cruise: Entertainment	8.5
Cruise: Activities Program	8.1
Cruise: Hospitality Standard	8.3
OVERALL RATING	124.9

+ Smart, contemporary profile. Similar interior layout and elegant decor to sister ship *Horizon*. Enlarged and enhanced forward observation lounge. Double-wide indoor promenade. Fine artwork throughout. Art deco hotel-like lobby, with two-deck-high ceiling. Soothing pastel colors and high-quality furnishings. Good library. Well-insulated cabins are nicely appointed, and have good closet and drawer space. Bathrooms are practical, with large shower areas. Suites are very tasteful, and have butler service. Excellent showlounge. Good seasonal, unobtrusive children's program. Children's playroom has a neat puppet theater.

— Expect lines for embarkation, disembarkation, shore excursions and buffets. Heavy doors to restrooms and outdoor decks. Most outside cabins on Bermuda Deck have lifeboat-obstructed views. No cushioned pads for deck lounge chairs.

Dining Good quality food, presentation and service. Large, elegant dining room has several tables for two. Chairs do not have armrests. Separate vegetarian and children's menu. Improved cabin service menu. Windsurf Café features good breakfast and luncheon buffets. The Grill serves fast-food items.

Other Comments For superb, value-for-money cruising in the Caribbean, this ship provides the benchmark for mainstream cruises and will almost certainly exceed your expectations.

448

SAIL SHIPS

mys Club Med I ★★★★+

OPERATES

7-DAY CARIBBEAN AND
EUROPE CRUISES

Cruise Line			Club Méditerranée
Former Names	-	Gross Tonnage	14,745
Builder	Ateliers et Chantiers du Havre (France)		
Original Cost			$140 million
Christened By			Mrs Silvie
Entered Service			Feb 1990
Interior Design			Pinto/Poyla
Country of Registry			Bahamas
Tel No	110-3117	Fax No	110-3117
Length (ft/m)			613.5/187.00
Beam (ft/m) 65.6/20.00		Draft (ft/m)	16.4/5.00
Type of Vessel			high-tech sail-cruiser
No. of Masts			5 (164 ft high)
Sail Area (sq ft/sq m)			26,910/2,500
Main Propulsion:			a) engines b) sails
Propulsion/Propellers		diesel (9,120kW)/2 (CP)	
Decks 8	Crew 178	Total Cabins	193
Pass. Capacity (basis 2) 386		(all berths) 413	
Pass. Space Ratio (basis 2) 38.1		(all berths) 35.7	
Officers			French
Size Range (sq ft/m)		188-321/17.5-29.8	
Outside Cabins 193		Inside Cabins	0
Single Cabins			0
Balcony Cabins 0		Wheelchair Cabins	0
Cabin Current			110/220 AC
Refrigerator			All cabins
Cabin TV Yes	VCR		No
Dining Rooms 2 (open seating)		Elevators	2

Casino	Yes	Slot Machines	Yes
Swimming Pools (outside)			2
Whirlpools	0	Gymnasium	Yes
Sauna/Steam Room Yes/No		Massage	Yes
Self-Service Launderette			No
Library			Yes
Watersports Facilities Aft platform, 12 windsurfers, 3 sailboats, 2 water-ski boats, 20 single scuba tanks, snorkels, 4 motorized watersport boats			
Classification Society			Bureau Veritas

RATINGS	SCORE
Ship: Condition/Cleanliness	8.2
Ship: Space/Flow/Comfort	8.0
Ship: Decor/Furnishings	8.6
Ship: Watersports Facilities	9.0
Cabins: Comfort/Facilities	8.4
Cabins: Software	8.0
Food: Dining Room/Cuisine	8.2
Food: Buffets/Informal Dining	7.6
Food: Quality of Ingredients	7.7
Service: Dining Room	7.6
Service: Bars	7.7
Service: Cabins	8.2
Cruise: Sail-Cruise Experience	7.2
Cruise: Entertainment/Activities	6.1
Cruise: Hospitality Standard	7.3
OVERALL RATING	117.8

+ Extensive watersports facilities and fine aft marina platform. Computer workshop. Golf simulator (provided instead of a gymnasium) incurs extra charge. Good public rooms. Cabins very well equipped, with plenty of storage space and 24-hour room service (but you pay for food). Six four-person cabins. Some 35 doubles are fitted with an extra pullman berth.

— Programmed activities under the direction of a large team of young, energetic GOs (Gentils Organisateurs), who have full run of the ship, are rather clown-like and amateurish.

Dining Two lovely dining rooms have tables for one, two or more. Open seating for all meals. The Odyssey Restaurant has a charming open terrace for informal meals. Afternoon tea is a delight. Open-air dining terrace. Cuisine is mainly French and Continental, but presentation needs improving. Beer and standard wines are included for lunch and dinner.

Other Comments One of a pair of the world's largest sail-cruisers is part cruise ship, part yacht. Larger version of the Windstar Cruises vessels. Five huge masts provide seven computer-controlled sails with a total area of 2,500 sq m. Superb for more upscale active singles and couples who might prefer casual elegance to the wilder vacation experience at some Club Med resorts. Cruise can be combined with a Club Med Village Vacation (Bora Bora and Moorea). No gratuities are expected or accepted, as at all Club Med resorts.

mys Club Med II ★★★★+

OPERATES
TAHITI AND SOUTH PACIFIC CRUISES

Cruise Line			Club Mediterranée
Former Names	-	Gross Tonnage	14,745
Builder	Ateliers et Chantiers du Havre (France)		
Original Cost			$145 million
Christened By			n/a
Entered Service			Dec 1992
Interior Design			Pinto/Poyla
Country of Registry			Wallis & Fortuna
Tel No	110-2173	Fax No	110-2173
Length (ft/m)			613.5/187.00
Beam (ft/m)	65.6/20.00	Draft (ft/m)	16.4/5.00
Type of Vessel			high-tech sail-cruiser
No. of Masts			5 (164 ft high)
Sail Area (sq ft/sq m)			26,910/2,500
Main Propulsion			a) engines b) sails
Propulsion/Propellers		diesel (9,120kW)/2 (CP)	
Decks	8	Crew 181	Total Cabins 196
Pass. Capacity (basis 2) 392			(all berths) 419
Pass. Space Ratio (basis 2) 37.6			(all berths) 35.1
Officers			French
Size Range (sq ft/m)			188-321/17.5-29.8
Outside Cabins	196	Inside Cabins	0
Single Cabins			0
Balcony Cabins	0	Wheelchair Cabins	0
Cabin Current			110/220 AC
Refrigerator			All cabins
Cabin TV	Yes	VCR	No
Dining Rooms	2 (open seating)	Elevators	2

Casino	Yes	Slot Machines	Yes
Swimming Pools (outside)			2
Whirlpools	0	Gymnasium	No
Sauna/Steam Room Yes/No		Massage	Yes
Self-Service Launderette			No
Library			Yes
Watersports Facilities Aft platform, 12 windsurfers,			
3 sailboats, 2 water-ski boats, 20 single scuba			
tanks, snorkels, 4 motorized watersport boats			
Classification Society			Bureau Veritas

RATINGS	SCORE
Ship: Condition/Cleanliness	8.2
Ship: Space/Flow/Comfort	8.0
Ship: Decor/Furnishings	8.6
Ship: Watersports Facilities	9.0
Cabins: Comfort/Facilities	8.4
Cabins: Software	8.0
Food: Dining Room/Cuisine	8.2
Food: Buffets/Informal Dining	7.7
Food: Quality of Ingredients	7.7
Service: Dining Room	7.6
Service: Bars	7.7
Service: Cabins	8.2
Cruise: Sail-Cruise Experience	7.2
Cruise: Entertainment/Activities	6.1
Cruise: Hospitality Standard	7.3
OVERALL RATING	117.9

+ Extensive watersports facilities and fine aft marina platform. Computer workshop. Golf simulator (provided instead of a gymnasium) incurs extra charge. Good public rooms. Cabins very well equipped, with plenty of storage space and 24-hour room service (but you pay for food). Six four-person cabins. Some 35 doubles are fitted with an extra pullman berth.

— Programmed activities under the direction of a large team of young, energetic GOs (Gentils Organisateurs), who have full run of the ship, are rather clown-like and amateurish.

Dining Two lovely dining rooms have tables for one, two or more. Open seating for all meals. The Odyssey Restaurant has a charming open terrace for informal meals. Afternoon tea is a delight. Open-air dining terrace. Cuisine is mainly French and Continental, but presentation needs improving. Beer and standard wines are included for lunch and dinner.

Other Comments One of a pair of the world's largest sail-cruisers is part cruise ship, part yacht. Larger version of the Windstar Cruises vessels. Five huge masts provide seven computer-controlled sails with a total area of 2,500 sq m. Superb for more upscale active singles and couples who might prefer casual elegance to the wilder vacation experience at some Club Med resorts. Cruise can be combined with a Club Med Village Vacation (Bora Bora and Moorea). No gratuities are expected or accepted, as at all Club Med resorts.

mys Le Ponant ★★★★+

OPERATES

VARIOUS CARIBBEAN AND
MEDITERRANEAN CRUISES

Cruise Line		Compagnie des Isles du Ponant	
Former Names	-	Gross Tonnage	1,489
Builder			SFCN (France)
Original Cost	n/a	Christened By	n/a
Entered Service			1991
Interior Design			Sterling Design
Country of Registry			France
Tel No	111-1406	Fax No	111-1406
Length (ft/m)			288.7/88.00
Beam (ft/m)	39.3/12.00	Draft (ft/m)	13.1/4.00
Type of Vessel			high tech sail-cruiser
No. of Masts			3
Sail Area (sq ft/sq m)			16,150/1,500
Main Propulsion			a) engine b) sails
Propulsion			diesel/sail power
Propellers			1 (CP)
Decks	3	Crew	30
Pass. Capacity (basis 2) 56		(all berths) 67	
Pass. Space Ratio (basis 2) 26.5		(all berths) 22.2	
Officers			French
Total Cabins			32
Size Range (sq ft/m)			140/13.0
Outside Cabins	32	Inside Cabins	0
Single Cabins			0
Balcony Cabins	0	Wheelchair Cabins	0
Cabin Current	220 AC	Refrigerator	All cabins
Cabin TV	No	VCR	No
Dining Rooms			1 (open seating)

Elevators			No
Casino	No	Slot Machines	No
Swimming Pools (outside)			0
Whirlpools	0	Gymnasium	Yes
Sauna/Steam Room	No/No	Massage	No
Self-Service Launderette			No
Library			Yes
Watersports Facilities		Aft marina platform,	
	windsurf, water-ski boat, scuba, snorkel		
Classification Society			Lloyd's Register

RATINGS	SCORE
Ship: Condition/Cleanliness	8.8
Ship: Space/Flow/Comfort	7.4
Ship: Decor/Furnishings	9.0
Ship: Watersports Facilities	8.8
Cabins: Comfort/Facilities	8.7
Cabins: Software	8.1
Food: Dining Room/Cuisine	8.5
Food: Buffets/Informal Dining	8.1
Food: Quality of Ingredients	8.0
Service: Dining Room	8.0
Service: Bars	7.7
Service: Cabins	8.0
Cruise: Sail-Cruise Experience	7.7
Cruise: Activities Program	7.6
Cruise: Hospitality Standard	8.0
OVERALL RATING	122.4

+ This captivating ship has plenty of room on her open decks for sunbathing. Features a watersports platform at the stern. Very elegant, no glitz interior design is clean, stylish and functional, and ultra-high-tech throughout. Three public lounges have pastel decor, soft colors and great European flair. Crisp, clean blond woods and pristine white cabins feature double or twin beds, mini-bar, personal safe, and private bathroom. All cabins feature portholes and crisp artwork.

— Cabin bathrooms are quite small. Cabins have limited storage space, and few drawers.

Dining The lovely Karukera dining room features complimentary wines and good food. There is fresh fish every day, and meals are true *affaires gastronomiques*. Charming outdoor café under canvas sail-cloth awning.

Other Comments Ultra-sleek, very efficient, this latest generation of sail-cruise ship has three masts that rise 54.8 ft (16.7 m) above the water line. One price fits all. Marketed mainly to young, sophisticated French-speaking passengers who love yachting and the sea. *Très* French, *très* chic. Gratuities are not "required," but they are expected.

sy Lili Marleen ★★★★+

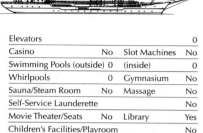

OPERATES

*CARIBBEAN, MEDITERRANEAN
AND BALTIC CRUISES*

Cruise Line		Peter Deilmann Reederei
Former Names	-	Gross Tonnage	750
Builder		Elsflether Werft (Germany)
Original Cost		DM16 million
Christened By		Gisa Deilmann
Interior Design		Partner Ship Design
Entered Service		July 1994
Country of Registry		Germany
Tel No	112-3465	Fax No	112-3466
Length (ft/m)			249.3/76.0
Beam (ft/m)	31.6/9.5	Draft (ft/m)	12.7/3.9
Type of Vessel		barkentine schooner
No. of Masts		3/16 manually furled sails
Sail Area (sq ft/sq m)		12,917/1,200
Main Propulsion		sail power
Propulsion/Propellers		diesel (660kW)/1 (CP)
Decks	3	Crew	25
Pass. Capacity (basis 2) 50		(all berths) 50
Pass. Space Ratio (basis 2) 15.0		(all berths) 15.0
Officers			German
Total Cabins			25
Size Range (sq ft/m)		96.8-129.1/9.0-12.0
Outside Cabins	25	Inside Cabins	0
Single Cabins			0
Balcony Cabins	0	Wheelchair Cabins	0
Cabin Current	220 AC	Refrigerator	No
Cabin TV	No	VCR	No
Dining Rooms	1	Sittings	Open

Elevators			0
Casino	No	Slot Machines	No
Swimming Pools (outside) 0		(inside)	0
Whirlpools	0	Gymnasium	No
Sauna/Steam Room	No	Massage	No
Self-Service Launderette			No
Movie Theater/Seats	No	Library	Yes
Children's Facilities/Playroom			No
Watersports Facilities			None
Classification Society		Germanischer Lloyd

RATINGS	SCORE
Ship: Condition/Cleanliness	8.7
Ship: Space/Flow/Comfort	8.0
Ship: Decor/Furnishings	8.7
Ship: Watersports Facilities	6.4
Cabins: Comfort/Facilities	8.1
Cabins: Software	8.5
Food: Dining Room/Cuisine	8.6
Food: Buffets/Informal Dining	8.1
Food: Quality of Ingredients	8.0
Service: Dining Room	7.8
Service: Bars	8.0
Service: Cabins	8.1
Cruise: Sail-Cruise Experience	9.1
Cruise: Activities Program	7.9
Cruise: Hospitality Standard	8.5
OVERALL RATING	122.5

+ This is a beautiful three-masted barkentine (one square-rigged and two gaff- or schooner-rigged masts), one of which is a 236-ft-high (71-m) mast. Timeless design that relies on the power of Nature most of the time. You can certainly take an active part with the sails, and even go up the rigging (at the captain's discretion). Oneness with the elements is exhilarating. Twin and double cabins are very comfortable. Bathrobes are provided for all passengers (on request). Has good amenities for passenger comfort.

— Little room on the open decks, as on any sailing vessel. No pool.

Dining Has a really charming dining room, and on many evenings dinner is often candlelit. Finest quality china and silverware. International cuisine with regional specialties, with much emphasis on hearty German cuisine.

Other Comments Only casual clothing is needed on this kind of cruise, which is a really relaxing way to travel. Currency is the Deutschmark. Gratuities and insurance not included.

sy Sea Cloud ★★★★★

OPERATES
7-DAY CARIBBEAN AND
EUROPE CRUISES

Cruise Line	Sea Cloud Cruises
Former Names	Antaria/Patria/Angelita/Hussar
Gross Tonnage	2,532
Builder	Krupp Werft (Germany)
Christened By	Mrs Marjorie Merriweather-Post
Entered Service	1931/1978 (restored)
Interior Design	Marjorie Merriweather-Post
Country of Registry	Malta
Tel No 125-6105 Fax No 125-6173	
Length (ft/m)	359.2/109.5
Beam (ft/m) 49.0/14.94 Draft (ft/m) 16.8/5.13	
Type of Vessel	4-masted barque
No. of Masts	4 (17.7 m)/(30 sails)
Sail Area (sq ft/sq m)	32,292/3,000
Main Propulsion	sail power
Propulsion/Propellers	diesel/1 (FP)
Decks 3 Crew 60	
Total Cabins	34
Pass. Capacity (basis 2) 69 (all berths) 69	
Pass. Space Ratio (basis 2) 37.2 (all berths) 37.2	
Officers	European
Size Range (sq ft/m)	102.2-409.0/9.5-38.0
Outside Cabins 34 Inside Cabins 0	
Single Cabins	0
Balcony Cabins 0 Wheelchair Cabins 0	
Cabin Current	110/220 AC
Refrigerator	No
Cabin TV No VCR No	

Dining Rooms		1 (open seating)	
Elevators			0
Casino	No	Slot Machines	No
Swimming Pools (outside)			0
Whirlpools	0	Gymnasium	No
Sauna/Steam Room	No/No	Massage	No
Self-Service Launderette	No	Library	Yes
Watersports Facilities		Snorkeling, water-skiing,	
		windsurfing	
Classification Society		Germanischer Lloyd	

RATINGS	SCORE
Ship: Condition/Cleanliness	8.8
Ship: Space/Flow/Comfort	8.2
Ship: Decor/Furnishings	8.8
Ship: Watersports Facilities	7.6
Cabins: Comfort/Facilities	8.1
Cabins: Software	8.5
Food: Dining Room/Cuisine	8.7
Food: Buffets/Informal Dining	8.1
Food: Quality of Ingredients	8.4
Service: Dining Room	8.3
Service: Bars	8.1
Service: Cabins	8.2
Cruise: Sail-Cruise Experience	9.2
Cruise: Activities Program	7.8
Cruise: Hospitality Standard	8.5
OVERALL RATING	125.3

+ Has plenty of deck space under the expanse of sail. Incredibly fine handcrafted interior, with antique furniture, original oil paintings, gorgeous carved oak paneling everywhere. Two owner's suites are lavish, with Chippendale furniture, gilt detailing, a real fireplace, and Italian marble bathrooms.

— Steep interior staircase, as on most sailing vessels.

Dining Elegant dining room (which is also the ship's library) has wood-paneled walls and a wood beam ceiling. Ample space at each table. Excellent Continental food and presentation, although choice limited. Good breakfast and lunch buffets. Wines included with lunch and dinner.

Other Comments The oldest and most beautiful tall ship sailing, and the largest private yacht ever built, constructed of the best materials. Her masts reach as high as a 20-floor building. Originally built for Marjorie Merriweather Post (the American cereal heiress), this lovely working sailing ship is now owned by a consortium of German yachtsmen and chartered to various operators. It is, in a single word, exhilarating. A special ship like no other, for the discerning few to relish the comfort and elegance of a bygone era. This is one of the world's most delightful travel and vacation experiences. I cannot recommend it highly enough.

sy Sir Francis Drake ★★

OPERATES

*3- TO 7-DAY UK/US VIRGIN ISLANDS
AND CARIBBEAN CRUISES*

Cruise Line			Tall Ship Adventures
Former Names			Godewind/Landkirchen
Gross Tonnage			450 DWT
Builder			(Germany)
Original Cost	n/a	Christened By	n/a
Entered Service			1917
Interior Design			n/a
Country of Registry			Honduras
Tel No			809-496-0914 (cellular)
Fax No			-
Length (ft/m)			162.4/49.50
Beam (ft/m)	22.9/7.00	Draft (ft/m)	9.1/2.80
Type of Vessel			topsail schooner
No. of Masts		3 (9 manually furled sails)	
Sail Area (sq ft/sq m)			1,968/600
Main Propulsion			sail power
Propulsion/Propellers			diesel/1 (FP)
Decks	2	Crew	14
Pass. Capacity (basis 2) 28		(all berths) 30	
Pass. Space Ratio (basis 2) 16.0		(all berths) 15.0	
Officers			British
Total Cabins			14
Size Range (sq ft/m)		80.0-120.0/7.4-11.1	
Outside Cabins	14	Inside Cabins	0
Single Cabins			0
Balcony Cabins	0	Wheelchair Cabins	0
Cabin Current			110/220 AC
Refrigerator			No

Cabin TV	No	VCR	No
Dining Rooms			1 (open seating)
Casino	No	Slot Machines	No
Swimming Pools (outside)			0
Whirlpools	0	Gymnasium	No
Sauna/Steam Room	No/No	Massage	No
Self-Service Launderette			No
Library			No
Watersports Facilities			None
Classification Society			Germanischer Lloyd

RATINGS	SCORE
Ship: Condition/Cleanliness	6.6
Ship: Space/Flow/Comfort	4.6
Ship: Decor/Furnishings	6.1
Ship: Watersports Facilities	3.8
Cabins: Comfort/Facilities	4.4
Cabins: Software	4.7
Food: Dining Room/Cuisine	5.5
Food: Buffets/Informal Dining	5.1
Food: Quality of Ingredients	5.8
Service: Dining Room	6.0
Service: Bars	6.0
Service: Cabins	6.2
Cruise: Sail-Cruise Experience	6.8
Cruise: Activities Program	5.6
Cruise: Hospitality Standard	6.2
OVERALL RATING	**83.4**

+ Authentic topsail schooner, restored to her original condition, and well appointed. Cozy chairs and benches on deck. More than a windjammer, this tall ship is a treasure for those who don't expect the service finesse offered aboard more contemporary ships. There is much wood paneling, brass fittings, and solid furniture. Cabins have various configurations, and a mixture of beds and upper bunks that are comfortable (for a sailing vessel). Carries snorkeling equipment. Passengers can, and often do, participate in hoisting the sails, but otherwise, there's little to do but relax, and her crew will help you unwind totally.

— Has steep interior stairways, as on most true sailing vessels. Constant music on deck is irritating.

Dining Charming dark-wood paneled dining room with wood-trimmed chairs and picture windows. Cuisine is decidedly casual Americana fare. Little choice for non-meat eaters, although the chef will try to accommodate requests. Food quality is barely adequate, although most passengers seem happy with it.

Other Comments You'll have a relaxing, unhurried vacation, in fairly comfortable but basic surroundings, aboard one of the last tall ships. This is for people who really like sailing ships and the hands-on experience this kind of vessel can provide.

sv Star Clipper ★★★★

OPERATES

7- AND 14-DAY CARIBBEAN CRUISES (YEAR-ROUND)

Cruise Line		Star Clippers
Former Names	-	Gross Tonnage 3,025
Builder		Scheepswerven van
		Langerbrugge (Belgium)
Original Cost		$30 million
Christened By		Ms Maria Krafft
Entered Service		May 1992
Interior Design		Struik & Hammerslag
Country of Registry		Luxembourg
Tel No 125-3210	Fax No	125-3206
Length (ft/m)		366.1/111.60
Beam (ft/m) 49.2/15.00	Draft (ft/m)	17.7/5.60
Type of Vessel		barkentine schooner
No. of Masts	4 (208 ft)/16 manually furled sails	
Sail Area (sq ft/sq m)		36,221/3,365
Main Propulsion		sail power
Propulsion/Propellers	diesel (1,030kW)/1 (CP)	
Decks 4	Crew 72	Total Cabins 79
Pass. Capacity (basis 2) 170		(all berths) 182
Pass. Space Ratio (basis 2) 17.7		(all berths) 16.6
Officers		European
Size Range (sq ft/m)		95-150/8.8-14.0
Outside Cabins	85	Inside Cabins 6
Single Cabins		0
Balcony Cabins	0	Wheelchair Cabins 0
Cabin Current		110 AC
Refrigerator		Category 1 cabins only
Cabin TV Yes	VCR	No

Dining Rooms		1 (open seating)
Elevators		0
Casino No	Slot Machines	No
Swimming Pools (outside)		2
Whirlpools 0	Gymnasium	No
Sauna/Steam Room No/No	Massage	No
Self-Service Launderette No	Library	Yes
Watersports Facilities	Waterski boat, sunfish,	
	scuba, snorkel, 8 Zodiacs	
Classification Society		Lloyd's Register

RATINGS	SCORE
Ship: Condition/Cleanliness	7.3
Ship: Space/Flow/Comfort	7.6
Ship: Decor/Furnishings	7.7
Ship: Watersports Facilities	6.6
Cabins: Comfort/Facilities	7.8
Cabins: Software	7.8
Food: Dining Room/Cuisine	6.3
Food: Buffets/Informal Dining	6.2
Food: Quality of Ingredients	6.4
Service: Dining Room	7.2
Service: Bars	7.1
Service: Cabins	7.2
Cruise: Sail-Cruise Experience	9.1
Cruise: Activities Program	6.8
Cruise: Hospitality Standard	7.3
OVERALL RATING	108.4

+ These true sailing ships with cruise accommodations evoke memories of the 19th-century clipper sailing ships. Accurate four-masted barkentine-rigged vessels have graceful lines, a superbly shaped hull and 63-ft-high (19.3-m) masts and 36,221 sq ft (3,365 m²) of sail. Absolutely breathtaking! Good for watersports lovers, these vessels have excellent sea manners. Sports directors provide basic dive instruction, albeit for a fee. Classic Edwardian nautical decor throughout is clean, warm, intimate and inviting. Paneled library has a fireplace, and chairs that are supremely comfortable. Well-equipped, comfortable, contemporary cabins. No lines. No hassle. "Sailing a Square Rigger" classes are now part of every cruise.

— These ships are not for the physically impaired, nor children. The internal stairs are steep, as in most sailing vessels. There is no room service. Pooled tipping system needs modification.

Dining Charming dining room is used for rather unimaginative buffet breakfasts and luncheons, and a mix of buffet and à la carte dinners. Poor seating arrangement. Cuisine is not gourmet, but is quite creative given the incredibly small galley space.

sv Star Flyer ★★★★

OPERATES

*7-DAY EUROPE AND SOUTHEAST
ASIA CRUISES*

Cruise Line			Star Clippers
Former Names	-	Gross Tonnage	3,025
Builder			Sheepswerven van Langerbrugge (Belgium)
Original Cost			$25 million
Christened By			Mrs Ann Krafft
Entered Service			Jul 1991
Interior Design			Struik & Hammerslag
Country of Registry			Luxembourg
Tel No	154-6232	Fax No	154-6231
Length (ft/m)			366.1/111.60
Beam (ft/m) 49.2/15.00		Draft (ft/m)	17.7/5.60
Type of Vessel			barkentine schooner
No. of Masts		4 (208 ft)/16 manually furled sails	
Sail Area (sq ft/sq m)			36,221/3,365
Main Propulsion			sail power
Propulsion/Propellers		diesel (1,030kW)/1 (CP)	
Decks	4	Crew	72
Pass. Capacity (basis 2) 170		(all berths) 182	
Pass. Space Ratio (basis 2) 17.7		(all berths) 16.6	
Officers			European
Total Cabins			85
Size Range (sq ft/m)			95-150/8.8-14.0
Outside Cabins	79	Inside Cabins	6
Single Cabins			0
Balcony Cabins	0	Wheelchair Cabins	0
Cabin Current	110 AC	Refrigerator	All cabins
Cabin TV	Yes	VCR	No

Dining Rooms		1 (open seating)	
Elevators			0
Casino	No	Slot Machines	No
Swimming Pools (outside)			2
Whirlpools	0	Gymnasium	No
Sauna/Steam Room	No/No	Massage	No
Self-Service Launderette	No	Library	Yes
Watersports Facilities		Waterski boat, sunfish, scuba, snorkel, 8 Zodiacs	
Classification Society			Lloyd's Register

RATINGS	SCORE
Ship: Condition/Cleanliness	7.3
Ship: Space/Flow/Comfort	7.6
Ship: Decor/Furnishings	7.7
Ship: Watersports Facilities	6.6
Cabins: Comfort/Facilities	7.8
Cabins: Software	7.8
Food: Dining Room/Cuisine	6.3
Food: Buffets/Informal Dining	6.2
Food: Quality of Ingredients	6.4
Service: Dining Room	7.2
Service: Bars	7.1
Service: Cabins	7.2
Cruise: Sail-Cruise Experience	9.1
Cruise: Activities Program	6.8
Cruise: Hospitality Standard	7.3
OVERALL RATING	108.4

It would have made more sense to have fewer passenger cabins and more room in the galley to provide a better dining experience than the present arrangement, which makes it very trying for any chef, even if provided with ingredients of a good standard. Dinner is à la carte, with a choice of just two entrees. A pasta dish would be a welcome, and simple, addition. Poor bread rolls, pastry items and fruits.

Tea and coffee should be, but is not, available 24 hours a day, particularly in view of the fact that there is no cabin food service at all. When it is available, only paper cups are provided (they should be real china).

Other Comments The staff are very casual, and often mix in areas that should be reserved for passengers. This is a carefree sailing cruise experience in a totally unstructured setting at a modest price. Take only casual clothes, as you won't need jackets, ties, high-heeled shoes, cocktail dresses, or the slightest hint of formal wear. *Star Clipper* and *Star Flyer* promote total informality. This is recommended for those that don't require much entertainment other than wind and sea.

mys Wind Song ★★★★+

OPERATES

7-DAY FRENCH POLYNESIA CRUISES
(YEAR-ROUND)

Cruise Line	Windstar Cruises
Former Names - Gross Tonnage	5,703
Builder	Ateliers et Chantiers du Havre (France)
Original Cost	$34.2 million
Christened By	Mrs Nadia Stolt-Nielsen
Entered Service	Jul 1987
Interior Design	Archiform Design/Marc Held
Country of Registry	Bahamas
Tel No 110-4270 Fax No	110-4271
Length (ft/m)	440.2/134.20
Beam (ft/m) 51.8/15.80 Draft (ft/m)	13.4/4.10
Type of Vessel	computer-controlled sail-cruiser
No. of Masts	4 (204 ft)/6 self-furling sails
Sail Area (sq ft/sq m):	21,489/1,996.4
Main Propulsion	a) engines b) sails
Propulsion	diesel-electric (1,400kW)
Propellers	1 (CP)
Decks 5 Crew	91
Pass. Capacity (basis 2) 148 (all berths)	159
Pass. Space Ratio (basis 2) 38.5 (all berths)	34.1
Officers	British
Total Cabins	74
Size Range (sq ft/m)	185-220/17.0-20.5
Outside Cabins 74 Inside Cabins	0
Single Cabins	0
Balcony Cabins 0 Wheelchair Cabins	0
Cabin Current 110 AC Refrigerator	All cabins
Cabin TV Yes VCR	Yes

Dining Rooms		1 (open seating)	
Casino	Yes	Slot Machines	Yes
Swimming Pools (outside)		1 (dip pool)	
Whirlpools	1	Gymnasium	Yes
Sauna/Steam Room Yes/No		Massage	Yes
Self-Service Launderette No		Library	Yes
Watersports Facilities		Aft marina platform,	
kayaks (2), sunfish sailboats (2), windsurf boards,			
waterski boat, scuba, snorkel, Zodiacs (4)			
Classification Society		Bureau Veritas	

RATINGS	SCORE
Ship: Condition/Cleanliness	8.2
Ship: Space/Flow/Comfort	7.8
Ship: Decor/Furnishings	8.3
Ship: Watersports Facilities	8.0
Cabins: Comfort/Facilities	8.2
Cabins: Software	8.3
Food: Dining Room/Cuisine	7.4
Food: Buffets/Informal Dining	7.0
Food: Quality of Ingredients	7.2
Service: Dining Room	7.6
Service: Bars	7.7
Service: Cabins	7.8
Cruise: Sail-Cruise Experience	8.1
Cruise: Activities Program	7.4
Cruise: Hospitality Standard	8.1
OVERALL RATING	117.1

+ Beautifully crafted interior with fine, blond woods, together with soft, complementary colors. Adequate open deck and sunning space. Cabins are all-outside one-price suites and come completely equipped. Bathrooms are a neat figure-of-eight shape. Watersports platform at stern. No scheduled activities make this a real relaxing vacation.

— Not much deck space, owing to the complex sail machinery. Constant whine from the ship's engine audible in most cabins. No bathtubs. Tiny dip pool. Ambiance could be warmer. Communication with the crew sometimes proves frustrating. Drinks prices are high.

Dining Charming, elegant dining room, with ocean views from large, picture windows. Creative and attractively presented *nouvelle cuisine*, but not up to the standard of the small luxury ships. Quality of ingredients needs upgrading. Attentive, friendly service throughout, but communication proves frustrating at times. Poor pastry items, breads and fruits.

Other Comments Long, sleek-looking craft that is part yacht, part cruise ship, with four giant masts and computer-controlled sails. One of three identical vessels (the fourth, *Wind Saga*, was never built). It will provide a relaxing, unstructured cruise experience that's just right for seven idyllic nights in sheltered areas. You'd be under sail about 40% of the time (conditions permitting). Gratuities "not required," but they are expected.

mys Wind Spirit ★★★★+

OPERATES
7-DAY CARIBBEAN AND
MEDITERRANEAN CRUISES

Cruise Line	Windstar Cruises
Former Names - Gross Tonnage	5,736
Builder Ateliers et Chantiers du Havre (France)	
Original Cost	$34.2 million
Christened By	Mrs Clara van der Vorm
Entered Service	Apr 1988
Interior Design	Archiform Design/Marc Held
Country of Registry	Bahamas
Tel No 110-4434 Fax No	110-4435
Length (ft/m)	440.2/134.20
Beam (ft/m) 51.8/15.80 Draft (ft/m)	13.4/4.10
Type of Vessel:	computer-controlled sail-cruiser
No. of Masts	4 (204 ft)/6 self-furling sails
Sail Area (sq ft/sq m)	21,489/1,996.4
Main Propulsion	a) engines b) sails
Propulsion	diesel-electric (1,400kW)
Propellers	1 (CP)
Decks 5 Crew	91
Total Cabins	74
Pass. Capacity (basis 2) 148 (all berths)	159
Pass. Space Ratio (basis 2) 38.7 (all berths)	36.0
Officers	British/Dutch
Size Range (sq ft/m)	185-220/17.0-22.5
Outside Cabins 74 Inside Cabins	0
Single Cabins	0
Balcony Cabins 0 Wheelchair Cabins	0
Cabin Current 110 AC Refrigerator	All cabins
Cabin TV Yes VCR	Yes

Dining Rooms		1 (open seating)	
Casino Yes	Slot Machines		Yes
Swimming Pools (outside)		1 (dip pool)	
Whirlpools 1	Gymnasium		Yes
Sauna/Steam Room Yes/No	Massage		Yes
Self-Service Launderette No	Library		Yes
Watersports Facilities		Aft marina platform,	
kayaks (2), windsurf boards (2), sunfish sailboats			
(2), water ski boat, scuba, snorkel, zodiacs (4)			
Classification Society		Bureau Veritas	

RATINGS	SCORE
Ship: Condition/Cleanliness	8.2
Ship: Space/Flow/Comfort	7.8
Ship: Decor/Furnishings	8.3
Ship: Watersports Facilities	8.0
Cabins: Comfort/Facilities	8.2
Cabins: Software	8.3
Food: Dining Room/Cuisine	7.4
Food: Buffets/Informal Dining	7.0
Food: Quality of Ingredients	7.2
Service: Dining Room	7.6
Service: Bars	7.7
Service: Cabins	7.8
Cruise: Sail-Cruise Experience	8.1
Cruise: Activities Program	7.4
Cruise: Hospitality Standard	8.1
OVERALL RATING	117.1

+ Nicely crafted, elegant nautical-themed interior. Light woods used throughout. No lines, no hassle. Outdoor deck space quite good unless full. All-outside suites are one price, well appointed, with a CD player and two portholes. Elegant main lounge, with crisp, stark colors. Good indoor-outdoor eatery. Recommended for watersports fans. Unstructured living at sea.

— Constant whine from the ship's generator audible in most cabins. Not much deck space, owing to the complex sail machinery. No bathtubs in cabins. Tiny "dip" pool. Interior colors a little cold. High drinks prices.

Dining Charming, elegant dining room, with ocean views from large, picture windows and tables for four, six or eight. Creative and attractively presented *nouvelle cuisine*, but not up to the standard of the small luxury ships. Quality of ingredients needs upgrading. Attentive, friendly service throughout, but communication proves frustrating at times.

Other Comments Sister to *Wind Song/Wind Spirit*. Part yacht, part cruise ship, with four giant masts and computer-controlled sails. Staff are very casual. This sail-cruise ship will provide relaxed, fairly refined surroundings, and cocoon you with seven nights of unstructured living, only partly under sail. Gratuities are "not required," but they are expected.

mys Wind Star ★★★★+

OPERATES
7-DAY CARIBBEAN AND
EUROPE CRUISES

Cruise Line		Windstar Cruises
Former Names	- Gross Tonnage	5,703
Builder	Ateliers et Chantiers du Havre (France)	
Original Cost		$34.2 million
Christened By		Mrs Louise Andren
Entered Service		Dec 1986
Interior Design	Archiform Design/Marc Held	
Country of Registry		Bahamas
Tel No 110-4266	Fax No	110-4267
Length (ft/m)		440.2/134.20
Beam (ft/m) 51.8/15.80	Draft (ft/m)	13.4/4.10
Type of Vessel	computer-controlled sail-cruiser	
No. of Masts	4 (204 ft)/6 self-furling sails	
Sail Area (sq ft/sq m)		21,489/1,996.4
Main Propulsion		a) engines b) sails
Propulsion	diesel-electric (1,400kW)	
Propellers		1 (CP)
Decks 5	Crew	91
Pass. Capacity (basis 2) 148	(all berths)	167
Pass. Space Ratio (basis 2) 38.5	(all berths)	34.1
Officers		British
Total Cabins		74
Size Range (sq ft/m)	185-220/17.0-22.5	
Outside Cabins 74	Inside Cabins	0
Single Cabins		0
Balcony Cabins 0	Wheelchair Cabins	0
Cabin Current 110 AC	Refrigerator	All cabins
Cabin TV Yes	VCR	Yes

Dining Rooms		1 (open seating)
Casino Yes	Slot Machines	Yes
Swimming Pools (outside)		1 (dip pool)
Whirlpools 1	Gymnasium	Yes
Sauna/Steam Room Yes/No	Massage	Yes
Self-Service Launderette No	Library	Yes
Watersports Facilities	Aft marina platform,	
kayaks (2), windsurf boards (2), sunfish sailboats		
(2), water ski boat, scuba, snorkel, Zodiacs (4)		
Classification Society		Bureau Veritas

RATINGS	SCORE
Ship: Condition/Cleanliness	8.2
Ship: Space/Flow/Comfort	7.8
Ship: Decor/Furnishings	8.3
Ship: Watersports Facilities	8.0
Cabins: Comfort/Facilities	8.2
Cabins: Software	8.3
Food: Dining Room/Cuisine	7.4
Food: Buffets/Informal Dining	7.0
Food: Quality of Ingredients	7.2
Service: Dining Room	7.6
Service: Bars	7.7
Service: Cabins	7.8
Cruise: Sail-Cruise Experience	8.1
Cruise: Activities Program	7.4
Cruise: Hospitality Standard	8.1
OVERALL RATING	117.1

+ Elegant, high-quality interior is beautifully crafted. Light woods used extensively. No lines, no hassle. Outdoor deck space quite good. All-outside suites are one price, well appointed and finished, with two portholes and even a CD player. Lots of wood trim everywhere. Elegant main lounge, with crisp, but stark colors. Recommended for watersports fans.

— Constant whine from the ship's engine audible in most cabins. No bathtubs in cabins. There's not much deck space, owing to complex sail machinery. Tiny pool. Interior colors a little cold. Communication with Indonesian crew often frustrating. High beverage prices.

Dining Charming, elegant dining room, with ocean views from large, picture windows. Creative and attractively presented *nouvelle cuisine*, but not up to the standard of the small luxury ships. The quality of ingredients should be upgraded. Attentive, friendly service throughout, but communication often proves frustrating. Poor pastry items, breads and fruits.

Other Comments One of three identical sisters that is part yacht, part cruise ship, this high-tech vessel has four tall masts with computer-controlled sails. She's a very comfortable ship throughout, and, with emphasis on refined privacy, will provide her passengers with a very relaxing, casual cruise experience, but only partly under sail. Gratuities are "not required," but they are expected.

The Ratings and Evaluations

CRUISE SHIP RATING SECTION
The ratings are provided in two ways:
1. The ratings by points and stars; numerically, from the highest to the lowest.
2. In the order of size; five divisions according to the number of passengers carried.

SHIP	CRUISE LINE	RATING	STARS
Europa	Hapag-Lloyd Cruises	136.5	★★★★★+
Royal Viking Sun	Cunard	136.5	★★★★★+
Sea Goddess I	Cunard	136.5	★★★★★+
Sea Goddess II	Cunard	136.5	★★★★★+
Seabourn Legend	Seabourn Cruise Line	136.5	★★★★★+
Seabourn Pride	Seabourn Cruise Line	136.2	★★★★★+
Seabourn Spirit	Seabourn Cruise Line	136.2	★★★★★+
Crystal Symphony	Crystal Cruises	135.3	★★★★★+
Crystal Harmony	Crystal Cruises	135.1	★★★★★+
Hanseatic	Hanseatic Tours	135.1	★★★★★+
Vistafjord	Cunard	134.8	★★★★★
Queen Elizabeth 2	Cunard (Grill Class)	134.7	★★★★★
Song of Flower	Radisson Seven Seas Cruises	133.8	★★★★★
Silver Wind	Silversea Cruises	133.4	★★★★★
Silver Cloud	Silversea Cruises	133.2	★★★★★
Asuka	NYK Cruises	128.7	★★★★★
Hebridean Princess	Hebridean Island Cruises	126.2	★★★★★
Radisson Diamond	Radisson Seven Seas Cruises	126.1	★★★★★
Sea Cloud	Sea Cloud Cruises	125.3	★★★★★
Oceanic Grace	Oceanic Cruises	125.2	★★★★★
Zenith	Celebrity Cruises	126.0	★★★★+
Century	Celebrity Cruises	124.8	★★★★+
Queen Elizabeth 2	Cunard (Caronia Class)	124.8	★★★★+
Minerva	Swan Hellenic Cruises	124.7	★★★★+

SHIP	CRUISE LINE	RATING	STARS
Horizon	Celebrity Cruises	124.6	★★★★+
Splendour of the Seas	Royal Caribbean Cruises	124.5	★★★★+
Legend of the Seas	Royal Caribbean Cruises	124.4	★★★★+
Oriana	P&O Cruises	124.4	★★★★+
Bremen	Hapag-Lloyd Tours	123.1	★★★★+
Aida	Deutsche Seetouristik	122.6	★★★★+
Sun Princess	Princess Cruises	122.6	★★★★+
Lili Marleen	Deilmann Reederei	122.5	★★★★+
Le Ponant	Compagnie des Isles du Ponant	122.4	★★★★+
Megastar Aries	Star Cruise	121.6	★★★★+
Megastar Taurus	Star Cruise	121.6	★★★★+
Royal Princess	Princess Cruises	120.3	★★★★+
Astor	AquaMarin Cruises	118.7	★★★★+
Club Med II	Club Mediterranee	117.9	★★★★+
Club Med I	Club Mediterranee	117.8	★★★★+
Star Princess	Princess Cruises	117.4	★★★★+
Berlin	Deilmann Reederei	117.3	★★★★+
Wind Song	Windstar Cruises	117.1	★★★★+
Wind Spirit	Windstar Cruises	117.1	★★★★+
Wind Star	Windstar Cruises	117.1	★★★★+
Sky Princess	Princess Cruises	116.9	★★★★+
Monarch of the Seas	Royal Caribbean Cruises	116.6	★★★★+
Majesty of the Seas	Royal Caribbean Cruises	116.4	★★★★+
Regal Princess	Princess Cruises	116.4	★★★★+
Sovereign of the Seas	Royal Caribbean Cruises	116.4	★★★★+
Veendam	Holland America Line	116.3	★★★★+
CostaRomantica	Costa Cruises	116.1	★★★★+
Langkapuri Star Aquarius	Star Cruise	116.1	★★★★+
Crown Princess	Princess Cruises	115.9	★★★★+
Ryndam	Holland America Line	115.6	★★★★+
Star Pisces	Star Cruise	115.5	★★★★+
Maasdam	Holland America Line	115.4	★★★★+
Statendam	Holland America Line	115.3	★★★★+
World Discoverer	Society Expeditions	115.2	★★★★+

SHIP	CRUISE LINE	RATING	STARS
Queen Elizabeth 2	Cunard (Mauretania Class)	114.8	★★★★
Norwegian Crown	Norwegian Cruise Line	114.7	★★★★
Nordic Empress	Royal Caribbean Cruises	114.7	★★★★
Windward	Norwegian Cruise Line	114.7	★★★★
Dreamward	Norwegian Cruise Line	114.6	★★★★
Meridian	Celebrity Cruises	114.6	★★★★
Royal Odyssey	Royal Cruise Line	114.3	★★★★
St. Helena	Curnow Shipping	114.3	★★★★
Marco Polo	Orient Lines	114.1	★★★★
Renaissance Five	Renaissance Cruises	114.1	★★★★
Renaissance Six	Renaissance Cruises	114.1	★★★★
Renaissance Seven	Renaissance Cruises	114.1	★★★★
Renaissance Eight	Renaissance Cruises	114.1	★★★★
Orient Venus	Japan Cruise Line	114.0	★★★★
Royal Majesty	Majesty Cruise Line	113.8	★★★★
Hong Kong Dragon Star	Topnew Cruises	113.3	★★★★
Island Princess	Princess Cruises	113.2	★★★★
Leeward	Norwegian Cruise Line	113.2	★★★★
Pacific Princess	Princess Cruises	113.2	★★★★
Americana	Ivaran Lines	112.9	★★★★
CostaClassica	Costa Cruises	112.5	★★★★
Inspiration	Carnival Cruise Lines	112.2	★★★★
Renaissance One	Renaissance Cruises	112.0	★★★★
Renaissance Two	Renaissance Cruises	112.0	★★★★
Renaissance Three	Renaissance Cruises	112.0	★★★★
Renaissance Four	Renaissance Cruises	112.0	★★★★
Imagination	Carnival Cruise Lines	111.2	★★★★
Cunard Dynasty	Cunard	111.1	★★★★
Norway	Norwegian Cruise Line	110.9	★★★★
Seaward	Norwegian Cruise Line	110.9	★★★★
Italia Prima	Nina Cruise Line	110.5	★★★★
Westerdam	Holland America Line	110.3	★★★★
Superstar Gemini	Star Cruise	110.2	★★★★
Nippon Maru	Mitsui OSK Passenger Line	110.1	★★★★
Arkona	Deutsche Seetouristik	110.0	★★★★
Nautican	Cruise Lines International	110.0	★★★★

SHIP	CRUISE LINE	RATING	STARS
Sensation	Carnival Cruise Lines	110.0	★★★★
Fascination	Carnival Cruise Lines	109.5	★★★★
Star/Ship Atlantic	Premier Cruise Lines	109.2	★★★★
CostaRiviera	Costa Cruises	108.7	★★★★
Polaris	Special Expeditions	108.5	★★★★
Maxim Gorki	Phoenix Seereisen	108.4	★★★★
Star Clipper	Star Clippers	108.4	★★★★
Star Flyer	Star Clippers	108.4	★★★★
Nieuw Amsterdam	Holland America Line	108.2	★★★★
Noordam	Holland America Line	108.2	★★★★
Song of America	Royal Caribbean Cruises	108.2	★★★★
Ecstasy	Carnival Cruise Lines	107.8	★★★★
Victoria	P&O Cruises	107.4	★★★★
Fuji Maru	Mitsui OSK Passenger Line	107.3	★★★★
Celebration	Carnival Cruise Lines	106.6	★★★★
Fantasy	Carnival Cruise Lines	106.5	★★★★
Jubilee	Carnival Cruise Lines	106.4	★★★★
Holiday	Carnival Cruise Lines	106.3	★★★★
Viking Serenade	Royal Caribbean Cruises	105.6	★★★★
Stella Solaris	Sun Line Cruises	105.5	★★★★
Caledonian Star	Noble Caledonian	104.9	★★★+
Bolero	Festival Cruises	104.8	★★★+
Star/Ship Oceanic	Premier Cruise Lines	104.7	★★★+
Black Prince	Fred Olsen Cruise Line	104.6	★★★+
CostaAllegra	Costa Cruises	104.5	★★★+
CostaMarina	Costa Cruises	104.5	★★★+
EugenioCosta	Costa Cruises	104.5	★★★+
Tropicale	Carnival Cruise Lines	104.3	★★★+
The Azur	Festival Cruises	104.0	★★★+
Song of Norway	Royal Caribbean Cruises	103.8	★★★+
Southern Cross	CTC Cruise Lines	103.3	★★★+
Yamal	Murmansk Shipping	103.2	★★★+
Carousel	Airtours Cruises	102.9	★★★+
Vistamar	Mar Line	102.7	★★★+
Rhapsody	StarLauro Cruises	101.8	★★★+

SHIP	CRUISE LINE	RATING	STARS
CostaPlaya	Costa Cruises	101.7	★★★+
Daphne	Costa Cruises	101.7	★★★+
Kazakhstan II	Delphin Seereisen	101.7	★★★+
Triton	Royal Olympic Cruises	101.6	★★★+
Olympic	Royal Olympic Cruises	101.3	★★★+
Sapphire	Thomson Cruises	101.3	★★★+
Cunard Countess	Cunard	101.1	★★★+
IslandBreeze	Dolphin Cruise Line	101.0	★★★+
Sun Viking	Royal Caribbean Cruises	100.8	★★★+
Rotterdam	Holland America Line	100.7	★★★+
Princess Danae	Arcalia Shipping	100.3	★★★+
Ocean Majesty	Majestic International Cruises	100.2	★★★+
Seawind Crown	Seawind Cruise Line	104.2	★★★+
Kapitan Dranitsyn	Murmansk Shipping	99.8	★★★
Monterey	Starlauro Cruises	99.6	★★★
Canberra	P&O Cruises	99.4	★★★
Orpheus	Royal Olympic Cruises	99.4	★★★
Bali Sea Dancer	P&O Spice Island Cruises	99.2	★★★
Albatros	Phoenix Seereisen	99.1	★★★
Symphony	StarLauro Cruises	99.1	★★★
Seawing	Airtours	98.9	★★★
Calypso	Tranocean Tours	98.0	★★★
OceanBreeze	Dolphin Cruise Line	97.6	★★★
Explorer	Abercrombie & Kent	97.5	★★★
Stella Oceanis	Royal Hispania Cruises	97.1	★★★
Don Juan	Royal Hispania Cruises	97.0	★★★
Royal Star	Star Line	97.0	★★★
Gripsholm	Tranocean Tours	96.7	★★★
Regina Maris	Phoenix Seereisen	96.7	★★★
Odysseus	Royal Olympic Cruises	96.2	★★★
SeaBreeze I	Dolphin Cruise Line	95.9	★★★
Constitution	American Hawaii Cruises	95.2	★★★
Independence	American Hawaii Cruises	95.2	★★★
Mermoz	Paquet Cruises	95.0	★★★
Aegean Dolphin	Dolphin Hellas Shipping	94.8	★★★

SHIP	CRUISE LINE	RATING	STARS
Royal Seas	Royal Seas Cruise Line	93.2	★★★
Yorktown Clipper	Clipper Cruise Line	93.1	★★★
Ausonia	Ausonia Cruises	92.5	★★★
Princesa Victoria	Louis Cruise Lines	92.5	★★★
Universe Explorer	World Explorer Cruises	92.3	★★★
Astra II	Neckermann Seereisen	91.7	★★★
Fairstar	P&O Holidays	91.5	★★★
Nantucket Clipper	Clipper Cruise Line	91.4	★★★
Princesa Marissa	Louis Cruise Lines	91.4	★★★
Enchanted Isle	Commodore Cruise Line	91.0	★★★
Kristina Regina	Kristina Cruises	91.0	★★★
Leisure World	New Century Tours	90.3	★★★
Azerbaydzhan	CTC Cruise Lines	90.2	★★★
Kareliya	CTC Cruise Lines	90.1	★★★
La Palma	Intercruise	89.8	★★+
Shota Rustaveli	Grandi Viaggi	89.7	★★+
Dolphin IV	Canaveral Cruise Line	89.6	★★+
Regal Empress	Regal Cruises	89.5	★★+
Funchal	Arcalia Shipping	89.3	★★+
Alla Tarasova	Quark/Marine Expeditions	89.1	★★+
Professor Khromov	Cruise Lines International	88.8	★★+
Andaman Princess	Cruise Lines International	88.2	★★+
Ivan Franko	Black Sea Shipping	87.0	★★+
Taras Shevcheko	PrimExpress Cruises	86.7	★★+
Princesa Amorosa	Louis Cruise Lines	86.3	★★+
Atalante	Paradise Cruises	85.8	★★+
Dimitri Shostakovich	Black Sea Shipping	84.8	★★
Konstantin Simonov	Baltic Line	84.8	★★
Mikhail Sholokhov	Far Eastern Shipping	84.8	★★
Astra	Caravella Shipping	84.7	★★
Carina	Phoenix Seereisen	84.3	★★
Sir Francis Drake	Tall Ship Adventures	83.4	★★
Antonina Nezhdanova	Far East Shipping	83.0	★★
Olga Sadovskaya	Pacific Cruise Company	82.3	★★

SHIP	CRUISE LINE	RATING	STARS
Queen Elini	Vergina Cruises	76.5	★
Klaudia Yelanskaya	Murmansk shipping	79.2	★

SHIPS NOT YET RATED

Carnival Destiny	Carnival Cruise Lines
CostaVictoria	Costa Cruises
Dawn Princess	Princess Cruises
Disney Magic	Disney Cruise Line
Enchantment of the Seas	Royal Caribbean Cruises
Galaxy	Celebrity Cruises
Grand Princess	Princess Cruises
Grandeur of the Seas	Royal Caribbean Cruises
Mercury	Celebrity Cruises
Rhapsody of the Seas	Royal Caribbean Cruises
Rotterdam VI	Holland American Line

APPENDIXES

The Cruise Industry: Milestones (1960–1997)

1960

Passenger shipping directories listed more than 30 ships operating transatlantic voyages for the better part of each year. Many ships were laid up in the ten-year period 1960–1970, and most were sold for a fraction of their value (or building cost). Most passenger lines simply went out of business or tried to survive by mixing transatlantic crossings with voyages south in search of the sun, which proved difficult for those without sufficient air-conditioning systems.

1961

Sun Line Cruises was founded by the late Charalambos A. Keusseouglou, who began his career at Home Lines, the immigrant carrier. He died in 1984, aged 64, after a 37-year cruise industry career.

1962

The Compagnie Générale Transatlantique's ss *France*, at 1,035 feet the world's longest passenger ship ever built, entered service between Le Havre and New York, in spite of the growing competition from the airlines.

1963

Cunard Line's *RMS Queen Elizabeth* made an experimental cruise from New York to the West Indies, which met with great success. This led to her being fitted with full air conditioning in a 1965/66 refit, as well as to more extensive cruising activities.

1965

P&O obtained the remaining shares of the Orient Steam Navigation Company. The new company became known as the Peninsular & Oriental Steam Navigation Company.

Princess Cruises was founded by Seattle entrepreneur and industrialist Stanley B. McDonald.

Sitmar Cruises started cruise operations from Sydney, Australia.

1966

Norwegian company Klosters Reederei formed a partnership with Miami businessman Ted Arison to market Caribbean cruises from Miami. Kloster provided the ship and Arison provided the passengers.

Commodore Cruise Line was founded by Sanford Chobol, and a single ship, *Boheme* (now *Freewinds*).

1967

Cunard announced the imminent withdrawal of both *Queen Mary* and *Queen Elizabeth*. *Queen Mary* was withdrawn from service on September 26 after completing 1,001 transatlantic crossings. She was sold to the City of Long Beach, California. She left Southampton on October 31, 1967 and has been in Long Beach been ever since she arrived.

1968

Cunard's *Queen Elizabeth* (at 83,673-grt, the world's largest ever passenger ship) was withdrawn from service in October. She had steamed a total of 3,472,672 miles and carried a total of 2,311,324 passengers (1,500,000 in peacetime, 811,324 in wartime) during her career.

Cunard Line refused delivery of the new *Queen Elizabeth 2* from her builders, John Brown, in December, owing to unacceptable turbine vibration levels. Repairs led to a five-month delay on her maiden transatlantic sailing to New York.

Boise Cascade bought Princess Cruises from its founder, Stanley B. McDonald, who re-purchased the line two years later.

1969

Lars-Eric Lindblad's *Lindblad Explorer* was launched expressly for close-in expedition cruising.

Royal Caribbean Cruise Line was founded January 31 by a consortium of Norwegian shipping companies, Gotaas-Larsen (actually it was American-owned), I.M. Skaugen, and Anders Wilhelmsen, and formally incorporated as Royal Caribbean Cruise Line A/S in Oslo. Edwin Stephan, who provided the initial concept and wisdom, was made President, and set up the Miami marketing arm of the company, which, at the end of 1968, ordered two new sister ships for delivery in 1970 and 1971.

The liner *United States* was laid up in November following a strike against the ship by the militant seamen's union, and the fact that the U.S. Government no longer wanted to subsidize the loss-making ship (which cost $118.8 million between 1955 and 1969).

1970

Royal Viking Line was founded by a consortium of three partners (Bergen Line, A.F. Klaveness, and Nordenfjeldske) who each contributed one ship (*Royal Viking Sea, Royal Viking Sky, Royal Viking Star*).

Germany's Norddeutscher Lloyd and Hapag (Hamburg American Line) merged on September 1. They chose the new name of Hapag-Lloyd.

1971

Cunard Line was sold to Trafalgar House Investments.

1972

Carnival Cruise Lines was formed by Ted Arison, following a disagreement with Knut Kloster, when both worked for Kloster's Norwegian Cruise Lines. After unsuccessfully trying to purchase Cunard's *Carmania* and *Franconia*, he learned of the availability of the *Empress of Canada*. The new company, funded by and operated as a subsidiary of the Boston-based American International Travel Service, Inc. (AITS). The company thus started with just one ship, *Mardi Gras* (ex-*Empress of Canada*). After a poor start (*Mardi Gras* ran aground on its first voyage, and competing company's ships even named a drink after her, called "Mardi Gras on the Rocks"), the company went from strength to strength, under Arison's aggressive direction, and went on to become the biggest success story of the contemporary cruise industry.

1973

Holland America Line withdrew sister ships *Veendam* and *Volendam* from service and laid them up, owing to the abundance of other cruise ships, high operating costs, a fall in the value of the U.S. Dollar, and a dramatic rise in fuel costs. The ships were placed under charter to Monarch Cruise Lines in 1976 for the sum of $5,000 each per day (*Veendam* became *Monarch Star*, *Volendam* became *Monarch Sun*). The Dutch-flag ships were re-registered in Panama and staffed by a multinational crew.

Sitmar Cruises began operations from the Port of Sydney, Australia, with a single ship, *Fairstar*, a converted troop carrier formerly operated by Bibby Line.

Deutsche Atlantik Line suspended operations. The company's *Hanseatic*, in service for only four years, was laid-up at Hamburg. In December, the intended sale of the ship to Ryutsu Kaiun KK of Japan for $25 million failed to materialize. She was instead sold to Robin International Corporation, New York, acting as buyers for the Black Sea Shipping Company of Odessa. The ship was renamed *Maxim Gorkiy* and is still in service for Phoenix Seereisen.

1974

P&O purchased Princess Cruises from its founder, Stanley B. McDonald, during the summer.

In July, the Compagnie Générale Transatlantique announced that after only 12 years of service, ss *France* was to be withdrawn from service with effect from October 25. She was losing money (being subsidized by the French government to the tune of $12 million a year). As the ship was about to berth in Le Havre on September 12, angry French trade unionists took over the ship from its officers and anchored her in the entrance channel, in protest to the impending loss of jobs. Passengers disembarked by tender. The ship docked on October 9 and was laid-up.

Royal Cruise Lines' first ship, *Golden Odyssey*, purpose-built to accommodate the equivalent passenger load of a Boeing 747 aircraft (425 passengers) was introduced. The company, founded by Pericles S. Panagopoulos in 1971, attracted a loyal U.S. west coast following.

1975

Princess Cruises' *Island Princess* and *Pacific Princess* became the "stars" in the American television show *The Love Boat*.

1977

World Explorer Cruises was founded and entered the cruise industry with one ship, the *Universe*.

Princess Grace of Monaco christened *Cunard Princess* at the Passenger Ship Terminal in March, the first time a passenger ship christening had taken place in the Port of New York.

Union-Castle/Safmarine, the South Africa-based shipping company, ceased passenger operations when its last vessel, *S.A. Vaal*, was sold to Carnival Cruise Lines in April.

Holland America Line announced it would take over the entire operation of Monarch Cruise Lines Inc. The two Monarch ships were handed back to Holland America Line in January, 1978.

1978

United States Cruises was formed by Mr Richard Hadley, who paid $5 million for the liner *United States*.

After an unsuccessful June 30 cruise from New York for new owners Venture Cruise Lines (also called America Cruise Lines), its *America* (ex-*Australis*) was arrested for debt and auctioned on August 28. Her previous owners, the Chandris Group, re-purchased the ship and renamed her *Italis*.

Royal Caribbean Cruise Line's *Song of Norway* was lengthened at the Wartsila shipyard in Helsinki. The *Nordic Prince* was lengthened at the same shipyard (March-June, 1980).

1979

American Hawaii Cruises was formed. Jimmy Carter, then President of the United States, signed a bill re-documenting *Independence* under the U.S.-flag. The new company began cruise operations on June 21, 1980, with *Independence*, joined by sister ship *Constitution* in 1982.

Special Expeditions founded by Sven-Olof Lindblad, son of Lars-Eric Lindblad, to provide expedition cruises.

Society Expeditions formed by a group of German investors under sole stockholder T.C. Schwartz, to manage and operate the adventure/expedition cruises of *World Discoverer*.

The liner *France* was purchased by Lauritz Kloster in June. The ship was taken to Bremerhaven and rebuilt for the Caribbean cruise trade by Hapag-Lloyd at Bremerhaven. She was renamed *Norway*, and transferred to the ownership of Norwegian Caribbean Lines in September, 1984.

1980

Sea Goddess Cruises was founded by Helge Naarstad. The first of two twin vessels, *Sea Goddess I* was delivered four years later, in 1984.

Denmark's DFDS (United Steamship Company) founded Scandinavian World Cruises to operate one-day cruises from Miami (the company subsequently became SeaEscape).

The International Organization of Masters, Mates and Pilots formed a joint venture company with Aloha Pacific Cruises. The company purchased the liner *Monterey* (the last U.S.-flag ship that qualified under the Jones Act to operate between American ports) for intended cruise service in Tahiti. The purchase went through in 1981. The union poured $5.7 million into the ship, for upkeep alone, between 1981 and 1986.

After a planned merger with Royal Viking Line failed in May, Norwegian America Cruises (formerly Norwegian America Line) was formed to manage *Sagafjord* and *Vistafjord*.

1981

Astor Cruises was formed in the UK, and began operations with a single ship, *Astor* (now *Arkona*).

1982

The British government chartered Cunard's *Queen Elizabeth 2* for use as a troop carrier for the famous Ghurka Regiment, among others, during the Falklands War between Argentina and Britain, at a rate of $225,000 per day. The ship eluded an Argentinean submarine sent to destroy her, due to the submarine's ineffectiveness in the icebergs close to the Falklands, and the speed of *QE2*. The government also chartered P&O Cruises' *Canberra* for use as a troopship as well as B&I Line's *Uganda*, used as a hospital ship.

Lindblad Travel, the company founded by Lars-Eric Lindblad in 1969, sold its *Lindblad Explorer*, and the rights to the Lindblad name, to Salen-Lindblad Cruising.

1983

Clipper Cruise Line (American cruise company) was founded by Barney Ebsworth in St. Louis.

Holland America Line ceased operating its lucrative New York-Bermuda sailings. The company moved from New York to Seattle.

Ocean Cruise Lines was founded by British entrepreneur Gerry Herrod, as an offshoot of Travellers, Europe's largest tour operator for Americans.

P&O appointed Jeffrey Sterling as chairman in order to fend off a takeover bid by Trafalgar House Investments, owners of Cunard Line.

Premier Cruise Lines was co-founded by Bruce Nierenburg and Bjornar Hermansen, both former executives of Norwegian Cruise Lines.

The B&I's *Uganda* was taken over by the British Ministry of Defence in January for two years for service between Ascension and the Falkland Islands. This ended passenger services for the British and India Steam Navigation Company.

Cunard's parent company, Trafalgar House, purchased Norwegian America Cruises (NAC) in May, together with *Sagafjord* and *Vistafjord*.

Salen-Lindblad Cruising's *Lindblad Explorer* became the first passenger ship to successfully navigate the Northwest Passage (in September), sailing 4,790 miles from Saint John's, Newfoundland to Point Barrow, Alaska. When the ship reached Point Barrow, the champagne flowed, and beards were shaved off (the crew had all vowed not to shave until that point). Lars Wikander provided the idea and planning for the 41-day cruise, which ended in Japan.

1984

Sundance Cruises, founded by Stanley B. McDonald, entered the industry with a single ship, *Sundancer*.

Carnival Cruise Line launched a $10 million television advertising campaign—the largest ever in the cruise industry. Two different 30-second spots were aired 133 times in the U.S.A.

An American investment group headed by J.H. Whitney & Company signed an agreement in principle in May for the purchase of Royal Viking Line and its three ships for $240 million. The sale did not go through, and Royal Viking Line was purchased by Kloster Cruise Limited, Oslo.

Regency Cruises was founded by Anastassios Kiriakidis, Fred Mayer and William Schanz. The company completed its initial public stock offering in June and began operations with one ship, *Regent Sea*.

Windstar Sail Cruises was founded in December by Karl Andren and Jacob Stolt-Nielsen to build and operate a fleet of three sail-cruise ships originally designed by Kai Levander, then of Wartsila shipyard in Helsinki,

Finland. Andren intended to re-launch the age of commercial sail.

Dolphin Cruise Line was founded by Peter Bulgarides and Paris Katsoufis (but actually owned by Ulysses Shipping, Piraeus).

Premier Cruise Lines, owned by the Greyhound-Dial Corporation, entered the industry with its first ship.

1985

The Chandris Group of Companies acquired Fantasy Cruises from GoGo Tours. Fantasy Cruises became known as Chandris Fantasy Cruises in the U.S.A., and Chandris Cruises in the U.K.

The first sailing ship designed for crewing by physically disabled passengers was launched at Wivenhoe, Essex on October 15. The sts *Lord Nelson*, owned by the Jubilee Sailing Trust, was named at Southampton, England, on May 9, 1986.

1986

Signet Cruise Line was founded in Norway by an investment group headed by Atle Brynestad. Owing to a lawsuit brought by an American who claimed the right to the name Signet, the company changed its name to Seabourn Cruise Line. The company's first ship, *Seabourn Pride*, entered service in December, 1988.

Eastern Cruise Lines, Western Cruise Lines, and Sundance Cruises merged to become Admiral Cruises.

Diamond Cruise Ltd. was founded in Helsinki, Finland, by Captain Offe Nyblin and his partner Christian Aspegren. They were to take delivery of *Radisson Diamond*, a semi-submersible twin-hulled vessel.

Cunard acquired Sea Goddess Cruises, together with the *Sea Goddess I* and *Sea Goddess II*, through a complex financial and management package negotiated with Norske Cruise A/S, whose 138 shareholders provided the funding for the construction and introduction of the new luxury yacht-ship concept.

1987

Carnival Cruise Lines made its first public stock offering.

Cunard's *QE2* was converted from steam turbine to diesel-electric power. It was the largest ever conversion in maritime history.

Society Expeditions purchased by German businessman Heiko Klein, chairman of Discoverer Reederei, which owns the vessels marketed and operated by Society Expeditions.

Kockums, the Swedish shipyard, ceased shipbuilding operations after the delivery of twin cruise ships for Carnival Cruise Lines, *Celebration* (1987) and *Jubilee* (1986).

Bahama Cruise Line changed its name to Bermuda Star Line.

Ocean Cruise Lines merged with Pearl Cruises.

The United States Public Health Service (USPH) resumed ship inspections January 1.

Holland America Line acquired a 50% share in Windstar Sail Cruises.

Norwegian Caribbean Lines changed its name and logo to Norwegian Cruise Line.

1988

Commodore Cruise Lines sold its *Boheme* (renamed *Freewinds*) to the Church of Scientology.

Crystal Cruises was formed as a wholly-owned company of Nippon Yusen Kaisha (NYK) of Japan, the world's largest shipping company. The company's first ship, *Crystal Harmony* entered service in July, 1990.

The three owning partners of Royal Caribbean Cruise Line (Gotaas-Larsen, I.M. Skaugen, Anders Wilhelmsen) decided, in March, to merge RCCL with the Gataas-Larsen-dominated Admiral Cruises (the Swedish company Axel Johnson group and the Finnish EFFOA group held 49%). Named Royal Admiral Cruises (later renamed Royal Caribbean Cruises) the new group was owned 36% by Gotaas-Larsen, and 28% each by Skaugen and Wilhelmsen, while Johnson/EFFOA held the remaining 8% of stock.

Home Lines ceased operations in April. Its two ships, *Atlantic* (1984) and *Homeric* (1986) were purchased by Holland America Line. The *Atlantic* was subsequently placed under long-term charter to Premier Cruise Lines.

Effjohn International purchased Bermuda Star Line in May for $17 million. Included in the deal were *Bermuda Star, Queen of Bermuda* and *Veracruz I.* The company was renamed BSL Cruises, Inc.

Sitmar Cruises (Societa Italiana Trasporti Marittimi), founded in 1938 by Alexandre Vlasov, was purchased by Princess Cruises (part of the P&O Group) for $210 million.

Carnival Cruise Lines' negotiations with Gotaas-Larsen to purchase its share in Royal Caribbean Cruise Line for $260 million came to light in August, following RCCL's administration moved from Oslo to Miami. At first, I.M. Skaugen and Wilhelmsen tried to pre-empt the Carnival offer. Later, Skaugen accepted a similar offer from Carnival. Wilhelmsen, the remaining partner in RCCL (28 per cent), pre-empted the Carnival offer of $567 million by going 50/50 with the Hyatt Hotel group of companies, owned by the Pritzker family of Chicago. The new joint owners paid the agreed amount five days before the deadline date of October 5th.

Holland America Line completed the purchase of Windstar Sail Cruises in March. Carnival Cruise Lines acquired Holland America Line in November, including its land-based hotel/transport operations, and Windstar Cruises, for $625 million, plus liabilities that pushed the purchase price effectively to $900 million.

1989

The Chandris Group of Companies announced the creation of Celebrity Cruises, which promptly ordered two new cruise ships, to be named *Horizon* and *Zenith*, from Meyer Werft shipyard in Papenburg, Germany. The company also planned to convert *Galileo* into *Meridian*, at the Lloyd Werft shipyard in Bremerhaven, Germany.

Meyer Werft, Papenburg, Germany, became the first shipyard to conduct a "chop and stretch" operation on a major cruise vessel in drydock when *Westerdam* (ex-*Homeric*) was lengthened in the same building shed as *Horizon*, under construction for Celebrity Cruises.

Renaissance Cruises was formed by Fearnley & Eger, the 120-year-old, Oslo-based shipping concern.

Showa Line entered the cruise

passenger market in Japan for the first time in 60 years with the introduction of its *Oceanic Grace*.

Mitsui OSK Line entered the cruise market in Japan for the first time in 50 years with its 23,340-grt, 600-passenger *Fuji Maru*.

The Panama Canal is now 75 years old.

Aloha Pacific Cruises went into bankruptcy and their single ship, *Monterey*, was put up for sale.

Wartsila Industries, Helsinki, Finland, one of the most famous and prestigious builders of cruise ships, collapsed in a tangle of financial problems. It was re-organized as Masa-Yards and is presently owned by Kvaerner of Norway.

1990

Ocean Cruise Lines was acquired by Croisières Paquet, itself owned by the French giant Accor leisure company.

Japan Cruise Line entered the cruise passenger market in Japan with its newbuild 21,906-grt, 606-passenger *Orient Venus*.

Aloha Pacific Cruises' *Monterey* was purchased by the Mediterranean Shipping Company, who chartered same to StarLauro Cruises.

Chandris Cruises introduced its new premium grade Celebrity Cruises product in April with the debut of the reconstructed *Meridian* and the brand new *Horizon*.

Delfin Cruises, established only one year earlier, ceased operations.

At the start of the Persian Gulf War, the U.S. Government chartered *Cunard Princess* for six months as a rest and relaxation center for U.S. service personnel. The ship was docked in Bahrain for the $31 million charter.

1991

EffJohn International, purchased Bermuda Star Line, together with its two ships, *Enchanted Isle* and *Enchanted Seas* as well as Crown Cruise Lines.

Carnival Cruise Lines acquired a 25% stake in Seabourn Cruise Line.

The Soviet cruise fleet was split into its constituent parts: Baltic Shipping Company (Russia), Black Sea Shipping Company (Ukraine), Estonian Shipping Company (Estonia), Far East Shipping Company (Russia).

In March, Fearnley & Eger, owner of Renaissance Cruises, announced voluntary liquidation and protection from its creditors. Renaissance Cruises was sold to the Cameli Group, controlled by Sebastiano Cameli (Italy), and Luxury Liners, Ltd., a holding company involving Norwegian shipowner Jorgen Jahre and controlled by Edward B. Rudner in the U.S.A.

Seawind Cruise Line began cruise operations with its single ship, *Seawind Crown* (ex-*Vasco da Gama*), after a 70%/30% interest purchase in the company by Swedish concern Nordisk, and Arcalia Shipping, Lisbon.

Nippon Yusen Kaisha (NYK) purchased Salen Lindblad Cruising.

Nippon Yusen Kaisha (NYK) Cruises introduced *Asuka*, the first cruise vessel to have been specifically designed for Japanese passengers.

New York-based Overseas Shipholding Group agreed to lend Kloster Cruise $175 million in exchange for a 50% stake in the company. The offer was later withdrawn.

1992

⚓ Society Expeditions ceased operation. Its two expedition vessels, *Society Explorer* and *World Discoverer* were placed on the sale/charter books.

⚓ Costa Cruise Lines introduced its new Euro-Luxe cruise concept with the debut of *CostaClassica*.

⚓ Admiral Cruises ceased operations. *Azure Seas* and *Emerald Seas* were sold to Dolphin Cruise Line and Sun-Fest Cruises, respectively.

⚓ Some 16 cruise ships were chartered for use as accommodation vessels in Barcelona for the 1992 Olympic Games (July 24-August 9). The ships: *Berlin, Club Med I, Crown Jewel, Crystal Harmony, Cunard Princess, Daphne, Golden Odyssey, Royal Majesty, Royal Viking Sun, Sally Albatross, Sea Cloud, Sea Goddess II, Seabourn Spirit, Star Clipper, Star Flyer, Vistafjord*.

⚓ Hurricane Andrew hit the south Miami area. Carnival Cruise Lines, with 600 of its staff made homeless, deployed the *Mardi Gras* for use as an accommodation ship.

⚓ The cruise division of The Chandris Group of Companies and Overseas Shipholding Group (OSG) signed an agreement on October 21 to form a joint venture company, Celebrity Cruise Lines, Inc. This involved Chandris supplying Celebrity Cruises' three ships, plus Fantasy Cruises' three, while OSG put up $220 million cash, with Chandris holding a 51% interest.

⚓ Chargeurs and Accor, French property and leisure industries group that own Paquet Cruises and Ocean Cruise Lines, bought a 23 per cent stake in Costa Crociere, the parent company of Costa Cruises, through a rights issue worth Lire 80 billion ($60 million). The Costa family's stake shrank from 40 to 31 per cent.

1993

⚓ In January, Carnival Cruise Lines announced a new subsidiary, FiestaMarina Cruises, specifically for the Spanish-speaking Latin American marketplace. Their ship, *FiestaMarina* (ex-*Carnivale*), would begin operations October 22 from San Juan.

⚓ Cunard and Effjohn announced a joint venture, good for 10 years, and created Cunard Crown Cruises.

⚓ American Family Cruises was announced by Bruce Nierenberg. The new company would initially use two Costa ships (*CostaRiviera* and *Eugenio-Costa*). Only *CostaRiviera* was converted into *American Adventure*.

⚓ In May, Rainbow Cruises purchased all the stock of Regency Cruises. Both companies were merged under the name Regency Cruises.

⚓ American Hawaii Cruises' secured lenders forced the line into involuntary bankruptcy in federal court in Honolulu. The company was purchased by the Delta Queen Steamboat Company.

⚓ Festival Cruises was founded by George Poulides and George Zoros, who re-acquired *The Azur*, on charter to Chandris Fantasy Cruises.

⚓ Kloster Cruise Ltd. signed a letter of intent to sell Royal Cruise Line and Royal Viking Line to ASA Investors, Inc. for $565 million. Royal Cruise Line ships: *Crown Odyssey, Royal Odyssey* and *Star Odyssey (Golden*

Odyssey was not included in the deal). Royal Viking Line ships: *Royal Viking Queen* and *Royal Viking Sun*. The deal was to be finalized in spring 1994, but subsequently collaped.

1994

Delta Queen Steamboat Company changed its corporate name to American Classic Voyages Company. The company owns American Hawaii Cruises and the Delta Queen Steamboat Company.

Festival Cruises started operations with one ship.

Trafalgar House, Cunard's parent company, signed an agreement to buy, for $170 million, the rights to the name Royal Viking Line, together with *Royal Viking Sun*. *Royal Viking Queen*, would go to Royal Cruise Line, to be renamed *Queen Odyssey*, on 1 January 1995.

In September, American Family Cruises ceased operations. The company's single ship, *American Adventure*, was returned to the Costa Cruises fleet, to be renamed *CostaRiviera*.

In September, FiestaMarina Cruises, a division of the Carnival Corporation, ceased operations.

Cycladic Cruises, based in Greece, ceased operations.

1995

British company Airtours Cruises bought *Southward* (from Norwegian Cruise Line) and *Nordic Prince* (Royal Caribbean Cruises) in 1994, and began operations March 1995.

Commodore Cruise Line was sold to International Cruise Finance.

Royal Venture Cruise Line was founded by Anastassios Kiriakidis.

1996

Royal Venture Cruise Line started operations with a single ship, *Sun Venture* (ex-*Ukraine*), then ceased operations abruptly. The company was then restarted as Royal Seas Cruise Line, using the same ship, but renamed *Royal Seas*.

Kloster Cruise (parent company of Norwegian Cruise Line and Royal Cruise Line) announced the closure of its Royal Cruise Line division. Two of the company's ships (*Crown Odyssey* and *Royal Odyssey*) went to sister company Norwegian Cruise Line; a third (*Star Odyssey*) went to Fred Olsen Cruise Lines as *Black Watch*; the fourth and smaller vessel (*Queen Odyssey*) went to Seabourn Cruise Line as *Seabourn Legend*.

Sunshine Cruise Lines ceased operations. The company's *Baltica* was acquired by Arcalia Shipping (and renamed *Princess Danae*).

Baltic Line ceased operations. The company's ships were acquired by other cruise lines.

Carnival Corporation, parent company of Carnival Cruise Lines, Holland America Line, Seaborn Cruise Line and Windstar Cruises, purchased 29.6 per cent share in Airtours plc, for approximately $310 million.

NEW OCEAN-GOING SHIPS TO DEBUT: 1997/1998/1999

Debut Date	Cruise Line	Name of Ship	Tonnage	Cost ($m)	Length (ft/m)	Cabins	Builder
April 1997	Royal Caribbean Cruises	Rhapsody of the Seas	75,000	275	834.0/254.2	1,000	Chantiers de l'Atlantique (France)
May 1997	Princess Cruises	Dawn Princess	77,000	300	856.0/261.0	1,050	Fincantieri (Italy)
June 1997	Costa Cruises	CostaOlympia	78,000	350	837.5/255.2	1,050	Bremer Vulkan (Germany)
June 1997	Hapag-Lloyd Tours	Columbus	14,000	n/a	472.4/144.0	210	MTW Schiffswerft (Germany)
Sept 1997	Royal Caribbean Cruises	Enchantment of the Seas	73,600	300	915.2/279.0	977	Kvaerner-Masa Yards (Finland)
Sept 1997	Holland America Line	Rotterdam VI	62,000	300	777.5/237.0	660	Fincantieri (Italy)
Sept 1997	Radisson Seven Seas Cruises	Paul Gauguin (prov.)	16,000	n/a	513.4/156.5	160	Chantiers de l'Atlantique (France)
Oct 1997	Princess Cruises	Grand Princess	104,000	385	935.0/285.0	1,300	Fincantieri (Italy)
Dec 1997	Celebrity Cruises	Mercury	73,850	320	852.0/259.0	900	Meyer Werft (Germany)
Jan 1998	Disney Cruise Lines	Disney Magic	85,000	325	718.5/219.0	1,200	Fincantieri (Italy)
Feb 1998	Carnival Cruise Lines	Elation	70,367	300	864.8/263.5	1,020	Kvaerner-Masa Yards (Finland)
Mar 1998	Star Cruise	Superstar Leo	74,500	350	879.2/268.0	1,000	Meyer Werft (Germany)
Apr 1998	Royal Caribbean Cruises	Vision of the Seas	75,000	275	915.2/279.0	1,000	Chantiers de l'Atlantique (France)
May 1998	Deilmann Reederei	Deutschland	22,000	160	573.4/174.8	318	Howaldtswerke Deutsche Werft (Germany)
May 1998	Silversea Cruises	unnamed	24,000	150	514.0/157.0	210	Francesco Visentini (Italy)
July 1998	Renaissance Cruises	unnamed	n/a	n/a	n/a	n/a	Chantiers de l'Atlantique (France)
Nov 1998	Carnival Cruise Lines	Paradise	70,367	300	864.8/263.5	1,020	Kvaerner-Masa Yards (Finland)
Nov 1998	Disney Cruise Lines	Disney Wonder	85,000	325	718.5/219.0	1,200	Fincantieri (Italy)
Dec 1998	Carnival Cruise Lines	Carnival Triumph	101,000	400	882.6/269.0	1,321	Fincantieri (Italy)
Feb 1999	Renaissance Cruises	unnamed	n/a	n/a	n/a	n/a	Chantiers de l'Atlantique (France)
Mar 1999	Princess Cruises	Sea Princess	77,000	300	856.0/261.0	1050	Fincantieri (Italy)
Apr 1999	Silversea Cruises	unnamed	24,000	150	514.0/157.0	210	Francesco Visentini (Italy)
Apr 1999	Star Cruise	Superstar Virgo	74,500	350	879.2/268.0	1000	Meyer Werft (Germany)
July 1999	Renaissance Cruises	unnamed	n/a	n/a	n/a	n/a	Chantiers de l'Atlantique (France)